# Prophetic Voices

## Editorial Advisory Committee

Rabbi Barbara AB Symons, *chair*

Cantor Dana Anesi, DMin
Rabbi Elizabeth Bahar
Cantor David Berger
Rabbi Sharon G. Forman
Rabbi Samantha G. Frank
Rabbi Alexander Grodensky
Rabbi Jan Katzew, PhD
Rabbi Karyn D. Kedar
Rev. Dr. David L. Morse
Rabbi Michael Namath
Rabbi Richard S. Sarason, PhD
Cantor Benjie Schiller
Rabbi Rachel Timoner
Rabbi Daniel G. Zemel

Rabbi Sonja K. Pilz, PhD, Rabbi Jan Katz,
and Rabbi Anne Villarreal-Belford
*Editors, CCAR Press*

Rafael Chaiken
*Director, CCAR Press*

Rabbi Hara E. Person
*Chief Executive, Central Conference of American Rabbis*

# Prophetic Voices

## Renewing and Reimagining Haftarah

*Edited by*
RABBI BARBARA AB SYMONS

*Foreword by*
RABBI JONAH DOV PESNER

CCAR
Press

CENTRAL CONFERENCE OF AMERICAN RABBIS
NEW YORK · 2023/5783

Copyright © 2023, Central Conference of American Rabbis
Printed in the U.S.A. All rights reserved. No portion of this book
may be copied in any form for any purpose without the written
permission of the Central Conference of American Rabbis.

LIBRARY OF CONGRESS CATALOGING-IN-PUBLICATION DATA
Names: Symons, Barbara AB, editor.
Title: Prophetic voices: renewing and reimagining haftarah / edited by
  Rabbi Barbara AB Symons; foreword by Rabbi Jonah Dov Pesner.
Description: First edition. | New York: Central Conference of American
  Rabbis (CCAR), 5783 = 2023. | Includes index. | Summary: "In Prophetic
  Voices, a diverse group of contributors--including rabbis, cantors,
  scholars, educators, activists, and poets--provide short commentaries on
  each haftarah. It presents alternative readings from Jewish texts
  biblical to contemporary. New haftarot for each Shabbat and holiday are
  included, plus haftarot for the Jewish American calendar, from Yom
  HaShoah to Pride Month to Martin Luther King Jr. Day. The readings are
  enhanced by scholarly essays placing the Prophets in historical context
  and examining the role of prophecy in Reform Judaism"-- Provided by
  publisher.
Identifiers: LCCN 2022054004 (print) | LCCN 2022054005 (ebook) | ISBN
  9780881233704 (paperback) | ISBN 9780881233711 (ebook)
Subjects: LCSH: Haftarot--Commentaries. | Reform Judaism.
Classification: LCC BM670.H3 S49 2023 (print) | LCC BM670.H3 (ebook) |
  DDC 296.8/341--dc23/eng/20221116
LC record available at https://lccn.loc.gov/2022054004
LC ebook record available at https://lccn.loc.gov/2022054005

10 9 8 7 6 5 4 3 2 1 0

Interior design and typography by Scott-Martin Kosofsky
at The Philidor Company, Rhinebeck, NY

Reform Judaism Publishing, a division of CCAR Press
Central Conference of American Rabbis
355 Lexington Avenue, New York, NY 10017
(212) 972-3636  info@ccarpress.org
www.ccarpress.org

# Contents

Foreword: The Haftarah Reading: The Leopard in Our Sanctuary     xvii
   *Rabbi Jonah Dov Pesner*
Acknowledgments     xxiii
Introduction     xxv
   *Rabbi Barbara AB Symons*
How to Use This Book     xxxi

## *Haftarah from Biblical Times to the Present*

Historical Context and Core Messages: Who Were the Biblical Prophets?     3
   *Rabbi Elizabeth Bahar*
Reading from the Prophets: The History and Significance of the Haftarah
   Readings in Rabbinic Judaism and in the Reform Movement     25
   *Rabbi Richard S. Sarason, PhD*
Connecting the Haftarah Readings with Social Justice Work: Reform
   Judaism from the Beginning of the Social Justice Movement to Today     39
   *Rabbi Lance J. Sussman, PhD*
The Prophetic Voice in the Reform Movement Today     49
   *Rabbi Rachel Timoner*
Contemporary Blessings for Prophetic Readings     55
   *Rabbi Samantha G. Frank and Rabbi Daniel G. Zemel*
Alternative Blessings     59
   *Rabbi Samantha G. Frank and Rabbi Daniel G. Zemel, Cantor David Berger,*
   *Cantor Margot E.B. Goldberg and Rabbi Barbara AB Symons*

## *Haftarot for the Weekly Torah Portions*

**GENESIS**     65
*B'reishit*     67
   Isaiah 42:5–43:10
     I Samuel 20:31–42
     Nehemiah 8:1–3; Rabbi Regina Jonas
*Noach*     71
   Isaiah 54:1–55:5
     "Tel Aviv: 1935," by Leah Goldberg
     "The Rainbow Haftarah," by Rabbi Arthur Waskow

*Lech L'cha*    77
   Isaiah 40:27–41:16
     "Traveler's Prayer," by Rabbi Sheila Peltz Weinberg
     "Let Go," by Alden Solovy

*Vayeira*    81
   II Kings 4:1–37
     Maimonides, *Mishneh Torah, Hilchot Mat'not Aniyim* 10:4
     From *Messengers of God: Biblical Portraits and Legends*, by Elie Wiesel

*Chayei Sarah*    86
   I Kings 1:1–31
   Jeremiah 1:11–19
     From *The Chosen*, by Rabbi Chaim Potok

*Tol'dot*    91
   Malachi 1:1–2:7
     From *Everyday Holiness*, by Alan Morinis
     "A Call to the Leaders of Islam for Peace and Brotherhood,"
       by Rabbi Ben-Zion Meir Hai Uziel and Rabbi Yitzhak HaLevi Herzog

*Vayeitzei*    96
   Hosea 12:13–14:10
     "Where Will I Find You," by Y'hudah HaLevi
     From "I and Thou," by Martin Buber

*Vayishlach*    101
   Hosea 11:7–12:12
     II Samuel 13:1–3, 5, 9–12, 14–16, 18–20
     "God Wrestler," by Rick Lupert

*Vayeishev*    107
   Amos 2:6–3:8
     Psalm 126:1–6; Babylonian Talmud, *Taanit* 23a

▶ *The First Shabbat of the Winter Cycle:* Shabbat of Thanksgiving    111
   Joshua 1:1–11, 5:1

*Mikeitz*    113
   I Kings 3:15–4:1
     *Sh'mot Rabbah* 18:12

▶ *The Second Shabbat of the Winter Cycle*    116
   Jeremiah 29:4–14

*Vayigash*    118
   Ezekiel 37:15–28
     Psalm 73:1–3, 21–28

▶ *The Third Shabbat of the Winter Cycle*                                 122
    Isaiah 2:1–5
*Va-y'chi*                                                               124
    I Kings 2:1–12
    Babylonian Talmud, *B'rachot* 12a
▶ *The Fourth Shabbat of the Winter Cycle:* Shabbat of New Year's        127
    Isaiah 56:1–7

**EXODUS**                                                               129
*Sh'mot*                                                                 131
    Isaiah 27:6–28:13, 29:22–23
      The Sephardic Tradition / Jeremiah 1:1–10
      Babylonian Talmud, *B'rachot* 63a; *Pirkei Avot* 2:6
*Va-eira*                                                                136
    Ezekiel 28:25–29:21
      "Pride," by Dahlia Ravikovitch
      Americans with Disabilities Act
*Bo*                                                                     142
    Jeremiah 46:13–28
      Zechariah 8:14–23
      From "Religion and Race," by Rabbi Abraham Joshua Heschel
*B'shalach*/Shabbat Shirah                                               146
    Judges 4:4-5:31
      From "My Parents' Lodging Place," by Yehuda Amichai
      "The Fourfold Song," by Rabbi Abraham Isaac Kook
*Yitro*                                                                  150
    Isaiah 6:1–7:6, 9:5–6
      *Pirkei Avot* 3:21
      From *Standing Again at Sinai*, by Judith Plaskow
*Mishpatim*                                                              155
    Jeremiah 34:8–22, 33:25–26
      "The New Colossus," by Emma Lazarus
      "The low road," by Marge Piercy
*T'rumah*                                                                160
    I Kings 5:26–6:13
      Song of Songs 3
      *Orchot Tzaddikim* 2:6
*T'tzaveh*                                                               164
    Ezekiel 43:10–27

Isaiah 61:1–4, 6–11

Psalm 122

*Ki Tisa*    169

  I Kings 18:1–39

    "Before the Statue of Apollo," by Shaul Tchernichovsky

    "K'hilah K'doshah," by Dan Nichols and Rabbi Michael Moskowitz

*Vayak'heil*    175

  I Kings 7:40–50

    "To be of use," by Marge Piercy

    From "When We Make Art Together, We Dream a Better World
      into Existence," by Caroline Rothstein

*P'kudei*    180

  I Kings 7:51–8:21

    Babylonian Talmud, *Gittin* 55a

    "Gods Change, Prayers Are Here to Stay," by Yehuda Amichai


**LEVITICUS**    185

*Vayikra*    187

  Isaiah 43:21–44:23

    From "Where Judaism Differs," by Rabbi Abba Hillel Silver

▶ *S'firat HaOmer*, Week 1:    190

  *Pirkei Avot* 1:1

*Tzav*    192

  Jeremiah 7:21–8:3, 9:22–23

    *Avot D'Rabbi Natan* 4

▶ *S'firat HaOmer*, Week 2:    195

  Babylonian Talmud, *M'nachot* 29b

*Sh'mini*    197

  II Samuel 6:1–7:17

    Job 38:1–6, 40:1–5

▶ *S'firat HaOmer*, Week 3:    201

  Babylonian Talmud, *Taanit* 7a; *Pirkei Avot* 4:15

*Tazria*    203

  II Kings 4:42–5:19

    From *Critique of the Gotha Program*, by Karl Marx, 1875

▶ *S'firat HaOmer*, Week 4:    206

  Babylonian Talmud, *Eiruvin* 13b; *Pirkei Avot* 5:20

*M'tzora*    208

  II Kings 7:3–20

  *Mishnah Yoma* 8:9

▶ *S'firat HaOmer*, Week 5:      211
   Babylonian Talmud, *Yoma* 35b

*Acharei Mot*      213
   Ezekiel 22:1–19
   From "To a Young Jew of Today," by Elie Wiesel

▶ *S'firat HaOmer*, Week 6:      217
   Babylonian Talmud, *Gittin* 6b; *B'rachot* 7a

*K'doshim*      219
   Amos 9:7–15
    "*V'ahavta*," by Marge Piercy

▶ *S'firat HaOmer*, Week 7:      222
   *Sh'mot Rabbah* 28:6

*Emor*      224
   Ezekiel 44:15–31
    Isaiah 1:11–17
    "Ready and Prepared," by Trisha Arlin

*B'har*      230
   Jeremiah 32:6–27
    Joel 4:9–21
    "The Horrors of Slavery," by Ernestine Rose

*B'chukotai*      236
   Jeremiah 16:19–17:14
    "Teach Me, O God," by Leah Goldberg
    "For Complete Healing," by Debbie Perlman

**NUMBERS**      241

*B'midbar*      243
   Hosea 2:1–22
    Psalm 136:1–9, 23–26
    From *Zohar* 1:15b; *Pardes Rimonim*, by Moses Cordovero

*Naso*      248
   Judges 13:2–25
    Psalms 67:2, 116:12, 104:1a, 118:5, 27:9, 18:29, 31:8, 42:3, 34:15, 42:6
    From "To Be a Jew: What Is It?" by Rabbi Abraham Joshua Heschel

*B'haalot'cha*      253
   Zechariah 2:14–4:7
    I Kings 19:1–8
    From "I Speak to You as an American Jew," by Rabbi Joachim Prinz

*Sh'lach L'cha* 257
 Joshua 2:1–24
  Psalm 91:1–12
  "The Silver Platter," by Natan Alterman
*Korach* 262
 I Samuel 11:14–12:22
  From *Ben-Gurion*, by Shimon Peres
  From *Jews and Words*, by Amos Oz and Fania Oz-Salzberger
*Chukat* 266
 Judges 11:1–33
  "Reciprocity," by Laura Eve Engel
  "You Are My Rock," by Moshe Lavee
*Balak* 270
 Micah 5:6–6:8
  "When Evil Darkens Our World," by Rabbi Chaim Stern
  "Bein Kodesh L'chol" / "Between the Holy and the Mundane," by
   Amir Dadon and Shuli Rand; Psalm 51:13–17
*Pinchas* 274
 I Kings 18:46–19:21
  II Samuel 21:8–14
  From "Bashert," by Irena Klepfisz
*Matot* 278
 Jeremiah 1:1–2:3
  From "Can Women Serve as Rabbis?" by Rabbi Regina Jonas
  From "Patriarchal Poetry," by Gertrude Stein
*Mas'ei* 284
 Jeremiah 2:4–28, 3:4 (Ashkenazic) or 2:4–28, 4:1–2 (Sephardic)
  Babylonian Talmud, *B'rachot* 29b; *T'filat HaDerech*
  From "Trees," by Leah Goldberg

**DEUTERONOMY** 289
*D'varim* 291
 Isaiah 1:1–27
  Babylonian Talmud, *Sanhedrin* 98a
  From "Take This Poem and Copy It," by Almog Behar
*Va-et'chanan*/Shabbat Nachamu 295
 Isaiah 40:1–26
  "*V'ahavta*," by Aurora Levins Morales
  "Tears, Too Close: A Prayer of Consolation," by Alden Solovy

*Eikev*                                                                301
  Isaiah 49:14–51:3
    "The Death of Adam," by Howard Schwartz
    "A Holy Nation," by Rabbi Regina Jonas

*R'eih*                                                                305
  Isaiah 54:11–55:5
    Jeremiah 5:20–31
    "Blessing and the Curse," by Rabbi Joe Black

*Shof'tim*                                                             310
  Isaiah 51:12–52:12
    Correspondence, Moses Seixas to George Washington, August 17, 1790
  ▶ Elul, Week 1: Wisdom of Solomon 1:1, 8:1–13, 21

*Ki Teitzei*                                                           315
  Isaiah 54:1–10
    Nachmanides on Deuteronomy 21:13
  ▶ Elul, Week 2: Maimonides, *Mishneh Torah, Hilchot Dei-ot* 1:4, 7

*Ki Tavo*                                                              319
  Isaiah 60:1–22
    From *When Bad Things Happen to Good People*, by Rabbi Harold S. Kushner
  ▶ Elul, Week 3: "Would an All-Powerful God Be Worthy of Worship?"
  by Rabbi Harold S. Kushner

*Nitzavim*                                                             324
  Isaiah 61:10–63:9
    Ezekiel 18:21–32
  ▶ Elul, Week 4: Nehemiah 6:1–13, 15

*Vayeilech*/Shabbat Shuvah                                             328
  Isaiah 55:6–56:8/Hosea 14:2–10; Micah 7:18–20; Joel 2:15–27
    Letter by Rabbi Stephen S. Wise, 1942
    "The Place Where We Are Right," by Yehuda Amichai

*Haazinu*                                                              332
  II Samuel 22:1–51
    Psalm 90
    "Two Candles," by Rabbi Zoë Klein

*V'zot Hab'rachah*                                                     337
  Joshua 1:1–18
    Micah 4:1–10
    Babylonian Talmud, *B'rachot* 16b

## Haftarot for the Traditional Jewish Calendar

*Shabbat Rosh Chodesh*     345
    Isaiah 66:1–13, 23
    Psalm 104:19–35
    "Split at the Root," by Adrienne Rich

*Shabbat Machar Chodesh*     350
    I Samuel 20:18–42
    From "Beautiful City," by Stephen Schwartz (from the musical *Godspell*)
    "Adoni," from *Beloved King* by J. Sylvan

*Rosh HaShanah*     355
    I Samuel 1:1–2:10
    Jeremiah 31:2–20
    "The Shofar's Calling," by Rabbi Israel Zoberman
    "The Judgment of Creation," by Aharon Berechiah of Modena, 1610
    From "Jews in the U.S.: The Rising Costs of Whiteness," by Melanie Kaye/Kantrowitz
    From "The Real Hero," by Yehuda Amichai
    For *Shabbat Shuvah*, see Vayeilech/*Shabbat Shuvah*, page 328

*Yom Kippur, Morning*     363
    Isaiah 57:14–58:14
    "Merger Poem," by Judy Chicago
    Leonard Fein, as quoted in a sermon by Rabbi Aryeh Azriel, 2011

*Yom Kippur, Afternoon*     367
    The Book of Jonah
    Babylonian Talmud, *B'rachot* 10a
    "I Remember You," by Rabbi Joe Black

*Sukkot, Day 1*     372
    Zechariah 14:7–9, 14:16–21
    "Be the Change," by Sue Horowitz
    "Beauty Dances," by Alden Solovy

*Shabbat Chol HaMo-eid Sukkot*     377
    Ezekiel 38:18–39:7
    From *The Essence of Judaism*, by Rabbi Leo Baeck
    "A Man in His Life," by Yehuda Amichai

*Simchat Torah*     381
    Joshua 1:1–18
    Nehemiah 8:1–10
    "Blessed Are You," by Ruhama Weiss, PhD

*Chanukah, Shabbat 1*                                                      385
    Zechariah 4:1–7
    "In Exile," by Emma Lazarus
    From "Some Notes on Jewish Lesbian Identity," by Melanie
    Kaye/Kantrowitz
*Chanukah, Shabbat 2*                                                      390
    I Kings 7:40–50
    Jeremiah 31:27–40
    "At Your Feet, Jerusalem," by Uri Zvi Greenberg
*Shabbat Sh'kalim*                                                         395
    II Kings 12:5–16
    Babylonian Talmud, *Sanhedrin* 17b
    From "Religion and Race," by Rabbi Abraham Joshua Heschel
*Shabbat Zachor*                                                           399
    Esther 7:1–10, 8:15–17
    Jeremiah 29:1–9
    Babylonian Talmud, *M'gillah* 7b
*Shabbat Parah*                                                            403
    Ezekiel 36:22–36
    "Esther," by Else Lasker-Schüler
    "And You Shall Draw Water . . . ," by Rabbi Sue Levi Elwell
*Shabbat HaChodesh*                                                        407
    Ezekiel 45:16–25
    From "The First Day of Pesach, 1857," by Rabbi David Einhorn
    "Book of Mercy #43," by Leonard Cohen
*Shabbat HaGadol*                                                          411
    Malachi 3:4–24
    "God's Beloved," Anonymous
    "Tefillah for *Agunot*," by Shelley Frier List
*Pesach, Day 1*                                                            416
    Isaiah 43:1–15
    "Reform Is Historical," by Rabbi Abraham Geiger
    "Discovery," by Ruth Brin
*Shabbat Chol HaMo-eid Pesach*                                             420
    Ezekiel 37:1–14
    Song of Songs 2:8–13, 5:2, 8:6–7, 13
    From the writings of Rabbi Dr. Shmuly Yanklowitz

*Pesach, Day 7*     425
    II Samuel 22:1–51
    Henrietta Szold's Letter to Haym Peretz, on Saying *Kaddish* for Her Mother
    "Passover's Peace Partners," by Rabbi Israel Zoberman
*Shavuot*     429
    Ezekiel 1:1–28, 3:12 and Isaiah 42:1–12
    "A *Ketubah* for Shavuot," by Rabbi Israel Najara
    "We All Stood Together," by Merle Feld
*Tishah B'Av*     434
    Jeremiah 8:13–9:23 and Isaiah 55:6–56:8
    "For the Anniversary of the Destruction of Jerusalem," by Rabbi David
    Einhorn
    From *Listening to Battered Women: A Survivor-Centered Approach to Advocacy*, by
    Lisa A. Goodman and Deborah Epstein

## Haftarot for the American Jewish Calendar

*Martin Luther King Day*     441
    From "Why We Went: A Joint Letter from the Rabbis Arrested in
    St. Augustine," 1964
*Tu BiSh'vat*     442
    Babylonian Talmud, *Taanit* 5b
*Black History Month*     444
    From "All the Things We Can Do with Hope," by Evan Traylor, 2019
*Presidents' Day*     445
    Proverbs 16:15–31
*Women's History Month*     447
    Esther 4:14; Speech by Rabbi Sally J. Priesand, Ordained as the
    First Female Rabbi at a Rabbinical Seminary, in June 1972
*International Women's Day*     448
    From "*Brown v. Board of Education* in International Context,"
    by Justice Ruth Bader Ginsburg
*Equal Pay Day*     450
    From "The Women of Reform Judaism Resolution on Pay Equity," 2015
*Transgender Day of Visibility*     451
    "Invisibility in Academe," by Adrienne Rich
*Baseball Opening Day*     452
    From "Kenneth Holtzman," Jewish Virtual Library
*Yom HaShoah*     454
    Ezekiel 37:1–14

*The Shabbat between Yom HaShoah and Yom HaAtzma-ut*　　　455
　Zechariah 4:1–14

*Yom HaAtzma-ut*　　　457
　The Israeli "Scroll of Independence" (*M'gillat HaAtzma-ut*)

*Earth Day*　　　458
　*Pirkei D'Rabbi Eliezer* 12:4, 6

*Lesbian Visibility Day*　　　460
　"I Shall Sing to the Lord a New Song," by Rabbi Ruth Sohn

*Mental Health Awareness Month*　　　461
　Jeremiah 20:7–18

*Jewish American Heritage Month*　　　463
　"Prayer for the Government" of the Reformed Society of Israelites,
　Charleston, South Carolina, 1825

*Mother's Day*　　　465
　"Women at the Head of the Class," by Jessica de Koninck

*Harvey Milk Day*　　　466
　From "The Hope Speech," by Harvey Milk

*Memorial Day*　　　467
　II Chronicles 10:1–11

*Gun Violence Prevention Day*　　　469
　Nachum 3:1, 3, 7, 18–19

*Beginning of Summer Camp*　　　470
　From *Next Generation Judaism*, by Rabbi Mike Uram

*Father's Day*　　　471
　"A Father's Blessing," from a Sermon by Rabbi Jerome Malino, 1974

*Pride Shabbat*　　　473
　Isaiah 58:1–12

*Juneteenth*　　　475
　From "Why Black Lives Matter to a People for Whom God Promised
　a Holy Place," by Graie Hagans

*Independence Day*　　　476
　Isaiah 1:11–7; Psalm 137:1–4

*Opening the Olympic Games*　　　478
　From "Exclusive: Aly Raisman Speaks Out on Sexual Harassment,
　Judaism, and Her Future," by Aiden Pink

*Labor Day*　　　480
　Speech by Rose Schneiderman, April 2, 1911, after the
　Triangle Shirtwaist Fire

*September 11*                                                                                        481
    "The Sandcastles," by Haim Gouri

*Bisexual Visibility Day*                                                                             482
    Ruth 1:12–22

*Breast Cancer Awareness Month*                                                                      484
    Psalm 27

*Domestic Violence Awareness Month*                                                                  486
    From "In the Midst of History," by Martin Buber

*Invisible Illness Awareness Week*                                                                   487
    From *Tomer Devorah* (*The Palm Tree of Deborah*), by Moses Cordovero

*National Coming Out Day*                                                                            488
    From "Coming Out: An Act of Love," by Rob Eichberg

*Indigenous Peoples' Day*                                                                            489
    From the speeches of Justice Raquel Montoya-Lewis

*Election Day*                                                                                        491
    I Samuel 8:4–6, 10–20

*Kristallnacht*                                                                                       492
    "The Salty Taste of Tears," by Rabbi Joe Black

*Veterans Day*                                                                                        494
    Judges 7:1–9

*Thanksgiving*                                                                                        496
    II Samuel 22:17–20, 38–51

*Kaf Tet B'November* (UN vote in favor of the Palestine Partition Plan)                               498
    Psalm 47

*World AIDS Day*                                                                                      499
    "Wingsong: For All the Lovers and Friends Who Died of AIDS,"
    by Maggid Andrew Elias Ramer

*International Human Rights Day*                                                                      501
    From the Universal Declaration of Human Rights Adopted by the
    General Assembly of the United Nations on December 10, 1948

*Secular New Year*                                                                                    502
    From "Three Calendars," by Shalom Aleichem


Sources and Permissions                                                                               505
Contributors                                                                                          517
Index of Commentary Authors                                                                           519
Index of Alternative Haftarah Authors                                                                 523

FOREWORD

# The Haftarah Reading:
# The Leopard in Our Sanctuary

*RABBI JONAH DOV PESNER*

IMAGINE THIS chaotic spectacle: It's the holiest day of the year. The temple is packed with worshipers; it is the most crowded of all the services. Families are wearing their finest clothing, and the sanctuary is decorated with beauty and ornament. The voices rise together in song and prayer, led by clergy whose petitions echo across eternity in a plea for forgiveness, blessings, and renewed life. Their piety is infused by the self-denial of the fast of Yom Kippur.

The people plead to God:

> When we fast, you say,
> Why do You pay no heed?
> *Why, when we afflict ourselves,*
> *do You take no notice?*
>> (Isaiah 58:3a)

Suddenly, from the back of the sanctuary, a booming voice shocks the room into silence, as it thunders the condemning charge:

> Because on your fast day you pursue your own affairs,
> while you oppress all your workers!
> Because you fasting leads only to strife and discord,
> while you strike with cruel fist!
> —Such a way of fasting on this day
> shall not help you to be heard on high.
> Is this the fast I have chosen?
> A day of self-affliction?
> Bowing your head like a reed,
> and covering yourself with sackcloth and ashes?
> Is this what you call a fast,
> A day acceptable to the Eternal?
>> (Isaiah 58:3b–5)

Security is alerted, and 911 is called. Law enforcement descends on the temple. The offending radical who has disturbed the traditional, institutional piety is taken into custody.

His offense? Calling out the hypocrisy of all those assembled.

The actual, original chaotic spectacle I have described occurred centuries ago and is recorded in Isaiah 58. The prophet continues his charge, with a positive call for the repair that is possible:

> Is not *this* the fast that I have chosen:
> to unlock the shackles of injustice,
> to loosen the ropes of the yoke,
> to let the oppressed go free,
> and to tear every yoke apart?
> Surely it is to share your bread with the hungry,
> And to bring the homeless poor into your house;
> when you see the naked, to cover them,
> never withdrawing yourself from your own kin.
> Then shall your light break forth like the dawn,
> and your healing shall quickly blossom;
> your Righteous One will walk before you,
> the glory of the Eternal will be your rear guard.
> Then, when you call,
> The Eternal will answer;
> when you cry, God will say: *Here I am.*
> (Isaiah 58:6–9)

Rabbi Arthur Waskow and many others have highlighted the ancient attempt by the prophet to disrupt society's oppressive hypocrisy and call attention to the plight of all those who suffer—particularly the most vulnerable—and the brilliance of the early Rabbis to assign Isaiah 58 as the haftarah reading for Yom Kippur, the holiest day of the year (and the day of maximal attendance!). However, Waskow also recalls a brilliant reflection by the great modern writer Franz Kafka, who, in Waskow's reformulation, said, "One day a leopard stalked into the synagogue, roaring and lashing his tail. Three weeks later, he had become part of the liturgy." Kafka understood that what is liturgically radical to one generation becomes rote to the next.

Think about it. You are sitting in synagogue, and a leopard wanders in, and prowls up and down the aisles. Screams. Flight. Hiding. Terror . . . Kafka understood the power of what Isaiah was doing: forcing the community to confront the reality of the world they hoped to ignore. A world of hunger, suffering, and oppression. It was as if a leopard had entered the sanctuary.

But Kafka also recognized the danger of these powerful, disruptive words becoming rote—and thus irrelevant. If we are being honest, many North American communities don't even take the time to read the text in English, which means almost no one understands the meaning of this text, let alone experiences it as a call to action.

On the one hand, Kafka is right—assigning Isaiah 58 to an annual ritual reading means we read it over and over and eventually miss its explosivity: the disruption and agitation it causes, demanding the community to confront the reality of the suffering of the world in which we live, and its accusation of hypocrisy and complicity, generation after generation.

On the other hand, think about what the Rabbis were doing: On the holiest day of the year—the day most of us show up and ask to be forgiven, ask to be inscribed in the Book of Life, as we suffer the delirium of fasting—on that day, the Rabbis require us to read Isaiah's words. To confront our own complicity. To reenact the moment when the leopard prowled through the sanctuary, setting off the pandemonium of a society that knows it has allowed selfishness, greed, and—worse—apathy to cause unthinkable suffering among other human beings. This is the power of the haftarah, embodied in Isaiah 58, read on Yom Kippur, the holiest day of the year, in the framework of the most attended service of the year.

Every Shabbat, every holy day, we have a chance to experience the haftarah reading as a call to action. As Rabbi Barbara AB Symons, the remarkable editor and visionary behind this commentary, writes in the introduction, "Its liturgical placement and literary power are the final push to open our hearts and minds—the closing argument before action."

This volume is making a demand: Let the haftarah reading once again be the leopard in the sanctuary. Let it roar and lash its tail; let it wake us up, make us outraged, and call us to action.

As a continual call to action, the haftarah reading is the voice of our prophetic ancestors, calling across generations, speaking truth to power, and echoing across centuries, saying:

> The world as it is—parched with oppression—is not the world as it
> must be.
> There is a better world—one overflowing with justice—if only we
> would make it so.

It is important to remember that Isaiah ends not with critique and condemnation, but rather with love and hope. His prophecy culminates with these words:

> If you banish the yoke from your midst,
> the menacing hand and evil speech,
> If you give yourself to the hungry,

and satisfy the needs of the afflicted;
then your light shall shine in the darkness,
and your night become bright as noon;
the Eternal will guide you always,
filling your throat with parched lands,
and renewing your body's strength;
you shall be like a garden overflowing with water,
like a spring that never fails.
Some of you shall rebuild the ancient ruins,
rebuilding the foundations of ages past.
You shall be called *Repairer of the breach*,
*Restorer of streets to dwell in*.
    (Isaiah 58:10–12)

But just as the ancient Israelites became desensitized to Kafka's leopard, too often we lose sight of the messianic promise of a truly just society. Too often we stop short with service programs of *tikkun olam* (repairing the world), however noble and important, like collecting food for the hungry, which have deadened us to the fast God truly requires of us.

It is not enough to share our bread with the hungry (though we must).
It is not enough to house one homeless person (though we must).

The leopard roars and Isaiah calls:
Lead with righteousness, march together.
Work for a world where there is no hunger;
strive for a day when there are no homeless,
dream of a time when all people live in peace,
and live as if it were no dream!

The most radical element of Isaiah's call
is that it strives for ultimate justice.
Isaiah's messianic charge
demands that we address
the root causes of injustice;
to transform the actual structures of despair,
and work for a time of complete healing.
The "repairing of the breach."

Every haftarah reading is another voice calling to us across history to remind us of our sacred obligation of *tikkun* (repair).

Now it is true that not every haftarah reading packs the social justice punch of Isaiah 58, and not every Jew sees *tikkun olam* as the ultimate objective of a Jewish life. So be it. Every person has the power of choice. As Rabbi Lance J. Sussman shows in his essay exploring the prophetic tradition in Reform Judaism, most Reform rabbis of the last century weren't civil rights activists (and even fewer Reform Jews were). Indeed, Rabbi Sussman notes that had it not been for Rabbi Emil G. Hirsch, the poignant declaration "In full accordance with the spirit of the Mosaic legislation, which strives to regulate the relations between rich and poor, we deem it our duty to participate in the great task of modern times, to solve, on the basis of justice and righteousness, the problems presented by the contrasts and evils of the present organization of society" would not have been included in the 1885 Pittsburgh Platform, the founding document of North American Reform Judaism.[1]

And yet. The idea for this volume came to us when hundreds of rabbis gathered in Chicago to collectively confront the moral crisis we faced in the United States in 2018. Those rabbis engaged thousands of cantors, other Jewish leaders, and allies across all lines of difference to heed the call of Micah, who charged that God requires us to "do justly, and love mercy, and walk humbly with your God" (Micah 6:8).

During the years over which this commentary was conceived and created, those rabbis, cantors, and Jewish leaders engaged hundreds of thousands of Reform Jews as they demanded racial justice, fought for voting rights, worked to end gun violence, advocated for reproductive rights, protected LGBTQ people, challenged mass incarceration, supported migrants and refugees, and stewarded God's sacred earth.

And then, the world confronted the most deadly pandemic in a century, and the United States experienced a racial reckoning catalyzed by the lynching of George Floyd by a white police officer, who had sworn an oath to protect and serve. Democracy came under direct threat as a white supremacist, violent mob sought to overturn a free and fair election. Violence rose against Jews, people of color, and other minority communities.

Nevertheless, week after week, rabbis, cantors, and other Jewish leaders led their communities. Often on Zoom, isolated in our homes, these remarkable Jewish leaders did more than read, chant, and interpret the haftarah. They applied it to the brokenness all around us, the suffering and inequity. Week after week they issued a call to action. Marches, protests, lobby visits, op-eds, voter education, civic engagement, letters to elected officials, volunteering, direct service work . . . the list goes on and on.

The haftarah cycle is still being written. This volume is evidence of that.

These efforts are all in the service of defining the centuries-old Jewish project: to stand in critique of the world as it is, and to call for collective action to build the world as it should be.

Every one of you has a choice.
You can "bow your head like a reed" (Isaiah 58:5)
or act against injustice like Isaiah.

Isaiah's promise is no less than ultimate. It is an eschatological vision of the time when all that is destroyed by human sin is restored by human achievement. The time when we are like a watered garden resplendent with beauty, bursting forth with life; the time when the gloom of suffering is illumined by the light of our deeds that shines forth; the time when the bones of our community are strong and we can truly be called "the repairers of the breach, the healers of a world shattered."

The haftarah is calling you to action.

NOTE
1. *Pittsburgh Platform* (1885), no. 8, https://www.ccarnet.org/rabbinic-voice/platforms/article-declaration-principles.

# Acknowledgments

Thank you to Rabbi Hara Person, Central Conference of American Rabbis Chief Executive, for realizing the CCAR's vision of supporting Reform rabbis and amplifying our voices. I am grateful that you entrusted me to do my part through this book.

Thank you to Rafael Chaiken, CCAR Press Director, for providing direction and oversight in your gentle yet professional way.

Rabbi Sonja K. Pilz, PhD, Editor: Thank you for partnering with me. Your scholarship, skill, boldness, and sense of humor shone through our thousands of emails and many Zoom calls—and given the pandemic, we have yet to meet in person! I have seen the many emails from our contributors thanking you for your brilliant edits, and I concur. You have helped me to find my voice not only between the covers of this book but beyond.

Rabbi Jan Katz and Rabbi Anne Villarreal-Belford, Editors: Thank you both for jumping right into this project with your scholarship, enthusiasm, and skill. This book is better because of you.

Thank you to Debbie Smilow, Press Operations Manager; Raquel Fairweather-Gallie, Marketing and Sales Manager; copy editor Debra Hirsch Corman; proofreader Michelle Kwitkin; cover designer Barbara Leff; and book designer Scott-Martin Kosofsky. Thank you to Leta Cunningham, former CCAR Press Publishing Assistant, and Chiara Ricisak, current CCAR Press Assistant Editor, whose email acumen enabled close to 180 contributors' voices to become part of this book. Thank you also to Cantor Shani Cohen, CCAR Press intern of summer 2020, for your fabulous feedback, writing, and encouragement. Thank you to Hagit Arieli-Chai, Professor of Hebrew Language at HUC-JIR, for her expertise. They say "it takes a village" and all of you are my village. Your skills are enabling all of the contributors to renew and reimagine prophetic voices, which in turn has the potential to better our shared world.

To the Editorial Committee: You brought your scholarship, pulpit experience, pastoral compassion and social justice work to this book, providing guidance from the outset by asking challenging questions. I only wish we had more time together so that I could have learned more from each of you.

Thank you to Rabbi Elizabeth Bahar, Rabbi Richard S. Sarason, PhD, Rabbi Lance J. Sussman, PhD, Rabbi Rachel Timoner, Rabbi Samantha G. Frank, Rabbi Daniel G. Zemel, Cantor David Berger, and Cantor Margot E.B. Goldberg for writing the introductory essays and alternative blessings. I have learned a tremendous amount from you, as will our readers. Your voices are the foundation upon which this book stands.

Thank you to Rabbi Jonah Dov Pesner for pausing from marching, speaking, meeting, and being the face of Reform Jewish advocacy in America in order to write the foreword. This book would not be complete without your voice.

To the over 170 contributors: thank you for saying "yes." Through your insightful, inspiring, and inclusive interpretations and alternative texts, our readers will deepen their knowledge about our prophets and the vastness of our people's literary gifts. Most importantly, thanks to you, they will be called to action. Thank you for your words of appreciation for this project; it is your scholarship and experience that renew and reimagine prophecy.

For the past sixteen years, Temple David of Monroeville, Pennsylvania, has shaped the rabbi I have become. The value of learning and commitment to tradition that Rabbi Jason Z. Edelstein (z"l) and the temple's founders championed and passed through the generations has strengthened our congregation and the Jewish people, myself included. As I say each year with renewed pride, I am honored to be your rabbi.

Rabbi Michael Szenes (z"l), my childhood rabbi at Temple Gates of Heaven in Schenectady, New York, you thought I could.

Cantor Margot E. B. Goldberg, for thirty-three years your voice—spoken and sung—has taught me, comforted me, and uplifted me. How could this book exist without you?

Diane Symons, from the moment I met you and Jerry (z"l) more than thirty years ago, you welcomed me into a family that lives Judaism through observance, values, traditions, and, of course, food.

Mom and Dad—June and Raymond (z"l) Benenson—you modeled temple leadership and commitment for me such that temple felt like a second home. Since my first pulpit, I have been trying to do that for others. In ways too lengthy to list, you are an inspiration to me. I love you.

Ron, Aviva, Ilana, Micah: Every single day I am thankful for and proud of each of you in your own way. During HUC-JIR Jerusalem, 1989, when Ron and I first met, I could not have dreamed that I would have the gift of you. That each of your voices is in this book is an illustration of the family that we are and the individuals that you are. I love you.

—*Rabbi Barbara AB Symons*

# Introduction

*RABBI BARBARA AB SYMONS*

WHEN I WAS a camper at the UAHC (now URJ) Kutz Camp Institute in the early 1980s, our songleaders—many of whom are now well-known cantors and rabbis—would sing, as they and their guitars were lifted into the air:

> Not by might and not by power
> But by spirit alone (*ruach*!)
> Shall we all live in peace!
> The children sing
> The children dream
> And their tears may fall
> But we'll hear them call
> And another song will rise . . .

We were all in: singing, standing, clapping, smiling, and craning our necks upward to see and hear prophetic voices—even if we had no idea that the lyrics were from Zechariah 4:6. The songleaders' embodiment, the prophet's words, Debbie Friedman's interpretation, and our shared enthusiasm lifted us all up. Anything was possible. That is what the haftarah can do: it can inspire us, and it can lift us up.

The word *haftarah* comes from the word for "conclusion." Usually, we speak of a haftarah reading as the portion from the second section of the Hebrew Bible, the Prophets, that we read or chant in our services after the Torah portion. It is the last word of sacred text before the closing blessing and the return of the Torah scroll to the ark. Its liturgical placement and literary power are the final push to open our hearts and minds—the closing argument before action. In the process of editing this volume, I have come to believe that the word *haftarah* is better translated as "punctuation." Haftarah readings can punctuate the Torah text or holiday—often with an exclamation point, sometimes with an implied question mark.

Yet, this last word is now straining to be heard. Often, the words and messages seem inaccessible and irrelevant to contemporary Jews and their lives. Throughout the years, I have seen congregants' and guests' eyes glaze over during the haftarah reading, which should be summoning us to action. Sometimes the haftarah reading is skipped altogether, even in our camps and national gatherings.

Though I had been playing with the idea for a book that would renew and reimagine the haftarah readings for the entire Reform Movement for quite some time, I finally gave voice to it when participants at the URJ Religious Action Center's Rabbinic Moral Leadership Conference in December 2018 were given time to suggest social justice steps forward. I shared my idea for the need of a new haftarah cycle so that the Reform Movement could reclaim the title "Prophetic Judaism." A small group of us began some preliminary work—and the rest is what you see before you!

"Renewing haftarah" occurs when rabbis, cantors, educators, scholars, students, artists, and activists of many backgrounds, ages, gender expressions, political convictions, nationalities, and writing styles offer contemporary, relevant interpretations for each standard Reform haftarah reading of the Jewish calendar as printed in the Plaut Torah commentary.[1] Each of these essays on the traditional haftarah reading concludes with a call to action in keeping with Abraham Joshua Heschel's words: "The prophet was an individual who said No to his society, condemning its habits and assumptions, its complacency, waywardness, and syncretism. . . . His fundamental objective was to reconcile man and God."[2]

"Reimagining haftarah" occurs when alternative prophetic voices are accompanied by contemporary teachings and reflections. "Alternative prophetic voices" are those Jewish voices that call us to sacred action. As Hillel said two thousand years ago, "If they are not prophets, they are children of prophets" (Babylonian Talmud, P'sachim 66b). These children of prophets paint for us a new vision of the messianic time: a world renewed and healed. Whenever we can consider saying the blessings before and after such an alternative reading—in a synagogue, on Zoom, while learning, and while marching—these children of prophets are calling out to us. This time, they are not limited to the all male, save a few, prophetic voices. Thus, the alternative prophetic voices include sections from the Prophets that we don't usually hear, plus sections from Psalms and Proverbs, Job and Ruth, Talmudic stories and teachings, debates and explanations, medieval and modern poetry, speeches and songs, and more. Both the breadth of alternative prophetic voices and the diversity of Jewish contributors make the statement that all Jewish voices are not only welcome—they are needed in order to teach the fullness of Torah and to make the Jewish people whole.

The final section of this book contains haftarah readings offered for the American Jewish calendar. This section includes both Jewish and American holidays and commemorations that do not traditionally have an accompanying haftarah. In it, we hear URJ president Rabbi Rick Jacobs's call to all Americans on the Fourth of July, the readings and essays for Memorial Day, Breast Cancer Awareness Month, Pride Month, and Earth Day, to name only a few of the forty-two.

There are many holidays and sacred moments that our diverse contributors felt should be included. Of course, we said "yes"! However, no book can include every holiday and commemoration. We invite you to discover a prophetic voice for additional days such as Sigd and the founding of the Union of American Hebrew Congregations.

Traditionally, there are certain times when the haftarah readings are related not to the Torah portion but rather to the time of year and are internally connected, week by week, to the nearby holiday—for example, from Rosh Chodesh Adar to Rosh Chodesh Nisan and the Shabbat before Passover and for the weeks surrounding Tishah B'Av. Three new cycles are a part of this volume: the weeks spanning Thanksgiving to Chanukah in the winter, the seven weeks of *S'firat HaOmer* (Counting of the Omer) in the spring, and the month of Elul in late summer as the High Holy Days approach. As the timing of the Torah portion cycle and holidays annually shifts, in the book these cycles are placed in close proximity to their intersection with the Torah portions. To determine the exact dates for the cycle in a given year, please consult a Hebrew calendar. A note about each:

- For the four-week arc from Thanksgiving through Chanukah, Rabbi Samantha G. Frank and Rabbi Daniel G. Zemel have selected haftarah readings from the Hebrew prophets that shed light on the tension between our individual and communal national and religious identities, helping us find our place in the American story in light of the Jewish story and vice versa.

- The period from Passover until Shavuot called the Omer cycle (*S'firat HaOmer*, the Counting of the Omer) connects the festival of our emancipation from bondage in Egypt (Pesach) to our entrance into the covenant forged at Mount Sinai through Torah (Shavuot). Seven weeks of counting end with the fiftieth day, which is Shavuot. In ancient times, Jews brought an omer, a "sheaf" of barley, to the Temple in Jerusalem daily during this period, beginning on the day after the first day of Passover. After the destruction of the Temple, other traditions arose to mark this period. In addition to counting the days by reciting a blessing and noting the day of the Omer each evening, many of us study a chapter of *Pirkei Avot* each Shabbat afternoon. In our alternative Omer cycle, Rabbi Amy Scheinerman offers rabbinic writings about the meaning of the Revelation at Mount Sinai and Torah learning in our lives as Jews.

- The third cycle leads up to Rosh HaShanah. The month of Elul is meant to be a time of self-reflection and examination, determining if we are living by our values, and beginning the difficult work of change and repentance. Over the course of those four weeks, Rabbi Alexander Grodensky uses ancient, medieval, and modern texts to help Jews prepare for the High Holy Days using the themes of the Jewish people's collective mission, wisdom, moderation, justice, and courage.

The introductory essays to this book ground, amplify, and enrich the prophetic voices gathered between its covers:

- In "Historical Context and Core Messages: Who Were the Biblical Prophets?" Rabbi Elizabeth Bahar introduces us to the heterogeneity of the historical context, personalities, and messages of the biblical prophets found in *N'vi-im*.
- In "Reading from the Prophets: The History and Significance of the Haftarah Readings in Rabbinic Judaism and in the Reform Movement," Rabbi Richard S. Sarason, PhD, traces how selections from prophetic books of the Bible became used as haftarah readings, laying out the fascinating evolution of the liturgical haftarah cycle from the first to the twenty-first century.
- In the middle of this process, we realized that Reform Judaism has been "prophetic" not only in regard to those liturgical readings, but also in the content of its most well-known sermons and social justice work. In "Connecting the Haftarah Readings with Social Justice Work: Reform Judaism from the Beginning of the Social Justice Movement to Today," Rabbi Lance J. Sussman, PhD, describes the way that the prophets' calls were used in sermons and social justice campaigns throughout the history of the Reform Movement in the United States.
- As a model of rabbinic social justice work, Rabbi Rachel Timoner writes passionately about the prophetic call to action in contemporary North America in "The Prophetic Voice in the Reform Movement Today."
- In "Contemporary Blessings for Prophetic Readings," Rabbi Samantha G. Frank and Rabbi Daniel G. Zemel explain the need for alternative haftarah blessings and offer their own. Other alternative blessings are provided by Cantor David Berger, Cantor Margot E.B. Goldberg, and myself. These better reflect the wide range of nontraditional prophetic voices gathered in this book, and are also appropriate to be said if it is neither Shabbat nor a festival.

Beyond a volume of traditional and alternative haftarah readings, this is also a compendium of Jewish literacy. It is an invitation to encounter new voices and texts and seek out the original sources. The essays are scholarly, empathic, uplifting, artistic, and inspiring—and they end with a call to you, the reader. In Rabbi Abraham Joshua Heschel's words, "Reading the words of the prophets is a strain on the emotions, wrenching one's conscience from the state of suspended animation."[3]

Prophetic voices should not be relegated to a few minutes on Shabbat or a festival, imprisoned on the bimah and remaining quiet the rest of the week. Whether they are chanted or read during worship or during a weekday study session, committee meeting, social justice rally, or interfaith gathering, each should be a call to action. Every single prophetic voice found within these pages punctuates the Torah text or holiday, in the spirit of the traditional haftarah blessings' own words and our re-translation: *likdushah*, "spirituality"; *limnuchah*, "comfort and care"; *l'chavod ultifaret*, "social justice work." Let us hear and let us act.

NOTES

1. W. Gunther Plaut, ed., *The Torah: A Modern Commentary*, rev. ed. (New York: Reform Judaism Publishing, an imprint of CCAR Press, 2005).
2. Abraham Joshua Heschel, *The Prophets* (New York: Harper & Row, 1962), xix.
3. Heschel, *The Prophets*, 7.

# How to Use This Book

THE PROPHETIC VOICES found within this book can be studied and shared in many ways and in many venues. Of particular import is that every single interpretation concludes with a call to action.

## Format

This book is composed of four parts:

1. Introductory Essays: These scholarly writings cover the background of the traditional prophets, the evolution of the haftarah cycle, the rise of prophetic Judaism, and modern applications. Since the goal is to hear prophetic voices on the bimah but not imprison them there, there are three sets of alternative blessings, which are better suited for many of the settings described below.

2. Haftarot for the Weekly Torah Portions: There are four offerings connected to each Torah portion. Two are contemporary interpretations of the standard Reform haftarah, and two are alternative prophetic voices that span Prophets, Writings, Talmud, poetry, speeches, and more, accompanied by interpretations.

3. Haftarot for the Traditional Jewish Calendar: For each of the Jewish holidays there are four offerings: two contemporary interpretations of the standard Reform haftarah, and two alternative prophetic voices accompanied by interpretations.

4. Haftarot for the American Jewish Calendar: These are commemorations on the American Jewish calendar—meaning secular holidays and Jewish holidays for which there is no traditional haftarah. For these, there is one innovative haftarah, accompanied by an interpretation.

## Haftarah Texts

The standard Reform haftarot are listed but not printed in this book, so you will need to find them in a *Chumash*, *Tanach*, or online source. We recommend Rabbi W. Gunther Plaut's *The Haftarah Commentary*, published by CCAR Press. All alternative haftarot are printed in this book.

## Haftarah Blessings

Because the alternative texts are taken from a multitude of sources beyond the Prophets section of the *Tanach*, the traditional blessings would not pair authentically. Further, because the expanded offerings of haftarot go beyond Shabbat and festivals, other blessings are more appropriate. There are three alternative sets of haftarah blessings in this book. (See the essay "Contemporary Blessings for Prophetic Readings," starting on page 55.) You are invited to explore them and consider which is the best fit depending on whether it is during a study session, on the bimah, at a march, or elsewhere, during Shabbat or festivals or other commemorations—or mix and match! Note that the final alternative set is considerably shorter and may be especially appropriate for a gathering such as a march or to be led by a person of any age with unique learning needs.

## Haftarah Cycles

Included in this book are three haftarah cycles (see facing page) that bring special attention to the time of year:

- Winter cycle: Thanksgiving to Chanukah
- Omer cycle (*S'firat HaOmer*): Pesach to Shavuot
- Elul cycle: the month leading up to Rosh HaShanah

The Winter and Omer cycles are placed in the book according to the approximate timing of when they would be read, but because of how the Hebrew lunar calendar interacts with the Gregorian solar calendar, they may not align with the same Torah portion each year. To determine the proper placement in a given year, consult a Hebrew calendar (e.g., hebcal.com). The Elul cycle will always align with the same *parashiyot*.

### USAGE SUGGESTIONS BY COHORT
*Here are some suggestions as to how to bring prophetic voices to your corner of the world.*

## Worship

In preparation for leading worship, first read the Torah portion and then the standard Reform haftarah from a *Chumash* or *Tanach* (citations are listed at the beginning of each *parashah* and holiday). Next look at the two modern interpretations with their calls to action, and read both alternatives with their interpretations and calls to action. Choose one as your haftarah.

Before the actual reading/chanting, share the background of the author of the haftarah text and the haftarah's connection to the Torah portion or holiday.

Consider setting the words—even English alternatives—to haftarah trope.

WINTER CYCLE

| | | |
|---|---|---|
| The first Shabbat of the winter cycle: Shabbat of Thanksgiving | Joshua 1:1–11, 5:1 | 111 |
| The second Shabbat of the winter cycle | Jeremiah 29:4–14 | 116 |
| The third Shabbat of the winter cycle | Isaiah 2:1–5 | 122 |
| The fourth Shabbat of the winter cycle | Isaiah 56:1–7 | 127 |

OMER CYCLE

| | | |
|---|---|---|
| S'firat HaOmer, week 1 | Pirkei Avot 1:1 | 190 |
| S'firat HaOmer, week 2 | Babylonian Talmud, M'nachot 29b | 195 |
| S'firat HaOmer, week 3 | Babylonian Talmud, Taanit 7a; Pirkei Avot 4:15 | 201 |
| S'firat HaOmer, week 4 | Babylonian Talmud, Eiruvin 13b; Pirkei Avot 5:20 | 206 |
| S'firat HaOmer, week 5 | Babylonian Talmud, Yoma 35b | 211 |
| S'firat HaOmer, week 6 | Babylonian Talmud, Gittin 6b; B'rachot 7a | 217 |
| S'firat HaOmer, week 7 | Sh'mot Rabbah 28:6 | 222 |

ELUL CYCLE

| | | |
|---|---|---|
| Elul, week 1 | Wisdom of Solomon 1:1, 8:1–13, 8:21 | 313 |
| Elul, week 2 | Maimonides, Mishneh Torah, Hilchot Dei'ot 1:4, 1:7 | 317 |
| Elul, week 3 | Harold S. Kushner, "Would an All-Powerful God Be Worthy of Worship?" | 322 |
| Elul, week 4 | Nehemiah 6:1–13, 6:15 | 326 |

### B'nei Mitzvah Students

Ask the family (note: not just the child) to read the Torah portion. They should then discuss the haftarot and blessings options with clergy and tutors months in advance, including haftarot on the proximate American Jewish calendar.

The haftarah that speaks most powerfully to the student should be studied in depth, including its author and the connection to the Torah portion or holiday. Note that the call to action may be an inspiration for a mitzvah project.

### Torah Study Groups

Choose from the alternatives which blessing to recite prior to study. Read the Torah portion and the standard Reform haftarah, and discuss what connects them. Learn a bit about the prophet of the standard Reform haftarah by reading the essay "Historical Context and Core Messages: Who Were the Biblical Prophets?" by Rabbi Elizabeth Bahar, or learn about the authors of the alternatives by accessing outside sources. Choose one or two haftarot to study each week in a multiyear cycle, or compare the four options all at once.

Consider what other prophetic voice could punctuate the Torah portion or holiday; this is an invitation to find your own voice.

### Adult Education

Choose from the alternatives which blessing to recite prior to study. Read and discuss each essay at the beginning of the book. After reading the Torah portion, study each successive haftarah or focus on the Jewish holiday cycle, the American Jewish calendar, or the special cycles. Each participant can be asked to choose a haftarah and present it to the class for study and discussion.

Collaborate with your temple's social action/social justice team, caring committee, ritual committee, or religious school by responding to one of the calls to action.

Consider what other special days on the American Jewish calendar deserve a prophetic voice and find one.

### Affinity Groups

(LGBTQ groups, Rosh Chodesh groups, women's groups, Women of Reform Judaism, Men of Reform Judaism, *chavurot*, etc.)

Discuss what you consider to be a "prophetic voice."

Look through the table of contents and choose alternative haftarot from anywhere in the book that speak to the group and/or seek out the holidays of particular interest to your group. Study those haftarot, discussing the interpretation and call to action.

Take a next step by considering what other prophetic voices could punctuate a Torah portion, Jewish holiday, or special observance on the American Jewish calendar.

## March/Community Gathering/Mitzvah Day

Based on that week's Torah portion or the American Jewish calendar, look at the prophetic voices and choose one that resonates with the theme of the day. You may choose to use that text's accompanying interpretation and call to action, or write your own interpretation and call to action. Begin and/or end with one of the creative blessings.

## Professional Development/Faculty Meetings/Board Meetings

Read the haftarah connected to that week's Torah portion or to an upcoming Jewish or American holiday, or choose a haftarah whose interpretation matches the goal of your meeting. Open the meeting with a presentation or by sharing the text and discussing the interpretation and call to action.

## Youth Group/Camp/Post-Confirmation

Ask teens what they remember about the haftarah they read/chanted if they became *b'nei mitzvah*. What was its impact on them? Invite them to look up their *parashah* in the book and discuss if any of the interpretations or alternates are meaningful. Discuss what makes a voice prophetic. Learn more about the authors of the alternate texts quoted in the book. Use the table of contents to see the variety of prophetic voices, and choose one or more to discuss. Then plan a mitzvah project based on its call to action. Create posters for social justice marches and programs that quote prophetic voices. Invite teens to set a prophetic voice—whether from the book or of their own choosing—to music.

# HAFTARAH
## from Biblical Times
## to the Present

# Historical Context and Core Messages
## Who Were the Biblical Prophets?

*Rabbi Elizabeth Bahar*

הִגִּיד לְךָ אָדָם מַה־טּוֹב
וּמָה־יְיָ דּוֹרֵשׁ מִמְּךָ
כִּי אִם־עֲשׂוֹת מִשְׁפָּט
וְאַהֲבַת חֶסֶד
וְהַצְנֵעַ לֶכֶת עִם־אֱלֹהֶיךָ.

*It has been told you, O mortal, what is good,*
*and what the Eternal requires of you—*
*Only this: to do justly,*
*and love mercy,*
*and walk humbly with your God.*
    —Micah 6:8

THESE PROPHETIC WORDS speak to us across generations—timeless words encouraging and prodding us to live up to the highest ideals of civilization politically, socially, and religiously. Yet other words of the prophets remain obscure, difficult to understand, and encased in imagery that no longer speaks to us. If we truly want to see ourselves as the heirs of these prophets, we need a more rounded and nuanced understanding of who they were and the messages they delivered. This essay will provide a brief introduction to the biblical prophets in their historical context, the nature of biblical prophecy, and the central messages of the biblical prophets.

## The Term "Prophet"
Let us begin with the meaning of the English word "prophet." It comes from the Greek *prophetes*, "one who speaks for" or "spokesperson," and expresses the understanding that the prophets "spoke for" God, delivering divine messages. The Hebrew term *navi*, on the other hand, most likely derives from Akkadian and means "one who has been divinely called."[1] Thus, the Hebrew term has a different connotation. Many of the Israelite and Judahite prophets most likely constituted

a professional class, associated with the royal court or its sanctuary. Another term for prophet in the biblical literature is "man of God," a term used with reference to Moses, Samuel, Shemaiah, Elijah, and Elisha.[2] Some prophets may have offered prophetic services for a fee, such as Samuel "the seer" to whom Saul went for consultation.[3] It is important to recognize that the individuals we know as biblical prophets constituted only a small portion of the overall larger institution at any given time.

A popular understanding of prophecy relates it to divination, the act of determining the will of the gods. In the ancient Near East, the phenomenon of divination existed among both the Israelites and other peoples.[4] Diviners used a variety of methods to determine the will of the gods, including the interpretation of the movement of the heavenly bodies, flights of birds, the appearance of animal livers and other organs, necromancy (consultation of the dead), dream interpretation, ecstatic experiences, visions, and the casting of lots, dice, and arrows.[5] Additionally, usage of sacred objects to understand the divine will is widely attested in ancient Israel among the priests;[6] they used the Urim and Thummim as well as the ephod, seeking "yes" or "no" answers.[7] Regardless of the method used, for the ancient Israelites the messages received were understood to come from God.[8] In this regard, it should be noted that prophets used objects to dramatize and visualize their messages, but not to receive them.

In addition, the biblical prophets were critical of mechanistic ritual. They challenged worship that was not accompanied by an inner disposition toward full obedience of divine commands.[9]

Although most of the prophets were men, there were women prophets as well. During the time of the monarchy, the best-known prophetess was Huldah.[10] Other women who are associated with prophecy are Miriam, Deborah, Noadiah,[11] and the unnamed wife of Isaiah.[12] It is interesting that both Ezekiel and Joel mention female prophets, but none are named.[13] Moreover, Joel has a vision of the restoration of Judah in which sons and daughters will have dreams and visions.[14]

## The Historical Context

Any discussion of the biblical prophets in their historical context requires an understanding of the literary medium through which their words and stories have been transmitted—a clear awareness of what biblical literature both is and is not. This literature does not report unmediated historical facts. Rather, the biblical narratives are essentially mythic and legendary stories of Israelite origins and historical experience that reflect a variety of political, religious, and ideological points of view. In their fully edited and compiled form in the biblical literature as we have it, they attempt to provide a coherent explanation for the rise and fall of the Israelite and Judean kingdoms. In what follows, I will offer a broad overview of the biblical books, prophets, and historical context. (For a complete timeline, see the table "The Prophets in Their Narrative and Historical Contexts" at the end of this essay.)

### The Former Prophets: Joshua, Judges, Samuel, and Kings

The Books of Joshua, Judges, Samuel, and Kings (traditionally known as the Former Prophets) comprise the main account we possess regarding the legendary history of ancient Israel. The Books of Joshua and Judges do not contain descriptions of prophets other than Joshua himself as the heir of Moses, and the prophetess Deborah as described in Judges. Judges narrates from the time of Joshua to Saul and, as argued by some scholars, is a contrasting account to that related in the Books of Samuel.[15]

The Books of I and II Samuel and I and II Kings contain narrative accounts about various prophets. Samuel is described as a seer (*ro-eh*) and a man of God (*ish haElohim*).[16] The prophets in both of these books were able to view and sense things remotely,[17] served as freelance consultants,[18] formed prophetic fellowships,[19] prepared to receive their message by induction of the correct technique,[20] performed wondrous acts,[21] restricted their audience to a small group or person (sometimes just the king),[22] performed strange deeds,[23] and made predictions.[24]

As biblical scholarship has matured, it has become increasingly clear that these books have an agenda. They were written through the lens of the Deuteronomic Historian supporting the Davidic monarchy.[25] Kings typically employed prophets as advisors in their service. Nathan, for example, appears as a court prophet during the reign of David. He famously delivers an oracle bestowing God's everlasting blessing upon the Davidic royal line: "Your house and your kingship shall ever be secure before you; your throne shall be established forever."[26] But he also calls David to task when the king unlawfully takes Bathsheba as his wife. To deliver his message in a dramatic form, he uses a parable, asking the king to judge the deed of a rich man who commandeers the lamb of a poor man, and thereby forces David to condemn himself ("That man is you!").[27]

### The Literary Prophets: Isaiah, Jeremiah, Ezekiel, Hosea, Joel, Amos, Obadiah, Jonah, Micah, Nahum, Habakkuk, Zephaniah, Haggai, Zechariah, and Malachi

Immediately following the narrative books of Joshua through Kings in the *Tanach* come the fifteen books of the so-called Literary Prophets, which comprise edited collections of their prophetic messages to the Kingdoms of Israel and Judah. These were transmitted as four separate scrolls—one each for the longer compilations of Isaiah, Jeremiah, and Ezekiel, as well as the scroll of the Twelve Minor Prophets, comprising the shorter compilations of Hosea, Joel, Amos, Obadiah, Jonah, Micah, Nahum, Habakkuk, Zephaniah, Haggai, Zechariah, and Malachi.

Amos and Hosea were contemporaries, although Hosea was the younger of the two. What we know of Amos comes from short biographical sections of his book. He was a shepherd from Tekoa[28] who prophesied during the time of King Jero-boam son of Joash (785–745 BCE) of Israel, roughly contemporary with King Uzziah of Judah. He prophesied primarily at the royal sanctuary of Bethel in the Northern Kingdom.[29] Amos prophesied the destruction of the Northern Kingdom, a prophecy that was fulfilled by the Assyrian destruction of Samaria in 722 BCE. Amos additionally spoke about a major earthquake, mentioned as well by Zechariah, though not dated precisely.[30] Hosea also prophesied during the reign of Jeroboam of Israel. He does not mention the destruction of Samaria in 722 BCE, though he does describe the events leading up to it. The Book of Hosea is divided into two main sections: the first tells of the prophet's marriage to a promiscuous woman, which functions as a metaphor for the relationship of God with Israel; the second section pertains to political and religious affairs of the Northern Kingdom in its final decades. Amos and Hosea reference the story of the Exodus and are both vehement in their criticism of the priests and their cult. Unlike Amos, Hosea does not dwell on the theme of social justice; rather he focuses on the political intrigue and rapid turnover of kings. Hosea also offers rich metaphorical language for God when he likens God to a jealous husband and a loving father.[31]

Isaiah and Micah were active in the Southern Kingdom of Judah at approximately the same time as Amos and Hosea were in the north. The prophet Isaiah lived and prophesied during the days of King Uzziah (783–742 BCE).[32] He describes the Syro-Ephraimite War[33] during the reign of King Ahaz and references a campaign of the Assyrian king Sargon against Philistia in 712 BCE.[34] Some of the oracles of Isaiah recall the preaching of Amos, since both insist on the futility of animal sacrifice.[35] The sacrificial cult is seen as a distraction from the real service of God, which is to defend the orphan and plead for the widow.

The Book of Isaiah, as it has come down to us, is a diverse compilation of materials from various periods. The book's first part (chapters 1–39) is associated with the prophet from the eighth century BCE, whereas chapters 40–66 transmit anonymous prophecies from the period of the Babylonian exile and its aftermath. Even so, later oracles are inserted into the first part of the book, such as the oracle against Babylonia describing a time after the Babylonians replaced the Assyrians as the dominating regional power.[36] In Isaiah 39, the story of the envoys from Babylon provides a bridge to the second half of the book, which addresses the exile. Therefore, it is possible to see a redactor's hand in this material.

Micah of Moresheth, a small town about twenty miles southwest of Jerusalem, was a contemporary of Isaiah. He lived during the time of Jotham, Ahaz, and Hezekiah. He focused much of his prophecy on the situation in Samaria and Jerusalem. Unlike Isaiah, he was not a royal prophet, but a rural prophet. He describes the need of Zion to writhe like a woman in labor before the city would be undone and its inhabitants forced to live in the fields.[37] The book ends with a prayer of hope that God will shepherd God's people toward restoration.

A series of oracles from the prophet Nahum relate to the fall of Assyria in 612 BCE, when Nineveh, the Assyrian capital, was destroyed by an alliance between the Medes and Babylonians.[38] The first oracle is one of assurance for Judah, describing a divine warrior supporting Judah.[39] Like Hosea, Nahum projects human emotion onto God (unlike Hosea, he does not distinguish which emotions are worthy of God and which are not). He is unique in that he offers no criticism of his own people but includes many oracles against the nations, thereby displaying Judahite nationalism.[40]

The narrative Book of Jonah, on the other hand, which likely is postexilic, uses Nineveh as a rhetorical foil to teach the value of repentance: if God accepts the repentance even of Israel's archenemies, so much the more so will God accept the repentance of Israel.

Zephaniah prophesied during the reign of Josiah and offered an oracle regarding the fall of Nineveh.[41] The main concern of his prophecy was not with Nineveh, however; it was with Jerusalem. The dominant motif is the Day of the Lord (discussed below) as a day of judgment and a festival day.

These prophetic narratives tend to cluster around great events and catastrophes that befell both the Kingdoms of Israel and Judah. Neither Nahum nor Zephaniah addressed issues arising from the shifts of power in the broader ancient Near East and the rising might of the Babylonians.

That situation was addressed by Jeremiah and after him by Habakkuk, both of whom prophesied in the context of an impending revolt against Babylonia. As power shifted, the Chaldeans of Aram became a dominating element in the Neo-Babylonian Empire. The empire, founded by Nabopolassar (626–605 BCE) and expanded by Nebuchadnezzar II, was the force that ultimately destroyed Jerusalem. Pharaoh Necho, in 609 BCE, led an army against this rising power. He was defeated at the Battle of Charchemish along the Euphrates River. King Josiah of Judah rode out to meet him at Megiddo, but the pharaoh killed him.[42] The victorious Babylonians now exerted control over Syria-Palestine.

Jeremiah was "the son of Hilkiah, one of the priests at Anathoth[43] in the territory of Benjamin."[44] He began to prophesy during the thirteenth year of King Josiah (627 BCE) and ended his prophecies around the time of the destruction of the Temple (586 BCE). The Book of Jeremiah is complex; it describes his scribe Baruch as writing down many of Jeremiah's prophecies as well as some biographical material. Jeremiah warns of the pending destruction of Jerusalem and of the Temple. Repeatedly, he calls for individuals to repent.[45] However, he also offers some hope for the future by purchasing a field in Anathoth[46] and demonstrating his belief in life beyond the destruction and a renewed covenant between God and God's people.[47]

Habakkuk offers a sustained reflection on the problems of injustice in Jerusalem:[48] "How long, O Eternal, shall I cry out and You not listen?"[49] Also Habakkuk resorts to a vision of the future to solve the problems of injustice occurring in the present.[50]

After Jerusalem was destroyed, the Judeans who were deported to Babylon struggled to create a life for themselves. The Book of Ezekiel opens with a superscription indicating that he wrote and prophesied outside of the Land of Israel in Babylon by the Chebar Canal in the land of the Chaldeans.[51] The book is highly structured: chapters 1–11 describe great, fantastic visions of God's glory, followed by a vision of God's glory departing from Jerusalem ahead of the city's judgment and destruction (chapters 12–24). There is a collection of oracles against foreign nations (chapters 25–32), with the remainder of the prophecies describing consolation and restoration (chapters 33–48). Unique to Ezekiel—a priest—are his priestly concerns; as in the Holiness Code of Leviticus, he does not distinguish between moral and ritual laws—he is concerned with holiness and purity.

Obadiah, the shortest book of the Bible, comprising only twenty-one verses, reflects on the conditions in Judah after the disaster. While there is no archaeological evidence of this, Edom is described as having entered into Jerusalem after the Babylonians to destroy what was left. Later, the Rabbis would use "Edom" as a code word for Rome. Also, Obadiah ends with a prophecy of the restoration of Judah and Jerusalem.

Historical circumstances continued to change following the ravaging of Judah and Jerusalem, the fulfillment of Jeremiah's and Ezekiel's prophecies. Only a small remnant of the people remained in the city.

Cyrus of Persia conquered Babylon, leading to its fall in 539 BCE. Again, the power structure of the ancient Near East changed. Cyrus restored shrines and worship and allowed the Judeans to return to their land and rebuild their sanctuary. In 538 BCE, they received back their Temple vessels.[52] The euphoria resulting from this policy is reflected in Second Isaiah (chapters 40–55). Persian imperial rule would remain in place until Alexander the Great's defeat of the Persians two centuries later.

The Books of Haggai and Zechariah, as well as the non-prophetic Book of

Ezra, describe the hardships of the Judean returnees upon entering an impoverished land during the reigns of King Darius (522–486 BCE) and King Artaxerxes I (465–423 BCE) of Persia. Haggai assumed that one of the reasons the people were struggling agriculturally was the lack of a centralized cult. However, in Haggai 1, the people were disputing if it was the right time to rebuild the Temple. The completion of the reconstruction came about seventy years after the destruction—a unifying moment for the community.

The prophet Zechariah is closely associated with Haggai, since they were both active at approximately the same time—while Zerubbabel was governor and Joshua the High Priest. The Book of Zechariah contains eight visions and one oracle. The prophet asserts that God will return to Judah if the people return to God. Also, Zechariah emphasizes that the purpose of prophecy is to bring warnings to the people and justify God's punishments of Judah. The Book of Zechariah begins a new genre that developed during the Second Temple period—apocalyptic literature.[53]

The final two prophets are Malachi (meaning "my messenger"; this may or may not be his proper name)[54] and Joel. The Book of Malachi contains six speeches and two appendixes. The prophet asks his listeners to examine everyday life, their relationship with God, and the cult at the Temple, encouraging them to follow the Torah and the laws of Moses.

Our last prophetic book is Joel. Though the Book of Joel appears between Hosea and Amos in the standard order, it most likely does so only for thematic reasons.[55] Scholars believe this book to be a postexilic work, as there is no king or historically identifiable event mentioned in the book. The book displays further apocalyptic motifs, comprising an additional bridge between prophetic works and apocalyptic writings.

## The Story of the Prophetic Books
### The Biblical Books in Their Time

During the eighth century BCE, there appeared to be a growth of literary elites associated with palace and temple administrations in both the Northern and Southern Kingdoms. These scribes wrote down prophetic oracles, which were used by the rulers in making decisions. Once written down, they were edited and augmented by later literary schools, including the so-called Deuteronomist school.[56]

This is also when the material that we now know as the Latter Prophets was collated. Unlike the entirely third-person narratives of the Former Prophets found in the Book of Kings (Elijah and Elisha), these later books are about and by individual prophets. In the Hebrew Bible, the books of the Major Prophets[57] and the

Minor Prophets[58] are roughly arranged in order of length (longest to shortest),[59] while the Book of Twelve appears to be arranged chronologically; the content of the first collection of prophets dates from the early Assyrian period—Hosea, Amos, Jonah, and Micah. Joel is undated but is placed before Amos because of its literary association with Amos. Obadiah is also undated. These are followed by Nahum, Habakkuk, and Zephaniah, dated from the later Assyrian period. Last are the three from the Persian period—Haggai, Zechariah, and Malachi.

Biblical prophetic literature includes three major literary categories:

1. Biographical material about the prophet written in the third person, indicating that the collection and editing of the material was done by someone other than the prophet himself. Stories about a prophet told by a third-person narrator often include intimate divine experiences that took place between the respective prophet and God. Recognizing that these moments occurred in private, how could they be wholly accurate in their transmission?

2. Autobiographical material written in the first person, supposedly written by the prophet himself. However, scholars now are beginning to question the authenticity of autobiographical material.[60]

3. Oracles or speeches delivered by the prophet, usually beginning with "an oracle of God," and continuing with "Thus says God. . . ." These oracles usually appear in poetic form.[61] They are words of God spoken through the mouth of the prophet.

All of the prophetic books should be considered anthologies with no clear principle regarding the arrangement of their texts. For example, the prophet's call is sometimes placed at the beginning of the book (as in the case of Jeremiah, Ezekiel, and Hosea), but it can also appear later in the text as in Amos (7:15) or Isaiah (chapter 6). Sometimes the material is arranged thematically. One example is the oracles against the nations, which are usually grouped together.[62]

### Rabbinic Perspectives

The Rabbis of late antiquity had an entirely different idea about the history of the prophetic books.[63] The Talmudic account of the order and authorship of the biblical books ascribes authorship of the Books of Joshua, Judges, Ruth, and Samuel to Samuel. They believed that the Book of Kings was written by Jeremiah. They understood the designation "Former [that is, Early] Prophets"[64] as related not to narrative chronology, but to authorship (who wrote what first). Regarding the number of prophets, the Rabbis also had their own distinctive ideas, which they most likely came to by simple enumeration.[65] According to the Rabbis of the Talmud, there were forty-eight prophets and seven prophetesses in Israel.[66] They also ordered the biblical books in a different way than later Jewish Bibles. The Rabbinic ordering of the prophetic material may have been based on their understanding of two types of prophetic discourse—the first being threats of punishment, predictions of calamity, and the destruction of Jerusalem; and the second, praises and commendation, hope, and comfort.[67] The Rabbis assigned all books to either of these two categories, based on their opening words. For example, for the Rabbis, the opening words of Second Isaiah, "'Comfort, My people, comfort them!' says your God,"[68] defined much of Second Isaiah altogether.

## Modern Scholarship

Most books of the Bible have come to be understood as composed over several stages and many centuries. They were shaped by different hands and include folklore, popular short stories, history, and more. Ancient editors were not concerned with consistency. As a result, we stumble over gaps, inconsistencies, and historical and geographical inaccuracies.

The history of biblical scholarship displays numerous attempts to come to terms with the composite nature of the text. In the nineteenth century, "literary criticism" of the Bible was understood as the process of separation of the various sources. Classic German scholar Julius Wellhausen (1844–1918) based his analyses on the tensions within the narratives of the text. Hermann Gunkel (1862–1932), regarded as the founder of form criticism, focused on the formal-generic and rhetorical characteristics of much smaller textual units. Gerhard von Rad (1901–71) and Martin Noth (1902–68) reacted to form criticism. Von Rad was best known for his work on the Pentateuch—more specifically, the final form of the so-called J, or "Yahwist," source localized to the Southern Kingdom. Noth demonstrated the editorial unity of the Deuteronomic History. While much of the scholarship listed above developed in Germany, there were also influential and diverse scholars in North America. William F. Albright (1891–1971) made extensive use of ancient Near Eastern literature as the context out of which the Bible emerged.[69] For William F. Albright and his student John Bright (1908–95), archaeology was believed essential for writing the history of the Bible.[70] More recently, the limits of archaeology have been discussed by Israel Finkelstein and Neil Asher Silberman in their book *The Bible Unearthed*.[71]

At the beginning of the twenty-first century, biblical scholarship was and is largely characterized by a diversity of methods, including literary criticism and sociology as knowledge. The Bible as literature is based on a movement called New Criticism, which began in the 1960s. It is formalistic in nature, meaning that it holds that the meaning of a text can be revealed through close examination of the text itself and without extensive research into its social, historical, and literary contexts. Robert Alter and Brevard S. Childs are two biblical scholars working with that premise.[72] Sociology of knowledge has shown that textual interpretation is never objective or neutral, but serves human interests and is shaped by them. Furthermore, the texts themselves reflect the ideological interests of their authors or scribes. Feminist scholarship has repeatedly pointed out the patriarchal assumptions in both biblical scholarship and authorship. Jewish scholars have pointed out the impact of Christian interpretations and assumptions on biblical scholarship. As a consequence, ever-richer readings and analyses have found their way into biblical scholarship.

## The Nature of Biblical Prophecy: What Are the Prophets' Messages?

What do these books and their stories actually tell us? Who are these biblical figures, what do they do, and what are their actual messages?

At some point in their lives, biblical prophets become aware of their mission through a calling from God, who tells them to *go forth*. Usually, the prophets first have to overcome feelings of inadequacy and gain an understanding of their task: they are to become mouthpieces for God. Many of them struggle with the magnitude of their task, realizing that it will be extremely difficult.

Once they accept their calling, the biblical prophets begin to share God's messages.

### The Covenant

The prophets call Israel to account for their disobedience to God and violation of the covenant (*b'rit*), or contractual relationship, between God and the people of Israel. A covenant is a contract between two parties—in this case between God and Israel. It can be most easily summarized as "You shall be My people, and I will be your God" (see, for example, Jeremiah 30:22). The first covenant, in Genesis, is made between God and Abraham. Abraham is promised abundant progeny for following God's instructions to uproot from the land of his fathers and follow God "to the land that I will show you."[73] This promise is extended to his descendants; the redemption of Israel from Egyptian slavery is described as its fulfillment (Genesis 12–25).

The subsequent covenant at Sinai (Exodus 19) is made with the entire Israelite people: God will bring them into the land, protect them, and grant them prosperity and blessing in exchange for their obedience to God's laws. Yet the covenant can be misinterpreted. The Israelites whom the prophets castigate assume that the proper fulfillment of their ritual obligations suffice to ensure God's favor and protection, and the Judeans assume that Jerusalem is inviolate as long as the Temple, God's earthly abode, stands in their midst. The prophets challenge these common assumptions: God's covenant requires more than ritual correctness; it requires social and economic justice. Similarly, the presence of God's earthly sanctuary in Jerusalem does not render it inviolable; only the people's obedience to the entirety of God's commandments—both ritual and ethical—ensures that.

The prophets seek to remind Israel of the terms of the covenantal arrangement—meaning that if one of the parties violates their agreement, then both parties are free from the arrangement. A brief examination of one such prophecy from Isaiah 5:1–7 illustrates this:

> Let me sing for my beloved. A song of my lover about his vineyard. My beloved had a vineyard on a fruitful hill. He broke the ground, cleared it of stones, and planted it with choice vines. He built a watchtower inside it, he even hewed a wine press in it; for he hoped it would yield grapes. Instead, it yielded wild grapes.
>
> "Now, then, Dwellers of Jerusalem and people of Judah, you be the judges between Me and My vineyard: What more could have been done for My vineyard that I failed to do in it? Why, when I hoped it would yield grapes, did it yield wild grapes?
>
> "Now I am going to tell you what I will do to My vineyard: I will remove its hedge, that it may be ravaged; I will break down its wall, that it may be trampled. And I will make it a desolation; it shall not be pruned or hoed, and it shall be overgrown with briers and thistles. And I will command the clouds to drop no rain on it."
>
> For the vineyard of the God of heaven's hosts is the House of Israel, and the seedlings God lovingly tended are the people of Judah. And God hoped for justice, but behold, injustice; for equity, but behold, iniquity!

In this prophecy, known as the Song of the Vineyard, Isaiah bids the people to consider that God planted and cared for the vineyard, the people Israel. While God tended to the vineyard, the grapes still failed to be domesticated. The grapes did not "behave." Isaiah here emphasizes the conditionality of the covenant: it was not only the ritual obligations that the Israelites had to fulfill, but also obligations to care for all members of their society.

### Breaching and Neglecting the Covenant

Frequently, the prophets engage in something like a covenantal lawsuit (*riv*). In the style of a legal suit brought in front of a court, the prophets first accuse Israel of having violated the Sinaitic covenant by engaging in idolatrous and immoral behavior and by relying on political alliances with foreign powers rather than on the sovereignty of Israel's God. Then, the Israelites are told to repent. Finally, the prophet announces the consequences of breaking the covenant, the frightening vision of the "Day of the Eternal" (see below). Each of these aspects of the law-court pattern—accusation, call to repent, and threat of destruction—presupposes an understanding of covenant and covenantal theology.

This pattern first appears in the Book of Hosea and is then repeated by several other prophets.[74] Hosea and Amos repeatedly accuse Israel of worshiping other gods, failing to show confidence in the God of Israel by making foreign alliances, building unnecessary fortifications, and denying (or impeding) social justice in the land.[75] Those violations of the covenant call forth the enactment of divine curses.

The prophets also argue that the people's sole focus on ritual compliance at the expense of social justice fails to fulfill God's will. Amos, Isaiah, Jeremiah, Hosea, Micah, as well as Psalms 50 and 51, all reject sacrificial offerings.[76] Other passages emphasize that ritual observance, while necessary, is less important than personal moral conduct.[77]

### Reestablishing the Covenant

The consequence of a violation of the covenant is destruction, depicted in the form of a "Day of the Eternal," first appearing in the prophecies of Amos. Subsequently, this became a central image in prophetic and apocalyptic literature.[78] The imagery is militaristic in nature, depicting God as a divine warrior who will come and fight against God's enemies.[79] There are two possible outcomes to this ultimate battle. The first of these is the fulfillment of the oracles of destruction against other nations.[80] The second possible outcome is the destruction of Israel among the enemies of God. Amos warns Israel that divine vengeance could be directed against them as well.[81]

The prophets also share their visions of the day when the chastened people of Israel will return to the observance of the covenant—the day on which God will receive them back and reestablish justice in the world. Another, postexilic motif is the comfort the prophets offer to the dispersed Israelites in Babylonia: God would restore the Davidic monarchy when God's anointed (*mashiach*), an ideal ruler descended from the House of David, would again rule over Israel. However, once the Judeans were permitted to return to their land, they were not allowed to establish themselves as an independent kingdom, but only as a Persian province and a temple-state governed by a High Priest. The hope for a restored powerful kingship was therefore transformed into a religious aspiration for the far future. According to Sheldon Blank, this transformation involved three conceptual shifts: "1) that God takes the initiative and gives to mankind His messianic king, 2) that the king, though a shoot of the tree of Jesse, is idealized—and especially as concerns his moral nature, and 3) that the ideal is universalized for the benefit of all mankind and all nature."[82]

## Concluding Thoughts

Studying prophetic literature is like examining a multilayered onion. In the words of the famous poet William Blake:

> To see a World in a Grain of Sand
> And a Heaven in a Wild Flower
> Hold Infinity in the palm of your hand
> And Eternity in an hour.[83]

It has often been said that the calling of the prophets was twofold: to afflict and challenge those who are comfortable, but also to comfort those who are afflicted and challenged. If we seek to be inspired today by the biblical prophets, this might be their primary lesson.

No other text from the ancient world has had as great an influence as the Bible. The primary voices regarding social justice come from the Hebrew prophets; however, one of the core messages of the Bible is its condemnation of idolatry. Idolatry is more than the worship of molten or carved imagery. Idolatry is an expression of the harmful human tendency to concretize and absolutize what is subjective, historical, relative, and ambiguous.

At times, ironically, we treat the Bible itself as an idol. Yet, biblical figures from Abraham to Job argued with God. As we read the prophetic texts, may we engage with God and with each other as they did: openly, righteously, and for the sake of a better and more harmonious world.

## *The Prophets in Their Narrative and Historical Contexts*
### A. The Prophets of Legend

**THE UNITED MONARCHY**

| King | Prophet |
|---|---|
| Saul, 1025–1005 BCE | Samuel acts as both a priest under Eli and a prophet with Saul |
| David, 1005–965 BCE | Nathan (II Samuel 12:1–15) is a critic of David's misbehavior |
| | Gad (II Samuel 24:10–14) transmits divine knowledge and judgment regarding the king |
| Solomon, 968–928 BCE | Ahijah (I Kings 11:29–40) prophesizes the division of the kingdom due to Solomon's worship of other gods; rise of the Ephraimite Jeroboam ben Nebat as ruler of the Northern Kingdom |

**THE DIVIDED MONARCHY**

| Israel (Northern Kingdom) | | | Judah (Southern Kingdom) | |
|---|---|---|---|---|
| King | Prophet | Major Events | King | Prophet |
| Jeroboam, 928–907 BCE | | Invasion of Shishak from Egypt, 924 BCE | Rehoboam, 928–911 BCE | |
| Nadab, 907–906 BCE | Shemaiah (I Kings 12:22–24) | | Abijam, 911–908 BCE | |
| Baasha, 906–883 BCE | Jehu (I Kings 16:1–4) | | Asa, 908–867 BCE | |
| Elah, 883–882 BCE | | Battle of Qarqar in Syria, 853 BCE | Jehoshaphat, 870–846 BCE | |
| Zimri, 882 BCE | | 7-day reign | | |
| Omri, 882–871 BCE | | Political coup | | |
| Ahab and Queen Jezebel, 871–852 BCE | Elijah/Elisha and Micaiah (I Kings 22) | | | |

## B. The Literary Prophets

**THE DIVIDED MONARCHY**

| Israel (Northern Kingdom) | | | Judah (Southern Kingdom) | |
| King | Prophet | Major Events | King | Prophet |
| --- | --- | --- | --- | --- |
| Jeroboam II, 788–747 BCE | Amos | | Amaziah, 798–769 BCE | |
| Zechariah, 747 BCE | | | Uzziah, 785–733 BCE | Isaiah (active during reigns of Uzziah, Jotham, Ahaz, and Hezekiah) |
| Shallum, 747 BCE | | | | |
| Menahem, 747–737 BCE | | | Jotham, 759–743 BCE | |
| Pekahiah, 737–735 BCE | Hosea | Syro-Ephraimite War (civil war between Northern and Southern Kingdoms) | Ahaz, 743/735–727/715 BCE | |
| Pekah, 735–732 BCE | | | | |
| Hoshea, 732–722 BCE | | Fall of Samaria, 722 BCE | Hezekiah, 727/715–698/687 BCE | Micah (active during the reigns of Jotham, Ahaz, and Hezekiah) |
| | | Sennacherib's invasion, 701 BCE | Manasseh, 698/687–642 BCE | |
| | | Assyria declines in the second half of the 7th seventh century BCE; Babylon asserts its independence | Amon, 641–640 BCE | Nahum |

## B. The Literary Prophets, cont'd.
### Judah (Southern Kingdom)

| Major Events | King | Prophet |
| --- | --- | --- |
| Battle of Charchemish on the Euphrates between Assyria and Babylonia (II Kings 23:29) | Josiah, 640–609 BCE | Zephaniah (active during the reign of of Josiah) Habakkuk Huldah (II Kings 22:14) Jeremiah |
| | Jehoiakim (Eliakim), 608–598 BCE | Jeremiah |
| First Babylonian siege of Jerusalem | Jehoiachin, 597 BCE | Jeremiah |
| Babylonians capture and destroy the Southern Kingdom, 586 BCE | Zedekiah (Mattaniah) 597–586, BCE | Jeremiah |

### The Persian Period, 539–332 BCE

| Major Events | King | Prophet |
| --- | --- | --- |
| Jews return to Judah from Babylon, 538 BCE | | Obadiah Ezekiel "2nd" Isaiah |
| Temple reconstruction, 520–515 BCE | | Haggai Zechariah "3rd" Isaiah |
| | Nehemiah is governor 445–433, BCE | Noadiah (Nehemiah 6:14) Joel Malachi |

NOTE: This table reflects the traditional timeline of the Jewish Bible; modern academic research has led to a reevaluation of these dates and events.

NOTES

1. Akkadian was spoken in ancient Mesopotamia from the eighth century BCE until about the third century BCE (Sheldon Blank, *Understanding the Prophets* [New York: UAHC Press, 1969], 40).

2. Deuteronomy 33:1; I Samuel 2:27; I Kings 12:22; II Kings 1:12, 5:8.

3. I Samuel 9:6–10, and note particularly v. 9: "Formerly in Israel, when a person went to inquire of God, they would say, 'Come, let us go to the seer,' for the prophet [*navi*] of today was formerly called a seer [*ro-eh*]."

4. Archaeological evidence exists for prophets in Byblos in Phoenicia, at Hamath and Mari in Syria, and Assyria. Furthermore, there are biblical references to prophets among ancient Israel's neighbors—specifically the 450 prophets of Baal and 400 prophets of Asherah (I Kings 18:19; II Kings 10:19).

5. "For the king of Babylon has stood at the fork of the road, where two roads branch off, to perform divination: He has shaken arrows, consulted teraphim, and inspected the liver" (Ezekiel 21:26). "The elders of Moab and the elders of Midian, versed in divination, set out. They came to Balaam and gave him Balak's message" (Numbers 22:7). "Then the Philistines summoned the priests and the diviners and asked, 'What shall we do about the Ark of the Eternal? Tell us with what we shall send it off to its own place'" (I Samuel 6:2). "Egypt shall be drained of spirit, and I will confound its plans; so they will consult the idols and the shades and the ghosts and the familiar spirits" (Isaiah 19:3). King Joash used arrows to ensure victory (II Kings 13:15–19). Saul consulted with the Witch of Endor (I Samuel 28:7–14).

6. Exodus 28:30; Leviticus 8:8.

7. To determine a course of action (I Samuel 30:7); to choose a leader (I Samuel 10:20–21); to determine a guilty party when the material evidence was inconclusive (I Samuel 14:41–42).

8. "Lots are cast into the lap; the decision depends on the Eternal" (Proverbs 16:33).

9. Amos 5:21–25; Isaiah 1:10–17, 66:1–4; Jeremiah 6:20–21, 7:21–26; Hosea 6:4–6; Micah 6:6–8; Psalms 50 and 51.

10. II Kings 22:14.

11. Exodus 15:20; Judges 4:4; Nehemiah 6:14.

12 Isaiah 8:3.

13. Ezekiel 13:17; Joel 3:1.

14. Joel 3:1–5 (in the Christian Bible, which divides up chapters and verses differently, this appears at the end of chapter 2).

15. The Book of Judges describes the need for a king and the problems the "judges" as leaders experience. It repeats the formula "in those days there was no king in Israel" four times in the final five chapters. It defines a proper king as an Othniel-like figure from Judah (Judges 3:7–11). The king cannot come from the Northern Kingdom nor from Gibeah (i.e., not Saul). The narrative in which the Israelites do ask for a king to replace the last chieftain ("judge") does not appear until I Samuel 8.

16. I Samuel 9.

17. II Kings 6:12: "Elisha, that prophet in Israel, tells the king of Israel the very words you speak in your bedroom."

18. I Samuel 9:6–8: Saul hires *ish Elohim* (a man of God) to help find his donkey.

19. I Samuel 10:10: Saul temporarily becomes an ad hoc prophet when he falls under the grip of ecstasy and joins a band of prophets (*chevel n'vi-im*).

20. II Kings 3:15: Elisha listens to music to prepare to receive prophecy. Others would enter dream states.
21. Elijah and Elisha are both depicted as miracle workers—they feed the masses with a small amount of food, revive the dead, find lost objects, make poisoned food safe, heal lepers, etc.
22. I Kings 17:1: Elijah the Tishbite from Gilead speaks to Ahab, king of the Northern Kingdom of Israel.
23. Elisha kills children who make fun of him (II Kings 2:23–25) and produces excessive amounts of oil for a needy widow in II Kings 4.
24. The former prophets predict the future, as in Elijah's final words to King Ahab, "As the Eternal lives, the God of Israel whom I serve, there will be no dew or rain except at my bidding" (I Kings 17:1), but that is not their primary focus.
25. Martin Noth in 1943 argued that this large literary unit was based on Deuteronomist ideology, which focused on the primacy of Jerusalem. His work has largely found acceptance by scholars to this day.
26. II Samuel 7:16.
27. II Samuel 12 (quote is v. 7).
28. Tekoa is located in Judah approximately ten miles south of Jerusalem.
29. Bethel was the southernmost edge of the Northern Kingdom, only ten to eleven miles north of Jerusalem.
30. Zechariah 14:5.
31. Hosea 11.
32. Isaiah 13–14.
33. This is stated in the introduction to the account of his inaugural vision, Isaiah 6. This vision is similar to that of Micaiah ben Imlah in I Kings 22. The ability of both of these prophets to see God seated on a throne is in opposition to a biblical tradition that mortals cannot see God and live, as described in Exodus 33:20.
34. Isaiah 7–8.
35. Isaiah 20.
36. Isaiah 1.
37. Micah 4.
38. Nahum is from an unknown location called Elkosh.
39. Nahum 1.
40. This same prophecy in the final chapters of Nahum offers imagery that is later picked up in the Christian Book of Revelation, where it describes divine vengeance against Rome.
41. Zephaniah is a descendant of Hezekiah, who may or may not be the king by that name. Zephaniah's father is named Cushi or Ethiopian. The early referencing of his genealogy ensures that he is not thought of as a foreigner.
42. II Kings 23:29 and Jeremiah 1. II Chronicles 35:20–27, on the other hand, suggests that Josiah was killed in battle.
43. Anathoth is located three miles northeast of Jerusalem. Solomon banished the priest Abiathar there after he supported Solomon's brother Adonijah (I Kings 2:26–27). Jeremiah is thought to be descended from this priestly line.
44. Jeremiah 1:1.
45. Jeremiah 3:14: "Turn back, rebellious children—declares the Eternal, since I have espoused you."

46. Jeremiah 32.

47. Jeremiah's eschatological picture differed from those of Amos and Isaiah. Amos thought that there would be agricultural bounty (Amos 9:13). Isaiah envisioned a wolf dwelling with a lamb (Isaiah 11:6–8). Jeremiah describes a new covenant inscribed on the hearts of those who engage it (Jeremiah 31:31–34).

48. This same opening oracle was interpreted five hundred years later in the Pesher Habakkuk from Qumran as referring to Rome. The authors of this commentary correlated the Babylonian military machine with that of Rome.

49. Habakkuk 1:2.

50. Habakkuk 2.

51. Ezekiel 1:1–3.

52. Ezra also describes how the King of Persia authorized the Jews to return and resume worship (Ezra 1).

53. "Apocalypse" is derived from the Greek word for revelation. In apocalyptic literature, revelation is described as mediated by an otherworldly being to a human being.

54. Malachi 3:1.

55. Amos 1:2 refers to God "roaring from Zion"; a similar verse appears in Joel 4:16.

56. The copying of this material was not simply "cold storage." This material was *used* and played a part in daily life. The purposes may have been literacy instruction, royal propaganda, or simply record keeping. In some cases, like those of psalms, songs, prayers, and priestly instructions, they may have been placed in a temple or court. Even within the biblical canon, interpretation of earlier material is found; later biblical books frequently mention or allude to earlier books and often modify or change the text.

57. The long books are considered the Major Prophets (Isaiah is sixty-six chapters, Jeremiah is fifty-two chapters, and Ezekiel is forty-eight chapters). The Christian tradition places the Book of Daniel after Ezekiel, but Jewish tradition places this book in the Writings section.

58. The Minor Prophets consist of shorter books, ranging in length from Hosea and Zechariah (fourteen chapters each) to Obadiah, which is only one chapter long.

59. Other religious texts, such as the letter of Paul in the Christian Bible and the suras of the Qur'an, are also arranged by length.

60. For example, the narrator in Amos 7:10–17 is not Amaziah, Jeroboam, or Amos.

61. They include covenant lawsuits (discussed below); oracles against the nations; judgment oracles, messenger speeches, songs or hymns, call narratives, laments, laws, proverbs, symbolic gestures, prayers, wisdom sayings, and visions.

62. Isaiah 13–23; Jeremiah 46–51; Ezekiel 25–32; Amos 1–2; Zephaniah 2:4–15; Zechariah 9:1–8; Obadiah and Nahum in their entirety. The origins of this type of oracle are obscure but may be related to specific oracles offered during a time of war (II Kings 13:17). The first appearance of these oracles occurs in the Book of Amos. They express the belief that God controls the entire world.

63. Babylonian Talmud, *Bava Batra* 14b–15a.

64. Those prophets described in the Books of Samuel and Kings who do not have books of their own.

65. Babylonian Talmud, *M'gillah* 14a.

66. The Rabbis of the Talmud and Rashi disagree on who are the male prophets. The accepted list is as follows: Abraham, Isaac, Jacob, Moses, Aaron, Joshua, Pinchas,

Elkanah, Eli, Samuel, Gad, Nathan, King David, King Solomon, Aidoin the Golah, Micha ben Yamla, Obadiah, Achiah Hashiloni, Yehu ben Hanani, Azaryah ben Oded, Haziel from B'nei Masni, Eliezer his cousin, Morishah, Hosea, Amos, Micah, Elijah, Elisha, Jonah ben Amittai, Isaiah, Joel, Nahum, Habakkuk, Zephaniah, Uriah, Jeremiah, Eziekel, Daniel, Baruch, Nariah, Sharyah, Machsiyah, Haggai, Zechariah, Malachi, Mordecai; female prophets: Sarah, Miriam, Deborah, Hannah, Abigail, Huldah, and Esther (Babylonian Talmud, *M'gillah* 3a, 14a).

67. Sheldon Blank, *Understanding the Prophets* (New York: UAHC Press, 1969), 87.

68. Isaiah 40:1.

69. William F. Albright, *From the Stone Age to Christianity* (Baltimore: Johns Hopkins University Press, 1957).

70. John Bright, *A History of Israel* (Louisville, KY: Westminster John Knox, 2000).

71. Israel Finkelstein and Neil Asher Silberman, *The Bible Unearthed: Archaeology's New Vision of Ancient Israel and the Origins of Its Sacred Texts* (New York: Free Press, 2001).

72. Brevard S. Childs, *Introduction to the Old Testament as Scripture* (Philadelphia: Fortress Press, 1979); Robert Alter, *The Art of Biblical Narrative* (New York: Basic Books, 1981).

73. Genesis 12:1.

74. "Hear the word of the Eternal, O people of Israel! For the Eternal has a case against the inhabitants of this land, because there is no honesty and no goodness and no obedience to God in the land. [False] swearing, dishonesty, and murder, and theft and adultery are rife; crime follows upon crime! For that, the earth is withered: everything that dwells on it languishes—beasts of the field and birds of the sky—even the fish of the sea perish" (Hosea 4:1–3).

75. Amos 2:6–7.

76. Amos 5:21–25; Isaiah 1:10–17, 66:1–4; Jeremiah 6:20–21, 7:21–26; Hosea 6:4–6; Micah 6:6–8.

77. I Samuel 15:22–23.

78. Malachi 3:19–21.

79. Jeremiah 46:10; Joel 2:11.

80. Isaiah 13:6, 13:9; Jeremiah 46:10; Ezekiel 30:3.

81. Amos 5:20.

82. Blank, *Understanding the Prophets*, 105.

83. William Blake, "Auguries of Innocence," in *Poets of the English Language* (New York: Viking Press, 1950), https://www.poetryfoundation.org/poems/43650/auguries-of-innocence.

*BIBLIOGRAPHY OF ADDITIONAL SUGGESTED SOURCES*

Blenkinsopp, Joseph. *A History of Prophecy in Israel*. Louisville, KY: Westminster John Knox, 1996.

Coogan, M.D., ed. *The Oxford History of the Biblical World*. New York: Oxford University Press, 1998.

Fishbane, Michael. *The JPS Bible Commentary: Haftarot*. Philadelphia: Jewish Publication Society, 2002.

Miller, Patrick. *The Religion of Ancient Israel*. Louisville KY: Westminster John Knox, 2000.

Nissinen, Martti. *Prophets and Prophecy in the Ancient Near East*. Atlanta: Society of Biblical Literature, 2003.

Peterson, David L. *The Prophetic Literature: An Introduction*. Louisville, KY: Westminster John Knox, 2002.

Podhoretz, Norman. *The Prophets: Who They Were, What They Are*. New York: Free Press, 2002.

Sweeney, Martin. *The Prophetic Literature*. Nashville, TN: Abingdon, 2005.

# Readings from the Prophets

## The History and Significance of the Haftarah Readings in Rabbinic Judaism and in the Reform Movement

*Rabbi Richard S. Sarason, PhD*

P UBLIC READING and study of the Torah on Shabbat has been a central religious activity among Jews at least since the origins of the synagogue as a place of communal gathering during the late Second Commonwealth period (roughly the late first century BCE). It is even older, in the synagogue setting, than regular public prayer, about which we have no evidence (at least in the Land of Israel) until after the Temple's destruction. A reading from the Prophets, as a counterpoint to and conclusion of the weekly Torah reading, is first known to us from early Rabbinic literature, developing in the second century CE.[1]

The Mishnah (ca. 200 CE) prescribes the practice on Shabbat mornings of "concluding [the reading of sacred Scripture] with the Prophets" (*maftirin banavi*; *Mishnah M'gillah* 4:1–3), from which language the activity derives its name, *haftarah*, meaning "conclusion" or "dismissal."[2] From the Mishnah and its accompanying *Tosefta*[3] we learn other details about how this "conclusion" was to be performed: the prophetic reading would be brief, generally no more than three verses in length, and the reader could skip around in the scroll, but not between scrolls (the Twelve Minor Prophets formed a single scroll, while Isaiah, Jeremiah, and Ezekiel each took up a full scroll).[4] The brevity of the prophetic reading here is in line with the brevity prescribed for the Torah reading as well: each of the seven Torah readers on Shabbat morning read minimally three verses apiece, and it would take between three and a half and four years to complete reading the entire Torah.[5]

What is not explicit in early Rabbinic literature is the rationale for a weekly prophetic reading. Some have suggested that it was motivated by a desire to "complete" the Torah reading with another, thematically complementary reading from the rest of Scripture—and that indeed is the rationale behind the medieval cycles of haftarah readings.

However, there is another possibility as well. It is noteworthy that early Rabbinic communal prayer heavily emphasizes petitions for divine redemption and the restoration of the Jewish people to their land, Temple, and sovereignty. This is also a major preoccupation of the Prophets. The canon of prophetic literature had been forged in the crucible of catastrophe and exile after the destruction of the First Temple: not only did it explain the loss of land, Temple, and sovereignty as a direct result of the people's disobedience to God's laws, but it also provided hope and reassurance for a future restoration if the now-chastened people returned to God and obeyed those laws. Such prophetic consolations embodying divine promises of redemption from the time of the first exile—most of them found in the last third of the Book of Isaiah—would have been deemed appropriately hopeful and uplifting to serve as conclusions to the public reading of Scripture in the wake of the second destruction and dispersal. (They are used in the same fashion to conclude rabbinic midrashic homilies with words of divine promise and encouragement.)

This surmise is borne out by the citation (*Tosefta M'gillah* 3:18) of Isaiah 52:3 as a permissible one-verse haftarah that is deemed both rhetorically and thematically complete in itself:

> For thus says the Eternal One:
> As you were sold for nothing,
> so you shall be redeemed without money.

It is also borne out by the content of the blessings that surround the haftarah reading.[6] There, the words of the prophets are lauded as true and trustworthy, while God is praised as just and faithful to fulfill them in the future. The prophetic words referred to, of course, are the divine promises of redemption to a repentant people.

Early Rabbinic literature does not yet know a fixed weekly cycle of haftarah readings (*Mishnah M'gillah* 3:6; *Tosefta M'gillah* 3:10).[7] Only the haftarot for the four special Sabbaths that precede Rosh Chodesh Nisan, the month in which Pesach falls, are specified (*Tosefta M'gillah* 3:1–4). These bear a thematic relation to both the occasion and the specified Torah readings for those Sabbaths that interrupt the otherwise continuous reading of the Torah.[8]

Haftarot for other special occasions appear for the first time in *P'sikta D'Rav Kahana*, a fifth-century midrashic compilation from the Land of Israel that expounds on scriptural readings for the Festivals, High Holy Days, and other special times. Here we find the cycle of haftarot that frame the Ninth of Av: the three of affliction preceding it, in which Isaiah and Jeremiah castigate the people for their backslidings, and the seven of consolation following it and leading up to Rosh HaShanah, in which the anonymous exilic prophet whose words form chapters 40–66 of the

Book of Isaiah promises divine redemption and restoration to the despondent exiles. This cycle is a liturgical enactment of the Rabbis' understanding of the Jewish historical experience as moving from destruction and catastrophe to redemption and renewal through acts of repentance. Thus, we also find here the haftarah for Shabbat Shuvah, the "Sabbath of Repentance" between Rosh HaShanah and Yom Kippur. These haftarot have been chosen because of their thematic relevance to the season or occasion; they are not related to any specific Torah readings (since none were ever specially designated for these Shabbatot).

By the seventh century, the Babylonian Talmud (*M'gillah* 30a, citing and elaborating on the tradition of *Tosefta M'gillah* 3:5–9) lists haftarot for all of the Festivals and High Holy Days, Chanukah, Purim, Rosh Chodesh, and fast days. A later gloss gives the Torah and haftarah readings for the second days of the Festivals in the Diaspora; these correspond pretty much to the traditional readings today. All relate thematically to the prescribed Torah readings and to the occasions on which they are read.

We know very little about specific haftarot for regular Shabbatot. Different Torah reading customs prevailed in the Land of Israel and in Babylonia. In the Land, it was customary to read shorter weekly passages (*s'darim*; sing., *seder* or *sidra*) and to take as long as four years to finish reading the entire Torah, while in Babylonia, the Torah would be read over the period of a year, which required longer weekly readings (*parashiyot*; sing., *parashah*). This means that there would have been more passages from the Prophets read as haftarot in the Land of Israel, though some might have served more than one Torah section.

A fascinating glimpse into passages read as haftarot in the Land of Israel in the late fifth and sixth centuries (at least in some places) comes from the liturgical poetry (*piyutim*) of Yannai and his successors, which has been preserved in the fragmentary prayer books and collections of the Cairo Genizah. These are multi-poem sequences (generally nine poems per week) that are recited during the Shabbat morning *Amidah*. They link the content of the week's Torah reading to the themes of the *Amidah*'s first three blessings and lead up to the recitation of the *K'dushah*. The first two poems in each cycle cite the first and second verses respectively of the week's Torah reading, while the third poem in the cycle cites the first verse of the haftarah. Generally, these align with the themes, and particularly with the first key words, in the Torah reading. For example:

1. For a Torah reading beginning at Genesis 8:15, "Go out of the ark," Yannai's haftarah is Isaiah 42:7, "To open eyes that are blind, to bring the captive out of confinement, those who sit in darkness, out of the dungeon." Metaphorically, this refers to God releasing Noah and

his family from their confinement in the ark, but also thematically to God's future redemption of Israel, bringing them forth from the confinement of exile. Additionally, there is verbal play between *tzei*, "go out," in the Torah reading and *l'hotzi*, "rescuing/bringing out," in the haftarah.

2. Similarly, for a Torah reading beginning at Genesis 16:1, "Now Abram's wife Sarai, who had not borne him a child," Yannai's haftarah is Isaiah 54:1, "Sing, O barren woman who has never given birth." The pairing is thematically apt; the prophet refers metaphorically to barren Jerusalem whose exiled children are destined to return to her. Again, there is verbal play: the phrase *lo yaldah/yaladah*, "she has not given birth," appears in *both* verses.

Note that in both cases, God's past actions on behalf of the Torah's protagonists serve as paradigms for, and assurances of, God's future actions on behalf of Israel, their descendants. Note, too, that neither of these Torah verses serves as the beginning of a weekly reading in the annual cycle. Isaiah 54 serves as a haftarah twice in the annual cycle, but never in conjunction with the story of Sarah.[9]

What has been remarked on in these examples in fact is characteristic of all the known haftarot of the so-called triennial cycle observed in the Land of Israel.[10] There is almost always a verbal link between the first or second verses of the Torah reading and the first verse of the haftarah. Additionally, the haftarah generally consoles with a promise of future restoration of Israel, a kind of messianic peroration, with or without a strong thematic link to the Torah reading.[11]

The annual cycle of Torah readings, which is current today, was customary in Babylonia and likely originated there, since it is unknown in Rabbinic literature from the Land of Israel. Both the Torah and haftarah readings in this cycle are longer than those of the triennial cycle. The relationship of the haftarot to the Torah readings is generally thematic. For example:

1. The Song of Deborah (Judges 5) is paired with the Song at the Sea (Exodus 15).
2. Isaiah's temple vision of God on the divine throne surrounded by heavenly beings (Isaiah 6) is paired with the revelation at Sinai (Exodus 19–20).
3. The story of Samson and his Nazirite vow (Judges 13) is paired with the laws of the Nazirite (Numbers 6).
4. The dedication of Solomon's Temple (I Kings 7–8) is paired with the dedication of the Tabernacle in the wilderness (Exodus 35–38).

However, the thematic link is sometimes superficial or based on an extended Rabbinic interpretation of the Torah portion. For example:

1. The story of Elijah (I Kings 18) is paired with the story of Pinchas (Numbers 25), on the basis of a Rabbinic tradition that Elijah *was* Pinchas, since both are described as having been particularly zealous for God.

2. Isaiah 40:27–41:16 is the haftarah for the story of Abraham's departure from Haran because 41:8 describes Israel as "offspring of Abraham My friend," but also because the Rabbis understood 41:2, "Who has roused [a champion] from the east, [one] whom triumph meets at every step," as referring to Abraham.

Often, as in the instance just noted, the connection between the haftarah and the Torah portion in the annual cycle is not evident from the first verse of either, unlike in the triennial cycle. The haftarot to the Book of Deuteronomy and the end of Numbers in the annual cycle are completely unrelated to their weekly Torah readings, because they comprise the ten prophetic readings of affliction and consolation that bridge the Ninth of Av and Rosh HaShanah, following the older custom from the Land of Israel.

Roughly, by the end of the ninth century, the traditional haftarah reading cycle as we know it today reached its basic form in Babylonia—and, notwithstanding some regional variations, remained fairly stable throughout the following centuries until, in the nineteenth century, a newly emerging movement began to question this ancient form and its messages.

The movement for religious reform in Judaism, beginning in Germany in the early decades of the nineteenth century and in America several decades later, was perhaps the most prominent early Jewish response to modern Western cultural and religious change, marked particularly by the reform of the public worship service. Early on, there was a move to abbreviate that service, partly to provide more time for edifying weekly sermons in the vernacular. A weekly Torah reading still took pride of place, but much shortened. To facilitate this, some communities (such as Hamburg and, under Rabbi Abraham Geiger, Breslau) by the 1840s and '50s were creating their own triennial cycles, whereby the entire Torah would be read over a period of three years without regard to the text divisions of the annual cycle. In some communities, such as Hamburg, the haftarah reading was eliminated in order to shorten the service. In others, such as Breslau, a brief prophetic selection was read by the rabbi. It is not clear from Geiger's 1854 prayer book whether this selection would have been chosen by him and whether it would have been read in Hebrew or German.[12]

Geiger was one of the first Reform thinkers to hold that a meaningful Judaism for the modern age must draw primarily upon the prophetic tradition emphasizing personal morality and social ethics. As Michael Meyer has written:

What Geiger preached from the pulpit and attempted to draw from all of its classical texts was what he called "Prophetic Judaism." The message of Israel's ancient Prophets, universalized beyond its original context, became for Geiger, as for the Reform movement, the most viable and important component of Judaism. The Prophets' concerns for the poor and downtrodden, their contempt for ritual acts unaccompanied by social morality, and their vision of peace for all humanity—these made Amos, Isaiah, Micah, and the others both timely and contemporary. Their ideals and faith in the one God as their source, Geiger argued, . . . were the eternal elements in Judaism.[13]

In their worship services, the Reform emphasis on prophetic social ethics was most evident in rabbinic sermons.[14] Its impact on haftarah selections can only be gauged from those published prayer books that listed such selections. The first such book was that of Rabbi David Einhorn, *Olat Tamid* ("A Perpetual Offering"), for Baltimore's Har Sinai Congregation in 1858.

Rabbi Einhorn compiled his own triennial cycle of Torah readings (159 in all) and chose a haftarah for each. Novel here is that he included selections from the Writings (particularly Psalms and Proverbs, but also Ruth, Daniel, Job, Ecclesiastes, Lamentations, and Chronicles) as well as from the Prophets (mostly the literary prophets—42 percent of the total—but occasionally Joshua, Judges, Samuel, and Kings). Expanding the range of haftarot to the Writings allowed Rabbi Einhorn to include a wider variety of edifying texts that exhort to, and exemplify, piety and right conduct. While not every selection deals with issues of morality or social ethics, most amplify and generalize whatever moral or religious themes are adumbrated in the brief Torah readings, to which all relate thematically. Here are a few examples:

1. For Genesis 2:18–24, the creation of the first woman from the first man, the haftarah is Proverbs 31:10–31, "A woman of valor who can find?"

2. For Genesis 3, the first humans' disobedience and their expulsion from the Garden of Eden, the haftarah is Ezekiel 18, the prophet's assertion that children will not be punished for the sins of their parents, but only for their own misdeeds (surely this is Einhorn rejecting the use of Genesis 3 to ground the Christian doctrine of original sin).

3. The haftarah for Genesis 17, God's renewal of the covenant with Abraham, is Jeremiah 31:27–37, the new covenant that will be made with Israel in the messianic era.

4. The haftarah for Genesis 18, the story of Sodom and Gomorrah, is Ezekiel 16:44–63, where Israel's backsliding is compared to that of

the Sodomites who, in their arrogance, refused to support the poor and the needy.

5. The two haftarot chosen for two readings from Leviticus 19 ("You shall be holy" and rules dealing with the stranger and fair weights and measures) appropriately deal with social ethics—Psalm 15 ("Eternal, who may sojourn in Your tent?") and Isaiah 2 ("Torah shall go forth from Zion and God's word from Jerusalem"), though only one of them is from the prophetic canon.

The 1894–95 *Union Prayer Book*, the first official liturgical publication of the CCAR, was heavily influenced by Einhorn but differs in its specific treatment of scriptural readings. In place of Einhorn's triennial cycle, *UPB* offers an annual Torah reading cycle of abbreviated readings that differ from those of the traditional annual cycle, although they follow the order of the Torah text. The readings were chosen for their edifying content; ritual laws were excluded, as were morally offensive narratives. There are, for example, many more weeks of brief readings from Genesis and only five highly selective readings from Leviticus (all dealing with social ethics or the festival calendar).[15] As with Einhorn, haftarot are drawn mostly from the literary prophets (80 percent), but also from the Writings (Proverbs, Job, Ecclesiastes, Ruth, Ezra, Nehemiah, Chronicles), and occasionally from Joshua, Samuel, and Kings. Unlike Einhorn, there are no haftarot from Psalms.[16] The haftarah selections have been chosen for their thematic relevance to the Torah readings, again mostly amplifying and generalizing whatever moral or religious themes are adumbrated in those excerpts. So, for example:

1. The haftarah for Genesis 4, the story of Cain and Abel, is Proverbs 3:11–12, "My son, despise not the chastenings of the Eternal . . . for whom God loveth, the Eternal correcteth even as a father the son in whom he delighteth."

2. The haftarah for Genesis 21, the story of the banished Hagar finding a well to slake Ishmael's thirst, is Isaiah 49:10, "Therefore with joy shall you draw water out of the wells of salvation."

3. The haftarah for Exodus 18, Jethro's arrival in the Israelite camp, is Isaiah 42:1, "Behold my servant, whom I uphold . . . I give thee for a covenant of the people, for a light of the Gentiles" (clearly mindful of the Rabbinic tradition that Jethro was a convert to the religion of Israel).

4. The haftarah for Exodus 20, the Ten Commandments, is Jeremiah 7:3, God requires ethical conduct and obedience rather than sacrifices, "Mend your ways and your actions, and I will let you dwell in this place."

The two revisions of the *Union Prayer Book* (from 1918 and 1940) revert to giving tables of scriptural readings, compiled respectively by Rabbis Kaufmann Kohler and Solomon B. Freehof. They both retain the *parashiyot* of the traditional annual Torah cycle but give multiple alternative brief readings from each *parashah*: between two and five in 1918, and consistently three in 1940, thereby creating the potential for a kind of triennial cycle within the annual cycle. Each alternative Torah reading within the *parashah* is provided with a haftarah. By and large, the variation between the two revisions with respect to Torah reading selections is minor; the haftarah selections vary a bit more—though the percentage of haftarot from the Prophets is virtually the same (48 percent in 1918, 46 percent in 1940). Once again, there are many haftarot from the Writings as well, including Psalms, Proverbs, Job, Ecclesiastes, Daniel, and Chronicles, as well as occasional haftarot from Joshua, Judges, Samuel, and Kings. It is not surprising that most of the chapters from the second part of Isaiah (40–66) are represented in the haftarah selections of both revisions.

Following are some examples of divergences between the two revisions in their selections of haftarot from the literary prophets:

1. For Genesis 22, the Binding of Isaac, the haftarah in 1918 is Isaiah 48:1–19, "I test you in the furnace of affliction" (v. 10), while in 1940 it is Micah 6:1–8, "It has been told you, O mortal, what is good" (v. 8). The latter passage has no direct connection to the Torah reading; it is simply a statement of religious and social ideals.

2. For Genesis 25:19–34, the young Jacob and Esau, the haftarah in 1918 is Isaiah 41:1–16, "Have no fear, you worm Jacob . . . I will help you" (v. 14), while in 1940 it is Malachi 1:1–11, "Is not Esau Jacob's brother? says the Eternal One. But I have loved Jacob, and hated Esau" (vv. 2–3). The latter is the beginning of the traditional haftarah for this *parashah* (*Tol'dot*); the former references Jacob in passing but also includes the theme of Israel as God's chosen servant.

3. For Exodus 6:2–13, where God reveals to Moses the divine proper name and promises to redeem the Israelites from Egyptian slavery, the haftarah in 1918 is Isaiah 42:5–17, "[I] made you a covenant people, a light to the nations" (v. 6), while in 1940 it is Ezekiel 28:25–29:16, "Set your face against Pharaoh king of Egypt" (29:2). While the latter is the traditional haftarah for this *parashah* (*Va-eira*), it also begins with God's promise to "[make] manifest My holiness there [the House of Israel] in the sight of the nations" (28:25). Both selections thus adumbrate the theme of Israel's special status in the sight

of the nations and are favorite proof texts for Reform understandings of the "mission of Israel."

4. For Leviticus 26:3–13, the blessings of the covenant, the haftarah in 1918 is Micah 6:1–8, "It has been told you, O mortal, what is good" (v. 8), and in 1940 it is Jeremiah 16:19–17:14, the traditional haftarah for this parashah (*B'chukotai*) which is a mixture of affliction and consolation.

It is noteworthy that, with two exceptions, the 1940 revision gives the traditional Ashkenazic haftarah (sometimes abbreviated) as the first option each week, which is not the case with the 1918 revision. This difference between the two should be understood in light of the reincorporation of more traditional texts and rituals generally in the 1940 revision.

That trend toward the inclusion of more tradition (as well as providing more options and more variety) increased over the next thirty-five years and is characteristic of the next CCAR liturgy, *Gates of Prayer* (1975). The table of scriptural readings for this prayer book, compiled by Rabbi A. Stanley Dreyfus, lists the traditional Torah readings *and* haftarah readings (both Ashkenazic and Sephardic) according to the annual cycle, but also gives multiple haftarah alternatives for each *parashah* (for a total of between two and nine options each week).[17] Once again, texts from the Writings (Psalms, Proverbs, Job, Ecclesiastes, Lamentations, Ezra, and Chronicles) appear among the options, and most of the selections are from the literary prophets. Here, for the first time, we find haftarah options that appear more than once and are associated with more than one Torah reading in the table. A revised and expanded version of this table, by Chaim Stern, appears in *On the Doorposts of Your House* (1994; rev. 2010) and contains yet further haftarah options. Like the *UPB* revisions and unlike Dreyfus, Stern subdivides each of the annual *parashiyot* into multiple shorter readings, between two and four, and provides haftarah options (sometimes more than one) for each of these short Torah readings. He also provides alternative Torah readings, mostly from Deuteronomy, for those portions of Exodus, Leviticus, and Numbers that deal with the building of the Tabernacle and the priestly cultic laws.[18]

Following are some examples of new additional haftarah options and some multiple reuses from the literary prophets in the Dreyfus and Stern lists:

1. For the story of the Tower of Babel in *Parashat Noach*, Dreyfus lists Isaiah 14:12–20, the fall of the mythical Heilel ben Shahar who once aspired to "climb to the sky and match the Most High"—a condemnation of hubris.

2. One of Dreyfus's haftarot for *Lech L'cha* is Joel 2:21–3:2, God's prom-

ise to repay Israel with prosperity for the famine caused by swarms of locusts. This likely is intended to align with Genesis 12:10–20, the famine in the land that prompts Abram's descent into Egypt. The haftarah ends with a favorite Reform text, in which God promises to pour out the spirit of prophecy upon all: "Your old shall dream dreams, and your young shall see visions" (Joel 3:1). Dreyfus then repeats this selection as an option for *Sh'mot*, the beginning of the story of Moses, including his call at the Burning Bush, and for Numbers 11, "Would that all the Eternal's people were prophets!" (v. 29) (here carrying forward the selection from the two revisions of *UPB*).

3. For the story of Jacob earning the name Israel in *Vayishlach*, Dreyfus gives Isaiah 44:6–21, where "one shall . . . take the name 'Jacob.' Another shall . . . be known as 'Israel'" (v. 5). Here, too, the haftarah concludes with a beloved Reform text: "For you are My servant, O Israel: I formed you, you are My servant" (v. 21), adumbrating the mission of Israel theme.

4. Jeremiah 31:23–36, a text of comfort and restoration promising a new covenant with Israel, is deployed four times by Dreyfus as a haftarah option: for Genesis 8, the rainbow covenant with Noah (where the haftarah begins at v. 31); for Exodus 19, the covenant at Sinai (where the haftarah begins at v. 23); for Exodus 34, the restoration of the covenant after the sin of the Golden Calf (where the haftarah begins at v. 31); and for Deuteronomy 29:9, *Nitzavim*, the renewal of the covenant before crossing the Jordan and entering the Land of Israel (where the haftarah begins at v. 27).

5. For Exodus 19, Stern flexibly supplies a selection of verses from Isaiah 42 (1–4), 45 (22–24), and 48 (17–19), which together adumbrate the mission of Israel theme: "This is My servant, whom I uphold" (42:1), "Turn to Me and be saved, all the ends of the earth" (45:22), and "If only you would heed My commands" (48:18).

6. Stern repeats this technique when supplying a haftarah for Deuteronomy 10:12–20, which itself is given as an alternative Torah reading for *Parashat Tzav* (dealing with cultic responsibilities of the priesthood). Deuteronomy 10:12–20 is a classic ethical-pious text, exhorting the Israelites to revere God and walk in God's paths by providing food and clothing for the needy and the foreigner; this is the kind of social behavior that is required by Israel's chosen status. The haftarah verses are Jeremiah 7:21–28, 8:7–9, and 9:22–23, which together form a concerted essay reiterating the Torah lesson: God

did not enjoin sacrifices upon Israel's forebears, but rather earnest devotion and imitation of God's acts of kindness, justice, and equity in the world.

7. Similarly, Stern gives selected verses from Zechariah (7:4–10, 8:16–19) to reinforce the ethical message of *K'doshim*, Leviticus 19:1–4 and 9–18: God does not want empty fasting, but rather true loyalty; compassionate conduct toward those who are socially and economically disadvantaged—the poor, the orphan, the widow, the stranger; and justice for all.

Noteworthy in the Stern list is its marked selectivity of verses. Whereas the *UPB* and Dreyfus lists give short, focused readings, they rarely skip around in or between chapters of the chosen book. Stern does this routinely, honing in on specific messages and their reiteration. In fact, were one looking for a haftarah list that consistently exemplifies the classical Reform themes of social justice and the mission of Israel, it would, ironically, be the most recent list, that of Stern from 1994/2010 rather than the older lists of Einhorn or the *Union Prayer Book*!

Finally, we come to the list of haftarot that is most frequently used in contemporary North American Reform congregations, that of W. Gunther Plaut in *The Torah: A Modern Commentary* (1981; revised edition, 2005).[19] Because the Plaut volume is a handy, all-in-one-book compilation with full Torah and haftarah texts on the page, it has easily surpassed the alternatives.[20] The haftarot in Plaut's volume, with few exceptions, are the traditional haftarot for each *parashah*, although many of them are shortened. The most glaring exception is the haftarah for Shabbat Zachor, the Sabbath before Purim. Here, instead of the traditional, rather bloodthirsty, haftarah from I Samuel 15:2–34, in which the Israelites under divine command slaughter all the Amalekites, and the prophet Samuel vivisects the Amalekite king Agag (for the Rabbis, the ancestor of Haman the Agagite), Plaut gives a selection from the Book of Esther (7:1–10, 8:15–17).[21] But he reinstates the traditional reading in his 1996 volume *The Haftarah Commentary*. He also gives fifty additional readings at the end of that volume, many from Psalms, that had appeared as alternatives on earlier Reform lists.

While the present volume continues broadly in the tradition of its predecessors, one of its aims is to reinvigorate the more creative and adventurous approach to choosing weekly haftarot on display most recently in the list of Chaim Stern. What in the Prophets and the Writings speaks to us today and also aligns interpretively and expansively with the message(s) of each week's Torah portion? What are the voices around us that augment our tradition? How can the words of our prophets and sages—their admonitions, hopes, dreams, and visions—come alive for us today, provoking and challenging, providing hope and comfort? These are the challenges to be explored and exemplified here.

NOTES

1. The earliest literary reference to Sabbath public readings from both the Torah and the Prophets in synagogues in fact is found in early Christian literature. Luke-Acts, generally dated to the end of the first or beginning of the second century CE and reflecting the social realities of its author's time more than those of its protagonists, depicts Paul speaking in a synagogue in Antioch of Pisidia in Asia Minor, "after the reading of the Law and the Prophets" (Acts 13:15) and Jesus standing up to read in a synagogue in Nazareth where "a scroll of the prophet Isaiah was given to him" (Luke 4:17). Since the latter reference does not mention a reading from the "Law," and the prophetic passage read by Jesus is germane to the author's theological message, the historical accuracy of its details is suspect. There is ample evidence, both literary (Philo and Josephus) and inscriptional, from the late Second Commonwealth period for public reading and study of the Torah on Sabbaths in synagogues, both in the Land of Israel and in Alexandria, Egypt.

2. *Mishnah M'gillah* 4:1–3 in fact states that "we do not conclude from the Prophets" when the Torah is read on Monday and Thursday mornings, Shabbat afternoons, Rosh Chodesh, and the intermediate days of the Festivals, thereby implying that this *was* to be done when the Torah was read on Shabbat and Festival mornings. (There is later evidence for a reading from the Prophets on Shabbat afternoons in some places.) The noun *haftarah* first appears later, in the Babylonian Talmud (*M'gillah* 30b) and in *Midrash T'hillim* (18:8, with reference to one of the blessings after the haftarah reading). The Aramaic verbal equivalent, *ashlam*, "conclude," appears in the Talmud of the Land of Israel (Jerusalem Talmud, *N'darim* 6:8, 40a = Jerusalem Talmud, *Sanhedrin* 1:2, 19a).

3. The *Tosefta* (third century CE) contains extra-Mishnaic traditions from the same period as well as early Mishnah commentary.

4. *Mishnah M'gillah* 4:4; *Tosefta M'gillah* 3:18–19.

5. Those called up to the Torah actually read from the scroll; Torah blessings were recited once only at the beginning and the conclusion of the entire reading.

6. The texts of these blessings first appear in Tractate *Sof'rim* (13:7–14), which is late (eighth century). The section of the text in which they are found (chapters 10–21) likely is later still, dating from some time prior to the eleventh century. In this context, it is noteworthy that the series of blessings following the haftarah reading includes petitions for the return of the exiles to Zion and for the restoration of the Davidic monarchy. These would later be omitted from most Reform prayer books.

7. Nor, for that matter, does it yet know a precisely demarcated weekly order of Torah readings; where these readings began and ended initially varied from place to place, and it could take close to four years to read the Torah in its entirety.

8. *Mishnah M'gillah* 3:5–9 additionally specifies the Torah readings for all the Festivals and High Holy Days, as well as for Chanukah, Purim, Rosh Chodesh, and fast days. The Mishnah's readings for the Festivals and Rosh HaShanah are different from, and briefer than, the ones that later became customary in Babylonia. Our current readings for Shavuot (Exodus 19) and Rosh HaShanah (Genesis 21) appear as alternative read-

ing traditions in *Tosefta M'gillah* 3:5–7. Later, Tractate *Sof'rim* (14:3–4) would additionally list appropriate psalms to be recited on each of these festive occasions.

9. It is the haftarah for Noah, since Isaiah 54:7 likens God's assurances of Israel's redemption to the divine promise never again to let loose the floodwaters. Additionally, it
serves as one of the seven haftarot of consolation.

10. "So-called" because in fact it took about four years to finish and may never have been
fully standardized.

11. Ben Zion Wacholder, in his prolegomenon to the reprint edition of Jacob Mann, *The
Bible as Read and Preached in the Old Synagogue*, vol. 1 (New York: Ktav, 1971), xxxi, determines that this characterization applies to a full 80 percent of the known "triennial"
haftarot and notes additionally that many of the haftarot "show a tendency to allego-
rize Torah passages into which later generations infused new meanings" (xxxiii). He
also remarks that a whopping 72 percent of these haftarot come from either Isaiah or
the Minor Prophets and that two-thirds of the haftarot from Isaiah are from the last
third of the book, the consolations of the anonymous exilic prophet.

12. Abraham Geiger, *Israelite Prayer Book for Public Worship* (title trans. from German;
Breslau: Verlag von Julius Hainauer, 1854). In his prayer book, Geiger provides a table
of triennial Torah readings, but does not list haftarot.

13. Michael A. Meyer, *Response to Modernity: A History of the Reform Movement in Judaism*
(New York: Oxford University Press, 1988), 95–96.

14. Meyer draws a critical distinction regarding Reform "Prophetic Judaism" between
Kant-inspired moral action at the level of individual conduct and an applied program
of social justice and social criticism. The former perspective was prevalent in both
Europe and America before the 1880s. Only in the late nineteenth and early twentieth
centuries did social activism begin to come to the fore in the American Reform pulpit, and this at the time of the Social Gospel movement in American Protestantism
and the Progressive movement in American politics. See Meyer, *Response to Modernity*,
286–89.

15. *The Union Prayer Book for Jewish Worship* (Cincinnati: CCAR, 1894-95). Unique among
the prayer books surveyed here, the 1895 *Union Prayer Book* provides, in 119 pages, the
full texts of its scriptural selections instead of listing them in a table. This was done to
obviate the need for freestanding Bibles in the synagogue, since there were then no
easily available authorized Jewish translations. With the Jewish Publication Society's
1917 release of *The Holy Scriptures*, this problem was solved, and subsequent revisions
of the *UPB* give tables of Torah and haftarah readings.

16. One haftarah, to Numbers 20, Moses's disobedience in striking the rock, is a compilation of verses from Proverbs, Psalms, and Isaiah. It is the only such compilation
haftarah in the list.

17. The table of scriptural readings was not included in the prayer book itself, on account
of that book's length, but appears in two supplementary volumes, *Gates of the House*
and *Gates of Understanding*, both published in 1977. Many of the alternative haftarot
derive from the 1940 *UPB*, a few from the 1918 *UPB*; the rest are new or derived from
"other sources" (unlisted; I have not been able to identify them, although they might
include lists prepared by the Liberal and Reform Movements in Great Britain or elsewhere in the World Union for Progressive Judaism).

18. Interestingly, Stern also provides an alternative reading from Deuteronomy for

*Parashat Bo*, which details the Ten Plagues. This narrative had also been omitted from the list of Torah readings in the 1895 *UPB*.

19. The first integral edition of this work was published in 1981, but the commentaries to Genesis through Numbers had previously been published separately in 1973 (Genesis), 1979 (Leviticus, by Bernard Bamberger; and Numbers), and 1981 (Exodus). The Deuteronomy volume was published separately in 1983 to complete the set. These separate volumes included alternative Haftarah selections in addition to the (sometimes abbreviated) traditional ones carried forward in the one-volume edition. (My thanks to my colleague Andrea Weiss for calling this to my attention.) Most of the alternative readings also appear in Dreyfus's list for *Gates of Prayer* or in Freehof's list for *UPB*, newly revised, but some do not.

20. The Plaut volume was in part designed to replace in Reform pews *The Soncino Press Pentateuch and Haftorahs*, edited by Dr. J.H. Hertz, dating originally to 1936–37, which provides a modern Anglo-Orthodox commentary on the traditional Torah and haftarah readings. The success of Plaut led the North American Conservative Movement to publish its own one-volume equivalent for synagogue use, *Etz Hayim: Torah and Commentary* (2001). The more recent URJ-published *The Torah: A Women's Commentary*, edited by Tamar Cohn Eskenazi and Andrea L. Weiss (2008), never intended to include haftarot in the scope of the project (communication from Andrea Weiss).

21. Selections from the Book of Esther also had been offered as the haftarah for Shabbat Zachor in both revised editions of the *Union Prayer Book*. In fact, Plaut initially offered the traditional haftarah selection from 1 Samuel 15 in his 1981 separate commentary volume on Exodus, changing this to Esther only in the 1983 single volume edition.

# Connecting the Haftarah Readings with Social Justice Work

## Reform Judaism from the Beginning of the Social Justice Movement to Today

*Rabbi Lance J. Sussman, PhD*

E XPLAINING THE RELATIONSHIP between the practice of reading the haftarah and the use of those specific texts by rabbis and others to help explicate Reform Judaism's embrace of social justice as part of its basic mission is not as easy a task as one might think. First, there is the long, complicated, and often ambivalent history of the liturgical haftarah reading in Reform practice, described by Rabbi Richard S. Sarason in the last chapter. Second, American Reform Judaism's view of social justice and how it incorporates ancient Israel's prophetic tradition into a modern, progressive, religious agenda is also very specific and requires historical analysis. Finally, how to create a new pathway that connects the haftarah readings with social justice in the future requires the creation of tools and a framework of understanding for contemporary Reform Judaism. Hopefully, this chapter will succeed in all three endeavors.

I want to begin by sharing my own experience with the haftarah readings, as I believe it is somewhat typical of the Reform Movement of the last half century. I was ordained by the Hebrew Union College–Jewish Institute of Religion (HUC-JIR) in 1980. For most of my rabbinic career, the haftarah readings have been problematic for me, both as source texts for sermons and as a part of worship services in the various synagogues I have served as a pulpit rabbi. On Shabbat mornings when there is no bar or bat mitzvah, it has been my personal practice for forty years to skip reading the haftarah. When we do have a bar or bat mitzvah and that student has reading issues, we often reduce the haftarah reading to a short passage to be read in English or, again, skipped altogether. In my congregational school, the Hebrew blessings over the haftarah readings are generally the last passages our students are asked to master in their preparation to become a bar or bat mitzvah. In my Saturday morning pre-service Torah study groups, I only occasionally include a haftarah reading, usually when its content is more compelling to adult learners than that of the actual Torah portion. Only on rare occasions do I preach or write an e-published weekly message on a verse from the haftarah readings. In my case, the only haftarah reading that truly stands as impactful in the Reform experience of the annual cycle of liturgical scriptural reading is read on the morning of Yom Kippur, Isaiah 58: "Is this not the fast have I chosen," the prophet asks rhetorically, "to loose the fetters of wickedness, to undo the bands of the yoke, and to let the oppressed go free?" (v. 6).[1]

In my own life, I can think of only three examples in which the words of a biblical prophet proved exceptionally important to me as a young Jew who always had a serious commitment to Jewish life. First, in my home synagogue, the former Temple Oheb Sholom, Baltimore, Maryland, the Torah service during my bar mitzvah began with a reading from Isaiah 2: "It will come to pass in the end of days," I began somewhat ironically, given Reform Judaism's rejection of the idea of building a third Temple in Jerusalem, "that the Temple of the Eternal will be firmly established as the heads of the mountains . . . [and] they shall beat their swords into plowshares" (2:2, 2:4).

Second, as a counselor in training (CIT) at Camp Harlam around 1970, I took a mandatory class taught by Rabbi Howard Bogot on the prophet Amos. "Howie," as we affectionately called him, brought the prophet Amos alive for me. Howie encouraged us to imagine what it would be like if the prophets were speaking their words today.

Finally, during my college years as a religious studies major, I took a class in the Hebrew Bible and was assigned Abraham Joshua Heschel's *The Prophets* (1962). I probably did not understand much of that book at the time, but all of a sudden, the prophets became powerful voices for me.

By contrast, I cannot recall a single "social justice" sermon during my childhood or adolescent years that made me want to put my *Union Prayer Book* back in the pew and hitch a ride to Alabama, although I am certain my childhood rabbis offered prophetic addresses and I, as a teenager, faithfully followed Dr. Martin Luther King Jr. on television and in the printed press and cheered him on literally as "my prophet." At the same time, I listened to endless family and neighborhood stories about "shvartzes" and complaints about Black violence against Jewish businesses in Baltimore's old former Jewish neighborhoods. I also accepted Jewish white flight to the suburbs as a consequence of the city's decline but did not see it as part of the problem of continued segregation in America.

The most dramatic embrace of the prophetic message I directly experienced during the forty years of my rabbinate was found not in texts, but in contemporary Reform Jewish art. I was called to the pulpit of Reform Congregation Keneseth Israel (KI), Elkins Park, Pennsylvania in 2001, whose one-thousand-seat sanctuary is framed by a massive series of stained glass windows. "The Prophetic Quest" by the artist Jacob Landau[2] was completed and dedicated in 1974. Landau's complex Peter Max–like work is purposefully colorful and fanciful, unlike more traditional, Tiffany-style stained glass windows. When fully understood, including their terse quotes from the prophets in Hebrew and English, the windows convey a powerful message of the primacy of the fight against social injustice. Ironically, the windows were commissioned just after the civil rights movement lost currency in the Reform Movement and traditionalism, mysticism, and feminism began reshaping Reform Judaism. Moreover, no attempt was made by the artist or the congregation to connect the windows and the haftarah readings. In 1974, it would have been hard to imagine anyone in the Reform Movement making that liturgical-ideological connection.[3]

My twenty-year experience of viewing the Landau windows has become complicated, as it quickly became clear to me in my first years at KI that our stained glass was not understood as an actual prophetic challenge to moral complacency but rather as ornamental, aesthetic, and a point of congregation pride. "Rabbi," I was told countless times, "I love our sanctuary windows. They are so beautiful, especially on Yom Kippur when the sunlight streams through them," casting a golden light across the sanctuary. Not once did anyone approach me to say, "Our windows' message about justice really moves me to protest, speak up, and march!" Instead, the response was always aesthetic, if not pietistic. Pun intended: our stained glass is more a window dressing than a call to action. However, verses from Torah like "Love your neighbor as yourself" (Leviticus 19:18), which has served as our congregational motto since 1847, and "Justice, justice you shall pursue" (Deuteronomy 16:20), which is featured in one of our small chapel's windows, remain the favorite "prophetic" teachings among my congregation's social activists.

Why has the late twentieth- and early twenty-first-century Reform Judaism I personally experienced been so ambivalent about the prophets and the haftarah readings?[4] The reality is that early Reform Judaism in both Germany and the United States did not focus on social justice issues. In the United States, where Reform was given expression already in 1824, it was not until after the arrival of Rabbi David Einhorn in 1855 that the issue of the abolition of slavery was raised. Like other Americans and American Jews, early American Reform Jews were deeply divided into pro-slavery, neutral, and abolitionist camps. In fact, Isaac Mayer Wise, widely viewed as the founder of American Reform Judaism, warned that abolitionists, because of their relationship with Christian missionaries, were actually dangerous to American Jews and that the abolition of slavery was not mandated by the Torah or the prophets.[5]

It was not until after the Civil War in 1865 that social justice gained currency among Reform rabbis. Rabbi Emil G. Hirsch, a son-in-law of Einhorn, successfully fought to have an eighth and final plank added to the 1885 Pittsburgh Platform. It stated, responding to the Social Gospel movement in American Christianity, that "in full accordance with the spirit of the Mosaic legislation, which strives to regulate the relations between rich and poor, we deem it our duty to participate in the great task of modern times, to solve, on the basis of justice and righteousness, the problems presented by the contrasts and evils of the present organization of society."

In time, "prophetic Judaism" became the Reform equivalent of the Social Gospel, broadening Reform Judaism's understanding of ethics to include both the individual and society at large. Hirsch's emphasis on economic issues and that of the Central Conference of American Rabbis (CCAR) on labor issues remained in place until World War I, when pacifism gained traction in the Reform Movement. During the Progressive era, less emphasis was placed on racial issues by the Reform Movement, although individual Reform Jews like Rabbi Stephen S. Wise and laypeople like Julius Rosenwald, a Chicago-based congregant of Emil Hirsch, started taking actions on behalf of African Americans.

Laypeople, one might suppose, would be less inclined than rabbis to supply prophetic proof texts in their social justice work. However, in understanding the history of social justice in the Reform Movement, it is important to note that lay leaders contributed as much to aligning Reform Judaism with progressive ideals as did the Reform Movement's rabbis. One driving force among the laymen was Kivie Kaplan (1904–75), who played the lead role in establishing the Religious Action Center in 1961 in Washington, DC. Kaplan also served as president of the NAACP for nine years, from 1966 to his death. Albert Vorspan (1924–2009), who headed the Commission on Social Justice and served as a vice president of the Union of American Hebrew Congregations, now the Union for Reform Judaism, was also a leading Reform voice for social justice after World War II.

Interestingly, in selecting items for their 2001 *The Reform Judaism Reader: North American Documents*, Professor Michael A. Meyer and Rabbi W. Gunther Plaut, two of the leading historians of Reform Judaism, picked a 1994 speech by a lay Reform activist, Evelyn Laser Shlensky (b. 1942), entitled "Jewish Faith and Social Justice," and not a rabbinic sermon. Shlensky ended her talk by stating, "I want people to understand that temples are places where Jews gather for prayer, for study, and for formulating plans to bring core Jewish values into the world: justice, mercy and peace."[6] She did not provide a prophetic text like Micah 6:8, "To do justly, and love mercy, and walk humbly with your God," from the haftarah reading for *Balak* (Numbers 22:2–25:9), to anchor her remarks.

Perhaps Meyer and Plaut did not include Joachim Prinz (1902–68) in their anthology because Rabbi Prinz, a member of the CCAR, was not serving a Reform pulpit when he gave his famous speech on August 28, 1963, in Washington, DC, just before Dr. King's famous "I Have a Dream" oration. In my opinion, Prinz's Washington speech may have been the single most important rabbinic statement on civil rights. "When I was the rabbi of the Jewish community in Berlin under the Hitler regime," Rabbi Prinz recalled, "I learned many things. The most important thing that I learned under those tragic circumstances was that bigotry and hatred are not the most urgent problem. The most urgent, the most disgraceful, the most shameful and the most tragic problem is silence."[7] According to Meyer, seventy Reform rabbis were present when Prinz spoke.

Meyer-Plaut's choice of a lay speech over a rabbinic sermon points to a larger issue in American historiography about the role of religion in American social justice movements. For example, some labor historians, like John R. Aiken and James R. MacDonald, have argued that the social gospel "movement had little influence on the labor movement" and concluded that "labor did not reject social 'gospellers' because they were unaware of them but, rather, because their tactics and ideas were considered inadequate."[8] More complicated is the relationship of lay and religious leadership in the civil rights movement after World War II. Not to detract from the leadership of Rev. Martin Luther King Jr. and other civil rights clergy leaders, but it is also important to remember that a whole spectrum of lay leaders and organizations from W. E. B. DuBois (1868–1963) to Thurgood Marshall (1908–93) and from the NAACP to the Congress on Racial Equality (CORE) and the Student Non-Violent Coordinating Committee (SNCC) all played leading roles in launching and sustaining the fight for civil rights for African Americans and others.

Although he taught briefly at the Hebrew Union College in Cincinnati from 1940 to 1945, when he first came to the United States, Rabbi Abraham Joshua Heschel (1907–72), like Prinz, mostly worked outside of the Reform Movement during his time in America. It is hard to point to a Reform rabbinic parallel to Heschel as an icon of the civil rights movement. Only a few scholars at HUC-JIR served as leading public proponents of social justice. Abraham Cronbach (1882–1965) came to Hebrew Union College in 1922 after serving as a congregational rabbi and prison chaplain. As a pacifist, he frequently clashed with the college's Board of Governors, especially after he urged that punishment for leading Nazis be limited. Later, he publicly defended the Rosenbergs.

Rabbi Eugene B. Borowitz (1924–2016), the leading Reform theologian during the closing decades of the twentieth century, who taught at HUC-JIR in New York, took a public though limited stand on civil rights. In 1964, two years after he began teaching at the College, Borowitz went with several rabbis to join Martin Luther King Jr. at a demonstration in Saint Augustine, Florida, following King's appeal to the CCAR for support. After fifteen rabbis were arrested for the crime of "integrated prayer," they asked Borowitz to write up an account of their time in jail. His report appeared on the front page of the *New York Times* and played an important role in further deepening the Reform Movement's commitment to social justice.

Rabbi Maurice Eisendrath (1902–73) served as president of the Union of American Hebrew Congregations (UAHC), beginning in 1946, for a thirty-year term. Best known for his opposition to the Vietnam War, Eisendrath strongly supported the civil rights movement, often over the opposition of southern rabbis and a variety of congregations. Eisendrath made civil rights one of the principle foci of the Reform Movement during his long tenure in office. He was in a unique position to rally both rabbis and lay leaders to the cause of civil rights and did so courageously and without hesitation.

In general, American Reform rabbis supported the civil rights movement through their preaching and by marching and demonstrating, often at great risk to their own safety. To a large extent, it was the marching, or what Abraham Joshua Heschel called "praying with his feet," which helped convey the seriousness and urgency of social justice to their congregants, perhaps even more than their preaching or writing. For example, Arnold Jacob Wolf (1924–2008), who worked as both a congregational rabbi and a Hillel director at Yale University, marched in Selma. Arthur J. Lelyveld (1913–96), rabbi of Fairmount Temple in Cleveland, was severely beaten by segregationists in Hattiesburg, Mississippi, in 1964. Israel Dresner (b. 1929), now emeritus of Temple Beth Tikvah in Wayne, New Jersey, has been called "the most arrested rabbi in America," having been jailed multiple times during the early 1960s, beginning with his participation in the Freedom Rides protests in 1961.

While a complete review of the sermons offered by Reform rabbis from 1945 to 1970 is beyond the scope of this chapter, the phrase "the Fatherhood of God and the brotherhood of man" was frequently employed as the essence of the theology of Reform Jewish social activism as much or exceeding the use of prophetic texts. Moreover, because of a need to present a variety of topics as well as to avoid controversy, Reform rabbis may not have preached as often on social justice in the post–World War II period as one might assume. Three collections of rabbinic sermons chosen randomly for this study produced surprising results:

- In his 1972 book, *Spoken and Heard: Sermons and Addresses*, Solomon B. Freehof (1892–1990), one of the giants of twentieth-century Reform Judaism, offers twenty-seven complete talks plus a number of excerpts. The sermons were written between 1938 and 1966. Remarkably, none of them addressed social justice topics.

- By contrast, in his 1982 book, Eugene J. Lipman (1919–94), who served both as a pulpit rabbi and the director of the UAHC's Commission on Social Justice during the course of his career, includes forty-one sermons, of which six were specifically on social justice, including one on the Vietnam War.
- Finally, Amiel Wohl (1930–2019), a pulpit rabbi and interfaith activist, published *Entrusted with the Word: Fifty Best Sermons* in 2012. Wohl's collection includes six sermons on Black-Jewish relations and one on the environment.

Although most were courageous in spirit and steadfast in purpose, it seems many Reform rabbis heeded the advice once offered to a young Florida-based Conservative rabbi by an elderly congregant. "If you want a successful career," the gentleman urged the young clergyman, "there are two things never to speak about from the pulpit: the first is Politics, the second is Religion."[9]

Finally, a word about social justice and the haftarah readings in American Reform publications over the last fifty years. In trying to understand my own experience, it is important to note that W. Gunther Plaut's *The Torah: A Modern Commentary* was not published until 1981. Prior to the Plaut *Commentary*, the vast majority of Reform synagogues used one of several editions of the Jewish Publication Society (JPS) Bible. The JPS Bibles came without commentary, often did not include the names of the weekly Torah portion, and provided no guide to the haftarah readings. By the 1960s, Reform's embrace of bar and bat mitzvah celebrations and the subsequent return to tradition necessitated a different kind of text for synagogue use.

The Plaut *Commentary* was originally designed to serve as a resource for synagogue study groups, although also, secondarily, as a liturgical publication. In the original Plaut *Commentary*, Shabbat and holiday haftarah readings were placed as a group at the end of each book in the Torah, not at the end of each portion. In 1996, according to then president-elect of the UAHC, Rabbi Eric H. Yoffie, the UAHC Press published *The Haftarah Commentary*, in part to draw attention to prophetic texts as a basis for social justice activism in the Reform Movement.[10] A revised edition of Plaut's original *The Torah: A Modern Commentary* was published in 2005. This time it was organized around the weekly portion and its accompanying haftarah.

*The Torah: A Women's Commentary*, edited by Dr. Tamara Cohn Eskenazi and Rabbi Andrea L. Weiss, was published by the URJ Press in 2008 in cooperation with the Women of Reform Judaism, the national organization of Reform Sisterhoods, primarily as a feminist study guide, this time without haftarah readings altogether.[11]

How can Reform Judaism do a better job of emphasizing its continued commitment to social justice and more fully root itself in both prophetic Judaism and the traditional liturgical experience? One possibility is for rabbis to regularly include the haftarah readings in their services and increase their utilization in their sermons and study groups. While social justice is not the only or necessarily even dominant theme in the haftarah readings (of which a number are not from prophetic literature per se), many of them contain powerful texts on social justice. To facilitate rabbinic "mining" of the haftarah, I have prepared the appended chart, "Social Justice Haftarah Readings: Select Verses." Hopefully, it will contribute to increased use of the haftarah in the Reform experience in the future and strengthen the Reform Movement's commitment to social justice as we journey deeper into the twenty-first century, with its many social, cultural, and religious challenges.

## Social Justice Haftarah Readings: Select Verses

**GENESIS**

| | | |
|---|---|---|
| B'reishit | Isaiah 42:6 | "called you in righteousness" |
| Noach | Isaiah 54:14 | "You shall be established in righteousness" |
| Tol'dot | Malachi 2:6 | "walked with Me in peace and equity" |
| Vayishlach | Obadiah 1:10 | "for violence done to your brother Jacob" (for Sephardim) |
| Vayeishev | Amos 2:6 | "sell the innocent for silver" |
| Va-y'chi | I Kings 2:5 | "shedding war-blood in peacetime" |

**EXODUS**

| | | |
|---|---|---|
| Yitro | Isaiah 9:6 | "supporting it, based on justice and right" |
| Mishpatim | Jeremiah 34:8 | "to proclaim liberty" |

**LEVITICUS**

| | | |
|---|---|---|
| Tzav | Jeremiah 9:23 | "I, the Eternal, practice kindness, justice, and righteousness in the earth" |
| Acharei Mot | Ezekiel 22:2 | "arraign the city of blood" |
| K'doshim | Amos 9:7 | "Are you not to Me . . . like the Cushites?" |

**NUMBERS**

| | | |
|---|---|---|
| B'midbar | Hosea 2:21 | "betroth you to Me in righteousness" |
| B'haalot'cha | Zechariah 4:6 | "not by might, nor by power" |

| Balak | Micah 6:8 | "only this: to do justly, and love mercy" |
| Pinchas | I Kings 19:12 | "a still, small voice" |
| Mas'ei | Jeremiah 4:2 | "in truth, in justice, and in righteousness" |

**DEUTERONOMY**

| D'varim | Isaiah 1:17 | "seek justice; relieve the oppressed" |
| Eikev | Isaiah 51:1 | "Listen to Me, all who pursue justice" |
| R'eih | Isaiah 54:14 | "You shall be established in righteousness" |
| Ki Tavo | Isaiah 60:17 | "I will make Peace your government" |
| Vayeilech/ Shabbat Shuvah | Hosea 14:3 | "accept the good" |
| Haazinu | II Samuel 22:22 | "I have kept the ways of the Eternal" |

**HOLIDAYS**

| Yom Kippur Morning | Isaiah 58:6 | "Is not this the fast I desire" |
| Yom Kippur Afternoon | Jonah 4:11 | "Should I, then, not have compassion" |
| Shabbat Chanukah | Zechariah 4:6 | "not by might, nor by power" |
| Shabbat HaGadol | Malachi 3:24 | "turn the hearts of parents to their children" |
| Tishah B'Av | Jeremiah 9:23 | "I, the Eternal, practice kindness, justice, and righteousness in the earth" |

NOTES

1. *The Union Prayer Book for Jewish Worship: Part II* (Cincinnati: Central Conference of American Rabbis, 1945), 243. In my current congregation, the poignancy of reading this text is reinforced by our custom of asking members who are United States federal judges to read it.

2. A full biography of Jacob Landau has yet to be written. For basic information, see http://www.jacoblandau.org/theartist.html.

3. Lance J. Sussman, "In Situ: A View of the Landau Windows from the Pulpit of Reform Congregation Keneseth Israel," in *The Prophetic Quest: The Stained Glass Windows of Jacob Landau, Reform Congregation Keneseth Israel, Elkins Park, Pennsylvania*, ed. David S. Herrstrom and Andrew D. Scrimgeour, Dimyonot: Jews and the Cultural Imagination (University Park: Penn State University Press, 2021).

4. On social justice in the Reform Movement, see Michael A. Meyer, *Response to Modernity: A History of the Reform Movement* (New York: Oxford University Press, 1988), 286–89, 309–14, 364–68.

5. L. J. Sussman, "Race, Social Justice and the Roots of American Reform Judaism: 1824–1860," *Reform Advocate* 12, no. 1: High Holy Days (September 2020): 3–6.

6. Michael A. Meyer and W. Gunther Plaut, *The Reform Judaism Reader: North American Documents* (New York: UAHC Press, 2001), 158.

7. Joachim Prinz, excerpted from a speech delivered at the March on Washington, August 28, 1963, http://www.joachimprinz.com/civilrights.htm.

8. John R. Aiken and James R. McDonnell, "Walter Rauschenbusch and Labor Reform: A Social Gospeller's Approach," *Labor History* 11.2 (1970): 131–150.

9. Quoted in Marc Saperstein, "'Rabbis, Stay Out of Politics': Social Justice Preaching and Its Opponents, 1848–2014," *Jewish Culture and History* 16, no. 2 (2015): 127–41.

10. Eric W. Yoffie, foreword to *The Haftarah Commentary*, ed. W. Gunther Plaut (New York: UAHC Press, 1996), vii–viii.

11. Communicated to the author by Rabbi Weiss by email, August 9, 2020: "Our focus was on creating a women's commentary on the Torah that brought together multiple voices on each Torah portion. We did not consider adding the haftarot."

# The Prophetic Voice in the Reform Movement Today

*Rabbi Rachel Timoner*

H UMAN BEINGS are adaptive creatures. We are able to live in the frozen tundra and the blistering desert. We are able to survive and recover from brutal violence, extreme hunger, prolonged imprisonment, and exile. Our bodies and minds seek homeostasis, continually balancing and rebalancing in response to changing conditions. I write this in the tenth month of a global pandemic, in which many of us have restructured our lives to exist almost entirely within our homes for a year. We adapt.

This adaptive capacity is essential for our survival and well-being. It also means that we become accustomed to the conditions of our world, even when those conditions should not be accommodated. We learn to tolerate intolerable injustice. Our initial shock at evil subsides. Obscene corruption becomes normal. Our shouts of indignation in response to blatant lies eventually fade. Our defiance against dehumanization wears off. In time, we are worn down. We rationalize. We minimize. We acquiesce. We grow silent. We look away. We give in. We give up. We wake up each day, we take showers, we make breakfast for our children, we tackle the to-do list. We go about our lives, and in the process we become complicit in the moral outrage to which we have become inured.

We see images of children torn from their parents' arms at the southern border. We see children in cages. Their cries haunt us. We do not sleep. We are tormented by their suffering. We weep, we write, we post, we march, we give money, we hold vigils, we get arrested, we reunite the few families we can. And then we see that the newly separated families are only a small fraction of the half a million immigrants detained every year, many of whom have been taken from their families. We get tired, or we feel defeated, or we feel overwhelmed by the magnitude and difficulty of the problem, or we get distracted by other crises, or we're not sure what else we can do, so we move on and in time we forget that there are still parents in cages and children longing to be held. Here, in our time, with our tax dollars.

We see a video in which a policeman nonchalantly but determinedly snuffs out the life of an innocent Black man for a sustained eight minutes and forty-six seconds at first, and now understood to be nine minutes and twenty-nine seconds. This is not the first murder of an innocent Black person by police that we have seen on video. We have been shown dozens. Most of us were not in the streets to grieve the deaths of Trayvon Martin, Eric Garner, Michael Brown, Tamir Rice, or Sandra Bland, but this time we fill the streets of every city in our country in outrage and grief over the deaths of George Floyd and Breonna Taylor. Led by the Black community, mostly Black youth, we sustain the protests for months. We read about our own racism, we train, we strive to change. We are overwhelmed the more we understand the all-encompassing and defining nature of the racism in our system. Our efforts seem too small to matter. We grow weary, we feel defeated, our attention shifts. The streets are quiet when more Black people are killed every month, the books sit on shelves, and many of us slip back into somnolence.

We could tell stories about mass incarceration, rape culture, the control of women's bodies and pervasive sexism, transphobia, the murders of trans women of color, homelessness, hunger, the extremes of wealth and poverty, homophobia, ageism, the degradation of our elders, voter suppression, the camps of asylum seekers at our border, the exploitation of debt, the normalization of greed, the barbarity of agribusiness, the despoilment of our earth, and so much more. How often when confronted with these failures of our society do we simply shake our heads and think, "That's how it is"? How many moral disengagements can we no longer even see?

This is why we need the Hebrew prophets. They reject compassion fatigue. They refuse normalization. They demand resensitization, reawakening, renewed disturbance. They will not tolerate our tolerance. They shout and scream and cry. They insult. They harangue. They plead. They threaten. And when we are exhausted, worn down, despairing and hopeless, when we have given up and given in, they comfort, they build up, they hold out hope, they promise redemption. They use every power of word and emotion to move us into action. Because they know that it is not primarily the active evildoers who enable the greatest crimes against humanity. It is those who strive to do good but who watch evil in passive or relenting silence.

Who are the prophets of today? How do we know a prophet when we hear one? If they're like their forebears, they will not tell us what we want to hear. If we are inactive out of perceived powerlessness, they will confront us with our power and our responsibility. If we are inactive because we like our comfort, they will shake us, roil us, skewer us, until we are no longer comfortable. They will often herald ideas whose time has not yet come. Their positions will sound radical, excessive, utopian. They will not shut up; they will not let us off the hook. They will obsess.

They will annoy, irritate, scare. They will make us feel ashamed. They will provoke defensiveness in us. Their urgency will feel unrealistic and unfair. We will want very much to dismiss them, and often we will, but there will be a tiny part of us that senses they are right.

Judaism demands a great deal of us, and for a reason. Our tradition claims that history has a direction and we are a part of it. Until redemption comes, we must not adapt to the sins of society, but be perpetually dissatisfied with the world as it is. In his chapter "The Dream and How to Live It" in his book *The Jewish Way*,[1] Rabbi Yitz Greenberg describes Judaism as a dialectic between dream and reality. The dream is portrayed in the first chapter of Genesis, where we see the Garden of Eden, a vision of the world in its perfect state: all life is interrelated and intertwined, humanity is living in harmony with the earth, and each human possesses the ultimate dignity of being created in the image of God. The Rabbis understood this to mean that every human being is unique, equal to every other, and of infinite value. This image of Eden became for the Jewish people our messianic vision, meaning that the world is moving toward this dream—toward harmony, dignity, equality, and the honoring of all life.

Judaism requires us to immerse ourselves in reality while clinging to the dream. As Jews we are to grapple with the world as it is, in its rank inequality, its obscene poverty, its cruel oppression, its wanton destruction of the natural world, and its routine degradation of human life. We are not to look away, we are not to pretend that this is an illusion, and we are not to wait it out for our time in heaven. We are to enter the muck of this world, all of its pain, all of its heartbreak, and all of its brokenness, while still holding onto the dream. We are never ever to give up on our vision of a world with equality, dignity, and harmony among all life; and we are never ever to give up on our role in bringing about that world.

So how do we sustain ourselves? This is the function of Shabbat. Six days a week we live in the world, striving to heal what is broken. But one day a week, we remember and immerse ourselves in the dream, living as if it is real. Shabbat is the day when we imagine what life will be like when all of our greatest longings for our world come true. That is why Shabbat is full of so much joy. We look at the world and we see our dreams fulfilled in it.

It is so important that we hear the voices of the prophets—biblical and contemporary—on Shabbat. The haftarah readings tie the prophetic call to the Torah, filling our sanctuaries with the voice of the prophets every week. Torah at its best is more than the scroll in the ark. It is a living conversation across time. The prophets apply Torah to their specific time, using the idioms, the grievances, and the metaphors of their time to respond to the real conditions of their world. They rebuke their listeners, holding out an image of the world that should be. They comfort their listeners, building up hope in redemption. They inspire their listeners, providing dreams in the dark.

We may be annoyed to be shaken from our quiet sleep. And yet, we too need dreams in the dark. We need sweet and fervent dreams of the world that's becoming. We must see them in all of their colorful imagery and vibrant illumination.

It can be painful to dream. We ache when we let ourselves really dream, because we feel our longing in its fullness. Dreaming is dangerous because we make ourselves vulnerable to disappointment, and disappointment can be crushing. As the poet Langston Hughes warns:

> What happens to a dream deferred?
> Does it dry up
> like a raisin in the sun? . . .
>
> Maybe it just sags
> like a heavy load.
>
> *Or does it explode?*[2]

It is risky to dream. It is easier to grow numb to what we're lacking, to forget about what we wish our lives or our world would be. But it is only our willingness to dream, and our commitment to turn our dreams into reality, that enable us to transform the conditions of our world.

Sometimes we hear debates in our congregations about "politics in the pulpit." We hear the assertion that the sanctuary should be reserved for spirituality, that there is no place for political matters in spiritual life. This distinction between politics (concerns about the polis, how the people govern themselves) and spirituality is unknown to the Torah or the prophets. The Torah is attempting to describe an ideal society, including matters of land and resource distribution, the relations between rich and poor, governance, taxation, dispute resolution, and the judiciary, along with the operation of the sacrificial cult. There is no separation between religion and politics in Torah. The prophets are primarily concerned with applying that ideal to the real conditions of their world, including failed allegiance to God right alongside economic injustice, oppression, the use of violence, and war.

Since 1885, the Reform Movement has consistently articulated an obligation to apply Torah through action to improve the social conditions of our time. The eighth plank of the 1885 Pittsburgh Platform declared, "In full accordance with the spirit of the Mosaic legislation, which strives to regulate the relations between rich and poor, we deem it our duty to participate in the great task of modern times, to solve, on the basis of justice and righteousness, the problems presented by the contrasts and evils of the present organization of society."[3]

The 1999 Pittsburgh Principles reinforced this foundation: "We bring Torah into the world when we strive to fulfill the highest ethical mandates in our relationships with others and with all of God's creation. Partners with God in *tikkun olam*, repairing the world, we are called to help bring nearer the messianic age. . . . We are obligated to pursue *tzedek*, justice and righteousness, and to narrow the gap between the affluent and the poor, to act against discrimination and oppression, to pursue peace, to welcome the stranger, to protect the earth's biodiversity and natural resources, and to redeem those in physical, economic and spiritual bondage. In so doing, we reaffirm social action and social justice as a central prophetic focus of traditional Reform Jewish belief and practice."[4]

Human beings will always be pulled by our adaptive nature to seek comfort and stasis. Communities will always hear voices that plead for quiet and calm, that want to prevent disruption and disequilibrium, that call for a spirituality devoid of politics. However, in alignment with Torah, the prophets, and the Reform Movement's platforms, our congregations ought to hear the biblical and contemporary prophetic voice speaking directly to us and our world every Shabbat, not only as admonition and rebuke, but also as encouragement and instigation to action.

Further, our action should not only be a reaction by those so moved, but should be collectively organized as a core function of the synagogue. The sins that our prophets bemoan, and the societal sins of our own time, are deep, complex, systemic, and long-lasting. Sins like cruelty to the stranger and the establishment of a caste system were here before we were born, and they will be here after we die. A surge of feeling inspired by compelling oratory will be insufficient to power or sustain our work, if it is to be effective. Rather, compelling oratory ought to reinforce existing structures and processes, infusing them with new energy. Congregations, led by their members in partnership with their clergy, ought to commit to particular changes they want to see in their societies, changes that reflect the prophetic mission and bring us closer to the messianic vision. This is not an ancillary activity of the Jewish community, but a core purpose for our existence.

Finally, it is not enough to hear radical, brave, and cutting-edge prophetic voices in our sanctuary. Often we will congratulate ourselves for making room for voices that make us uncomfortable, as if the courage to speak and hear the words is enough. The courage to speak and hear the words is important, essential even, but it is not enough. In fact, the words should be a support for the work, and not the other way around. The work—the organizing, the action, the prophetic work itself—is how change happens: slowly, methodically, persistently, tenaciously. The prophetic message reminds us why we do the work; it inspires and reenergizes us when the road is long, when we tire, and when we fail or feel defeated. The prophetic message sometimes convinces those not yet active to join the effort and may reinforce the will of those who are wavering. But the prophetic message is not the work itself and must not be confused with it. In *Pirkei Avot*, in the same chapter that finds Rabbi Tarfon teaching that it's not upon us to complete the work nor are we free to desist from it, Rabbi Chanina ben Dosa says, "Anyone whose good deeds exceed their wisdom, their wisdom will endure; but anyone whose wisdom exceeds their good deeds, their wisdom will not endure" (*Pirkei Avot* 3:12). Our deeds must exceed our wisdom.

Yes, Jews are particularly adaptive creatures, and that has kept us alive. We adapt, and we also do not adapt. We live right in the midst of reality, never turning away from the shattered shards of our world. But we also tether ourselves to our vision, loyal always to the conviction that our world as it is cannot be accommodated, but that the world that should be—a world of justice, freedom, dignity, equality, and harmony among all life—is on its way. As Reform Jews, that means we have work to do six days a week, prophetic work, work inspired every Shabbat by the unfurling dreams of the haftarah readings and the knowledge that we are part of making those dreams real.

NOTE
1. Irving Greenberg, "The Dream and How to Live It: Shabbat," *The Jewish Way: Living the Holidays* (NJ and Jerusalem: Jason Aronson Inc., 1988), 127–181.
2. Langston Hughes, "Harlem" (1951), in *The Collected Works of Langston Hughes* (Columbia, MO: University of Missouri Press, 2002).
3. "Declaration of Principles: 'The Pittsburgh Platform,'" Central Conference of American Rabbis, 1885, www.ccarnet.org/rabbinic-voice/platforms/article-declaration-principles/
4. "A Statement of Principles for Reform Judaism," Central Conference of American Rabbis, May, 1999, www.ccarnet/org/rabbinic-voice/platforms/article-statement-principles-reform-judaism/

# Contemporary Blessings
# for Prophetic Readings

RABBI SAMANTHA G. FRANK AND RABBI DANIEL G. ZEMEL

OVER THE PAST two and a half years at Temple Micah in Washington, DC, we have been engaged in an exploratory, experiential, and spiritual endeavor: "The Haftarah Project."

Our inherited haftarah reading system is a product of a number of historical developments and changes, and it does not always speak to our time. In an era when people did not own books or scrolls, the selection of haftarah readings accompanying the Torah reading represented a process of editing and molding both the content of the Torah portion and the entire prophetic tradition. However, often the traditional haftarah readings require decoding for the modern reader or listener to understand their relevance. Often, the haftarah selection is connected to the Torah reading simply by one Hebrew word, which may or may not be read aloud on a particular Shabbat morning, and even if the word is read aloud, it may not be understood by the worshiper. In each case, however, the historical selection was made based on the assumptions, reasons, and needs of the time and place. We decided to make our own assumptions, reasons, and needs the basis of new, contemporary selections. While we read the Torah linearly each year, we wanted to be free to make individual and community-based choices when it comes to the prophetic readings. We read each Torah portion and drew out contemporary themes and questions and explored which biblical texts might elucidate them. We gave ourselves permission to dispense with haftarah readings that no longer spoke to us or to provide two readings when multiple themes were worth exploring. Thus we began a project of exploring which of the traditional haftarah readings deserved to be retained, what liturgical framing they might require, and which texts we might add to the traditional haftarah reading cycle.

Based on the premise that reading prophetic texts is intended to be edifying but is all too often a point of disconnect for the worshiper, we asked ourselves what changes were necessary to bring to this Shabbat morning moment the *kavod* (honor, dignity) it deserves:

1. Reform Judaism prides itself on being inspired by the words of the Hebrew prophets, yet too few Reform Jews are actually familiar with those words. Reform Jews know that there are Jewish texts that drive their commitment to social justice, and we thirst for texts beyond *Tzedek, tzedek tirdof* ("Justice, justice shall you pursue"; Deuteronomy 16:20). American Reform Jews today are engaged in civic discourse and care about a myriad of social issues. We wished for our liturgical experience to speak to the social times in which we live. While the biblical texts do not always share our vocabulary, many prophets speak clearly and powerfully about our social justice obligations. The biblical prophets clearly articulate a vision of inclusion even for the most downtrodden and ignored, reminding us again and again that we are responsible to one another. In making our selections, we sought out those texts.

2. However, social justice texts are not the only biblical stories that are too rarely told in the Reform synagogue. We wanted to include stories ranging from the relatively unknown and understudied women of the Bible to the widely known story of David and Goliath.

3. In addition to a robust consideration of social justice themes and a reintroduction of many of the narrative sections of our prophetic books, we hoped to create a reading cycle that included meaningful offerings for both the educated Jew as well as the non-Jewish member of the *kahal* (community). We sought for our new haftarah selections to rise to the level that Isaiah proclaimed when he called God's "House . . . a house of prayer for all people" (Isaiah 56:7). Our commitment was to speak to the atheist, agnostic, and believer alike. We tried to provide an appropriate framing for our new selections that offered a way in for all the members of our community.

4. Given that we live by the American calendar and celebrate American holidays like Independence Day, Juneteenth, Thanksgiving, and Pride Month, we felt that our haftarah readings should speak to these moments as well, so we expanded on the traditional cycle.

5. As we went to work selecting new haftarah readings, it dawned on us that there was little point to including them in the service if we didn't call attention to the change. Otherwise, we ran the risk that people simply sat through the new readings as they had sat through the old ones on any given Shabbat morning. The service leader needed to direct new energy and attention to our new readings. Therefore, we wrote new haftarah blessings that we read aloud together as a con-

gregation in English. The blessings remind us that each of us has a role in engaging with tradition, making it our own, and passing it on.

6. A blessing was not the only way in which we wanted to draw people's attention to the changes that we were making. Each new reading, as well as each traditional reading that remained, needed description: an explanation of the text, why it was chosen, and its relevance to us today. This description provided the much needed context for the ritual experience of reading the haftarah.

7. Speaking of experience, we also wondered about the liturgical arc of the service and the traditional placement of the haftarah reading. What might be an appropriate ritual frame for that reading, traditionally placed right after the climactic moment of the reading from the *sefer Torah*? Its current position seems to make it a liturgical afterthought. We reinvigorate this moment with the reading of new blessings and have experimented with reading the haftarah earlier in the service, after the blessing for the study of Torah.

We have come to believe that the haftarah could be an inspiring, challenging, and spiritual moment—not only in worship, but wherever Jews gather to express our values and faith. We want to introduce you to three different sets of alternative blessings over prophetic readings for our time. We hope that these blessings and texts inspire you to deepen your Jewish journey toward justice, compassion, and the discovery of the sacred.

# Alternative Blessings

*Alternative Haftarah Blessings by Rabbi Samantha G. Frank*
*and Rabbi Daniel G. Zemel*

**Alternative Blessing before the Haftarah—A**

Blessed are You, Adonai our God, whose spirit inspired our prophets, and whose spirit inspires us to thoughtfully discern their words. Each generation that has come before us has taught and made our prophets' words their own. Thank you for *binah*, "understanding," and *dei-ah*, "knowledge": for the opportunity to choose the holy words that we pass on to the next generation.

**Alternative Blessing before the Haftarah—B**

בָּרוּךְ אַתָּה יְיָ אֱלֹהֵינוּ מֶלֶךְ הָעוֹלָם,
אֲשֶׁר בָּחַר בְּסוֹפְרִים טוֹבִים,
וְרָצָה בְדִבְרֵיהֶם הַנֶּאֱמָרִים בֶּאֱמֶת וָצֶדֶק.
בָּרוּךְ אַתָּה יְיָ, הַבּוֹחֵר בַּתּוֹרָה וּבְמֹשֶׁה עַבְדּוֹ,
וּבִנְבִיאֵי הָאֱמֶת וָצֶדֶק.

*Baruch atah, Adonai Eloheinu, Melech haolam,*
*asher bachar b'sofrim tovim,*
*v'ratzah v'divreihem, hane-emarim be-emet vatzedek.*
*Baruch atah Adonai, habocheir baTorah uvMosheh avdo,*
*uvinvi-ei ha-emet vatzedek.*

Blessed are You, Adonai our God, Ruler of the world,
who chose great scribes to record scrolls and words of truth,
faithfulness, and justice.
Blessed are You, Adonai, for the revelation of your Torah,
for Moses your servant, and for prophets of truth and righteousness.

**Alternative Blessing after the Haftarah**

Thank You, O God, whose spirit inspired the prophets of old, and whose spirit inspires us to live with intention. God, You call to us to be our best. You call us to justice, mercy, and care for the oppressed. Blessed are You, Adonai our God, who gives us the ability to discern, to live, to inspire, and to do Your work.

## *Alternative Haftarah Blessings and Commentary*
## *by Cantor David Berger*

### Alternative Blessing before the Haftarah

בָּרוּךְ אַתָּה יְיָ אֱלֹהֵינוּ מֶלֶךְ הָעוֹלָם,
אֲשֶׁר בָּחַר בַּחֲכָמִים טוֹבִים
וְרָצָה בְדִבְרֵיהֶם הַנֶּאֱמָרִים בֶּאֱמֶת.
בָּרוּךְ אַתָּה יְיָ, הַבּוֹחֵר בַּתּוֹרָה וּבְמשֶׁה עַבְדּוֹ,
וּבְיִשְׂרָאֵל עַמּוֹ, וּבַחֲכָמֵי הָאֱמֶת וְהַצֶּדֶק.

*Baruch atah, Adonai, Eloheinu Melech haolam,*
*asher bachar* bachachamim *tovim*
*v'ratzah v'divreihem hane-emarim be-emet.*
*Baruch atah, Adonai, habocheir baTorah uvMosheh avdo,*
*uvYisrael amo,* uvachachamei *ha-emet v'hatzedek.*

Praise to You, Adonai our God, Sovereign of the universe,
who has chosen faithful *sages* to speak words of truth.
Praise to You, Adonai, for the revelation of Torah, for Your servant Moses,
for Your people Israel, and for *sages* of truth and righteousness.

This alternative blessing makes only one change to the words of the traditional blessing. It replaces, in two occurrences, the word *navi* (prophet) with *chacham* (sage). In the introduction to *Sefer Mitzvot Gadol*, Moses ben Jacob of Coucy (thirteenth century, France), writes:

"From the day that vision and prophecy ceased, and the Holy Spirit [of prophecy] departed from the Jewish people, the Holy One of Blessing raised up the *sages*, who were the students of the prophets, to guide the Jewish people through good instruction, and they spread Torah throughout the Jewish people, and their students, and the students of their students continue to this very day."

As Moses ben Jacob described, with the end of the age of prophecy, the task of guiding and inspiring the Jewish people toward greater ethical, moral, and spiritual heights falls to the *chachamim*, the "sages." While the term *chachamim* is frequently understood to mean the sages of the Talmudic era, Moses ben Jacob asserts that its relevance continues into "this very day."

It is with this understanding of *chacham*, as the next step in the chain of prophetic leadership of our people, that this revised blessing has adopted "sage" in place of "prophet."

## Alternative Blessing after the Haftarah on Shabbat

בָּרוּךְ אַתָּה יְיָ אֱלֹהֵינוּ מֶלֶךְ הָעוֹלָם,
צוּר כָּל הָעוֹלָמִים, צַדִּיק בְּכָל הַדּוֹרוֹת,
הָאֵל הַנֶּאֱמָן, הָאוֹמֵר וְעֹשֶׂה, הַמְדַבֵּר וּמְקַיֵּם,
שֶׁכָּל דְּבָרָיו אֱמֶת וָצֶדֶק.
עַל הַתּוֹרָה, וְעַל הָעֲבוֹדָה, וְעַל הַחֲכָמִים,
וְעַל יוֹם הַשַּׁבָּת הַזֶּה, שֶׁנָּתַתָּ לָנוּ, יְיָ אֱלֹהֵינוּ,
לִקְדֻשָּׁה וְלִמְנוּחָה, לְכָבוֹד וּלְתִפְאָרֶת.
עַל הַכֹּל, יְיָ אֱלֹהֵינוּ, אֲנַחְנוּ מוֹדִים לָךְ,
וּמְבָרְכִים אוֹתָךְ, יִתְבָּרַךְ שִׁמְךָ בְּפִי כָּל חַי
תָּמִיד לְעוֹלָם וָעֶד.
בָּרוּךְ אַתָּה יְיָ, מְקַדֵּשׁ הַשַּׁבָּת.

*Baruch atah, Adonai, Eloheinu Melech haolam,*
*tzur kol haolamim, tzadik b'chol hadorot,*
*haEl hane-eman, haomeir v'oseh, ham'dabeir um'kayeim,*
*shekol d'varav emet vatzedek.*
*Al haTorah v'al ha-avodah, v'al hachachamim,*
*v'al yom haShabbat hazeh, shenatata lanu, Adonai Eloheinu,*
*likdushah v'limnuchah, l'chavod ultifaret.*
*Al hakol, Adonai Elohainu, anachnu modim lach,*
*um'varchim otach, yitbarach shimcha b'fi kol chai*
*tamid l'olam va-ed.*
*Baruch atah Adonai, m'kadeish haShabbat.*

Praise to You, Adonai our God, Sovereign of the universe,
Rock of all creation, Righteous One of all generations,
the faithful God whose word is deed, whose every command
is just and true.

For the Torah, for the privilege of worship, for the *sages*,
and for this Shabbat that You, Adonai our God,
have given us for holiness and rest, for honor and glory:
we thank and bless You.

May Your name be blessed forever by every living being.
Praise to You, Adonai, for the Sabbath and its holiness.

## Call to Action—Insertion into the Blessing after the Haftarah

תַּעְזְרֵנוּ[1] יְיָ אֱלֹהֵינוּ, לִשְׁמֹעַ אֶת חָכְמַת[2] עֲבָדֶיךָ,
וּלְהַקְשִׁיב לְדִבְרֵי קְדוֹשֶׁיךָ.
בִּמְהֵרָה נַעֲבֹד לְתַקֵּן אֶת עוֹלָמֶךָ,
לִהְיוֹת רֹדְפֵי צֶדֶק מְבַקְשֵׁי יְיָ.[3]
זַכֵּנוּ לִשְׁמֹר וְלַעֲשׂוֹת מִשְׁפָּט,[4]
לִלְמֹד וּלְלַמֵּד אַהֲבַת חֶסֶד,
וּלְהַצְנִיעַ לֶכֶת עִם אֱלֹהֵינוּ.

*Ta-azreinu Adonai Eloheinu, lishmoa et chochmat avadecha,*
*ulhakshiv l'divrei k'doshecha.*
*Bimheirah na-avod l'takein et olamecha,*
*lih'yot rodfei tzedek m'vakshei Adonai.*
*Zakeinu lishmor v'la-asot mishpat,*
*lilmod ul'lameid ahavat chesed,*
*ulhatznia lechet im Eloheinu.*

Help us, Adonai our God, to hear the wisdom of Your servants and
to attend to the words of Your holy ones. Speedily, may we labor
toward the repair of Your world and become pursuers of justice,
seekers of Adonai. Grant us the merit to be guardians and doers
of justice, students and teachers of the love of mercy, so as to walk
humbly with our God.

The call to action reflects directly on the intended effect of the haftarah text.
Abraham Joshua Heschel wrote that "the purpose of prophecy is to conquer
callousness, to change the inner person as well as to revolutionize history" (*The
Prophets* [New York: Harper & Row, 1962], 17). We read texts of haftarah not only
for the beauty of their composition or the craft of their poetry, but to inspire us to
transform ourselves and our world. This blessing, modeled on words and phrases
from the biblical prophets, makes explicit the call to action inherent in all haftarah
readings.

1. This section is modeled on
the third blessing in the received
sequence of blessings following
the reading of the haftarah.
2. According to I Kings 5:14.
3. Isaiah 51:1.
4. Following Micah 6:8.

## Alternative Blessing after the Haftarah on Weekdays
## (the Days of the American Jewish Calendar)

עַל הַתּוֹרָה, וְעַל הָעֲבוֹדָה, וְעַל הַחֲכָמִים, וְעַל יוֹם הַתְּפִלָּה\
הַהֲכָנָה\וְהַהַפְגָּנָה\הַלִּמּוּד\וְהַהִתְקַהֲלוּת\הַחֲגִיגָה\הָאֲבֵלוּת הַזֶּה,
שֶׁנָּתַתָּ לָנוּ, יְיָ אֱלֹהֵינוּ, לַעֲשִׂיָּה וְלִשְׁמִיעָה,[1] לְכָבוֹד וּלְתִפְאָרֶת.
עַל הַכֹּל, יְיָ אֱלֹהֵינוּ, אֲנַחְנוּ מוֹדִים לָךְ, וּמְבָרְכִים אוֹתָךְ,
יִתְבָּרַךְ שִׁמְךָ בְּפִי כָּל חַי תָּמִיד לְעוֹלָם וָעֶד.
בָּרוּךְ אַתָּה יְיָ, מְקַדֵּשׁ עַמּוֹ יִשְׂרָאֵל עַל יְדֵי[2] חַכְמֵי אֱמֶת וָצֶדֶק.

*Al haTorah, v'al ha-avodah, v'al hachachamim, v'al yom hat'filah/*
*hahachanah/hahafganah/halimud/hahitkahalut/hachagigah/ha-aveilut hazeh,*
*shenatata lanu, Adonai Eloheinu, la-asiyah v'lishmiah, l'chavod ultifaret.*
*Al hakol, Adonai Eloheinu, anachnu modeim lach, umvarchim otach,*
*yitbarach shimcha b'fi kol chai tamid l'olam va-ed.*
*Baruch atah Adonai, m'kadeish amo Yisrael al y'dei chachamei emet vatzedek.*

For the Torah, for the privilege of worship, for the sages, and for this
day of
Prayer/Preparation/Protest/Study/Gathering/Celebration/Grieving
that You, Adonai our God, have given us for action and for attention,
for honor and glory: we thank and bless You. May Your name be
blessed forever by every living being.
Praise to You, Adonai, who sanctifies the people Israel through sages
of truth and righteousness.

The closing benediction above for the reading of haftarah on weekdays offers
seven options for the type of day one is marking with this ritual reading. More
invitation to creativity than exhaustive list, this is an opening to define and declare
what is the special nature of this particular day on which haftarah will be recited.
If none of the seven options correctly describes the moment, choose whatever
descriptive terms seem most appropriate. The closing blessing, rather than celebrating God as the One who sanctifies the occasion as in the received blessings,
praises God for sanctifying the Jewish people through the chain of wisdom and
inspiration that extends from our earliest ancestors to the great sages of today
and into the future.

1. Based on Exodus 24:7, when the Israelites responded
"*naaseh v'nishmah.*"
2. This final blessing based on *Birkat Eirusin*, the blessing
of engagement at a Jewish wedding.

## *Alternative Haftarah Blessings*
### *by Cantor Margot E.B. Goldberg and Rabbi Barbara AB Symons*

### Alternative Blessing before the Haftarah

יְהִי רָצוֹן מִלְפָנֶיךָ, יְיָ אֱלֹהֵינוּ וֵאלֹהֵי אִמוֹתֵינוּ וַאֲבוֹתֵינוּ
שֶׁתְּחַדֵּשׁ וּתְחַזֵּק אֶת־יָדֵינוּ קְדוּשָׁה מְנוּחָה,
כָּבוֹד וְתִפְאֶרֶת בְּעוֹלָמֵנוּ:
הַשְׁמִיעֵנוּ | אֶת־קוֹלוֹת הַנְּבִיאִים
וְהַנְּבוּאוֹת שֶׁאַתָּה בָּחַרְתָּ,
בְּכָל עֵת וּבְכָל מָקוֹם: וְנֹאמַר, אָמֵן.

*Y'hi ratzon milfanecha, Adonai Eloheinu veElohei Imoteinu va-Avoteinu*
*shet'chadeish ut'chazeik et yadeinu k'dushah m'nuchah,*
*kavod, v'tiferet b'olameinu.*
*Hashmi-einu et kolot hanviim*
*v'hanvu-ut she-atah bacharta,*
*b'chol et uvchol makom. V'nomar, Amen.*

May it be Your will, Adonai our God and God of our mothers and fathers,
to renew and strengthen through our hands holiness, rest,
honor, and glory[1] in our world.
May we listen to the prophets and those prophetic voices
you have chosen, at any given moment,
and in any given place.[2] And let us say: Amen.

### Alternative Blessing after the Haftarah

הָאֵל הַנֶּאֱמָן, הָאוֹמֵר וְעוֹשֶׂה נִשְׁמַע וְנַעֲשֶׂה.

*HaEl hane-eman, haomeir v'oseh nishma v'na-aseh.*

Faithful God whose word is deed,[3] we will hear and we will act.[4]

---

1. From the traditional haftarah blessings.
2. *Makom*: literally "place," also a name of God.
3. From the traditional haftarah blessings.
4. Based on Exodus 24:7, a reminder of the covenant at Sinai.
Here the words are reversed, in our attempt to parallel God,
who spoke first and then acted.

# *Haftarot for the Weekly Torah Portions*

## *GENESIS*

# B'reishit
## Genesis 1:1–6:8

## Traditional Haftarah Reading:
## Isaiah 42:5–43:10

## One God, One Task
### RABBI SETH M. LIMMER

THE DIVINE POWER of the Creation is the theme linking the opening *parashah* of our Torah to its haftarah portion. In Genesis, God creates the heavens and the earth, and in Isaiah, we are reminded that Divine Power still maintains—and can overturn, if needed!—the cosmic balance of our universe. And lest the reader wonder what happened in history before this *B'reishit* ("In the beginning . . ."), Isaiah teaches what Torah omits: he confirms that no other deity was formed before God, nor will there ever be any other. God is the One who formed and illuminated our universe.

Isaiah's powerful passage links the One God of Creation to the one task of humanity: to lead righteous lives that bring even more divine light to our often benighted world. In contrast to the cosmic universalism of Genesis 1, the prophet Isaiah introduces a dose of particularism: the Jewish people were fashioned to be a covenant people, a light to other nations. Paradoxically, our particular mission is about universal goals: to unshackle all who are in chains, to bring all those suffering in the darkness out into the light of hope and liberation. The One God of the Jewish people calls us to one task: leading lives of righteousness for the sake of all of us!

## Invited to Contribute
### RABBI MAYA Y. GLASSER

THE HAFTARAH READING for the very first Torah portion reiterates its themes of creation and the bond between God and God's people. God reminds us that it is God who made us and created us in the divine image.

However, just like Adam and Eve and Noah's peers made their mistakes, Isaiah states that we have continued to make mistakes throughout human history. Our mistakes—traditionally "sins"—in neglecting our obligation to take care of our-selves and the world we inhabit, and, most significantly, in forgetting our sacred bond with the Eternal, continue to be displeasing to our God, who threatens to destroy all that God has created.

However, we have reason to hope. In Psalm 96:1, God invites us to *shiru l'Adonai shir chadash*, "sing to the Eternal a new song." We are invited to create from scratch—not only to take care and maintain, but also to contribute and better. Just like God, we too have the potential to create. Each of us is capable of being God's partner. Each of us is capable of working toward a better world. The prophet Isaiah tells us to have no fear, because God is with us. We are called to be kind to one another, recognize our own power as humans made in God's image, and sing the song that is unique and beautiful within each of us.

## *Alternative Haftarah Reading:*
## *I Samuel 20:31-42*

[Saul said to his son Jonathan,] "As long as the son of Jesse lives on earth, neither you nor your rule will be secure. Now go and have him brought to me—he deserves to die!"

But Jonathan spoke up and said, "Why should he be killed? What has he done?"

Then Saul threw his spear at him to kill him, and Jonathan realized that his father was determined to kill David. So Jonathan got up from the table in a rage and ate nothing on the second day of the new month, out of his hurt for David, and because his father had shamed him.

In the morning, Jonathan went out to the field as he and David had agreed; with him was a young boy. He said to the boy, "You run and find the arrows that I shoot." The boy ran, and he shot an arrow beyond him. When the boy reached to where the arrow shot by him had fallen, Jonathan shouted to him, saying, "The arrow is further on." And Jonathan shouted to the boy, "Quick, hurry up, don't stand still!" And the boy collected the arrows and returned to his master. Only Jonathan and David understood what was happening; the boy who served him suspected nothing.

Then Jonathan gave his weapons to the boy and said, "Take this back to town." When the boy had gone, David got out of his hiding place to the south [of the Ezel Stone], and he bowed down to the ground three times. They kissed each other and wept together, David weeping uncontrollably. And Jonathan said to David, "Go in peace; we two have taken a binding oath, that the Eternal will be between us and between our descendants forever!"

# A World Full of Love

*RABBI ELIZA McCARROLL*

THESE TORAH AND HAFTARAH selections are each filled with the characteristic tension of rivalry:

1. *Parashat B'reishit* includes the infamous tale of Cain murdering his brother Abel after his offering to God is not accepted—as opposed to that of his brother.

2. Our haftarah reading tells a different story, in which King Saul is hunting his royal rival, David. However, David's closest associate, who happens to be Saul's son, Jonathan, helps him to hide, and this concealment effort saves David's life. When David and Jonathan finally reunite, they weep in joy. The haftarah reading concludes with the verse "The Eternal will be between us and between our descendants forever!" (I Samuel 20:42).

As these texts sit in sharp contrast to each other, they provide a lesson in how to get through tumultuous times. On the one hand, the Torah portion shows us that vengeance is fruitless, that it ultimately leaves us living in a colder and lonelier world. On the other hand, the Book of Samuel teaches us that to protect and care for one another can lead to a world that is full of love and connection.

May we all aspire to be a part of this latter world, one that is good and right in the eyes of God.

## Alternative Haftarah Reading:
## Nehemiah 8:1-3; Rabbi Regina Jonas

The Book of Nehemiah describes the teaching of Torah in the fifth century BCE to men and women, equally, as it is written:

> The entire people assembled as one in the square before the Water Gate, and they asked Ezra the scribe to bring the scroll of the Teaching of Moses with which the Eternal had charged Israel. On the first day of the seventh month, Ezra the priest brought the Teaching before the congregation, men and women and all who could listen with understanding. He read from it, facing the square before the Water Gate, from the first light until midday, to the men and the women and those who could understand; the ears of all the people were given to the scroll of the Teaching. (Nehemiah 8:1-3)

Millennia later, Rabbi Regina Jonas reflected on becoming the first woman ordained as a rabbi, living and teaching Torah to all:

> I hope the time will come for all of us in which there will be no more questions on the subject of "woman": for as long as there are questions, something is wrong.... God has

*placed abilities and callings in our hearts, without regard to gender. Thus, each of us has the duty, whether man or woman, to realize those gifts God has given. If you look at things this way, one takes woman and man for what they are: human beings.*

# Telling the Full Version of Jewish History

### RABBI MARY L. ZAMORE

CONSIDERED TO BE the first female rabbi, Regina Jonas was ordained by Rabbi Dr. Max Dienemann in Berlin in 1935. She was tragically murdered at Auschwitz in 1944—the end of not only her life but also of the opportunity to become a living role model to women aspiring to be rabbis.

Dienemann performed the ordination on behalf of the Liberaler Rabbiner-Verband (Conference of Liberal Rabbis) when Jonas's seminary, the Hochschule für die Wissenschaft des Judentums (Academy for the Science of Judaism), following the death of her faculty mentor, refused to have her sit for the final examination to qualify for ordination. Therefore, hers was a private, not a seminary, ordination, proving that a woman could be a rabbi, but not opening a path for more women to study and be ordained. This haftarah reading combines three verses from the Book of Nehemiah—also quoted in Jonas's rabbinical thesis, a halachic treatise titled "Can Women Serve as Rabbis?"—with some of Jonas's own writing.

There has been confusion regarding the exact date of Rabbi Jonas's death. Today, we mark her *yahrzeit* on Shabbat *B'reishit*, as she was transferred to Auschwitz, the Nazi extermination camp, on October 14, 1944. That very day, in 1944, was Shabbat *B'reishit*.

In marking Rabbi Jonas's *yahrzeit*, we dedicate ourselves to telling the fullest version of Jewish history, celebrating the lives and struggles of Jews of all gender identities.

# *Noach*
## Genesis 6:9–11:32

## Traditional Haftarah Reading:
## Isaiah 54:1–55:5

## Come to Me
*BRANDON POLAND*

IN THE BEGINNING of *Parashat Noach*, we are told that Noah is a righteous man in his generation and above reproach (Genesis 6:9). However, at the end of this Torah portion, Noah drinks wine, grows drunk, and exposes himself in his tent (Genesis 9:21).

The Book of Isaiah is a powerful juxtaposition to *Parashat Noach*, as it speaks to everything that happens to those of us who are addicts and alcoholics after we drink, grow drunk, and expose ourselves. Isaiah 51:19 states it quite clearly: "These two things have befallen you: devastation, destruction—who will console you?" Further on: "They were despised, shunned by all, a people of suffering, familiar with disease" (53:3).

The lives that addicts and alcoholics lead aren't pretty, whether they are Jewish or not.

Addiction is a disease that is progressive and deadly. However, there is hope. There are ways out of that despair. Today, there are treatment centers and twelve-step meetings all over the world that are dedicated to helping anyone seeking recovery. Even though wrack and ruin, drunkenness and exposure happen to addicts and alcoholics, there is hope. There is recovery. There is a reconciliation back to righteousness—and back to God.

For many people in recovery, specifically those who work a twelve-step program, this work is done to get us closer to a God we understand and whose presence we can feel in our day-to-day lives.

The haftarah reading accompanying *Parashat Noach* ends with this: "Open your ears and come to Me; hearken and you shall live" (Isaiah 55:3). What a relief it was for me.

# Finding Comfort in Ancient Texts

## Rabbi Sharon G. Forman

IN THE LOW-LYING tidewater area of Virginia where I grew up, a river, bay, lake, pond, or ocean was never far from sight. When heavy rain fell, streets and lawns vanished under bubbling waves. Perhaps this memory of water easily covering the face of the earth is one of the reasons why this Torah portion, *Parashat Noach*, fascinates me. Without any hesitation, God puts an end to "all flesh" (Genesis 6:13) because of their violence. In a charming detail in a grim tale, God closes the ark's door, sealing in the small family and their zoo, as they ride out an annihilating storm.

The portion's traditional haftarah reading presents poetry from the prophet Isaiah (eighth century BCE) with a message of hope, growth, and renewal. Confronted with a text from close to three millennia ago, it is not surprising that we bump into difficult language and sexist themes. Isaiah explains that Israel is like a disgraced woman whose crimes include being barren, widowed, or simply cast off.

However, if a reader is ready to work through these disturbing metaphors, great beauty can be gleaned. The prophet also provides comfort and care when he reminds a storm-tossed nation of its everlasting covenant with God. He proclaims that comfort, peace, justice, faithfulness, and learning are possible. Like a storm, anger can and will subside. Peace and harmony will replace fear and violence. Even the most destructive catastrophe will end in due time, and the possibility for healing and harvest eclipses the darkness.

Isaiah offers a message of supreme optimism and hope. Oppressive conditions can change for the better. A rainbow will sparkle out of the water droplets. So, too, internal storms of despair and hopelessness are finite. The rainbow that shines after these emotional upheavals emanates from each precious soul, just as the glowing carbuncles emit their own beautiful light.

## Alternative Haftarah Reading: "Tel Aviv: 1935," by Leah Goldberg

The masts on the roofs of the houses were just
Like the masts on Columbus's boat
And each raven that stood on their tip
Heralded a new continent.

And the backpacks of the travelers went by in the street
And the language of a strange land

Sliced through the hot day
Like the blade of a cold knife.

How can the air of the small city
Bear so many
Childhood memories, loves that had fallen,
Rooms that were emptied somewhere?

Like photographs blackening inside a camera
The pure winter nights turned into
Rainy summer nights beyond the sea
And gray mornings of capital cities.

And the sound of each step drums behind your back
The marching song of a foreign army,
And it seems—if you were just to turn your head back, and in the sea
The church of your city floats.

## Nostalgia, and the Disruption of Migrations

### CANTOR SARAH GRABINER

WHAT DOES IT MEAN to be out at sea? To be floating on a flood and not to know where you will find landfall? How does it feel to arrive at a new land?

Leah Goldberg describes the experience of some arrivals to pre-state Tel Aviv. Their first glimpses of the shores of the new land are tinged with melancholy and nostalgia for the places they left behind. She conflates the ancient Flood, the biblical return to the Promised Land, Columbus's fifteenth-century voyage, and her own pre-1948 immigration experience.

In *Parashat Noach*, we do not learn about the protagonist and his family's emotions in the midst of their traumatic leaving of all that they knew before. Whether or not Goldberg set out to write a midrashic exposition on Noah and the Flood, the story of the twentieth-century wanderers that she illuminates in "Tel Aviv: 1935" is full of diluvian references: the masts, the boats, the raven, the new continent.

*Parashat Noach* concludes with the building of the Tower of Babel and the diversification of human language. Goldberg refers to the babble of tongues spoken in the strange land as part of the confusion and disorientation of arriving in a new place.

With this twentieth-century piece of Hebrew poetry from Leah Goldberg, we may reconsider *Parashat Noach* from a more humanistic, empathetic standpoint. What memories of the pre-Flood world did Noah and his family carry with them? How do journeys and migrations define our ancient, contemporary, and future narratives and lives, as individuals and as a community?

## Alternative Haftarah Reading:
## "The Rainbow Haftarah," by Rabbi Arthur Waskow

You, My people, burnt in fire,
still staring blinded
by the flame and smoke
that rose from Auschwitz and from
    Hiroshima;

You, My people,
Battered by the earthquakes
of a planet in convulsion;

You, My people,
Drowning in the flood of words and
    images
That beckon you to eat and eat,
to drink and drink,
to fill and overfill your bellies
at the tables of
the gods of wealth and power;

You, My people,
Drowning in the flood of words and
    images
That—poured unceasing on your eyes
    and ears—
drown out My words of Torah,
My visions of the earth made whole;

Be comforted:
I have for you a mission full of joy.
I call you to a task of celebration.

I call you
to make from fire not an all-consuming
    blaze
But the light in which all beings see each
    other fully.
All different,
All bearing One Spark.

I call you to light a flame to see more
    clearly

That the earth and all who live as part
    of it
Are not for burning:
A flame to see
The rainbow
in the many-colored faces
of all life.

I call you:
I, the Breath of Life,
Within you and beyond,
Among you and beyond,
[That One Who dwells between you
    and me]
That One Who breathes from redwood
    into grizzly,
That One Who breathes from human into
    swampgrass,
That One Who breathes the great
    pulsations of the galaxies.
In every breath you breathe Me,
In every breath I breathe you.

I call you—
In every croak of every frog I call you,
In every rustle of each leaf, each life,
I call you,
In the wailings of the wounded earth
I call you.

I call you to a peoplehood renewed:
I call you to reweave the fabric of
    your folk
and so to join in healing
the weave of life upon your planet.
I call you to a journey of seven
    generations.

For seven generations past,
The earth has not been able to make
    Shabbos.

And so in your own generation
You tremble on the verge of Flood.
Your air is filled with poison.
The rain, the seas, with poison.
The earth hides arsenals of poisonous
    fire,
Seeds of light surcharged with fatal
    darkness.
The ice is melting,
The seas are rising,
The air is dark with smoke and rising
    heat.

And so—I call you to carry to all peoples
the teaching that for seven generations
the earth and all her earthlings learn to
    rest.

I call you once again To speak for Me,
To speak for Me because I have no voice,
To speak the Name of the One who has
    no Name,
[To speak on behalf of those without a
    Voice of their own]
To speak for all the Voiceless of the
    planet.

Who speaks for the redwood and the
    rock,
the lion and the beetle?

My Breath I blow through you into a
    voicing:
Speak for the redwood and the rock,
the lion and the beetle.

I call you to a task of joy:
For seven generations,
this is what I call for you to do:

To make once more the seasons of your
    joy
into celebrations of the seasons of the
    earth;

To welcome with your candles the dark
    of moon and sun,
To bless with careful chewing
the fruits of every tree
For when you meet to bless
the rising juice of life
in every tree trunk—
I am the Tree of Life.

To live seven days in the open, windy
    huts,
And call out truth to all who live beside
    you—
You are part of the weave and breath of
    life,
You cannot make walls to wall it out.

I call you to a covenant between the
    generations:
That when you gather for a blessing of
    your children
as they take on the tasks of new
    tomorrows,
You say to them, they say to you,
That you are all My prophet
Come to turn the hearts of parents
and of children toward each other,
Lest my earth be smashed in utter
    desolation.

I call you
To eat what I
call
kosher:
Food that springs from an earth you do
    not poison,
Oil that flows from an earth you do not
    drain,
Paper that comes from an earth you do
    not slash,
Air that comes from an earth you do not
    choke.

I call you to speak
to all the peoples,
all the rulers.

I call you to walk forth before all nations,
to pour out water that is free of poison
and call them all to clean and clarify the
    rains of winter.
I call you to beat your willows on the
    earth
and shout its healing to all peoples.

I call on you to call on all the peoples
To cleanse My Breath, My air,
from all the gases
that turn My earth into a furnace.

I call you to light the colors of the
    Rainbow,
To raise once more before all eyes
That banner of the covenant between Me,
and all the children of Noah and
    Naamah,

and all that lives and breathes upon the
    Earth—
So that
never again,
all the days of the earth, shall
sowing and harvest,
cold and heat,
summer and winter,
day and night
ever cease!

I call you so to love the Breath of Life—
For love is the fire
That blazes in the Rainbow.

I call you so to live for seven generations
As in the days when you went forth from
    slavery;
So in these seven generations
The earth will bring forth manna,
The bread of joy and freedom—
And all earth can sing together
Songs of Shabbos.

## A Guide to Prevent Destruction

### Maggid Marques Hollie

"The only thing they have to look forward to is hope. And you have to give them hope." This is the Torah of Harvey Milk. While these exact words do not appear in *Parashat Noach*, the central theme of the Flood and its aftermath is just that—hope. In the Flood narrative, the sign of hope is the rainbow, a symbol that has become a beacon of safety.

Even though our text tells us explicitly that God will not destroy the earth again with a flood, I have often wondered if we, humanity, will be responsible for the next round of destruction. Are we paying attention?

By listing historic examples of humanity's capacity for destruction, "The Rainbow Haftarah" is both a cautionary tale and a guide to prevent us from bringing flood-like destruction on ourselves. If we engage our senses to hear, see, and feel the divinity that surrounds and fills us; if we speak words of life to and for the voiceless; if we love—each other and this earth we inhabit; and if we recognize our role, our responsibility, within and toward the mysteries of life, then not only can we prevent more destruction, but we can actively bring healing.

# *Lech L'cha*
## Genesis 12:1–17:27

## Traditional Haftarah Reading:
## Isaiah 40:27–41:16

### God Is by Our Side
#### EMILY DANA

"MY WAY IS HIDDEN from the Eternal, my claim is ignored by my God," reads Isaiah 40:27.

The path ahead seems uncertain. Similarly, in Genesis, Abraham's path is uncertain. He is told to *lech l'cha*, to "go forth" (Genesis 12:1), without truly knowing where the journey would lead him.

This week's haftarah reading is one of care and comfort. Just as a parent may remind a child that they love them or as a spouse may remind their partner, here, Isaiah is reminding the people that the God they believe in is still the God they began believing in in *Parashat Lech L'cha*. God is still the God of the morning liturgy "who gives strength to the weary" (*Mishkan T'filah*, 38), still the God of the *Sh'ma* and Its Blessings "who chooses Your people Israel" (62), and still the God of the *Hashkiveinu* in the evening who "spread[s] over us the shelter of Your peace" as we lay down (18). God is by our side on all of our journeys; we just have to trust.

When we remember that God will be our "help" (Isaiah 41:14), we will be comforted throughout our battles, metaphorical ones as well as physical ones. We will always be reassured. We may not always have a firm grasp on where we are going, but we will always be assured that we are going to a place that God will show us.

### Going Forth toward the Promised Land
#### RABBI JEFFREY SIRKMAN

What do you do when you feel like the world's caving in?
Where do you turn when there are so many problems out there—and
  in here—you're not sure where and how to start?

With all the challenges we face, not knowing exactly where life is
  leading us,

or even how to get there,
we are actually following in the footsteps of Abraham and Sarah.
In the Torah portion of this week, *Parashat Lech L'cha*, God calls our
 founding family to
"*lech*—go forth . . ." (Genesis 12:1),
but never tells them just where they are supposed to get to . . .

Sounds familiar?

Thankfully, the haftarah reading gives us
just the guidance we need.
"Have no fear; I will help you. Have no fear, you worm Jacob. I will
 help you" (Isaiah 41:13–14).

Sounds a bit severe! Why would God call us a "worm"?

Maybe because the challenges we face
can at times make us feel helpless, insignificant,
like a lowly worm. But don't miss the key message:

No matter how daunting the world—how overwhelming;
too big for any of us to really make a difference,
The Holy One is still holding your hand . . .
Which means you have more power than you think.

Your life journey is immeasurably important. It may even be sacred.
And every step leads you closer to the Promised Land.

## *Alternative Haftarah Reading:*
## *"Traveler's Prayer," by Rabbi Sheila Peltz Weinberg*

A prayer for the journey
We could say it every day
When we first leave the soft warmth of our beds
And don't know for sure if we'll return at night.
When we get in the trains, planes, and automobiles
And put our lives in the hands of many strangers
Or when we leave our homes for a day, a week, a month or more—
Will we return to a peaceful home? Untouched by fire, flood, or crime?
How will our travels change us?
What gives us the courage to go through the door?

A prayer for the journey
For the journey we take in this fragile vessel of flesh.
A finite number of years and we will reach

The unknown where it all began.
Every life, every day, every hour is a journey.
In the travel is the discovery,
The wisdom, the joy.
Every life, every day, every hour is a journey.
In the travel is the reward,
The peace, the blessing.

# May God Be with Us On Our Journeys

### *RABBI FAITH JOY DANTOWITZ*

*Parashat Lech L'cha* includes God's call to Abram to go forth and journey to a place that God will show him. We, too, are called by God, by loved ones, by employers, by adventure, by sorrow, and for an array of reasons, to go forth in our lives.

The traditional haftarah reading, Isaiah 40:27–41:16, emphasizes that God will be with us on our journeys: "Have no fear, for I am with you . . . I will give you strength, I will help you. . . . For I, the Eternal your God, hold you by the hand; and I say to you: Have no fear; I will help you" (Isaiah 41:10, 13).

Each day of our lives is a journey, be it simple or grand. Rabbi Sheila Peltz Weinberg's "Traveler's Prayer," inspired by a prayer in the Babylonian Talmud (*B'rachot* 29b) beautifully articulates that we are all travelers benefiting from God's support. We should approach our daily journeys with an openness to imagine the potential a new day offers, whether we are excited or whether our hearts ache with the pain of the past year. Whether we feel called by God like our ancestor Abram, respond to a loved one's call, are divinely inspired, or are traveling without intention—may we face life's daily journeys in a spiritual manner, and may our journeys include sweetness. May God be with us on our journeys.

## *Alternative Haftarah Reading: "Let Go," by Alden Solovy*

Let go.
Let it all go.
Let go of the darkness
That ties you to empty ideas.
Let go of the fear
That binds you to false gods.
Let go of the chains
That imprison you in foreign lands.

Follow God's voice
To an unseen horizon.
Follow God's command
To an unknown destination.
Surrender to the truth
That God summons you
To a sacred calling,
To Torah,
To mitzvot,
To healing the world.
Surrender to the wisdom
Of letting go,
Letting it all go,
So that glorious mystery
Will open before you,
So that life will become an adventure
In the palm of
God's hand.

## Bravery, Openness, and a Yearning for God's Presence
### RABBI JOSEPH R. BLACK

The beautiful poem "Let Go," by Alden Solovy, encapsulates the essence of *Parashat Lech L'cha*.

For us to truly understand the power and importance of God's command to Abram and Sarai, we need to have personally experienced the fear, anticipation, wonder, and trepidation of leaving all that we know in order to embark on a journey into the unknown. "Let Go" reinforces the power of such a leap of faith.

Our progenitors faced an existential crisis of sense and understanding of self when they discovered that the spiritual paths on which they had traveled all their lives no longer were sustainable. In hearing God's call to "go forth" (Genesis 12:1) and leave behind all that was familiar in pursuit of a new paradigm of divine partnership, they entered new and unknown territory. There was no road map—only the promise of a new beginning.

Our tradition teaches that Abram and Sarai "acquired" souls—that is: followers—in the land of Haran. They were successful because they embodied potential: potential for goodness, meaning, and purpose in the way that they treated others and sought out God's presence. Their faith ensured that they would never be alone, but rather "in the palm of God's hand."

Bravery, openness, and a yearning for God's presence—what is your recipe to embrace your true potential?

# *Vayeira*
## Genesis 18:1–22:24

## Traditional Haftarah Reading:
## II Kings 4:1–37

## Welcoming Guests, Visiting the Sick
### *Rabbi Faith Joy Dantowitz*

PARASHAT VAYEIRA begins and ends with stories of *malachim*, "angels" or "God's messengers," appearing. The first passage in Genesis 18 (Genesis 18:1–5) shows the angels visiting Abraham following his circumcision—the biblical text from which we derive the mitzvah of *bikur cholim*, "visiting the sick." The mitzvah of *hachnasat orchim*, "welcoming guests," is derived from the following biblical scene: Sarah prepares food to welcome the three men/angels of God (18:6–8)—but then only laughs in disbelief when she hears that supposedly she will give birth to a son (18:12). In the final chapter of the *parashah*, Genesis 22, an angel of God calls out to Abraham to stop him from slaying his son Isaac (22:10–11). God appears here as protector—yet, it had also been God's instruction that led Abraham to the brink of sacrificing his son.

In the haftarah reading, the same two mitzvot are present:

1. *Hachnasat orchim*: Elisha the prophet visits a wealthy woman of Shunem, who provides him food and lodging (II Kings 4:8). Her kindness touches Elisha, who, upon learning she has no children, promises her a son the following year. She asks that he not delude her—her lack of trust is similar to that of Sarah in the Torah portion. However, just like Sarah, the woman does give birth to a son (4:17).
2. *Bikur cholim*: The child of the woman from Shunem grows up. One day, he falls ill and dies (II Kings 4:18–20). The woman then insists on finding the "man of God," Elisha (4:21–22). She tells him that her son has died and convinces him to follow her home and revive the child. He miraculously brings the boy back to life (4:33–37).

In our darkest times, God is with us. God is there to provide comfort and care and even, like the third angel in the *parashah*, to stay our hand from inflicting harm. God's presence is often felt through acts of *g'milut chasadim*, "acts of loving-kindness," which are often the acts of dear friends and extended family.

## Working Together toward Redemption

*Rabbi Leah Rachel Berkowitz*

The Shabbat before my father died, I listened to a bar mitzvah read the story of Elisha and the miracle of the oil (II Kings 4:1–7). In this rare moment of respite, during three weeks of shuttling quietly between the synagogue and the ICU, I found comfort in Elisha's promise: "You and the children can live on what remains" (4:7). It felt as if he had taken my hand and said, "You're going to be okay."

Elisha's miracle isn't flashy, and it doesn't solve the systemic injustice that is the subject of the widow's *tzaakah* (outcry; II Kings 4:1). We might have preferred that the prophet denounce the institution of debt slavery that threatens her children or propose a universal basic income to protect *all* vulnerable families. Instead, Elisha has her gather empty jugs from her neighbors, and he fills them with oil that she can sell to sustain her family.

Elisha makes the widow self-sufficient, removing the shame of perpetually relying on handouts. But he also does something important for her community. He requires the widow to ask for what she needs. Her neighbors must bear witness to both her family's private sorrow and this systemic injustice.

A prophet might bring about a miracle, but ordinary people must also play a role in redemption.

### Alternative Haftarah Reading:
### Maimonides, Mishneh Torah, *Hilchot Mat'not Aniyim 10:4*

Anyone who gives *tzedakah* to a poor person with a scowl and causes them to be embarrassed, even if they gave a thousand *zuz* [gold pieces], they have destroyed and lost any merit thereby.

Rather, one should give cheerfully, with happiness and empathy for their situation, as it is said (Job 30:25): "Did I not weep for the unfortunate? Did I not grieve for the needy?"

And they should speak to them words of sympathy and comfort, as it is said (Job 29:13): "I gladdened the heart of the widow."

# Eagerness, Enthusiasm, Joy, and Empathy

*RABBI ERIN BINDER*

The opening scene of *Vayeira* is a well-known one: Abraham welcomes three strangers into his tent; he and Sarah provide for them shelter and sustenance; and in turn, these strangers tell Abraham that his ninety-year-old wife will conceive a child. Sarah overhears this prediction and laughs (from which we get the name "Isaac," meaning "to laugh" in Hebrew). While the miracle of Sarah's conception is central to our narrative, Abraham's eagerness and enthusiasm in welcoming these strangers is also striking. Not only does he rush to greet and bring them in, but he also urges his household to use the choicest ingredients for their meal and to hasten in its preparation.

Throughout the stories of the Torah, we are told time and again that we ought to perform acts of loving-kindness because those are part of the mitzvot commanded to us by God—usually with the framing that we were once strangers in Egypt and know the plight of the less fortunate. However, the intentions and details of our fulfilling these mitzvot are just as important, if not more so, than the acts themselves. In Maimonides's *Mishneh Torah*, a whole chapter is devoted to one's intention and exact behavior when giving *tzedakah*. Even if you give the most generous of gifts, he says, if you cause shame or discomfort to the person you are giving to, it negates the value of the mitzvah.

We make this world holy and whole when we treat each other with kindness, integrity, and respect. Each human being, regardless of their wealth or station, is created in the image of God. We have a long way ahead of us before we can claim true equity and equality, but every act matters. Our faith and tradition guide us to give, but it is up to us to do so with open hearts, the eagerness and enthusiasm of Abraham and Sarah, and the joy and empathy of Maimonides.

## *Alternative Haftarah Reading:*
## *From* Messengers of God: Biblical Portraits and Legends, *by Elie Wiesel*

At the end of his struggle, which Job recognized as being lost in advance—for how can a human being hope to defeat God?—Job discovered a novel method to persevere in his resistance: he pretended to abdicate before he even engaged his battle.

Had he remained firm, had he discussed the divine arguments point by point, one would conclude that he had to concede defeat in the face of his interlocutor's rhetorical superiority. But he said yes to God, immediately. He did not hesitate or procrastinate, nor did he point out the slightest contradiction. Therefore, we know that in spite or perhaps because of appearances, Job continued to interrogate God. By repenting sins he did not commit, by justifying a sorrow he did not deserve, he communicates to us that he did not believe in his own confessions; they were nothing but decoys. Job personified human beings' eternal quest for justice and truth—he did not choose resignation. Thus he did not suffer in vain; thanks to him, we know that it is given to [human beings] to transform divine injustice into human justice and compassion.

Once upon a time, in a faraway land, there lived a legendary man, a just and generous man who, in his solitude and despair, found the courage to stand up to God. And to force [God] to look at [God's] creation. And to speak to those [human beings] who sometimes succeed, in spite of [God] and of themselves, in achieving triumphs over [God], triumphs that are grave and disquieting.

What remains of Job? A fable? A shadow? Not even the shadow of a shadow. An example, perhaps.

## The Power of Silence

### Rabbi Suzanne Singer

Two of the most disturbing texts in the Hebrew Bible are the *Akeidah*—the Binding of Isaac—and the Book of Job. In both, the central figure is righteous but is tested by a capricious God. God seems insecure about whether Abraham and Job love and obey God without reservation and devoid of self-interest. So God subjects them to unconscionable suffering, offering them a reprieve only at the very last moment. God demands that Abraham sacrifice his beloved son Isaac as a burnt offering and, making a bet with the Prosecuting Angel, God allows Job to be stripped of wealth, health, and children, hoping to prove that despite these tragedies, Job will not curse God.

Interestingly, both our heroes ultimately employ the same strategy in the face of this extreme injustice: silence. Not that either of them has any compunction about challenging God. Abraham argues forcefully with God over the destruction of Sodom and Gomorrah (Genesis 18–19), and Job spends more than thirty chapters demanding an explanation for his suffering. But in both cases, the disputation is based on reasoning: Abraham argues that if there are at least ten righteous people in Sodom, everyone should be spared, and Job makes a clear and compelling case for his innocence.

However, following God's speeches from the whirlwind, Job announces he will "yield" or "relent"—the verse (42:6) is very difficult to translate—and he falls silent. In the face of God's might and power, Job, a mere human being, is no match. There is no argument to be made. Similarly, sacrificing his son is so far out of the realm of the ethics Abraham has internalized, his only alternative is to be dumb-struck—literally—in response. But does silence mean defeat and surrender?

Elie Wiesel certainly does not think so. He points out that this silence is but a ruse. By keeping quiet and seeming to accept his fate, Job exposes the cruelty and the absurdity of God's actions; and so does Abraham, in my view. But we must ask: Does God really make bets with angels? Would God really ask us to murder our child? I believe that the authors of our Bible told these stories to reflect the reality that life is often arbitrary and unfair, whether or not God is to blame. And they are offering us a consolation: no matter what, rebellion is always an option, whether through argument or through silence. And through rebellion, we are able to preserve our dignity as human beings.

# *Chayei Sarah*
## Genesis 23:1–25:18

## Traditional Haftarah Reading:
## I Kings 1:1–31

## Growing Closer in Times of Change
### SHARON R. KELLER, *PhD*

THE TORAH PORTION *Chayei Sarah* takes us from Abraham burying his wife, Sarah, to Isaac and Ishmael burying their father, Abraham. In the interim, both Isaac and Abraham marry, and Abraham has more children; after Abraham's death, Isaac receives God's blessing.

The associated haftarah reading (I Kings 1:1–31) tells of the last days of King David and the palace intrigue that results. Adonijah, David's son with Haggit, understandably assumes he is heir to the throne and acts accordingly. However, Solomon's mother, Bathsheba, another wife of the dying king, has other ideas! The pericope ends with David's swearing to Bathsheba that Solomon, and not Adonijah, will inherit the throne and rule after him.

The haftarah reading is linked to the Torah portion by the phrase "old, well advanced in years," describing both Abraham and David, respectively (Genesis 24:1; I Kings 1:1). But equally important is their thematic connection, of change and transition—within a family, between different generations, and between the carriers of power. With change and transition come expectations, and these need to be assessed with care. Especially within families, the family members can either find closeness to each other (Isaac and Ishmael) or find themselves pushed apart (Adonijah and Solomon).

Change is inevitable. It is our responsibility to meet the challenges presented by change and build each other up rather than tear each other down.

# Friends at Our Deathbeds

*Rabbi Tom Alpert*

In *Parashat Chayei Sarah*, old age encounters mortality in the scene of Abraham's death (Genesis 25:8). The same happens in the haftarah reading: there, King David is "old, well advanced in years" (I Kings 1:1), the same phrase the Torah uses to describe Abraham's last days. Both David and Abraham face the end of their lives and work hard to ensure their legacies.

The haftarah reading tells us that David is always cold (I Kings 1:1). His courtiers bring him a beautiful young woman named Abishag to sleep beside him, warming the king but not being intimate with him (I Kings 1:3–4).

Robert Frost, in his poem "Provide, Provide," writes a modern midrash on Abishag's story. Abishag is pictured as she, too, would be of old age: a former Hollywood star (it is a midrash, after all) whose physical beauty has faded and who can find no livelihood other than to wash the outside steps of a building. Frost, realistically and perhaps cynically, advises others to accumulate wealth to avoid this indignity. He ends:

> Better to go down dignified
> With boughten friendship at your side
> Than none at all. Provide, provide!

The term "Boughten" was a folk expression of Frost's northern New England. It meant that a product was "Store-bought," and therefore inferior to what was crafted at home. But while genuine, homemade friendship would have been better, the poet advises taking even the shoddy comfort of boughten friendship rather than being abandoned in old age.

As Frost writes elsewhere in this poem, the end of life is often hard. However, if we look out for each other, and especially for the most vulnerable among us, we can give those facing the hardship of dying real friendship, not just the boughten kind. Others in turn will make sure that we will not be abandoned when our time comes.

## *Alternative Haftarah Reading:*
## *Jeremiah 1:11-19*

And the word of the Eternal came to me, saying:
"What do you see, Jeremiah?"
And I said: "I see a branch of an almond tree."
The Eternal then said to me:

You see well: "I am like an almoner
[dispensing] My word to be fulfilled."
The word of the Eternal came to me a second time:
"What do you see?"
And I said:
"I see a boiling pot whose face
is tipped away from the north."
And the Eternal One said to me:
"Out of the north shall disaster break forth
over all the people of the land."

I am calling all the kings of the north—says the Eternal One; each one will set up his throne facing the gates of Jerusalem, and all its surrounding walls, and all the cities of Judah. I will deliver My verdict against them for all their evil deeds, for they have forsaken Me, and have sacrificed to other gods, and prostrated themselves before the work of their own hands.

So you, gird your loins, get up and speak to them all that I have commanded you. Do not lose your nerve because of them, or I will unnerve you before them! I am making you this day a fortified city, an iron pillar, and [like] bronze walls against the whole land, against the kings of Judah, against its leaders, priests, and people of the land. They shall attack you, but they shall not overcome you, for I am with you to keep you safe, says the Eternal One.

# Stepping into One's Legacy

## ILANA Y. SYMONS

*Parashat Chayei Sarah* is not about the life of Sarah. On the contrary, it begins with Sarah's death and burial and then transitions to the narrative of her son, Isaac. At the outset of the *parashah*, Isaac is alone, physically and emotionally. He has just lost his mother, his greatest source of comfort, and narrowly avoided sacrifice at the hand of his father. Isaac is called a young man, *naar*, by his father at the foot of Mount Moriah. He is in distress and without a clear path forward. He knows there is a great legacy waiting for him but has not yet claimed it as his own.

Jeremiah begins his narrative in a similar place. He calls himself a young man, *naar*, at the beginning of his journey. God tells Jeremiah that God chose him in the womb to be a prophet. Despite this great legacy waiting for him, Jeremiah is hesitant to claim it as his own, saying he does not yet know how to speak. However, with God's guidance, Jeremiah sees visions of prophecy for the first time: an almond tree and a boiling pot. Slowly, he eases into his role. With a figure to guide him and ensure his protection, Jeremiah steps into his legacy.

As *Chayei Sarah* progresses, it becomes clear that Isaac also has forces guiding and protecting him. His father's servant goes in search of a wife for the young man; the woman chosen, Rebekah, is the only person who brings him comfort after his mother's death. When his father dies at the end of the parasha, Isaac officially becomes the story's protagonist. Abraham's covenant with God, stipulating that he will be a great nation, is realized through his son. Like Jeremiah, Isaac's feelings of aloneness and inadequacy are real, but they are tempered by those who support him into his new role. If we envisioned a dialogue between Isaac and Jeremiah, we might see two men empathizing about being afraid but tough; lonely but supported; unsure about themselves but resolved to continue the legacies for which they were destined. Isaac and Jeremiah demonstrate that we are not as weak as we might feel, even in our lowest moments, if only we can identify the forces that guide us from grief to comfort, from doubt to confidence, from childhood to maturity. In doing so, may we also take up the legacies set before us.

## Alternative Haftarah Reading: From The Chosen, by Rabbi Chaim Potok

Human beings do not live forever, Reuven. We live less than the time it takes to blink an eye, if we measure our lives against eternity. So it may be asked what value is there to a human life. There is so much pain in the world. What does it mean to have to suffer so much if our lives are nothing more than the blink of an eye? . . . I learned a long time ago, Reuven, that a blink of an eye in itself is nothing. But the eye that blinks, that is something. A span of life is nothing. But the man who lives that span, he is something. He can fill that tiny span with meaning, so its quality is immeasurable though its quantity may be insignificant. Do you understand what I am saying? A man must fill his life with meaning, meaning is not automatically given to life.

It is hard work to fill one's life with meaning. That I do not think you understand yet. A life filled with meaning is worthy of rest.

# A Life Filled with Meaning Is Worthy of Rest

### RABBI ILANA GREENFIELD BADEN

Chaim Potok's powerful passage reminds us that it is up to each of us to make our lives into something meaningful—so that when our days on earth end, we and our loved ones may take solace in knowing that our time with them was meaningful.

It is interesting that while the Torah portion *Chayei Sarah* begins with the account of this matriarch's death, the opening words are "Sarah lived to be one hundred years and twenty years and seven years—such was the span of Sarah's life" (Genesis 23:1). Accordingly, the name of the portion is "The Life of Sarah," not "The Death of Sarah." Moreover, our Sages, notably Rashi, have commented that the word "years" is repeated in this opening sentence, emphasizing the fact that Sarah lived every stage of her life with purpose and virtue.

This phrasing in our Torah portion teaches us that as overwhelming as death may be, we are encouraged to focus on the life that was lived, rather than the life that was lost. In other words, "A life filled with meaning is worthy of rest" (*The Chosen*, 205).

# Tol'dot
## Genesis 25:19–28:9

## Traditional Haftarah Reading:
## Malachi 1:1–2:7

### Lovers of the Virtuous

RABBI DR. SHMULY YANKLOWITZ

PARASHAT TOL'DOT, with its descriptions of Isaac's and Rebekah's uneven, unfair, polarizing, and ultimately destructive way to love each of their sons, Jacob and Esau, can be troubling to the contemporary reader. How can parents feel such a way about their own children, and how can God love a part of God's own Creation, the Edomites (Esau's tribe), less than God loves the tribe of Jacob?

Those descriptions are foreign to our ideas and values about parenting and community building. However, here, in the Book of Malachi, we see that God especially loves the tribe of Levi. We see that God loves the virtuous. Yes, God loves all divine creations, but those who choose to live justly are more intimately connected. What do we learn that God loves here?

- B'rit hachayim v'hashalom, "a covenant of life and peace" (Malachi 2:5): God wants our commitment to life and peace.
- Yirat HaShem, "awe for God" (v. 5): We are invited not to have all the answers, but to live with spiritual wonder, theological uncertainty, and sacred reverence.
- Torat emet, "a teaching of truth" (v. 6): We should be radically committed to truth.
- Avlah lo nimtza, "no wrong was found" (v. 6): One must not only reject injustice, but stand up robustly in its defiance.
- B'shalom uv'mishor, "walked in peace and equity" (v. 6): Social justice is not an abstract ideology; rather, we must incorporate our deepest moral principles into our words and actions—every day.

Indeed, we may wish for egalitarian love and worth. But we learn here that while everyone has human dignity, we should indeed never forget the ethical models we're striving to live by each day.

# Unconditional Love Within

*RABBI LISA SARI BELLOWS*

In *Parashat Tol'dot*, we read of Isaac and Rebekah's twin sons, Esau and Jacob, and their competition for their father's love and blessing. Our haftarah portion begins with a reminder that God not only had rejected Esau in the past, but also, indeed, rejected the entire people of of Edom (Esau's offspring) to that day.

In our haftarah portion, God speaks to the people of Israel of the unconditional love God has shown to them, yet the people neither remember these acts of love nor feel God's love in their hearts. We read, "'I have loved you,' says the Eternal One. But you say, 'How have You shown Your love for us?'" (Malachi 1:2). The people demand to see "proof" of God's love.

There are times when we feel forgotten and unloved, just like the Israelites. A reminder of God's great love can be found in the daily morning liturgy in the *Ahavah Rabbah* (Great love) blessing, which speaks to God's abundant, overflowing, and unconditional love. Additionally, whenever we feel that we need proof for that unconditional love, we can also turn within, for the unconditional love we seek to feel can be found within us.

Think of a moment when you have either experienced unconditional love from a family member, friend, mentor, even a beloved pet—and think of a moment of love that you gave to someone else. It doesn't have to be the perfect moment, just a moment when you have given or have felt love. We can find comfort in an unconditional holy love that is within us, always.

## *Alternative Haftarah Reading:*
## *From* Everyday Holiness *by Alan Morinis*

When asked how he had had such an impact as a great sage and leader in the twentieth-century Jewish world, the Chafetz Chaim answered, "I set out to try to change the world, but I failed. So I decided to scale back my efforts and only try to influence the Jewish community of Poland, but I failed there, too. So I targeted the community in my hometown of Radin, but achieved no greater success. Then I gave all my effort to changing my own family, and failed at that as well. Finally, I decided to change myself, and that's how I had such an impact on the Jewish world."

# Standing at the Crossroads

### RABBI PETER RIGLER

*Parsahat Tol'dot* tells the story of two brothers—twins who struggle with one another, deeply entrenched in their respective viewpoints. The brothers are doomed from the start to never hear one another, to never work together, and to never feel any sense of connection. This is a story about missed opportunities for connection, friendship, and growth. We are asked not to judge Jacob and Esau, but to look inward to see where we close off the possibility that someone else's opinion or way of life could be correct. We often use this story as a lesson about how two nations need to reconcile with one another and how families need to come to peace. I think we also need to view it as a personal invitation for change.

Jacob stands on a tributary of the Jordan River, about twenty-five miles north of the Dead Sea at, *Maavar Yabok*. This can be read to mean "passageway of the Jabok river" or alternatively "the transition point." Jacob is at a crossroads in his life. He is destined for greatness as he inherits the legacy of Abraham, Sarah, and Isaac. Yet Jacob feels unworthy, struggling to feel legitimate with an identity that he usurped from Esau. Before Jacob can move forward to change the world and become the progenitor of our people, he must first contend with this transition point where he stands.

To take on the tasks of improving anything or anyone else, we can best prepare by looking inward to find our own sense of self. Once Jacob wrestles and embraces his own life, he is ready to face the challenges and joys that lay ahead. How do we embrace the crossroads that are presented to find a better path in our own lives and world?

## *Alternative Haftarah Reading:*
## *"A Call to the Leaders of Islam for Peace and Brotherhood,"*
## *by Rabbi Ben-Zion Meir Hai Uziel*
## *and Rabbi Yitzhak HaLevi Herzog*

21 Kislev, 5708 [December 4, 1947]

A Call to the Leaders of Islam for Peace and Brotherhood.

To the Heads of The Islamic Religion in the Land of Israel and throughout the Arab lands near and far, Shalom U'Vracha:

Brothers, at this hour, as the Jewish people have returned to its land and state, per the word of God and the prophets in the Holy Scriptures, and in accordance with the decision of the

United Nations, we approach you in peace and brotherhood, in the name of God's Torah
and the Holy Scriptures, and we say to you:

Please remember the peaceful and friendly relations that existed between us when we lived
together in Arab lands and under Islamic Rulers during the Golden Age, when together we
developed brilliant intellectual insights of wisdom and science for all of humanity's benefit.
Please remember the sacred words of the prophet Malachi, who said: "Have we not all one
Father? Did not one God create us? Why do we break faith with one another, profaning the
covenant of our ancestors?" (Malachi 2:10).

We were brothers, and we shall once again be brothers, working together in cordial and neighborly relations in this Holy Land, so that we will build it and make it flourish, for the benefit of all
of its inhabitants, without discrimination against anyone. We shall do so in faithful and calm
collaboration, so that we may all merit God's blessing on the land, from which there shall
radiate the light of peace to the entire world.

Signed,
Rabbi Ben-Zion Meir Hai Uziel
Rabbi Yitzhak HaLevi Herzog

## Respect among the Nations

### RABBI PHILIP J. BENTLEY

In this week's *parashah*, *Tol'dot*, Jacob and Esau meet many years after Jacob stole
Isaac's blessing from his brother. Esau is a violent man, and Jacob has reason to
fear this meeting. He takes several measures to appease his brother, and their
meeting is warm and nonviolent. Even if Esau still holds hard feelings toward
Jacob, he is willing to move forward in peace.

Zionism and the State of Israel have always hoped for acceptance in the Middle East. In 1919, at Versailles, Chaim Weizmann (who would become Israel's
first president) and Emir Feisal created an agreement that included this hope:
"His Royal Highness the Emir Feisal, representing and acting on behalf of the
Arab Kingdom of Hedjaz, and Dr. Chaim Weizmann, representing and acting
on behalf of the Zionist Organization, mindful of the racial kinship and ancient
bonds existing between the Arabs and the Jewish people, and realizing that the
surest means of working out the consummation of their natural aspirations is
through the closest possible collaboration in the development of the Arab State
and Palestine."

"A Call to the Leaders of Islam for Peace and Brotherhood," our alternative
haftarah, was written in Arabic six months before Israel's independence by Israel's
two chief rabbis, expressing the hope that Israel would be welcomed as one of the
newly independent states in the region.

The Declaration of Independence of Israel confirmed this hope again: "We offer peace and amity to all neighboring states and their peoples and invite them to co-operate with the independent Jewish nation for the common good of all."

Israel is the Jewish state, and that means, even if we have never lived there, we are connected to it. Those concerned with justice, peace, and the environment in the Middle East need to be informed and supportive of Israeli organizations that reflect their opinions. That includes the Reform Movement.

# *Vayeitzei*
## Genesis 28:10–32:3

## Traditional Haftarah Reading:
## Hosea 12:13–14:10

### Trusting in Order to Trust

*Rabbi Cantor Jordan Shaner*

JACOB'S MARRIAGE begins in betrayal—as Hosea reminds us, "Israel served for a wife . . . he kept watch [of sheep]" (Hosea 12:13). That is to say, Israel fell in love and worked seven years to marry Rachel, only to find Leah under the bridal veil. Jacob was betrayed by Laban, his father-in-law.

Likewise, in the haftarah reading, God is portrayed as having cared for the people Israel through the generations, watching over them, and sending Moses to shepherd them (Hosea 12:14), only to have the people stray after idols.

Both stories end in the shocking realization that what we think we know about each other does not guarantee that we will not sometimes be surprised, disappointed, and even shocked to discover another truth about the people we live with. The question that Hosea makes us ask is: How can we establish trust, especially in the most intimate relationships?

The prophet Hosea suggests that trusting someone means accepting that we cannot guarantee the outcome of any relationships, including our relationship to God. However, we are still invited to enter them and to give both ourselves and others a chance to grow and become more trustworthy.

Thus, the Book of Hosea concludes here with a trust-inspiring image: the cypress, which neither produces fruit nor changes with the seasons. The cypress is evergreen. We may grow impatient over its boring stability, longing for change. Nevertheless, the prophet reassures us that it is this Tree of Life that will sustain us: "I am a luxuriant cypress, from which your fruit is found" (Hosea 14:9). The trust that grows through commitment is its own nourishing reward.

# To See Your Face Is Like Seeing the Face of God

*RABBI JADE SANK ROSS*

*Parashat Vayeitzei* and its haftarah reading from the Book of Hosea are connected through the theme of distance. In *Vayeitzei*, Jacobs flees from home after impersonating and receiving the blessing meant for his brother Esau. For the first time, Jacob, the mild-mannered homebody (Genesis 25:27), leaves his family and is far from all that was familiar to him. In the Book of Hosea, the Israelites have abandoned their faith in God and failed to see God's presence in their lives. In both the *parashah* and the haftarah reading, distance is the result of a broken relationship. What relationships are broken in our lives? How is brokenness distancing us from our loved ones and from God?

According to Hosea, whenever we are distant from God, we are also distant from our best selves. When we misplace our faith and trust, when we take the gifts of life and loving-kindness for granted, and when we fail to act with goodness and justice, we are not only distant from God, we are also distant from those we love and from the people we can be. The same is true vice versa: when there is brokenness in our relationships with each other, there is a fracture in our relationship with God.

However, Hosea also teaches that there is hope for healing: "I the Eternal have been your God ever since the land of Egypt. I will let you dwell in your tents again as in the days of old" (Hosea 12:10). Ultimately, no matter the distance, God is always close to us, and we are always capable of return and healing. Similarly, we know that upon reuniting with his brother to make amends, Jacob embraces Esau and says, "To see your face is like seeing the face of God" (Genesis 33:10).

In healing our relationships with each other, we can once again see God in our lives. To come close to God is to embrace each other.

## Alternative Haftarah Reading:
## "Where Will I Find You," by Y'hudah HaLevi
### Translated by Peter Cole

*Where, Lord, will I find you:*
*your place is high and obscured.*
*  And where*
*    won't I find you:*
*  your glory fills the world.*

You dwell deep within—
  you've fixed the ends of creation.
You stand, a tower for the near,

refuge to those far off.
You've lain above the Ark, here,
  yet live in the highest heavens.
Exalted among your hosts,
  although beyond their hymns—
    no heavenly sphere
      could ever contain you,
  let alone a chamber within.

In being borne above them
   on an exalted throne,
you are closer to them
   than their breath and skin.
Their mouths bear witness for them,
   that you alone gave them form.
Your kingdom's burden is theirs;
   who wouldn't fear you?
    And who could fail
      to search for you—
who sends down food when it's due?

I sought your nearness.
   With all my heart I called you.
And in my going out to meet you,
   I found you coming toward me,
as in the wonders of your might
   and holy works I saw you.

Who would say he hasn't seen
   your glory as the heavens'
     hordes declare
       their awe of you
   without a sound being heard?

But could the Lord, in truth,
   dwell in men on earth?
How would men you made
   from the dust and clay
fathom your presence there,
   enthroned upon their praise?
The creatures hovering over
   the world praise your wonders—
    your throne borne high
     above their heads,
   as you bear all forever.

# God Is Already Halfway to Us

### ABIGAIL POGREBIN

In *Parashat Vayeitzei*, God appears to Jacob in a dream and reaffirms the covenant made with Abraham—that God will be a stalwart companion on the journey of the Jewish people toward progeny and the Promised Land (Genesis 12–17). When Jacob wakes up, he utters these words: "Truly, the Eternal is in this place, and I did not know it!" (Genesis 28:16).

Jacob's simple exclamation reminds us of the many times we have essentially stumbled over God's presence without having realized that it was there all along. So many of us describe searching for spirituality and not knowing where to look. But especially during the acute crises of the COVID-19 pandemic—when we saw the decency of strangers, the quiet heroism of frontline workers, the peaceful gatherings of thousands taking a knee in the street, the Zoom shivahs and synagogue outreach to the homebound—we were reminded that God appears in the most mundane moments, if only we pay closer attention.

Medieval poet Y'hudah HaLevi's "Where Will I Find You" echoes our current disquiet and dislocation. The comfort of Jacob's words—"The Eternal is in this place"—answers HaLevi's cry (and ours):

   I sought Your nearness.

With all my heart I called You.
And in my going out to meet You,
I found You coming toward me.

Maybe the lesson of both this *parashah* and this poem is that spirituality is found where you "did not know it," to use Jacob's words. And that when we go out to meet God, we discover God is already halfway to us.

## Alternative Haftarah Reading:
## From I and Thou, *by Martin Buber*

The You encounters me by grace—it cannot be found by seeking. But that I speak the basic word to it is a deed of my whole being, is my essential deed.

The You encounters me. But I enter into a direct relationship to it. Thus the relationship is election and electing, passive and active at once. An action of the whole being must approach passivity, for it does away with impartial actions and thus with any sense of action, which always depends on limited exertions.

The basic word I-You can be spoken only with one's whole being. The concentration and fusion into a whole being can never be accomplished by me, can never be accomplished without me. I require a You to become; becoming I, I say You.

All actual life is encounter.

The relation to the You is unmediated. Nothing conceptual intervenes between I and You, no prior knowledge and no imagination; and memory itself is changed as it plunges from particularity into wholeness. No purpose intervenes between I and You, no greed and no anticipation; and longing itself is changed as it plunges from the dream into appearance. Every means is an obstacle. Only where all means have disintegrated encounters occur.

# Infused into Our Every Interaction

### CANTOR SHANI COHEN

For Buber, the fundamental state of being is relational. This elemental state of connecting with the world around us does not rely on knowledge, experience, or even feeling; it requires only one's whole, unmediated presence. Both parties must be open to the relationship. In *Parashat Vayeitzei*, the *sulam* (ladder) in Jacob's dream can be read as illustrating the tangible relationship between Jacob and God. In Buber's words, "longing itself is changed as it plunges from the dream into appearance."

Like Buber, I do not trust the human mind to always act rationally and responsibly, nor do I believe that we can rationally understand the mysteries of this world. Buber describes the incorporeal God through the compelling lens of relationship, be it a person-to-God connection or a person-to-person relation (which I would describe as the communal experience of God). Buber imagines an ideal world that values relationships based on love and interpersonal responsibility (*I and Thou*, 66).

Sometimes, when I am alone and close my eyes, I feel a swell of emotion I can only understand as God. I have also had extraordinary moments of connection during prayer services, when I forget about the boundaries I put up between myself and others. God is not an entity separate from human beings, but within and a part of who we are, infused into our every interaction with the world.

The image of connecting to God and to everything around us brings us back to Jacob's dream. Many commentators explain that Jacob came upon "the place" by surprise. Jacob's dream encounter with God was not the product of intense effort or careful planning. Rather, he happened upon the holy place by surprise, only realizing its sanctity after the fact.

Like Jacob, we encounter God when we allow ourselves to be changed by our relationships. The more we approach the world from the perspective of I-Thou, the more love and responsibility we will feel for others, seeing within each encounter the divine spark.

# *Vayishlach*
## Genesis 32:4–36:43

## Traditional Haftarah Reading:
## Hosea 11:7–12:12

## Love and Deceit
### AARON DB TOROP

THIS PASSAGE in Hosea directly references Jacob's encounter with an angel, the most obvious connection between this traditional haftarah reading and *Parashat Vayishlach*. But other more subtle references emerge as well: Hosea mentions Beth El, a different location where God appears to Jacob in this *parashah*; Hosea describes the angel that Jacob wrestled with as weeping, and while in the *parashah* the angel does not cry, Jacob and Esau do when they meet. Lastly, Hosea proclaims the name of God, just as names are key narrative components of *Vayishlach*.

Love and deceit are central themes in both Hosea's and Jacob's stories and teachings. Just as Jacob's deceitful taking of the birthright and his father's blessing ends in a loving, weeping embrace with Esau, so too does Hosea's description of the people's deceit and turning away from God end in a loving reunion. Hosea portrays the people, referred to as both Ephraim and Israel, as constantly defecting from God, but God cannot bring Godself to destroy the people. A midrash in the Babylonian Talmud (*Taanit* 5a) takes this love one step further, with God's status reflecting that of Israel. The midrash teaches that God will not enter *Y'rushalayim shel malah* (the heavenly Jerusalem) until God can enter *Y'rushalayim shel matah* (the earthly Jerusalem). After the destruction, God too is in a version of heavenly exile, unable to enter *Y'rushalayim shel matah* or *malah* until the redemption. God's identification with Israel demonstrates the robustness of God's love and concern.

From Hosea and Jacob, we learn about the possibility of maintaining love even through immense frustration and conflict. Rabbi Yosei bar Chanina teaches in *B'reishit Rabbah* (54:3) that love without rebuke is not love. However, love must have more than rebuke to overcome conflict and deceit. Our love for each other must be modeled on God's love for Israel: based on emotional identification, necessitating growth and change through conflict, and remaining eternal.

# Struggle and Return to Wholeness

### MICAH SYMONS

In the Book of Hosea, the prophet calls for a reinvigoration of the people's relationship with the Divine. He invokes two episodes from Jacob's life: one of Jacob grabbing his brother Esau's heel in the womb (Genesis 25:26); and the other of Jacob wrestling with the angel, who afterward renames him Israel (Genesis 32). The latter comes from *Parashat Vayishlach*. Hosea interestingly does not recall the exchanging Esau's birthright for Jacob's bowl of lentil soup (Genesis 25:29–34).

"Now, then, you must [truly] turn back to your God" (Hosea 12:7): The theme of return is common throughout the Jewish liturgy, be it on the High Holy Days ("Take us back, Adonai; let us come back to You") or as part of our traditional weekday *Amidah* ("Return us to Your Torah").

What does it mean to "return" in the twenty-first century? To what are we returning?

Hosea's prophecy references Jacob's struggle with the divine being. The evening before encountering his brother Esau for the first time in years, Jacob wrestles with this being, who, after dislocating Jacob's hip, renames him Israel—because he "struggled with God and with human beings, and [he has] prevailed" (Genesis 32:29).

The world we inhabit is broken. Individuals are targeted for their skin color, gender identity, religion, and so on; people are more concerned with proving their point than bettering the world; individualism runs supreme. Hosea's words call us to return to a way of being where our struggles serve a higher purpose. As the Rabbis taught, "Any dispute that is for the sake of heaven will endure" (*Pirkei Avot* 5:20).

In the eyes of Hosea, we are called to engage in dialogue whose only purpose will be to bring the world we live in now closer to its divine ideal. By being in meaningful struggles with both God and humanity, we will return to "steadfast love and justice" (Hosea 12:7).

## *Alternative Haftarah Reading:*
## *II Samuel 13:1–3, 5, 9–12, 14–16, 18–20*

*This happened sometime afterward: Absalom son of David had a beautiful sister named Tamar, and Amnon son of David became infatuated with her. Amnon was so distraught because of his [half-]sister Tamar that he became sick; for she was a virgin, and it seemed impossible to Amnon to do anything to her. Amnon had a friend named Jonadab, the son of David's brother Shimah; Jonadab was a very clever man. . . . Jonadab said to him, "Lie down in your bed and pretend you are sick. When your father comes to see you, say to him, 'Let my sister Tamar come and give me something to eat. Let her prepare the food in front of me, so that I may look on, and let her serve it to me.'" . . . After everyone had withdrawn, Amnon said to Tamar, "Bring the food inside and feed me." Tamar took the cakes she had made and brought them to her brother inside. But when she served them to him, he caught hold of her and said to her, "Come, lie with me, sister." But she said to him, "Don't, brother. Don't force me. Such things are not done in Israel! Don't do such a vile thing!" . . . But he would not listen to her; he overpowered her and lay with her by force.*

*Then Amnon felt a very great loathing for her; indeed, his loathing for her was greater than the passion he had felt for her. And Amnon said to her, "Get out!" She pleaded with him, "Please, don't commit this wrong; to send me away would be even worse than the first wrong you committed against me." But he would not listen to her. . . . His attendant took her outside and barred the door after her. Tamar put dust on her head and rent the ornamented tunic she was wearing; she put her hands on her head, and walked away, screaming loudly as she went. Her brother Absalom said to her, "Was it your brother Amnon who did this to you? For the present, sister, keep quiet about it; he is your brother. Don't brood over the matter." And Tamar remained in her brother Absalom's house, forlorn.*

# Hard Conversations

### Rabbi Ayala Ronen Samuels, PhD

The Ashkenazic haftarah reading (Hosea 11:7–12:12) mentions the successful struggle of Jacob with the angel in our Torah portion (Genesis 32:29). It is an enigmatic speech that both criticizes the descendants of Jacob for being cunning like their father and, at the same time, offers comfort to them, the children of God. The text addresses the entire people of Israel as "Jacob." The Sephardic haftarah reading for *Vayishlach* focuses on God's promise to avenge Esau and his people, Edom (Obadiah 1:18), and establishes the siblings' rivalry as eternal—a mirror for historic tensions between Jews and gentiles.

As an alternative to these traditional readings, I suggest the story of Amnon and Tamar—a horrifying tale about King David's eldest son, Amnon, who desires his sister Tamar, invites her to his room, rapes her, and then throws her out of his room and his life. Inevitably, this story reminds us of the story of the torture of Dinah, Jacob's only daughter (Genesis 34).

Reading either or both of those stories in synagogue, as well as in bar and bat mitzvah classes, may spark conversations that are hard to have in most families and communities, as they touch upon topics like sexual assault, incestuous relationships, the silencing of victims, and gender hierarchies and their violent expressions, then and now. The two stories also bring up the issue of revenge and its consequences. The "deed that was done to Dinah," as the Rabbis referred to it, results in a horrible slaughter in Shechem (Genesis 34:25–31) and in the disappearance of what might have been the thirteenth tribe of Israel: the tribe of Dinah. The rape of Tamar motivates Absalom, Tamar's brother, to murder Amnon and start his vengeful alliance with the king of Geshur against David (II Samuel 13:23–39). While the Torah forbids revenge (Leviticus 19:18), the brothers of Dinah and of Tamar choose revenge of the attackers over rehabilitation of the victims.

We need to be brave and forthcoming by introducing these conversations into our spiritual spaces. The introduction of this haftarah reading to Shabbat Vayishlach can help us do it.

*In recent years, Israeli society has begun to publicly and openly address issues of violence against women. Within MARAM—the Israeli Council of Progressive Rabbis—a group of women founded B'not Dinah, "Dinah's Daughters." The group's main purpose is to fight the violence against women.*

*Under the leadership of Rabbi Ayala Ronen Samuels and Rabbi Ayala Sha'ashua-Miron, the Israeli Reform Movement instituted the Sabbath of Parashat Vayishlach as Shabbat Dinah—a day dedicated to fighting violence against women. In the service, before saying the Mourner's Kaddish, the names of women murdered in the past year are recalled. The alternative haftarah reading is II Samuel 13:1–14 (above) and Isaiah 60:15:*

> *Whereas you have been forsaken,*
> *Rejected, with none passing through,*
> *I will make you a pride everlasting,*
> *A joy for age after age.*

> —Rabbi Yehoram Mazor

## Alternative Haftarah Reading: "God Wrestler," by Rick Lupert

Your name shall no longer be called Jacob, but Israel,
because you have commanding power

After a night of stranger wrestling
After the he donkeys and she donkeys
were wrapped in fraternal paper to
make up for the inadequacy of the stew
After the wives were sent across the river
After the unnamed wrestler caused
a permanent limp with just a finger.
After the unnamed wrestler glowed

until the break of dawn
until the break of dawn
After Jacob kicked holy butt
After Jacob told the stranger his name
After the stranger was coy about his name.
Then, Jacob got a new name
Then, Jacob became the wrestler
Then, Jacob became Israel
And the rest of us
after the donkeys
and the wives, and the river
Never forgot that name
put it on our business cards
Speak it out loud whenever
we're asked
who we are.

# Our Names, Ourselves

### RABBI BARBARA AB SYMONS

Jacob is renamed—twice—in this *parashah*. In the midst of this holy wrestling match, Jacob is asked his name and after he responds, he is told, "No more shall you be called Jacob, but Israel ... for you have struggled with God and with human beings, and you have prevailed" (Genesis 32:29). When Jacob in turn asks for the angel's name, he is told in the very next verse "Why do you ask my name?" and the being departs. Later in the portion, God tells Jacob: "Jacob are you called no more, for Israel is your name!" (Genesis 35:10).

Jacob is given the name Israel and then God reiterates it. Perhaps he had to hear it directly from God, not from an angel. Perhaps God needed to make sure that Jacob earned it, and once Jacob passed the trial period, he could keep the name Israel—though this is questionable given that he misled Esau and given his silence when his daughter Dinah was raped. It also must be noted that "Israel" is not used as consistently as "Jacob" throughout the rest of his life, though as the poem says, it does become ours.

We read in the midrash:

"A person has three names:
one that they are called by their father and mother;
one that people know them by,
and one that they acquire for themself." (*Kohelet Rabbah* 7:3)

The name we are given links us to past generations, solidifying the chain of tradition. The name that others call us is of their own invention. It takes work to acquire a name for oneself: It means being victorious in the wrestling match between our evil inclinations and our good inclinations. It means living our obituaries, not our resumes—focusing on relationships and values rather than academic achievement or professional advancement. It means acting with justice and compassion in our daily, moment-by-moment interactions at home and on our way.

We are not only called by our name; our name calls us.

# *Vayeishev*
## Genesis 37:1–40:23

## Traditional Haftarah Reading:
## Amos 2:6–3:8

## Walking Together

*RABBI ALONA LISITSA, PhD*

AMOS WAS A PROPHET from the Southern Kingdom of Judah, who was called to bring the words of God to the Northern Kingdom of Israel. He lived and prophesized in the first part of the eighth century BCE, which was a period of economic prosperity, territorial expansion, and relative peace and stability. However, Amos brought to the king Jeroboam II and his court a disturbing message of destruction. He rebuked the rich and prosperous for their neglect of the poor and the needy (Amos 2:6). His words resonated strongly among the lavishly living elites of his days.

We read the Book of Amos as a warning not only to the elites of his day, but also as a reminder of Joseph's brothers' transgression. As they sold Joseph for twenty pieces of silver (Genesis 37:28–29) and were punished in the future (Genesis 42:6–7), so would the corrupted rich of Israel be punished in the future (Amos 2:13–16). Amos says to Israel that her closeness to God does not entail any privilege, but to the contrary, "You alone have I known of all the families of the earth—therefore I will punish you for all your iniquities" (Amos 3:2). Other nations, rebuked in the first chapter for the atrocities they committed in times of war, will be punished too; but the people of Israel will be held accountable for the injustices they committed during the times of peace!

Both Joseph's brothers and the people of Israel among whom Amos lived are accountable for their moral corruption. The covenant with God presupposes obligations not only toward God, but also toward our entire community. Those who are in the covenant with God are in the covenant with each other; the covenant with God is a warranty for the covenantal community in which we live. "Do two walk together without having arranged it?" (Amos 3:3). Walking together with God is walking with each other—meeting, seeing, and caring. Indifference is perceived as a crime against God, and the Kingdom of Israel will be destroyed because of the indifference of the rich to the sufferings of the poor—those who have nothing.

To meet, see, and care—to walk together as one people: *kein y'hi ratzon*, "may it be God's will."

# Called to Speak

*RABBI PAUL J. CITRIN*

The prophet Amos (eighth century BCE) was one of the great truth-tellers in ancient Israel. He rebuked the powerful for exploiting the poor and the weak. His charge that the people in power "sell the innocent for silver, the needy for a pair of sandals" (Amos 2:6) awakens us to the deed of Joseph's brothers centuries earlier. Recall that in *Parashat Vayeishev*, they threw Joseph into a desert pit, with the intention to sell him (Genesis 37:28–29).

Amos confronts the Israelites' decline in personal morality and social ethics. He reminds them that God freed them from enslavement in Egypt, led them to Canaan, and raised up among them guiding prophets. Yet, the people have not kept their commitment to live by the ethical laws of Torah.

Some Israelites thought of themselves as "the chosen people." They believed God would never abandon them despite their intolerable crushing of the poor. Amos states that the opposite is true. Because of God's saving and intimate relationship with Israel, God expects more of them (Amos 3:2). God threatens dire punishment particularly because the prophets have taught what is expected of them. Amos chastises them like a roaring lion (v. 4). When the Eternal speaks, the prophet must transmit the frightening message (v. 8).

Today, some of us denigrate as fake news the efforts by the media to paint a picture of our flawed society. Cruel efforts are afoot to litigate against the plans of many of our political leaders for affordable, available health care for millions. Rabbis address failures of social ethics and empathy but are frequently silenced by the criticism that their sermons are too "political." Yet, Amos models for us the core and essence of Jewish leadership and values. We must speak truth to power, protect the poor, and look deeply into our own behavior and commitments. Only by means of responding to the call for social justice can we bless our lives with honor and glory.

## *Alternative Haftarah Reading:*
## *Psalm 126:1–6; Babylonian Talmud,* Taanit 23*a*

In the Book of Psalms, we are asked to dream of redemption:

A song of Ascents:
When the Eternal brought back those who returned to Zion,
we were like those who dream—
our mouths shall be filled with laughter,
our tongues, with songs of joy.
Then shall they say among the nations,
"The Eternal has done great things for them!"
The Eternal will do great things for us
and we shall rejoice.

Restore our fortunes, O Eternal,
like watercourses in the Negeb.
Those who sow in tears
shall reap in joy.
Though they go along weeping,
carrying the seed-bag,
they shall come back with songs of joy,
carrying their sheaves. (Psalm 126:1–6)

Millennia later, the Talmud teaches about a specific dreamer:

Rabbi Yochanan said: "All the days of the life of that righteous man, Choni, he was dism tressed over the meaning of this verse: 'A song of Ascents: When the Eternal brought back those who returned to Zion, we were like those who dream' (Psalm 126:1). He said to himself: Is there really a person who can sleep and dream for seventy years? One day, he was walking along the road when he saw a certain man planting a carob tree. Choni said to him: 'This tree, after how many years will it bear fruit?' The man said to him: 'It will not produce fruit until seventy years have passed.' Choni said to him: 'Is it obvious to you that you will live seventy years, that you expect to benefit from this tree?' He said to him: 'That man himself found a world full of carob trees. Just as my ancestors planted for me, I too am planting for my descendants.'" (Babylonian Talmud, *Taanit* 23a)

# To Live as in a Dream
### RABBI JOSEPH B. MESZLER

In this week's Torah portion, we encounter a famous dreamer, Joseph. In Psalm 126, we are all asked to be dreamers. Returning to Zion is like a dream come true. This psalm is sung before the Blessing after Meals, *Birkat HaMazon*, on Shabbat. It contains four of the most beautiful and poetic words ever written in Hebrew:

*Hazorim b'dimah b'rinah yiktzoru*, "Those who sow in tears shall reap in joy" (Psalm 126:5). This is a song of hope; before the State of Israel instituted "HaTikvah" ("The Hope") as its national anthem, the Jewish people sang this psalm.

Hope, however, is hard to hold onto. The Talmud story tells us about a righteous person—a tzaddik—named Choni who simply could not fathom the dream of returning from exile ever coming true. He looked back to the previous exile from Israel, which lasted seventy years, and wondered: How could anyone say that such hardship passed by like a dream?

He learns something crucial from an old man planting carob trees: to commit to the dream means to know that you may not live to see the dream's fulfillment, but your descendants might. Just as we have received from those who came before us, we work and live for those who will come after us. *Midor lador*, "from generation to generation"—that is not just how we survive, but that is how we thrive, during exile or any other difficult time. We commit to a larger vision of hope and work together toward it, even if we may never live to see the result. That's what it means to live "as in a dream."

## THE FIRST SHABBAT OF THE WINTER CYCLE:
### SHABBAT OF THANKSGIVING

### *Alternative Haftarah Reading:*
### *Joshua 1:1–11, 5:1*

After the death of Moses, the servant of the Eternal, the Eternal said to Joshua son of Nun, Moses's attendant, "My servant Moses is dead; come now, come across this [river] Jordan, you and all this people, and go into the land that I am giving to the people of Israel. As I promised Moses, I am giving you every foot of ground you step on. Your borders [shall reach] from the desert [in the south] and the Lebanon [in the north] to the great River, the river Euphrates [in the east]—[that is] all the land of the Hittites—and to the Great Sea in the west. As long as you live, no one shall be able to stand against you. I will be with you as I was with Moses. I will never fail you or leave you.

"Be strong and of good courage, for you must bring this people into possession of the land that I swore to their ancestors to give to them. Only be strong and of good courage in observing faithfully all the Torah that Moses My servant commanded you; do not turn away from it to the right or to the left: then you shall do well wherever you go. Let the book of this Torah never depart from your mouth; meditate on it day and night, taking care to carry out all that is written in it. Then shall you be successful in your enterprise, and then shall you do well. Have I not enjoined you? Be strong and of good courage, do not be afraid or disheartened, for I, the Eternal your God, am with you wherever you go."

Then Joshua gave these orders to the officers of the people: "Go through the camp and tell the people: Get provisions ready, for within three days you are going to cross the Jordan to take possession of the land that the Eternal your God is giving you to possess!" . . .

When all the kings of the Amorites on the western side of the Jordan, and all the kings of the Canaanites near the sea, heard how the Eternal had dried up the waters of the Jordan for the sake of the Israelites until they crossed over, they lost heart, and no spirit was left in them because of the Israelites.

## Meeting Our Best—and Our Worst
### Rabbi Samantha G. Frank and Rabbi Daniel G. Zemel

From the week of Thanksgiving through New Year's Day, Americans participate in seasonally appropriate social rituals: from enjoying Thanksgiving meals with family and friends and watching parades, to exploring the history of Native populations and the effects of colonialism, to attending holiday parties. The winter season is special. Homes are decorated with lights, and in Jewish homes, *chanukiyot* are lit, latkes are eaten, and dreidels are spun. At this time of year, Jews are particularly aware of how we seamlessly participate in American culture, and we are particularly aware of our differences.

On Thanksgiving, we pause to express gratitude for our lives and reflect on the stories that we tell about the founding of America, as well as the story about who we wish to be as American Jews. The critical engagement with our history is linked to the creation of our future. Telling the truth about our history requires us to be courageous in confronting truths previously suppressed or ignored. The American story is a story of conquest and cultural clash.

We find echoes of our own story in the Book of Joshua as the Israelites enter what for us is the Promised Land, but what was also a land already inhabited. In preparation for their entry into the land, Joshua, the Israelites' new leader, is enjoined twice by God: *chazak ve-ematz*, "be strong and of good courage" (Joshua 1:6, 1:9). He and the Israelites need strength not only for this new step of the journey. Rashi tells us that they need different kinds of strength: physical strength (Rashi on Joshua 1:6), strength to observe the commandments (Rashi on Joshua 1:7), and mental strength in preparation for war (Rashi on Joshua 1:8–9).

How might the Israelites—and how do we—reconcile the Torah's injunction *V'ahavta l'rei-acha kamocha*, "Love your neighbor as yourself" (Leviticus 19:18), with the injunction to make war on the current inhabitants of "their" land? In Joshua, chapter 5, we learn the effect of the Israelite conquest on the native people: they grow faint of heart. The Israelites' strength has a direct negative impact that is both physical and spiritual on the native inhabitants to the land.

In this story, we meet our best and our worst all at once. How do we enact repair? The first step is in acknowledging the truths of our stories: sometimes our success means causing loss and pain to others. Taking the first step to acknowledge this enables us to move forward with integrity and to enact deeper repair and change. In this spirit, a congregation might choose to learn about the First Peoples who lived on the land in their community. A congregation might also choose Native poetry to read alongside this haftarah reading. Some communities may have the opportunity to form relationships with the Indigenous Peoples in the area.

# Mikeitz
## Genesis 41:1–44:17

## Traditional Haftarah Reading:
## I Kings 3:15–4:1

## When Is a Dream Not Just a Dream?
### RABBI SARAH BERMAN

IN *PARASHAT MIKEITZ*, Joseph interprets Pharaoh's dreams, and together they help the Egyptian people prepare to weather a famine. The week's haftarah reading also opens on the heels of a dream—Solomon's dream of meeting God, who grants the new king the wisdom, discernment, and sound judgment he requests and even the wealth and glory he does not.

Solomon's wisdom is tested immediately, but not with a case of property, legal status, or religious practice—topics of political importance to a ruler. Rather, this heartbreaking case pits two women against each other, both claiming to be the mother of the same child. In adjudicating this case, the new king shows himself sensitive to more than just his own concerns. Like Joseph and Pharaoh before him, he uses his power of state to help his people, sending a child home with the child's loving parent. The reading ends calling Solomon "king over all Israel" (I Kings 4:1), recognition that he has passed this first test.

In his dream, Solomon seeks wisdom instead of wealth and uses that gift to help his people. What examples do we see today of leaders who use their status to help people, rather than for personal gain? A strong social safety net, protected voting rights, disarmament treaties, even new parks and streetlights, all can indicate leaders who—like Solomon, Joseph, and Pharaoh—use their positions to improve the lives of those under their care.

## Between Dreams and Reality
### RABBI MAX CHAIKEN

Just as *Parashat Mikeitz* opens with a dreaming king, so does our haftarah reading, where King Solomon awakens from a dream. While the Pharaoh must eventually bring in Joseph to interpret the haunting images of his dreams, Solomon awakens blessed with wisdom itself, granted directly from God.

As the haftarah reading continues, we hear a story meant to demonstrate the king's wisdom. Two new mothers, both sex workers, approach Solomon after the baby of one of them has died, while the baby of the other is still alive. Both claim the living child as her own. Solomon's proposition to cut the baby in half reveals the true mother. Importantly, all of Israel sees the wisdom granted by God to Solomon as he is able to settle the terrible conflict.

Our dreams remain a potent force for inspiration and introspection to this day. Through interpretation of the dreams in our sleep or through working toward a dream that encapsulates all of our aspirations, we constantly connect our dreams to our lived reality. Joseph's interpretation of the symbolism of Pharaoh's dreams helps him plan for famine, so people don't starve. The wisdom Solomon found in his dream helps him resolve a life-threatening conflict, even if we might cringe at his method, suggesting the mothers split the baby in half.

While we don't read about the new mothers' dreams, I wonder about them. The passage calls us to consider, reflect, and interpret our dreams. Which of your dreams might turn into a source of wisdom?

## Alternative Haftarah Reading:
### Sh'mot Rabbah 18:12

And on the day that they went down to Egypt, on that same day did they go out. And on that day Joseph went out from jail. Hence this night is a joyful occasion for all of Israel, as it is written (Exodus 12:42), "That was for the Eternal a night of vigil." In this world, God made a miracle for them at night, since it was a temporary miracle, but in the future to come, this night will become a day, as it is stated: "And the light of the moon will be like the light of the sun and the light of the sun will be seven times, etc." (Isaiah 30:26)—like the light that the Holy One, blessed be God, created at first and hid in the Garden of Eden.

## Freeing the Light

### Rabbi Heather Miller

The Torah portion of *Mikeitz* centers around Joseph's life. It is always read during Chanukah, the Festival of Lights. This midrash tells us that three light-filled days of redemption occurred on the same date years apart: (1) Joseph was freed from jail, (2) the Israelites went down to Egypt to escape famine, and (3) the Israelites left Egypt to escape oppression. Each of these miracles is a great light itself.

From this, we learn that each time redemption takes place, light is unlocked. When we are free, each of us can shine our own unique light in the world. Redemption occurs when light that is hidden within each of us is set free.

In what ways can we work to ensure that everyone, especially the oppressed, famished, and incarcerated, has the opportunity to shine their light? What might we gain from ensuring that they do?

## THE SECOND SHABBAT OF THE WINTER CYCLE

### *Alternative Haftarah Reading: Jeremiah 29:4–14*

Thus said God of heaven's hosts, the God of Israel, to the whole community which I exiled from Jerusalem to Babylon: Build houses and live in them, plant gardens and eat their fruit. Take wives and beget sons and daughters; and take wives for your sons, and give your daughters to husbands, that they may bear sons and daughters. Multiply there, do not decrease. And seek the welfare of the city to which I have exiled you and pray to the Eternal in its behalf; for in its prosperity you shall prosper.

For thus said the God of heaven's hosts, the God of Israel: Let not the prophets and diviners in your midst deceive you, and pay no heed to the dreams they dream. For they prophesy to you in My name falsely; I did not send them—declares the Eternal.

For thus said the Eternal: When Babylon's seventy years are over, I will take note of you, and I will fulfill to you My promise of favor—to bring you back to this place. For I am mindful of the plans I have made concerning you—declares the Eternal—plans for your welfare, not for disaster, to give you a hopeful future. When you call Me, and come and pray to me, I will give heed to you. You will search for Me and find me, if only you seek Me wholeheartedly. I will be at hand for you—declares the Eternal—and I will restore your fortunes. And I will gather you from all the nations and from all the places to which I have banished you—declares the Eternal—and I will bring you back to the place from which I have exiled you.

## When Exile Becomes Homeland

Rabbi Samantha G. Frank and Rabbi Daniel G. Zemel

In this season of holiday celebrations, we are particularly aware of what we share with the majority Christian culture and of what differentiates us. While Chanukah and Christmas share some essential themes (hope amid darkness, the reality of miracles), at Christmastime particularly we are more than ever aware of our differences.

The Hebrew Bible is the story of the Israelite journey, from home to exile, and then back to home. For American Jews, America is our home. Fittingly, this reading from the prophet Jeremiah reminds us that our task is to create roots where we are. What was once thought of as "exile" may actually be home.

The American ideal is the flourishing of many cultures. We can invest in our lives and in our neighbors' lives with joy and hope. We are instructed to plant gardens, build homes, have children, and seek the welfare of the city in which we live (Jeremiah 29:5–7). In other words, we ought to embrace life and work for harmony. Jeremiah calls us to partner with others, for our differences need not be divisive. What can you do to help a newer immigrant community feel as settled as we do?

# *Vayigash*
## Genesis 44:18–47:27

## Traditional Haftarah Reading:
## Ezekiel 37:15–28

## My Messianic Dream
### Rabbi Denise L. Eger

T HE PROPHET EZEKIEL delivers a message of hope and unity. This haftarah reading speaks to the messianic ideal of the unification of the Jewish people: one God and one people.

Called by God, Ezekiel is tasked with a ritual of bringing together two engraved sticks and binding them as one. One stick will be engraved with "for Judah and the Israelites associated with it," and the second will have engraved "Joseph's—the stick of Ephraim—and all the House of Israel associated with it" (Ezekiel 37:16). This prophetic ritual is an image for a message of hope and consolation: God will bring back together the dispersed people. Just as the two sticks would become one, the Northern and the Southern Kingdoms would be reunited one day.

These are powerful images while living in exile, as Ezekiel did. He had lived through the destruction of the First Temple in 587 BCE and was exiled to Babylonia. As the leader of the community in exile, he needed to lift their spirits and nourish the hope for their eventual return to the Land of Israel. His vision relays God's promise of reunification and unity for all who were longing to return to Zion.

There is a sublime beauty to this passage chosen as the haftarah reading for *Parashat Vayigash*. In our Torah portion, Joseph, now second to rule in all of Egypt, is reunited with his brothers, including his brother Judah, who was the one to have suggested that Joseph be sold into slavery rather than be killed. Joseph and Judah reunite. The beautiful scene of reunification in *Parashat Vayigash* is hinted at in Ezekiel's vision: The descendants of Joseph, embodied in the tribes of Ephraim and Manasseh, were part of the Northern Kingdom. The tribe of Judah, descendants of Judah, was part of the Southern Kingdom. Just like the two brothers in the Torah portion and the two sticks of the haftarah reading, the two kingdoms of Israel and Judah will be reunited one day. This is Ezekiel's message.

Ezekiel's prophecy rings true today, too. When we as a people get over our divisions, the messianic ideal will be realized. The promise of God's *b'rit shalom*, "covenant of peace" (Ezekiel 37:26), is based on the unity of our people. The Rabbis teach that the Second Temple was destroyed in 70 CE because of *sinat chinam*, "baseless hatred," of Jew against Jew. This vision is the antidote to that hatred and reminds us of the principle of *ahavat Yisrael* and *K'lal Yisrael*: "love of the people Israel" and that we are one people—the "Community of Israel." One day, we will be able to return in love to the Land of Israel, bringing us into communion with the one God.

This messianic ideal expresses a universal respect of one Jew for another regardless of how they practice their Judaism—or not. Rather than exclude one another from our minyanim because we are of the "wrong" gender, sexual orientation, or denomination, this messianic ideal will allow everyone to bring the offerings of their heart into the community of our people.

The promise of a *b'rit shalom*, a "covenant of peace," includes other nations and people. However, as long as there is infighting among us, how can we seek peace with others? This is the challenge behind the biblical statement "Love your neighbor as yourself" (Leviticus 19:18). We are asked to love both our neighbor who is from our own tribe and people, as well as our neighbor who is from a different background and people. Ezekiel's hope is that we learn to love our own people, creating one strong people Israel—so that the olive branch of peace may be extended to all the nations in friendship and strength.

# [Re]Building Bridges

### *RABBI BILL S. TEPPER*

It's difficult not to be affected by the narrative of *Parashat Vayigash*, with its emotionally charged reunion of Joseph and his brothers.

The haftarah reading for *Vayigash* is about a reunion, too. Just as Joseph and his brothers embrace in understanding, our prophet Ezekiel—thanks to the "two sticks" God commands him to hold so that they may be as one in his hand (Ezekiel 37:17)—envisions the moment when the Northern and Southern Kingdoms are a united Jewish kingdom. Ezekiel's "two sticks" parallel the "dry bones" shown to him by God at the beginning of chapter 37, from which a reborn House of Israel will arise. Scholar Michael Coogan writes, "The prophet's utopian program for rebuilding Jerusalem and the Temple remained an unrealized dream; at the same time, it most certainly contributed to keeping the hope of redemption alive."

Both the *parashah* and the haftarah reading teach us that pain and suffering are the prices paid by a divided Jewish people. Though millennia would pass before the State of Israel would become a reality, Ezekiel—endeavoring to comfort his fellow exiles in Babylon—offers hope that this extraordinary event will unfold. It is in our hands, today, to broaden his vision to make space for our neighbors and their needs and visions that are different from ours.

May we honor our differences and not render them incendiary. May we learn from one another and from our own missteps. May we build, and rebuild, bridges.

## Alternative Haftarah Reading:
### Psalm 73:1–3, 21–28

A psalm of Asaph.

Yes, God is good for Israel,
For the wholesome of heart;

As for me, my feet had almost strayed,
I almost slipped at every step—
For I am jealous of the boastful ones.
I see the peacefulness of wicked people.

For my heart was fermenting, like rising dough,
I was stabbed in my inmost parts.
But I was a dimwit, I did not know—
I was an animal in Your presence.

Still, I am always with You,
You have grasped my right hand.
You guide me with Your counsel,
And afterward, You take me with glory.
Who but You is there for me in heaven?
And being with You, I have no other desires on earth.
Though my flesh and my heart be spent,
The rock of my heart and my portion is God—forever.
For behold, those who are far from You shall perish;
You destroy all who wander away from You.
As for me, the nearness of God is good for me,
I have made the Superior, God, my refuge,
That I may tell my tale of Your creative works.

# Between Feeling and Acting

*RABBI RUTH ADAR*

In *Parashat Vayigash*, the family of Israel is reunited after many years. The brothers who had been so envious of Joseph that they sold him into slavery have seen the pain they caused Jacob; no doubt, hot-headed youth has given way to a more mellow adulthood. Time and experience have been Joseph's teachers, too; in the face of suffering, he decides to become a better person.

Psalm 73 might have been written by Joseph's brothers. They had been envious of Joseph, because their father Jacob spoiled and favored Joseph as a child. They acted on their anger and envy and sold their brother into slavery, telling Jacob that Joseph was dead. Yet God did not abandon them for their sins; indeed, they live to reunite with Joseph and Jacob, who has also grown wiser in the meantime.

The psalm begins with a statement of faith, but immediately turns to confession: the Psalmist has envied the prosperity enjoyed by wicked people. So envious had the singer been that they wrote, "My mind was stripped of its reason, my feelings were numbed" (Psalm 73:21). In a moment of introspection, the Psalmist sees the emptiness of a wicked life and the person they would become if they chose it. They see, too, that while they were cultivating evil thoughts, God never lost faith in them and was ever present even when they were completely unaware of it.

Envy is a very understandable and common emotion. In this world, we are not all equally endowed with talent, resources, or luck. Envy is also poisonous: it tempts us toward sin. The writer of Psalm 73 reminds us that while we may feel the emotion, we are called to step back from sinful speech or action. When we do that, God will be waiting for us—because God is always there.

## THE THIRD SHABBAT OF THE WINTER CYCLE

### *Alternative Haftarah Reading: Isaiah 2:1–5*

The word that Isaiah son of Amoz prophesied concerning Judah and Jerusalem.

In the days to come,
the Mount of the Eternal's House
shall stand firm about the mountains
and tower above the hills;
and all the nations shall gaze on it with joy.
And the many people shall go and say:
"Come,
let us go up to the Mount of the Eternal,
to the House of the God of Jacob;
that God may instruct us in God's ways,
and that we may walk in God's paths."
For instruction shall come forth from Zion,
the word of God from Jerusalem.
Thus God will judge among the nations
and arbitrate for the many peoples,
and they shall beat their swords into plowshares
and their spears into pruning hooks:
Nation shall not take up
sword against nation;
they shall never again know war.

## Bring Light to an Issue

*Rabbi Samantha G. Frank and Rabbi Daniel G. Zemel*

What better way to welcome Chanukah than through the prophet Isaiah's promises of joy and instruction to walk by God's light? In light we see hope, possibility, and the end of war. Isaiah prophesies, "They shall beat their swords into plowshares and their spears into pruning hooks: Nation shall not take up sword against nation; they shall never again know war" (Isaiah 2:4).

At this time of the year, close to the winter equinox, we are reminded that it is our task to create light, no matter how dark it is outside our homes. This passage also includes the words of our Torah service, meant as a pathway toward a peaceful future: *Ki miTziyon teitzei Torah udvar Adonai miYrushalayim,* "For Torah [instruction] shall come forth from Zion, the word of the Eternal from Jerusalem" (Isaiah 2:3).

As Reform Jews, we believe that God's word can be heard everywhere. We believe that our synagogues and houses of gathering are spaces in which we can access profound sanctity, inspiration, comfort, and hope. It is our responsibility to bring forward these messages and pass them on through study and intentional action.

Together we can light the world with goodness and fairness. Bring light to an issue: Find something new to study and share it with others. Discover another local community's concern and build a bridge.

# *Va-y'chi*
## Genesis 47:28–50:26

## Traditional Haftarah Reading:
## I Kings 2:1–12

## Torah Is Connection
### *Rabbi Ashley Barrett*

LOSING OUR PARENTS is an experience that impacts us for the rest of our lives. However daunting and tough the experience of that loss is, it also unites us with most of humanity. We all must face loss at one point or another in our lives. Loss is a simple fact of life, as old as humanity, as old as time.

As Jacob nears the end of his life in the Torah portion, so too does King David in the haftarah reading. Both have the opportunity to acknowledge that they will soon "go the way of all the earth" (Genesis 47:28–49:29; I Kings 2:2).

Our ancestors Jacob and David both have the privilege to give voice to a final message, too. David leaves Solomon with the reminder "Keep faith with the Eternal your God, walking in God's ways, carrying out the laws, commandments, rules of justice, and directions of God" (I Kings 2:3). The dying king connects his final blessings and warnings to the observance of God's laws. He sends his son on a journey of both mourning and Torah study.

David's final words remind us that even in the darkest of times, engaging with Torah can always bring us back to a sense of connection, tradition, and wholeness. Through the study of Torah, we are connected to our community, to the Holy One, and ultimately to the memory of those we have lost.

## Passing on Your Ethical Will
### *Rabbi Stacey Blank*

In the haftarah reading, David lies on his deathbed and passes on his advice, requests, and blessings to his son Solomon, who will succeed him as the king of Israel.

This scene reflects the Torah portion in which Jacob lies on his deathbed and passes on his blessings to his twelve sons.

These passages are the inspiration for what we call today an "ethical will." In addition to dividing up the physical estate, throughout the ages Jews have left their children a document outlining their values and the spiritual heritage they wish to pass on to the next generations.

For example, the renowned Torah commentator Ramban wrote a letter that he asked his son to read once a week. He gave advice like "Be accustomed always to speak calmly to everyone at all times. Thus you will be saved from anger, a terrible attribute that causes people to sin." The tradition of writing an ethical will can inspire us, first of all, to live a life of exemplary values. Then, we can write our own ethical will to pass on to the generations to come.

Material inheritance is temporary. Spiritual inheritance is truly eternal.

### *Alternative Haftarah Reading:*
### *Babylonian Talmud,* B'rachot *12a*

On Shabbat they add a blessing for the outgoing priestly watch. What is the one blessing? Rabbi Chelbo said: The outgoing priestly watch said to the incoming priestly watch: "May the One who caused the Name to dwell in this house cause love and camaraderie, peace and friendship to dwell among you."

## A Blessing for Moments of Transition

### RABBI JESSICA K. BAROLSKY

The Torah portion *Va-y'chi* tells the story of the end of Jacob's life and includes his blessings for Joseph's sons, Jacob's grandsons, Ephraim and Manasseh, as well as for each of Jacob's twelve sons. As the Book of Genesis comes to a close, Jacob dies, and all Egypt mourns his passing. This passage is a blessing for a time of transition, as the outgoing watch shares its hope for the incoming watch.

The words from the Babylonian Talmud sheds light on another, much more ritualized moment of the transition of power. When the members of the priestly watch would pass the watch to another group each week, they would say this blessing. The blessing reminds us of the importance of coming together, even when we have different perspectives, as we pass in the night—literally or figuratively. Rabbi Adin Steinsaltz explains that tasks in the Temple were sometimes determined by competition, and that this blessing had therefore additional importance for the priests as they attempted to overcome professional disagreements.

As we work to improve our world, we will often encounter different opinions and styles. This blessing reminds us that we can, that we must, nonetheless remember that all those we encounter are created in the divine image and that they, too, are deserving of blessing. As power shifts from one watch to another— or, as in the Torah portion, from one generation to another—this blessing can show us a way to make those transitions peacefully, intentionally, and beautifully.

## THE FOURTH SHABBAT OF THE WINTER CYCLE:
## SHABBAT OF THE SECULAR NEW YEAR

### *Alternative Haftarah Reading:*
### *Isaiah 56:1-7*

Thus says the Eternal One:
"Maintain justice and do what is right,
for My salvation is close at hand,
and revealed shall be My vindication."
Happy is the one who does this,
the person who holds fast to it—
who keeps the Sabbath lest it be profaned,
who keeps from all wrongdoing.

Never more let the foreigner who has joined the Eternal say,
"The Eternal will keep me apart from God's people."
And nevermore let the eunuch say,
"I am but a withered tree."
For thus says the Eternal One to those eunuchs
who keep My Sabbaths
and choose what pleases Me
and hold fast to My covenant:
"In My House, within My walls,
I will give you a monument and a name
better than sons and daughters;
I will give you an everlasting name
that will never be cut off.
As for the foreigners who join themselves to the Eternal
in love and service
who keep the Sabbath lest it be profaned,
and hold fast to My covenant:
I will bring them to My holy mountain
and make them joyful in My house of prayer.
[I will accept] the burnt offerings and sacrifices they offer on My altar;
for My house
shall be called a house of prayer for all peoples."

# May We Find Unity and Peace

*RABBI SAMANTHA G. FRANK AND RABBI DANIEL G. ZEMEL*

On the Shabbat closest to the New Year, Isaiah's words focus on that which unie fies us. Though we have passed the winter equinox and days are beginning to lengthen, the cold of winter is upon us. Spring is still far away. Yet these rhythms of the natural world need not prevent us from gathering in meaningful ways or from seeing what unites us.

In this prophecy, God reminds us that God's home is meant to be a house of prayer for all peoples—no one is excluded from the way of righteousness. God's greatest wish for humanity is that we might find unity and peace.

The secular year guides so much of our lives, and at this moment, as we greet the secular new year, we pray for the good of the American polity. Just as our houses of worship are meant to be open to all, it is our role to advocate that American society provide equitable pathways of success for all. Praying for unity must be followed by taking action and working to advance the causes of justice. None are excluded from our or God's vision.

Join or help form a coalition on an issue of local concern. Examples include advocacy to the school board or parks department or cleaning up the watershed. The possibilities are endless.

# *Haftarot for the Weekly Torah Portions*

## *EXODUS*

# Sh'mot
### Exodus 1:1–6:1

## Traditional Haftarah Reading:
## Isaiah 27:6–28:13, 29:22–23

### Potential for Redemption
#### RABBI MAYA Y. GLASSER

BOTH *PARASHAT SH'MOT* and its haftarah reading begin with a lot of doom and gloom. In the Torah, the people have been enslaved in Egypt for generations; in the haftarah, the prophet Isaiah is intent on delivering a foreboding message about how the people are enslaving themselves by ignoring their covenant with God. Whereas the people in Egypt toil and labor through no fault of their own, the horrors described in the Book of Isaiah occur as a result of the people's own actions.

Like our ancestors, we too constantly face both challenges that are out of our control and those resulting of our own choices. How can we comfort one another when we, at the same time, have to struggle with those challenges? How can we do the hard work of taking care of ourselves and others while acknowledging our own responsibilities and mistakes?

Those difficult questions have no ultimate and universal answers, but the haftarah reading reminds us that God is always present in our lives, through the good times, as well as through the doom and gloom. That reassurance gives us the comfort and safety we need to face and overcome our own mistakes. Just as God eventually redeemed us from enslavement, so too do we have ability to redeem ourselves by being reflective of our choices and accessing the divine power within.

### Return and Renewal
#### RABBI PAUL J. CITRIN

The haftarah reading accompanying *Parashat Sh'mot* contains numerous references to national and international events the contemporary reader might not be familiar with. In spite of our growing knowledge about the world Israel inhabited in Isaiah's days, the late eighth century BCE, even contemporary scholars have often written, "Meaning of Hebrew uncertain." None of the foregoing should discourage us from looking for the timeless and universal messages in Isaiah's words. Isaiah begins his message with hope for Israel's future. At the time, the enemy, Assyria, is at the gates. Isaiah believes that the Assyrians are the rod of God's punishment for Israel's idolatry and faithlessness to the ethical laws of Torah. Yet, Isaiah assures the people of Israel that repentance, ridding themselves of idolatrous beliefs and rituals, and living by the laws of the Torah will result in an ultimate renewal of Israel; the scattered and exiled people will eventually return home again. The theme of renewal and return links the words of the prophet Isaiah to the narrative of *Sh'mot*, which anticipates the return from Egypt.

The return that Isaiah envisions is not only the physical return of the Kingdom of Israel. His hope is that the people will restore its spiritual commitment to the one God and to the ethical laws of Torah.

Throughout the thirty-five hundred years of our people's history, these timeless qualities have sustained us: our hope for the future, the conviction that we can renew ourselves and do better, and the commitment to live our lives according to the laws of Torah. If these three qualities form a measuring stick, how do we as individuals, as congregations, and as a people measure up?

## *Alternative Haftarah Reading:*
## *From the Sephardic Tradition—Jeremiah 1:1–10*

The words of Jeremiah son of Hilkiah, one of the priests of Anatot in the territory of Benjamin. The word of the Eternal came to him in the time of King Josiah son of Amon of Judah, in the thirteenth year of his rule, and during the rule of King Jehoiakim son of Josiah of Judah, and until the end of the eleventh year the rule of King Zedekiah son of Josiah of Judah, when, in the fifth month, Jerusalem went into exile.

> The word of the Eternal came to me, saying,
> "Before I formed you in the womb, I knew you;
> before you were born, I set you apart;
> I have appointed you a prophet to the nations."
> And I said,
> "Oh! Eternal God:
> I do not know how to speak;
> for I am only a youth."
> The Eternal said to me,
> "Do not say, 'I am only a youth,'

for wherever I send you, you must go;
and whatever I command you, you must speak.
Have no fear of them,
for I am with you to keep you safe!"
—says the Eternal One.
The Eternal then reached out God's hand and touched my mouth,
and [the Eternal] said to me,
"Behold, I put My words in your mouth!
See, I have appointed you this day
[to speak] to nations and kingdoms,
to uproot, to pull down,
to destroy, to root out,
[but also] to build and to plant."

# What Is Your Calling?

### RABBI PAUL J. CITRIN

What does it mean to have a calling or to be called? *Parashat Sh'mot* and the above extract from the Sephardic haftarah reading, Jeremiah 1:1–2:3, suggest an answer.

At the Burning Bush, Moses receives a divine call to liberate Israel from Egyptian bondage. Even though he demurs five times from accepting the call, God does not relent. Eventually, Moses's call would be not only to free Israel, but also to form them into a covenanted community, marking the beginning of peoplehood.

Six hundred years later, Jeremiah receives a divine call to guide Israel through the destruction of the Kingdom of Judah and the Temple and the subsequent exile to Babylon. Jeremiah witnesses the temporary ending of peoplehood and tries to offer hope in the midst of national disintegration.

Like Moses, Jeremiah initially demurs from his call, even though God promises to protect and sustain him. Both Moses and Jeremiah perceive their calling through images of fire: Moses hears the divine call at the bush that is aflame but not consumed (Exodus 3; Jeremiah describes his need to act and speak as a raging fire shut up in his bones (Jeremiah 20:9).

We are called when we feel deeply obligated to fulfill a task sacred to us. Frontline pandemic workers, schoolteachers, and social workers surely feel a calling to do their holy work. The author James Baldwin said it this way: "You have to go the way your blood beats. If you don't live the only life you have, you won't live some other life, you can't live any life at all."

Being alert and responsive to our calling gives us a life of sanctity and fulfillment.

## *Alternative Haftarah Reading:*
## *Babylonian Talmud, B'rachot 63a; Pirkei Avot 2:6*

Bar Kappara taught, "If the price of the merchandise has declined, jump and purchase from it; and where there is no man, there be a man; where there is no one to fill a particular role, accept that role upon yourself." Abayei said, "Infer from this that where there is a man, there do not be a man."

[The Gemara asks:] Isn't Abayei's conclusion obvious? [The Gemara explains:] This statement is only necessary in a case where there are two who are equal. Although you, too, are suited to fill that role, since another qualified person is already filling that role, allow them to succeed. (Babylonian Talmud, *B'rachot* 63a)

Hillel used to say: An ignorant person cannot be fearful of sin; an unlearned person cannot be scrupulously pious; the bashful person cannot learn, and the quick, impatient person cannot teach; anyone excessively occupied in business cannot become a scholar. In a place where there are no men, strive to be a man. (*Pirkei Avot* 2:6)

# Know Your Place
### Rabbi Jay Asher LeVine

These two teachings from Rabbinic tradition mention an *ish*, translated literally as "man." However, the intent is to refer to someone of good character and capable leadership, regardless of gender. Throughout *Parashat Sh'mot*, we find not only the word *ish*, but multiple people who fit those qualities of moral leadership, both men and women:

- In Exodus 1, the Israelites become enslaved, and the new Pharaoh seeks their diminishment by ordering the midwives to murder all newborn boys. Shiphrah and Puah, however, "fear God" (1:17) and secretly thwart the decree, saving countless lives.
- In Exodus 2:1–10, Miriam watches over her baby brother Moses as he floats down the Nile and into the compassionate hands of Pharaoh's daughter. At a time when no one else would protect and adopt a Hebrew boy, these two women step up, ensuring the future liberation of the Israelites.
- In Exodus 2:11–25, a grown Moses, nurtured by women who exemplify moral character, repeatedly acts to fight oppression, leading to his personal exodus from Egypt until he is later commissioned to be God's prophet. His first action for justice ties most closely with our Rabbinic texts. After seeing an Egyptian taskmaster beating an

enslaved Israelite, Moses "turned this way and that and, seeing that there was no *ish*, he struck down the Egyptian and hid him in the sand" (2:12). On the surface, Moses looks around to see if anyone will observe his violent act. But some commentators connect *ish* to someone of moral leadership. See, for example, *Vayikra Rabbah* 32:4.

It is on you to act. Sometimes that means you must respond to the circumstance even though it isn't your style, your strength, your desire, or what you've prepared for. If no one else is there but you, rise to the occasion. Other times, though, you should become aware of the way you can strategically participate in a collaborative effort. You may not need to and maybe shouldn't take on some specific roles, because others already are. Be clear about your leadership and allyship, and figure out the most effective role to take.

# Va-eira
## Exodus 6:2–9:35

## Traditional Haftarah Reading:
## Ezekiel 28:25–29:21

## Coming Home

*RABBI GERI NEWBURGE*

THE NARRATIVE of *Parashat Va-eira* opens with God's instructions to Moses to confront Pharaoh. *Va-eira* then recounts the first plagues afflicting Pharaoh and all other Egyptians, while Pharaoh's heart hardens with each plague. The connection of the haftarah's reading to the *parashah* is found in Ezekiel's prophecy of Egypt's destruction at the hands of the Babylonian king Nebuchadnezzar—the very same king who cast the Jewish people from their homeland in 587 BCE. Ezekiel perceives of Egypt and the Pharaoh as the oppressors of the Israelites, and he predicts Egypt's fall from glory. The haftarah reading offers a hopeful message of restoration for the people of Israel, with the assurance of a return to the Promised Land.

Ezekiel's prophecy opens with powerful words about the dispersal and return of the Jewish people (Ezekiel 28:25) to their land. The same language is echoed several verses later in regard to the Egyptians: they too were scattered, and they too shall return to their land (29:13–14). This message of return is comforting, especially for those forced from their home. Moreover, Ezekiel makes clear that even the former oppressors, as well as the formerly oppressed, will be restored to their lands. His message is one of forgiveness.

When we are scattered from our communities or from ourselves—physically, emotionally, or spiritually—we find ourselves marginalized and powerless, lonely, and stripped of our resources and the reassurances they provide.

Who in our congregations and among the Jewish people is scattered and needs to be gathered back? There are many individuals, once connected to the Jewish community, who have distanced themselves, for any number of reasons. They would benefit from hearing Ezekiel's message that they can return to and have a place at home. This message is just as important today as it was for our ancestors.

# Redemption Will Triumph

*Rabbi Douglas Kohn*

It is always exciting to encounter a text from the Book of Ezekiel. The prophet uses language alternatively like a sword, a tickle, a challenge, or a dream, and the reader is carried from one image to yet another new encounter—sometimes experiencing sudden, unexpected shifts.

In the haftarah reading for *Parashat Va-eira*, the link to the Torah portion is evident: the prophet excoriates Egypt and the Pharaoh for again bringing devastation on Israel, though this time on Jerusalem and the Kingdom of Judah, whom he abandoned facing impending Babylonian attacks. Ezekiel offers God's angry words, "I am against you, Pharaoh king of Egypt" (Ezekiel 29:3). After describing the destruction God will bring upon Egypt, the prophet adds, "Then all who dwell in Egypt shall know that I am the Eternal" (29:6).

Yet, an unexpected, exciting parallel unfolds. Later in the haftarah, the reader is treated to an astonishing twist: "For thus said the Eternal God: 'At the end of forty years, I will gather the Egyptians from the peoples among whom they were scattered, and I will restore Egypt's fortunes" (Ezekiel 29:13–14). Just as God redeemed Israel after forty years in the wilderness, so too God will redeem the Egyptians!

Ezekiel's message is one of hope, justice, and redemption: enemies do not remain eternal enemies. There is potential to turn enmity into a renewed relationship of neighborly partnership. The late Anwar Sadat came to Jerusalem in 1977, in Israel's fortieth year, bringing a message of peace, hope, and justice. The haftarah reading reminds us of our abiding hope that redemption will triumph over enmity.

We have daily opportunities to bring redemption to the four corners of our world. We do not need to wait for God to enact redemption—we can bring it about ourselves. Showing kindness to a short-tempered boss, listening patiently to a neighbor whose politics are oppositional, changing our minds on sensitive matters—these are all little moments of redemption: from little matters of redemption, to grand gestures of Egyptian premiers.

Thus, today, the texts of Ezekiel and Exodus elide, charging us to be bearers of redemption in the conflicts and challenges of our own day—that we might take the astonishing steps toward peace!

### *Alternative Haftarah Reading:*
### *"Pride," by Dahlia Ravikovitch*

Even rocks crack, I'm telling you,
and not on account of age.
For years they lie on their backs
in the heat and the cold,
so many years,
it almost creates the illusion of calm.
They don't move, so the cracks stay hidden.
A kind of pride.
Years pass over them as they wait.
Whoever is going to shatter them
hasn't come yet.
And so the moss flourishes, the seaweed
whips around,
the sea bursts forth and rolls back—
and still they seem motionless.
Till a little seal comes to rub up against the rocks,
comes and goes.
And suddenly the rock has an open wound.
I told you, when rocks crack, it comes as a surprise.
All the more so, people.

# The Cracking Foundations of Human Pride
### Rabbi Jamie Gibson, MAHL, DD

*Va-eira*, the second *parashah* of the Book of Exodus, begins with the long-awaited confrontation between God (through Moses) and Pharaoh, the man-god of Egypt. Pharaoh barely deigns to listen to Moses's call to let God's people go. He believes that they are his permanent possession. He orders his magicians to replicate the miracles produced by Moses. He will not be moved. His pride blinds him to the cracking foundation under his feet. His pride keeps him from seeing that this battle will destroy his very rule, not only his ownership of our ancestors as slaves.

In the traditional haftarah reading, Ezekiel puts words into Pharaoh's mouth: "My River is mine, I made it for myself" (Ezekiel 29:3). For Moses and Ezekiel, it is Pharaoh's pride that must be broken so that God's people might be free and able to flourish.

The poet Dahlia Ravikovitch compares this pride to a seemingly immovable rock, one that can withstand all elements and endure, or so it seems. But in the end, when it is touched by something as light as a single seal, it begins to give way until it is shattered.

People, too, Ravikovitch says, are shocked to realize their cracking foundation, when their pride has blinded them for decades to their weakness and folly. Pharaoh is doomed before the plagues even start. He just doesn't see the cracks until it is too late.

God defeats the evil built on human pride. Just as God's word endures, human evil does not last. The poet gives us hope that we, too, will be saved from the cruel pride of the oppressor—even when we are the oppressors of ourselves. In the end, as the poet writes, "When rocks crack, it comes as a surprise. All the more so, people."

We cannot give up the struggle against the evil works of prideful men and women, and of pride itself. They will not endure, but we must. They will crack, but we will not. We must never lose our fervor to fight oppression, evil, and pride in our own day, even if it will not crack and be destroyed until tomorrow.

## *Alternative Haftarah Reading: Americans with Disabilities Act*

The Congress finds that

(1) physical or mental disabilities in no way diminish a person's right to fully participate in all aspects of society, yet many people with physical or mental disabilities have been precluded from doing so because of discrimination; others who have a record of a disability or are regarded as having a disability also have been subjected to discrimination;

(2) historically, society has tended to isolate and segregate individuals with disabilities, and, despite some improvements, such forms of discrimination against individuals with disabilities continue to be a serious and pervasive social problem;

(3) discrimination against individuals with disabilities persists in such critical areas as employment, housing, public accommodations, education, transportation, communication, recreation, institutionalization, health services, voting, and access to public services;

(4) unlike individuals who have experienced discrimination on the basis of race, color, sex, national origin, religion, or age, individuals who have experienced discrimination on the basis of disability have often had no legal recourse to redress such discrimination;

(5) individuals with disabilities continually encounter various forms of discrimination, including outright intentional exclusion, the discriminatory effects of architectural, transportation, and communication barriers, overprotective rules and policies, failure to make modifications to existing facilities and practices, exclusionary qualification standards and criteria, segregation, and relegation to lesser services, programs, activities, benefits, jobs, or other opportunities;

(6) census data, national polls, and other studies have documented that people with disabilities, as a group, occupy an inferior status in our society, and are severely disadvantaged socially, vocationally, economically, and educationally;

(7) the Nation's proper goals regarding individuals with disabilities are to assure equality of opportunity, full participation, independent living, and economic self-sufficiency for such individuals; and

(8) the continuing existence of unfair and unnecessary discrimination and prejudice denies people with disabilities the opportunity to compete on an equal basis and to pursue those opportunities for which our free society is justifiably famous, and costs the United States billions of dollars in unnecessary expenses resulting from dependency and nonproductivity. . . .

Congress finds that:

(1) in enacting the Americans with Disabilities Act of 1990 (ADA), Congress intended that the Act "provide a clear and comprehensive national mandate for the elimination of discrimination against individuals with disabilities" and provide broad coverage;

(2) in enacting the ADA, Congress recognized that physical and mental disabilities in no way diminish a person's right to fully participate in all aspects of society, but that people with physical or mental disabilities are frequently precluded from doing so because of prejudice, antiquated attitudes, or the failure to remove societal and institutional barriers.

# All Bodies Are Whole

### RABBI ELLIOT KUKLA

The Torah reminds us that what we think of as weaknesses may in fact be strengths. In *Parashat Va-eira*, God again tells Moses that he is to be the spokesperson for the Jewish people, leading them out of slavery in Egypt to freedom and into the Promised Land. Moses objects, saying that he is one "who gets tongue-tied" (Exodus 4:10) (literally "uncircumcised lips"; Exodus 6:12). Some commentators believe that Moses had a stutter, whereas others believe he had a learning disability or a phobia that made public speaking hard. What is clear is that Moses has some sort of speech disability *and* that he is chosen to speak on behalf of the entire Jewish people.

An alternative haftarah reading is the groundbreaking text of the American with Disabilities Act from 1990, which changed the lives of people with disabilities in this country. The ADA removes many barriers to employment for people with mental and physical disabilities and legislates that reasonable accommodations be made to create access to public spaces. This legislation was passed due to the efforts of countless disabled activists. On March 13, 1990, the night before Congress was set to vote on the ADA, disabled activists cast aside their wheelchairs and other mobility aids and crawled up the Capitol steps. The "Capitol Crawl" was a physical demonstration of how inaccessible architecture impacts people with disabilities.

Moses is a perfect model of what happens when you create pathways for people with disabilities to access leadership. When Moses says that he cannot deliver the divine message due to his speech impediment, instead of choosing a new leader, God appoints Aaron to be his speaking aid as a "reasonable accommodation." Moses's disability leads him to be humble in the face of the Divine and to work collaboratively with his siblings to deliver God's message. As contemporary disabled activists Patricia Berne and Aurora Levins Morales say, "All bodies are unique and essential. All bodies are whole. All bodies have strengths and needs that must be met. We are powerful not despite the complexities of our bodies, but because of them."

# *Bo*
## Exodus 10:1–13:16

## Traditional Haftarah Reading:
## Jeremiah 46:13–28

### We Swarm the Streets for Justice

*Rabbi Natalie Louise Shribman*

THE PROPHET JEREMIAH preaches against the power of Egypt, which will be overcome by King Nebuchadnezzar of Babylon. A day of disaster is upon Egypt; it will be shamed. God will punish Pharaoh and all those who rely on him, casting a nationwide "plague" on the land (Jeremiah 46:23). The message concludes with words of reassurance and deliverance for the Israelites.

This haftarah reading mirrors *Parashat Bo* three times. First, Jeremiah's foretelling of the attack on Egypt mirrors the remaining three plagues of locusts, darkness, and the death of the firstborns in the time of Moses (Jeremiah 46:23–26). Second, Jeremiah tells the Egyptians to equip themselves for exile, just as the Israelites are preparing to leave Egypt to journey to the Promised Land (46:19). Third, the Israelites are witness to God's power and deliverance yet again, as they witness Egypt's ultimate destruction (46:13–26).

Today, we are facing many different forms of oppression by many different forms of personal "Egypts." We fight these oppressions by swarming the streets in protest, shedding light on areas of ignorance, and taking nonviolent actions such as voting. We are using our power to become deliverers of peace as we continue on our journey of making the world right and just.

### Speaking Up to Power

*Rabbi Elizabeth Bahar*

Jeremiah, a prophet living just before the fall of the First Temple during the promising reign of King Josiah (640–609 BCE), whose prophecies were intended to push the Israelite people toward a restoration of the Davidic monarchy, offers several series of prophecies against Egypt (Jeremiah 46–51) as well as against Israel itself (Jeremiah 1–25). This haftarah reading is one of a series of prophecies against Egypt, delivered following Egypt's loss at the battle of Carchemish. Egypt's fall is understood by Jeremiah as God's punishment for the killing of King Josiah in the battlefield of Megiddo.

Jeremiah's contemporaries are put in an overwhelming position. They are striving to survive, while the leadership, the best king according to the prophet Jeremiah, has just been murdered and their society is threatened by inherent tensions caused by class differences between the elites (priests and politicians) and farmers. Yet, Jeremiah speaks up. He reprimands those in power who sought political alliance with Egypt, mocking the Pharaoh by calling him a "Big Noise Who Has Missed His Chance" (Jeremiah 46:17).

In the latter part of the haftarah reading, Jeremiah shifts focus. We learn that God reassures Israel that "[God] will save you" (Jeremiah 46:27). The Sages, notably Rabbbi David Kimchi (1160–1235, Narbonne, France) connect the Torah portion and the haftarah reading in order to deliver a specific message: While we read the story of our enslavement in Egypt in the *parashah*, we hear about Egypt's eventual destruction. There will be justice.

Jeremiah reminds us that while things may seem overwhelming and we might be full of dread, we can gain strength from even the challenging moments of our history and realize that we have an obligation to speak up, use our voice to better the world around us, and ensure that everyone's voice is heard.

## *Alternative Haftarah Reading: Zechariah 8:14–23*

For thus said the God of heaven's hosts: Just as I planned to afflict you and did not relent when your fathers provoked Me to anger—said the God of heaven's hosts—so, at this time, I have turned and planned to do good to Jerusalem and to the House of Judah. Have no fear! These are the things you are to do: Speak the truth to one another, render true and perfect justice in your gates. And do not contrive evil against one another, and do not love perjury, because all those are things that I hate—declares the Eternal.

And the word of the God of heaven's hosts came to me, saying, Thus says the God of heaven's hosts: The fast of the fourth month, the fast of the fifth month, the fast of the seventh month, and the fast of the tenth month shall become occasions for joy and gladness, happy festivals for the House of Judah; but you must love honesty and integrity.

Thus said the God of heaven's hosts: Peoples and the inhabitants of many cities shall yet come—the inhabitants of one shall go to the other and say, "Let us go and entreat the favor of the Eternal, let us seek the God of heaven's hosts; I will go, too." The many peoples and the multitude of nations shall come to seek the God of heaven's hosts in Jerusalem and to entreat the favor of the Eternal. Thus said the God of heaven's hosts: In those days, ten people from nations of every tongue will take hold—they will take hold of every Jew by the corner of their cloak and say, "Let us go with you, for we have heard that God is with you."

# Being a Role Model

### Rabbi Charles Middleburgh, PhD

Zechariah, the eleventh of the Minor Prophets, is known to us from the haftarah reading of the first Shabbat of Chanukah; yet, that extract is only a taste of the riches to be mined in the book. This text speaks of a post-punishment time for Israel, when, their sins expiated, they go from strength to strength. They will earn God's trust and blessing by speaking the truth to each other; and by judging with scrupulous honesty, they will remove the stain of previous falsehoods. By doing what God loves, rather than what God hates, they will create among themselves a place where the Divine Presence may comfortably dwell, and the people will have earned this closeness.

We talk of being a "nation of priests," a "treasured people," but Zechariah reminds us that this special status only comes from doing God's will so as to be worthy of God's presence. Zechariah goes even further than Isaiah and Micah: instead of the nations streaming to Jerusalem to worship God there, in Zechariah's vision the nations stream to the people themselves and ask for their help in approaching God. Because the people of Israel live godly lives, they are worthy of this mission.

Only by being true to the teachings of our faith can we become godly, can we be true role models to others, can we fulfill our own covenantal relationship with God.

## Alternative Haftarah Reading:
## From "Religion and Race," by Rabbi Abraham Joshua Heschel

At the first conference on religion and race, the main participants were Pharaoh and Moses. Moses' words were: "Thus says the Lord, the God of Israel, let My people go that they may celebrate a feast to Me." While Pharaoh retorted: "Who is the Lord, that I should heed this voice and let Israel go? I do not know the Lord, and moreover I will not let Israel go."

The outcome of that summit meeting has not come to an end. Pharaoh is not ready to capitulate. The exodus began, but is far from having been completed. In fact, it was easier for the children of Israel to cross the Red Sea than for a Negro to cross certain university campuses.

Let us dodge no issues. Let us yield no inch to bigotry, let us make no compromise with callousness.

In the words of William Lloyd Garrison, "I will be as harsh as truth, and as uncompromising as justice. On this subject [slavery] I do not wish to think, to speak, or to write with moderation. I am in earnest—I will not equivocate—I will not excuse—I will not retreat a single inch—and I will be heard."

Religion and race. How can the two be uttered together? To act in the spirit of religion is to unite what lies apart, to remember that humanity as a whole is God's beloved child. To act in the spirit of race is to sunder, to slash, to dismember the flesh of living humanity. Is this the way to honor a father: to torture his child? How can we hear the word "race" and feel no self-reproach?

# Our Exodus

### *Rabbi Seth M. Limmer*

Dr. Martin Luther King Jr. was among the initial audience hearing Rabbi Abraham Joshua Heschel compare the struggle against American racial injustice to the biblical campaign against Pharaoh's oppression, a campaign that culminates in this week's Torah portion.

Throughout history, the Exodus narrative has served as a frame for many peoples seeking their own freedom, from the struggle against slavery in the United States to liberation theology in Latin America. In *Exodus and Revolution*, Michael Walzer explains how the archetypes of Pharaoh, Moses, and the Israelites are relied upon by many revolutionaries as ways to understand and shape their place in history. All people long to march in freedom toward their own land of promise. Heschel underscores this lesson: the meaning of our Exodus from Egypt can only be complete when all experience the same liberation.

Heschel knew that the moral fate of the Jewish people was intertwined with the American struggle for racial justice. Reminding us that we can dodge no issues, Heschel compels us to work for racial justice—true equality and protection under the law, meaningful reparations for a rapacious history—as a Jewish obligation. Just as Heschel famously claimed, crossing the Edmund Pettus Bridge on Shabbat, that he was "praying with his feet," here he teaches us that working to end racial injustice is a Jewish obligation, a commandment, a mitzvah. In perfect prophetic style, Heschel challenges us with provocative questions, demanding we answer through our individual actions.

# *B'shalach*/Shabbat Shirah:
## Exodus 13:17–17:16

## Traditional Haftarah Reading:
## Judges 4:4–5:31

## Raising Our Souls through Song
### CANTOR SUSAN CARO

THE ONLY FEMALE JUDGE whose story is recounted in the Bible is Deborah, who stands out as an exception to all the other judges, both as a woman and as a prophet for an entire generation.

Both the Torah and haftarah readings present to us situations of confrontation: in the Torah portion, Moses and the people of Israel face Pharaoh; and in the Book of Judges, Deborah faces Sisera and the Canaanite army. In each narrative, when victory is won, the leaders celebrate in song, and both songs extol God's strength and presence in the deliverance of the people. However, Deborah also praises the dedication of the people. She sees victory not just in God's hands, but in the hands of humans: "When people volunteer themselves, praise the Eternal" (Judges 5:2).

To live as holy beings is to live with clear intention and paths. We are dedicated to evoke God's presence in our lives. In this week's texts, that pledge is expressed in song. The physicality of raising and opening our voices, of bursting out in song, expresses pure joy and gratitude. The Song of Deborah calls out, "Rouse yourself and sing a song!" (Judges 5:12). We are to fill our mind and body with the vibrancy of song to walk through this world with awareness and clarity.

When we sing of God's holiness, we lift our souls from the mundane to the holy, able to experience a moment of God's presence.

## Humans Lead Us to Redemption
### CANTOR RHODA J. HARRISON, PhD

I admit it. I'm a cantillation geek. One of my favorite things to do as a cantor is chant Torah. Chanting *Shirat HaYam* (the Song at the Sea), with all of its musical detours, each year on Shabbat Shirah, is a highlight of the Torah cycle.

The haftarah reading for Shabbat Shirah also contains a song, the Song of Deborah (Judges 5:2–31). There are clear parallels between Moses's *Shirat HaYam* and Deborah's Song that make the partnering of the poems an obvious choice:

- Moses and Deborah both serve as judges to their communities.
- Moses and Deborah both lead their people to victory over an enemy.
- Both poems are very old, much older than the narratives into which they have been embedded.

However, there is a key difference between these songs that makes them ideal companions for Shabbat Shirah:

- The *shirah* (singing) of Moses is all about God—celebrating God, even through the cantillation, as ultimate victor.
- Deborah's Song doesn't have those festive musical detours. Instead, it has us. Deborah's Song acknowledges the role humanity has had to play in the story.

The Song of Deborah celebrates God while at the same time highlighting the human characters involved in securing this redemptive moment in history.

## *Alternative Haftarah Reading: From "My Parents' Lodging Place," by Yehuda Amichai*

My mother was a prophet and didn't know it.
Not like Miriam the prophetess dancing with cymbals and tambourines,
not like Deborah who sat under the palm tree and judged the people,
not like Hulda who foretold the future,
but my own private prophet, silent and stubborn.
I am obliged to fulfill everything she said
and I'm running out of lifetime.
My mother was a prophet when she taught me
the do's and don'ts of everyday, paper verses
for one-time use: You'll be sorry,
you'll get exhausted, that will do you good, you'll feel
like a new person, you'll really love it, you
won't be able, you won't like that, you'll never manage
to close it, I knew you wouldn't remember, wouldn't
forget give take rest, yes you can you can.
And when my mother died, all her little predictions came together
in one big prophecy that will last
until the vision of the end of days.

# The Prophecies of Our Parents

## RABBI PAMELA WAX

*Shirat HaYam*, the "Song at the Sea," featured in *Parashat B'shalach*, is introduced by Moses. It is followed by a prose section about Miriam's response to that song. Not only does Amichai's poem invoke Miriam, but it also mentions the prophet Deborah, whose song is contained within the traditional haftarah for *B'shalach*.

In the *parashah*, the two prophets—Moses and Miriam—bracket *Shirat HaYam*, a song to the God of victory and celebration for having survived the enemy's pursuit. Miriam adds dance and musical instruments to singing and celebration.

In this section of a longer poem, Yehuda Amichai celebrates his mother, his "own private prophet," who, like many of the prophets of old, was wise, demanding, encouraging, and even, at times, demeaning. He is aware that he has not yet fulfilled all her wishes for him—what he calls her "little predictions"—which, after her death, added up to "one big prophecy" that is eternal and will likely never be fulfilled. Amichai's poem is filled with longing and sadness for a life that is not long enough to accomplish the "yes you can you can."

Amichai invites us to consider the prophets and the role of prophecy in our own lives, particularly that of female role models—like his mother—who succeeded the prophets Miriam, Deborah, and Hulda. He reminds us that there is not one way to be a prophet and that our own parents may, in fact, be the closest any of us will ever come to knowing one. He invites you, his readers, to consider what your parents imparted to you.

## *Alternative Haftarah Reading:*
## *"The Fourfold Song," by Rabbi Abraham Isaac Kook*

There is a person who sings the song of the Self, and within themselves, they find everything, complete spiritual satisfaction.

And there is a person who sings the song of the Nation. They step forward from their private self, finding it narrow and insufficiently developed. They yearn for the heights. They cling with a sensitive love to the entirety of the Jewish nation and sing with it its song. They share in its pains, and are joyful in its hopes, speak with exalted and pure thoughts regarding its past and its future, and investigate its inner spiritual nature with love and a wise heart.

And there is a person whose soul is so broad that it expands beyond the border of Israel, to sing the song of humanity. This soul constantly grows broader with the exalted totality of humanity and its glorious image. They yearn for humanity's general enlightenment, looking forward to its supernal perfection. From this source of life, they draw all of their thoughts and insights, their ideals and visions.

And there is a person who rises even higher until uniting with all existence, with all creatures, and with all worlds, singing together with all of them. This is the person who, engaged in the Chapter of Song every day, is assured that they are a child of the world-to-come.

And there is a person who rises with all these songs together in one ensemble so that they all give forth their voices, they all sing their songs sweetly, each supplies its fellow with fullness and life: the voice of happiness and joy, the voice of rejoicing and tunefulness, the voice of merriment and the voice of holiness.

The song of the soul, the song of the nation, the song of humanity, the song of the world—they all mix together with this person at every moment and at all times.

And this simplicity in its fullness rises to become a song of holiness, the song of God, the song of Israel, the song that is simple, doubled, tripled, quadrupled, the "Song of Songs of Solomon" which is the song of the Ruler whose very name is Peace.

# The Song of God

## Rabbi Daniel Kirzane

*Parashat B'shalach* contains *Shirat HaYam*, "Song at the Sea," giving the Shabbat on which it is read the name Shabbat Shirah, the "Sabbath of Song." Another song—the Song of Songs of Solomon—is connected with *Shirat HaYam* because both are recited on the festival of Pesach. The teaching of Rabbi Abraham Isaac Kook (1865–1935), the first Ashkenazic chief rabbi of British Mandatory Palestine, draws on the deep biblical and midrashic traditions of singing to express his vision of messianic harmony.

The Fourfold Song of Holiness follows a classic Jewish literary structure: while it appears at first to depict a hierarchy, the final section undermines the reader's assumptions. The fourth song is not the best; rather, the ideal is to blend all four songs—the song of the self, the song of the nation, the song of humanity, and the song of existence—into a single chorus.

A midrash on *Shirat HaYam* teaches, "In the messianic age, Israel will utter song, for it says, 'Sing unto the Eternal a new song; for God has worked wonders' (Psalm 98:1)" (*Sh'mot Rabbah* 23:5). This "new song" is transcendent, surpassing in beauty all other music.

There are times when we need to focus on the individual, created in the image of God. There are some times when we honor particular groups, and others when all of humanity takes precedence. And there are times when we heed the earth itself first and foremost. None of these can be our exclusive concern, and we live our best lives when seeking to balance them all.

# Yitro
## Exodus 18:1–20:23

## Traditional Haftarah Reading:
## Isaiah 6:1–7:6, 9:5–6

## Responding to God's Call
### CANTOR GABRIELLE CLISSOLD

I learned this haftarah reading for my bat mitzvah because my synagogue did not allow women to chant Torah. Later, in my first pulpit, after months of study and focus with a student on his Torah portion, we began learning the text and chant of his haftarah. As I chanted the opening words, *Bishnat mot hamelech Uziyahu* "In the year that King Uzziah died" (Isaiah 6:1), realization struck: this was my portion!

God speaks through Isaiah. Gods tells us about purification, humility, and the holy chorus of angels, saying, "Go and tell this people: Hear again and again—but without understanding; look again and again—but without perceiving" (Isaiah 6:9). Many of us think, "I understand, I am worthy, my heart is pure!"; however, I maintain that we are probably not as worthy as we think. Isaiah 6:9 speaks to me. It helps me to connect to the words of a prayer: "Purify our hearts to serve You in truth" (*v'taheir libeinu l'ovd'cha be-emet*; in the fourth blessing of the Shabbat *Amidah*). Moses was a humble man (Numbers 12:3); God spoke to and through Moses for this reason.

Today, we will only be able to hear God's voice when we listen to pure and humble messengers. Different from Moses, Isaiah is humble but does not try to escape from God's call: "Then I heard the voice of my Liege saying, 'Whom shall I send? Who shall go on Our behalf?' And I said, 'Here am I; send me'" (Isaiah 6:8). Never forgetting, we must start with a pure heart. Then we can fulfill our calling.

## Through Limitations to Holiness
### RABBI DEBRA BENNET

"*Kadosh, kadosh, kadosh!*" ("Holy, holy, holy"; Isaiah 6:3)—with these words, the haftarah reading for *Parashat Yitro* sets the tone: it is all about our connection with God's holiness. At first, Isaiah's vision appears as a lofty dream, disconnected from reality. Yet, the texts of both the haftarah and the Torah reading become more expansive, demonstrating possible connections between God's holiness and human behavior:

1. The Torah describes Moses's incapability of leading the people all by himself. He attempts to resolve all their problems on his own, until his father-in-law shows him his limitations and encourages him to rely on others.

2. The Torah also speaks about the limitations of the people as a whole. In Exodus 19:12, God says, "You shall set bounds for the people round about, saying, 'Beware of going up the mountain or touching . . . it." God places restrictions on who can encounter and how they can encounter God.

3. The haftarah reading shows Isaiah, who embraces his own limitations, giving way to greater gratitude. In Isaiah 6:5, the prophet cries, "I am a man of impure lips . . . yet these eyes of mine have seen [God]."

By becoming aware of our own limitations, we can connect with holiness:

1. Moses makes a choice, choosing holiness, to strengthen the community.

2. When God says in the Torah, "You shall be to Me . . . a holy nation" (Exodus 19:6), the people make a choice, choosing holiness when they respond, "All that the Eternal has spoken, we will do!" (19:8).

3. And Isaiah makes this choice. He embraces the life of a prophet and guides the people to holiness. As the community lays vanquished, merely a "stump," Isaiah tells them that this stump "shall be a holy seed " (Isaiah 6:13).

We may often feel despair knowing that we are limited, unworthy beings, but our tradition reminds us that we too are holy—with all our limitations a holy seed is implanted within each of us, destined to grow and connecting us with the holiness of God.

## *Alternative Haftarah Reading:*
### Pirkei Avot *3:21*

Rabbi Elazar ben Azaryah says:
If there is no Torah, there is no worldly occupation [*derech eretz*];
if there is no worldly occupation [*derech eretz*], there is no Torah.
If there is no wisdom, there is no fear of God;
if there is no fear of God, there is no wisdom.

If there is no knowledge, there is no understanding;
if there is no understanding, there is no knowledge.
If there is no flour, there is no Torah;
if there is no Torah, there is no flour.

# Torah and *Derech Eretz*

### RABBI ERIN BINDER

The moment of Revelation at Sinai is arguably one of the peak moments of the story told in the Torah. With every single member of the community present and prepared, the Israelites encounter God and receive the Ten Commandments. While the Ten Commandments serve as the basis for the Jewish faith (belief in one God, rejection of idol worship, and the keeping of Shabbat), they also are the basis for how we put that faith into action with one another (don't steal, lie, murder, envy, etc.).

*Pirkei Avot*, a book in the Mishnah full of wisdom from our Sages, amplifies what it means to live a life of meaning, both as Jews and in relationship with one another. In *Pirkei Avot* 3:21, Rabbi Elazar ben Azaryah's opening line takes us right back to the moment of Revelation: "If there is no Torah, there is no *derech eretz*." *Derech eretz* is tricky to translate, sometimes offered as "right conduct," "worldly occupation," or "social order," and literally meaning "way of the land." It is here, in this *derech eretz*, in this land, in this society, and through our behavior, that we engage with each other and God in ways guided by and befitting of Torah.

This mishnah reminds us that everything is interconnected. The improv community calls it the "Yes, and," acknowledging that there is always much to build on and draw from without changing the subject. Each of these pairings are not polar opposites, but rather they lift each other up and build the foundation for the next pairing. None of the learning or experience of Judaism happens in a vacuum—the stories and laws of Torah need to be in constant dialogue with the world we live in—and more importantly, the world we live in is framed by Torah.

How can we take care of our spiritual sustenance while also paying attention to our moral and physical needs?

## *Alternative Haftarah Reading:*
## *From* Standing Again at Sinai, *by Judith Plaskow*

There can be no verse in the Torah more disturbing to the feminist than Moses' warning to his people in Exodus 19:15, "Be ready for the third day; do not go near a woman." For here, at the very moment that the Jewish people stands at Mount Sinai ready to receive the covenant—not now the covenant with individual patriarchs but with the people as a whole—Moses addresses the community only as men. The specific issue is ritual impurity: An emission of semen renders both a man and his female partner temporarily unfit to approach the sacred (Leviticus 15:16-18). But Moses does not say, "Men and women do not go near each other." At the central moment of Jewish history, women are invisible. It was not their experience that interested the chronicler or that informed and shaped the Torah. . . . We . . . cannot redefine Judaism in the present without redefining our past, because our present grows out of history. The Jewish need to reconstruct the past in light of the present converges with the feminist need to recover women's history within Judaism. Knowing that women are active members of the Jewish community in the present, . . . we know that we were always part of the community—not simply as objects of male purposes but as subjects and shapers of tradition. To accept androcentric texts and contemporary androcentric histories as the whole of Jewish history is to enter into a secret collusion with those who would exclude us from full membership in the Jewish community. It is to accept the idea that men were the only significant agents in Jewish history when we would never accept this (still current) account of contemporary Jewish life. The Jewish community today is a community of women and men, and it has never been otherwise. It is time, therefore, to recover our history as the history of women and men, a task that will both restore our own history to women and provide a fuller Jewish history for the Jewish community as a whole.

# All Voices
### *Rabbi Seth M. Limmer*

Judith Plaskow has written powerful feminist responses to the disturbing exclusion of women from the divine Revelation in this week's Torah portion. "You should not go near a woman" (Exodus 19:15) is a text we modern Jews committed to equity must approach with a "hermeneutic of suspicion," which Rita Felski defines as "reading texts against the grain and between the lines, of cataloging their omissions and laying bare their contradictions."

Reading between the lines of the Book of Exodus, we can infer that over six hundred thousand women stood at Sinai. As Plaskow teaches, "The Jewish need to reconstruct the past in light of the present converges with the feminist need to recover women's history within Judaism." It is our obligation to uncover—against the grain and between the lines—the presence, stories, and legacy of *all* those who stood at Sinai but whose experiences have not been recorded.

Plaskow teaches, "It is time, therefore, to recover our history as the history of women and men, a task that will both restore our own history to women and provide a fuller Jewish history for the Jewish community as a whole." Today, we expand her teaching: It is time to restore Jewish history for the Jewish community as a whole, by including all voices: female, male, trans, gender-nonconforming, and nonbinary Jews. It is our task to make Jewish history complete by uncovering and creating the stories of every individual so precious to Jewish life. Which marginalized voices will you work to amplify?

# *Mishpatim*
Exodus 21:1–24:18

## Traditional Haftarah Reading:
Jeremiah 34:8–22, 33:25–26

## Justice, Freedom, and Equality

*Rabbi Uri Regev*

T HE HAFTARAH reading focuses on the laws of a Hebrew slave, with which
the *parashah* opens. The liberal Jewish reader must not read the words of the
haftarah as just reflecting the prophets' social and religious critique of their time.
Instead, we should follow their inner spirit, that which transcends their time. We
must translate their words into our ever-evolving reality.

The Torah and the prophets were revolutionary for their time, but reality has
since changed. The core values of Judaism—"Justice, justice shall you pursue!"
(Deuteronomy 16:20)—must serve as a basis for our rereading of God's will. We
no longer live in the reality of slavery, but severe bondage of various kinds prevails.
The Torah and the prophet cry out against bondage, and this should guide us as
we decide to forge our path as individuals, as a community, and especially as Jews
living in the Jewish state, Israel.

Liberal readers should be open to understanding the prophet's harsh prediction not only as expressing God's punishment for transgressions, but also as a
warning regarding the natural disintegration and demise of societies unmoored
from the foundations of justice, freedom, and equality. We must expand and fil-
ter the commandments of the Torah and the words of the prophets through the
prism of contemporary values.

We should follow the model of the Sages, who at times ascribe to the words of
Torah a meaning opposite of the literal reading. In doing so, they anchor their
progressive interpretation in reading into the Torah the revolutionary democratic
principle "Follow the majority" even as the original biblical verse literally says the
opposite! Exodus 23:2 states: "You shall not side with the mighty to do wrong—
you shall not give perverse testimony in a dispute so as to pervert [justice]."

# Collective Responsibility

## MICAH SYMONS

*Parashat Mishpatim* immediately follows the giving of the Ten Commandments at Mount Sinai. Here we have the first *parashah* exclusively consisting of commandments given from the Divine to the people of Israel. Everything from the rights of slaves to compensation in the event of manslaughter to the *Shalosh R'galim* (the Three Pilgrimage Festivals) is covered. The haftarah reading, coming from the Book of Jeremiah, features a rebuke from the Divine after the Israelites refuse to release their slaves during the Sabbatical year, violating a commandment issued in *Mishpatim*.

*Mishpatim* offers rules and guidance for how individuals can and should take responsibility for their own actions. The haftarah reading broadens this theme to include the collective of Israelite society. Jewish tradition provides us with tools with which we can address past actions, notably the "big three" conjured during the High Holy Days: *t'shuvah* (repentance), *t'filah* (prayer), and *tzedakah* (acts of justice). And yet, even our *machzor* makes clear that the Days of Awe are intended for *individual* judgment. How can we make sure that the human-human relationships ensuring the health and justice of our communities remain intact?

The very beginning of the haftarah selection gives us a hint. We are told that the Israelites initially made an agreement with King Zedekiah to release their slaves, before going back on their word. The king of Israel failed to uphold both the letter of the law and the covenant made with his constituents. While the failure to observe a divinely inspired law is certainly problematic, it is the breach of a human relationship that is perhaps of greater concern.

Why is this so? For one, the kingship of ancient Israel was born out of human—not divine—imagination. The people voluntarily surrendered a measure of power in order to have a single figurehead to rule and represent the nation. Second, even in the days of explicit Divine-human interaction, God spoke primarily to prophets and kings. The overwhelming majority of relationships—then as now—were between people.

The takeaway here is that the most authentic way to maintain our human relationships is by keeping our word. King Zedekiah made an agreement with the people that was not upheld by both sides: the people reclaimed their slaves, and King Zedekiah did not enforce the initial contract.

Only when we keep our word will our relationships endure. We must ensure accountability and mutual trust so central to all our relationships.

## *Alternative Haftarah Reading:*
## *"The New Colossus," by Emma Lazarus*

Not like the brazen giant of Greek fame,
With conquering limbs astride from land to land;
Here at our sea-washed, sunset gates shall stand
A mighty woman with a torch, whose flame
Is the imprisoned lightning, and her name
Mother of Exiles. From her beacon-hand
Glows world-wide welcome; her mild eyes command
The air-bridged harbor that twin cities frame.
"Keep, ancient lands, your storied pomp!" cries she
With silent lips. "Give me your tired, your poor,
Your huddled masses yearning to breathe free,
The wretched refuse of your teeming shore.
Send these, the homeless, tempest-tost to me.
I lift my lamp beside the golden door!"

# The Jewish Commitment to the Immigrant
### RABBI DOUGLAS KOHN

Scores of laws are recorded in *Parashat Mishpatim*, ranging from religious to criminal, civil behavior to domestic conduct. In the middle of this catalogue of commandments, we find this singular verse, "You shall not wrong nor oppress a stranger, for you were strangers in the land of Egypt" (Exodus 22:20). Reminding us of the stranger's or immigrant's plight and our own association with them, this verse has become part of the enduring ethics and sensitivities of a meaningful Jewish life.

Thus, it should not surprise us that the foremost American voice for the forlorn, homeless, immigrant refugee is the voice of a Jewish woman in New York City: Emma Lazarus, a young poetess and essayist, was moved by the suffering of immigrants crowding into New York in the early 1880s, including thousands of Eastern European Jews. As an almost sole beacon of light in the night herself, she wrote and organized incessantly, becoming the leading activist for immigrant rights and nascent Zionism.

In 1883, responding to an effort to raise money for the pedestal of the monumental statue *Liberty Enlightening the World*, which Lazarus would retitle *Mother of Exiles* and we now know as the Statue of Liberty, Lazarus wrote "The New Colossus" for a fundraising art exhibit. Her sonnet coined signature phrases: "A mighty woman with a torch," "the imprisoned lightning," "Give me your tired, your poor," and "Send these, the homeless, tempest-tost to me."

Lazarus died in 1887 at age thirty-eight, before the poem was affixed to the pedestal that she helped establish, but her poem redefined "for you were strangers in the land of Egypt" and defined the American Jewish commitment to the immigrant. Now, it is up to us to bring Emma Lazarus's sonnet, and her legacy, to life in our generation!

## Alternative Haftarah Reading:
## "The low road," by Marge Piercy

What can they do
to you? Whatever they want.
They can set you up, they can
bust you, they can break
your fingers, they can
burn your brain with electricity,
blur you with drugs till you
can't walk, can't remember, they can
take your child, wall up
your lover. They can do anything
you can't stop them
from doing. How can you stop
them? Alone, you can fight,
you can refuse, you can
take what revenge you can
but they roll over you.

Two people can keep each other
sane, can give support, conviction,
love, massage, hope, sex.
Three people are a delegation,

a committee, a wedge. With four
you can play bridge and start
an organization. With six
you can rent a whole house,
eat pie for dinner with no
seconds, and hold a fund raising party.
A dozen make a demonstration.
A hundred fill a hall.

A thousand have solidarity and your own
    newsletter;
ten thousand, power and your own paper;
a hundred thousand, your own media;
ten million, your own country.

It goes on one at a time,
it starts when you care
to act, it starts when you do
it again and they said No,
it starts when you say We
and know who you mean, and each
day you mean one more.

# Working and Playing Together toward Holiness

### Rabbi Barbara Rosman Penzner

*Parashat Mishpatim* details the Jewish covenantal ideal that first appears in *Parashat Noach*, when we are given the universal obligation to create a society based on and accountable to a system of laws. In *Parashat Mishpatim*, "criminal and civil statutes" (*mishpatim*) are couched in religious language, giving the Jewish people the framework and regulations for being a *goy kadosh*, a "holy people" (Exodus 19:6) in covenant with the Divine. When Moses reads the words of this covenant to the people, they respond wholeheartedly, "All the things that the Eternal has commanded we will do!" (Exodus 24:3).

The poem "The low road," by Marge Piercy, describes the power of working together toward the holy pursuit of amplifying the voice of moral conscience. The playful aspects of the poem remind us that joy and beauty are essential for human connections to flourish, just as the Torah portion ends with the surprising image of Moses, Aaron, Aaron's sons, and the elders ascending to join God for their own private celestial dinner party (Exodus 24:9–11).

Spiritual activism brings people together to transform our world into a place of godliness. This passage urges us to participate, educate, advocate, demonstrate, legislate, appreciate, and celebrate—and thereby elevate the lives and souls of countless others.

# T'rumah
## Exodus 25:1–27:19

## Traditional Haftarah Reading:
## I Kings 5:26–6:13

## The Temple Within:
## How We Embody Our Holy Places

### CANTOR LISA LEVINE

THE TIME we are living in is unprecedented, and so was the age of King Solomon, who began his twenty-year-long building project of the First Temple 480 years after our people escaped slavery in Egypt.

In the desert, years before Solomon's time, God commands, "Let them make Me a sanctuary that I may dwell among them" (Exodus 25:8).

Today, neither of these sanctuaries stand; they belong to times when our people struggled for peoplehood and sovereignty. They also belong to an age of idol worship.

The unique concept of having the capacity to carry God within us, in our hearts and as our moral and spiritual compass, has been paramount to our survival. Our sanctuaries, as suggested in the Torah, are within us. This is where holiness abides. At the time of an epidemic, we find ourselves separated from our communities. Our Zoom rooms have become our sacred spaces. We have expanded our vision of the *Mishkan* to include our living rooms and our hearts. Our sense of presence and peoplehood exists right where we are.

May the light of Eternal healing and hope continue to burn brightly within.

## Light Shining from the Inside Out

### RABBI LISA SARI BELLOWS

In *Parashat T'rumah*, God asks the Children of Israel to bring gifts for the building of the *Mishkan*, the portable sanctuary, so that God "might dwell among them" (Exodus 25:8). In our haftarah reading, we read of King Solomon's building of the *Beit HaMikdash*, the Temple in Jerusalem.

King Solomon, a man of wisdom, builds the Temple with help from his friend, King Hiram of Tyre (I Kings 5:26). Details and descriptions of the Temple's construction fill this portion; about constructing the Temple's windows, we read, "They are wide inside and narrow outside" (I Kings 6:4).

Usually, for maximum light to enter, windows are narrow inside and wide outside! Rabbi Chanina teaches that the Temple windows were made in this unusual way so that light would go out from inside the Temple into the world (*Vayikra Rabbah* 31:7).

And so it is with each of us. We are the sanctuary in which God dwells; holy beings created in God's image; vessels for God's light. When we are still enough to notice the sanctity that is heart, mind, body, and breath, we, like the windows of the *Beit HaMikdash*, allow the divine light to shine from the inside into the world.

## *Alternative Haftarah Reading:* *Song of Songs 3*

Upon my couch at night
I sought the one I love—
I sought, but found him not.
"I must rise and roam the town,
through the streets and through the squares;
I must seek the one I love."
I sought but found him not.
I met the guards
who patrol the town.
"Have you seen the one I love?"
Scarcely had I passed them
when I found the one I love.
I held him fast, I would not let him go
till I brought him to my mother's house,
to the chamber of her who conceived me.
I adjure you, O maidens of Jerusalem,
by gazelles or by hinds of the field:
Do not wake or rouse
love until it please!
Who is she that comes up from the desert
like columns of smoke,
in clouds of myrrh and frankincense,
of all the powders of the merchant?
There is Solomon's couch,

encircled by sixty warriors
of the warriors of Israel,
all of them trained in warfare,
skilled in battle,
each with sword on thigh
because of terror by night.

King Solomon made him a palanquin
of wood from Lebanon. He made its posts of silver,
its back of gold,
its seat of purple wool.
Within, it was decked with love
by the maidens of Jerusalem.
O maidens of Zion, go forth
and gaze upon King Solomon
wearing the crown that his mother
gave him on his wedding day,
on his day of bliss.

# A Place of Perfect Union

### Rabbi Audrey R. Korotkin, PhD

Exodus 26:31–37 describes the making of the inner curtain (the *parochet*) and the outer curtain for the Tabernacle. The *parochet* "shall serve you as a partition between the Holy and the Holy of Holies" (Exodus 26:33)—presumably a measure to keep humans separated from God's dwelling place.

"Rabbi Akiva said: . . . All the writings are holy but the Song of Songs is the holy of holies" (*Mishnah Yadayim* 3:5). Such proclaimed one of our greatest sages, explaining why this collection of erotic love poetry belonged in the Hebrew biblical canon. In describing Song of Songs using the same phrase—*kodesh kodashim*—that is used to describe the inner sanctuary where the Ark of the Covenant was kept and God's presence was believed to dwell, Rabbi Akiva connects the Song of Songs to this week's Torah portion.

Chapter 3 of Song of Songs, like the traditional haftarah reading from I Kings, focuses on King Solomon (whom tradition assumed to be the author of Song of Songs). However, it describes not Solomon's Temple, but his royal bedroom. Like the *Mishkan* in the Torah, this space is treated as *kodesh*, in the sense that it is "set apart" from prying eyes. Richly decorated in fine wood, posts of gold and silver, and spun yarns in the style of the *Mishkan*, the bedchamber is the setting for the palanquin, or sedan chair. The text describes it with the term *ratzuf* (v. 10), a construction term for closely joining two elements, which carries the connotation of perfect union.

The human love depicted in Song of Songs is interpreted by the Rabbis as an allegory of the love between God and Israel. The parallel place of *ratzuf* in the *Mishkan* is its own Holy of Holies, around which the *parochet* is drawn like a wedding canopy. This text invites us to envision that the purpose of this richly embroidered curtain is not for separation between the people and their God, but for privacy for the eventual perfect union of the bride, Israel, and her groom, the Holy One.

## Alternative Haftarah Reading:
### Orchot Tzaddikim 2:6

And a person must conduct themselves in their dealings with people and in money matters with even greater care for their interests than the law demands (beyond the letter of the law), and all their transactions with people should be with humility and gentleness. And the essence of modesty is that they should be humble before those who are in a lower position than they. For example, to their help and their household, and to those poor who obtain their sustenance or benefit from them—to those from whom they never need or expect any favors, and whom they do not fear.

# Be Exceedingly Humble
### RABBI DAVID OLER, PhD

*Parashat T'rumah* is the quintessential Torah portion concerning ritual objects. It provides descriptions of the design of the Tabernacle, later followed in the First and and Second Temples in Jerusalem, and of the artifacts that were used. Exodus 25:8 states, "And let them make for Me a sanctuary that I may dwell *among them*," suggesting that it is not the sanctuary or the ritual objects that are inherently holy, but that the potential for holiness and the experience of the Divine is within and among the people.

Over the course of Jewish history, Mussar, a body of ethical literature building on biblical and Rabbinic texts, evolved, which fosters a movement toward moral righteousness. *Orchot Tzaddikim (Paths of the Righteous)* is part of this genre. The selection here, from this anonymous five-hundred-year-old text, is an example of the emphasis on humility in Mussar literature.

Acting humble in the face of authority is often an expression of codependency and fear, but being modest and gentle toward those less powerful than ourselves is consistent with the Torah's emphasis on providing for the needy and loving the stranger and with the Rabbinic dictum to "be exceedingly humble" (*Pirkei Avot* 4:4).

# T'tzaveh
## Exodus 27:20–30:10

## Traditional Haftarah Reading:
## Ezekiel 43:10–27

## The Steps toward Wholeness
### RABBI GERI NEWBURGE

THE TORAH PORTION *T'tzaveh* lays out detailed plans for the construction of the *Mishkan* (Tabernacle) and the various components required to outfit it. Similarly, the haftarah reading echoes God's command to the prophet Ezekiel to rebuild the Temple in Jerusalem. Like Moses, Ezekiel speaks from outside the Promised Land, but with a message of hope for restoration.

As Ezekiel conveys the measurements of the Temple, he also instructs on the "laws" (*torot*; Ezekiel 43:12) and "rules" (*chukot*; v. 18) of sanctifying the building. Each aspect of Ezekiel's prophecy speaks to the ritual observance in the reestablished Temple—for its consecration, as well as for its future use.

While some may see trivial or meaningless detail, Ezekiel's words offer the reader a sense of renewed spirituality. The steps taken for rebuilding the Temple, our most sacred Jewish space, are also steps for rebuilding ourselves and for seeing ourselves as active parts of God's holiness. We may consider the twelve steps of recovery programs, each step a necessary part toward completeness. In fact, the final offering mentioned in the haftarah is the *sh'lamim* (well-being) offering; the root of this Hebrew word pertains to "wholeness" (*sh'leimut*).

When we follow the steps of life that take us beyond ourselves, connecting us in meaningful and sacred ways to loved ones, our community, and God, we can rebuild ourselves and our sense of spirituality in wholeness.

## Begin with the Vision
### RABBI VALERIE LIEBER

This haftarah portion, like the Torah portion, reveals the dimensions of the altar the community will build.

The prophet Ezekiel begins with rebuke. He shares the plans for the next Temple with the exiled Jewish people. Ezekiel uses the tangible architectural plans to ground a panicking, pain-struck population. Focusing their energy on the concreteness of lengths and widths comforts the overwhelmed exiles, and the vision of an altar whose hearth can bring the Jews close to God's power and forgiveness encourages them. Wisely, Ezekiel first presents a larger vision of beauty, holiness, and a shared mission and only then breaks the work into its component parts, to make sure that no one is paralyzed by the magnitude of the rebuilding.

In our days, too, we need to begin with large visions, with the assessments of our own responsibilities, and with the possibility of repentance. However, when large-scale societal transformation is necessary, it is easy to be paralyzed by the mere size of the project.

For example, as we examine and attempt to transform our culture from a racist society to an egalitarian one, white Jews have to begin their work by assessing their own responsibility and then break the work into achievable components. We know that while we do our work, others are busy with theirs, too.

## *Alternative Haftarah Reading: Isaiah 61:1–4, 6–11*

The spirit of the Eternal God is upon me,
because the Eternal has anointed me;
God has sent me as a herald of joy to the humble,
to bind up the wounded of heart,
to proclaim release to the captives,
liberation to the imprisoned;
to proclaim a year of the Eternal's favor
and a day of vindication by our God;
to comfort all who mourn—
to provide for the mourners in Zion—
to give them a turban instead of ashes,
the festive ointment instead of mourning,
a garment of splendor instead of a drooping spirit.
They shall be called terebinths of victory,
planted by the Eternal for God's glory.
And they shall build the ancient ruins,
raise up the desolations of old,
and renew the ruined cities,
the desolations of many ages....

While you shall be called "Priests of the Eternal,"
and termed "Servants of our God."
You shall enjoy the wealth of nations,
and revel in their riches.
Because your shame was double—
people cried, "Disgrace is their portion!"—
assuredly,
they shall have a double share in their land,
joy shall be theirs for all time.
For I the Eternal love justice,
I hate robbery with a burnt offering.
I will pay them their wages faithfully,
and make a covenant with them for all time.
Their offspring shall be known among the nations,
their descendants in the midst of the peoples.
All who see them shall recognize
that they are a stock the Eternal has blessed.

I greatly rejoice in the Eternal,
my whole being exults in my God,
who has clothed me in triumph,
and wrapped me in victory,
as a bridegroom whose head is adorned,
as bride who bedecks herself in finery.
For as the earth brings forth its blossoms,
as gardens spring into flower,
so the Eternal God
will make a glorious victory
spring up before all the nations.

## Building a Personal Relationship with God

### Rabbi Debra Bennet

In *Parashat T'tzaveh*, we read of the sanctification of the priests in their role as communal leaders in the Tabernacle. The Torah portion captures the awe-inspiring transformation of these individuals into holy intermediaries between the people and God. However, priesthood only lasts as long as the Tabernacle and Temples stand. The destruction of the Temples eventually creates opportunities for other individuals to become the leaders of our people. Isaiah 61:1–4 and 61:6–11 as an alternative haftarah portion captures this evolution of leadership.

In the Exodus text, Aaron and his sons are mediators between the Divine and the individual Israelite, offering sacrifices to God. Due to their work, the Israelites know the Eternal our God. Isaiah 61 describes the powerful reality of being one who is appointed by God. At a time the priests still carry out God's commandments in the Temple, Isaiah describes the fulfillment of God's commandments in the world outside the holy structure. He says, "The spirit of the Eternal God is upon me, because the Eternal has anointed me" (Isaiah 61:1).

Through the presence of this leader, the people build a relationship with God. In fact, Isaiah foresees a time when the people will "be called 'Priests of the Eternal,' and termed 'Servants of our God'" (Isaiah 61:6). The prophet allows for the people to become leaders with access to God. They are the new priests and servants. Isaiah makes space for a new generation of leaders and for every Jewish individual to create a personal relationship with God.

We answer that call today, carrying forward a connection with God that beckons us to strive to make the world a better place.

## *Alternative Haftarah Reading: Psalm 122*

A Song of Ascendings, Of David.
I rejoice when they said to me:
"We are going up to the House of Adonai"—
Our feet standing
In your gates, Jerusalem,
Jerusalem rebuilt,
Like a city joined together!

For up to it tribes would travel,
The tribes of Yah—testimony for Israel,
To sing praise to the name Adonai.
For there sat seats for judgment,
Thrones for the House of David.

Pray for the peace for the City of Peace:
May those who love you find repose.
May there be peace in your palace,
Respite on your ramparts.
For the sake of my brothers, my sisters, my friends,
Let me say: Peace within you.
For the sake of the House of Adonai our God,
Let me seek your good.

# We Can Be the Hands of God

*Rabbi David E. Ostrich*

In *Parashat T'tzaveh*, we read about the intricate details of fashioning the *Mishkan* and its equipment and utensils. The text is very specific—perhaps even tedious. However, getting something right requires paying attention to the details. In a big project, it can be helpful to step away and consider the grander design and purpose that will eventually evolve. Psalm 121 reminds us to look up and remember the One to whom our labors are dedicated—the One with whom we are constructing a relationship: "I turn my eyes to the mountains; from where will my help come?" (Psalm 121:1).

Psalm 122 reminds us of that purpose: we are building an ideal place. The Rabbis hear the phrase "Jerusalem rebuilt, like a city joined together" (Psalm 122:3) as a description of two Jerusalems: one on earth and imperfect, and another one in heaven and ideal (Babylonian Talmud, *Taanit* 5a).

How do we make our Jerusalem as wondrous as the one in heaven? By praising the name of the Eternal, by establishing and listening to the thrones of justice, by praying for peace and well-being, and by seeking the good for everyone (Psalm 122:4–6, 8). We can be the hands of God; we can bring the blessings of heaven to all the earth.

# Ki Tisa
## Exodus 30:11–34:35

## Traditional Haftarah Reading:
## I Kings 18:1–39

## Faith, Courage, and Convictions
### RABBI DAN LEVIN

FEW FIGURES in Jewish tradition embody heroism more than Elijah the Prophet. Elijah witnesses with revulsion Queen Jezebel and King Ahab's embrace of the cult of Baal and the erosion in the Northern Kingdom of Israel's commitment to the Eternal. Despite the horrific persecution of God's prophets, Elijah steps forward to force a showdown.

The haftarah inspires us to step forward when injustice and evil abound. The hero Obadiah, who saved one hundred prophets of Israel from Ahab and Jezebel, encounters Elijah, who bids him to announce to Ahab that he is ready for a confrontation. Elijah's challenge to the prophets of Baal makes a mockery of their pathetic ritual before proving the true power and presence of the Eternal.

The echoes of our Torah portion ring out so loudly. Moses steps into the breach to confront the Holy One to save his people despite their slide into idolatry (Exodus 32:11–13) and then steps up against his people, grinding their false god to powder and returning his people to God (32:26–27).

Both Elijah and Moses drew on their faith, courage, and convictions to stand up to their own people and proclaim the essential truths they knew. Even the single one against the many who stands up, unwavering, and steps forward can inspire the people to join the side of the right and good and call out, as they did before Elijah, "*Adonai hu haElohim*—the Eternal alone is God!" (I Kings 18:39).

# Whatever It Takes

*SEBASTIAN SLOAN (BAR MITVZAH 2020)*

In my portion, God tells Elijah to confront King Ahab. However, Elijah is seen as cukoo. Yet, Ahab has already been screwing up, with his land of Samaria suffering from increasing famine. Ahab sends Obadiah to search for more grass to keep the animals alive.

On his search, Obadiah, to his surprise, encounters Elijah. Instead of delivering a big speech, Elijah does a Michael Jordan move, simply stating, "I'm back" (okay, maybe not just that, but very similar). Elijah is being searched for all across the land. His own people had turned against him. Obadiah fears that "Elijah's God" would make Elijah disappear, leaving Obadiah to be killed by Ahab. Elijah then tells him that he would confront Ahab himself.

Ahab then encounters Elijah, and they both start to roast each other (not the physical way). Elijah calls Ahab out and says that all of the prophets of both Baal and Asherah shall come to Mount Carmel so that he can prove to them that the Eternal One can light a fire—like a YouTube challenge video: Elijah is the only one representing God, while 450 other prophets follow Baal. The 450 prophets call upon Baal for hours, yet, there is no sign, sound, or fire. Elijah then takes twelve stones, one for each tribe of the sons of Jacob, and builds an altar. He then has four jars of water poured onto the altar and calls upon God, praising God, and asking for a sign. Lightning strikes into the altar, which proves to the people that the Eternal alone is God.

What I got out of this portion, besides that Ahab needs to read a "Leadership for Dummies" book, is the confidence and grit of Elijah. I find this portion very relatable to our time. Through hardships and betrayal, Elijah does whatever it takes to make God's name heard. Like Elijah, the protesters and activists marching in the streets, demanding change and wanting their voice to be heard, are persevering through struggles, hardships, and social injustice. Ahab sent armies to find Elijah, just because he praised a different God, just because he stood with the Eternal One. The government has sent the National Guard to stop protesters just because they're stating the truth, just because they're saying that Black Lives Matter.

This is the haftarah for *Ki Tisa*, which is on a similar topic. The Jewish people start to praise a Golden Calf, and Moses was one of the only ones still praising the Eternal. Moses and Elijah are both at the bottom of the barrel, they both are left behind, yet they both do whatever it takes to make their voice heard, to make God's name heard. And just like Moses and Elijah, the BLM protesters are doing whatever it takes to make change come. Whatever it takes. Wow, this sounds like Avengers Endgame.

## *Alternative Haftarah Reading:*
## *"Before the Statue of Apollo," by Shaul Tchernichovsky*

I have come before you, forever-forgotten God,
God of the moons of old and other days,
Ruling over the fresh streams of humanity,
Waves of strength with the abundance of ages!
God of a generation of the glorious and giants in the land,
Who subdues with his arm even the borders of those who dwell on high
As a seat of heroes amongst his children with a crown
Of laurel leaves on their proud forehead,
Vanquishing his idols and it seemed to them,
As if he added even more to the secret of the rulers of the earth;
A generation of God in the land, drunk on the abundance of life,
A stranger to a sick nation and to the house of pain.
God of youth, glorious, lush, the epitome of beauty,
Dominator of the sun and the mysteries of life
In the dark haze of poetry and in the treasuries of its shades,
In the sea of melodies in its thousands of its waves;
God of the joy of life in all its wealth and its glory,
Its power and the hidden artistries of its adornment.

I have come before You—do You recognize me?
Here I am, the Jew: we have argued since time began! . . .
From the waters of the ocean between the dry land
The depths stretched out between us fall short
Of filling their mouth with their tumultuous multitude.
The heavens and the breadth of the deserts are too small
To mend the breach, that separates
The Torah of my ancestors from the law of those who worship You.
Your eyes see me! Since I have distanced myself
Departing from all that went before me
And after me, on the path that a mortal trod,
Here I am, the first to return to You,
In this moment I have become weary of the perishing of the generations,
At this time I will break the shackles of the soul,
My living soul, cleaving to the earth.
The people have become old—and their God has become old with them!
Emotions are stifled by those who lack strength,
They have arisen to life from being shut up since generations ago.
The light of God is mine! The light of God! In me every bone cries out,
Life, O life! Every bone, every sinew.

The light of God and life!

And I have come before you.

I have come before you, before your statue I bow.
Your statue—a symbol of the light of life;
I prostrate, I bow to the good, to the exalted,
To that which is lifted up in the entire world,
To that which is glorified amongst all creation,
To that which is high up with the secret of secrets of all existence,
I bow to life, to strength, and to beauty,
I bow to all forms of grace, that
Human carcasses and the rotten seed of humanity have stifled,
Those who rebel against life from my Rock the Almighty,
O God, God of the wondrous desert,
O God, God of the conquerors of Canaan in a whirlwind,
And they bound God up with the straps of the t'fillin.

# Natural, Wild, Desert-Dwelling, Ancient Passion

## CANTOR SARAH GRABINER

The story of the Golden Calf in *Parashat Ki Tisa* casts an indelible mark on Jewish history. We are reminded of the terrible deed in our liturgy and folklore, so that we might learn from the error of the Israelites' idolatry, never to be repeated. However, there is a hazier distinction between what does and does not constitute idolatry than the stark biblical narrative assumes.

When Shaul Tchernichovsky published his epic poem, in adoration of a statue of Apollo in 1899, he was castigated as "the Hellenist" for his supposedly idolatrous position. But was he attempting to worship Apollo in a blasphemous act of irreverence? Or to mock Judaism's legalistic obsession with idolatry? Or to show appreciation for a beautiful statue?

Tchernichovsky sought a return to what he saw as the true, intrinsic core of Judaism. He bemoaned the legalistic, ivory towers of cerebral, Rabbinic tradition and yearned for the natural, wild, desert-dwelling, ancient Israelite passion. The controversial final line of this poem, in which he accuses the dullness of the antiquated Jewish establishment, overly focused on ritual and commandments, of strangling God with their t'fillin, expresses this most dramatically.

Tchernichovsky glorifies Apollo as the epitome of strength, youth, and beauty. These are the attributes of ancient Greek culture with which he wanted to reinvigorate the tired tribes of Judah. He challenged Judaism's aversion to images, portrayed in the often-quoted saying of the nineteenth-century historian Heinrich Graetz that "paganism sees its gods, Judaism hears Him." This poem poses these questions: Have we forgone opportunities for beauty and vibrancy in our purging of every trace of potential idolatry? Can we admire that which falls outside our tradition without succumbing to worship of the profane? May we tread the line delicately, appreciating beauty, strength, and vitality, while avoiding turning these attributes into gods in and of themselves. This is the nuance of the prohibition against idolatry that we must learn by reading this *parashah* alongside Tcherni-chovsky's hundred-year-old call.

### Alternative Haftarah Reading: "K'hilah K'doshah," by Dan Nichols and Rabbi Michael Moskowitz

Each one of us must play a part
Each one of us must heed the call
Each one of us must seek the truth
Each one of us is a part of it all
Each one of us must remember the pain
Each one of us must find the joy
Each one of us
Each one of us

*K'hilah k'doshah . . .*

Each one of us must start to hear
Each one of us must sing the song
Each one of us must do the work
Each one of us must right the wrong
Each one of us must build the home
Each one of us must hold the hope

Each one of us
Each one of us

*K'hilah k'doshah . . .*

It's how we help
It's how we give
It's how we pray
It's how we heal
It's how we live
It's how we help
It's how we give
It's how we pray
It's how we heal
It's how we live

## We Have a Choice to Make

RABBI SHARYN H. HENRY

When the Israelites feared that Moses had abandoned them at the foot of Mount Sinai after God's revelation of Torah, they panicked. The text tells us that they gathered to construct the Golden Calf, using the word *vayikaheil* (Exodus 32:1). This particular form of the word for "community" is reserved for those places in the Torah where people are gathering for something menacing or problematic.

In next week's portion, the people gather again to create a community. This time the word is *vayak'heil*, which has a positive connotation. This time the entire Israelite nation has gathered as a community to begin to hear the instructions for building the *Miskhan*, the portable sanctuary that will accompany them throughout their sojourn in the wilderness.

People gather; we make community, all the time. And each time we gather, we have a choice to make: Will our gathering be for the good? Will we gather to bring about understanding? Will our community gather to work for justice? Will our community pray together and share with one another and provide shelter and safety for ourselves and others? Will we create holiness within our gatherings and allow God's presence to dwell with us?

Jewish singer-songwriter Dan Nichols and Rabbi Michael Moskowitz encourage us to gather to create holy communities of understanding, respect, and love. Let us listen to their call.

# Vayak'heil
Exodus 35:1–38:20

## Traditional Haftarah Reading:
I Kings 7:40–50

## Cultivating the Gifts from God
*Cantor Margot E. B. Goldberg*

THE TORAH PORTION and haftarah reading share the topic of building a sacred space. The Torah portion begins with Moses telling the people that they are to observe Shabbat, and it then moves on to building the Tabernacle, the *Mishkan*—the place where God will reside and sacrifices will take place while wandering in the wilderness. The building directions are detailed and require great artistry.

In the haftarah reading, we hear about the process of building the First Temple in Jerusalem. We are introduced to Hiram, who is a skilled coppersmith, and the details of what he will build.

When wandering in the wilderness, the Israelites needed organization and direction. Creating a central place for God to reside and the Israelites to look to for comfort and direction helps this fledgling group become a community. In the accompanying haftarah reading, King Solomon is trying to establish himself as the ruler of Israel by building the Temple in Jerusalem.

We are all created *b'tzelem Elohim*, "in the image of God," to be God's partners in creation. As we grow and mature, skills and passions develop and become hobbies and/or livelihoods. In this week's Torah portion and haftarah reading, we learn that skilled artisans have been identified for specific tasks in the building of both the *Mishkan* in the wilderness and the Temple in Jerusalem. Some might say that these artisans' talents come from God.

Each individual has to cultivate their talents and embrace their passions. This is the first step in our partnership with God. God presented the detailed instructions for the *Mishkan* so that everyone could lend their unique gifts in their own way.

# Finding Our Creative Capacity

*RABBI JORDANA SCHUSTER BATTIS*

Just as *Parashat Vayak'heil* describes the construction of the *Mishkan* (the Tabernacle, the "dwelling" for God) in the wilderness by Moses with the craftsman Bezalel, this haftarah reading offers the parallel construction of *Beit Adonai* (the First Temple, "House of the Eternal") by Solomon with the artisan Hiram. The passages share vocabulary, including many of the words describing Bezalel and Hiram—each was filled with *chochmah*, "wisdom"; *t'vunah*, "ability"; and *daat*, "knowledge." What's more, both passages contain echoes of the first account of Creation, when God engaged in the work of making order and artistry from the tumult.

Through these parallels, this haftarah signals the power and centrality of the Temple as the dwelling place for God in humans' midst, a miniature creation within Creation.

If the Temple stands for the Tabernacle, which stands for the cosmos, then we—ourselves made in the image of God—are reminded here that we, too, are creators, like God. This haftarah reading calls us to remember that God can dwell among us wherever we build our own *mikdashei m'at*, "holy dwellings in miniature," bringing holiness into our midst wherever we journey. We can understand our creative capacity as being patterned on Creation itself, in all its complexity and contrasts: tent fabrics giving way to columns, primeval waters giving way to water bowls.

## Alternative Haftarah Reading:
## "To be of use," by Marge Piercy

The people I love the best
jump into work head first
without dallying in the shallows
and swim off with sure strokes almost out of sight.
They seem to become natives of that element,
the black sleek heads of seals
bouncing like half-submerged balls.

I love people who harness themselves, an ox to a heavy cart,
who pull like water buffalo, with massive patience,
who strain in the mud and the muck to move things forward,
who do what has to be done, again and again.

I want to be with people who submerge
in the task, who go into the fields to harvest
and work in a row and pass the bags along,
who are not parlor generals and field deserters
but move in a common rhythm
when the food must come in or the fire be put out.

The work of the world is common as mud.
Botched, it smears the hands, crumbles to dust.
But the thing worth doing well done
has a shape that satisfies, clean and evident.
Greek amphoras for wine or oil,
Hopi vases that held corn, are put in museums
but you know they were made to be used.
The pitcher cries for water to carry
and a person for work that is real.

# The Work of the World

*DANIELLE KRANJEC*

With the destruction of the Second Temple in 70 CE, the nature of what it meant to serve the Divine on behalf of *Am Yisrael* (the people of Israel) was forever changed. As we have replaced the Temple service with the service of the heart, so too must we revisit our prophetic writings and their interpretation.

*Vayak'heil's* discussion of the construction of the *Mishkan* is paralleled in its haftarah reading, which focuses on the construction of the Temple, with its heavy-beyond-measure bronze implements and decorations and its golden ornaments and component pieces. With no Temple and no Temple service, how do we understand the physicality of these ritual objects transformed along with the service of the heart?

Perhaps the "work of the world," in the words of Piercy, infused with the holiness of a shared vision and commitment to the actions that sustain our people and our human lives on a daily basis, can take the place of that bronze and gold. Perhaps we, who "jump into the work headfirst," have taken the place of the artisan Hiram and King Solomon.

### Alternative Haftarah Reading:
### From "When We Make Art Together, We Dream a Better World into Existence," by Caroline Rothstein

Art may be the—or at least a—catalyst, gateway, door that can save us. . . .

The tabernacle is God's art project for the Israelites to find a common purpose and cause by collaborating, by co-creating, and by taking their scattered voices and molding some kind of harmony amidst the cacophony of wandering in the desert.

. . . God is our teacher. Our arts educator. Art provides a house—a container, a place, a shared space—where we can come together with our multifaceted narratives and intersectional identities and collectively dwell and find literal common ground. We don't have to agree. We don't have to have the same beliefs. But we do ask ourselves to show up, together, as one.

Art can offer us a model of how expression itself is a means of amalgamating and dreaming into existence the kind of community, nation, world we are together looking to build. Let's be honest. It's a mess right now—both the world and this American project—this attempt at a nation. It's a mess because it was founded, as we know it today, through some super-duper messy means. But that doesn't mean it has to fail. That doesn't mean we can't still learn to dwell. . . .

Art is a call to action. Art is a language for the soul. In modeling our own feelings and experiences through this particular dialect, we give each other permission to break open and free.

Like the tabernacle was a sanctuary we made to learn how to share space, so too can the art we create now and in the generations to come be where and how and why we dwell into wholeness.

Art has saved my life. And art has saved civilizations and humanity time and time again. And while we've had countless dire times before as a species and a planet, I'd say it's especially urgent now. I think that art can save us all. I think if we center our faith around expression, we might make it out of this masterpiece of a cultural, climate, cataclysmic thunderstorm alive.

## With Skill and Confidence

### Rabbi Jordan Helfman

To take raw materials and turn them into a finished product requires both a skill and a confidence that makes me envious of artists. The building of the Tabernacle and later the Temple must have been nerve-racking tasks. Kind of like, Caroline Rothstein points out, the building of our society.

This parallel between architecture and society reminds me of the early Reform synagogue choice to place Moorish revival architecture over a cathedral base, blending both into an idea of what sacred Jewish space might look like. The cathedral-like elements helped the community fit in with the surrounding cultures, and the Moorish elements reinforced their sense of their unique Jewish identity. Rothstein focuses not on the work of the master artists and architects, but rather on how all in society contribute toward a perfect union of narratives and identities in this sacred task of co-creation.

I am frightened by the immensity of the task to be partners with God in building a more just world through word and action, through synagogue and software architecture. What happens if we get something wrong? Caroline Rothstein's writing reminds me that while I often choose not to act because I might not get everything right, the process of building society is collaborative.

May we all find our our brave voices and participate in this collective project, striving to make it a little more perfect of a union between God and us.

# P'kudei
### Exodus 38:21–40:38

## Traditional Haftarah Reading:
## I Kings 7:51–8:21

## The Yearning to Feel Home
*RABBI PETER RIGLER*

SYMPTOMS CAME from nowhere. She sat in her hospital room while they tried to figure it all out. The symptoms got worse and the tests gave no clues. The day the doctor finally came to share the diagnosis, the day it ceased to be a mystery and took on a name, we found comfort. It wasn't over, but the connection to a name meant "possibilities for action." We felt grounded. We felt like we had found a home for the moment.

That yearning to feel home is powerful. It has served as a driving force in our tradition. In *Parashat P'kudei*, we finally complete the building of the Tabernacle, which creates a physical dwelling place for God in the wilderness. We know that we still have a long journey ahead—but how nice it is to have a place to feel at home! This desire to draw near to the center, to arrive, and to feel connected and belonging also lies at the center of the haftarah portion, which describes the completion of an even grander project, the Temple of Solomon in Jerusalem.

Both the Torah portion and the haftarah reading offer a home to ground our wandering spirits. In the case of the Temple of Solomon, it is built as a permanent structure, something that already Solomon's father, King David, had wanted to complete.

As students of history, we know that the wandering will continue and that even this seemingly permanent home, just like the Tabernacle, is actually far from being permanent.

When we are ill, we feel like we are wanderers. Healing isn't solely connected to medical care. It also takes place in our connection to those who heal, our caregivers, or God, or even just in language. In finding a name for the illness, we finally felt like we could begin to build hope and to ground ourselves again.

# The Ark: Bringing Holiness into Our Lives

*RABBI VICTOR S. APPELL*

Unlike many other haftarah readings, the haftarah portion for *P'kudei* does not include a litany of transgressions and punishments. Rather, it is a celebration of the completion of the Temple in Jerusalem, echoing the completion of the Tabernacle recounted in this week's Torah portion. This great architectural undertaking, conceived by King David, is finally completed by his son, King Solomon.

Of great importance is the Ark, which will house the stone tablets that Moses placed in the Tent of Meeting. With the destruction of the First Temple, the Ark and the tablets disappear. Though several midrashim imagine that the Ark was hidden in a safe place, we have no such proof.

Yet, for us, the Ark has not really disappeared. Rather, it has become the center of synagogue worship. Whether the ark in our prayer spaces containing the Torah scrolls toward which we focus our prayers is permanent or temporary, elaborate or simple, like our ancestors, we consider it to be holy. In front of the open ark we name babies, bless those becoming *b'nei mitzvah*, and seek solace on our holiest of days.

Even if we are not standing in front of an ark, we can infuse our lives with sacredness through the objects that bring holiness into our lives. Just like an ark, a piece of Judaica or Jewish artwork can be the focus of our prayers. In those moments of prayer, we transcend time and can imagine ourselves standing shoulder to shoulder with every Jew who has sought a connection to the Divine.

## *Alternative Haftarah Reading:*
## *Babylonian Talmud,* Gittin 55a

The mishnah teaches that Rabbi Yochanan ben Gudgeda further testified about a stolen beam that was already built into a building and said that the injured party receives the value of the beam but not the beam itself. With regard to this, the Sages taught in a *baraita* (*Tosefta Bava Kama* 10:5): "If one robbed another of a beam and built it into a building, Beit Shammai says: 'That person must destroy the entire building and return the beam to its owners.' And Beit Hillel says: 'The injured party receives only the value of the beam but not the beam itself, due to an ordinance instituted for the sake of the penitent.' In order to encourage repentance, the Sages were lenient and required the robber to return only the value of the beam." The mishnah was taught in accordance with the opinion of Beit Hillel.

# The Foundations of Our Actions

### Rabbi Michael L. Feshbach

*Eileh p'kudei haMishkan,* we read in Exodus 38:21: "These are the records of the Tabernacle, the Tabernacle of the Pact, which were drawn up at Moses's bidding." The Torah commands that careful records be kept and an accounting made of material and funds, to show that it was not misused. Moses is able to proclaim, against any suspicion, that his hands are clean, that the work was done honestly, that he pocketed no profit and bore no taint of corruption.

In the Babylonian Talmud, *Gittin* 55a, we read of an astonishing argument. Material has been procured through theft; a building erected with stolen goods. Something must be done! *L'shem tiferet,* "for the glory of God," justice demands restitution be made.

But how? The item holds up an entire structure.

Pure justice would say it must be returned. "So," say the followers of Shammai, "the thief should return it. The same beam. The fact that a whole house would have to come down, that's not the rightful owner's problem. Blame for damage caused falls only on the thief."

But the followers of Hillel object. Here damage cascades far beyond the original offense. What incentive could there be for one who did something wrong to make things right? Far better to figure out the value of the wood and repay the equivalent amount. It might not be pure justice. But it maximizes the amount of good for everyone.

Which is all fine, except for this: what if an entire community—a whole country, even—is built on the value of stolen beams?

We face, in our lives and our countries, a realization and a reckoning. Much of what we have is built neither on fairness nor on justice. May we be open to reflection, repentance, reconciliation, and perhaps even "reparation," to make right the wrongs that are so subtly embedded in the lives we enjoy.

## *Alternative Haftarah Reading: "Gods Change, Prayers Are Here to Stay," by Yehuda Amichai*

> Bird tracks in the sand on the seashore
> like the handwriting of someone who jotted down
> words, names, numbers and places, so he would remember.
> Bird tracks in the sand at night
> are still there in the daytime, though I've never seen
> the bird that left them. That's the way it is
> with God.

# Traces in the Sand

### RABBI JILL PERLMAN

P'kudei is the last parashah of the Book of Exodus. It concludes momentously with the physical presence of God settling over the newly completed Tent of Meeting. God's cloud—and pillar of fire by night—was undeniably and undoubtably present. God was *there*. Oh, how wonderful it must have been to live in the black and white of God's existence splayed out right before you, all doubt washed away. Today, many of us live in the gray, seeking to tie strings of meaningful experiences together to glimpse an image of the Divine. Certainty settles over the few, while the rest of us wrestle for understanding.

Yehuda Amichai wonders along with us in his poem about bird tracks in the sand. These tracks, he tells us, are perhaps like a memory aid. They could be the evidence of the act of someone who has noticed us, knows our name, and marked it down so that they would not forget. In the Torah, we are told time and again that God "remembers" us. While that may prompt the question "Did God forget us?" another reading on "remember" is that it is the act of paying close attention. When God remembers, God is focusing on us, our joy or perhaps our plight; God is seeing us. But then again, Amichai is just playing with an image, musing on a theology, and the ultimate judgment is ours.

The poem's speaker claims to have never seen the bird that left the tracks. What are the tracks, if any, that are left behind by the miraculous? Tracks in the sand are easy to erase. All that is needed is a wave, the wind, or feet paying no mind. Is that the way it works with us as well? In a day and age when God's presence no longer descends from heaven by cloud or fire, is it possible to discover the Divine unseen before the traces disappear?

Amichai's poem hints at the signs of God all around us, the presence that lands for just a moment before taking off again. Amichai allows us to imagine God trying to remember the details of our lives. As we root around in the sand for God's notes about us, we must admit that we too need to jot down words, names, numbers, and places so that *we* can remember God. Somewhere along the way, we have forgotten the Divine and how properly to seek God out. Bird tracks in the sand by the seashore are evocative of the search for meaning and the elusive feeling of finding certainty only to have it be washed away in the next wave. Yet with each new day comes another opportunity for the search and, with it, the possibility of glimpsing even for a moment the bird that left its tracks.

# *Haftarot for the Weekly Torah Portions*
## *LEVITICUS*

# *Vayikra*
## Leviticus 1:1–5:26

## Traditional Haftarah Reading:
## Isaiah 43:21–44:23

## Come Back to Me

*CANTOR SARAH GRABINER*

THE BOOK OF LEVITICUS begins with a list of commanded sacrifices: the well-being, meal, guilt, sin, and restitution offerings. Our first *parashah* of the sacrificial rites clarifies their common purpose: to evoke "atonement" for our sins. The verb *l'chapeir* (to make expiation), familiar from the "Day of Atonement," Yom Kippur, appears eleven times in the text of our *parashah*. As such, the haftarah focuses on a time when the Children of Israel failed to make restitution and Isaiah's response of prophetic outrage.

Isaiah's reproach emphasizes the benefits of the covenant between God and God's people and the risks of not fulfilling our ancient sacrificial obligations. However, in the middle of the text of the haftarah reading, the tone shifts: Indeed, as humans, we err, but forgiveness is always possible. God speaks, uncommonly, in the first-person singular: *Anochi, anochi*—"I, I am the One who blots out your transgressions" (Isaiah 43:25), and later, "I have swept away your transgressions like a cloud, your sins like like a thick cloud; return to Me" (44:22). These verses are central to our Yom Kippur liturgy, recited at least four times throughout the day.

It can be difficult to connect with the God of Leviticus, the God of blood-and-guts sacrifices. Yet, we embrace the first-person singular relationship asserted in this haftarah, which reminds us of the possibility of *t'shuvah*, of "return and redemption." In this way, we find assurance—not only on Yom Kippur but also throughout the year. God always awaits our resolve to change.

# The Path to Blessing

*RABBI BILLY DRESKIN*

*Vayikra* (Leviticus 1–5) presents the Torah's recipe for building a relationship with God through a system of sacrificial offerings that provided ancient Israel with a very specific and navigable path. Combined with the observance of the ethical mitzvot delineated elsewhere in Torah, this is how one earns God's blessing.

As our haftarah reading from the Book of Isaiah indicates, Israel opts for a different and disappointing path, worshiping arrogance and self-indulgence as they fashion iron and wood into idols (Isaiah 44:9–20). Isaiah is possibly lamenting the majority of Israelites who declined King Cyrus of Persia's invitation to return from Babylonia to the Promised Land. He writes with remorse, "They kindle a fire and bake bread; and they make a god and bow down [to it]" (44:15).

I cannot help but see our own world reflected in these words. The ever-continuing need for a racial justice movement reminds us that despite all the sources of learning and guidance available to us, we cling to small-minded ideas of superiority and domination. We continue to endanger the lives of others with our high-risk behavior; we choose death over life, again and again resisting simple prescriptions for healthy living that can easily bring these threats to heel. Not Torah alone but so many of humanity's sacred teachings offer us "a very specific and navigable path" to blessing—yet we stubbornly refuse.

God is hopeful, however, that Israel will rekindle the relationship. "Return to Me, for I have redeemed you" (Isaiah 44:22). May we be among those who stay the course, partnering with God and the ideals that God represents, to help rebuild a world of goodness and well-being for all.

## Alternative Haftarah Reading:
## From "Where Judaism Differs," by Rabbi Abba Hillel Silver

Judaism admonished men not to despair of the future, nor of their own strength, nor of mankind's inexhaustible spiritual resources nor of God's cooperation. Long and hard is the way, but there is a way, and there is a goal.

The moral life and human aspirations are the "sacraments" of Judaism. It recognizes no others. There are no beliefs which "save" men. There are no ceremonial or ritual acts the very performance of which bestows supernatural grace and saving power. There are visible symbols in Judaism, signs of the covenant, memorials of fidelity, but no sacraments. From earnest and faithful quest of the good life, in all ways, great or small, flow all divine grace and power.

# Do Not Despair of the Future

*RABBI DANA EVAN KAPLAN, PhD*

In this Torah portion, God sets forth the laws of animal sacrifice, explaining that different sacrifices serve different functions. God teaches Moses about the different types of offerings, what they should consist of, and under what circumstances they should be offered. These teachings are an elaborate description of biblical ritual. Ritual is a sequence of religious actions that are performed in a prescribed manner for a particular theological purpose. From the establishment of the First Temple (and possibly even earlier) to the destruction of the Second Temple more than a thousand years later, the major public Jewish rituals were performed primarily in the Jerusalem Temple.

Once the Second Temple was destroyed, the Sages developed new forms of ritual designed to replace the sacrifices that had been offered in the Temple. While the Sages who were alive at the time were shocked and horrified by the destruction of the Temple, they did not waste valuable energy on endless ruminations on the terrible tragedy that had befallen them.

As Rabbi Abba Hillel Silver reminds us, they did not despair of the future. There might be a long, arduous struggle ahead, but humankind has the spiritual resources, with the help of God, to accomplish almost anything. Central to Rabbi Silver's argument is the fact that in Judaism, the sacrifices were not essential for salvation. They were important public rituals that helped all to respond to the events of human existence in religiously meaningful ways, but they were not essential for the nullification of moral or ethical failings or for the restoration of spiritual purity. While the destruction of the Second Temple was a terrible tragedy, the Sages were able to take what Silver calls "visible symbols" from preexistent Jewish sources and practices as well as to create new "memorials of fidelity" in order to help all people develop an approach to faithfully pursue a life filled with divine grace.

Judaism places a heavy emphasis on living a good life, a life devoted to public welfare as well as personal happiness. As Reform Jews in twenty-first-century America, we understand that living a moral and ethical life are the only religious sacraments that we have. We agree with Rabbi Silver that beliefs do not bestow divine saving power upon humans. Judaism is urging us to take advantage of our short lives to do something good in concrete terms for our fellow human beings and for the world.

S'FIRAT HA-OMER, WEEK 1
THE FIRST SHABBAT AFTER THE BEGINNING OF PASSOVER

## *Alternative Haftarah Reading:*
## Pirkei Avot *1:1*

Moses received Torah at Sinai and transmitted it to Joshua, Joshua [transmitted it] to the elders, the elders [transmitted it] to the prophets, and the prophets [transmitted it] to the Members of the Great Assembly. They said three things: "Be patient in [the administration of] justice, raise many disciples, and make a fence round the Torah."

# Ongoing Revelation

*RABBI AMY SCHEINERMAN*

Beginning on the second night of Passover, the festival of our redemption, we begin a countdown to Shavuot, the celebration of God's revelation of Torah to Israel. Liberation from bondage paved the way for Israel to freely enter a covenant of obligation with God at Sinai. In the imagery of the mystics, we travel a spiritual path throughout the time of *S'firat HaOmer* (the Counting of the Omer), preparing ourselves to receive Torah anew in our hearts and lives.

When Moses ascended Mount Sinai a second time following the calamity of the Golden Calf, God instructed him, "Write down these commandments, for in accordance [*ki al pi*] with these commandments I make a covenant with you and with Israel" (Exodus 34:27). In the Talmud, Rabbi Yochanan explains that "the majority [of Torah was transmitted] orally [*al peh*] and the smaller part [was transmitted] in writing" (Babylonian Talmud, *Gittin* 60b). Rabbi Yochanan is speaking of the two Torahs given at Mount Sinai: the Written Torah (*Torah Shebichtav*, i.e., the Five Books of Moses) and the Oral Torah (*Torah Sheb'al Peh*, i.e., Mishnah and Talmud). The seven passages offered to accompany the Torah readings during the period of the Omer are accordingly drawn from *Torah Sheb'al Peh*, the Oral Torah.

The first mishnah of *Pirkei Avot*, which is a tractate of the Oral Torah and functions as its introduction, accords divine authority and a chain of transmission for *Torah Sheb'al Peh*, the oral tradition. The Sages tell us that God revealed the Oral Torah at the same time and in the same place God gave Moses the Written Torah. Unlike the Written Torah, which was written down immediately, the Oral Torah was transmitted orally from generation to generation and only committed to writing by the Talmudic Sages between the third and sixth centuries CE. From the vantage point of history, we know that the Sages of Babylonia and *Eretz Yisrael* wrote the Babylonian Talmud and the Jerusalem Talmud during this period, but they understood their work to be genuine Torah, ongoing revelation. The very idea of Oral Torah affirms the growing and evolving nature of Torah and our relationship with it. The mishnah says that Moses received "Torah"—not "the Torah"—from God.

On Shavuot, we will not only reenact the giving of the Torah at Mount Sinai, but also spiritually recommit ourselves to learning and living Torah. The three precepts promulgated by the Members of the Great Assembly address the roles the Sages held to be primary for them: as judges, helping people resolve their differences and adjudicating civil, criminal, and personal matters; as teachers, conveying and expanding Torah in the lives of Jews; and as legislators, determining how Jews should fulfill their covenant with God under changing conditions of life.

We, too, are students and custodians of Torah in our lives. The sage Ben Bag Bag taught, "Turn it over and over—everything is in it. Scrutinize it and and grow old and gray with it, but do not turn away from it, for there is no better portion than it" (*Pirkei Avot* 5:26). How can you recommit yourself to Torah?

# Tzav
## Leviticus 6:1–8:36

## Traditional Haftarah Reading:
## Jeremiah 7:21–8:3, 9:22–23

## Communicate in Sacred Ways

### Rabbi Maya Y. Glasser

PARASHAT TZAV focuses mainly on sacrificial rituals that bind the Israelites closer together as a community and, on an individual level, bring the people who partake in them closer to God. Its haftarah reading, though, finds the prophet Jeremiah using a particularly negative tone when he speaks on God's behalf. God has found that the people have ceased to perform these sacrificial rituals to strengthen the community. They are disregarding God's presence among them and neglecting their sacred covenant with the Divine.

There is not much that is comforting or reassuring about this section of the Book of Prophets. It is difficult, and even painful, to relate to a God who is incredibly disappointed in us and angry about our actions. However, the Torah and haftarah readings together remind us that relationship building is all about intention. It is not so much about the individual sacrifices that God asks of us in the Torah, but about how we live, knowing that each of us is holy and capable of communicating in sacred ways. The rituals do not have to be performed exactly right—as long as we have an intentional mindset.

The end of the haftarah reading reminds us that fulfillment lies in our relationships and in our lifelong quest to seek and communicate with God's presence in our world.

## Kindness, Justice, and Equity

### Rabbi Rachel L. Joseph

Fittingly, the Rabbis chose to pair a haftarah text that strongly condemns Temple service and sacrifice with a Torah text dedicated to praising the very same details.

The haftarah text begins with a rebuke from God: "Add your [whole] burnt offerings to your other sacrifices and eat the meat! But when I brought your ancestors out of the land of Egypt, I neither spoke to them about burnt offerings or sacrifices" (Jeremiah 7:21–22). Jeremiah calls out the people for their empty rituals. He is reminding us that the sacrificial system is not the goal of the covenant, but rather, a vehicle through which the people can express their relationship with God. When performed in the context of broader concerns, this leads to a powerful conclusion: "Let not the wise glory in their wisdom, . . . but let them who glory, glory in this: that they understand and know Me—that I, the Eternal, practice kindness, justice, and righteousness in the earth; for in these do I delight" (Jeremiah 9:22–23).

What an important lesson in Jewish values! What does God want from us? Not empty, meaningless ritual; God wants us to *act* in this world with kindness, justice, and righteousness—a message that rings true not only in the time of Jeremiah but especially today.

### Alternative Haftarah Reading:
### Avot D'Rabbi Natan 4

SIMEON THE RIGHTEOUS WAS AMONG THE LAST OF THE MEN OF THE GREAT ASSEMBLY. HE USED TO SAY: ON THREE THINGS THE WORLD STANDS—ON THE TORAH, ON THE TEMPLE SERVICE, AND ON ACTS OF LOVING-KINDNESS.

*On the Torah: how so? Lo, it says,* For I desire mercy and not sacrifice, the knowledge of God rather than burnt offerings *(Hosea 6:6). Hence we see that the burnt offering is the most beloved of sacrifices, for the burnt offering is entirely consumed by the flames, as it is said,* And the priest shall make the whole smoke on the altar *(Leviticus 1:9), and elsewhere it says,* And Samuel took a suckling lamb, and offered it for a whole burnt offering unto the [Eternal] *(I Samuel 7:9). But, the study of Torah is more beloved by God than burnt offerings. For if a man studies Torah he comes to know the will of God, as it is said,* Then shalt thou understand the fear of the [Eternal], and find the will of God *(Proverbs 2:5). Hence, when a sage sits and expounds to the congregation, Scripture accounts it to him as though he had offered up fat and blood on the altar.*

## Acts of Loving-Kindness
### RABBI MARK H. LEVIN, DHL

While our Torah portion focuses on the ritual sacrifices that maintain God's covenant with Israel, the traditional haftarah reading poses the profound question of whether ritual without fidelity to God suffices. Israel deceived God even while slaughtering the Levitical offerings—but what does God require of us? Jeremiah arrives at the conclusion that "kindness, justice, and righteousness" (Jeremiah 9:23) are needed in addition to sacrifices.

The early sage Simeon the Righteous famously holds that the world sits on a three-legged stool of Torah study, worship (including sacrifices), and acts of loving-kindness (*Pirkei Avot* 1:2).

Another tannaitic text, *Avot D'Rabbi Natan*, expands that thought. The most cataclysmic moment in Jewish history, the Second Temple's destruction, brought the entire sacrificial system to a screeching halt. Rabbi Yochanan ben Zakkai, at the very moment of transition, abandons the burning Temple in Jerusalem, symbolizing the sacrificial system, and heads with his disciple Y'hoshua to Yavneh—symbolizing the Rabbinic system that would replace the sacrificial system of the Temple.

Y'hoshua, recognizing that the very foundation stone of God's covenant with Israel lays in ruins, is overcome with grief. However, his teacher, Rabbi Yochanan ben Zakkai, recognizes that "we have another atonement . . . acts of loving-kindness." The replacement for the sacrificial system is *g'milut chasadim*, "acts of loving-kindness." The ethical treatment of all human beings will become the foundation stone of the renewed covenant between God and Israel.

### Alternative Haftarah Reading:
### Babylonian Talmud, M'nachot 29b

Rav Y'hudah said in the name of Rav: When Moses ascended to the heavens, he saw God sitting and tying crowns to the letters [of the Torah]. Moses asked, "What is staying Your hand?" God replied, "There is a man who will be in the future, after many generations, named Akiva ben Yosef, who will find in every jot and tittle mounds of halachot." Moses said, "Master of the universe, show him to me!" God said, "Turn around." Moses turned around and [found himself] in the eighth row of students in Rabbi Akiva's academy, but he had no idea what they were saying. His strength deflated. The class asked Rabbi Akiva about a certain matter, "From where do we know this?" He replied, "It is a law transmitted to Moses at Sinai." Moses's mind was put at ease. [Moses] turned to God [and asked], "If You have someone like this, why are You giving the Torah through me?" God said, "Silence! This is what arose in My mind!" Moses continued, "Master of the universe! You showed me his Teaching, now show me his reward." God said, "Turn around." He turned around and saw that Rabbi Akiva's flesh was being weighed out in the marketplace. Moses confronted God: "This is Torah and this is its reward?!" God said, "Silence! This is what arose in My mind!"

## On the Shoulders of Giants

*RABBI AMY SCHEINERMAN*

In this dramatic Rabbinic story, the Sages imagine the moment just prior to God's giving the Torah to Moses on Mount Sinai. God is adding *tagin*, the only decorative flourishes that may be added to a Torah scroll; the Rabbis imagine God "tying" them to the letters. Not every Torah scroll has *tagin*; these calligraphic additions are not required and do not change the meaning of the words. Yet God adds them because God recognizes that in the future, Rabbi Akiva will derive interpretive meaning from every jot and tittle of Torah. Rabbi Akiva, a seminal Rabbinic figure who established methods of halachic exegesis and rabbinic hermeneutics still employed today, was the Rabbinic "Second Moses."

The story suggests that Rabbi Akiva, thanks to his vast and deep interpretative abilities, will surpass even Moses in comprehending Torah. According to Jewish tradition, Rabbi Akiva was brutally martyred by the Romans (Babylonian Talmud,

*B'rachot* 61b). The story expresses the view that Torah study is indeed rewarding in itself, but we should not expect it to be rewarded in a worldly sense.

We all stand on the shoulders of giants, and Torah's meanings thereby grow and expand. Torah is never finished; it continues to grow and evolve thanks to the modes of interpretation Rabbi Akiva and the Sages pioneered and due to the continuing contributions of every generation. According to midrash, "When God's voice came forth at Mount Sinai, it divided itself into seventy human languages, so that the whole world might understand it. All at Mount Sinai—young and old, women, children, and infants—understood according to their ability. Moses, too, understood only according to his capacity, as it is said, 'Moses spoke and God answered him with a voice' (Exodus 19:19). With a voice that Moses could hear" (*Sh'mot Rabbah* 5:9). Torah is for all of us.

What might be your unique contribution to the ongoing revelation of Torah?

# Sh'mini
## Leviticus 9:1–11:47

## Traditional Haftarah Reading:
## II Samuel 6:1–7:17

## Acknowledging the Gifts of Others
### RABBI MICHELLE MISSAGHIEH

*P*ARASHAT SH'MINI tells of two of Aaron's sons, Nadab and Abihu, who, on the opening day of the sacrificial cult in the Tabernacle, bring "strange fire" to the scene and are punished with death. The haftarah reading describes a similarly upsetting moment: When King David and his entourage set out to bring the Ark of God to Jerusalem, the oxen carrying the Ark let it drop, and Uzzah puts his hand out to prevent it from falling. He immediately dies, having forgotten that it was forbidden to touch the Ark.

In this haftarah reading, good intentions are often unappreciated or punished. Uzzah is the son of Abinadab, and Abinadab is the man who housed the Ark of God in his home after it was brought back by the Israelites from the Philistines (I Samuel 7:1–2). After watching his father guard the Ark with great care, it makes sense that he, Uzzah, would be the one to reach out and prevent it from falling on the ground. But God does not see it that way. Uzzah's good intention of caring for the Ark is ignored, and he is struck with death.

After this distressing event, Obed-Edom the Gittite takes the Ark into his home for three months. However, it seems like King David never thanks him for his graciousness. It is God, not David, who blesses Obed-Edom (II Samuel 6:10–11). David takes Obed-Edom's hospitality for granted and fails to acknowledge his generosity.

In a third scene, Michal, Saul's daughter, David's first wife, sees David approaching Jerusalem leaping and whirling with joy, exposing his body. Instead of recognizing her husband's ability to unabashedly celebrate by using his whole body and voice, she looks down on him with contempt (II Samuel 6:16). David's ability to rejoice is rejected.

The haftarah reading is calling on us not to ignore, overlook, or reject other people's contributions and gifts toward us and the world. Instead, we are called to acknowledge, celebrate, and be grateful for the many ways our fellow human beings enrich our lives with their care, generosity, and joy.

# A Lesson in Self-Restraint

### Rabbi Paul J. Citrin

*Parashat Sh'mini* introduces the idea of religious fanaticism as a road to human disaster. God strikes dead two of Aaron's sons, Nadab and Abihu, because their enthusiasm to serve God blots out their understanding of the rules of *Mishkan* rituals. The young priests perish because they allow their ardor to overcome their self-restraint.

In the haftarah reading, we read about several other examples of misplaced fervor:

1. Uzzah reaches out to grab the Ark to save it from falling off a wagon. In his devotion to the Ark's well-being, he forgets the prohibition against physical contact with it and is struck dead.
2. When David brings the Ark to Jerusalem and sacrifices animals every six paces, he dances like someone entranced. Michal, David's wife, chastises him for his embarrassing lack of restraint. From the day that Michal mocked and criticized him, David never approaches her again. She remains childless. David punishes Michal for reminding him to restrain himself—he is not capable of accepting her rebuke and containing his anger.
3. When David decides to honor God by building a Temple in which to house the Ark, God reminds David that the Ark and the divine spirit have always dwelt in a simple tent. God restrains David by forbidding him to build a glorious Temple, thereby bridling David's burgeoning ego.

Religion and faith traditions require restraint in order to avoid fundamentalism and literalism. Leaders in religion, politics, and business require restraint to prevent the manipulation and exploitation for the sake of their own empowerment. Individuals do well to exercise restraint in the face of enticing opportunities to grasp power and thereby taking it away from the powerless—in our business, in our consumption behavior, and in our daily encounters. The virtue of self-restraint is summed up by Rabbi Ben Zoma: "Who is strong? One who subdues one's base instincts" (*Pirkei Avot* 4:1).

## *Alternative Haftarah Reading: Job 38:1-6, 40:1-5*

Then the Eternal replied to Job out of the tempest and said:

Who is this who darkens counsel,
speaking without knowledge?
Stand up straight like an adult;
I will ask and you will inform Me.
Where were you when I laid the earth's foundations?
Speak if you have understanding.
Do you know who fixed its dimensions or who measured it with a line?
Onto what were its bases sunk?
Who set its cornerstone? . . .

The Eternal said in reply to Job:

Shall one who should be disciplined complain against Shaddai?
The one who arraigns God must respond.

Job said in reply to the Eternal:

See, I am of small worth; what can I answer You?
I clap my hand to my mouth.
I have spoken once, and will not reply;
twice, and will do so no more.

# Living with the Question— in Solidarity with Each Other

### Rabbi Joseph B. Meszler

In the Torah portion *Sh'mini*, Aaron faces the unspeakable horror of losing two of his sons, Nadab and Abihu. They brought "alien fire" to God's altar and were incinerated as a consequence (Leviticus 10:1–2). While Moses offers pious words of consolation, the Torah says that "Aaron was silent" (Leviticus 10:3).

In this haftarah from the Book of Job, Job has suffered similar tragedy: the loss of first his wealth, then his home, then his children, and finally his health. His friends offer pious words to him in a farce of consolation. They claim that if he is suffering, he must have done something to deserve it. Unlike Aaron, Job is not silent (at first) but instead rejects this explanation openly. He knows he has done nothing to deserve this. Job, and the storyteller of this book, refuses to blame the victim. When Job finally calls God to account, the unbelievable occurs: God shows up. God does not answer Job's charges directly. The Eternal declares that God is the Creator of the whole universe, and in response to the overwhelming Divine Presence, Job feels infinitesimally small. He falls into an over-awed silence.

The silence of Aaron and the parable of Job highlight the human experience of undeserved suffering. We do not have answers, and even God's answer in the Book of Job is not a rational explanation, but merely a description of God's presence.

God did not abandon Aaron in the wilderness, and the Infinite One appeared to Job. We, too, may not know why there is so much pain in the world. We can, however, still feel the presence of the Creator, and we can live in solidarity with each other.

## Alternative Haftarah Reading:
### Babylonian Talmud, Taanit 7a; Pirkei Avot 4:15

Rav Nachman bar Yitzchak said, "Why are words of Torah likened to a tree, as it is stated, 'It is a tree of life to them who hold fast to it' (Proverbs 3:18)? This verse comes to tell you that just as a small piece of wood can ignite a large piece, so too, small Torah scholars can sharpen great Torah scholars." And this is what Rabbi Chanina said: "I have learned much from my teachers and even more from my friends, but from my students I have learned more than from all of them." (Babylonian Talmud, *Taanit* 7a)

Rabbi Elazar ben Shamua taught, "Let the honor of your student be as dear to you as your own, and the honor of your colleague as the reverence for your teacher, and the reverence of your teacher as the reverence of heaven." (*Pirkei Avot* 4:15)

# Teachers and Students
### RABBI AMY SCHEINERMAN

Torah learning is nurtured by a positive atmosphere for study and constructive relationships between learners and teachers.

For our Sages, Torah study was a central obligation of Jewish life and core path of spirituality. Ideally, all Jews engage in Torah learning. During the period of *S'firat HaOmer*, as we retrace our ancestors' route to Mount Sinai, we meditate on the role of Torah study in our lives and recommit ourselves to learning.

The image of a tree is highly evocative. A tree is a living, breathing, growing organism. So, too, is Torah when we "hold fast to it," studying its words along with the interpretations of those who came before us and offering our own. Rav Nachman bar Yitzchak, however, employs the image of the tree in another, creative way, to focus our attention on the power of engaging in *talmud Torah* (Torah study) in *chavruta*, that is, "together with others." In choosing a study partner or group, we might be concerned that we are "small pieces of wood," insignificant students of Torah. Rav Nachman assures us, however, that a beginning or less accomplished student of Torah has much to offer a more established student of Torah, just as a small piece of wood can kindle a larger piece.

Rabbi Elazar ben Shamua's teaching emphasizes the centrality of one's learning relationships, with both students and teachers. Both students and teachers deserve our respect and attention. Each offers a spiritual pathway to the Divine.

While the Rabbis recognized the hierarchy of a teacher-student relationship, they also recognized that life often juggles or inverts the expected order of things. The Chasidic master Rabbi Menachem Mendel of Kotzk taught, "If you truly wish your children to study Torah, study Torah in their presence and they will follow your example. Otherwise they will not study Torah, but simply instruct their children to do so."

Why are respect and reverence core to the relationship between teacher and student?

# Tazria
## Leviticus 12:1–13:59

## Traditional Haftarah Reading:
## II Kings 4:42–5:19

### The First, Small Step

*RABBI JESSICA K. BAROLSKY*

Tazria, the favorite Torah portion of dermatologists everywhere, tells about skin afflictions and what to do about them. The haftarah reading takes up the theme of skin conditions and shares a story about Naaman, a general from Aram, who had that same affliction. The reading from II Kings is part of a series of miracle stories about the prophet Elisha, the disciple of Elijah. The portion opens with a story in which Elisha multiplies loaves of bread for a crowd, reminding the reader that Elisha is a prophet and a miracle man. The story then tells of Naaman, a general from Aram, who has *tzaraat*, the skin disease discussed in *Tazria*. While the Israelites treated *tzaraat* with isolation, Naaman continues to go on raids and lead the army. His wife's servant, an unnamed girl captured from Israel, suggests that he visit the Israelite prophet Elisha, and through the kings, the connection is made.

Naaman expects fireworks and miracles. Instead, Elisha sends a message telling Naaman to bathe seven times in the Jordan River—a much smaller river than the ones Naaman has closer to home. Naaman rants. His servants encourage him to try it anyway: they have come this far, and immersing is easy. After the inevitable miracle, when the lowly Jordan River clears his skin, Naaman converts to Judaism, pledging his allegiance to the Eternal, the God of the Israelites.

It seemed too easy to bathe in the river seven times. Naaman is so certain it won't work that in a fury, he almost doesn't even try, until his servants point out that if he was prepared to go through a much more complicated ritual, why would he not try something easy?

Robert Alter explains, "It is a great thing that can be effected through an easy act." We have all inflated problems—and solutions—in our minds, assuming that giant problems can be solved only through grand actions. Sometimes, we are wrong. The big change for Naaman was not bathing in the Jordan River, but rather becoming an Israelite; unbeknownst to him, immersing was only the first step. First steps are hard, no matter their size. Naaman reminds us that they do not have to be big to be impactful. All we have to do is take that first step. Small steps can change everything.

## No More Than My Space, No Less Than My Place

*Rabbi Elizabeth Bahar*

This haftarah reading consists of two episodes out of fifteen depicting Elisha, a prophet during the reign of King Jehoram (851–842 BCE), engaging in miraculous deeds. The first miracle is known as the Miracle of the Loaves (II Kings 4:42–44), when Elisha is able to use a small amount of food that is offered to him to feed a hundred people. The second miracle depicts a story of a miraculous healing: Naaman, an Aramean commander, is a leper, who is advised by his wife's Israelite servant girl to seek a cure from a prophet in Samaria.

Elisha's servant takes Naaman to Elisha's house, where he is prescribed to immerse himself seven times in the Jordan River. Naaman is at first angry, because he was expecting an elaborate ceremony, but in the end he listens to the advice of his servants and follows Elisha's prescription. He is cured and chooses to pray to the Eternal. He understands that his healing comes from the God of Israel (Malbim on II Kings 5:8).

Elisha's humility and the simplicity of his actions remind us that we need to know our place in the world and allow others to have a place as well. We are not called to perform grandiose actions. We are called to fulfill our calling with both humility and dignity. In the words of Alan Morinis, "No more than my space, no less than my place."

### Alternative Haftarah Reading:
### From Critique of the Gotha Program, *by Karl Marx, 1875*

In a higher phase of communist society, after the enslaving subordination of the individual to the division of labor, and therewith also the antithesis between mental and physical labor, has vanished; after labor has become not only a means of life but life's prime want; after the productive forces have also increased with the all-around development of the individual, and all the springs of cooperative wealth flow more abundantly—only then can the narrow horizon of bourgeois right be crossed in its entirety and society inscribe on its banners: From each according to [their] ability, to each according to [their] needs!

# What We Can—What We Need

*RABBI MICHAEL L. FESHBACH*

We read in *Parashat Tazria* that a woman was supposed to bring a certain kind of offering after giving birth. But if her means were not sufficient for one kind of animal, she was to bring other, more affordable animals instead (Leviticus 12:8).

The above haftarah is a controversial excerpt from a much-maligned figure, one who was not a practicing Jew but who had Jewish roots: Karl Marx. Marx was not the first to reflect on the words at the end of this reading. Over time, we have learned that the societies founded on the teachings of Marx have proved corrupt, flawed, and particularly perilous for Jews. That does not mean, however, that the idea of "From each according to their ability, to each according to their needs" is without merit. Indeed, in our pursuit of justice and a better world, the idea of giving what we can and being able to find the support that we need is crucial.

Think of Social Security, Medicare, Medicaid, and the general idea of insurance: putting into a pot what we can, having something to draw on when we need it. What are our responsibilities to the society, the community, the country we live in? Yes, what can we do for our country? But, also, what can we expect? What, as members of a community, should we be able to count on for that community to do for us?

## *Alternative Haftarah Reading:*
## *Babylonian Talmud, Eiruvin 13b; Pirkei Avot 5:20*

Rabbi Abba [the name of the rabbi known as Rav] said in the name of Shmuel: "The schools of Hillel and Shammai debated for three years. One side claimed, 'The law is as we say,' and the other side claimed, 'The law is as we say.' A heavenly voice called out, 'Both are the words of the living God, but the law is according to the school of Hillel.' Inasmuch as both are the words of the living God, why did the school of Hillel merit that the halachah be established according to their opinions? Because they [the disciples of Hillel] were peaceful and humble and would study the teachings of the school of Shammai. What is more, they would mention the opinion of the school of Shammai before their own."(Babylonian Talmud, *Eiruvin* 13b)

Every dispute that is for the sake of heaven will in the end endure. But [a dispute] that is not for the sake of heaven will not endure. Which is the controversy that is for the sake of heaven? Such were the controversies of Hillel and Shammai. And which is the controversy that is not for the sake of heaven? Such was the controversy of Korach and all his congregation. (*Pirkei Avot* 5:20)

# For the Sake of Heaven

*Rabbi Amy Scheinerman*

Judaism is an interpretive tradition. At the core is our sacred literature. We study our texts to extract religious meaning and spiritual guidance for our lives. We study the interpretations of those who came before us and generate our own interpretations to pass on to future generations, ever increasing the pool of commentaries that constitute Torah. Disagreement and debate promote deeper inquiry, sharpened reasoning and thereby increase learning, but as both texts remind us, they must be kept within proper boundaries and serve the higher purpose of learning.

Questioning and debating are integral to the process of study and interpretation because they stimulate the refinement of our ideas as well as new insights. Disagreement is inevitable, and how we handle our disagreements makes a world of difference: it matters whether we reject and belittle or respect and embrace our intellectual partners and adversaries. The Rabbis held up the early sages Hillel and Shammai, along with their disciples, as exemplars of appropriate and constructive Jewish debate and disagreement. Talmud records more than three hundred disagreements between the school of Hillel and the school of Shammai. Just as a heavenly voice called out in their day that each expressed "words of the living God," we are challenged to accord those with whom we disagree in the realm of *talmud Torah* (Torah study) respect for uttering "words of the living God." The Rabbis tell us that Beit Hillel's opinions were accepted when it was necessary to make a decision for the community because of their humility and civility, attributes as needed today as then.

There may still be times when a disagreement grows so rancorous, it threatens to taint the views expressed. When this happens, it becomes necessary to step back and consider the dispute and the disputants. *Pirkei Avot* offers us a way to evaluate the legitimacy of the controversy: Is it for the sake of heaven? Or is it about the egos, reputations, or status of certain participants? Korach, who mounted a rebellion against Moses and Aaron to satisfy his urge for power and status (Numbers 16:1–35), met a violent end. Hillel and Shammai are revered Rabbinic figures.

When we are humble and respectful in the course of debate and our motivation is "for the sake of heaven," our viewpoint is lent greater Jewish legitimacy. How can we learn to disagree respectfully?

# M'tzora
## Leviticus 14:1–15:33

## Traditional Haftarah Reading:
## II Kings 7:3–20

## Each of Us Can Make a Difference
### *Rabbi Nicole Roberts*

LIKE THE *PARASHAH*, this haftarah reading begins with the *m'tzora* (one afflicted with skin disease) who has been cast outside the community's walls. In fact, here we read of four Israelites who have been made to stay outside the gates of the city, so as not to infect anyone else.

Being cast outside the gates is, essentially, a death sentence for the four. Knowing they have nothing to lose, they decide to go over to the enemy's camp. The camp has been abandoned, but there they find food, riches, horses, and donkeys—all left behind by their enemies. They return to tell the Israelite king about all they have found, and the food, riches, and animals help save Israel from famine.

From this haftarah reading, we learn that we should never disregard our fellow human beings. Even those who are sick and may not recover may still make a difference to the fate of our people—perhaps even become our salvation.

## Rush Out of the Gates!
### *Cantor Brad Hyman*

The beginning of our haftarah reading introduces us to four men who are afflicted with what we believe to be a version of leprosy (*m'tzora*). Like the rest of the inhabitants of Samaria, they are being held at siege by outside forces, including the Arameans, who have caused the prices of precious resources to soar beyond what is accessible for the besieged population. However, because of their disease, they get cast out of the city, ignored, unseen, and unheard.

Rather than simply die where they are, they decide to take their chances by fleeing to the nearby camp of the Arameans, who might serve them a better fate. Upon arrival at the camp of the Arameans, the four men find the camp deserted.

They eat and drink and take what they can. Furthermore, they decide to inform the court of King Jehoahaz of their fortunate find. The four men, with absolutely nothing and suffering from a skin affliction, suddenly become seen and heard because they bring not only good news, but, ultimately, salvation.

What is the lesson of this story? There are many who live far from our own gaze. While we spend a great deal of time convincing ourselves that "it is not us," in a heartbeat it very well could be. We must all strive to be the person who does not wait to profit from someone else's pain, but rather the person who rushes out to the gates and beyond to help those who are crying out to be seen and heard and to help them up and out of their affliction.

### Alternative Haftarah Reading: *Mishnah* Yoma 8:9

Rabbi Akiva said, "Fortunate are you, O Israel! Before whom do you purify yourselves? And who purifies you? Your Parent in heaven! As it is said: 'I will pour pure water upon you and you will be purified' (Ezekiel 36:25); and it is further said: 'The hope [*mikveh*] of Israel is Adonai' (Jeremiah 17:13). Just as a *mikveh* purifies the impure, so too does the Holy One of Blessing purify Israel."

# Bathe in Water

### RABBI RONALD B. B. SYMONS

How scary it must have been back then to notice a growth on your body with discoloration. Back in the day, you entrusted your journey from impurity toward purity to the priest (as doctor), who followed a ritual of first checking the inflammation and then isolating the person.

How scary it must have been back then to notice a plague on your house, the place where your family lays their heads. Back in the day, you entrusted your journey from impurity toward purity to the priest (as building/health inspector), who followed the ritual of removing infected stones and examining the growth.

How scary it must have been back then to notice a discharge from your body in the most private of places. Back in the day, you entrusted your journey from impurity toward purity to the priest (as urologist or gynecologist), who followed a ritual of checking the discharge.

Throughout it all, the priest used water for sacrifices, to wash clothing, and to wash the person. In all three cases, the journey from impurity to purity was made through water. In our day, with infections and viruses that we cannot see but whose effect alters our way of life, and with homes whose water pipes bring poison into the bodies of our most vulnerable neighbors, the fears of yesteryear are alive and menacing still. Luckily, today we can rely on science to help us through our challenges. And yet, there is something about the simplicity of water, in addition to the complexity of science, that brings renewal. Even today.

Rabbi Akiva understood the spiritual impact of water. In our day, when science has run its course and, God willing, all is well, we can allow the waters of a traditional *mikveh*, a stream, river, lake, or ocean to give us *tikvah*, "hope," in all the ways we need it.

*S'FIRAT HAOMER*, WEEK 5

## *Alternative Haftarah Reading:*
## *Babylonian Talmud,* Yoma 35b

Our Rabbis taught [in a *baraita*]: "The poor person, the wealthy person, and the sensual person come to be judged [by the heavenly court]. To the poor person they say, 'Why did you not engage in Torah [study]?' If the poor person says, 'I was poor and preoccupied with my sustenance [i.e., earning a living],' they say to the poor person, 'Were you poorer than Hillel?' They said about Hillel the Elder that each and every day he would work and earn a half-dinar. He would give half to the guard at the House of Study and use half for his sustenance and the sustenance of his family. Once, he did not find work to earn a wage, and the guard of the house of study did not allow him to enter. He ascended [to the roof] and suspended himself to sit on the edge of the skylight in order to hear the words of the living God from the mouths of Sh'maya and Avtalyon. They said that that day was the eve of Shabbat at the winter solstice and snow fell upon him from the sky. When the dawn arose, Sh'maya said to Avtalyon, 'Avtalyon, my brother, every day the house of study is filled with light, but today it is dark. Is it perhaps cloudy today?' They focused their eyes and saw the figure of a man in the skylight. They ascended and found him on [buried in] three cubits of snow. They extracted him, bathed him, rubbed him down with oil, and placed him near the fire. They said, 'This man is worthy of Shabbat being desecrated on his behalf.'"

# The Value of Torah Study

### Rabbi Amy Scheinerman

The Talmud preserves the teaching of Rabbi B'naah that Torah study enhances our lives—emotionally, physically, and spiritually: "Rabbi B'naah taught: 'For those who engage in Torah study for its own sake, it will be an elixir for life, as it says, 'It is a tree of life to those who hold fast to it' (Proverbs 3:18); and it says, 'It shall be a cure for your body, a tonic for your bones' (Proverbs 3:8); and it says, 'For whoever finds Me finds life' (Proverbs 8:35)" (Babylonian Talmud, *Taanit* 7a). Accordingly, our Sages encouraged us to make Torah learning a central pillar of our lives.

This priority is reinforced by imagining that after we die, we will be required to account for how we have spent our lives. The story of the lengths to which Hillel went to learn, despite all the limitations that poverty imposed upon him, and hearing how the sages of his day responded to his earnest desire and willing sacrifice to learn Torah can inspire us to find time for learning.

*Pirkei Avot* 1:6 tells us that Y'hoshua ben P'rachyah taught: Throughout the generations, Jews have understood that Jewish tradition rests on the foundation of our sacred texts and the remarkable structure of the interpretative tradition built on that foundation. We study Torah for our own personal spiritual, ethical, and religious growth and also to convey the tradition of Jewish values to future generations.

# *Acharei Mot*
## Leviticus 16:1–18:30

## Traditional Haftarah Reading:
## Ezekiel 22:1–19

## Don't Let Evil Sneak In

### RABBI JILL JACOBS

BEHOLD, JERUSALEM is soaked in blood. The prophet Ezekiel excoriates the people for the sins that have defiled the city and brought on disgrace and exile. These include the incest and sexual violence prohibited in *Parashat Acharei Mot*, as well as the ethical sins mentioned in next week's *parashah*, *K'doshim* (these two *parashiyot* are often read together, but are paired with a different haftarah when they are combined). In the repeated accusations of bloodshed, we find, too, an echo of the *parashah*'s repeated reminder that blood is life and that it must be treated with the appropriate care.

The dystopian tone of this haftarah reading fulfills the Torah's warning "You shall not pollute the land in which you live; for blood pollutes the land, and the land can have no expiation for blood that is shed on it, except by the blood of the one who shed it" (Numbers 35:33). The people have shed blood and now suffer the consequences. Fault for this tragedy falls squarely in the hands of the leaders: "Every one of the leaders of Israel among you uses his strength in order to shed blood" (Ezekiel 22:6).

Yet, the midrash identifies the sin of these leaders not as literal bloodshed, but rather as a culture of bribery that leads to an unjust and deadly system:

> A judge who sets their heart on a bribe becomes unable to perceive justice and cannot adjudicate honestly. Rabbi Eliezer said, "It says here, 'Every one of the leaders of Israel among you uses his strength [*z'ro-o*] in order to shed blood' (Ezekiel 22:6). They stretched out [*poshtin*] their arms [*z'ro-oteihen*] under the corners of their garments to take a bribe." Rabbi Abahu said, "Anyone who takes a bribe worth a *p'rutah* [very small amount of money] from another is called wicked." . . . Rabbi Chama bar Oshaya said, ". . . The one who takes a bribe corrupts justice, . . . causes Israel to be exiled from their land, and brings hunger into the world." (*Tanchuma Shof'tim* 7:1)

Through reversal of letters within *shofeit* (judge) and *posheit* (stretch out), and based on the biblical use of the word *z'roa*, "arm," as a metaphor for strength, the Rabbis here suggest that the leaders' sin was to surreptitiously and regularly take small bribes, which distorted their judgment just enough to lead to a complete corruption of the justice system.

It is easy to condemn major transgressions such as bloodshed and murder and to attribute to them the destruction of the Temple and the exile. But the Rabbis suggest that it is the evil that sneaks in much more furtively—in the form of the accumulation of tiny everyday acts of corruption, like the bribe of a single *p'rutah*—that creates a culture of injustice and inequity that ultimately crumbles the very foundations of society. We must learn to call out evil—even if it is in the form of small corruptions—in order to ensure that our society remains both stable and just.

# We Are Capable of Change

### Rabbi Philip J. Bentley

*Acharei Mot* includes a detailed account of the Yom Kippur rituals in the Tabernacle, followed by a list of sexual prohibitions. The accompanying haftarah reading is from the Book of Ezekiel, denouncing the people of Israel for their sins, including government corruption, failure to honor parents, oppression of strangers, violations of Shabbat, idolatry, and most of all, violations of women.

The sin of sexual mistreatment of women is listed together with bloodshed and idolatry (according to Maimonides, one should prefer to die rather than commit one of those three sins [*Mishneh Torah, Hilchot Y'sodei Torah* 5:4]). The prophet Ezekiel then says that in order to be cleansed of those severe sins, the Jewish people would suffer, dispersed among the nations of the world, as their claim to the Land of Israel was always dependent on their moral behavior.

Yom Kippur gives us a chance to repent and change. In Judaism, it is a basic principle that God created no illness without a cure, as well as that human beings are capable of change.

We are never allowed to hurt other people—neither physically nor emotionally. Learn from your mistakes and you will become a better person.

## Alternative Haftarah Reading:
### From "To a Young Jew of Today," by Elie Wiesel

You are seventeen and confused. You are Jewish without knowing why. You don't even know what it means to be Jewish: your friends are not, and your parents just barely. You are not religious, yet not fasting on Yom Kippur makes you feel inexplicably uneasy. . . . Real or apparent, your contradictions trouble you and you ask me to help you untangle them. In short: what does being a Jew mean in these times and to what does it commit you? . . .

For me to be a Jew, in my eyes, constitutes not a problem . . . but a situation. I am Jewish because I am Jewish. And not because my existence is a problem for those who are not. . . . To be a Jew, therefore, is to ask a question—a thousand questions, yet always the same— of society, of others, of oneself, of death and of God. Why and how survive in a universe which negates you? Or: How can you reconcile yourself with history and the graves it digs and transcends? Or: How should you answer the Jewish child who insists: I don't want to suffer, I no longer want to suffer without knowing why. Worse: How does one answer the child's father who says: I don't want, I no longer want, my son to suffer pain and punishment without knowing that his torment has meaning and will have an end? And then, the big questions, the most serious of all: How does one answer the person who demands an interpretation of God's silence at the very moment when . . . any . . . Jew or non-Jew . . . has greater need than ever of His word, let alone His mercy? . . .

To be a Jew today, therefore, means: to testify. To bear witness to what is, and to what is no longer. One can testify with joy—a true and fervent joy, though tainted with sadness— by aiding Israel. Or with anger—restrained, harnessed anger, free of sterile bitterness—by raking over the ashes of the holocaust. For the contemporary Jew . . . , there can be no theme more human, no project more universal.

# With Anger, Authenticity, and Joy
### RABBI ANDREW BUSCH

*Parashat Acharei Mot* begins with the story of the deaths of two of Aaron's sons, Nadab and Abihu, and then continues with a wide-ranging list of mitzvot. In a different type of intergenerational message, Elie Wiesel's essay challenges the post-Shoah generation with a multifaceted set of obligations. In the mid-1960s, Wiesel wrote his essay "To a Young Jew of Today" and published it in his book *One Generation After*. At the time of this open letter's publication, Wiesel's son was not yet born. Yet the survivor and prophetic teacher is addressing his son's generation. His essay is grounded in post–World War II and pre-1967 doubts regarding Jewish identity and Zionism. However, its message is clear: while the historical specifics may vary, the Jewish obligations remain constant. Young and older Jews responded to Wiesel's challenge to reject negative images of Judaism and his encouragement to connect with Israel while navigating its imperfections.

Today, we still embrace the Jewish impulse to ask questions, "a thousand questions," and "bear witness" to history and present. Being angry at times is part of the process and encourages us to live our Judaism with authenticity and joy. May Wiesel's words spur us to embrace an unapologetic Jewish life of wide-ranging and joyous social justice work. May our approach be thoughtful, active, and impactful.

## Alternative Haftarah Reading:
## *Babylonian Talmud,* Gittin 6b; B'rachot 7a

Rabbi Evyatar came across [the prophet] Elijah and said to him, "What is the Holy Blessed One doing [right now]?" [Elijah] said to him, "God is engaged in studying the episode of the concubine in Gibeah." [Rabbi Evyatar] asked [Elijah], "What is God saying [concerning this passage]?" [Elijah] said to him, "[God is saying,] 'Evyatar, My son, says this, and Yonatan, My son, says that.'" [Rabbi Evyatar] said to [Elijah], "God forbid! Is there uncertainty in heaven?!" [Elijah] said to him, "Both these and those are the words of the living God." (Babylonian Talmud, *Gittin* 6b)

Rabbi Yochanan says in the name of Rabbi Yosei: "How do we know that the Holy Blessed One prays? Because it says: 'Even them will I bring to My holy mountain and make them joyful in My house of prayer' (Isaiah 56:7). It does not say 'their prayer' but rather 'My prayer.' Thus [we learn] that the Holy Blessed One prays." What does God pray? Rav Zutra bar Tovyah said in the name of Rav: "May it be My will that My mercy may suppress My anger, and that My mercy may prevail over My [other] attributes, so that I may deal with My children through the attribute of mercy and, on their behalf, stop short of the limit of strict justice."(Babylonian Talmud, *B'rachot* 7a)

# Study and Prayer
### RABBI AMY SCHEINERMAN

For our Sages, Torah and prayer are central to Jewish living, so much so that they envisioned God engaged in both learning and prayer. How better to affirm the divine quality of these endeavors?

The Babylonian Talmud recounts several occasions when rabbis encounter the prophet Elijah, who, according to tradition, did not die. Upon finding Elijah, Rabbi Evyatar is burning to know what God does and so asks, "What is God doing this very minute?" The remarkable response from Elijah is that God is studying Scripture, just as we Jews do (the story of the concubine of Gibeah is recounted in

Judges 19–21). Even more, God studies the opinions of people who study Torah, engaging in our ongoing interpretative tradition.

The Babylonian Talmud also asserts that just as God studies Scripture as we do, God prays as we do. The proof supplied by Rabbi Yosei turns on a clever interpretation of Isaiah 56:7. The phrase "My house of prayer" (*beit t'filati*) is more literally translated "the house of My prayer," implying that God prays. What is more, God recites a prayer each of us would do well to recite daily; it could be paraphrased, "May I act today with compassion and suppress my anger and tendency to judge so that I treat everyone I encounter today with mercy."

Teaching us that God studies and prays as people study and pray does not reduce God to a human, but rather elevates our study and prayer to the level of divine activities. The religious goal of *Imitatio Dei* ("emulating God") is possible because we are *imago Dei*—*tzelem Elohim*, the "image of God." We fulfill our divine potential through acts of *chesed* (loving-kindness), *tzedek* (justice), *tzedakah* (righteousness), and *rachamim* (compassion)—which we learn through Torah study and reinforce through prayer.

# K'doshim
## Leviticus 19:1–20:27

## Traditional Haftarah Reading:
## Amos 9:7–15

## Holy Lives of Honor
### Rabbi Seth M. Limmer

AMOS'S WORDS engage with the *parashah's* themes to create a dialogue about distinction: in *Parashat K'doshim*, Israel is called upon to distinguish itself *from* other nations through its sexual boundaries and to distinguish itself *among* all people through its holy conduct. Amos's rebuke that the Children of Israel are in essence no different from Philistines or Arameans reminds us that Judaism determines sacred status not by birth, but by deed. Israel's connection to God, although born of history, is determined by our behavior; Israel's status is not based on its election. Moral, religious, even sexual behaviors are what will make us a holy people—a "nation of priests" (Exodus 19:6)—or have us fall from divine favor.

Just as the *parashah* juxtaposes the abominable with the sacred, so too does Amos contrast those who lead lives of sin with those dedicated to the holy. Amos claims not only that God pays attention to human behaviors, but also that God holds every person accountable for their deeds. Each of us is shaken like a pebble in a sieve to see if we pass divine muster (Amos 9:9). Like *Parashat K'doshim*, Amos calls each of us to live a holy life of honor: to display our concern for the honor of others in all of our deeds; to dispense honor to every other human being created in the divine image.

## Living Up to the Prophet's Call
### Rabbi Matt Friedman

If we were to try to look for a condensed version of the entirety of the messages of the Pentateuch and the paired readings from the Prophets, the texts of *Parashat K'doshim* and Amos are the best places to start. *Parashat K'doshim* provides not only the code for a just and righteous society, but also its underlying philosophy. This week's selection from the Book of Amos is the quintessential prophetic reading. It includes words of admonition, evidence of failed behavior, a description of punitive consequences, and the promise of hope and forgiveness. The structure of Amos's words is a model to guide the sentiments of a group of adults as well as to raise one's children. Failure is followed by an unavoidable and unpleasant aftermath; however, forgiveness and hope are always within reach.

In our own day, the reading from the Book of Amos emphasizes once again the importance of maintaining our ethical standards and our efforts to live according to them. At times, this goal might appear quite distant, but we must nonetheless not give up. We are not allowed to let go of the belief that we can achieve our goals.

## *Alternative Haftarah Reading: "V'ahavta," by Marge Piercy*

So you shall love what is holy
with all your courage, with all your passion
with all your strength.
Let the words that have come down
shine in our words and our actions.
We must teach our children to know and understand them.
We must speak about what is good
and holy within our homes
when we are working, when we are at play,
when we lie down and when we get up.
Let the work of our hands speak of goodness.
    Let it run in our blood
and glow from our doors and windows.

We should love ourselves, for we are of G-d.
We should love our neighbors as ourselves.
We should love the stranger, for we
were once strangers in the land of Egypt
and have been strangers in all the lands of the world since.
Let love fill our hearts with its clear precious water.
Heaven and earth observe how we cherish or spoil our
    world.
Heaven and earth watch whether we choose life or choose
    death.
We must choose life so that  our children's children may live.

Be quiet and listen to the still small
voice within that speaks in love.
Open to that voice, hear it, heed it and work for life.
Let us remember and strive to be good.
Let us remember to find what is holy
within and without.

# Find It Within and Find It Without

*Rabbi Daniel Kirzane*

All human beings have the potential for holiness, and *Parashat K'doshim* lays out how we can realize that potential. Marge Piercy (b. 1936) likewise reminds us that holiness is not simply a state of being; it is the by-product of fulfilling sacred duties. Even the simple instruction to "love your neighbor as yourself," for instance, first requires the hard work of loving ourselves.

To "work for life" is a struggle with inner and outer dimensions. As Hillel (first century CE) expressed it, "If I am not for myself, who will be for me? But if I am [only] for myself, what am I? And if not now, when?" (*Pirkei Avot* 1:14). Every day, we must live for ourselves, *and* we must live for others. Loving ourselves is connected to loving our children, which is connected to loving the stranger, which is connected to loving the world. To be holy is to love what is holy, to find it "within" and to discover it "without."

The liturgist Chaim Stern (1930–2001) reminds us that ours is "a world far from wholeness and peace" (*Mishkan T'filah*, 15, 57). Our sacred task is to bring healing to the world, and we do our best work when we ourselves are healed. The prophet Jeremiah prays, "Heal me, Eternal, and I will be healed" (Jeremiah 17:14)—read not "I will be healed," but "I will heal." Both diligent self-care and opening ourselves to the help of others are necessary in the long and difficult quest for redemption.

## *S'FIRAT HA-OMER*, WEEK 7

### *Alternative Haftarah Reading:*
### Sh'mot Rabbah *28:6*

"God spoke all these words, saying" (Exodus 20:1). Rabbi Yitzchak said, "At Mount Sinai, the prophets of each and every [future] generation received what they were to prophesy. For thus Moses told Israel, '[I make this covenant . . . not with you alone,] but with those who stand here with us this day before the Eternal our God, and also with those who are not here with us this day' (Deuteronomy 29:14). [Moses] did not say, 'Who are not standing here with us this day,' but rather, 'Who are not here with us this day,' [in order to include] souls that are destined to be created, but do not yet exist. For although they did not exist at the time, each received what was to be theirs."

## Every Day (A)New

*RABBI AMY SCHEINERMAN*

On Shavuot, we stand again at Mount Sinai and receive the Torah anew. Tradition holds that in the verse in Deuteronomy 29:14, God asserts that the covenant includes not only the Israelites standing arrayed at the foot of the mountain but also those "who are not here with us this day." It includes all of us, both those born into Jewish families and those who choose to become Jews. We all stood together at Mount Sinai. As the midrash specifies that the prophets yet to be born were endowed with their prophetic messages as part of Revelation, so too was each of us endowed at Mount Sinai with the wisdom we need to learn and transmit Torah and find meaning in living as Jews. On Shavuot, the commemoration of God's giving Torah, the focus in equally on our receiving Torah.

Rabbi Shlomo Ephraim Luntschitz, the sixteenth-century author of *K'li Yakar*, offered an insightful and inspirational commentary on Leviticus 23:16, which describes the omer, the sheaves brought to the Temple each day for seven weeks from Passover until Shavuot: "You must count until the day after the seventh week—fifty days; then you shall bring an offering of new grain (*minchah chadashah*) to the Eternal." Rabbi Luntschitz, focusing on *minchah chadashah*, explains, "The Torah must be new for each person every day as the day that it was received from

Mount Sinai. For the words of Torah shall be new to you, and not like old matters, which the heart detests. For, in truth, you are commanded to derive novelty each and every day."

What new kind of Torah have you discovered today? And yesterday? How can you stay open to receiving more?

# *Emor*
## Leviticus 21:1–24:23

## Traditional Haftarah Reading:
## Ezekiel 44:15–31

## Holiness and Justice
### *Rabbi Peter Rigler*

T HE TORAH PORTION of *Emor* is part of the priestly ritual instructions that are detailed throughout the Book of Leviticus. There are a myriad of detailed descriptions of how, when, and what the priests are required to do. It is no surprise that the connection to the haftarah is established on the basis of yet another description of the role of the priests: the prophet Ezekiel lays out the role of the priests for what he hopes will be an eventual Third Temple, where we can again practice the rituals performed by the priests.

It would be easy to miss that both the Torah and haftarah readings are about more than physical structures or a return to them. Instead, found within both is an emphasis on the foundational laws to create a functional society. *Emor* details that "you shall have one standard for stranger and citizen alike: for I the Eternal am your God" (Leviticus 24:22). There is no room for corruption. Justice is essential. Rashi comments on this verse by saying, "I am the God of all of you. Just as I join My name with you, so do I join My name with the alien ones."

In other words, we are all God's children. We will all be judged equally.

In the Torah portion, the priests are reminded of the fact that their role is just as sacred as any other person's role. In the haftarah reading, the priests are told, "They are to teach My people the difference between the holy and the common" (Ezekiel 44:23).

Also the haftarah reading describes a communal holiness. This community as a whole is envisioned as just and holy for all.

Prophets like Isaiah and Jeremiah wrote in the Land of Israel. Ezekiel lives as a foreigner in a strange land. He struggles with the question of what it means to live in the Diaspora. His words are addressed to a community who must reconfigure not only their religious practices but also the ethical concerns of their community. The vision of the Third Temple serves as a mystical source of hope for a people struggling, guided by priests who try to ground them in holiness and justice.

Ezekiel's words help us envision not only a Third Temple but also a time when holiness and justice are experienced by all. This call for justice is more than a yearning; it is an ethical concern for a holy community.

## Separate and Special

### Rabbi Geri Newburge

*Parashat Emor* begins with detailed instructions to the *kohanim* (priests) for their daily personal and professional lives and continues with descriptions of the appropriate procedures for sacrifices and festivals. The haftarah reading from Ezekiel echoes the guidelines for the *kohanim*, dictating their dress, marital relations, and ritual purity.

These rules were established by God in order to elevate those who served—first in the *Mishkan*, and later in the Temple in Jerusalem. Midway through the haftarah reading, Ezekiel states that the priests "are to teach My people the difference between the holy and the common" (Ezekiel 44:23). Only when they themselves appreciate the difference between the commonplace and the sacred are the priests able to instruct the Israelites.

While modern sensibilities may lend themselves to a resentment of the text as exclusionary, and Reform Judaism rejects the concept of a restricted priesthood, the Hebrew word *kodesh*, found in Ezekiel 44:23, in its simplest form means "separate" but is generally understood to mean "holy." "Holiness" is often evoked when something is different or separate from everything else.

Separation has positive and negative connotations. When something is set apart as special, such as a food or a relationship, that separation adds sanctity and elevates it to a more meaningful status. When something is set apart because it is different, that separation leads to exclusion and derision.

Ezekiel's prophecy teaches and reinforces the former and invites the reader to cultivate opportunities to sanctify time and space, thereby enhancing one's spiritual and religious life.

## *Alternative Haftarah Reading: Isaiah 1:11–17*

"What are your many sacrifices to Me?"
says the Eternal One.
"I am sated with the rams you bring as burnt offerings,
with the fat of your fine animals;
I take no delight in the blood of bulls or lambs or goats.
When you come to seek My presence,
who asked this of you,
to trample My courts?
Bring Me no more futile offerings;
incense is an abomination to Me.
New moon and sabbath,
the calling of assemblies:
I cannot endure festivities
along with evil.
I hate your your new moons, your festival days:
they are a burden to Me;
I can bear [them] no more.
When you stretch out your hands,
I will avert My eyes from you;
however much you pray,
I will not listen,
while your hands are filled with blood.
Wash yourselves; cleanse yourselves;
put your evil doings away from My sight.
Cease to do evil,
learn to do good,
seek justice; relieve the oppressed.
Uphold the orphan's rights;
take up the widow's cause."

# Aiding the Wronged and Learning to Do Good
### Abigail Pogrebin

*Parashat Emor* is a blueprint for observance, including stringent directives on purity, sacrifices, proper meat, bread, Sabbath rest, and atonement.

But our prophet Isaiah reminds us that the rules take us only so far. God doesn't want just obsessive piety; God seeks selfless activity. There's a higher Jewish value placed on deeds than on devotion. God cares more about what we're doing than how we're praying: "What are your many sacrifices to Me?" says the Eternal One. "I am sated with the rams you bring as burnt offerings, with the fat of your fine animals; I take no delight in the blood of bulls or lambs or goats. . . . Bring Me no more futile offerings; incense is an abomination to Me" (Isaiah 1:11–13).

Incense is an abomination? Really? *Parashat Emor* tells us just the opposite, enumerating in painstaking detail how to offer the proper fire and sacrifices. Why is Isaiah contravening God's message?

Maybe, more accurately, Isaiah is not contradicting God's directives but clarifying them: Don't get so caught up in the minutiae of worship. Look harder at who you're helping. There's religiosity in rescue. Isaiah continues a few verses later, "Learn to do good, seek justice; relieve the oppressed. Uphold the orphan's rights; take up the widow's cause" (Isaiah 1:17).

As we read *Parashat Emor*'s dictates in the modern moment—when the call to do our part is as pressing as ever—perhaps Isaiah reminds us to make sure we're doing the heavier lift: relieving the oppressed and learning to do good.

### *Alternative Haftarah Reading: "Ready and Prepared," by Trisha Arlin*

I invite you to cover yourself with your tallit.
Imagine that everything outside your tallit is mundane
And everything inside it, especially you, is kadosh,
holy and separate.
Close your eyes,
Breathe regularly,
Everything is God
So if every breath is a holy interaction, then
Every breath is a prayer.
You go to the door to the room you are in,
Imagine that you open the door and step outside
And you find yourself in a quiet meadow in May.
Everywhere you look are wildflowers and grasses,
Birds singing, tall trees in the distance.
And you see that there is a small house a short walk away,
With a door but no windows.
You reach the house
You walk quickly around it
And you realize, this is your Holy of Holies,
Where you are the Kohen Gadol, the high priest.

You get to the door, you touch it,
It is warm and mysterious.
You open the door and go inside,
Close the door behind you,
Realize that though there are no windows it is brightly lit.
And now you see there is a small pool of running water
And you remember, this is your mikvah.
You realize you are completely yourself here,
So you take off your clothes
And you step into this mikvah and go under the water.
Baruch atah Adonai Eloheinu ru'ach ha olam, asher kid'shanu bemitzvotav,
    vetzivanu al hat'vilah.
Bless the One-ness, Breath of the Universe, sanctifying us with God's
    obligations, obliging us to immerse.
Dunk yourself again, and this time
Create up your own blessing,
This one for your family and friends.
Dunk yourself again, and make up another blessing,
This one for your community and your world.
Leave the water.
There's a lovely fluffy towel.
Dry yourself off.
Dress yourself and imagine that you are ready
    for holiness, for action, for change.
Now you can leave your Holy of Holies,
Walk out the door through the meadow,
You see your door, re-enter your room,
You are back to yourself
With the tallit covering your head,
Joined with all the other holy ones
Everyone
In the Holy Wholeness.

## Stepping behind the Curtains

*Rabbi Sonja K. Pilz, PhD*

In a world polarized and polarizing, possibly the last things we might look for in our spiritual tradition are labels of hierarchy and separation. The categories into which the Rabbis divided the people (*kohanim*, *l'viyim*, *yisrael*, women and minors, Jews of disability and androgynity, and non-Jews) seem offensive, harmful, and useless in our current world.

And yet, in moments of humility, we might find ourselves using similar categories: the wealthy and educated versus the poor, activists versus bystanders, traditional versus liberal, healthy and beautiful versus overweight, more versus less Jewish—all are categories that we are regularly exposed to. We grow accustomed to these categories, integrating them into our thoughts and actions, and if not for arbitrary, sudden moments of awareness, we live quite comfortably with them over long stretches of time.

Liturgical poet Trisha Arlin invites us to go onto an inner journey. What if we dunked ourselves into clearing and cleansing waters? What if we left behind all categories except for those established in Leviticus 16: our friends and family (16:6); the immediate spaces we inhabit (16:16); and the broader (in our context, globalized) community we live in (16:21)? If we confessed our natural desire to care most for those we love and live with, could we come to a new awareness of our connection with the life unfolding all around us, even in the most remote corners of the earth?

May our awareness flow like water. May we step into and out of the categories of care. May we find ways to refresh our souls and eyes in our synagogues, through texts old and new.

# B'har
## Leviticus 25:1–26:2

## Traditional Haftarah Reading:
## Jeremiah 32:6–27

## Buying Land While Facing Destruction
### RABBI STEPHEN WEISMAN

The traditional haftarah reading for *Parashat B'har* has two parts:

1. God tells Jeremiah that his cousin Chanam-el will visit him and request that Jeremiah redeem his family's land in Anatot—and Chanam-el does arrive at the prophet's house. Jeremiah, recognizing God's will, redeems the land while imprisoned in Jerusalem for prophesying the impending downfall of Jerusalem. He gives the deed to his aide, Baruch, along with instruction to preserve it safely in an earthen jar.

2. Jeremiah offers a prayer, praising God's role in creation and Jewish history, marveling over God's faith with future generations, symbolized by God's request that he purchase his cousin's land.

This reading follows the Torah's laws regarding the Sabbatical and Jubilee years. In particular, it invokes the laws protecting land holdings in Leviticus 25:25–28 and our servitude to God in 25:55. The haftarah reading adds depth and significance to the Torah portion, which was becoming less accessible to a more and more urban Jewish community.

The haftarah's message is clear: just as God saved our faithful ancestors from Egyptian slavery by purchasing our lives from the Egyptians and providing a path to our freedom in our own land, so, in Jeremiah's time, and even while warning of the impending destruction, God promises to eventually give that land back to us—when we have earned it through our work on ourselves and when we will have brought justice to the world.

# A Life in Dignity

*Rabbi Isabel de Koninck*

In the haftarah reading for *Parashat B'har*, the prophet Jeremiah's cousin Chanam-el comes to visit him, pleading for Jeremiah to buy his land. Jeremiah knows that the purchase would be a financial loss (he had prophesied the impending Babylonian exile) but purchases the land anyway, according to the laws of land redemption found in *Parashat B'har*.

The laws of land redemption ensure that communal resources are martialed to support those in dire straits to remain in their homes in dignity. Regarding Leviticus 25:25, Rabbeinu Bachya suggests that what makes the law of land redemption work is compassion. He maintains that people are able to fulfill these financially arduous obligations only because of the deep compassion they feel for their kin.

In today's world, where the ancient ties of tribal kinship have long since vanished and where familial ties may not be our most sacredly held relationships, the haftarah reading prompts us to inquire: Who are our kinfolk? Who do we trust enough that we could, in our hour of greatest need, go to them and expect them to help us? For whom would we be willing to endure significant personal expense in order to ensure that they are able to survive and thrive in dignity?

## *Alternative Haftarah Reading: Joel 4:9–21*

Proclaim this among the nations:
Prepare for battle!
Arouse the warriors,
let all the fighters come and draw near!
Beat your plowshares into swords,
and your pruning hooks into spears!
Let even the weakling say, "I am strong."
Rouse yourselves and come,
all you nations;
come together
from roundabout.
There bring down
your warriors, O Eternal!
Let the nations rouse themselves and march up
to the Valley of Jehoshaphat;
for there I will sit in judgment

over all the nations roundabout.
Swing the sickle,
for the crop is ripe;
come and tread,
for the winepress is full,
the vats are overflowing!
For great is their wickedness.

Multitudes upon multitudes
in the Valley of Decision!
For the day of the Eternal is at hand
in the Valley of Decision.
Sun and moon are darkened,
and stars withdraw their brightness.
And the Eternal will roar from Zion,
and shout aloud from Jerusalem,
so that heaven and earth tremble.
But the Eternal will be a shelter to God's people,
a refuge to the children of Israel.
And you shall know that I the Eternal your God
dwell in Zion, My holy mount.
And Jerusalem shall be holy;
nevermore shall strangers pass through it.
And in that day,
the mountains shall drip with wine,
the hills shall flow with milk,
and all the watercourses of Judah shall flow with water;
a spring shall issue from the House of the Eternal
and shall water the Wadi of Acacias.
Egypt shall be a desolation,
and Edom a desolate waste,
because of the outrage to the people of Judah,
in whose land they shed the blood of the innocent.
But Judah shall be inhabited forever,
and Jerusalem throughout the ages.
Thus I will treat as innocent their blood
which I have not treated as innocent;
and the Eternal shall dwell in Zion.

# Proclaim Liberty Throughout All the Land Unto All the Inhabitants Thereof

*RABBI STEPHEN WEISMAN*

My choice for an alternative haftarah reading for *Parashat B'har* is inspired by thirty years of work with *b'nei mitzvah*. Summarizing *B'har* is challenging enough for twelve-year-olds. So much of its content has no connection to their lives. Asking them to pick what they want to read and teach about invariably leads them to select the opening verses, so they can focus on the words of Leviticus 25:10, inscribed on the Liberty Bell: "Proclaim Liberty Throughout All the Land Unto All the Inhabitants Thereof."

The words in this closing poem of Joel, especially Joel 4:10 ("Beat your plowshares into swords, and your pruning hooks into spears"), are an inversion of the more familiar, idyllic, and well-known teachings of Isaiah 2:4 and Micah 4:3. Yet they are neither bellicose nor hateful. They promise God's continuing love and support even in exile.

One may envision America's founders reading these verses from the Book of Joel in the early days of the Revolutionary War, seeking encouragement. In connection with the words they chose for the Liberty Bell, Joel's verses are a strong support for social justice initiatives.

## *Alternative Haftarah Reading:*
## *"The Horrors of Slavery," by Ernestine Rose*

It is utterly impossible for us, as finite beings, with the utmost stretch of the imagination, to conceive the depth and immensity of the horrors of slavery. I would that, instead of speaking and listening to-day, we could all sit down in perfect silence, and each and every one of us ask ourselves what is it to be a slave? . . .

We have the evil among us; we see it daily and hourly before us; we have become accustomed to it: we talk about it; but do we comprehend it—do we realize it—do we feel it?

What is it to be a slave?

Not to be your own, bodily, mentally, or morally—

that is to be a slave.

Ay, even if slaveholders treated their slaves with the utmost kindness and charity;

if I were told they kept them sitting on a sofa all day and fed them with the best of the land,

it is none the less slavery;

for what does slavery mean?
To work hard, to fare ill, to suffer hardship, that is not slavery;
for many of us white men and women have to work hard, have to fare ill,
    have to suffer hardship, and yet we are not slaves.
Slavery is not to belong to yourself—to be robbed of yourself.
There is nothing that I so much abhor as that single thing—to be robbed
    of one's self. . . .

The same mother earth has created us all; the same life pervades all;
the same spirit ought to animate all.
Slavery deprives us of ourselves.
The slave has no power to say, "I will go here, or I will go yonder."
The slave cannot say, "My wife, my husband, or my child."
He does not belong to himself, and of course cannot claim anything whatever
    as his own.
This is the great abomination of slavery, that it deprives a man of the common
    rights of humanity stamped upon him by his Maker.

## Ensuring *D'ror*
### CANTOR RHODA J. HARRISON, PhD

"Proclaim Liberty Throughout All the Land Unto All the Inhabitants Thereof" (Leviticus 25:10)—this is the Levitical verse that found its way onto America's Liberty Bell, a national symbol of independence. In the context of *Parashat B'har*, the verse introduces the instructions for the Jubilee year's release of one's material purchases, including land, loans, and people.

The choice of the word *d'ror*, translated on our national bell as "liberty," is of interest. Most often when referring to "freedom" (such as the setting free of a slave or servant), the Bible uses the word *chofesh*, a term that in Modern Hebrew retains the notion of freedom. When school lets out, *chofesh*, "vacation," begins.

So, why *d'ror*? Why not *chofesh*? The eleventh-century French commentator Rashi views *d'ror* as specifically the freedom from living under someone else's rule, an understandable interpretation given the reality of Jewish life in medieval France. Thirteenth-century grammarian Rabbi Avraham Bedersi argues that *chofesh* implies solely a reduction of servitude, whereas *d'ror* represents its total abolition. Later scholars add that while *chofesh* marks the absence of labor for a limited period of time, *d'ror* implies that a person has become his or her own master.

Ernestine Rose, an outspoken nineteenth-century feminist and abolitionist, abhorred the notion of slavery. Her writings, like this prophetic selection, further the biblical notion of *d'ror*. She understood that the proclamation of liberty throughout the land must apply eternally and universally to everyone, no matter the color of their skin or their gender.

Especially in today's world, where the shackles of slavery are not necessarily visible, Rose's words inspire us to fulfill the ideals of the Jubilee year by ensuring *d'ror* throughout the land to all its inhabitants.

# B'chukotai
## Leviticus 26:3–27:34

## Traditional Haftarah Reading:
## Jeremiah 16:19–17:14

### God Will Welcome Us Back

*Rabbi Erin Boxt*

PARASHAT B'CHUKOTAI begins with the supposition that the Israelite nation will follow or walk in the ways of God's commandments and thus be rewarded or blessed. However, if the Children of Israel choose not to observe God's laws and turn away from Torah, they will be cursed.

The haftarah reading comes from the prophet Jeremiah, who, in his agonizing visions of the destruction of Jerusalem, foretold the exile of Israel to Babylonia in 587 BCE. Although Jeremiah alerted the Israelites of the curses that would transpire against them, the final verse of Jeremiah's vision in this haftarah section speaks of his willingness and desire to return to God, through healing:

> *R'fa-eini Adonai*
> *v'eirafei*
> *hoshi-eini*
> *v'ivashei-ah*
> *ki t'hilati atah.*
>
> Heal me, Eternal One!
> [Only] then shall I be healed.
> Save me!
> [Only] then shall I be saved:
> for You are my praise.
>     (Jeremiah 17:14)

Even though *B'nei Yisrael* (the Children of Israel) turn away from God time and time again, as long as we return to God as in days of old, God will welcome us back with open arms, healing us in our pain and agony along God's way.

# In Moments of Doubt

### CANTOR SHANI COHEN

In *Parashat B'chukotai*, God promises peace and prosperity if the people of Israel follow God's commandments, and war and famine if they do not. Yet Jeremiah's struggles seem to put God's promise into question, or at least throw a wrench into the system. The prophet is extremely troubled. He wants to believe that God is trustworthy and beneficent, but cannot understand why he is being punished. He finally calls out, "Heal me, Eternal One! [Only] then shall I be healed. Save me! [Only] then shalll I be saved" (Jeremiah 17:14). Jeremiah intensifies his petition by using the verb *r'fa*, "heal," in the first phrase and the verb *hoshi'a*, "save," in the second phrase of his prayer.

We all have moments when we doubt our core beliefs and lose our sense of self, overwhelmed with the evils of the world. Like Jeremiah, we might find ourselves calling out, "Why me? Why now?" Back in verses 10–11, God reassures Jeremiah that there is a divine plan and that, despite all appearances, in the end everyone will get what they deserve.

Jeremiah's God is not one of parental love, but rather the source of both life and death, an all-powerful, all-knowing judge. Faced with Jeremiah's struggles, can we trust in this God, even when the world seems to be filled with corruption and greed? What gives you hope in God, and what inspires you to move from doubt to accountability?

## *Alternative Haftarah Reading: "Teach Me, O God," by Leah Goldberg*

Teach me, O God, a blessing, a prayer
on the mystery of a withered leaf,
on ripened fruit so fair,
on the freedom to see, to sense,
to breathe, to know, to hope, to despair.

Teach my lips a blessing, a hymn of praise,
as each morning and night
You renew Your days,
lest my days be as the one before;
lest routine set my ways.

# Filling Our Lives with Blessing

*Rabbi Reena Spicehandler*

In many years *B'chukotai* is joined to *B'har*, which immediately precedes it, to form a double Torah portion. When that occurs, only the haftarah for *B'chukotai* is read. *B'chukotai* lays out the consequences of obeying or disobeying God's laws, the blessings and curses that result. The idea of a God who curses us is both frightening and objectionable for contemporary readers. Perhaps we can focus instead on finding blessings in our lives and working to transform perceived curses into blessings as well.

Leah Goldberg's poem suggests ways to transform our daily lives so that they are filled with blessing. In this way we can heighten awareness of living in God's house all the days of our lives (Psalm 27:4).

## *Alternative Haftarah Reading: "For Complete Healing," by Debbie Perlman*

Like a pure crystalline tone,
Sounding in the deepest fear of night
So will You call to me
To leave this land of my distress.

O let me turn to You
Let me loose the steel bands of my dread
And listen for the ringing
Of Your summons.

How can I leave with so much undone?
How can I move away from this place
And follow, fearless, into the strength
Of Your concern for me?

I am only Your creation
Striving to create my own remembrance,
To leave this world with knowledge
Of my passage through it.

So soon You call me to Your harmonies,
To close my manuscript,
To sing unaccompanied
These notes of my life, the final hymns.

Still my terror with clear notes, Righteous One;
Quiet me with a silken melody,
That by accepting Your judgement,
I might turn to sing with You.

# Blessings and Curses

### *CANTOR ALANE S. KATZEW, BCC*

A cartoon by Paul Palnik depicting a multitude of blessings and curses was steady company in my childhood home, and now it adorns the wall in my house as reminder of the dynamic of all human life; its ups and downs are a given. Sometimes we find ourselves in deep valleys of sadness, and other times we stand elated upon mountaintops of joy. The artist injects humor into this notion of blessings and curses, or in today's psychobabble, "opportunities and challenges" ("May your heart, mind, soul, and spirit be filled with knowledge, wisdom, kindness, love, truth, peace, strength, and light"; "May a huge corned beef sandwich land on and crush your car").

In this week's *parashah*, *B'chukotai*, we are taught that by following God's covenant, we will be blessed, and if we stray, our lives will be cursed. When illness overtakes us, both physically and spiritually, adopting an attitude of gratitude is documented as being palliative. Ultimately, when we are alone and all pretense is gone, we must accept that we are not in control. Only the grace of God and our faith can bring comfort. The prophet Jeremiah states:

> Heal me, Eternal One!
> [Only] then shall I be healed.
> Save me!
> [Only] then shall I be saved:
> for You are my praise.
> (Jeremiah 17:14)

Debbie Perlman's poem "For Complete Healing" speaks of this naked vulnerability and finding meaning in God's comfort. In the quiet and stillness, alone with our thoughts, Perlman reminds us that God is still with us in our distress, dread, fear, and solitude. Perlman's words harmonize the experiences of our ancestors; their collective song rings true throughout the generations of the Torah, the prophets, and our time.

Even on the precipice of life and death, if we are open to God's presence, then we can hear God's call, pray for redemption, accept God's omnipotence, and still hold onto hope for healing.

# *Haftarot for the Weekly Torah Portions*

## *NUMBERS*

# B'midbar
## Numbers 1:1–4:20

## Traditional Haftarah Reading:
## Hosea 2:1–22

### You Will Call Me "My Person"
#### RABBI CANTOR JORDAN SHANER

PARASHAT B'midbar begins the record of the Israelites' forty-year journey through the wilderness with a census—literally, a "counting of heads" (Numbers 1:2). In the haftarah reading, the prophet Hosea consoles the divided kingdoms of Israel and Judah with a vision of a time when their populations will be uncountable, but united under a single head (Hosea 2:2).

Despite this image of unity under a powerful ruler, Hosea dispels the notion that God wants this power over the people. The people believe that divinity is all about power—the power of a master over a slave or of a patriarchal relationship, in which the parties use and abuse each other. They worship that power through idolatry.

Generally, idolatry is ridiculed in the Hebrew Bible as an absurd and backward practice—an absurd belief that a piece of wood or stone can answer prayers—but Hosea makes clear that the people hold a deeper and more insidious belief: the real idolatry is not just worshiping statues, but the kind of power dynamics these statues represent. The people, whom God freed from slavery, have continued to call God *Baali*, "My Master" (Hosea 2:18), thereby maintaining their own status as "slaves of." Their trust in power reduces religious ritual into an unseemly, wooden transaction. As *Baali*, God becomes the Great Vending Machine in the Sky. Flatter the King, the Husband, the Master, and He will give me "my bread and my water," give me "my wool and my linen, my oil and my drink" (2:7).

Ultimately, what God wants is not to be worshiped, honored, or flattered, but known, loved, and partnered with—as the prophet reminds us: "You will call Me *Ishi*—'My Person'—no longer will you call Me *Baali*—'My Master'" (Hosea 2:18). Hosea turns us toward an image of intimate partnership through faith. For that reason, the words of this haftarah reading adorn many couples' *ketubot*: "I will betroth you to Me in faithfulness, and you shall know the Eternal" (Hosea 2:22).

# Against the Vision of an Abusive God

### RABBI VALERIE LIEBER

While the Torah portion counts the people for the census, the haftarah reading promises that the Jews will be incalculably numerous. Within twenty-two verses, the language of Hosea veers from horrifying to exalted. His extended metaphor of God as a betrayed husband and the Jewish people as an adulterous wife is deeply disturbing to us today. However, it was a powerful and useful metaphor for his listeners because they could empathize with God and understand the effects of their idolatry.

As postmodern listeners, we hear an abusive spouse perpetrating classic domestic violence. Hosea's God privately and publicly shames the "wife" Israel. God threatens, intimidates, and coerces; uses tactics of emotional and economic abuse; and abandons the "children." And then, with regret, God seeks reconciliation and promises never to abuse her again.

This is a textbook pattern of spousal abuse. Hosea's personal experience of adultery colors his language about God; this is Hosea's vision of God, but it need not be ours. We shouldn't accept this vision of an abusive God. Nor should we allow this God's abuse to justify human abusers. It is important to recognize domestic violence and teach young adults to recognize it, shun it, and support institutions that assist the abused.

## Alternative Haftarah Reading: Psalm 136:1–9, 23–26

Give thanks to Adonai, who is good,
*For eternal is God's covenantal love;*
Give thanks to the God of gods,
*For eternal is God's covenantal love;*
Give thanks to the Majesty of majesties,
*For eternal is God's covenantal love;*

To the Maker of great wonders all alone,
*For eternal is God's covenantal love.*
To the Maker of the heavens through understanding,
*For eternal is God's covenantal love;*
To the Spreader of the earth over the waters,
*For eternal is God's covenantal love.*
To the Maker of great lights,
*For eternal is God's covenantal love*

The sun for sovereignty by day,
*For eternal is God's covenantal love.*
The moon and stars for sovereignty by night,
*For eternal is God's covenantal love.*

Who took note of us when we were low,
*For eternal is God's covenantal love,*
And tore us away from out oppressors,
*For eternal is God's covenantal love;*
Giver of bread to all flesh,
*For eternal is God's covenantal love.*

Give thankful praise to the God of heaven,
*For eternal is God's covenantal love!*

# God's Steadfast Love Is Eternal

### Rabbi David E. Ostrich

*B'midbar* tells us of the challenges and opportunities in the wilderness. Sometimes, as we shall read over the next several weeks, we do not respond well to those challenges and opportunities—focusing on the problems more than the blessings. Psalm 136 reminds us of the continuing presence of God in our lives. At every step along the way, God is with us—doing justice, soothing pain, setting free, giving light, lifting up, taking care, inspiring and challenging us: *Ki l'olam chasdo,* "God's steadfast love is eternal" (Psalm 136)—God's loving-kindness and attention are constant!

Most of us are intelligent enough to see that "the glass is half empty." May we all be hopeful and perceptive enough to see that it is also "half full."

Read the psalm and notice the attention God gives us in moments both good and bad. Look at the high points and the low: "Who took note of us in our degradation, God's steadfast love is eternal!" (Psalm 136:23). As we go through the complexities of our lives, may we look for God's presence and guidance—and eternal possibility. Even when we are in the wilderness, God is with us.

## *Alternative Haftarah Reading:*
## *From Zohar 1:15b; Pardeis Rimonim, by Moses Cordovero*

The letters [of the Torah and vowels] follow their melody, oscillating, like soldiers after their king. The letters are body, the vowels are spirit. Their motions follow the movements and stand in place. When a melody of Torah notes moves, the letters and vowels follow. When it pauses, they cease and stand in place.

The letters are the animus (*nefesh*), the vowels are the spirit (*ru'ah*) to the animus, which is the letters, and the accents/cantillation are the soul (*n'shamah*) of the spirit of the animus. . . . The vowels ride on the letters, like a rider on a horse, but their subtlety, which is greater than the letters', cannot dwell in the material substance of letters but rather in their echoes, which follows the letter's articulation. . . . The cantillation does not come into contact with a letter but rather rides on top of the vowels, the hidden echo. One must bring great attention to this from oneself, since it cannot be explained in writing, only mouth to mouth.

## The Invisible That Enlivens Our World

### Rabbi Jay Asher LeVine

*Sefer B'midbar*, the Book of Numbers, opens with an eye to order. The Israelites, only recently freed from slavery, dwell in a wilderness near Mount Sinai. Soon they are to enter a new land. Difficult confrontations are inevitable. God commands Moses to take a census (Numbers 1), to have the people arrange themselves by tribe in marching formation (Numbers 2), and to count the Levites and assign to them a special role of priestly leadership (Numbers 3–4). Each of these actions provides a sense of strength in numbers, clarity in structure, and readiness to take the next step together.

This process of organizing the community and detailing an elaborate division of labor could be applied to any mundane group of people. Any gathering of more than one individual requires some level of sorting out who goes where and who does what.

However, this is no ordinary group of people. The Israelites represent a *k'hilah k'doshah*, a "holy community," and the ordering we read about in this *parashah* points to spiritual dynamics as well as practical logistics. The *Zohar* and later Moses Cordovero offer beautiful, poetic meditations on order and movement, central themes of the whole book of Numbers. In the *Zohar* text, one might imagine the Israelites as the letters of Torah (a connection Rabbi Levi Yitzchak of Berditchev explicitly makes), and the music by which we chant the letters into motion as the invisible Divine Presence accompanying the camp and signaling when to settle and when to march. Cordovero adds the insight that the cantillation marks do not touch the letters. Some necessary distance remains between the physical and spiritual realms, as is made clear when God urges for great care in the interaction with the *Mishkan* and its contents, "so that they [the Kohathites] do not come in contact with the sacred objects and die" (Numbers 4:15).

Out of a text that apparently describes the Israelites assembling into military formation, we find a reflection on the invisible that enlivens the visible, and the intricate act of seeking balance and harmony in community and in relationship to the Divine.

Whenever we build a holy community—a community not only to accomplish goals in this world but also suggesting the possibilities of a better world to come—how we join together and and also honor the space in between us makes all the difference.

# *Naso*
## Numbers 4:21–7:89

## Traditional Haftarah Reading:
## Judges 13:2–25

### A Blessing of Wholeness

*RABBI MATT FRIEDMAN*

THIS READING from the Book of Judges describes the encounters of the unnamed wife of Manoah and Manoah himself with an angel of God:

1. In the first instance, an angel appears to Manoah's wife and tells her that he is aware of her infertility but that she will have a son and must from now on abstain from wine, intoxicants, and impure food. Additionally, the son will be a Nazirite. The woman shares this prophecy with Manoah, and he prays to meet the man so he can ask for instruction regarding raising the boy.

2. The angel appears for a second and final time to Manoah's wife, who runs to get Manoah. The angel reiterates the prohibitions for Manoah's wife. She then gives birth to Samson.

Traditionally, the pairing of this haftarah reading with *Parashat Naso* is described as being based on the description of the Nazirite vow process in the *parashah*; however, there are other themes and connections. The pain and sadness of infertility are recurrent topics; fertility is seen as a reward for faith in God. The most widely known element of this *parashah* is the Priestly Benediction (Numbers 6:24–26), which seeks God's blessing upon the people, graciousness, and shalom. The Hebrew word *shalom* is most often translated as "peace"; however, the root of the word also means "wholeness" and "completeness." In the story told in the haftarah reading, the birth of their son creates a sense of wholeness for Manoh and his wife. It represents the fulfillment of God's blessing—which is why we use those words to bless our children on Shabbat.

How do we find wholeness and fulfillment in our lives when we are denied a core need? Is it possible for us to be agents of fulfillment for other people if we ourselves are lacking? Is so, how?

# Rejecting the Bond

*Rabbi Michael F. Lewis*

In *Parashat Naso*, the Torah lays out the laws of the Nazirite vow, limiting a person from drinking wine, touching impure objects like dead bodies, and getting haircuts. It is not surprising that the haftarah reading for *Parashat Naso* tells us the story of Samson, the *Tanach*'s most in depth narrative about a *Nazir*. Unlike the *parashah*, which describes the *choice* an individual makes to become a *Nazir*, Samson is assigned this role in utero. Samson attempts to break the bonds of this vow, ripping apart a lion in the middle of a vineyard (contact with wine) and killing many enemies (contracting impurity). Many women try to literally bind Samson up. Yet in breaking those bonds, Samson shows the frustration with his fate being "bound" as a *Nazir*, symbolizing his attempt to reject his path.

Ultimately, Samson represents the Jewish people. In the time of the Judges, the Israelites were assigned the impossible task to rid the land of idolatry, child sacrifice, and a social system that enabled some humans to rule others as gods. They, too, rejected their bond with God—they did not want to feel bound.

Despite myriad moments in which our biblical ancestors rebelled and tried in frustration to throw off their bond to the Eternal, our tradition survives. We continue to be bound by our status as Jews and have a specific task in the world as "others." There may be moments when we want to escape our responsibility, but like Samson, we are eternally bonded to the fundamentals of what and who we are.

We can also understand Samson's role as describing queer experiences: Individuals in the LGBTQ community often feel tied by chemistry established in utero that impacts who we are and how we present in the world. While there may be moments when queer people feel frustrated by their own self and being, we can learn from the story of Samson that we cannot run away from such an integral part of our identity. Instead, we must embrace both our identities—Jewish and queer—and remind society of the importance of treating the "other" with the respect they deserve.

*Alternative Haftarah Reading:*
*Psalms 67:2, 116:12, 104:1a, 118:5, 27:9, 18:29,*
*31:8, 42:3, 34:15, 42:6*

May God show grace to us and bless us,
May the Holy One shine the divine countenance among us—selah!

What can I return to Adonai
For all your favors unto me?

Praise Adonai, O my being,
Adonai, my God, You are grand indeed!

From within the narrow space I cried out: Yah!
The Holy One answered me in Yah's expansive space.

Do not hide Your face from me; do not thrust aside Your servant in anger;
You have ever been my help!

For You light my lamp;
Adonai, my God, You make my darkness glow!

I delight, I rejoice in Your covenantal love,
For You have seen my affliction,
You know intimately the sufferings of my life.

My being thirsts for God, for the living God:
When shall I arrive and appear at the face of the Almighty?

Negate evildoing; rather, do good—
Seek peace and harmony-pursue them!—

Why are you bowed down, O my being, moaning within me?
Hope in God, for I will yet sing praise
For the deliverance God's presence brings.

# The Priestly Blessing

### Rabbi Max Chaiken

While the traditional haftarah reading for *Parashat Naso* focuses on the connection to the laws of the *Nazir* (a Jewish ascetic), this alternative reading offers a personal response to the Priestly Benediction, Numbers 6:24–26. Millennia old, these oldest words of blessing in our Torah continue to inspire us. We offer them to our children, to wedding couples, when closing prayer services, and at many other occasions. These words are words of hope and promise—a wish that the Eternal One will offer blessing and protection, enlightenment, mercy, and peace.

The verses above form a compilation, or florilegium, of verses from the Book of Psalms as a response to the words of the blessing in Numbers. The opening verse uses language very similar to the Priestly Benediction found in the *parashah* but speaks in the first person *plural*. These lines form an invocation and a connection to that blessing, reminding us that we are not alone as we seek to live lives worthy of blessing, protection, and the Divine Presence.

The following three stanzas speak in the first person, with each stanza relating in theme to its respective line in the Priestly Benediction. Together, this compilation reminds us of our agency and partnership in our relationship with God, our source of life. Only the third verse speaks in the third person, as if the pray-er or reader is beginning an inner dialogue—a "pep talk" reminding themself that our actions help us bring about the Divine Presence in our world and our lives.

Read together, this alternative sacred text creates a new piece of liturgy, affirming our power to bring about the blessings of the Priestly Benediction in partnership with the Divine.

How can you do that in your relationships and communities?

### Alternative Haftarah Reading:
### From "To Be a Jew: What Is It?"
### by Rabbi Abraham Joshua Heschel

Why is my belonging to the Jewish people the most sacred relationship to me? . . .

For us as Jews there can be no fellowship with God without the fellowship with Israel. Abandoning Israel, we desert God. . . . Judaism is not only a certain quality in the souls of individuals but primarily the existence of the community of Israel. . . . Our share in holiness we acquire by living in the Jewish community. What we do as individuals is a trivial episode; what we attain as Israel causes us to grow into the infinite.

## On the *Nazir*

#### Rabbi Jeffrey Sirkman

How do we, as Jews, grow in holiness?
If you ask a Nazirite (a Jewish ascetic), she might suggest not raising
    a glass in *l'chayim*,
not joining in communal celebrations, and—if you are faced with a
    death in the family—
not even taking part in the funeral.
In essence,
abstaining from the care, the connection we share.

Why in the world would a man or woman in ancient Israel decide to
    become a Nazirite?
Knowing that the customary time limit in the Torah for the Nazirite
    vow was a thirty-day commitment,
in the light of today's practices, it does not look as peculiar anymore.
Do you know anyone who has ever gone on a weeklong detox, cutting
    out whole food groups,
or maybe even a thirty-day cleanse?
The goal is to reboot the body, promoting a hormonal and psychological
    balance that can lead to inner renewal. The question is, at what expense
    does that happen?
Our teacher Rabbi Lawrence Kushner called us as Jews "a hopelessly
    communal people."
To become the human beings we must,
to grow in holiness, we need each other.
Feeding the hungry,
tending to the sick,
lifting up the fallen,
being there for our families,
we share the human care that brings our covenant,
and God's presence to life.
What vow could be more valued,
more holy,
than that?

# B'haalot'cha
## Numbers 8:1–12:6

## Traditional Haftarah Reading:
## Zechariah 2:14–4:7

## Inner and Outer Change

*RABBI ALONA LISITSA, PhD*

THE GOLDEN MENORAH is mentioned in both the Torah portion and in the vision of Zechariah, the haftarah reading for this week, which is also the reading for Shabbat Chanukah.

Zechariah has a vision of Joshua, the High Priest, wearing filthy garments. The High Priest seems to be accused by the Accuser but defended by God (Zechariah 3:1–2). Then his garments are changed to new and clean ones: "See, I have taken off your iniquity and am giving you something new to wear" (3:4). The sins and iniquities of the priests, symbolically represented by the filthy garments of the High Priest, are removed and forgiven.

God's forgiveness is accompanied by a simple external change. Those external markers are necessary. The internal process is incomplete without external markers, and external markers are insufficient if they are not accompanied by deep internal processes. Frequently, we are drawn to focus on the internal and spiritual—the journey and its meaning—and perceive it as sufficient. God's message to Zechariah is that there should always be a visible, external parallel to the internal process. The High Priest is ritually clean, absolved of any iniquity, and his garments mirror his internal state only when he is pure and beautiful both from inside and from outside.

One of the teachings of Zechariah's prophesy then is to remind us that our garments and our appearance are important, no matter how external and superficial they seem to be. They reflect our internal world. Our actions, even routine ones, reflect our internal spiritual processes and changes. Just as the High Priest could not enter the Holy of Holies and perform the sacred worship as long as his clothes were dirty, so are we in need of a visible expression through actions to affirm our deeper internal intentions.

Changing ourselves and changing our appearance are signs of true inner changes expressed in action. May it be the divine will that we succeed.

# Refraining from Violence and Corruption

RABBI PHILIP J. BENTLEY

*Parashat B'haalot'cha* begins with describing the design of the menorah. The haftarah reading includes a vision of a golden menorah, too: "He said to me, 'What do you see?' I said, 'I see a lampstand all of gold'" (Zechariah 4:2). (This is why the text is also read on Shabbat Chanukah.)

Zechariah writes at the time of the restoration of Jerusalem and its Temple (around 520 BCE). Here, he gives advice to the High Priest and to the appointed head of government, Zerubbabel. The most famous verse of this haftarah reading is "Not by might, nor by power, but by My spirit—says the God of heaven's hosts" (Zechariah 4:6). The sentence is a warning to Zerubbabel not to engage in armed struggle against the Persian Empire. The rabbis who selected the haftarah reading accompanying this week's *parashah* chose it for the week of Chanukah not only because it mentions the menorah, but also because they saw that the Hasmonean family rebelling against the Greek Empire was a corrupt dynasty that would eventually give Judea to the Romans.

It is noteworthy that the Jewish people survived two millennia in exile. We can learn from our unique history: During two millennia in which Jews frequently suffered violence, we did not respond with violence. So, we learned the ways of survival without resorting to violence.

In responding to life's challenges, consider how to do that without resorting to force. "Not by might, nor by power" tells us we can succeed through working with people rather than against them. As a wise man said, "There is no way to peace. Peace is the way."

## Alternative Haftarah Reading:
### I Kings 19:1–8

When Ahab told [Queen] Jezebel all that Elijah had done, and how he had put all the prophets [of Baal] to the sword, Jezebel sent a messenger to Elijah, who said: "May the gods do this to me and more if by this time tomorrow I have not done the same thing to your life as you did to the life of one of them!"

Fearing this, Elijah fled at once for his life. He came to Beersheba, in [the territory of] Judah, and there he left his servant behind. He went on a day's journey into the wilderness. He came and sat under a broom-bush and prayed for death, saying, "It is too much! Take my life now, Eternal One; I am no better than my forebears."

He lay down under the bush and fell asleep. Suddenly an angel touched him and said, "Get up and eat!" He looked around and there, beside his head, was a cake baked on hot stones and a jar of water! After eating and drinking, he lay down again and slept. The angel of the Eternal came a second time and woke him, saying, "Get up and eat, or the journey will be too much for you." He got up and ate and drank, and that meal gave him enough strength to walk forty days and nights as far as the mountain of God at Horeb. There he went into a cave and spent the night. . . .

## How Healing Comes

*Rabbi Barbara AB Symons*

At the end of *B'haalot'cha*, Miriam is struck with leprosy, apparently for speaking against Moses's wife, but probably more so for challenging his leadership. The climax of the story is when big brother and High Priest Aaron demands that Moses pray for her recovery. Five Hebrew words make up Moses's entire prayer—in translation: "O God, pray heal her" (Numbers 12:13).

In this alternative haftarah reading, we meet up with Elijah the Prophet, who, after being mortally threatened by Queen Jezebel, seems to have given up. Leaving his servant as did Abraham (Genesis 22:5), he flees into the wilderness Moses-like (Exodus 3:1) and sits under a bush and prays to die Jonah-like (Jonah 4:6–9). God's messenger shows up, reaches out, and touches him, then brings him food and drink. The angel brings more food and drink the next day. Then Elijah arises, begins to care for himself, and ultimately resumes his prophetic work.

How powerful a model for us: Healing comes through personal contact—a hand on a shoulder, holding a hand, a hug. Healing comes through not just offering but actually bringing food and drink, and doing it again the next day, and the day after if needed. We who pray for healing recognize that it is only in partnership with God that true healing comes. It is time to reach out to the people on your *Mi Shebeirach* list and bring comfort, care, and resources.

## *Alternative Haftarah Reading: From "I Speak to You as an American Jew," by Rabbi Joachim Prinz*

I speak to you as an American Jew.

As Americans we share the profound concern of millions of people about the shame and disgrace of inequality and injustice which make a mockery of the great American idea. As Jews we bring to this great demonstration, in which thousands of us proudly participate, a two-fold experience—one of the spirit and one of our history.

In the realm of the spirit, our fathers taught us thousands of years ago that when God created man, He created him as everybody's neighbor. Neighbor is not a geographic term. It is a moral concept. It means our collective responsibility for the preservation of man's dignity and integrity.

From our Jewish historic experience of three and a half thousand years we say: Our ancient history began with slavery and the yearning for freedom. During the Middle Ages my people lived for a thousand years in the ghettos of Europe. Our modern history begins with a proclamation of emancipation.

It is for these reasons that it is not merely sympathy and compassion for the Black people of America that motivates us. It is above all and beyond all such sympathies and emotions a sense of complete identification and solidarity born of our own painful historic experience. When I was the rabbi of the Jewish community in Berlin under the Hitler regime, I learned many things. The most important thing that I learned under those tragic circumstances was that bigotry and hatred are not the most urgent problem. The most urgent, the most disgraceful, the most shameful and the most tragic problem is silence.

# Miriam, Aaron, and the Cushite Woman

### Rabbi Dena A. Feingold

In *Parashat B'haalot'cha*, Moses's siblings, Aaron and Miriam, speak out against Moses for having married a Cushite woman. Since Cush was an African nation, perhaps Ethiopia or Sudan, the implication is that Miriam and Aaron opposed Moses's interracial marriage. God is incensed with Miriam and Aaron for questioning Moses's prophetic wisdom in this or any matter. Miriam, in fact, is stricken with a skin ailment that turns her skin white as a punishment.

This alternative haftarah reading is an excerpt from a speech by Rabbi Joachim Prinz, delivered at the March on Washington in 1963, when Dr. Martin Luther King Jr. gave his "I Have a Dream" speech. Echoing God's criticism of Aaron and Miriam for their prejudices, Prinz's message spoke to American Jews in his time about their role in combating "bigotry and hatred." Speaking from his own experience, having served as a rabbi in Berlin during the Holocaust, Prinz exhorts his contemporaries that Jews must show a profound sense of identification with the injustices experienced by Blacks in America due to our own "painful historic experience." It is not only morally insufficient to silently oppose prejudice; rather, says Prinz, "the most urgent, the most disgraceful, the most shameful and the most tragic problem is [our] silence."

Prinz's words challenge us as Jews in our day. How can we confront our inner biases and speak out when we encounter racism and injustice?

# Sh'lach L'cha
## Numbers 13:1–15:41

## Traditional Haftarah Reading:
## Joshua 2:1–24

### Risk and Reward
#### RABBI BILL S. TEPPER

RISK-TAKING and the strong will to survive and grow are at the center of *Parashat Sh'lach L'cha*. The spirit of this text imbues the accompanying haftarah reading from the Book of Joshua.

In both the *parashah* and the haftarah reading, Israelite scouts journey to Canaan. In *Parashat Sh'lach L'cha*, Joshua and Caleb proceed forward. In the haftarah reading, two unnamed scouts encounter Rahab, a prostitute, who acknowledges Israel's relationships with the Divine and the Promised Land. In exchange for Rahab's aid, the scouts promise not to harm either her or her household once the Israelite conquest unfolds.

The Babylonian Talmud (*M'gillah* 14b) teaches that Rahab, in the aftermath of this experience, converted to Judaism, married Joshua, and—as a further reward—had nine of her descendants become prophets and prophetesses, including Jeremiah and Huldah.

The bravery of Joshua and Caleb—just as the bravery of two unnamed scouts—ensures Israel's survival and eventual arrival home. The unnamed Israelite scouts and Rahab—just as Joshua and Caleb—engage peril. But only by way of taking risks are knowledge and reward acquired. And only with such unwavering nerve may we usher in the future for which we are intended.

### Rahab and the Spies
#### RABBI JUSTIN KERBER, BCC

There's many a story where someone, fleeing for their life, is offered a hiding place by an unlikely hero who comes to their aid at the critical moment: a white American hides a fugitive slave from pursuers; a Pole or a German looks the other way when a fleeing Jewish family hides in their barn or cellar.

The story of Rahab, the harlot who hides the Israelite spies sent by Joshua to reconnoiter the Promised Land before the invasion, is such a story. At great personal risk, she hides them from the authorities and then bets on their side's victory in the conflict she knows is coming.

I imagine myself on different sides of this story, depending on the circumstances under which we live. At times, I identify with the desperate one in need of a hiding place. At other times, I see myself as the one who quietly provides it. And yet, until recently, I could never fully imagine finding myself in such a dire situation.

In our story, Joshua will soon order the sounding of the shofar at Jericho and win the crucial battle. The sound of the shofar reverberates within me as I write this in an unexpected way: Awake! Prop up your own walls of equal justice under the law! Value the democratic institutions that have kept you safe! If you must flee, you cannot assume there will be a Rahab to hide you.

## *Alternative Haftarah Reading: Psalm 91:1–12*

One who dwells in the hidden place of the Most High,
Who spends the night in the shade of Shaddai:
I say to Adonai, my refuge and my stronghold, My God:
I trust in You,
For the Holy One will save you from the trap of the hunter,
From the ruinous plague.
ike branches on a sukkah
God will cover you with outstretched pinions,
And beneath holy wings
Will be your refuge.
God's truth is our shield and buckler,
So do not be afraid of the terror of the night,
Of arrows flying by in daytime,
Of the plague that stalks in darkness
Or the horror that ravages at noon.
A thousand may fall at your side,
Ten thousand on your right hand—
Nothing shall touch you.
Only look with your eyes,
And see the payback of the wicked!

For You, Adonai, are my refuge;
And when you, my friend, make the Most High
Your dwelling-place,
No harm will happen to you,
No calamity will draw near to your tent.
For God will command the angels to you,
To guard you in all your ways;
They shall carry you upon their hands
Lest your foot be struck with a stone.

# Human Angel-Messenger

### *Rabbi Ruth Adar*

Moses sends twelve scouts into the Land of Israel. After forty days of exploration, ten of them report that the land is indeed rich and fertile but that its inhabitants are dangerous giants. The people panic at this news, refusing to enter the Land and demanding to return to Egypt. Joshua and Caleb, the two dissenting scouts, say, "If pleased with us, the Eternal will bring us into that land, a land that flows with milk and honey, and give it to us" (Numbers 14:8). God, furious with faithless scouts, decrees that out of all the Israelites who left Egypt, only Joshua and Caleb will eventually enter the Land.

Psalm 91 is a song that Joshua and Caleb might have sung, in an attempt to reassure the Israelites not to fear, because God would protect them in the conquest of the Land. It is filled with vivid images that seek to express the tender love God has for the faithful of Israel: God is their shelter, their fortress, who will save them from harm. The avian imagery for both the people and God in verses 3–4 is striking: the people fear "the fowler's trap," but God will shelter them "under God's wings." No matter how terrible the situation, God will protect the faithful. Then, in verses 11–12, God orders angels "to guard you wherever you go," an image that would inspire the idea of a guardian angel.

A modern reader might scoff: How can anyone take this psalm seriously? Where are the protecting angels? Rabbi Richard N. Levy, in his commentary on the Book of Psalms, reminds us that the Hebrew word for "angel" also means "messenger." Is it possible for us to see the people who have helped us in times of need as the angel-messengers of a loving God?

When we are in trouble, this psalm encourages us to pray that we will recognize the human helpers through whom the love of God is made manifest.

### *Alternative Haftarah Reading:*
### *"The Silver Platter," by Natan Alterman*

And the land grows still, the red eye of the sky slowly dimming over smoking frontiers

As the nation arises, torn at heart but breathing, to receive its miracle, the only miracle

As the ceremony draws near, it will rise, standing erect in the moonlight in terror and joy

When across from it will step out a youth and a lass and slowly march toward the nation

Dressed in battle gear, dirty, shoes heavy with grime, they ascend the path quietly

To change garb, to wipe their brow
They have not yet found time. Still bone weary from days and from nights in the field

Full of endless fatigue and unrested,
Yet the dew of their youth is still seen on their head

Thus they stand at attention, giving no sign of life or death

Then a nation in tears and amazement
will ask: "Who are you?"

And they will answer quietly, "We are the silver platter on which the Jewish state was given."

Thus they will say and fall back in shadows
And the rest will be told in the chronicles of Israel.


# Determination

### Rabbi Morley T. Feinstein, *z"l*

At the beginning of *Parashat Sh'lach L'cha*, God empowers Moses to select twelve scouts to check out the Land of Israel. Moses picks the very best, one per tribe, including Joshua and Caleb. Unfortunately, upon their return, the first ten scouts are disheartened both by God's and Moses's leadership and by their own self-doubt. They perceive of themselves as grasshoppers too tiny for the task of entering and conquering the Land of Israel.

Caleb and Joshua want to take the land. Both have faith in God and in Moses. God uplifts the supporters and eventually destroys the detractors.

On November 29, 1947, following the United Nations approval of the Partition Plan, the Israeli poet Natan Alterman overheard a celebratory crowd at Cafe Kassit quoting Israel's soon to be president Chaim Weizmann, who had placed a somber note onto the joy: "The State will not be given to the Jewish people on a silver platter." Alterman realized that gaining the land would require sacrifice and death.

Both texts remind us of the promise of the Jewish homeland and the determination necessary to make it a reality. There are a pair of protagonists: the biblical heroes Joshua and Caleb, and the sacrificial bearers of the platter, an Israeli girl and boy. The list of tribal enemies in the biblical age foreshadows both the perpetrators of the Shoah and those who will attack Israel in the War for Independence. In the Book of Numbers, the ten demoralized spies view Israel as a choice that they can turn down. Jews in 1947, post-Shoah, see Zionism as an imperative. They are willing to sacrifice everything, including their lives, in order to redeem the Jewish people and the Jewish homeland.

May we continue to have the faith and determination of Joshua and Caleb.

# Korach
## Numbers 16:1–18:32

## Traditional Haftarah Reading:
## I Samuel 11:14–12:22

## Power for Community

### RABBI JORDAN M. PARR

WHO GETS TO LEAD? In a simplified view of our democratic process, leaders are the ones whom voters choose. If a person wants to be a leader, he or she must stand before the people—and the people must approve. And if a person does not want to lead, he or she is not forced into an unwanted choice.

Of course, in the biblical world, it is the Almighty who chooses the leaders of Israel, like God chooses Moses to lead the Israelites out of Egypt and to the edge of the Land of Israel. Still, at first sight, Korach and his followers seem to ask a legitimate question: "Why not me? Why can't I, Korach—a Levite—lead? And who are you, Moses, to lead us?"

However, our tradition does not support Korach's revolution. According to Rashi (on Numbers 16:1), Korach separates himself from the rest of the community, claiming all the power for himself—and this is the link to our haftarah reading. In I Samuel 11:14–15, we read: "Samuel said to the people, 'Let us all go up to Gilgal and there renew the kingship.' So all the people. . . ." Notice the language here: "Let *us all* go to Gilgal. . . . So *all* the people. . . ." The contrast with Korach could not be starker. Under Saul, the people as one dedicate themselves to live under a king whom God has appointed. They declare that their king is subject to the law of Torah, as well as they themselves.

When a person tries to accumulate power for their personal benefit, they are doomed to failure. But when we work together, for the benefit of all, we are doing God's work. Power for the sake of power leads to ruin. Power for the sake of the community leads to community.

# A Respectful Transition of Leadership

*EMMA DUBIN*

*Parashat Korach* deals with a swelling of anger from a faction of Israelites demanding their share of the leadership. The ensuing power struggle leaves thousands dead; and the leader of the revolution, Korach, becomes Judaism's archetype of the self-serving agitator, exemplifying an argument not for the sake of heaven but for self-advancement.

This week's haftarah reading presents an alternative model of challenging leadership. The prophet-judge Samuel, up to that point Israel's de facto political and religious leader, is agitated over the inauguration of Saul, Israel's first king. The transition of leadership from Samuel to Saul represents Israel's transformation from theocracy to monarchy. In spite of God's acquiescence to the nation's clamor for a king, Samuel is furious, seeing it as a betrayal of God—and of himself.

Samuel's speech contains a certain recognition that his resistance to the anointing of a king may be viewed as defensive and self-promoting. Echoing Moses in this week's *parashah*, Samuel affirms his own integrity, asking rhetorically whom he has mistreated. The people reply that he has been nothing but just. Then Samuel calls for a miracle: thunder and rain during the dry harvest season.

Why does God provide the miracle, seemingly reinforcing Samuel's authority? Perhaps God, too, sees the people's desire for a king as a betrayal. Yet God consented to anointing Saul. Saul is already king, and in contrast to the power struggle displayed in our *parashah*, no deaths have occurred (so far) in the process of Israel's political restructuring.

Therefore, perhaps the thunderstorm is God's simple affirmation of Samuel's righteousness. God grants Samuel a miracle because he asked for a sign of God's approval. Through the thunderstorm, God communicates to all that Samuel has served well. Israel's transition to new leadership is not an indictment of Israel's former leader. Thus, God grants Samuel his miracle—and Israel its king.

There are moments in which we need to help a loved one save face while navigating a difficult change. Have you lived through such moments?

## Alternative Haftarah Reading:
## From Ben-Gurion, *by Shimon Peres*

Of the thousand-odd Jewish families in Vishneva, almost half went on aliyah before the Holocaust. In my mother's family all four of her sisters, together with their husbands and children, made it to Eretz Yisrael. But my beloved and revered grandfather stayed behind and was burned alive in his synagogue by the Nazi Einsatzgruppen. I will never forget his words to me on the station platform when my mother, my brother, and I set out for Palestine. (My father, Yitzhak Persky, had gone on ahead and established himself in Tel Aviv before bringing us over.) My zeide embraced me and said, "My child, one thing above all else: Always be a Jew."

Looking back on that period of profound agitation and dramatic change in Jewish history, the period that produced Ben-Gurion and a whole generation of pioneers, I would say, first, that the Jewish people is a fighting people. The Jews' greatest contribution to history is dissatisfaction! We're a nation born to be discontented. Whatever exists we believe can be changed for the better. The Jews represent permanent revolution in the world. However small a nation we may be, we are the flag-bearers of revolution.

# The *K'dushah* (Holiness) of Complaining

### Rabbi Michael L. Feshbach

*Parashat Korach* tells a twisted tale of rebellion and insurrection, but several things seem clear: part of what is being contested is civil and political leadership, and some of this is religious authority (Numbers 16:3, 10). Moses, Aaron, and Miriam have a hard time in the Book of Numbers, facing discontent on many levels. But to some extent, this hardship—absorbing the heat and living with discontent—is an essential element of leadership. When Moses does not absorb, deflect, and redirect this discontent—when, in fact, he screams at people simply because they are asking for water—he demonstrates that he has temporarily forgotten the implications of being a leader.

Shimon Peres captures elements equally essential to Jewish life. Jews whine. And complain. As the joke says, "A server approaches a group of Jews after a meal and asks, 'Was anything okay?'" Peres notes that what may be a hardship to leaders is something essential, and important, for the people as a whole: to challenge, to question, to push . . . and to be dissatisfied—even if we may not always be right and we may not always get what we want.

Progress, improvement, and building a better world depend entirely on finding fault, noticing weakness, wanting things to be better, and working to make it happen. We are not an easy people. We can push and we can demand. And—at least some of the time—thank God for that!

## *Alternative Haftarah Reading:*
## *From* Jews and Words, *by Amos Oz and Fania Oz-Salzberger*

Jewish continuity has always hinged on uttered and written words, on an expanding maze of interpretations, debates, and disagreements, and on a unique human rapport. In synagogue, at school, and most of all in the home, it has always involved two or three generations deep in conversation.

Ours is not a bloodline, but a textline. There is a tangible sense in which Abraham and Sarah, Rabban Yohanan, Glikl of Helm, and the present authors [and readers] all belong to the same family tree.

# God in Words
### *Rabbi Jay Asher LeVine*

*Parashat Korach* tells a story of rebellion and power struggle masquerading as a quest for equality. Korach, a Levite, and the Reubenites Dathan, Abiram, and On accuse Moses and Aaron, "You have gone too far! For all the community are holy, all of them, and the Eternal is in their midst. Why then do you raise yourselves above the Eternal's congregation?" (Numbers 16:3). "We are all the same," they say, "so we deserve the same power as you."

This conflict serves as the exemplar of disagreement that shatters community. "Any dispute that is for the sake of heaven will endure; but one that is not for the sake of heaven will not endure. What sort of dispute was for the sake of heaven? The dispute between Shammai and Hillel. And which was not for the sake of heaven? The dispute of Korach and his company" (*Pirkei Avot* 5:20). Because the challenge comes from a Levite excluded from the elite priestly roles of Aaron and his family and from Reubenites, whose tribe had its birthright stripped from it, the disagreement seems to stem from priestly and tribal power dynamics. Hillel and Shammai, on the other hand, disagree over matters of halachah and textual interpretation.

Amos Oz and Fania Oz-Salzberger offer a new take on the teaching in *Pirkei Avot*: any disagreement that truly lives in a passion for words, their meanings, and their applications becomes part of our cultural heritage for generations to come. The bloodline disputes that motivate Korach and his band separate members of the same family; textual disputes become part of the record we study—and in that study we discover ourselves to be part of the family. This ongoing and expansive conversation is not only for the sake of heaven, but also, as Abraham Joshua Heschel once wrote, it helps us to discover "the heavenly in the Torah," when we encounter God and each other—as our conversation partners, our family, and in our words.

# Chukat
## Numbers 19:1–22:1

## Traditional Haftarah Reading:
## Judges 11:1–33

## The Diminished Value of a Human Life

### RABBI GERI NEWBURGE

THE BIBLICAL TEXTS of *Chukat* and its accompanying haftarah reading are connected through the description of wars with the Amorites, first during Moses's leadership in the wilderness and then in the time of Jephthah, one of the judges enumerated in the prophetic book of the same name.

Jephthah is known to be a great warrior but is also a social outcast because of his questionable parentage. In their hour of need, his brethren plead with Jephthah to lead them into battle, and he agrees to come to their rescue, but only on condition that if he is triumphant he will become the leader of the clan.

The story of Jephthah is a story of rejection and acceptance. When we first meet Jephthah, he is fleeing from home as a result of taunts about his lesser status by his half-brothers. When his brothers track him down to lead them, he questions their motives, holding them accountable for their abusive treatment. Now able to negotiate from a position of power and successful in battle, Jephthah negotiates a new status for himself. Yet in his quest for acceptance Jephthah makes a rash vow, offering a sacrifice to God of the first thing that comes from his house to greet him upon return from his victorious conquest.

What is not included in the haftarah reading, for many reasons articulated by the Sages, is the remaining text of the Jephthah narrative: his only child, an unnamed daughter, is the first to greet him when he returns. She agrees to be sacrificed, after requesting time to be with other women and mourn her maidenhood. The value of the daughter's life is diminished in order to maintain her father's new-won acceptance by God and the community.

Humanity continues to struggle with these same lessons of rejection and acceptance, and the prophetic calls to justice remind us that people should not be accepted or rejected based on the color of their skin, religious affiliation, gender identity, sexuality, or political leanings.

# Neither Hero nor Villain

*Rabbi Maya Y. Glasser*

Both the Torah and haftarah readings address protagonists who have had rocky journeys. In a very eventful Torah portion, one among many events is Moses striking a stone in the middle of the desert to make water, which prevents him from entering the Promised Land. The haftarah reading tells the story of Jephthah, who is first shunned by his tribe because of his lineage and then begged to come back and help them in battle. He attempts peaceful negotiations with the enemy king, and when that does not work, Jephthah invades the land, ultimately winning.

Both the Torah and haftarah readings pose questions of how our actions influence who we become and how we can gain redemption. In the Torah, despite Moses's leadership, God tells him that he will not be able to enter the place he has worked so hard to enter. In the haftarah reading, Jephthah has an opposite trajectory, where first he is cast aside and then he becomes a hero.

These two stories remind us that life is complicated and that people can be flawed while still providing many contributions to their communities. The challenge is not to characterize people as only a hero or only a villain, and instead to look beyond single events to gain a broader perspective on who they are and their contributions to their people.

## *Alternative Haftarah Reading: "Reciprocity," by Laura Eve Engel*

And who bites for a living.
And who skims the scrape off whose knee.
And who warm milks who into evening.
And who pops whose blister, the skin bright for popping.
And who shields who from the shadow's big tree.
And who bends whose face into a picture of sadness.
And who hangs the frame in place on the wall
and who watches and helps with the crooked.
And who makes the coffee and whose mouth does it burn.
And whose mouth falls apart from the burn and who kisses it.
And who builds up the show with its shiny guitars and who stays home.
And who whines like a bird and who like a toothache.
And who blames it on distance and who on the front yard.
And who sends who to the bottom of a sweet drink.
And who shames who into yes-making.
And who cops a feel and who an out.

And who talks to the weather and who to the dog.
And who to the dog says who took him out last time.
And who sees the news and who thinks it's about who.
And who lights some matches to flick them at who.
And who makes a noise like the time who was crying.
And who cries for who and who cries for who.

# Intimacy, Complexity, and Entanglement with Those We Love

### Rabbi Daniel Kirzane

*Parashat Chukat* recounts the deaths of Miriam and Aaron, the two people closest to Moses. The relationships among these siblings were deep and complex, surfacing untold emotions in Israel's leader, now alone, when they die. Engel's poem, drawing inspiration from Yom Kippur's *Un'taneh Tokef*, also reflects themes of vital intimacy, both beautiful and dark. She invites us to consider our own roles in the cycles of life.

When Miriam risks her life to watch over the infant Moses, she embodies *Ruach Hakodesh*, the Holy Spirit (*Sh'mot Rabbah* 1:22). And when Moses prays for her to be healed—even after she has critiqued him—his prayer ascends *b'ruach*, with spirit (Rabbeinu Bachya on Numbers 12:13). When Aaron witnesses the tragic death of his oldest sons, Moses offers cold and insufficient comfort; now, when Aaron dies, Moses solemnly invests his third-born with the mantle of the priesthood.

There are things we do for family that we wouldn't do for anyone else, but we also have the power to hurt those who are closest to us unlike anyone else. These intimate human connections reflect the divine sparks that bind us to those we love—"who cries for who and who cries for who." When we aspire to our best selves, we strive to bring positive and constructive reciprocity into our most intimate relationships.

When a loved one dies, we honor their life by remembering the fullness of their days. Every person has healed and hurt, and the closer we look, the more texture we perceive in a loved one's life. Like Moses at the graves of his sister and brother, we need not bury our pain nor suppress the difficult chapters of the past. Rather, we seek to see ourselves bound up in their life, to see the reciprocities given and received, and to consider how their impact on us lives on in the relationships we continue to maintain. We ask not only "who shall live and who shall die," but also who, while still living, "makes the coffee and whose mouth does it burn"?

## *Alternative Haftarah Reading:*
## *"You Are My Rock," by Moshe Lavee*

I spoke to you so many times / I told you / I told you again / I was trying to explain / rock / rock / are you listening? / Damn you, rock / move already, rock / answer me already / I'm speaking to you, rock / are you listening, rock? / I have a stick, rock / I can also hit / I do not like to hit, rock, I do not believe in it rock / I am a man of words, rock, are you listening, rock? / I have hands, rock, and they are strong, rock, I can also hit / rock, look, rock, can you see the fingers, rock? / can you feel, rock, I am touching, rock, I am touching you, rock, do you feel it? / My fingers, rock / so gentle, rock /stroking / rock / probing / searching / rock /move already, rock / respond / say something / get mad at me, rock / tell me I have no water. I have no wetness, I do not want. / This fist, rock, this fist I shall smash into you / I have hands / and hard fingers / that know how to hit, rock / I have a stick / I can / rock / I can without being confused / hit you with the stick, rock. / But I do not want to , rock, I do not want to hit, rock, I am speaking, rock, I am stroking, you feel, rock, move already, say something, respond already, rock rock rock / trach! / Blast! / AMEN SELAH.

# Talking to the Rock

### Rabbi Lea Mühlstein

The incident of Moses and the rock, which is described in *Parashat Chukat*, is one of the reasons given by the text for why Moses was prevented from entering the Promised Land. According to the medieval commentator Rashi, Moses was punished for hitting the rock instead of talking to it.

In his poem, Moshe Lavee imagines the fruitless dialogue between Moses and the rock. The poet elegantly uses the repetition of the word *sela* (rock) to paint a picture of an increasingly desperate Moses. The poem reaches its climax not simply with the shattering of the rock but with a clever wordplay in the Hebrew, which connects *sela* (the rock) to *selah*—a word almost impossible to translate but which, in its biblical use, is often interpreted as a calling to pause and listen—a beautifully ironic ending to the description of a rock that seems to be stone-deaf.

In the poem, Moses seeks to effect change through words, but just as we experience in some of our social justice work, words are not always enough. Moses here is a reluctant activist, hesitant to take matters into his own hands. The tension between the physical act of hitting the rock as a grievous sin or a simply necessary means to save society is felt throughout the poem. It will resonate with many Jewish social activists as we reflect on the limits of our public actions.

# Balak
## Numbers 22:2–25:9

## Traditional Haftarah Reading:
## Micah 5:6–6:8

### Returning to the Covenant

*Rabbi Rachel Axelrad*

T HE HAFTARAH READING envisions a restored Israel after the impending
destruction of Jerusalem. While the people attempt to appease God through
offerings (Micah 6:6), the prophet Micah calls on them to return to their original covenant with God; a covenant based on "rectitude" (2:7). Micah reminds
the people of Balak's plot against them and the blessing that was put in Balaam's
mouth: "How fair are your tents, O Jacob, your dwellings, O Israel!" (Numbers
24:5).

He then continues to speak about the spirituality of divine forgiveness in the
following verses. In Micah 6:7, the prophet speaks about Israel's desire to bring
burnt offerings and the offering of their firstborns. The line "Should I give my
firstborn for my transgression, the fruit of my body [*p'ri vitni*] for my own sin?"
is usually considered to refer to child sacrifices, but it can also be understood as
referring to the womb, invoking the notion of compassion, care, and protection—expressing the desire of the sinner to return to the behavior prescribed in
the divine covenant and be sheltered again by a compassionate, caring, and protective Deity. The nation yearns to return to God's loving embrace.

The prophet Micah instructs the nation of Israel to "do justly, and love mercy,
and walk humbly with your God" (Micah 6:8). These acts represent the part of
the covenant that is dearest to God—a people that acts compassionately. In
return, the people will be blessed with that which is dearest to them: God's loving-
kindness, care, and protection.

# The Divine Will and the Human Deed

*RABBI SETH M. LIMMER*

Two prophecies of Micah connect directly to *Parashat Balak*, as the prophet literally invokes our episode from the Book of Numbers. The first is Micah 6:5: "Remember what Balak king of Moab planned, and how Balaam son of Be'or answered him." In his recounting of Israel's sacred history (6:3–6:4), Micah places special prominence on this tale, using it as evidence of divine righteousness that foils the wicked plans of Israel's enemies. We learn this lesson in chapter 6, but it helps explain the backdrop of chapter 5, which illustrates the salvation that will come to the remnant of Israel and the concomitant punishment unleashed upon the idolatrous nations.

In the second prophecy connected to the *parashah*, Micah's message moves from an invocation of God's continuing care for Israel (Micah 5:6–8) to the metaphorical filing of legal claim against Israel for failing to follow divine paths (5:9-6:2). The listener is reminded that past beneficence will not guarantee future protection (3:4); only righteous action can ensure Israel continues to find divine favor. Micah is clear about divine demands on human life: to bring about justice and mercy in all our deeds, to bend our own will to follow divine paths (Micah 6:8). Ritual considerations are cast aside in favor of each and every human being engaging in the work of repairing our world.

## *Alternative Haftarah Reading:*
## *"When Evil Darkens Our World," by Rabbi Chaim Stern*

When evil darkens our world, let us be the bearers of light.
When fists are clenched in self-righteous rage, let our hands be open for
  the sake of peace.
When injustice slams doors on the ill, the poor, the old and the stranger,
  let us pry the doors open.

Where shelter is lacking, let us be builders.
Where food and clothing are needed, let us be providers.
Where knowledge is denied, let us be champions of learning.

When dissent is stifled, let our voices speak truth to power.
When the earth and its creatures are threatened, let us be their guardians.
When bias, greed, and bigotry erode our country's values, let us proclaim
  liberty throughout the land.

In the places where no one acts like a human being,
let us bring courage;
let us bring compassion;
let us bring humanity.

# Turning a Curse into a Blessing

*Rabbi Sara Rae Perman*

The conclusion of the traditional haftarah reading for *Parashat Balak* tells us that God requires us to do justice, love goodness, and walk humbly with God. The *parashah* itself tells of how Balaam was hired to curse the people of Israel. Instead, he ends up blessing the Israelite people. How does a curse become a blessing?

On October 27, 2018, eleven Jews at prayer were horribly murdered in the Tree of Life-Or L'Simcha Synagogue in Pittsburgh, Pennsylvania. Others were injured. And the entire Jewish community, the entire city of Pittsburgh and beyond, were shaken beyond belief. The curse of hate had become a cruel tragedy that affected so many. How to turn this curse into a blessing?

One of the families who lost loved ones has, indeed, turned the curse into a blessing. Along with the special needs agency Achieva, the family of the intellectually challenged Cecil and David Rosenthal, who were among the eleven murdered, established "Love Like the Boys." The idea is to do random acts of kindness because David and Cecil, "the boys," as described by their sister, Diane, in her eulogy, were "innocent like boys, not hardened like men oftentimes become with age and experience." Both brothers were known for always being willing to help others, sometimes through actions, sometimes just with words.

You too can "love like the boys." You too can turn a curse into a blessing.

## Alternative Haftarah Reading:
## "Bein Kodesh L'chol" / "Between the Holy and the Mundane," by Amir Dadon and Shuli Rand; Psalm 51:13–17

Israeli singers and composers Shuli Rand and Amir Dadon share their deep sense of yearning for wholeness and rest in their song "Between the Holy and the Mundane":

> Between reality and madness
> It is all coming back to me.
> Even the place from whence I came
> Has no peace in it.
> And the journey is heavy
> And a little too much for me.
> I need to grow out of it
> And that's it—
> To grow out of it and
> That's it.
> I live between the holy and
> The mundane.

PSALM 51:13–17

Do not cast me away from Your presence,
And Your holy spirit do not take away from me!
Bring back to me the joy of Your deliverance,
And let a generous spirit uphold me.
    I will teach the rebellious Your ways,
      And sinners will come back to You.
Rescue me from blood-guilt,
O God, the God of my deliverance,
That my tongue may sing of Your justice.
Adonai, open up my lips
That my mouth may declare Your praise.

# Word of Blessings, Word of Curses

### SASHA DOMINGUEZ

*Parashat Balak* focuses on the Moabite king Balak and the prophet Balaam, who is hired by Balak to curse the nation of Israel. Balaam tries to curse Israel but is incapable of doing so and instead blesses Israel three times. The main message of the *parashah* seems to be that the God of Israel is the supreme ruler of the universe.

However, I chose the two parts of the alternative haftarah reading above to focus on *the means* this story uses to deliver its message: words and language. What do a blessing and a curse have in common?

In the song "Bein Kodesh l'Chol," "Between the Holy and the Mundane," the seeming tensions between religious and secular culture in Israeli society are addressed. The distinctions between *kodesh* and *chol*—or, in the case of *Parashat Balak*, the differences between blessings and curses—are at times difficult to grasp because they are so nuanced. Seemingly, blessings and curses are opposites. However, blessings and curses are both passionate words one wishes upon another.

I imagine the words of the song by Rand and Dadon going through Balaam's head after the events described in *Parashat Balak*: exhausted by internal struggles—struggles we all face—trying to find adequate words to express the strong emotions evoked by the words of both blessings and curses. The words of Psalm 51 open up a way to give space to those emotions, by directing us to focus, praise, and reflect.

*Parashat Balak* makes the point that words matter. The words we speak and their reception by others carry real emotional weight. It is our duty to find the blessings and curses that need to be spoken in our own lives—and to utter them.

# *Pinchas*
## Numbers 25:10–30:1

## Traditional Haftarah Reading:
## I Kings 18:46–19:21

## The Prophet and the Sisters
### CANTOR LISA LEVINE

THE TRADITIONAL haftarah reading for *Parashat Pinchas* features Elijah the Prophet, who flees for his life after rising up in protest against the worshipers of Baal. He walks forty days and nights to Mount Horeb, where he enters a cave to rest for the night. God visits him and asks what he is doing there. Elijah responds: "I have always been devoted to You, only to You. But the people of Israel have broken their covenant with You." (I Kings 19:10).

Elijah's passion for change and his belief in God are his fuel for rebellion and fight for justice.

In the Torah portion *Pinchas*, the daughters of Zelophehad—Mahlah, Noah, Hoglah, Milcah, and Tirzah—use their strength and faith to stand up against Moses and challenge the inheritance system. After the death of their father, when land is being portioned out, the brotherless sisters are determined to receive their due and fight to change the system!

Today, we join those who are protesting and rebelling against systemic racism that has prevented equality. May we continue to learn the lessons of our prophets and biblical role models who stood up with the faith, courage, strength, and determination that are needed to effect the changes so desperately needed in our world today.

## Being a Voice in the Face of Brokenness
### RABBI RACHEL GREENGRASS

In *Parashat Pinchas*, God is angry, watching the Israelite leadership be anything but leaders. When a chieftain from the house of Simeon takes a Moabite princess to have sex with her in front of the Tent of Meeting, God instructs Moses to slay all the idol-worshippers. In this moment, Pinchas gets up onto his feet, follows the couple, and impales them while they are coupling. This sacrifice is enough. God's anger is soothed, the plague stops.

Four hundred years later, once again, seduction has led Israel astray. King Ahab, seduced by his wife Jezebel to worship Baal and Asherah, allows the slaughter of the prophets of the Eternal, attempting to wipe our faith off the face of the planet. Elijah, being one of the hundred who survive, climbs Mount Carmel and challenges four hundred and fifty priests of Baal to a duel where each would offer their sacrifices and see which god would accept them. The false priests cut themselves and dance ecstatically, but their god does not bring down fire to accept their sacrifice. Then Elijah digs a hole, covers his sacrifice in water, and prays. God accepts his sacrifice. All the people see and believe once again. They slaughter all four hundred and fifty priests of Baal.

There can be no doubt that Pinchas and Elijah were religious heroes. They stepped into the void at a time when the nation was facing religious and moral crisis and palpable divine anger. Yet these zealots leave the reader, both ancient and modern alike, "uncomfortable." God gives Pinchas "My covenant of peace" (Numbers 25:12), meaning that he will never again have to act the part of a zealot. As for Elijah, God tells him to appoint Elisha as his successor.

Zealotry is an understandable reaction to our broken world, and our faith calls us not to stand idly by but to be a light unto the nations. It is easy to look at Pinchas and Elijah and believe that they are models of what God wants from us. However, when we look closer, we see that they got it only half right. They were right to stand up and act but wrong in the violence they did in God's name. As a result, one was eternally blessed with peace, never being permitted to even come in contact with the dead again, and the other lost his power. We learn that even in the moments that capture the height of idolatry and immorality, in a society completely gone astray, God does not want violence. God wants us to be God's voice—the still, small voice.

## *Alternative Haftarah Reading: II Samuel 21:8–14*

Instead, the king took Armoni and Mephibosheth, the two sons that Rizpah daughter of Aiah bore to Saul, and the five sons that Merab, daughter of Saul, bore to Adriel, son of Barzillai, the Meholathite, and he handed them over to the Gibeonites. They impaled them on the mountain before the Eternal; all seven of them perished at the same time. They were put to death in the first days of the harvest, the beginning of the barley harvest. Then Rizpah, daughter of Aiah, took sackcloth and spread it on a rock for herself, and she stayed there from the beginning of the harvest until rain from the sky fell on the bodies; she did not let the birds of the sky settle on them by day or the wild beasts [approach] by night. David was told what Saul's concubine Rizpah, daughter of Aiah, had done. And David went and took the bones of Saul and of his son Jonathan from the citizens of Jabesh-gilead, who had made off with them from the public square of Beth-shan, where the Philistines had hung them up on the day the Philistines killed Saul at Gilboa. He brought up the bones of Saul and of his son Jonathan from there; and he gathered the bones of those who had been impaled. And they buried the bones of Saul and of his son Jonathane in Zela, in the territory of Benjamin, in the tomb of his father Kish. And when all that the king had commanded was done, God responded to the plea of the land thereafter.

# It Only Takes One

### RABBI PAMELA WAX

In *Parashat Pinchas*, Mahlah, Noa, Hoglah, Milcah, and Tirzah—the five daughters of Zelophehad, who, as females, had no claim to their deceased father's share in the land—stood before Moses and the Israelite community to demand a stake on behalf of their father: "Let not our father's name be lost to his clan just because he had no son!" (Numbers 27:4). God decreed that their plea was just. In speaking truth to power, these five women were able to change inheritance law to include transfer to daughters if a father had no sons.

In II Samuel 21:8–14, Rizpah (who, like the five sisters, is identified by her father's name despite her status as a concubine to a king, as well as a mother) also speaks truth to power in order to perform the mitzvah of *kibud hameit*, "honoring the dead," by standing watch over them from the time of the barley harvest in early summer until the time of the rains in autumn. A woman *without* power speaks truth to power. Rizpah's story is therefore a perfect feminist companion piece to the Toraitic story of the five sisters. Where they used eloquent words to argue their case, Rizpah uses nonverbal civil disobedience to make hers. Just as God had responded positively to the five sisters, so does God respond positively to the events that Rizpah sets in motion.

Rizpah's story reminds us of the eternal value of *kibud hameit* and its significance to Jewish life since biblical times. It also speaks powerfully about taking a stand against injustice, the impact that just one person can have, and the importance of questioning authority and speaking truth to power.

May Rizpah be an inspiration to those of us who wonder, "What can I, one person, possibly do to make a difference?" It only takes one.

## *Alternative Haftarah Reading:*
## *From "Bashert," by Irena Klepfisz*

These words are dedicated to those who died
because death is a punishment
because death is a reward
because death is the final rest
because death is the eternal rage
These words are dedicated to those who died

*Bashert*
. . .
These words are dedicated to those who survived
because life is a wilderness and they were savage
because life is an awakening and they were alert
because life is a flowering and they blossomed
because life is a struggle and they struggled
because life is a gift and they were free to accept it

These words are dedicated to those who survived

*Bashert*

# What They Might Have Told Us

### CANTOR ABBE LYONS

In "Bashert," Irena Klepfisz names small and large aspects of different people's trajectories during the Holocaust, both of those who died and of those who survived. She gives voice to their stories.

In *Parashat Pinchas*, as in quite a few other episodes in the Torah, first in Egypt and then during the forty years of wandering, we hear about many who died and also about many who survived. Few if any individuals are named, and reasons are not always given for these mass deaths, though the plague mentioned in *Parashat Pinchas* is attributed to acts of sexual immorality and idolatry by Israelite men with Moabite women at Baal Peor. The plague kills twenty-four thousand Israelites, until God is shocked into stopping it by the zealotry of Pinchas's assassination of Zimri, an Israelite man, and Cozbi, a Midianite woman. Following this event, the Israelites are told to attack the Midianites, and later they will kill Midianite men, women, and girls.

Not only the stories of those who died are missing, but also the stories of those who survived, and whether they were traumatized or empowered by their experiences.

Klepfisz's poem can help us begin to imagine some of the things they might have told us. Let us begin imagining.

# Matot
## Numbers 30:2–32:42

## Traditional Haftarah Reading
## Jeremiah 1:1–2:3

## Do Not Fear

*Rabbi Dana Evan Kaplan, PhD*

WHEREAS THE HAFTARAH readings accompanying most of the Torah portions have a thematic connection, the haftarah readings of the three Shabbatot between the seventeenth of Tammuz and the ninth of Av are prophecies that in various ways forewarn the Children of Israel that the First Temple in Jerusalem would be destroyed. This is because, chronologically speaking, the seventeenth of Tammuz is the day on which Jerusalem's walls were breached, and the ninth of Av is the day on which the First Temple (as well as the Second Temple) was destroyed.

In this selection from the Book of Jeremiah, the prophet is told that God had chosen him to be a prophet even before he was born (Jeremiah 1:5). Jeremiah, apparently realizing the danger that this would put him in, tells God that he cannot become a prophet because he does not know how to speak well, since he is only a youth (1:6). God delivers two visions to Jeremiah: The first is of a branch from an almond tree, to symbolize that God is committed to bringing the prophecies to fruition (1:11–12). The second vision is a boiling pot whose face is tipped away from the north (1:13–15), which would have been immediately understood by Jeremiah's contemporaries as referring to the military threat from Babylonia.

Despite the imminent threat that the second prophecy represents, the selection is full of reassurances. God remembers that the Children of Israel were devoted to the divine covenant, willingly leaving Egypt to go into "the wilderness in a land not sown" (Jeremiah 2:2).

Jeremiah's message for us today is that in spite of all of the adversity we may face, God loves us and remains faithful to our covenant. We should remain strong and brave, working actively to make the world a better place, without fear of retribution. God is with us.

# Listening to the Next Generation

*RABBI JESSICA K. BAROLSKY*

The haftarah reading for *Matot*, the opening chapter of the Book of Jeremiah, does not directly relate to the Torah portion's description of the campaign into Midian and its aftermath; instead, it is the first of the three haftarot of affliction read on the Shabbatot from the seventeenth of Tammuz (when the Babylonian army breached the city walls of Jerusalem) to the ninth of Av (when the Temple was destroyed). This haftarah reading contains God's call of Jeremiah to prophecy and the beginning of Jeremiah's prophesying Jerusalem's destruction.

Even in this rather depressing haftarah reading, we can find much hope. Like so many other prophets, Jeremiah first resists the call to service. Like Moses (Exodus 4:10), he claims not to speak well—in his case, because he is "only a youth" (Jeremiah 1:6). God encourages him, reminding him that he must simply follow God's command and speak the words God gives to him. God promises to keep him safe and protected (1:7–8).

Jeremiah's call reminds us to listen to those around us, especially to the young. Our children will inherit the world that we create and shape today. While Jeremiah might still be a child, a "youth," he is the one God chooses to carry God's message to the people.

Jeremiah's message is not only one of destruction and war, but also one of eventual hope. God tells Jeremiah, "See, I have appointed you this day [to speak] to nations and kingdoms, to uproot, to pull down, to destroy, to root out, [but also] to build and to plant" (Jeremiah 1:10). Our children know that whatever destruction and uprooting happens during our lifetimes, it will be their responsibility to continue to build and to plant in the future.

No matter how old or young we are, we can find a child, a young person, who might not seem to have authority—yet. Listen to them. Like the people living with Jeremiah, we have to listen to what excites, scares, and worries them about their future. We must encourage them to lead, to speak out, to help build and plant our shared world. We must learn from Jeremiah's struggles to stand together and help make a better future happen.

## Alternative Haftarah Reading:
## From "Can Women Serve as Rabbis?"
## by Rabbi Regina Jonas

"Wise women" who are *ra'uy* [worthy] *lehorot* [to teach] thus are given the right to make decisions. So there apparently were in fact women who, in addition to possessing intelligence—for that alone did not suffice—had acquired the professional knowledge and applied it, as emerges from the citation above. The only thing is, there were relatively few. Their entire work as household "supervisor" is a *pasken* [interpreter and adjudicator of Jewish law]. This is possible for in this area she knows something; no one else can represent her and therefore she had the chance to demonstrate in practice that she can summon the requisite understanding and seriousness for such matters.

If she now has a career as a rabbi and must make decisions in other areas in which she has studied, then nothing revolutionary has happened. With the seriousness that her job entails, she puts into practice something that women long were allowed to do in the household, only to a greater extent; but it lies within the same level and therefore does not offend Jewish sensibilities. It is written that "one relies upon women" so it is not foreign to Judaism if this "support" is broadened from the narrow, permitted range into a larger one of *pasken*, to which in principle there is no objection.

I believe that the question of whether a woman may make halachic decisions as a Rabbinerin may very clearly be seen as permitted, and it is not necessary to continue to linger over this matter.

# Laying Foundations

### RABBI AUDREY S. POLLACK

*Parashat Matot* opens with vows and legal scenarios that question the validity of promises made by women. Our text asserts that a male is held responsible for the vows that he makes to God and for oaths and pledges made to another man. The Torah questions whether a woman possesses independent authority. If she still lives in her father's household, he has the right to annul or cancel her vows and oaths under certain circumstances. If her husband learns of a vow or commitment that she has voluntarily made prior to marriage and he does not object, her obligations remain in force. If upon hearing them, he objects, he has the power to annul her vows and oaths. But if he annuls them later, he is responsible for the consequences. She is under the authority of her father or her husband. A widow or divorcee alone have the authority and independence to be responsible for their own promises.

*Parashat Matot* is sandwiched in between the two *parashiyot* of *Pinchas* and *Mas'ei*, which bring us the story of the daughters of Zelophehad. In *Pinchas*, Zelophehad's daughters ask to be their father's inheritors, since he died without sons. In *Mas'ei*, the decision is revised, maintaining the right for the daughters to inherit, but restricting their marriages to within the tribe, lest their father's lands be transferred out of the tribe of Manasseh.

The halachic reasoning that restricts women from serving as valid witnesses and from possessing their own authority and that exempts women from certain mitzvot is rooted in *Matot* and in other biblical texts. These Torah portions give us a glimpse of the struggle and the glimmers of hope for "half the kingdom" of Israel—the women. These laws and rules have stood as part of the foundational arguments against the equality of women in the synagogue and the ordination of women rabbis.

In 1930, Regina Jonas submitted her halachic treatise "Can Women Serve as Rabbis?" as the completion of her studies in Berlin, Germany. Her thesis legitimized the rabbinical role for women, including numerous quotations in Hebrew and lengthy Talmudic citations as the underpinning of her argument. Rather than rejecting traditional halachah, Jonas's claims were grounded in Jewish law. Her thesis advisor was satisfied "that according to [Jewish law] . . . a woman can be appointed to rabbinical office." However, the head of the school at the time was not convinced. It was not until four years later that she achieved her life's dream: Rabbi Max Dienemann agreed to administer the rabbinical exam that the seminary had not permitted her to take, and she officially became Rabbi Regina Jonas.

It would take seven years more for Rabbi Leo Baeck to certify her ordination. Rabbi Regina Jonas's story was all but lost to history in the ashes of the Shoah. Surviving male colleagues who knew her story never spoke of her. Her papers were found tucked away in an archive after the fall of the Berlin Wall. Rabbi Regina Jonas's legacy lives on in her work and in the foundation she laid for the generations of women who followed her into the rabbinate.

## Alternative Haftarah Reading:
### From "Patriarchal Poetry," by Gertrude Stein

Patriarchal poetry is the same as Patriotic poetry is the same as patriarchal poetry is the same as Patriotic poetry is the same as patriarchal poetry is the same.
Patriarchal poetry is the same. . . .
Let her be to be to be to be let her be to be to be let her to be let her to be let her be to be when is it that they are shy.
Very well to try.
Let her be that is to be let her be that is to be let her be let her try.
Let her be let her be let her be to be to be shy let her be to be let her be to be let her try.
Let her try. . . .
To be shy.
Let her be.

Let her try. . . .
Let her be shy.
Let her
Let her
Let her be.
Let her be shy.
Let her be let her try. . . .
Let her try
Let her let her try to be let her try.
Let her try.
Just let her try.
Let her try.
Never to be what he said. . . .
Not to let her to be what he said not to let her to be what he said.
Never to be let her to be never let her to be what he said. Never let her to be
what he said. . . .
Patriarchal she said what is it I know what it is I know I know so that I know
what it is I know so I know. . . at first it was the grandfather then it was not that
in that the father not of that grandfather and then she to be to be sure to be
sure to be I know to be sure to be I know to be sure to be not as good as that.
To be sure not to be sure to be sure correctly saying to be sure to be that. It
was that. She was right. It was that.
Patriarchal poetry.

# Patriarchal Expectations

### Rabbi-Cantor Elana Rosen-Brown

In *Parashat Matot*, we read, "Those are the laws that the Eternal enjoined upon
Moses between a husband and his wife, and as between a father and his daughter
while in her father's household by reason of her youth" (Numbers 30:17). This is
just one text of many in the Torah that affirms strict gendered expectations and
hierarchical relationships. And while countless feminist scholars have reframed,
resisted, reclaimed, and reimagined Torah in meaningful ways, we still can't fully
escape the principle starting point: the patriarchal nature of the text.

In "Patriarchal Poetry," Gertrude Stein similarly exposes hierarchical gendered
biases in poetics, as commentators on the Torah have been doing for decades. In
the middle of "Patriarchal Poetry" with "Let her try," Stein attempts to re-create
patriarchal poetry by renaming and reclaiming it. And yet, the poem as a whole
skillfully demonstrates her claim that we can't mount a critique fully outside the
poetics of what we critique. The patriarchal frame into which we are born remains

always part and parcel of the critique. However, we can shake up patriarchy's confidence by playing with identification, as Stein does so brilliantly.

Beyond their obvious connection, Stein's "Patriarchal Poetry" and *Parashat Matot* are paired for an additional purpose. We read *Parashat Matot* around the month of August, close to the time we observe International Childfree Day on August 1. International Childfree Day seeks to foster respect for the childfree choice. Honoring International Childfree Day with this haftarah reading is one way to celebrate and affirm the choice not to have kids equally to the choice to become a parent.

Those who choose not to have kids regularly report being met with suspicion. Women in particular note the shaming they encounter. Progressive Jewish institutions and communities are not exempt from this behavior. In fact, implicitly promulgating the commandment of *p'ru ur'vu* ("be fruitful and multiply"; Genesis 1:28) through the blessings at a *b'rit* or prying questions after services are just some of the ways that we, as a Jewish community, have remained within the patriarchal framework of Judaism while simultaneously critiquing it.

As we celebrate International Childfree Day, we commit to making a bigger space within the Jewish community to affirm reproductive choice. We acknowledge the ways patriarchal expectations of prescribed gender roles and family constellations still continue to dominate many Jewish spaces.

# Mas'ei
## Numbers 33:1–36:13

## Traditional Haftarah Reading:
## Jeremiah 2:4–28, 3:4

### The Life-Giving Force of the Eternal
*Rabbi Rachel Axelrad*

THIS HAFTARAH reading is for the second week before Tishah B'Av. The nation of Israel is instructed to "hear the word of the Eternal. . . that they moved away from Me [God]" (Jeremiah 2:4-5) and to look forward to their "return to Me [God]" (Jeremiah 4:1). Additionally, both the haftarah reading and the Torah portion discuss a woman's capacity to make valid vows.

Jeremiah's overall mission was to destroy the community and then to plant it anew. This is evident in his frequent use of metaphors for femininity and fertility, simultaneously seen as morally impure and life-giving. For example, in Jeremiah 2:7 he says that "you came and defiled My land," while in 2:20 he warns that "on every high hill, under every leafy tree you lie sprawling as a harlot."

While the haftarah reading focuses on the negative, the additional concluding verses of hope offset the negative tone. Ultimately, the vision of the renewal of the nation (its metaphorical replanting) brings out the positive aspects of feminine fertility and God's forgiveness. Jeremiah's mission, to pull down and then plant, ties the beauty of feminine fertility to the life-giving force of the Eternal, emphasizing the feminine aspect of the Holy One.

In Jeremiah 2:13, God describes Godself as "the Fountain of Living Waters." This is the essential basis for fertility, for life itself. The feminine aspect of fecundity is directly related to the source of life and living waters, thus channeling God's feminine aspect.

# To Do the Next Right Thing

*Rabbi Jordana Schuster Battis*

The haftarah reading for *Mas'ei* is the second haftarah of affliction we read in the weeks before Tishah B'Av. The connection here is not to the *parashah* but to the time of year, which marks the fall of Jerusalem and the ancient Temple. These weeks are traditionally observed with mourning rituals for the Temple itself and with commemoration of the Jewish people's fateful disregard for each other.

Jeremiah's words admonish the people, saying that like their ancestors, they have brazenly abandoned God and covenant, in defiance of what they know well: that they are only here because of the bounty God has bestowed upon them. Only in the final verse(s) of this selection (the verses are placed here out of context, in order to end the haftarah selection on a consoling note) does Jeremiah express hope that rightness may yet be restored.

As we sit with our discomfort with this haftarah's accusations and depiction of a punishing God, we may find that we bristle in part because something deep in the text rings too true, at a time when disregard of basic care and compassion seem to run rampant in our world. What moral voice are we ignoring, even as it rings in our ears? Jeremiah reminds us that it is on us to do the next right thing in the moment we are in, whether tomorrow we live or die.

## Alternative Haftarah Reading:
### *Babylonian Talmud,* B'rachot *29b;* T'filat HaDerech

And when you set out on a journey, consult with your Creator, and then set out. [The Gemara asks,] "What is the meaning of 'Consult with your Creator, and then set out'?" Rabbi Yaakov said that Rav Chisda said, "That is the traveler's prayer." (Babylonian Talmud, *B'rachot* 29b)

> *T'filat HaDerech*
> May it be Your will, our God and God of our ancestors,
> that You lead us in peace and help us reach our destination
> safely, joyfully, and peacefully.
> May You protect us on our leaving and on our return
> and rescue us from any harm,
> and may You bless the work of our hands,
> and may our deeds merit honor for You.
> Praise to You, Adonai, Protector of Israel.

# Not Alone

### RABBI SARA RAE PERMAN

When I was in college, I first learned of *T'filat HaDerech*, the prayer for a journey. I was with two Orthodox friends, who recited it while we were on a road trip. One mentioned that they knew of someone who had left out the traditional part asking God to protect them from wild beasts, as that person believed it no longer applied to people in this modern age. As the individual who had left out the section on wild beasts was traveling by car, the car was struck by a deer. So much for eliminating the part of the prayer asking for protection from wild beasts.

*Parashat Mas'ei* is about the journey the Israelite people took during their forty years in the wilderness. Their journey took them from Raamses near Egypt to the steppes of Moab overlooking the Land of Israel. Their journey had its ups and downs, from crossing the Sea of Reeds, to getting the Torah, to experiencing rebellions and deaths. Journeys can be exciting. They can also be scary. They can be of short duration or last a lifetime. We don't always know what we will experience on our journey; that is as true for us as it was for our ancestors.

A prayer before a journey may not necessarily protect us, but it offers us comfort. It is a reminder that we are not alone on our journey, no matter where it may take us and no matter what we may experience along the way.

## *Alternative Haftarah Reading: From "Trees," by Leah Goldberg*

### Cypress

Here I will not hear the call of the cuckoo
Here the tree will not wear a snowcap
But under the shadow of those cypresses
All my childhood, which came back to life.

The ring of the needles: Once upon a time . . .
I will call homeland to the wide expanse of snow
To the ice, [to the] greening bordering the brook,
to the language of a poem in a strange land.

Perhaps only migrating birds know
When they are hanging between heaven and earth
This pain of the two homelands.

With you, I have been planted twice
With you, I have sprouted, oh cypresses
But my roots lie in two different landscapes.

# Roots and Wings

## RABBI JAVIER E. CATTAPAN

*Parashat Mas'ei* is marked with variations of the Hebrew root *nun-samech-ayin*, meaning "to set out, to journey, to march." More than forty times we are reminded that the Jewish people's sojourn in the wilderness of Sinai was that of a migrant people, suspended between their physical and their aspirational homelands. Goldberg's poem also uses this same verb in the image of the migrating birds who "hang" between two polar opposites. The space they inhabit is the realm of in-between, the air. Goldberg imagines that birds, being both air and earth creatures, feel the tension as a painful reminder that they are not fully either.

Originally published in 1955 as part of Goldberg's book *Barak HaBoker* (Morning Lightning), this poem is one of a group of three titled "Trees" (the other two are "Eucalyptus" and "Castor-Oil Tree"). "Cypress" is written in the classic form of an Italian sonnet (in 1953, Goldberg translated selected poems by Petrarch). In the opening stanza, the poet describes the place where she is living as both not her birthplace and a place of rebirth. The conifers, so prevalent in the forest around the Baltic Sea, appears to be the link between the two lands. The Mediterranean cypress found around Israel are of a different variety than those that can tolerate copious amounts of snow, but both are conifers and resemble each other.

The frozen landscape described in the second stanza alludes to Northern Europe, but line 8 of the poem seems ambiguous: The homeland is both birthplace and "a strange land" (cf. Exodus 2:22, referring to Egypt, and Psalm 137:4, referring to Babylon as "land of the alien"). The sestet makes the poet's ambiguity of her patriotic feelings clear: even a committed immigrant cannot escape the realization of having two homelands. Speaking to the cypresses, the poet finally admits a fundamental difference between her and the tree: whereas the trees are anchored to the soil, the poet-immigrant accomplished the unnatural feat of having roots in two different places.

Those of us who are immigrants know that feeling very well. Migrants, both voluntary and forced ones, cannot cut themselves off completely from the land that saw them grow, even if that same land, at one point, turned on them. Immigrants come to America with their homeland wrapped around their tongue. We sound and dress differently. There are those who question the migrants' loyalty to their new land. Yet, like the poem indicates, also in the new land we can be planted, grow roots, and sprout. Migrants become part of their land; it becomes their homeland, our homeland.

The idea of treating the migrant fairly, the "stranger," as the Torah calls them, is deeply rooted in the experience of the Jews journeying through the wilderness of

Sinai. The experience of their *masa'ot* teaches us empathy for the migrants' difficult feelings of having two homelands. It makes us sensitive to their plight so that we will act in a way that values, acknowledges, and, more importantly, celebrates their journeys as something that adds value to ours.

# Haftarot for the
# Weekly Torah Portions
## DEUTERONOMY

# D'varim
## Deuteronomy 1:1–3:22

## Traditional Haftarah Reading:
## Isaiah 1:1–27

## Continuing the Story
### RABBI MAYA Y. GLASSER

WHAT ARE THE STORIES we tell ourselves about ourselves? Both *Parashat D'varim* and its accompanying haftarah reading invite us to look back on the history of our people and reflect on how it may shape our present and our future.

While in the *parashah* Moses is reviewing the wanderings of the Israelites in the desert, in the haftarah, through the prophet Isaiah, God is reminding us of all of the ways in which we have done wrong since then. However, though parts of our story are already completed, there is still potential to change the overall narrative. God implores us, "Cease to do evil, learn to do good, seek justice; relieve the oppressed" (Isaiah 1:16–17).

As contemporary Reform Jews, one of our strongest mandates is to participate in the work of *tikkun olam* and leave the world better than we found it. This is the legacy that we want to leave, and God empowers us to do so. The story of our people continues with us, and we, like the generations before us, are striving to do good, be just, and help those in need. We retell ourselves these narratives over and over, so that we can learn from those who came before us, build on their work, and pave the way for the next chapter.

## Focus on Social Justice, Not Meaningless Rituals
### RABBI MORDECAI FINLEY

The haftarah for the Torah portion *D'varim* begins a series of ten haftarah readings that are connected not to the respective Torah portion, but rather to the calendar. The ten haftarot are divided into three of "affliction" and seven of "consolation." These haftarah readings link Tishah B'Av, the date of the destruction of both Temples, to Rosh HaShanah and the rest of the Days of Awe. The most important thing to know about the haftarah reading for *Parashat D'varim* is the moment when it is chanted: on the Shabbat just before Tishah B'Av.

The haftarah reading of this week contains the dreadful condemnation of the Judeans, using chilling metaphors of bodily diseases and descriptions of a desolate and abandoned land. Literally, it is magnificent, magnificent in its horror. What has offended the God of Isaiah so much to bring the imminent destruction and exile? Insincere prayer and the reliance on rote forms. Isaiah's prophecy expresses God's disgust of the mendacity, the pretensions. Say it true, or don't say it all. What does God want in place of this deceitfulness? "Cease to do evil, learn to do good, seek justice; relieve the oppressed" (Isaiah 1:16–17). Focus on social justice, not meaningless rituals.

And here, we pause. On this Shabbat before Tishah B'Av, are we to feel smug? Fine, we go to services, but do we break our hearts before the Divine? We engage in good deeds and fight for justice, laudably, yes, but do we demand enough spiritually of ourselves? Do we love God, with all our heart and might? What does that actually mean? Isaiah might say, to us in particular, "Figure that out as if your life depends on it."

## Alternative Haftarah Reading:
### Babylonian Talmud, Sanhedrin 98a

Rabbi Joshua ben Levi met the prophet Elijah, who was meditating at the entrance to the cave of Rabbi Shimon bar Yochai. "When will the Messiah come?" asked Joshua. "Ask him," replied Elijah. "The Messiah is at the gates to the city, sitting among the poor, the sick, and wretched. Like them, he changes the bandages on his wounds, but he does so one bandage at a time. He says, 'I may be needed at any moment.'"

Then Joshua went to meet the Messiah and greeted him, saying, "Peace be upon you, my master and teacher," and the Messiah replied, "Peace be upon you, son of Levi." Joshua then asked, "When will you be coming?" and was told, "Today!" Joshua went back to Elijah and was asked what the Messiah said. "'Peace be upon you, son of Levi,'" Joshua replied. Elijah told him that it meant that he and his father would have a place in the world-to-come. Joshua said that the Messiah had not told him the truth, because he had promised to come today but he didn't come. Elijah explained, "This is what he said to you, 'Today'—if you will hearken to his voice."

## Being a Part of Redemption
### Rabbi Kerry M. Olitzky

Shabbat Chazon—"the Shabbat of Vision"—is oddly named, since it always precedes Tishah B'Av, the date that marks the destruction of the ancient Temples in

Jerusalem, as well as other tragic events in Jewish history. On the eve of massive destruction, we are directed to see beyond it.

This notion has propelled the Jewish people throughout its journey. For us, history is not a recording of events. Rather, it is a path toward the ultimate redemption of the world. Our history has a purpose to it. Our reading reminds us that we can't merely wait for this redemption. Instead, we have to be part of it. We have to be the ones to bring messianic redemption to the world through our actions.

The text from the Babylonian Talmud is a teaching of Rabbi Y'hoshua ben Levi, who lived in the first half of the third century CE, and references Shimon bar Yochai, purported to be the author of the mystical *Zohar* text. Bar Yochai hid in a cave for twelve years to avoid capture by the Romans. The text highlights the role of the prophet Elijah, who is associated with messianism, for it is he, says Jewish tradition, who will announce the Messiah.

This text reflects what is perhaps unique about Jewish liberation theology: it is we who will usher forth the messianic period through our personal acts. It is through our personal deeds that we will be redeemed—and so will the world.

## Alternative Haftarah Reading:
### From "Take This Poem and Copy It," by Almog Behar

Take this poem and copy it in your handwriting on a piece of paper and insert words from your soul between the words your hands copied. And notice the additions made by the words from your hands and the subtractions made by punctuation, the spaces and the lines which are broken within your life. Take this poem and copy it a thousand times and distribute it to people on the city's main street. And say to them I wrote this poem this is a poem I wrote this is a poem I wrote this I wrote this poem I wrote this I wrote this I wrote. Take this poem and put it in an envelope and send it to the one your heart desires and include a short letter with it. And before you send it change its title and at the end add rhymes of your own. Sweeten the bitter and enrich the spare and bridge the cracked and simplify the clumsy and enliven the dead and square the truth. A person could take many poems and make them his. Take this very poem and make only this one yours for even though it has nothing special which ignites your desire to make it yours it also has no possessiveness of the kind which says a man's poems are his property and his only and you have no right to meddle or ask anything of them but this is a poem which asks you to meddle with it to erase and to add and it is given to you freely for free ready to be changed by your hands. Take this poem and make it yours and sign your name on it and erase the previous name but remember it and remember that every word is poetry is the offspring of poetry and poetry is the poetry of many not one. And someone after you will take your poem and make it his and command those after him the children of poets take this poem and copy it on a piece of paper and make it yours in your handwriting.

# Pens in Hand

*RABBI JILL PERLMAN*

*Parashat D'varim* begins the first in a series of speeches Moses shares with the people as they prepare to enter the Promised Land. This is Moses's opportunity to share his final guidance with the Children of Israel, since he won't be accompanying them on the next stage of their journey. In an earlier *parashah*, God had informed Moses that his time was coming to an end. This place, this threshold between the wilderness and what will become Israel, will be his final stop. What does a leader like Moses say in their last chance to impart wisdom to their people? What does anyone say, knowing that their next words will be their last words?

*D'varim* literally translates as "words"—and words have extraordinary power. Words create worlds. After all, language was the mechanism through which God created everything: the earth and all who dwell upon it. In his poem "Take This Poem and Copy It," Almog Behar plays with and points to the power of words and even more so to memory and legacy. When the speaker in Behar's poem urges us as the readers to take this poem, copy it down, and make it our own, we are reminded that legacy is never ours alone. True legacy occurs when someone uses our lives as models and adds their name to our life's project. Enduring legacy occurs when ego disappears and we realize that it's the process of passing down that matters far more than authorship, my name, or your name. Others will work on our poem, interweaving new words with our own. Our story is not meant to sit on a shelf collecting dust; no, it is meant to be read and then rewritten. I want a coffee ring right smack in the middle of my poem because it will have meant that my people will have pored over my pages. We don't share our stories, speak our speeches, live our legacies so that our name alone endures; it is the content that matters and the chain that links me to you and to all that have come before and all that will come after.

What humility to say: take my poem and meddle with it! What a joy to revel in the permission—and the obligation!—to take the stories that have come before and interpret them anew. Moses shares his story with the people because he wants them to own and live his words. He can't possibly imagine all that will befall the Children of Israel in the future, but he knows that he is linked to them always through this moment.

So too with all of us. Let us live our lives as poems that will live on the lips of our descendants, reworked and reimagined. Pens in hand, let us write a guiding legacy that will link us to the next generation.

# *Va-et'chanan*/Shabbat Nachamu
### Deuteronomy 3:23–7:11

## Traditional Haftarah Reading:
### Isaiah 40:1–26

## Much-Needed Messages
### RABBI KERRY M. OLITZKY

ISAIAH 40:1–26 is read on the Shabbat following Tishah B'Av, a date on the Jewish calendar with which many of us struggle. Our discomfort is not simply a result of the various calamities marked by this day and faced by the Jewish people over the course of its journey through history. Our distress emerges from the traditional blame of the destruction of the ancient Temple in Jerusalem on the Jewish community and its *sinat chinam* (baseless hatred). The marking of this date also implicitly includes the desire to rebuild Jerusalem and the Temple.

In a time in which we have seen a rebuilt—and reunited—Jerusalem, this haftarah reading hardly seems to be the stuff out of which prophetic Judaism is made. Read on what is called Shabbat Nachamu (the Sabbath of Comfort), this reading is the first of the so-called haftarot of consolation (*sheva d'nechemata*).

It is this prophetic message of comfort—made explicit in the first words of the haftarah portion—that is sorely needed in this postmodern period of alienation and isolation. Perhaps the desire to rebuild the Temple is but a metaphor to suggest that we long to be closer to the Divine and that God may be closer to us, reminiscent of the Torah verse, "And let them make Me a sanctuary *but* I will dwell among them" (Exodus 25:8). By listening to others with our hearts, and by offering *ahavat chinam* (unconditional love) to those who also seek the Divine, we can indeed make room for God.

# Be Comforted—and Comforting

RABBI MATT FRIEDMAN

This reading is assigned to coincide with the first Shabbat after Tishah B'Av. The haftarah readings for the preceding three weeks are referred to as the haftarot of affliction. They share the reiterating of the failures of the people and prophesize punishment by God. The observance of Tishah B'Av focuses on the destructions of the First and Second Temples and other crushing events throughout Jewish history.

This haftarah reading begins the series of the haftarot of consolation taking place over seven weeks, setting the stage for the period of self-assessment in the Jewish calendar, Rosh HaShanah and Yom Kippur. Its opening words are among the most powerful of prophetic literature: "'Comfort My people, comfort them!' says your God" (Isaiah 40:1).

In the Torah portion, *Va-et'chanan*, Moses makes a final plea to God to be allowed to enter the land of Canaan. However, God rejects Moses's request and only allows him to ascend a mountain and see the land from afar. God further instructs Moses not to revisit the topic. Despite his disappointment, Moses continues to provide instruction and guidance to the people.

Often, it is easy to not see the broader impacts of our lives and deeds. The message of the haftarah cycle of consolation and Moses's continued loyalty and love of his people teach us to be sentient with our words and deeds. What we do and say matters—we can comfort, and then we will find comfort, too.

## Alternative Haftarah Reading:
## "V'ahavta," by Aurora Levins Morales

Say these words when you lie down and when you rise up,
when you go out and when you return. In times of mourning
and in times of joy. Inscribe them on your doorposts,
embroider them on your garments, tattoo them on your shoulders,
teach them to your children, your neighbors, your enemies,
recite them in your sleep, here in the cruel shadow of empire:

Another world is possible.
Thus spoke the prophet Roque Dalton:
All together they have more death than we,
but all together, we have more life than they.
There is more bloody death in their hands
than we could ever wield, unless

we lay down our souls to become them,
and then we will lose everything. So instead,

imagine winning. This is your sacred task.
This is your power. Imagine
every detail of winning, the exact smell of the summer streets
in which no one has been shot, the muscles you have never
unclenched from worry, gone soft as newborn skin,
the sparkling taste of food when we know
that no one on earth is hungry, that the beggars are fed,
that the old man under the bridge and the woman
wrapping herself in thin sheets in the back seat of a car,
and the children who suck on stones,
nest under a flock of roofs that keep multiplying their shelter.
Lean with all your being towards that day
when the poor of the world shake down a rain of good fortune
out of the heavy clouds, and justice rolls down like waters.

Defend the world in which we win as if it were your child.
It is your child.
Defend it as if it were your lover.
It is your lover.

When you inhale and when you exhale
breathe the possibility of another world
into the 37.2 trillion cells of your body
until it shines with hope.
Then imagine more.

Imagine rape is unimaginable. Imagine war is a scarcely credible rumor
That the crimes of our age, the grotesque inhumanities of greed,
the sheer and astounding shamelessness of it, the vast fortunes
made by stealing lives, the horrible normalcy it came to have,
is unimaginable to our heirs, the generations of the free.

Don't waver. Don't let despair sink its sharp teeth
Into the throat with which you sing. Escalate your dreams.
Make them burn so fiercely that you can follow them down
any dark alleyway of history and not lose your way.
Make them burn clear as a starry drinking gourd
Over the grim fog of exhaustion, and keep walking.

Hold hands. Share water. Keep imagining.
So that we, and the children of our children's children
may live.

# The World Is Our Child; the World Is Our Lover

*RABBI GILA COLMAN RUSKIN*

*V'ahavta* is one of the first prayers that Jewish children learn to recite, conveniently chanted according to the Torah trope. "Convenient" because "teach it to your children when you sit, walk, lie down, and rise up" foreshadows the day when that child will ascend to the bimah to chant from the Torah itself when they become a b'nei mitzvah and a responsible Jewish young adult.

Aurora Levins Morales reminds us in her stirring and prayerful poem that it is not enough for us to pass on to our children's children's children the ancient tales of the Torah or the rulings of the Talmud. Loving God with all our heart, soul, and might calls us to work and fight for radical social justice. War, rape, genocide, greed, and poverty appear in this poem as harsh realities that must be confronted and diminished by those who love God and seek to bring about a world based on God's principles of compassion and justice.

It's not enough to just sweetly chant *V'ahavta* with Torah trope; *V'ahavta* must stir us to action with the urgency present in this poem. The world is our child; the world is our lover. And our passion must rise to defend and redeem it.

## *Alternative Haftarah Reading: "Tears, Too Close: A Prayer of Consolation," by Alden Solovy*

These tears are too close to my eyes,
Ready to burst forth
For the sorrow that surrounds us.

These tears are too close to my heart,
Ready to burst forth
For the pain that surrounds us.

These tears are too close to my soul,
Ready to burst forth
For the heartbreak that surrounds us.

נַחֲמוּ נַחֲמוּ עַמִּי יֹאמַר אֱלֹהֵיכֶם,
כִּי נִחַם יְיָ צִיּוֹן.

*Nachamu, nachamu ami, yomar Eloheichem,*
*Ki nicham Adonai Tziyon.*
Comfort, comfort My people, says your God,
For God will comfort Zion.

Well of compassion,
Comfort of generations,
Let us cry together
For all that has been lost,
And all that
Might have been.

אָנֹכִי אָנֹכִי הוּא מְנַחֶמְכֶם,
וְרַב שְׁלוֹם בָּנָיִךְ.

*Anochi anochi hu m'nachemchem,*
*V'rav sh'lom banayich.*
It is I, it is I who comforts you,
And great shall be your children's peace.

Yearning,
Still yearning,
For solace and consolation,

Yearning,
Still yearning,
With hope and faith,

Yearning,
Still yearning,
For healing to flow free.

קוּמִי אוֹרִי כִּי בָא אוֹרֵךְ,
כִּי הֶהָרִים יָמוּשׁוּ וְהַגְּבָעוֹת תְּמוּטֶינָה
וְחַסְדִּי מֵאִתֵּךְ לֹא יָמוּשׁ.
וּמַלְאַךְ פָּנָיו הוֹשִׁיעָם
בְּאַהֲבָתוֹ וּבְחֶמְלָתוֹ הוּא גְאָלָם.

*Kumi ori ki va oreich,*
*Ki heharim yamushu v'hag'vaot t'mutenah*
*V'chasdi mei-iteich lo yamush.*
*Umalach panav hoshiam*
*B'ahavato uv'chemlato hu g'alam.*

Arise, shine, for your light has dawned,
For mountains may move and hills be shaken
But My kindness shall not be removed from you.
And the angel of God delivered them,
In love and mercy God redeemed them.

# "Comfort, Comfort . . ."

*RABBI LEA MÜHLSTEIN*

In "Tears, Too Close: A Prayer of Consolation," Alden Solovy adopts a literary technique favoured by *paitanim* (Jewish liturgical poets) throughout the ages: weaving together quotes from each of the seven haftarot of consolation to form the biblical backbone of the prayer. The prayer captures the atmosphere of Shabbat Nachamu, expressing our human yearning for consolation. Almost anyone can relate to emotions welling up even when we are not prepared for them.

The image of God that the prayer paints for us beautifully encapsulates the ambivalence of the opening words of *Haftarat Nachamu* (Isaiah 40:1), which leaves doubt as to whether it is us or God who is in need of comfort: "Comfort, oh comfort My people." Fitting for the accompanying Torah portion, which includes both the *Sh'ma* and the Ten Commandments, the motif of God weeping with humanity adds spiritual depth to the meaning of our covenantal relationship with God: just like we ask God not to give up on us, we are asked not to give up on God. And just as the Psalmist reminds us that those who sow in tears will reap in joy (Psalm 126:5), the prayer leads us from sorrow to hope.

Can you think of a time when prayer helped you transpose sorrow to hope?

# Eikev
## Deuteromony 7:12–11:25

## Traditional Haftarah Reading:
## Isaiah 49:14–51:3

## You Will Be Okay

### EMILY DANA

IF THE TORAH portion of *Eikev* is the "wound," the "tough love" of telling us as Jews how to behave, the haftarah portion is designed to do the opposite.

The haftarah reading is a reassurance that we are not forsaken by our God. As any of us know, Judaism is, among other things, a religion of the law—but Isaiah doesn't seem too concerned with that law! Rather, he is unwaveringly faithful that God will help him by giving him open ears (Isaiah 50:5) and "a skilled tongue" (Isaiah 50:4). Isaiah notices that we are given gifts by God, even if we are not always able to see them.

The prophet also tells us that whenever we lose our trust, we should look to our history: "Look back to Abraham your father, and to Sarah who bore you! When I called him he was alone, but I blessed him and made him many" (Isaiah 51:2). We can use the past as reassurance for the present and the future. At all times, "the Eternal will comfort Zion" (Isaiah 51:3). We will be okay; our people will be okay—because God is here to comfort us.

## God as a Mother

### RABBI AUDREY R. KOROTKIN, PhD

This week's haftarah reading, like the rest of the seven readings *d'nechemta* (of comfort) is designed to lift up the worshiper from the depths of despair to the promise of forgiveness and redemption. All seven readings come from the anonymous prophecies of the so-called Second Isaiah (Isaiah 40–66), representing material from during and just after the Babylonian exile (587–538 BCE).

The unbreakable bond between mother and child is the core metaphor of this lengthy poetic passage, invoking the loving, immanent presence of the *Shechinah*, the female aspect of God, who travels with the people of Israel wherever they may find themselves (Babylonian Talmud, *M'gillah* 29a)—even into forced exile.

As the poem opens, it is this maternal manifestation of Israel's God who comes to comfort the collective Zion as she laments that "the Eternal [*Adonai*] has forsaken me" (Isaiah 49:14). Zion is reminded that *Adonai* is only one aspect of God: "Can a mother forget her babe, or stop loving the child of her womb?" she is asked (49:15). The phrase "stop loving" is rendered as *meiracheim*, from the same root as *rechem*, the "womb" itself. Just as it is usually physically and emotionally very rare for a mother to be separated from her child, it is equally almost impossible for the *Shechinah* to forget or forsake Israel.

The future of Zion's children is repeatedly assured (Isaiah 49:20–22, 25), and the haftarah's final section reminds us that this future is promised eternally by the mother of them all: "Look back to Abraham your father, and to Sarah who bore you!" (Isaiah 51:2). Passed from the secure embrace of one mother (Sarah) to another (*Shechinah*), Zion will always be God's beloved.

## Alternative Haftarah Reading: "The Death of Adam," by Howard Schwartz

Adam lay in his tent, surrounded by his many sons and daughters. He had lived to be nine hundred and thirty when the sickness had seized him, and now even the days that had been numbered were drawing to an end. His first wife, Lilith, had left him long ago, and Eve, whom God had created for him from his own rib, had been dead for more than two centuries. In their last years, Adam's memory of their life inside the Garden had become blurred, and when he had finally forgotten the lost splendor Eve had died of grief, and the burden of bearing a memory was too great for a single survivor. Now Adam alone was left. And strange to say, among the children of his children, there were those who had come to doubt the story of his origin, who could not bring themselves to believe that one father and mother had given birth to so many. But his sons and daughters had always shielded him from these skeptics, and among them, the years he had toiled outside the gate that the angel still guarded were burned into their memory, as was the story of the death of Abel, his second son, and the punishment of Cain, his first. And now only Cain and Abel, among his many children, were missing. Instead it was Seth, himself an old man, who bent over his bed and spoke in his ear. But Adam had come to a place where he could not turn back. The words of his oldest living son were lost to him. Neither did he notice the presence of the angel that had entered the room. His eyes had turned inward. At the last moment, a luminous light passed through them and a bright glow surrounded his face. And at that very moment even those who had been uncertain that he was, in fact, the first father, felt the past become a blank wall behind them, and knew that the first era was finally past.

# Life Is Giving Rise to More Life

*Rabbi Beth L. Schwartz*

*Parashat Eikev* promises God's blessings of fertility and health in return for observing and living according to God's "rules" (*mishpatim*): God will "bless you and multiply you—blessing your issue from the womb" (Deuteronomy 7:13). Of the first ten generations of humanity, Adam lived to see the births of eight generations of offspring (Genesis 5:3–25). If Adam, long before the years of bondage, exodus, and revelation, experienced the blessings of knowing these generations, how much the more so can we, the children of the covenant, appreciate its rewards?

The midrash fills in the fullness and end of Adam's life: an example of the blessings of fertility and fecundity. It reminds us in particular of the commandment to honor our parents, as Seth bends over his dying father's bed. The presence of the angel at the moment of death is a sign of God's compassion and gentle care for Adam, the first human being, and of the permission for the living to attend to life. Seth, Adam's sole surviving son, is present at his father's last moments. He too has seen the blessings of fertility and remembers the line of Adam's descendants. Their presence shows us a glimpse of our own continuity, as far back as we can remember, and as far back as Creation itself.

The midrash also helps us to understand that the transition of living memory to historical memory is a natural process and that older memories, now less poignant, still endure and are part of our collective identity—life giving rise to more life, despite the loss.

## *Alternative Haftarah Reading: "A Holy Nation," by Rabbi Regina Jonas*

Our Jewish people was planted by God into history as a blessed nation. "Blessed by God" means to offer blessings, lovingkindness and loyalty, regardless of place and situation. Humility before God, selfless love for His creatures, sustain the world. It is Israel's task to build these pillars of the world—man and woman, woman and man alike have taken this upon themselves in Jewish loyalty. Our work in Theresienstadt, serious and full of trials as it is, also serves this end: to be God's servants and as such to move from earthly spheres to eternal ones. May all our work be a blessing for Israel's future (and the future of humanity). . . . Upright "Jewish men" and "brave, noble women" were always the sustainers of our people. May we be found worthy by God to be numbered in the circle of these women and men. . . . The reward of a mitzvah is the recognition of the great deed by God.

# Providing Strength and Comfort

*RABBI DENA A. FEINGOLD*

During the weeks following Tishah B'Av and leading up to Rosh HaShanah, we read seven haftarot of consolation. On this Shabbat, traditionally, the second of these seven haftarot of comfort is read. In addition, on this Shabbat, the words of *Parashat Eikev* teach us that there is reward for following God's mitzvot.

Rabbi (Fräulein Rabbiner) Regina Jonas, the first female rabbi in history, served the Jewish community of Germany in the 1930s and '40s. She was ordained in Berlin and taught and preached there and in other German cities until she was transported to Terezin (Theresienstadt) in the Czech Republic in 1942. Records in the archives of Terezin show that in spite of the circumstances, Rabbi Jonas continued to teach, preach, and serve in a pastoral care role to bring comfort and inspiration to her fellow Jews interned in the camp.

The text above, found in a collection titled "Lectures by the only female rabbi, Regina Jonas," is taken from notes for a sermon she delivered in Terezin. Even in the midst of a hopeless situation where any reward for following God's commandments must have seemed remote, Jonas encouraged her followers to lead a life devoted to the mitzvot: "The reward of a mitzvah is the recognition of the great deed by God." In a time where little consolation was to be found, Rabbi Jonas continued to find the strength and the words to comfort her people. She died in Auschwitz in 1944.

How will you provide strength and comfort to others when you are suffering yourself?

# R'eih
## Deuteronomy 11:26–16:17

## Traditional Haftarah Reading:
## Isaiah 54:11–55:5

## A Future of Beauty, Peace, Wisdom, and Glory
### Rabbi Joseph B. Meszler

JERUSALEM is not just a geographic location in the Hebrew Bible. It is an allegory for a future of hope.

The traditional haftarah reading for this week continues the theme of consolation after the destruction of the Temple in Jerusalem, marking the third week of a series of seven haftarot. As such, it is not connected to the Torah portion. Four main ideas are contained in these verses from Isaiah:

1. Jerusalem will not only one day be rebuilt, but also its walls will be encrusted with gemstones, superseding the original beauty of the city (Isaiah 54:11–12).
2. Any weapon that is wielded against the inhabitants of this future Jerusalem will not succeed, indicating peace and security (54:14–17).
3. Isaiah calls upon his audience to accept his wisdom, which will satisfy their hunger and thirst, as opposed to their current idolatry, which leaves them empty (55:1–2).
4. Finally, he promises a future ruler from the House of David, based on "an everlasting covenant" when nations they do not even know will come to show tribute and honor God (55:3–5).

At the moment the speech is delivered, Jerusalem is an "unhappy, storm-tossed soul, with none to comfort you" (Isaiah 54:11), but Isaiah paints a picture of a future Jerusalem restored, representing beauty, peace, wisdom, and glory. We must never give up the hope for such a future for all of us.

# Establishing Righteousness

### RABBI MAX CHAIKEN

This passage from the Book of Isaiah marks the third of seven haftarah readings of consolation. In the weeks following Tishah B'Av, the day of Jewish mourning, these passages are designed to offer "comfort," *nechamah*, to our people in a time of unthinkable loss, sadness, and despair. The opening verse even uses the phrase "storm-tossed" souls (Isaiah 54:11) to describe the people of Israel, reminding us that whatever storms we have weathered ourselves, we too are deserving of comfort and hope.

While the traditional reading may have been chosen because of this hopeful and comforting message, it also fits quite powerfully to the *p'shat*, the "plain meaning," of the weekly Torah portion with which it is paired. *R'eih* begins with a reminder that if we observe our covenant with the Divine, blessings will ensue. If we do not, curses will follow. Isaiah then reminds us that even after we inevitably fail to keep the covenant perfectly, God will forgive and take us back.

Isaiah's words also connect directly with several of the commandments found in *R'eih* concerning the establishment of economic justice in our society. The portion teaches that "the stranger, the fatherless, and the widow in your settlements shall come and eat their fill, so that the Eternal your God may bless you in all . . . you undertake" (Deuteronomy 14:29), and continues to teach about the remission of debts. At the beginning of chapter 55, Isaiah reminds us that creating such a society is, in fact, part of the "everlasting covenant" (Isaiah 55:3) that God will keep with us. "Come, all who are thirsty, come for water; even if you have no money, come buy food and eat: come buy food without money, wine and milk without cost" (55:1).

Therefore, this traditional haftarah reading both consoles us and calls us to action. God will take us back even when we have fallen short of creating a world of justice, but we must continue to work for a day when all who are hungry will eat, and our people and our world will "be established in righteousness" (Isaiah 54:14).

## *Alternative Haftarah Reading: Jeremiah 5:20-31*

Tell this to the House of Jacob
and make it heard in Judah:
Hear this, foolish people,
with no heart,

whose eyes won't see,
whose ears won't hear:
Shouldn't you show more reverence for Me?
—says the Eternal.
Before Me, shouldn't you shudder?
I drew a boundary of sand for the sea,
an eternal limit that cannot be broken.
Waves may crash, they cannot get through;
they may make noise, but they cannot pass.
But this people has a stubborn and rebellious heart;
they obstinately go off course.
They have not taken to heart:
"We should show more reverence to the Eternal our God,
the One who gives rain,
early and late in its time,
with weeks designated for the harvest
protecting us."
Your wrongdoings have these off course,
your sins have blocked bounty from you.
For among My people are found the wicked,
who wait like hunters for a bird trap to spring,
setting snares for people.
Like a crate full of fowl,
so their houses are filled with falsehood.
That is how they have grown powerful and rich!
They have become grossly swollen,
with wickedness beyond limit.
They do not judge justly for the orphan;
the poor cannot even get their case heard.
Should I not respond in kind to such?
—says the Eternal.
To this kind of nation
will I not avenge My spirit?
An atrocious catastrophe
has happened in the land:
the prophets prophesy lies,
the governing priests enable them,
and My people actually love it!
But what will you do in the end?

# True and False Prophets

*RABBI JOSEPH B. MESZLER*

The Torah portion *R'eih* speaks of false prophets.

While there will always be people who claim God-given authority, the Torah explains that this is a test of our wisdom and the integrity of society. The prophet Jeremiah says that his generation has failed this test spectacularly. False prophets are in charge. They are empowered and enabled by a ruling priestly class. Worst of all, the people wildly applaud for these pretenders with love and adoration. Jeremiah's words indict everyone who participates in this corruption. The wealthy and powerful prey on the poor, the downtrodden have no recourse, and God is going to call the nation to account. The prophet concludes with a haunting question: How do you think this will end?

God is depicted as the One who sets and enforces boundaries. Just as the sea has a limit, God demands restraint from us and threatens us with consequences. The people's impudence and foolish lack of fear of the divine judgment will bring disaster.

We too get tested by prophets, false and true. False prophets are only as powerful as we let them be. True prophets call us to justice and integrity. It is on us to respond to their call.

## Alternative Haftarah Reading: "Blessing and the Curse," by Rabbi Joe Black

Deuteronomy 11:29: When the Eternal your God brings you into the land that you are about to enter and possess, you shall pronounce the blessing at Mount Gerizim and the curse at Mount Ebal.

> When you walk into the land
> When you cross that sacred stream
> Be careful where you stand—at Ebal or at Gerizim.
> When you come into the valley
> Bring your best—expect the worst
> Listen for the tally: Is it blessing? Is it curse?
>
> For things are seldom the way they seem
> Yesterday's promise is tomorrow's dream
> And dreams become the glue that binds the universe.
> They can help us tell the difference
> between the blessing and the curse.

When you plant your meager offering
When you sow your precious seed
As you gather in the blessing luck and labor have decreed—
You must ask yourself this question:
Are things better? Are they worse?
What is it that I gather? Is it blessing? Is it curse?

And the mountains scream their thunder
And the rivers greet the roar
And the force can pull you under
As the crowd screams out for more
Yes the moon will get you thinking,
And the sun can quench your thirst
Just be careful what you're drinking: Is it blessing? Is it curse?

# Finding the Concealed Good

## Rabbi Elyse D. Frishman

Before entering the land to conquer it, six of the twelve tribes stood on Mount Ebal and six stood on Mount Gerizim, facing each other. In the valley between stood the Levites, who turned first toward Gerizim and uttered blessings, then toward Ebal and uttered curses. After each blessing or curse, all twelve tribes declared together, "Amen!" Then, everyone brought stones, coated them with plaster, and inscribed the words of Torah in seventy languages upon them. And then they slept.

Who receives a blessing, and who a curse? Each of us, depending not on where we stand, but on what we understand.

The blessings and curses were declared while the people were preparing for battle to conquer the land. Saying "Amen!" together, all realized the shared impact. In order to achieve greater clarity of intention and with hope for a blessing, they wrote down the Torah in every known language. Was it the whole Torah? Perhaps it was just the most famous verse "Love the other as yourself" (Leviticus 19:18).

No life battle leaves one unscathed. Everyone experiences curses. Yet it's taught that curses are concealed good.

How does one reach enlightenment? Move from battle into service. Sign each deed with the holy, blessed signature of love.

# Shof'tim
## Deuteronomy 16:18–21:9

## Traditional Haftarah Reading:
## Isaiah 51:12–52:12

### Awake, Shake Off the Dust
#### RABBI LISA SARI BELLOWS

IN *PARASHAT SHOF'TIM*, God commands the Israelites to pursue justice. This week's haftarah reading, the fourth of the seven haftarot of consolation read during the weeks following Tishah B'Av, describes God as a judge.

The prophet Isaiah begs Israel to "shake off the dust and rise up" (Isaiah 52:2). The Israelites need consoling after the destruction of the Temple. They are in exile. They have lost everything and the life they once knew and are in tremendous despair. Isaiah seems to know that true consolation also needs to convey a renewed sense of purpose. Before he urges the people to rise from their despair, he reminds them that they are "pursuers of justice" (Isaiah 51:1). This is their purpose. The world needs them. They are not allowed to give up.

To pursue justice is a sacred and spiritual act that begins with deeply connecting to the self, to others, and to the Holiness, which both surrounds us and dwells within us. To rise from a state of hopelessness, we need to settle into stillness, settling in and settling down. From this place we may then rise again with a new awareness that we have both the capacity and the potential to heal and bring justice into our own lives and the world.

### *Anochi, Anochi!*
#### RABBI DOUGLAS KOHN

*Parashat Shof'tim* opens with its unforgettable pronouncement "Justice, justice shall you pursue" (Deuteronomy 16:20), as powerful for its very message as it is for its poetic repetition: *Tzedek, tzedek tirdof.* This doubling is not only a reinforcement, but also a poetic charge, and the words stick in the emotional memory of the reader.

The text from the Book of Isaiah doubles down on the textual doubling. In our haftarah passage, the prophet commences, *Anochi, Anochi,* "I, I am the One" (Isaiah 51:12); then later, *Hitor'ri, hitor'ri,* "Rouse yourself, rouse yourself!" (51:17); still later, *Uri, uri,* "Awake, awake!" (52:1); and, finally, *Suru, suru,* "Depart, depart!" (52:11).

Though the themes of the Torah and prophetic passages elide in their search for a just society living under God's justice, the genius of these parallel passages lies in their linguistic echoes. Just as one can never forget the sound of *Tzedek, tzedek!,* the reader is captivated by the repetition of repetitions. Shlomo Alkabetz, our mystic of Safed who penned the *L'chah Dodi,* incorporated Isaiah's anaphoras in his signature Shabbat love poem, offering a mnemonic device as well as spiritual inspiration.

Today, as much as seeking a society of God's justice is compelling, finding a salve in the poetic craftsmanship and cadence of our sacred texts, mirroring each other—from Torah to haftarah to siddur—offers spiritual comfort and continuity that buoy and lift up the reader: *Anochi, Anochi!*

## Alternative Haftarah Reading: Correspondence, Moses Seixas to George Washington August 17, 1790

To the President of the United States of America
Sir:

Permit the children of the Stock of Abraham to approach you with the most cordial affection and esteem for your person & merits—and to join with our fellow citizens in welcoming you to NewPort.

With pleasure we reflect on those days—those days of difficulty, & danger, when the God of Israel, who delivered David from the peril of the sword—shielded your head in the day of battle:—and we rejoice to think, that the same Spirit who rested in the Bosom of the greatly beloved Daniel enabling him to preside over the Province of the Babylonian Empire, rests and ever will rest, upon you to discharge the arduous duties of Chief Magistrate in these States.

Deprived as we heretofore have been on the invaluable rights of free Citizens, we now with a deep sense of gratitude to the Almighty disposer of all events behold a Government, erected by the Majesty of the People—a Government which to bigotry gives no sanction, to persecution no assistance—but generously affording all Liberty of conscience, and immunities of Citizenship—deeming every one, of whatever Nation, tongue, or language equal parts of the great government machine; —This so ample and extensive Federal union whose basis is Philanthropy, Mutual confidence and Public Virtue, we cannot but acknowledge to be the work of the Great God, who ruleth in the Armies of Heaven, and among the inhabitants of the Earth, doing whatever seemeth him good.

For all these Blessings of civil and religious liberty which we enjoy under an equal benign administration, we desire to send up our thanks to the Ancient of Days, the great preserver of Men—beseeching him that the Angel who conducted our forefathers through the wilderness into the promised Land, may graciously conduct you through all the difficulties and dangers of this mortal life;—And, when, like Joshua full of days and full of honour, you are gathered to your Fathers, may you be admitted into the Heavenly Paradise to partake of the water of life and the tree of immortality.

Done and Signed by the order of the Hebrew Congregation in NewPort, Rhode Island August 17th 1790.

Moses Seixas, Warden

## Deeming Every One Equal

### Rabbi Douglas Kohn

*Parashat Shof'tim* famously opens with the words *Tzedek, tzedek tirdof*, "Justice, justice shall you pursue!" (Deuteronomy 16:20). This simple yet powerful command has compelled Jews to address seats of power and seek the transformation of our communities for millennia. It also finds an eternal echo in the words of an historic letter from America's earliest days.

Summer 1790: President George Washington was on a "Thank You" tour, visiting the newly established states to offer gratitude for their support during the years of war and anxiety. In Newport, Rhode Island, the Jewish community eagerly welcomed the new leader to their beautiful synagogue, where Washington had met earlier with Rochambeau to plan the campaign on Yorktown. They presented the first president with a timeless and beautifully written missive on the meaning of being Americans and Jews, seeking justice and religious freedom as enshrined in the First Amendment.

Penned by their cantor, Moses Seixas, the letter evokes King David, Joshua, and Daniel; calls the Almighty for blessings; and notably describes "a government which to bigotry gives no sanction, to persecution no assistance." It was a phrase repeated back to the Jews of Newport in Washington's reply of August 21, 1790, and would become a staple in defining the American experiment—in Seixas's words: "deeming every one, of whatever Nation, tongue, or language equal parts of the great government machine."

How can we make sure to live up to those ideals today?

## Alternative Haftarah Reading:
## Wisdom of Solomon 1:1, 8:1-13, 21

Love righteousness, you who judge the earth; think of the Eternal One in goodness, and seek God with integrity of the heart. . . .

Indeed, Wisdom spans the world from end to end mightily and governs all things well. Her I loved and sought after from my youth; I sought to take her for my bride and was enamored of her beauty. She adds to nobility the splendor of companionship with God; even the Ruler of all loved her. For she leads into the understanding of God, and chooses God's works. If riches are desirable in life, what is richer than Wisdom, who produces all things? And if prudence is at work, who in the world is a better artisan than she? Or if one loves righteousness, whose works are virtues, she teaches temperance and prudence, justice and fortitude, and nothing in life is more useful than these. Or again, if one yearns for wide experience, she knows the things of old, and infers the things to come. She understands the turns of phrases and the solutions of riddles; signs and wonders she knows in advance and the outcome of times and ages. So I determined to take her to live with me, knowing that she would be my counselor while all was well, and my comfort in care and grief. Because of her I have glory among the multitudes, and esteem from the elders, though I am but a youth. I shall become keen in judgment, and shall be a marvel before rulers. They will wait while I am silent and listen when I speak; and when I shall speak the more, they will put their hands upon their mouths. Because of her I shall have immortality and leave to those after me an everlasting memory. . . . And knowing that I could not otherwise possess her unless God gave it—and this, too, was prudence, to know whose gift she is—I went to the Eternal One and besought God.

# On Wisdom

### Rabbi Alexander Grodensky

The verses from the Book of Wisdom of Solomon offer a poetic contemplation on Wisdom as the spouse of God. Wisdom is an important virtue that any person, but especially judges, should possess. *Parashat Shof'tim* talks specifically about its importance for judges, kings, and prophets; the text is also used as the scriptural basis for rabbinic authority (Deuteronomy 17:9).

Wisdom is, according to the noncanonical book Wisdom of Solomon, the basis of all virtues. Wisdom, or prudence, is the quality of having experience, knowledge, and good judgment, especially in practical matters: to know what to do, and how and when to do it. The Babylonian Talmud (*Sotah* 3a) states that people commit sins because of their spirit of "foolishness" (*ruach sh'tut*), for if they had the wisdom to know the consequences of their sins, they would not sin at all.

This alternative haftarah reading opens a cycle of four weeks leading up to Rosh HaShanah during the month of Elul. This alternative cycle in turn stands in relation to the overall course of the Jewish year. From Passover to Shavuot, we prepare ourselves to receive Torah; after receiving it on Shavuot, we try to live according to its precepts, at least as a community—the House of Israel—and to build a community based on Torah's lofty values; after Tishah B'Av, we expand our horizon and go beyond the communal to the universal, into the wider world; on Rosh HaShanah, we reflect on our success and failure to live according to Torah.

Especially this time of the year is a time of reflection on our virtues, four of which became classical in the Western world: wisdom, justice, temperance, and courage. While reflecting on these universal virtues that we share with other cultures, we learn to connect to the universal teachings of our tradition. Leading up to Rosh HaShanah, the birthday of humanity, we may use these weeks to deepen our studies of Jewish thought on these virtues and, at the same time, find ways in which we, as members of humanity, may participate in the general moral advancement of all humanity.

# Ki Teitzei
## Deuteronomy 21:10–25:19

## Traditional Haftarah Reading:
## Isaiah 54:1–10

## God Takes You Back in Love
### RABBI AUDREY KOROTKIN, PhD

ALTHOUGH EACH of the seven haftarot of consolation offers the promise of redemption of Israel to their land, this fifth—and shortest—of them compellingly assures permanent redemption between God and Israel: "So now I promise never again to be angry with you or rebuke you. Though the mountains may depart and the hills be removed, My love shall never depart from you" (Isaiah 54:9–10).

This is the renewal of the eternal Abrahamic covenant of unbreakable loyalty (Genesis 15:1–15), not the Siniatic covenant that depends on the behavior of the people. Perhaps now that God has meted out the ultimate punishment of exile for breaching the latter, and now that the people have suffered mightily and repented wholeheartedly, it is time for God to guarantee the people that the initial *b'rit* (covenant) will nevertheless stand forever.

This eternal covenant with the children of Abraham and Sarah is, of course, at the core of Israel's identity—it is a given. Additionally, we see that God gives leave to Isaiah to speak of the Eternal One in clearly anthropomorphic terms: God is showing God's "face" again (Isaiah 54:8) and allows Israel to experience this immediate outpouring of divine love, expressed in human metaphors. Only God's true beloved would receive such a gift.

## The Loving Parent
### CANTOR SARAH GRABINER

Isaiah 54:1–10 constitutes the fifth of the seven haftarot of consolation between Tishah B'Av and Rosh HaShanah, rising up from destruction to renewal. While *Parashat Ki Teitzei* lays out a host of civil and religious laws, dealing with rebellious children to ritual purity, the haftarah reading speaks to our deepest personal experiences.

All human beings know the feeling of shame, loss, and abandonment, be it by a parent, the Divine Presence, or as a result of social or societal pressure and strain. Isaiah invokes the metaphor of childlessness and familial loss, deepening the metaphor of the parent-child relationship between Israel and God that will be emphasized as the High Holy Days approach.

While acknowledging the emotional brokenness we can experience, the prophetic tradition implores us to remember that shame can be overcome and connection reignited. We come away from this haftarah reading with the certainty that change is possible and that better days lie ahead. As Psalm 30:6 declares, "One may lay down weeping at nightfall, but at dawn there are shouts of joy." The God of this passage is a God who promises that love and kindness will always return.

### Alternative Haftarah Reading: Nachmanides on Deuteronomy 21:13

The Book of Deuteronomy provides guidelines on how to take a captive woman as a wife during wartime:

> When you [an Israelite warrior] take the field against your enemies, and the Eternal your God delivers them into your power and you take some of them captive, and you see among the captives a beautiful woman and you desire her and would take her to wife, you shall bring her into your house, and she shall trim her hair, pare her nails, and discard her captive's garb. She shall spend a month's time in your house lamenting her father and mother; after that you may come to her and possess her, and she shall be your wife. (Deuteronomy 21:10–13)

Millennia later, in Spain in the thirteenth century, Nachmanides comments on Deuteronomy 21:13, "lamenting her father and mother":

> She is being forced to convert against her will, and they do not ask her if it is her desire to forsake her faith and be converted to Judaism . . . rather, the [prospective] husband will tell her that she will observe the law of Israel against her will and that she will forsake her own. And this is the reason that "she laments her father and mother," for she is forsaking her people and her god.

# Wholeheartedly and without Any Pressure

*RABBI AUDREY R. KOROTKIN, PhD*

Nachmanides's understanding of why the captive woman essentially enters a period of mourning speaks to the heart of what it should mean to become Jewish—to embrace our faith, our way of life, and our community *wholeheartedly* and not by force. One cannot be forced to convert to Judaism—or really to any religion. We think of King Ferdinand and Queen Isabella's attempt to convert the Jews of Spain to Christianity by force—and then to unleash the Inquisition to persecute, torture, and kill those Conversos suspected of continuing to practice Judaism in secrecy. They ended up expelling all of them in 1492—an expulsion that eventually led to the earliest Sephardic Jewish communities in America.

This captive woman is in mourning, not just for her family but for what they represent: her personal history, her way of life, and her faith. In fact, while the month of formal mourning will pass and she will remove her widow's garb, her former identity remains a part of her forever.

This is why the moment when someone becomes a member of the Jewish people is both a moment of personal choice and a moment of Jewish communal responsibility. We need to make sure that the prospective convert is embracing Judaism *wholeheartedly* and with full knowledge and intent and without any pressure—and then welcome them with open arms.

---

*ELUL, WEEK 2*

## *Alternative Haftarah Reading:*
## *Maimonides,* Mishneh Torah, Hilchot Dei-ot *1:4, 7*

The straight path is the mean disposition found in each and every tendency of all the human tendencies. Such tendency is removed from both extremes an equal distance, and is not nearer to one than to the other. Therefore have the wise of yore commanded that a person should ever review their tendencies, estimate them, and direct them toward the middle-path so that they will be sound in body. How may one do it? One should not be an excitable person, easily angered; nor like the dead without feelings, but adopt a middle-course, not to become indignant, save only at something big which is worthy enough to be angry at, so that the like should not be done another time. Likewise shall one not crave for aught save the things which the body requires, and without which it is impossible to be, as the subject is spoken of: "The righteous eats to their heart's content" (Proverbs 13:25). Likewise shall one not continue to fatigue themself in their affairs, save to acquire what is necessary for them to live on for the time being as the subject is mentioned, saying: "Better the little that the righteous has" (Psalm 37:16). One should not be too close-fisted, nor yet squander their money, but give within the means of their hand, and lend accordingly to the needy. One should not be too optimistic and playful, nor too pessimistic and mournful, but spend all of their days in good cheer and with a pleasant countenance. So should one measure all the rest of their tendencies. And this path is the path of the wise. Every person whose tendencies are mean tendencies of the middle-course is called wise. . . .

And how may a person accustom themself in these tendencies so that they be permanent with them? One should try once, repeat it, and do a third time the things one is called upon to do in harmony with the tendencies of the middle-course, and repeat the practice continuously until the doing it will be accomplished with slight effort, and they will not be burdensome upon them, then will the tendencies be a fixed part of their being. And because the Creator is termed by these attributes which are the middle-way, this way is called the Eternal's way.

# On Temperance

## RABBI ALEXANDER GRODENSKY

Maimonides is one of the vocal proponents of the golden mean, the "middle way," avoiding any extremes. According to him, any one of our tendencies toward an extreme, however good this extreme may be, is inappropriate, whether in physical or in spiritual matters. Following the middle way demands thorough examination, self-control, and temperance in all spheres of life.

The "middle way," or "mediocracy," got its negative connotation at the end of the seventeenth century, when revolutions and scientific breakthroughs began to change the world we inhabit. Earlier on, "mediocracy" was understood as a neutral term, as something well-balanced, secure, predictable, and even beautiful (e.g., the "golden ratio," the highest standard of beauty in the European Renaissance). In fact, mediocracy, in the sense of "balance," does not oppose creativity; on the contrary, only through repetition and attention to detail are we capable of creating pieces of art, technology, and even successful communication.

*Parashat Ki Teitzei* is full of rules restricting uncontrolled passions, especially those directed at sexuality and the exercise of power. Certain regulations are in blatant contradiction to our current understanding of fairness and moderation. This haftarah reading can serve as an opening for a conversation on toxic masculinity (any array of cultural, often unspoken, norms on masculinity and traditional stereotypes of male domination that can harm society and men themselves).

What kind of men do we want to be?

# Ki Tavo
Deuteronomy 26:1–29:8

## Traditional Haftarah Reading:
Isaiah 60:1–22

## Between Light and Darkness
### RABBI JORDAN HELFMAN

The haftarah's promised messianic time, when *shalom* (peace) and *tzedakah* (righteousness) are the governing forces in the life of God's people (Isaiah 60:17), functions as an affirmation of the rewards promised for right conduct in *Parashat Ki Tavo* (Deuteronomy 26:12–19, 28:1–14) and as a balm to the curses promised if God's laws are not followed (Deuteronomy 27:15–26, 28:15–68). This connection may be incidental, as this haftarah reading is in place as the sixth of the seven haftarot of consolation.

The hidden light of God bursts forth in this postexilic poetic vision of a world redeemed, illuminating a people of Israel whose radiance reflects over a world in which violence and destruction are no more. One of the most striking ideas is that "your people shall be righteous, all of them, and possess the land forever" (Isaiah 60:21), which shows that each one of us not only is created in the image of God, but also has the potential to be a righteous luminary.

James Madison, the slaveholding founding father of America, famously wrote in the Federalist Papers (51): "If men were angels, no government would be necessary," and I often find myself trapped in the wary and wearying search for the darkness in humankind. And so, I find great comfort in this alternative vision, the search instead for the righteous light in myself and others, just waiting to be amplified in the days to come.

## The Measure of Our Deeds
### RABBI PAUL J. CITRIN

Magnificent metaphors of light, material riches, and spiritual wholeness infuse the words of the Book of Isaiah. The author of Isaiah chapters 1–39, though, has a heavy message of punishment and doom to deliver. The Isaiah who is the author of chapters 40–55 preaches the future restoration to the Jews of the Babylonian exile (sixth century BCE).

The Isaiah author of this haftarah reading and of chapters 56–66 may have come back with the exiles to the Land of Israel. He envisions a community that basks in God's eternal light of Torah and blessing. The light of Israel's communal commitment to righteousness will attract the attention and presence of foreign nations. Wealth will come with the foreigners who will flock to Zion.

*Parashat Ki Tavo* was very clear that obedience to the divine commandments yields abundant blessing. Curses and dire punishments are the result of injustice and idolatry. In the haftarah reading, Isaiah remembers that Israel's exile was due to the people's disobedience, arousing God's anger. Now that the people of Israel has paid its debt to God and has learned from its punishment, Isaiah shares his vision of a national future blessed by God and of blessing for the entire human family.

The exalted and glorious literary style of this haftarah does not remove for us the theological question: Does God actually reward or punish us physically and materially according to our deeds? Perhaps in Israel's early days as a young ethical monotheistic nation, such a literal theology was necessary to encourage compliance with God's will.

However, only two thousand years ago, Rabbi Ben Azzai taught, "The reward of fulfilling a religious duty is the fulfillment itself" (*Pirkei Avot* 4:2). Such a theology, we moderns and post-moderns may readily accept, thereby basking in the divine light.

## Alternative Haftarah Reading:
## From When Bad Things Happen to Good People,
### by Rabbi Harold S. Kushner

The idea that God gives people what they deserve, that our misdeeds cause our misfortune, is a neat and attractive solution to the problem of evil at several levels, but it has a number of serious limitations. As we have seen, it teaches people to blame themselves. It creates guilt even where there is no basis for guilt. It makes people hate God, even as it makes them hate themselves. And most disturbing of all, it does not even fit the facts. . . .

Belief in a world to come where the innocent are compensated for their suffering can help people endure the unfairness of life in this world without losing faith. But it can also be an excuse for not being troubled or outraged by injustice around us, and not using our God-given intelligence to try to do something about it. The dictate of practical wisdom for people in our situation might be to remain mindful of the possibility that our lives continue in some form after death, perhaps in a form our earthly imaginations cannot conceive of. But at the same time, since we cannot know for sure, we would be well advised to take this world as seriously as we can, in case it turns out to be the only one we will ever have, and to look for meaning and justice here.

# Blessings and Curses

## Rabbi Sharon G. Forman

As the parchment wrapped around the left dowel of the Torah scroll rolls across to the weighty side of the Torah, we reach one of its final portions, a stern warning about human conduct in the Land of Israel:

- The Israelites are required to share their bounty with the Levite, the stranger, the orphan, and the widow.
- Those who commit idolatry, insult parents, change neighbors' borders, misdirect the blind, subvert the rights of the vulnerable, commit sexual offenses, accept bribes, or refuse to uphold God's teachings will be subject to a horrific litany of dramatic curses.
- Blessings will rain upon those who keep the commandments.

In his book about suffering, Rabbi Harold S. Kushner considers the traditional Jewish attitude regarding reward and punishment. The loss of his teenage son to a rare disease inspired him to grapple with the meaning of his faith and Torah. Rabbi Kushner speaks to his readers about the fact that kind, decent people can experience grief, disappointments, and catastrophes that appear almost curse-like. Living a moral life filled with justice and mercy will help a person achieve goodness, yet in spite of everyone's best efforts, bad things also happen to good people.

Rabbi Kushner does not see the inherent unfairness of this human reality as a reason to abandon one's faith or quest for goodness. On the contrary, the Torah portion reminds us of our responsibilities. When God cannot always provide bountiful blessings, we are required to assist our families, communities, and our world through our own actions. Life's difficulties are baked into the fabric of existence, and our pain can often lead us to bring about healing.

## Alternative Haftarah Reading: "Would an All-Powerful God Be Worthy of Worship?" by Rabbi Harold S. Kushner

"Shall not the God of Justice practice what He preaches?" . . . We recall the old trilemma: God is good. God is powerful. Evil is real. Most theologians, amateur and professional, solve the problem by denying the reality of evil. ("There was a good reason for what happened. God knows what He is doing. In the long run, you'll be better off for it.") Some deny that God is good as we have been taught to understand the meaning of this word. ("God cannot be limited by considerations of human need or morality. God's mind works in different ways than ours do.") I choose to solve the trilemma by asking, "What's so great about being all-powerful?" Some power is undoubtedly good, and utterly powerless people may become desperate. But total power is bad. Power isolates. I cannot imagine God worthy of worship who thrives on a diet of groveling obedience. . . . We can fear an all-powerful God, but we cannot love Him, because love exists between equals, entities who if not matched in power at least have a mutual need for each other. . . . [David Griffin] said, "Maybe God is all-powerful but God's power is not the power to coerce but the power to enable." In other words, God can do anything, but only through human and other instruments. I thought that was a remarkable insight, and responded by saying, "That's why, so often in the Bible and afterwards, God is portrayed by fire—at the Burning Bush, in the Eternal Flame before the Ark, etc." Fire is not an object: fire is a process, the process by which the latent energy in a lump of coal or a log of wood is turned into actual energy. God is like fire, liberating the potential energy in each of us. . . . God is not found in the flood or the earthquake; God is found in the ability of people to transcend themselves, to risk their lives to save their neighbor from the flood, to rebuild their ravaged communities after the earthquake.

# On Justice

### Rabbi Alexander Grodensky

The virtue of justice—treating all human beings equally with fairness and kindness, regardless of their status—is the theme of this week. *Parashat Ki Tavo* presents to us one of the most disturbing questions of monotheism:

- The logic of the Deuteronomist is quite straightforward: if you obey the commandments, you will be blessed, and a long list of curses awaits those who disobey.
- The reverse, then, is also true: if you suffer, you deserve it.

This naïve theology not only is foreign to our lived experiences of the suffering of the righteous, but with its potential for blaming the victim and the afflicted, it also maintains any unjust status quo and opens the door for any abuse of power.

Moreover, this theology portraits God as a harsh judge who seems to ignore the most basic principles of justice and adequacy. How can an all-powerful, all-knowing, all-benevolent God allow evil in our world?

Kushner addresses this harmful theology—and shows a way to liberate ourselves from our all-powerful fantasies reflected on God.

When do you fall in line with the Deuteronomistic theology? How would your thoughts and behavior toward others change if you were to give it up?

# *Nitzavim*
## Deuteronomy 29:9–30:20

## Traditional Haftarah Reading:
## Isaiah 61:10–63:9

### Rejoice and Reflect
#### CANTOR SUSAN CARO

This is the seventh of the haftarot of consolation, a pretty upbeat selection from the Book of Isaiah saying that Jerusalem's and Israel's redemption from her enemies is at hand. This is just the sort of message we need to hear right before Rosh HaShanah as we are on our spiritual journey toward wholeness, with more internal work still to do.

In our Torah portion, we are standing, all together, hearing the divine call across the generations to enter the Promised Land in truth. In the haftarah reading, Isaiah begins by calling upon us to rejoice: "I greatly rejoice in the Eternal; My whole being exults in my God" (Isaiah 61:10).

However, this is not just a party; Isaiah speaks about a deep, substantial, lasting joy. In Isaiah 63:9, he says, "Afflicted in their affliction, the divine Presence saved them. In love and pity God redeemed them, carried them, and raised them high in all times past." This, too, is part of the sacred covenant between us and God: When Israel suffers, God suffers with us.

Through embracing joy with our whole being, and knowing that God mirrors our own vulnerability, we become ready for the work of *t'shuvah* (repentance).

Let us both rejoice and reflect.

### Do Not Be Still
#### RABBI ERIC S. GURVIS

We come to Shabbat Nitzavim at a peak moment, standing on the threshold of a new year. Our hearts and souls open wide as we reflect on our lives. As we open ourselves to the possibility that *t'shuvah* (repentance) holds for resetting our lives, relationships, and priorities, both our Torah and haftarah portions call us to account (Deuteronomy 29:9; Isaiah 62:1).

Commenting on Isaiah 62:1, the medieval French commentator Rashi states that "For Jerusalem's sake I will not be still" should be understood as "I will not sit at ease without doing a thing, rather I will be diligent to save them."

In our time, we have borne witness to a rising crescendo of protest and unrest surrounding the lack of equity before the law, the ongoing injustice of racism and prejudice, economic injustice, and more. Our haftarah reminds us that silence is complicity. At the threshold of a new year, it demands not only that we speak out, but also that we take action. We must not only reflect upon our lives and repent for our misdeeds. We must also commit to taking action to create lives of justice.

## *Alternative Haftarah Reading: Ezekiel 18:21–32*

Moreover, if the wicked one repents of all the sins that they committed and keeps all My laws and does what is just and right, they shall live; they shall not die. None of the transgressions they committed shall be remembered against them; because of the righteousness they have practiced, they shall live. Is it My desire that a wicked person shall die?—says the Eternal God. It is rather that they shall turn back from their ways and live.

So, too, if a righteous person turns away from their righteousness and does wrong, practicing the very abominations that the wicked person practiced, shall they live? None of the righteous deeds that they did shall be remembered; because of the treachery they have practiced and the sins they have committed—because of these, they shall die.

Yet you say, "The way of the Eternal is unfair." Listen, O House of Israel: Is My way unfair? It is your ways that are unfair! When a righteous person turns away from their righteousness and does wrong, they shall die for it; they shall die for the wrong they have done. And if a wicked person turns back from the wickedness that they practiced and does what is just and right, such a person shall save their life. Because they took heed and turned back from all the transgressions that they committed, they shall live; they shall not die.

Yet the House of Israel say, "The way of the Eternal is unfair." Are My ways unfair, O House of Israel? It is your ways that are unfair! Be assured, O House of Israel, I will judge each one of you according to their ways—declares the Eternal God. Repent and turn back from your transgressions; let them not be a stumbling block of guilt for you. Cast away all the transgressions by which you have offended, and get yourselves a new heart and a new spirit, that you may not die, O House of Israel. For it is not My desire that anyone shall die—declares the Eternal God. Repent, therefore, and live!

# Turning Back

RABBI AMY L. MEMIS-FOLER

*Nitzavim*, a Torah portion that falls right before Rosh HaShanah, contains the expression "turning," "turning back," or "repenting" multiple times. The theme of *t'shuvah*, "repentance," connects beautifully to this time of year, as well. However, the accompanying traditional haftarah reading is not connected to the portion; it is one of the seven haftarot of consolation following Tishah B'Av. Therefore, this traditional haftarah reading from Isaiah misses the opportunity to inspire us to turn—to turn back and repent—at this time of year.

Ezekiel 18:21–32 offers a terrific parallel to the message of return in *Nitzavim* as well as of the upcoming *Aseret Y'mei T'shuvah* (Ten Days of Repentance). The prophetic text suggests that one who does righteous deeds will live, whereas one who does wicked deeds will die. If, however, one "turns away" from one's wicked deeds, one will certainly live.

*Nitzavim*, in addition to its multiple references to *t'shuvah*, also offers us the lesson to choose life: "I call heaven and earth to witness against you this day: I have put before you life and death, blessing and curse. Choose life—if you and your offspring would live—by loving the Eternal your God, heeding God's commands, and holding fast to [God]" (Deuteronomy 30:19–20). Ezekiel, too, focuses on this message: "For it is not My desire that anyone shall die—declares the Eternal God. Repent, therefore, and live!" (Ezekiel 18:32).

Which acts are true expressions of "turning back" from one's (wicked) ways and toward life?

---

*ELUL, WEEK 4*

## Alternative Haftarah Reading: Nehemiah 6:1-13, 15

When word reached Sanballat, Tobiah, Geshem the Arab, and the rest of our enemies that I had rebuilt the wall and not a breach remained in it—though at that time I had not yet set up doors in the gateways—Sanballat and Geshem sent a message to me, saying, "Come, let us get together in Kephirim in the Ono valley"; they planned to do me harm. I sent them messengers, saying, "I am engaged in a great work and cannot come down, for the work will stop if I leave it in order to come down to you." They sent me the same message four times, and I gave them the same answer. Sanballat sent me the same message a fifth time by his servant, who had an open letter with him. Its text was: "Word has reached the nations, and Geshem too says that you and the Jews are planning to rebel—for which reason you are building the wall—and that you are to be their king. Such is the word. You have also set up prophets in Jerusalem to proclaim about you, 'There is a king in Judah!' Word of these things will surely reach the king; so come, let us confer together."

I sent back a message to him, saying, "None of these things you mention has occurred; they are figments of your imagination"—for they all wished to intimidate us, thinking, "They will desist from the work, and it will not get done." Now strengthen my hands!

Then I visited Shemaiah son of Delaiah son of Mehetabel when he was housebound, and he said,

> "Let us meet in the House of God, inside the sanctuary,
> and let us shut the doors of the sanctuary, for they are coming to kill you,
> by night they are coming to kill you."

I replied, "Will a man like me take flight? Besides, who such as I can go into the sanctuary and live? I will not go in." Then I realized that it was not God who sent him, but that he uttered that prophecy about me—Tobiah and Sanballat having hired him—because he was a hireling, that I might be intimidated and act thus and commit a sin, and so provide them a scandal with which to reproach me. . . .

The wall was finished on the twenty-fifth of Elul, after fifty-two days.

# On Courage

### RABBI ALEXANDER GRODENSKY

The last week before Rosh HaShanah is devoted to the virtue of courage, or fortitude, which entails being neither timid nor foolhardy, but doing the right thing *under all circumstances*.

In *Parashat Nitzavim* and the following *parashah*, *Vayeilech*, Moses encourages the people to stay on the chosen way under all circumstances and empowers them and the next generation of leadership to be strong and resolute. In this haftarah reading, we meet Nehemiah, who persistently resists the pressure of his enemies during the implementation of his mission to rebuild the wall of Jerusalem.

The wall is not only important for the defense of the city—it should also be read as a symbol for inner strength and resilience.

# *Vayeilech*/Shabbat Shuvah
## Deuteronomy 31:1–30

## Traditional Haftarah Reading:
## Isaiah 55:5–56:8

## Traditional Haftarah Reading for Shabbat Shuvah:
## Hosea 14:2–10; Micah 7:18–20; Joel 2:15–27

## That Which We Utter

### Rabbi Shira Gluck

U*unshal'mah farim s'fateinu*—One of the most evocative images in the traditional haftarah reading for Shabbat Shuvah, this curious phrase in Hosea 14:3 has been subject to two common translations since antiquity: "We shall offer the bulls of our lips," a reference to the sacrifice of bovines in the Temple precinct; or, as a few ancient interpretations put it, "the fruits of our lips." Whichever translation you prefer, both have the same essential meaning: that which we utter is the most precious offering we can bring to the Divine.

Notice that it doesn't say "prayers," "praises," or "supplications." Just like ritual sacrifice, fixed liturgy is at risk of becoming rote and sterile—disconnected from the spirit or sentiment of the individual—and our texts caution us against this (see *Mishnah B'rachot* 4:4).

This warning is a thread that runs through the entire season of *t'shuvah*, from the weeping and wailing of Tishah B'Av to the potent cry of Elul's daily reading of Psalm 27: "My heart calls to you: 'Seek my face' and I will seek Your face, O God." It is exquisitely articulated in the story of Hannah pouring out her heart before God in the haftarah reading for the first day of Rosh HaShanah, and culminates in the haftarah of Yom Kippur morning in which God expresses contempt for empty rituals and performed piety absent of true feeling.

In this reading, the prophet Hosea reminds us that the most meaningful offerings we can bring are those of our own lips, minds, and hearts—seeking personal connection and return to the Divine unmediated by scripted rituals.

# Take Words with You

*RABBI DR. SHMULY YANKLOWITZ*

On Shabbat Shuvah, the Shabbat that falls between Rosh HaShanah and Yom Kippur, the tradition is to read a haftarah portion assembled from three different books of the Prophets: Hosea, Micah, and Joel. Usually, we read from only one book for a haftarah portion, but here we are allowed to combine teachings from *T'rei Asar* (the Twelve "Minor" Prophets). This haftarah is truly an amazing moment in the Jewish calendar. It allows us, on the Shabbat in between the holiest of days in the Jewish calendar, to reflect on our direction for the coming year. The theme can be summed up by the first word of the haftarah, for which this Shabbat is named: *Shuvah!* Return! (Hosea 14:2).

The haftarah instructs us to "take words with you" (Hosea 14:3). We have no belongings, memories, or awards to show. But if we leave our place and turn back, turn around, and turn inward, what shall we bring? What are we allowed to take on such a journey? We just bring our words: our transcendent words of prayer, our difficult words of apology, our words of yearning; words from the mind, words from the heart. We are, at this time of year, our words. But these words only carry integrity if they are accompanied by renewed actions. In our behavior, we must elevate the vulnerable and downtrodden, advocate for the forgotten, and bring light during times of darkness.

We return to God because God is our model for living with mercy. It is only through kindness that we are granted the ability and opportunity to transform ourselves. It is precisely this element of freedom—the freedom to change, to grow, to become!—that makes us godly. By returning to God, we return to the well of deepest human potential.

## Alternative Haftarah Reading:
## Letter by Rabbi Stephen S. Wise, 1942

I am almost demented over my people's grief... and still I must add, I do not lose faith—my faith that we will, in part, because of these awful sacrifices, march on to a decenter, juster, and, it may be, a warless world. Faith, as we both know, isn't a thing to be reasoned about. One has it, or one has not. You and I both have it. Both of us see the Divine, even from far off, toward which all creation moves, though it move haltingly, painfully and, perhaps it must be so, sacrificially.

# Faith Isn't a Thing to Be Reasoned About

*RABBI STEPHEN A. WISE*

Shabbat Shuvah is an auspicious time, between Rosh HaShanah and Yom Kippur, to peer deeply into our souls as we are in the midst of *Aseret Y'mei T'shuvah*, the Ten Days of Repentance. This Shabbat marks the midway point—a time to ask: Have we done enough? Is there time to do more? As we consider our lives in the grand scheme of things, we might take the opportunity to delve into the words of Rabbi Stephen S. Wise, founder of the Jewish Institute of Religion and the Stephen Wise Free Synagogue, among other achievements as a leading American rabbi during the 1920s and '30s.

Wise's thousands of letters, sermons, and thoughts were born out of a profoundly religious spirit. In the midst of World War II, he received bits of information about the horrors of the Holocaust and the treatment of his brothers and sisters in Europe. Sadly, few heeded his warnings of disaster for world Jewry. In 1942, he wrote the above to his friend John Haynes Holmes.

In this prophetic paragraph, Wise acknowledges his deep sadness over the murder of Jews in Europe but also denies a loss of faith. He hopes and prays for the day when war will end, while acknowledging that "faith isn't a thing to be reasoned about." We might wonder, especially as we stand between Rosh HaShanah and Yom Kippur, about our faith, about the presence of God in our lives, if our repentance really matters. Wise would remind us that the Divine sometimes is far off, but we are all in some ways connected through the act of Creation. As our liturgy says, God determines "who shall live and who shall die"; we cannot possibly comprehend our existence and the time we have. But we certainly have a role to play in the script of what befalls us. We can make moments of clarity by connecting with those we hurt, by apologizing, by forgiving others if they approach us in sincerity. On this Shabbat, let us take the opportunity to renew our faith, in our fellow human beings, in God, and in ourselves.

## Alternative Haftarah Reading:
## "The Place Where We Are Right," by Yehuda Amichai

From the place where we are right
flowers will never grow
in the spring.

The place where we are right
is hard and trampled
like a yard.

But doubts and loves
dig up the world
like a mole, a plow.
And a whisper will be heard in the place
where the ruined
house once stood.

# Spiritual Gardeners

## *Rabbi Shira Gluck*

Shabbat Shuvah is the fulcrum of our High Holy Days—a turning point between Rosh HaShanah, the Day of Judgment, and Yom Kippur, the Day of Atonement. On this day, we entreat God to move from the seat of judgment to the seat of compassion so our *t'shuvah* may be accepted. But Yom Kippur grants us atonement only for sins against God, not for those against our fellow humans (*Mishnah Yoma* 8:9). The work of *Aseret Y'mei T'shuvah* (Ten Days of Repentance, from Rosh HaShanah to Yom Kippur) is to seek forgiveness from others and—perhaps the more difficult task—to offer forgiveness to those who seek it from us. In both cases, we, like God, must be willing to move ourselves from a position of judgment to one of compassion.

Amichai diagnoses the desire to be right as a condition that leaves us barren. Earth that is trampled down and hardened does not allow any sprout of life to break through; humans who are unyielding will never grow. The trampled courtyard is a powerful metaphor for the way we harden ourselves to the perspectives and, ultimately, the humanity of others. When we are convinced that we are right and someone else is wrong, we run roughshod over the possibility of connection. Always insisting on being right, we become self-righteous. Amichai's remedy for this ailment is to loosen our grip and allow for a healthy amount of self-doubt. We don't always need to be right, and chances are that over the course of our lives, each of us is right and wrong in equal measure. But when we make space for uncertainty, we also make room for love. This is the essence of the Ten Days of Repentance: to open our hearts to the possibility that we are not perfect, that we are not always right, and to seek repair. Thus we are able to both ask others for forgiveness *and* give it to those who ask it of us.

On Shabbat Shuvah, we are called to be spiritual gardeners—to break up the hardened earth of our hearts, pull out the roots of certainty, and plant seeds of love.

# Haazinu
## Deuteronomy 32:1–52

## Traditional Haftarah Reading:
## II Samuel 22:1–51

## Songs of Salvation

*Cantor Kenneth J. Feibush*

Parashat Haazinu contains the Song of Moses, a poem written in a special two-column layout with short verses. Moses's poem is part of the final lesson before the Children of Israel enter the Promised Land after forty years of wandering in the desert. He recounts how God demonstrates love by redeeming the Children of Israel from slavery and leads them to defeat many enemies. This bookends the Song at the Sea in Exodus 15:1–18, which extols God's miracle of parting the sea and the victory over Pharaoh's armies forty years prior.

The reading from II Samuel is also called the Song of David. Its layout is similar to the Song of Moses: a special poetic layout with short verses. This poem offers similar messages too: God as salvation, God defeating foes, and wonder at God's might. Similar to the Song of Moses, the Song of David stands out from the rest of II Samuel in format and language and could possibly be interpolated from another source. Indeed, the structure is nearly identical to Psalm 18.

There is a special connection between this haftarah and the calendar, since it is often read around the High Holy Days. We look inward, reflect on our past, and start to work on self-improvement for the year to come. To attune us for the High Holy Days, we too sing special praises to God, as David does in his song.

This is also the time of the year when the school year begins, and many begin new jobs—two exciting but daunting prospects. We might, as David does, call out from our personal depths and anxiety and look to God for support. For David, God was the main player behind all events. So, God would also be the one to deliver him from personal despair.

However, we live in an era shaped by postmodernist thought and the covenant theology as proposed by Dr. Eugene Borowitz (1924–2016): While we know that we have individual autonomy, we still believe in an evolving relationship with

God. Just like any relationship, it ebbs and flows with different experiences in our life. Sometimes we are able to connect to God's saving powers; sometimes we are not. With all the changes in our lives, the steadiness of our reading cycles allows us to take stock of ourselves, work on our weaknesses, draw comfort from our strengths—and sometimes break into praise. In those moments of praise, we can emulate David with our own words, using spontaneous prayers of the heart or the liturgy of our tradition for inspiration.

## God Is a Rock

### RABBI AUDREY S. POLLACK

Both the Torah portion and the haftarah reading consist of poems of praise of God's greatness and generosity. God's song to the Israelites in *Haazinu*, recited by Moses, reflects on God's protection in providing sustenance despite the people's many faults, weaknesses, and imperfections. God remains faithful and reliable. David's song in the haftarah is a hymn of praise and thanksgiving he sings to God after having been saved from the hands of his enemies.

Both songs describe God as *tzur* (rock), connoting stability, shelter, security, and protection. In the *parashah*, God is praised for protecting the whole nation, despite the peoples' failings; in the haftarah reading, David sings of his personal deliverance from his enemies as a reward for his faithfulness to God.

Every time we move from praying the *Sh'ma* and Its Blessings to praying the *Amidah*, the "Standing Prayer," we chant *Tzur Yisrael, kumah b'ezrat Yisrael*, "Rock of Israel, rise in support of Israel," and we rise and step into an even more intimate conversation with God (*Mishkan T'filah*, 72).

The prayer for the State of Israel begins with the words *Tzur Yisrael v'go-alo*, "Rock and Redeemer of Israel" (*Mishkan T'filah*, 377).

Our relationship with God is both personal and communal. The strength and stability of that relationship is the foundation on which we live our faith.

## *Alternative Haftarah Reading:*
## *Psalm 90*

A prayer of Moses, man of God.

Adonai, You have been a refuge for us in each generation.
Before the mountains were birthed
And You had labored with the earth and the world—
From the first eternity to the last, You are God.

You return each of us to the crushed state from which You made us,
From which You say, "Return, children of the earth."
For a thousand years in Your eyes
Are like yesterday, which passes;
They are like a short watch in the night.
You sweep them away—asleep are they;
In the morning like grass they sprout;
In the morning it blossoms and sprouts,
In the evening it is cut off and dries up.
For we are consumed in Your anger,
We are terrified by Your wrath.
You have set our iniquities before You,
Our secret sins, into the light of Your countenance.
For all our days are spent in Your wrath;
We finish up our years like a sigh.

The days of our years have seventy years in them—
With strength, eighty years—
Their pride is toil and sorrow,
It is shorn quickly, and we fly off.
Who knows the strength of Your anger,
Or Your fury, as fierce as the fear of You?
So let us know how to make our days count,
And sum them up in a heart of wisdom.

Return, Adonai—how long?!
Have compassion on Your servants!
Satisfy us every morning with Your covenantal love,
That we may sing for joy, delighting in all our days!
Delight us in proportion to the days You have afflicted us,
To the years we have looked at pain.
Let Your work appear to Your servants,
And Your glory be over Your children.
Let the pleasantness of Adonai our God be upon us,
And the work of our hands—establish it upon us;
The work of our hands, establish it upon us.

# Making a Holy Difference

*RABBI DAVID E. OSTRICH*

In the Torah reading, Moses's last message to Israel reminds us of the wonders of our relationship with God. Selfless and dedicated to our holy mission, Moses talks about God instead of himself.

In Psalm 90, "A prayer of Moses, the man of God" (verse 1), Moses parallels this message with a prayer: "Return, Adonai—how long?! Have compassion on Your servants!" (verse 13). Moses prays that everyone might have a sense of God's presence in their lives: "Let the pleasantness of Adonai our God be upon us" (verse 17). Just as he has felt God's guiding spirit in his life, he yearns for everyone to feel a similar connection with the Divine.

He also prays, on behalf of all the Jewish people, that our contributions to *tikkun olam*, the "perfection of the world," will make a difference: "The work of our hands, establish it upon us" (verse 17). May we make a holy difference in our world.

## *Alternative Haftarah Reading: "Two Candles," by Rabbi Zoë Klein*

On Shabbat we would light two candles,
one for remembering Shabbat
and one for observing Shabbat.
Tonight, we light two candles.
   This one is for Building One,
    and this one is for Building Two,
this one for the Pentagon,
and this one for Pennsylvania,
   This one is for those on American Airlines,
    and this one for those on United Airlines.
this one for the hundreds of firefighters
and this one for the hundreds of police,
   this one for all the men
    and this one for all the women
this one for all the girls,
and this one for all the boys,
   and these candles for the husband and wife
   who leapt out of the tower holding hands,
this one for our luck running out,

this one for the New York skyline,
   this one for the walking wounded,
   this one for the critically wounded,
this one for the survivors,
this one for the dead,
   this candle for Building One,
   this candle for Building Two.

# God, Shabbat, and the Rekindling of Life

### RABBI SARA RAE PERMAN

Most of the Torah portion *Haazinu* is written as two columns. The two columns came to represent to me the Twin Towers. In 2001, *Haazinu* was read on the Shabbat after Yom Kippur (September 29), a little more than two weeks after the horror that shook our county. The traditional haftarah reading, II Samuel 22:1–51, is a song of David after he was rescued from his enemies, including King Saul. In both the Torah portion and the haftarah reading, God is described as a rock.

The almost three thousand deaths that took place that September morning left many of us asking, "Why?"; many of us trying to understand, "Where was God?"

Rabbi Klein wrote this poem to bring solace to those who filled our synagogues on the Shabbat after 9/11. We read *Haazinu* exactly eighteen days after the attack on our country. The number eighteen, written in Hebrew letters as חי, represents "life." The Torah and haftarah readings remind us that in times of unbearable pain God is our rock and that Shabbat too can bring us comfort at the end of a week of pain. With God as our rock and with Shabbat, we can rediscover life.

# V'zot Hab'rachah
## Deuteronomy 33:1–34:12

## Traditional Haftarah Reading:
## Joshua 1:1–18

### Be Strong and of Good Courage
#### RABBI JAY ASHER LEVINE

THE HAFTARAH reading accompanying the Simchat Torah reading *V'zot Hab'rachah*, unique among the prophetic readings, not only echoes the Torah portion thematically, but continues the story directly. The first chapter of the first book of Prophets follows the last chapters of Torah. In the Torah portion, Moses dies before reaching the Promised Land, having been told earlier, "You shall not go across" (Deuteronomy 31:2). In the haftarah reading, Joshua is instructed to "come across" (Joshua 1:2). A key theme recurs throughout the reading: "be strong and of good courage" (Joshua 1:6–7, 9, 18). Moses, the servant of God, has died, but Joshua, servant of the servant, will lead the people to success. Moses leaves his teaching to Joshua, and Joshua contemplates it day and night.

On Simchat Torah, we ritualize a paradox: After we read about Moses's death, we immediately return to read the opening words of the Book of Genesis. The cycle of Torah is eternal, inhabiting mythological time. Yet through the haftarah reading, we boldly step forward and out of that mythical cycle, entering the historical arc leading to our present moment.

We know that the Promised Land will be imperfect, that exile is a possibility, and that encountering the present with all its hope and suffering and joy requires courage and bravery. Through it all, we are never alone, "for I, the Eternal your God, am with you wherever you go" (Joshua 1:9).

### Be Strong and of Good Courage
#### RABBI DANA EVAN KAPLAN, PhD

The Torah portion *V'zot Hab'rachah*, which is read on Simchat Torah, is the final portion in the Book of Deuteronomy and ends with Moses's death after God lets him see the land of milk and honey that will be given to the Children of Israel.

Joshua, son of Nun, is filled with the spirit of wisdom and is therefore accepted by the Children of Israel as Moses's successor. Nevertheless, the Torah ends by stating that never again would there be a prophet like Moses, who had known God face to face.

As the haftarah reading, the beginning of the Book of Joshua continues the Torah's chronicling of the Children of Israel's search for the Holy Land. The transition from Torah to haftarah is driven home by the repeated use of the expression *chazak ve-ematz*, which means "be strong and of good courage." God urges Joshua to be strong and of good courage so that he can lead the Children of Israel into the land of milk and honey, as well as to observe faithfully all of the Torah and not to be afraid or disheartened—God will be with Joshua wherever he goes. This parallels the three times that Moses encourages Joshua with the same words in the Book of Deuteronomy (3:28 and 31:7, 23).

We need to take this exhortation to heart. "Be strong and of good courage" is one of the most profound teachings in the entire Torah. By spending concentrated time focusing on these character traits, we can determine what it means to us to be strong and to be brave and how we can take steps to put these exhortations into action.

## *Alternative Haftarah Reading: Micah 4:1-10*

In the days to come,
the Mount of the Eternal's House shall stand
firm above the mountains;
and it shall tower above the hills.
The peoples shall gaze on it with joy,
and the many nations shall go and shall say:
"Come,
Let us go up to the Mount of the Eternal,
to the House of the God of Jacob;
that God may instruct us in God's ways,
and that we may walk in God's paths."
For instruction shall come forth from Zion,
the word of the Eternal from Jerusalem.
Thus God will judge among the many peoples,
and arbitrate for the multitude of nations,
however distant;
and they shall beat their swords into plowshares
and their spears into pruning hooks.

Nation shall not take up
sword against nation;
they shall never again know war;
but every person shall sit
under their grapevine or fig tree
with no one to disturb them.
For it was the God of heaven's hosts who spoke.
Though all the peoples walk
each in the names of its gods,
we will walk
in the name of the Eternal our God
forever and ever.

In that day
—declares the Eternal—
I will assemble the lame [sheep]
and will gather the outcast
and those I have treated harshly;
and I will turn the lame into a remnant
and the expelled into a populous nation.
And the Eternal will reign over them on Mount Zion
now and for evermore.

And you, O Migdal-eder,
outpost of Fair Zion,
it shall come to you:
The former monarchy shall return—
the kingship of Fair Jerusalem.

Now why do you utter such cries?
Is there no king in you,
have your advisors perished,
that you have been seized by writhing
like a woman in travail?
Writhe and scream, Fair Zion,
like a woman in travail!
For now you must leave the city
and dwell in the country—
and you will reach Babylon.
There you shall be saved,
there the Eternal will redeem you
from the hands of your foes.

# Educate, Recognize, and Engage, Engage, Engage

*Rabbi Burt E. Schuman*

Before his death, Moses has transferred his authority to Joshua to ensure continuity. Moses's final words to the Israelites are words of blessing and profound hope for their future.

The passage from the Book of Micah is also a vision of hope and reconciliation. What distinguishes the passage from Micah from the Torah portion is its vision not only of peace and continuity, but of pluralism and change: "Though all the peoples walk each in the names of its gods, we will walk in the name of the Eternal our God, forever and ever" (Micah 4:5). Micah promises that "every person shall sit under their grapevine or fig tree with no one to disturb them" (4:4), a huge and powerful *nechemta* (comfort) in an age of such suffering and pain.

Our traditional perspectives on American history, including Jewish history, have often been skewed by false narratives. In my generation, we were exposed to many of those because our teachers and textbooks presented a patriotic ethos imbuing "patriotic" and "American" values. All too often, those narratives were flawed and unrealized.

- In the South, "Reconstruction" *de jure* enfranchised large numbers of African Americans, gave them the right to vote, offered educational opportunities at every level from from elementary education and basic literacy to university degrees, and gave rise to a new professional and political class. In reality, this so-called era of "Redemption" was a time of disenfranchisement, economic oppression, brutality, violence, and wholesale murder.
- Native Americans were increasingly deprived of their culture.
- Latinx Americans were increasingly impoverished and subject to increasing exploitation and isolation.
- The so-called model minorites of Chinese, Japanese, and Korean immigrants were subject to exclusionary and discriminatory laws and riots and—in the case of Japanese-born citizens and Japanese Americans on the West Coast—suffered brutal conditions and humiliations in internment camps.
- Beginning in the mid-nineteenth century, succeeding generations of Jews faced discrimination in hotels and other public accommodations, at the workplace, and in many neighborhoods, especially planned neighborhoods in cities and suburbs.
- Other groups of immigrants, like Italians, Poles, Hungarians, Croatians, Romanians, and Greeks, suffered intense discrimination

caused by the fears and hatred of Nordic "old-stock" Americans, which led to severe immigration restrictions in both 1921 and 1924.

We continue to witness the horrors of systemic, institutional racism, resegregation, homelessness, food insecurity, depressed wages, dying industrial and farming communities, and the most dysfunctional system of medical care in the industrialized world. We need to educate ourselves, follow the lead of neighborhood activists, recognize our own inherent privileges, and engage, engage, and engage.

Let us march to the tunes of *Gesher Tzar M'od*, *Ani V'atah*, and *Olam Chesed Yibaneh*, daring ourselves to actively bring about a less fearful and kinder world. Let us march to the words of the prophet Micah: "All the peoples [will] walk in the names of its gods; we will walk in the name of the Eternal our God forever and ever" (Micah 4:5).

## *Alternative Haftarah Reading:*
## *Babylonian Talmud, B'rachot 16b*

When Rabbi Elazar finished his prayer, he said as follows: "May it be Your will, Eternal our God, that You cause love and friendship, peace and camaraderie to dwell in our lot. Make our borders numerous with students, cause us to succeed to our ends with hope, and put our portion in the Garden of Eden. Set up for us good friends and a good inclination in Your world. May we rise early and may we find the expectations of our hearts to have awe in Your name, and may the manifestation of our souls come before You for good."

When Rabbi Yochanan finished his prayer, he said as follows: "May it be Your will, Eternal our God, that You notice our shame and see our troubles, that You dress Yourself with Your mercy, cover Yourself with strength, and wrap Yourself with Your loving-kindness. Strengthen Yourself with Your grace, and may Your attributes of goodness and humility come before You." . . .

When Rav finished his prayer, he said as follows: "May it be Your will, Eternal our God, that You give us long life, a life of peace, a life of goodness, a life of blessing, a life of livelihood, a life of personal freedom, a life with fear of wrongdoing, a life without shame or humiliation, a life of wealth and honor, a life in which we have love for Torah and awe for heaven, a life in which You fulfill for us all the wishes of our heart for good."

# To Deepen Our Own Prayers

### RABBI JESSICA K. BAROLSKY

*Parashat V'zot Hab'rachah* contains the final chapters and verses of the Torah, the end of Moses's final blessing to the Israelites. This alternative haftarah reading from the Babylonian Talmud, *B'rachot* 16b, is a collection of blessings that different rabbis said at the end of their daily prayers.

We often think of prayers and blessings as scripted. We can open any siddur and find a full service of prayers; Jewish tradition has fixed blessings for almost every occasion; in any synagogue across the world, we recite many of the same words. But blessings have not always been so fixed; the ancient rabbis each had their own unique way to end their prayers each day. The Talmud preserves not only Rabbinic discussions about Jewish law, but also stories about the rabbis who had those discussions and those rabbis' personal customs. Each one of them, we learn, had a different way to conclude their daily prayers. Their words can guide us to consider different perspectives on prayer, reminding us of the importance of personal prayer.

Each of us comes to pray with different needs, perspectives, anxieties, and desires, and our prayers should reflect our differences. May their words inspire us to deepen our own prayers, to form the words that express our deepest feelings, fears, hopes, and gratitude.

# Haftarot for the Traditional Jewish Calendar

# Shabbat Rosh Chodesh
## Traditional Haftarah Reading:
## Isaiah 66:1–13, 23

## Giving Birth to Light
### Rabbi Emily E. Segal

In this special haftarah reading, Isaiah looks ahead from the Babylonian exile to the rebirth of the Israelites and to Jerusalem restored. God is portrayed as a midwife, coaching Jerusalem through labor, enabling her to (re)birth the people Israel without a single pang of pain. Jerusalem then nurses the Israelites with milk of consolation and glory.

This strong, feminine imagery is striking and infrequent in *Tanach*, especially in reference to God, and therefore makes for a strong link to the holiday of Rosh Chodesh, traditionally considered a special holiday for women (see *Pirkei D'Rabbi Eliezer* 45, referencing Exodus 32:3). As the month begins with the tiniest sliver of light emerging from darkness, we are drawn to consider what might be delivered through this narrow passage into the days ahead.

At all times, even in our times of darkness—as in the moments just before the month begins—we have been growing and nurturing light within ourselves: the light of peace; the light of learning; the light of love. Through our labor pangs, with God as our midwife, we can bring that light out into the world, illuminating it all.

## Seeing the Gifts of Everyone
### Rabbi Elizabeth Bahar

Chapter 66, the final chapter of the Book of Isaiah, brings to conclusion prophecies mentioned in chapter 1 of the book as well as the Deutero-Isaiah prophecies (chapters 40–66).

Read on the Sabbath coinciding with the beginning of a new lunar month, this haftarah reading is linked to the festival of Rosh Chodesh primarily because of Isaiah 66:23: "And from new moon to new moon. . . ." So as not to end the haftarah on a negative note, as verse 24 depicts the consequences of those who rebel against God, verse 23 is repeated as we complete the reading in our synagogues out loud.

"And from among them too I will choose priests and Levites, says the Eternal One" (Isaiah 66:21). Who is Isaiah speaking about here? He is speaking about non-Jews who come to worship with the Israelites. He says that he will make some of them priests and Levites. Isaiah's voice yells at us that we are all worthy of God's love. People who have the desire to pray together shall do so. In a messianic era yet to be entered, all of us will be *inspired* to work together. Therefore, a new day will come when we will see the gifts of every group of people regardless of where they come from in the world—regardless of race or class. On this day, we will go on a pilgrimage, and all the nations will come to Jerusalem to worship God on the Sabbaths and new moons.

Perhaps, if we allow the radical words of Isaiah to reach us, we will not need to wait until the nations can come to worship in Jerusalem, but will instead work every day to ensure that everyone feels welcome and that every voice is heard.

## *Alternative Haftarah Reading: Psalm 104:19–35*

God made a moon for seasons;
the sun knows the time to go in.
You decree darkness—and it is night,
when all the creatures of the forest crawl about,
the young lions roar for their carrion,
and seek their food from God.
The sun rises—they withdraw,
and spread out in their lairs.

Human beings go forth to their work,
to their labor, until evening.

How many are Your works, Adonai!
All of them You made with wisdom!
The earth is full of Your creatures.

This is the sea—great and many hands wide!
There—creeping things without number,
wild things, little ones and big ones.
There go the ships,
and Leviathan, this creature You formed to play in the sea—

all of them wait for You
to give them their food in its time.

You give to them, they go gathering,
You open Your hand—they are given good aplenty.

You hide Your face, they are terrified,
You cut off their breath—they perish,
and to their dust they return.
You send forth Your breath, they are created anew
and You renew the face of the ground.
Let the glory of Adonai last forever,
let Adonai rejoice in divine works,
who looks upon the earth and it trembles,
who touches the mountains and they smoke.

Let me sing to Adonai during my lifetime,
let me sing praise to God while I still am!
Let my meditation rest sweetly upon the Holy One—
I will rejoice in Adonai!
Let sinners cease from the earth
and wicked people be no more;
Praise Adonai, O my being,
*Hall'lu-Yah*, Praise Adonai!

# Filling the World with Song

### *Rabbi Debra J. Robbins*

The Torah portion for Rosh Chodesh is filled with the messy details of animal sacrifices offered in biblical times at the start of each new month. Those sacred gifts of the people were turned into smoke—a prayer of gratitude to God—by the priests.

The traditional haftarah reading is the concluding chapter of Isaiah, chosen for its penultimate verse, the prophetic vision that "from new moon to new moon . . . all flesh shall come to worship [God]" (Isaiah 66:23). Psalm 104 (read in its entirety in some communities following the Psalm of the Day) offers a soaring vision of the majesty of the world while at the same placing the power to praise back into the hearts and mouths of each person.

Each month, a sliver of moon emerges. Each moon is unique, expanding and contracting to keep pace with the sun (Psalm 104:19) and secure our human holy days in their places. The Hand of Holiness (104:28), like gravity, holds all of creation in one holy cycle (104:24). We feel fear and grief (104:29), embrace renewal as the earth does (104:30), tremble like mountains, and rejoice (104:32). We sing with voice, breath, and deeds (104:33) and turn from wrong (104:35), for this is our work (104:23). We give thanks to our Creator, wrapped in light (104:2). This month, each month, at each season of our lives, we affirm with joy: With all my soul, with all I've got, in the face of a universe of grandeur, in awe, I praise: "Hallelujah!" (104:35).

The Rabbis of the Talmud imagined that some angels offer words of *k'dushah* (holiness) only once every seven years; some once in fifty years; some only once, with only a single word. But we humans can fill our mouths and minds, yes, our entire world, with words of holiness, with psalms, prayers, poems, and songs of praise for God at all times (Babylonian Talmud, *Chulin* 91b). While it is possible any time and every day, there is no time more powerful to rise to the challenges of increasing *k'dushah* in our lives and our world than as each new month begins, on Rosh Chodesh, with words from Psalm 104.

## *Alternative Haftarah Reading: "Split at the Root," by Adrienne Rich*

Sometimes I feel I have seen too long from too many disconnected angles: white, Jewish, anti-Semite, racist, anti-racist, once-married, lesbian, middle-class, feminist, expatriate Southerner, split at the root: that I will never bring them whole. I would have liked . . . to bring together the meanings of anti-Semitism and racism as I have experienced them and as I believe they intersect in the world beyond my life. But I'm not able to do this yet. . . . I feel the history of denial within me like an injury, a scar—for assimilation has affected my perceptions, those early lapses in meaning, those blanks, are with me still. My ignorance can be dangerous to me, and to others. Yet we can't wait for the undamaged to make our connections for us; we can't wait to speak until we are wholly clear and righteous. There is no purity, and in our lifetimes, no end to this process . . . every aspect of my identity will have to be engaged. The poet who knows that beautiful language can lie, that the oppressor's language sometimes sounds beautiful. The woman trying, as part of her resistance, to clean up her act.

## On Women and the Moon

### Cantor Abbe Lyons

Each of us has a multifaceted identity within a much larger context. In "Split at the Root," Adrienne Rich challenges us not to shy away from the contradictions and intersections of our identities and to respond to how they shape us and our lived experiences.

The holiday of Rosh Chodesh, the new moon, is, in its own way, split at the root. Portrayed as a reward for the refusal of the Israelite women to contribute their earrings to the idolatry of the Golden Calf (*Pirkei D'Rabbi Eliezer* 45:4–5), this women's holiday is quite different from Shabbat, when women typically end up being responsible for chores such as preparing meals, doing the dishes, and taking care of children. In fact, "women" as a category are conspicuously absent from the Ten Commandments, which specify that you (masculine singular), your sons and daughters, manservants and maidservants, and animals must rest on Shabbat. Rosh Chodesh can inspire women to take the time to rest; at the same time, it reminds us that we, as women, are somehow in a biblical category separate and unequal to others.

Adrienne Rich shows us the importance of continuing to explore, appreciate, and critique not only the festival of Rosh Chodesh, but the ways human beings both uplift and oppress one another across the generations.

When do you find tradition oppressing? When do you find it uplifting?

# Shabbat Machar Chodesh
## Traditional Haftarah Reading:
## I Samuel 20:18–42

## Love That Grows
### Rabbi Cantor Kim Harris

ON THE SHABBAT preceding the new moon, we read this poignant story of deep and growing love, which begins on the morrow of the new moon.

In a field (a place symbolizing God's creative power), David and Jonathan come together one last time, the sky deep and dark, with only a growing sliver of moon for light. Realizing that this moment may be the last they share, the two kiss, embrace, and weep. Jonathan says to David, "Go in peace; we two have taken a binding oath, that the Eternal will be between us and between our descendants forever" (I Samuel 20:42). The word "between" tells us that God is present in that relationship.

As the light of the moon grows, so the creative power of God is made manifest. God's presence grows with them and between them, affirming their sacred relationship.

As the moon grows ever larger and radiant, so may our relationships grow deeper and brighter with each passing day.

## About That Which Is Missing
### Cantor Sarah Grabiner

At first glance, there is one obvious reason to read this haftarah the day before a new moon; it states, "Tomorrow is the New Moon" (I Samuel 20:18). The passage is prescribed for the Shabbat before a Sunday Rosh Chodesh in the Babylonian Talmud (*M'gillah* 31a), an apparently obvious tradition of antiquity.

However, with this opportunity to contemplate the lunar cycle and this biblical selection, what might we learn?

We begin in the midst of the beautiful and tumultuous tale of David and Jonathan. The text tells of how David will not appear at the next day's feast. If we look up on this Shabbat, before the first sliver of the new moon, we see the darkest expanse. While David is missing from the table, the moon is absent from the sky. We are aware of that which is lacking in our lives, that which is hidden in the darkness—relationships, opportunities, and reconciliations. The new moon comes and goes, and David, the symbol of the messianic age of perfection and redemption, is still missing.

How much imperfection still fills the world in which we live?

By the end, Jonathan and David embrace in love. Whether we read this as a romance or as the love of loyal, devoted friends, the dark night before the new moon is brightened by the hope of an unlikely, precious relationship. Let us find new light waxing in this special Shabbat before Rosh Chodesh.

## Alternative Haftarah Reading: From "Beautiful City," by Stephen Schwartz (from the musical Godspell)

Out of the ruins and rubble,
out of the smoke,
out of our night of struggle
can we see a ray of hope?
One pale thin ray reaching for the day . . .

We can build a beautiful city.
Yes we can, yes we can.
We can build a beautiful city,
not a city of angels,
but we can build a city of man. . . .

When your trust is all but shattered,
when your faith is all but killed,
you can give up, bitter and battered . . .
Or you can slowly start to build . . .

A beautiful city.
Yes we can, yes we can.
We can build a beautiful city,
not a city of angels,
but finally a city of man.

# Friendship and Renewal

*RABBI MAYA Y. GLASSER*

In the traditional haftarah for Machar Chodesh (I Samuel 20:18–42), we read a story of flight and destruction that leads to renewal and hope. David and Jonathan develop a strong relationship rooted in trust in God and in one another. King Saul condemns David to death, but Jonathan ultimately helps David escape that harsh sentence. A situation of despair becomes one of trust and growth because of a dedicated friendship.

Both the haftarah and the time during which it is read take place with the dawning of the new moon, which symbolizes potential for rebirth and for moving forward even in the darkest situations. Though King Saul is determined to destroy David, the bond between Jonathan and David and their undeterred faith in God help David to survive and later himself become the king of Israel.

These song lyrics from Stephen Schwartz's "Beautiful City," too, point to the power of faith during hard times. Everyone experiences difficulties; even the mighty King David had to endure extreme trials before he became a monarch. There is much chaos and destruction in our world, yet sometimes we only need one ray of hope, or light from the new moon, to give us the strength to go on. For me, lyrics like these and stories like this haftarah portion serve as those rays of light. These texts are a reminder that I am not alone, even in my darkest moments. Singing is a way for me to find meaning and activate my hope that I can overcome obstacles. Though our people's stories and songs cannot change anything in and of themselves, they can provide us with solidarity as well as moments to discover and rediscover the wisdom of tradition. It is in our interactions with our sacred texts, both the ancient *Tanach* stories and the modern works that reflect their themes, that we can find holiness. As the moon reminds us, there is always potential for renewal.

## *Alternative Haftarah Reading:*
## *"Adoni," from* Beautiful King *by J. Sylvan*

"Adoni" takes place directly after David kills Goliath. When King Saul and the soldiers run off after the retreating Philistines, Prince Jonathan sees his chance to approach the shepherd. ("Adoni" means "my lord.")

JONATHAN: I've never seen anyone take up and wield a stone that then took down a giant. Standing near naked, without a shield, yet so absolutely defiant. Please,

take my cloak, you have to be cold. Have you . . . borne the blade of a man?
I'd be glad honored, that is—if you'd hold my armor and sword in your hand.
Here's my bow.

DAVID: Adoni . . .

JONATHAN: Here's my tent, come with me.

DAVID: . . . Adoni . . . I cannot say no to you. You are my lord. Whatever
you wish I will do.

JONATHAN: If you don't want to—

DAVID: That's not what I said.

JONATHAN: I leave the decision to you. Alone you defeated a great enemy that
no one among us could kill. If anything, I should be bending my knee and
begging for whims of your will.

DAVID: Stand up please,

JONATHAN: (You look good from down here.)

DAVID: Adoni.

JONATHAN: (I mean, my cloak, it suits you.)

DAVID: I'm no lord.

JONATHAN: Well, how should we—

DAVID: Adoni, I'll carry your cloak, your sword, and your shield, now take off
your tunic and belt.

JONATHAN: I'll give you my everything, nothing concealed.

DAVID: Now lie on the place where you knelt.

DAVID: Love can't help us, really.

JONATHAN: It won't stop these wars.

DAVID: I'm not here for easy release.

JONATHAN: I think that my soul could get bound up with yours. And maybe,

BOTH: between us,

DAVID: some peace.

JONATHAN: Go slowly.

DAVID: Adoni.

JONATHAN: Now show me what's holy . . .

DAVID: Adoni.

# The Holiness of Love

### RABBI GILA COLMAN RUSKIN

If the COVID-19 pandemic had not shut down Broadway and other theater productions in March 2020, *Beloved King* by J. Sylvan would already be celebrated as
modern midrash on the relationship between David and Jonathan. Their saga, the
most extensive and descriptive love story in the entire Bible, was already portrayed

in nineteenth-century stained glass windows in Scotland, a German woodcut in 1700, and an illuminated Italian manuscript in 1300. Now it would have taken up a life in this contemporary art form: the American stage musical.

The song "Adoni" highlights the utter devotion of Jonathan toward David, despite the impossible quandary of being King Saul's (who seeks David's demise) son. The conversation between them occurs on the darkest night before the new month, when it is easiest to hide. Their erotic attraction is here characterized as "holy."

Sixteenth-century Spanish mystic John of the Cross viewed their friendship as the model for divine love: "The love Jonathan bore for David was so intimate that it knitted his soul to David's. If the love of one man for another was that strong, how much more could be our soul's love for God?"

# Rosh HaShanah

NOTE: *Due to variations in which Torah and haftarah readings are read in different communities, readings for the first and second days are combined into one section.*

## Traditional Haftarah Reading: I Samuel 1:1–2:10

## Prayer and Gratitude

*RABBI SANDRA J. COHEN*

POOR HANNAH. On Rosh HaShanah, we read how every year, when her family went to Shiloh, Elkanah, her husband, would give portions to Peninnah and each of her sons and daughters, but to Hannah only one portion, because she had no children. Elkanah does not understand her grief: "Am I not worth more to you than ten sons?" (I Samuel 1:8).

Hannah prays. Fervently, she asks God for a child. The Rabbis, moved by her devotion, consider her a model for silent prayer (Babylonian Talmud, *B'rachot* 31a). Hannah, like Sarah in the Torah reading of the same day (Genesis 21:1), is "remembered" by God (I Samuel 1:19), and they each are given a son. In their own way, each gives that child back to God:

- Sarah's child, Isaac, is brought up to Mount Moriah by his father Abraham, saved only at the last moment from being slaughtered as a sacrifice (Genesis 22).
- Hannah, however, promises her child to God in a different way: she makes him a *nazir*, "a person set apart for God." At the age when she weans him, she brings him back to Shiloh. There, he grows up with Eli the priest, serving God in the Temple at Shiloh.

While unnamed in the text, this boy is Samuel the prophet. He would become the anointer of kings, the guardian of the Ark of the Covenant. Hannah's prayer was answered more fully than she could know.

When we pray with full hearts, truly open to God, we too might become part of something bigger than ourselves; the words of our hearts may set in motion blessings for years to come—for ourselves, for our communities, even for those we do not know.

# I See You

### RABBI BARBARA AB SYMONS

Hannah is childless and heartbroken. Her husband Elkanah has children with his other wife, Peninnah, but none with her. Though he loves Hannah deeply, Elkanah does not understand her sadness. He asks her a rhetorical question, "Am I not worth more to you than ten sons?" (I Samuel 1:8).

Eli the priest, seeing her praying silently while her lips are moving, also does not understand her. He too asks her a rhetorical question: "How long will you persist in drunkenness? Put away your wine—get rid of it" (I Samuel 1:14).

Only Peninnah understands Hannah's pain—and in response, she taunts Hannah so viciously that Hannah weeps and cannot eat anymore.

Three people interact with Hannah: two do not see her pain; one is only making it worse. As each of the men is unable to understand how Hannah is feeling, and the woman lacks empathy and compassion, Hannah's pain seems either invisible or unimportant. Her sense of isolation is deepening as her pain is ignored. The seeming invisibility of Hannah's pain brings to mind an interview in the *Guardian* with Robin DiAngelo, author of *White Fragility*, who says, "The problem with white people is that they just don't listen. In my experience, day in and day out, most white people are absolutely not receptive to finding out their impact on other people. There is a refusal to know or see, or to listen or hear, or to validate." What makes Hannah invisible is not her skin color; what makes Hannah invisible is that her husband, the priest Eli, and her co-wife Peninnah all refuse to know, see, listen to, hear, or validate her. Let us begin the new year by doing the internal work necessary in order to be ready to know, see, listen to, hear, and validate others.

# Traditional Haftarah Reading:
# Jeremiah 31:2–20

## Receive Us Back in Love

### RABBI SANDRA J. COHEN

"A voice is heard in Ramah . . . Rachel weeping for her children, refusing to be comforted" (Jeremiah 31:15)—thus, the bittersweet nature of the haftarah for the second day of Rosh HaShanah. Two themes run through the Jeremiah's words, braided together in one verse, as in life: distress at God's chastening the Jewish people, and greater joy at God's promise to forgive.

This haftarah reading, read on Rosh Hashanah at the beginning of the Yamim Noraim, the days between Rosh HaShanah and Yom Kippur, comes to us at a time of self-reflection and repentance. "Help me return—and I will return," the haftarah has us say (Jeremiah 31:18).

Our passage, however, also points to the joy at the end of the period, after we will have atoned for our sins, as individuals and as a community. The great commentator Rashi connects the haftarah reading with the holiday by quoting the final verse: "I will receive him [Ephraim] back in love" (Jeremiah 31:20). The theme of mercy flows through the Rosh HaShanah services, especially in the Shofar Service of *Zichronot*, "Remembrance."

This is the promise of atonement: when we move toward God, God will smooth the highways, gather in the scattered, and "receive [us] back in love."

# Compassion and Love

## Rabbi Lisa Sari Bellows

The haftarah portion for the second day of Rosh HaShanah echoes the themes of the holiday: repentance and reconciliation. The prophet Jeremiah gives hope to the people that the Northern and Southern Kingdoms will reunite and worship together at the Temple in Jerusalem.

At the beginning of our portion, God says, "With an everlasting love I have loved you; indeed, with a love that is faithful [loving-kindness], I draw you near" (Jeremiah 31:3). God's assurance of love is strong and straightforward. And as the people repent and turn toward God with tears and longing, God again embraces them with words of kindness and love: "With weeping, they will come; with compassion, I will guide them" (Jeremiah 31:9). The people long for a physical reunification, for coming together to Jerusalem. Their longing is also spiritual: their hearts long to feel connected and close to God.

In the Babylonian Talmud, we read, "Even if the gates of prayer are shut, the gates of tears are not" (*Bava M'tzia* 59a). God's answer to our tears is to embrace us with love and compassion.

During periods of return, of *t'shuvah* (repentance), it is especially important to give ourselves compassion and love, for this is the way toward *shalom*, "wholeness and peace."

## Alternative Haftarah Reading:
## "The Shofar's Calling," by Rabbi Israel Zoberman

"In the seventh month
on the first day of the month,
there shall be a sacred assembly,
a cessation from work,
a day of commemoration
proclaimed by the sound
of the Shofar." (Numbers 29:1)

The ram's horn cut off,
to proclaim the brokenness
of the heart,
only what's incomplete
may sound the yearning
to be whole.

# Returning to Wholeness

### RABBI PETER J. HAAS

On the second day of Rosh HaShanah, we continue our reading from Genesis from the day before, now listening to the story of the Binding of Isaac in Genesis 22. This story of near extinction and salvation is echoed poignantly in the haftarah reading for this day, drawn from Jeremiah 31. The prophet Jeremiah had seen the Northern Kingdom disappear and now sees the Southern Kingdom of Judah face potential extinction as well.

The leaders of the community have been exiled; the community is broken. However, as Jeremiah tells us in these short hymns that make up this chapter, not all is lost. As in the case of Isaac, there will be divine intervention and the people, like Isaac, will go on to a renewed life. There may even be a direct allusion to Abraham and Isaac in Jeremiah 31:9, "For I have become like a father to Israel, and Ephraim is My firstborn."

Jeremiah is telling his broken and scattered people that a return to wholeness is both possible and assured if the people completely repent. As Jeremiah 31:18 says, "You have disciplined me . . . and I have been disciplined. Help me return—and I will return." As we move from the broken to the whole, may we, as Rabbi Zoberman's poem calls upon us, "sound the yearning to be whole."

## *Alternative Haftarah Reading:*
## *"The Judgment of Creation," by Aharon Berechiah*
## *of Modena, 1610*

It is a general principle on which all teachers agree, just as we see in the order of prayers set by the men of the Great K'nesset, that every person is judged on Rosh HaShanah on all of their acts and thoughts as to whether they will die or live, whether they will be healthy or sickly, whether they will be hungry or sated, and so with all that happens in the world such as whether or not there will be rain, and concerning crops and the fruit of trees. Of all that is found in the world, nothing is exempt from being judged on Rosh HaShanah. And all of them on account of the actions of humanity, for all of them were created only for the sake of humanity, and all of them are sustained by [humanity's] strength and life, as it is said, "As surely as I have established My covenant with day and night—the laws of heaven and earth." The Torah was established only for the sake of Israel. Furthermore, it is written, "You have made [humanity] master over all Your handiwork" (Psalm 8:7). Therefore [humanity] was created after all the work of Creation so that [humanity] found a completely set table.

# Responsible for It

### Rabbi Philip J. Bentley

This alternative haftarah is the opening passage of a sermon delivered on Rosh HaShanah 5309 (1610). Aharon Berechiah of Modena (1549–1639) was a kabbalist. He is most famous for his *Ma'avar Yabbok*, which is a Jewish Book of the Dead that describes the journey of the soul after death.

Here, he expands on the idea of judgment on the Jewish New Year to include every living person. As in the *Un'taneh Tokef* prayer, this preacher says that the destiny of every human being is determined on this day. However, he takes this belief a lot further. Not only are people judged, but nature itself, the health of our planet, is suffering under our failures; it is judged "with us" and according to human conduct. Genesis 2:15 says, "God Eternal took the man, placing him in the Garden of Eden to work it and keep it." We should see the natural world as being created to meet all our needs. We are therefore responsible for it. As we read in a midrash:

> When God created the first human, God took him and showed him all the trees of the Garden of Eden and said to him: "See My works, how beautiful and praiseworthy they are. And everything that I created, I created it for you. Be careful not to spoil or destroy My world—for if you do, there will be nobody after you to repair it." (*Kohelet Rabbah* 7:13)

How we use the resources of Creation matters. We must not assume that someone or something will fix a spoiled Creation environment, not even God. In our everyday lives at home, at work, and wherever we are, we should be conscious of avoiding waste, destruction, and pollution.

### Alternative Haftarah Reading:
### From "Jews in the U.S.: The Rising Costs of Whiteness,"
### by Melanie Kaye/Kantrowitz

What happens if . . . I assert my right to choose and not suffer for it. To say, I choose: my lesbianism and my Jewishness. Choose to come out, be visible, embrace both. . . . I could have kept the name Kaye, and never once at Christmas—in response to the interminable "what are you doing for . . . ? have you finished your shopping?"—never once answer, "I don't celebrate Christmas. I'm a Jew." I could lie about my lover's gender. I could wear skirts uncomfortably. I could bleach my hair again, as I did when I was fifteen. . . . I could remain silent when queer or anti-Semitic jokes are told, when someone says "you know how they are." I could endure the pain in the gut, the hot shame. I could scrunch up much, much smaller.

## Sarah as a Shofar

### CANTOR KAREN WEBBER, MSM, CPRS

My relationship with my husband Abraham was over at dawn this morning, when I heard them both rise, and he didn't even say goodbye. He knows I would have yelled, "Do not lay a hand on my son! Take me!" But he didn't take me. At that moment, I felt alone in my marriage, alone and ignored.

All Isaac saw and felt that day, I experienced in my own body. I became one with him. My feet blistered as we walked up the mountain. When Abraham laid me down and tied me to the altar, I became smaller. When he raised the knife, something in me broke. Something in me died.

I became the ram's horn. With one long cry of t'kiah, and staccato wails of t'ruah, I crossed over. The shofar wakes us to injustice, injury, and invisibility.

Many think I died of sadness. I didn't. I died of years of stuffed feelings turned rage.

So, dear women, speak up, do not be silent. Go out. Choose to be seen, to be heard, to be loved, in all your broken wholeness.

## Alternative Haftarah Reading:
### From "The Real Hero," by Yehuda Amichai

The real hero of The Binding of Isaac was the ram,
who didn't know about the collusion between the others.
He was volunteered to die instead of Isaac.
I want to sing a memorial song about him—
about his curly wool and his human eyes,
about the horns that were so silent on his living head,
and how they made those horns into shofars when he was slaughtered
to sound their battle cries
or to blare out their obscene joy.

I want to remember the last frame
like a photo in an elegant fashion magazine:
the young man tanned and pampered in his jazzy suit
and beside him the angel, dressed for a formal reception
in a long silk gown,
both of them looking with empty eyes
at two empty places,

and behind them, like a colored backdrop, the ram,
caught in the thicket before the slaughter.
The thicket his last friend.

The angel went home.
Isaac went home.
Abraham and God had gone long before.

But the real hero of The Binding of Isaac
is the ram.

## *Bal Tashchit*
### RABBI SARA RAE PERMAN

On the second day of Rosh HaShanah we traditionally read the story of the *Akeidah*, "the Binding of Isaac." Instead of sacrificing Isaac, as God had asked of him, Abraham sacrificed a ram found caught by its horns in a thicket. The poet Amichai suggests the real hero was the ram.

What purpose did this sacrifice serve? A midrash in *Pirkei D'Rabbi Eliezer* 31:13 suggests that all parts of the ram were used for something: the ashes were the foundation of the inner altar; the sinews were used in David's harp; the ram's skin was used as clothing for Elijah; one horn was blown at Mount Sinai; and the other horn will be used in the future to announce the messianic age. Judaism knows the concept of *bal tashchit*, "not to waste." Everything has a purpose. Amichai makes us look at the ram in a different way. With the beginning of a new year, we are expected to look at our lives in a different way, too.

What can we do to be more careful with the precious resources with which we have been blessed?

For Shabbat Shuvah, see *Vayeilech*/Shabbat Shuvah, page 328.

# *Yom Kippur, Morning*
## Traditional Haftarah Reading:
## Isaiah 57:14–58:14

## Is This the Fast I Desire?

*RABBI DANIEL B. MEDWIN*

YOU DID SOME THINGS wrong this year. Now is the time to reflect on them and express remorse. You're looking for Me, but you're doing it wrong.

On the holiest day of the year, all you can think about is how hungry you are, while someone who works for you doesn't have adequate health care, parental leave, or a good pension.

You think a day of dressing up and not eating is what I care about? This is what I want you to be doing:

1. Fight injustice in the world, and treat people fairly.
2. Release anyone falsely imprisoned, or with a harsh maximum sentence, and a record that will follow them for the rest of their lives.
3. Free the people in your very own city who are living like slaves.
4. Feed hungry people here and all over.
5. Give shelter to those experiencing homelessness, or support a homeless shelter.
6. And most importantly, never ever let your family down. You must always be there for them, and they will do the same for you.

Then, when you seek a connection to Me and the universe, you will find Me. You will be honoring and drawing from ancient wisdom, and the legacy of your impact will last well beyond your time. You will be responsible for helping people to stroll down the street, rather than march down it.

Then you will feel a sense of connection to everyone and everything. Your life will be filled with meaning and joy. And your connection to Judaism will be a source of healing and nourishment.

# Ritual and Ethical Action

*RABBI SANDRA J. COHEN*

On Yom Kippur morning, Isaiah's voice rings out: "Is this the fast I desire?" (Isaiah 58:5). Starving bodies; sackcloth and ashes? No, God explains. God looks for a fast wherein the oppressed go free, we share our bread with the hungry, clothe the naked, and take the needy into our homes.

Reading this as progressive Jews, we often have a moment of self-satisfaction. See, God does not ask for empty ritual; God seeks ethical action! This is why so many non-Orthodox Jews do not observe any fast days other than Yom Kippur. Even disregarding theological issues (Tishah B'Av and the seventeenth of Tammuz commemorate the Temple's destruction, which is not very meaningful to the theology of many contemporary Reform Jews), fasting itself just does not seem to be a very relevant or appealing practice. And after all, Isaiah said that God doesn't need our fasts, as long as we take care of the poor.

But this misinterprets Isaiah's message. His message is that God asks for both ritual *and* ethical behavior. Our fasting, our ritual behavior, should lead us to ethical behavior indeed—but those rituals still matter! They bring us together, remind us of our history, connect us to God, and mark times of holiness. Thus renewed, we reenter the world and work to heal it.

## *Alternative Haftarah Reading: "Merger Poem," by Judy Chicago*

And then all that has divided us will merge.
And then compassion will be wedded to power
And then softness will come to a world that is harsh and unkind.
And then both men and women will be gentle.
And then both women and men will be strong.
And then no person will be subject to another's will.
And then all will be rich and free and varied.
And then the greed of some will give way to the needs of many.
And then all will share equally in the earth's abundance.
And then all will care for the sick and the weak and the old.
And then all will nourish the young.
And then all will cherish life's creatures.
And then all will live in harmony with each other and the earth.
And then everywhere will be called Eden once again.

# The Work We Need to Do

*RABBI PHILIP J. BENTLEY*

Many cultures transmit a vision of a perfect age, but ours is a vision of a perfect future. We call that the messianic age.

In the Garden of Eden, everything needed for human life was there for the taking. Eve and Adam worked, but they were assured of a successful outcome. They made love.

Then, when they were cast out and we became fully human, we had to work without any certainty of a good outcome. The pain and distress in the world we know is a challenge. How do we respond to sickness, war, injustice, and hatred? How do we, as the song goes, "get back to the garden"? We call our efforts *tikkun olam* (repairing the world). Rabbi Abraham Joshua Heschel taught that God needs us to do this work.

The ideal world described by Judy Chicago requires each of us to do something to make the vision of a fixed world into a reality. As Rabbi Tarfon taught, "The day is short, the task is abundant, the laborers are lazy, the wage is great, and the Master of the house is insistent. . . . You are not required to complete the task, yet you are not free to desist from it" (*Pirkei Avot* 2:20–21).

## Alternative Haftarah Reading:
## Leonard Fein, as quoted in a sermon
## by Rabbi Aryeh Azriel, 2011

The Jewish community has no more urgent interest than the energetic pursuit of its values. Our values are not merely grace notes to our lives; they are our purpose. . . . The central American Jewish problem of our time is not anti-Semitism, inter-marriage specifically, or assimilation in general.

It is a problem with boredom, the fact that for very many American Jews, the experience of being Jewish does not seem to be about anything—not, at any rate, about anything that matters very much.

Many Jews are simply unable to fill in the blank in the sentence that begins with the words "It is important that the Jews survive in order to . . ." In order to what? In order to survive? Lots of luck: send out an invitation to the young that reads: "Please come survive with us," and see how many RSVP. . . .

I can think of no single statement to which more Jews throughout the centuries, and even today, would subscribe, no sentence more accurately and comprehensibly captures the most fundamental Jewish insight, than that this, our world, God's world is not working the way it was meant to—and that to be a Jew is to know that, somehow you are implicated in its repair.

The complete sentence then will read: "It is important that the Jews survive, in order to help repair this fractured world." ...

There is mending to be done—healing, fixing, repairing. That is the Jewish calling, our historic vocation, and the education we offer our children. ...

Judaism is not only our passive birthright, it is our active conviction. ... The rich religious culture that we have been bequeathed and that we are privileged to bequeath to our children and they to theirs is not a contemplative culture. In the end, it is not the services we attend that will sustain us; it is the services that we perform. For us, Shabbat was never meant as a stopping place, it was meant as a resting place, a place to re-gather our energies, to take up again, and forever, God's work in this world.

It is the work of clothing the naked and feeding the hungry, of embracing the stranger and freeing the captive, and smashing the idols; it is to insure the work of justice. That is the Torah that we are instructed to do. That is the Torah that drives us.

# God's World Is Not Working the Way It Was Meant To

### RABBI SUZANNE SINGER

We are told that prophecy ended with Ezra in the fifth century BCE. I disagree. Listen to these words of Leonard Fein, a true modern prophet, calling us to return to our mission as Jews. Does his voice not resonate with what Abraham Joshua Heschel describes in *The Prophets*: "Their words are onslaughts, scuttling illusions of false security, challenging evasions, calling faith to account, questioning prudence and impartiality"?

The traditional haftarah reading from the Book of Isaiah has challenged us for centuries. Yet, still today, we stray. Still today, we require the passionate, insistent, fierce voice of the prophets, old and new, to shatter our complacency, to dismantle our indifference.

Isn't Leonard Fein's challenge, just like Isaiah's, critical at Yom Kippur, a day of profound reckoning? We must allow this message to pierce our conscience. Then we will heed the cry of the needy and take action to fight poverty, to demand justice. As Leonard Fein reminds us, the synagogue is not meant to be a sanctuary where we escape from the world's problems. Rather, it is a place to fortify ourselves for the work of justice. This is who we are meant to be. This is what we were meant to do.

# Yom Kippur, Afternoon
## Traditional Haftarah Reading:
## The Book of Jonah

## The Strangers Shall Be as Your Citizens
### Rabbi Erin Boxt

DURING THE YOM KIPPUR afternoon service, it is traditional to read the Book of Jonah. Many lessons can be gleaned from Jonah's story. Jonah faces the ultimate choice—do I save myself or do I save the others?—when he demands the sailors hurl him into the sea, thus calming the stormy waters. The sailors initially refuse, not wanting to be found guilty of shedding Jonah's blood.

The dilemma Jonah faces is one that we face time and time again today: do we sacrifice our own happiness for the sake of others? In today's "me, me, me" world, it is often too easy to turn a blind eye to the suffering of others. However, as we read in the Holiness Code on Yom Kippur:

> When strangers reside with you in your land, you shall not wrong them. The strangers who reside with you shall be to you as your citizens; you shall love each one as yourself, for you were strangers in the land of Egypt. I am the Eternal your God. (Leviticus 19:33–34)

The passages from Leviticus and the Book of Jonah teach us the importance of loving others and treating everyone with respect and kindness. Just as Jonah chose to put himself in danger rather than save himself, let us strive to work toward a better tomorrow in which everyone's wants and needs are equal.

## How the Light Gets In
### Rabbi Phil M. Cohen, PhD

For refusing to head over to Nineveh and do God's bidding—namely, suggesting that repentance is superior to destruction—it's well-known that Jonah found himself lodging for a time in the belly of a large fish. At first Jonah sulked, "Why me, God? Couldn't you have picked someone else?" To these questions Jonah was met by silence. He continued sulking.

In Rashi's commentary on Exodus 19:11, he points out that time has no meaning in the Torah. Past and future flow into one another like two streams meeting. So it is not surprising that on the second day of his sojourn in the fish Jonah heard the strains of poetry from what we would call "another time":

Ring the bells that still can ring
Forget your perfect offering
There is a crack, a crack in everything
That's how the light gets in.

And since Jonah had nothing to do but contemplate, he considered those words while resting on the innards of that big fish.

"Maybe so," Jonah the prophet thought. "Maybe we're all in this muddle together, including my own people, including the boatmen who bent over backward to save me, including those wretched Ninevites whom I'm supposed to warn. We're all cracked, damaged, worn out from too much living in an imperfect world. Maybe it's through our very damaged condition that the light God infused into the world sneaks in, unifies us, and bears the potential to make us whole and bring some peace."

Jonah stood up, did what he could to wipe off the fish muck stuck to his clothes, and announced to God that he was prepared to move on and do his job. Thus did the big fish vomit Jonah onto the shore, whereupon he got on with things and brought a modicum of light into this cracked world.

## *Alternative Haftarah Reading: Babylonian Talmud, B'rachot 10a*

Every chapter that was dear to David, he began with "happy is" and concluded with "happy is." He opened with "happy is," as it is written: "Happy is the person who has not walked in the counsel of the wicked or stood in the way of sinners or sat in the dwelling place of the scornful" (Psalm 1:1). And he concluded with "happy," as it is written at the end of the chapter: "Pay homage in purity, lest God be angry, and you perish on the way when God's anger is kindled suddenly. Happy are those who take refuge in God" (Psalm 2:12). We see that these two chapters actually constitute a single chapter.

With regard to the statement of Rabbi Y'hudah, son of Rabbi Shimon ben Pazi, that David did not say Hallelujah until he saw the downfall of the wicked, the Gemara relates: There were these zealots in Rabbi Meir's neighborhood who caused him a great deal of anguish. Rabbi Meir prayed for God to have mercy on them, that they should die. Rabbi Meir's wife, B'rurya, said to him: "What is your thinking? On what basis do you pray for the death of these hooligans? Do you base yourself on the verse, as it is written, 'Let sins cease from the land' (Psalm 104:35), which you interpret to mean that the world would be better if the wicked were destroyed? But is it written, 'let sinners cease'? 'Let sins cease,' is written. One should pray for an end to their transgressions, not for the demise of the transgressors themselves.

Moreover, go to the end of the verse, where it says, 'And the wicked will be no more.' If, as you suggest, transgressions shall cease refers to the demise of the evildoers, how is it possible that the wicked will be no more, that is, that they will no longer be evil? Rather, pray for God to have mercy on them, that they should repent, as if they repent, then the wicked will be no more, as they will have repented."

Rabbi Meir saw that B'rurya was correct and he prayed for God to have mercy on them, and they repented.

## Not Against the Sinners, but Against Sinning

*Rabbi Sharon G. Forman*

On Yom Kippur afternoon, as the metaphorical gates of repentance begin to close, worshipers contemplate the topics of sinning and forgiveness. Although a colorful tale, the customary haftarah reading from the Book of Jonah merely tells the story of an anti-prophet who flees from responsibility, cares less for human life than for a plant, and is skeptical of the human capacity for transformation and redemption.

Another possibility for a meaningful and thought-provoking haftarah is this excerpt from the Babylonian Talmud. Here, the Rabbis discuss the moral courage, optimism, and compassion of Rabbi Meir's wife, B'rurya. B'rurya stands up to conventional thought in an era in which only men were sages. Her husband, Rabbi Meir, prays for the downfall and even the death of the wicked. B'rurya, basing her argumentation on a verse from the Book of Psalms and using her grammatical expertise, proves that the end of sinning is more desirable rather than the end of the sinners themselves. She encourages Rabbi Meir to understand that our prayers should focus on changing transgressors rather than hurting them. This statement becomes even more profound when examined in the context of B'rurya's personal life: both of her parents were murdered by the Romans in brutal fashion. She speaks up for those individuals who commit sins even though her own life was scarred by the cruelty of others.

Instead of wishing away those individuals who carry out crimes, we can learn from B'rurya's example to focus on redemption, education, and hope. We can look at this country's criminal justice system with fresh eyes. Instead of wishing for the death or disappearance of those individuals who stand outside of the law, we can work toward the elimination of crime and the creation of a fair and just society for all.

## *Alternative Haftarah Reading:*
## *"I Remember You," by Rabbi Joe Black*

I remember you . . .
How we stood at the foot
of that mountain,
covered with soot
from all the fire and the smoky cloud
I remember you . . .
we stood side by side
trying to hide,
our eyes and our ears
from the power of the shofar blast so loud.
I remember you . . .
It's been a while—we've gone our separate ways
you seem so foreign to me
and I know that you think me strange

But no matter how we live our lives
There comes a moment of awe and surprise
And maybe even some compromise
when we remember
how we stood together
at the foot of that mountain
so long ago.

For I heard the sound
And you heard it too
And though we may seem different
In all that we do
When we remember that place
where God spoke face to face
Our steps we retrace
to the foot of that mountain
So long ago.

I remember you, and I know it's not too late
We are bound—not by hate but by our memory.
I remember you—do you remember me?
Through the smoke and all the lies as the fire testifies
I'm not the enemy
I remember you . . .
It's been a while—we've gone our different ways
you seem so foreign to me

and I know that you think me strange

But no matter how we live our lives
There comes a moment of awe and surprise
And maybe even some compromise
when we look in each other's eyes
and recognize
how we stood together
at the foot of that mountain
so long ago.

# To Remember and Be Remembered

### *Rabbi Joseph Edelheit*

Rabbi Joseph R. Black's "I Remember You" invites us to imagine a lost relationship. These words "sing" to us even without hearing the music; the repetition of the phrase "I remember you . . ." opens each individual's past.

Yom Kippur requires that we spend time evaluating our past behavior for the sake of the future. By the afternoon, we usually are already tired, hungry, and distracted, anticipating the end of the service. "I Remember You" revives us. We are getting ready to remember those whose names we put on the *Yizkor* list; the lyrics take us each back to our own treasured experiences of when we "stood side by side" with someone who is now gone. We are also getting ready to ask God to remember us, because we each admit that "it's been a while—we've gone our separate ways," the Holy One whispering to us, "I remember you, and I know it's not too late."

The Torah teaches us that *zachor* (remember) requires *shamor* (keep). Especially today, we are commanded to do more than merely remember the ones we lost— we must honor and celebrate their memory as a source of hope and strength with which to embrace the future. Before the *N'ilah* service ends, "we [will] look in each other's eyes and recognize how we stood together at the foot of that mountain so long ago." Our memories will give us the strength to move forward.

May we remember and be remembered as the year begins.

# *Sukkot, Day 1*
## Leviticus 23:33–44

## Traditional Haftarah Reading:
## Zechariah 14:7–9, 16–21

### There Will Be No More Strangers
*Rabbi Cantor Jordan Shaner*

Sukkot celebrates the beginning of the rainy season—the renewal of life-giving water after a long period of dry weather. In the traditional haftarah reading for the first day of Sukkot, the prophet Zechariah consoles us with a vision of a time when living waters will flow freely out of the Mount of Olives, bringing life to both East and West (Zechariah 14:8). In that time, distinctions will cease. Fresh water will irrigate the land year-round, regardless of the winter rainfall. The heat of the day will be cooled, and the dark of the night will be brightened. There will be no more inequality between rich and poor. There will be no more distinction between Jew and gentile: "there will be no more Canaanite in the house of the Eternal" (Zechariah 14:21)—not because the Canaanite would be exiled as a stranger, but because she is welcomed as family.

The holiness of Zechariah's vision is pervasive. The secular and the sacred will be one and the same: "even the bells on the horses shall be inscribed 'holy'" (Zechariah 14:20). Our tendency to divide and separate the human experience into categories, including holiness and profanity, is important for helping us understand that experience. Even so, the purpose of faith is not to maintain those distinctions, but to look beyond them. As we celebrate our festival, we have the opportunity to extend our sense of belonging beyond our immediate family to include complete strangers—those with whom we disagree or whose experience is radically different from our own. Like the sheltering sukkah, in which we are neither entirely inside nor outside, not entirely comfortable and complacent nor vulnerable to the elements, the vision of Zechariah brings together opposing forces, not for division, but to realize anew the truth that Israel has long attested: "In that day, the Eternal will be One, and God's name will be One" (Zechariah 14:9).

# In the World-to-Come . . .

*RABBI PAULA JAYNE WINNIG*

There is a blessing that is said at the end of Sukkot: "May it be Your will, Eternal, our God and God of our ancestors, that just as I have stood up and dwelled in this sukkah, so may I merit next year to dwell in the sukkah covered with the skin of the Leviathan." This curious passage is connected to Sukkot due to the traditional haftarah reading, which sees this as an expression of what will happen when the world is redeemed and all people are whole and secure.

In the traditional haftarah reading for the first day of Sukkot, Zechariah imagines a united world of peace and abundance, the future pilgrimage to Jerusalem and Temple worship on Sukkot, and a shared sense of holiness. None of these really connect to the meaning or give explanation for the blessing of having a sukkah covered with the skin of the Leviathan. However, the Talmud makes this connection:

> Rabbi Yochanan says, "In the future, the Holy One, blessed be God, will make a feast for the righteous from the flesh of the Leviathan. . . . The remaining part of the skin of the Leviathan, the Holy One, blessed be God, spreads it on the walls of Jerusalem, and its glory radiates from one end of the world until the other end. As it is stated: 'And nations shall walk in your light, and kings at the brightness of your rising' (Isaiah 60:3)." (Babylonian Talmud, *Bava Batra* 75a)

The Leviathan is connected to the messianic age. The sukkah covered with its skin becomes the hall of a festive banquet for all the righteous to feast and rejoice together.

The Book of Job (chapters 40–41) marvels at the wondrousness of this creature Leviathan and the special power of God to have created and tamed it for service to God. God's reply to Job's complaints and questions often leaves people frustrated, especially regarding Job's real questions about the meaning and cause of pain and suffering.

We all want answers to these same questions throughout our lives. We want to know why we live in a world without proper shelter for all God's people. During Sukkot, when we dwell in our temporary, fragile shelters, we learn to relate, at least for a while, to the pain and suffering of those less fortunate than we are.

The Book of Job is never read in connection to a holiday, perhaps because people were afraid that the very idea of questioning God might cause people to lose faith. Job, however, can be read as the most meaningful of biblical books for today's world. It takes on our very real existential questions—Why is there pain and suffering? Why do some people who are undeserving get things they should not? Is there real equality and justice?—and Job explores the fallacy of the belief in a strict plan and destiny for the world.

The Book of Job reminds us that the ways of the world and the ways of God are not so easily discerned; we learn to expect less and do more, without knowing if we will gain any reward for doing so. At the end of the book (chapter 42), Job recants and admits that he did not know as much about the way the world works as he thought he did. The Rabbis' call for a sukkah made of the skin of the Leviathan connects us to their vision of the time of redemption for all God's creatures—human, animal, and mythic—a time when we will be understanding and compassionate to all.

## *Alternative Haftarah Reading: "Be the Change," by Sue Horowitz*

CHORUS:
God created this whole world, God created this whole world
God created this whole world in seven days
And what have you done today?

It's taught that we are created, created in the image
The power and the blessing rest within our hands
When we awake each morning, the world is open to us
The power and the blessing rest within our hands

The chaos and injustice in news reports and daily papers
The power and the blessing rest within our hands
Our eyes are open wider, our hearts are open wider
The power and blessing rest within our hands

It's action and intention and community and invention
That are the tools of creation
Be the change you want to see in the world,
the change you want to see in the world.
Be the change.

Hey, be the change, what have you done today?

# What Have You Done Today?

### Rabbi Lev Baesh

In Leviticus 23:42, we are taught "to live in booths" to remind us that God makes the rules: "You shall live in booths seven days; all citizens in Israel shall live in booths, in order that future generations may know that I made the Israelite people live in booths when I brought them out of the land of Egypt, I the Eternal your God."

I don't believe in that model of divine authority; however, I do believe in using our biblical and Rabbinic stories and metaphors—like the sukkah—as a teaching tool.

The song "Be the Change" by Sue Horowitz reminds us to consider that the world wasn't created by us, individually or collectively. She reminds us to keep thinking of something bigger and more powerful than ourselves. She hopes to broaden and deepen our vision, so that we can move past our usual thoughts—while at the same time reminding us that we do have the responsibility and chance to create greater change in the world.

When we say "God the Creator," we remind ourselves that we are not responsible for the maintenance and absolute betterment of the world, but we are called to play a part in those tasks.

"What have you done today?" The song asks us not only about our individual achievements and creations, but also about our part in creating change and maintaining Creation.

"What have you done today?"

## *Alternative Haftarah Reading:*
## *"Beauty Dances," by Alden Solovy*

Beauty dances
With us
Whenever we build
A tabernacle
To God's holy name.

Love sings
With us
Whenever we rejoice
In gladness
On God's festive days.

Peace cries
With us
Whenever we yearn
In prayer
For God's holy shelter.

Come,
Let us build this place,
This tabernacle where we praise,
With all of our hearts,
God's pardon and promise.

Let us build this place,
Where we delight,
With thanksgiving and wonder,
In God's bounty and gifts.

Come,
Let us build this place,
This *sukkat shalom*,
This shelter of peace,
Where beauty dances
And love sings.
Where peace cries out:
Build, build,
You Children of Israel,
A tent of holiness,
Strong and true.
Build it in your heart,
In your home,
In your life,
In God's world.

# Ingathering

*RABBI PAUL KIPNES*

As raging fires burn down our beloved homes, as horrific hurricanes and ferocious floods destroy houses we once thought impervious to peril, as predatory loan practices preclude too many from attaining or retaining the dream of owning a home of their own, here comes Sukkot to open our eyes and hearts. Sukkot reminds us that what was abiding—before and after the fires, floods, and unfair financing—was only the "tent of holiness" we built, strong and true, in our homes, in our lives, and in God's world: a tent, but not a permanent structure.

Sukkot then is a countercultural celebration, prodding us to push through the façade of permanence to grasp the intangible impermanence of our lives. Sukkot goads us to dwell in fragile booths open to the skies, fleeing the mundane materialism that makes us think that our possessions and willpower will protect us. Only there, in the booths, will we gain a clear perspective on the truly transitory nature of our belongings. Only there will we "delight, with thanksgiving and wonder," finally feeling the permanence that lies in "God's bounty and gifts."

That is the secret of Sukkot, the Festival of Ingathering: As we gather in the fruits of our labors, we labor to feel gathered in by God's redemption. Only then will we truly feel God's protective love.

# Shabbat Chol HaMo-eid Sukkot
## Traditional Haftarah Reading:
## Ezekiel 38:18–39:7

### God's Shelter
#### RABBI EMILY E. SEGAL

IN THE TORAH portion for Shabbat Chol HaMo-eid Sukkot, God comforts Moses, offering him reassurance following the Israelites' sin of the Golden Calf. The traditional haftarah portion contains Ezekiel's vivid and violent prophecy of a future war with Israel's enemies, Gog and Magog, promising that God will defeat them with a crushing blow. Ezekiel reassures the Israelites following the destruction of the First Temple with the promise of future redemption through God's continued care and favor, clearing enemies from their path, and bringing them back in forgiveness.

While *Tanach* describes military victories in terms of God's favor of the Israelites, the fact remains that in order to conquer their enemies, the Israelites still needed to march into battle, to strategize and fight to secure their victory. God did not act alone; rather, it was the marriage of the Israelites' military action and God's favor that enabled them to succeed.

Similarly, we are the ones who need to do the work. We must open our eyes and our hearts to those who are vulnerable, providing reassurance and assistance to our fellow human beings in need of shelter, an amplified voice, and justice. With God at our side, may we find the strength to do so.

### Gratitude, Wonder, and Peace
#### RABBI JORDANA SCHUSTER BATTIS

It is not clear why end-times and a great final battle of redemption are themes of a number of the festival haftarot. In this case, it may be that our passage from Ezekiel is supposed to remind us of the great Sukkot celebration that the prophet Zechariah says will follow the final victory at the end of all days (14:16).

In the traditional haftarah reading for Shabbat Chol HaMo-eid, Ezekiel assures his readers that the time will come when Israel's enemies will be defeated; when

God will display power over earth, people, and wildlife; when God will triumph and be known by all; and when the Land of Israel will be purified through the blood and burial of its enemies.

This is a somewhat gruesome selection to be read within the holiday dubbed Z'man Simchateinu, "the time of our joy." However, the passage can take on a different significance as we sit in our fragile sukkot, those physical manifestations of our fragility and of the power of choosing trust in a world beyond our control: embracing our vulnerability, we can choose exhilaration in lieu of fear. In the fierceness of this choice, we might find ourselves dreaming of revenge, yes, such as Ezekiel prophesies—but we might also arrive at something beyond that: gratitude, wonder, and a world that joins together in praise and peace at last.

## Alternative Haftarah Reading:
## *From* The Essence of Judaism, *by Rabbi Leo Baeck*

Human beings seem to be bordered by loneliness on every side. One seems to stand in the midst of the world, in infinite space and in endless time. Together with this loneliness of time and space, there arises the loneliness of fleeting, finite life coerced by causality. This is the feeling of being forsaken and subject to the inevitable. Without God life is a lonely darkness, even for the one who is in the midst of many others and even for the one who enjoys pleasures and power. It is the loneliness of the one whose soul is far from all that is real, eternal and sublime. In this forlorn state one trembles with despair when seeking to answer those questions about life that one cannot evade.

It is precisely from this fear that there arises the yearning for that illuminating and harmonizing One who is the creator of all eternity. The person who knows this yearning is lifted out of their forlornness; their night is filled with light and their soul redeemed from despair. Whoever knows themself to be bound to the one and eternal God knows no loneliness, for their life is never solitary. No matter how intimately we may come into contact with our fellow human beings we still remain alone in our innermost soul, for every person is unique upon earth and loneliness is part of individuality. But in God our life finds its peace.

## God Can Provide Us with Hope
### Rabbi Dana Evan Kaplan, PhD

The Torah reading for Shabbat Chol HaMo-eid Sukkot includes Exodus 34:22, which specifically commands the Children of Israel to celebrate the Feast of Weeks with the first offering of the wheat harvest and the Feast of Ingathering [Sukkot] at the turn of the year. The reading begins after the calamity of the Golden Calf and the subsequent smashing of the first set of the Ten Commandments. God summons Moses back to the top of Mount Sinai in order to work on a new set of tablets, but Moses seems to feel completely alone and adrift. In order to reassure himself, he asks to see God. As he is told that no one can see God and live, he takes shelter behind a rock, and God passes in front of him.

Leo Baeck, a German Reform rabbi who survived the Holocaust, speaks of a spiritual loneliness that is foreshadowed by Moses's sense of isolation on Mount Sinai. Rabbi Baeck utilizes the Psalms, which refer to the soul as "the lonely one" (22:21 and 35:17). Moses's soul appears to be lonely. Even though God is near, his soul yearns for a direct connection with the Divine. Rabbi Baeck connects the social loneliness that so many people in his time felt with the absence of God in their lives. He argues that it is precisely when people reach this nadir of hopelessness that they confront the need for a personal relationship with God. Out of the isolated darkness may arise a yearning for an illuminating and harmonizing God who is able to help us lift ourselves out of our despair. God can be a tremendous source of inspiration for many of us. God can provide us with hope.

As we celebrate the intermediate days of Sukkot, we remember the insecurity of wandering throughout the desert, living in fragile booths, and relying on manna for daily sustenance. In a very different way, our lives today are equally fragile. We have seen how unexpected events can destabilize societal structures that we thought were extraordinarily stable, if not permanent. Our task is to search for a God that can bring us a sense of security in an insecure world.

## *Alternative Haftarah Reading:*
## *"A Man in His Life," by Yehuda Amichai*

A man doesn't have time in his life
to have time for everything.
He doesn't have seasons enough to have
a season for every purpose. Ecclesiastes
was wrong about that.

A man needs to love and to hate at the same moment,
to laugh and cry with the same eyes,
with the same hands to cast away stones and to gather them,
to make love in war and war in love.

And to hate and forgive and remember and forget
to set in order and confuse, to eat and to digest
what history
takes years and years to do.

A man doesn't have time.
When he loses he seeks, when he finds
he forgets, when he forgets he loves, when he loves
he begins to forget.

And his soul is experienced, his soul
is very professional.
Only his body remains forever
an amateur. It tries and it misses,
gets muddled, doesn't learn a thing,
drunk and blind in its pleasures
and in its pains.

He will die as figs die in autumn,
shriveled and full of himself and sweet,
the leaves growing dry on the ground,
the bare branches already pointing to the place
where there's time for everything.

# Remembering the Shortness of Our Days

### *Rabbi Sara Rae Perman*

Traditionally we read Ecclesiastes on the Shabbat of Sukkot. In "A Man in His Life," Yehuda Amichai has reworked the traditional text, reminding us about the fleeting nature of time, as did Ecclesiastes's author. Sitting in the sukkah as the days grow shorter, we remember how short time is. Just as the sukkah suggests the fragility of our homes and our lives, this poem reinforces the idea that our lives do not last forever. Sukkot, Ecclesiastes, and the poem all urge us to avoid neglecting the things we need to do. While we may not be able to do it all, we can still accomplish a lot; we can still make a difference. As Rabbi Tarfon teaches in *Pirkei Avot* 2:20: "The day is short and the task is abundant." While the High Holy Days were a chance to reflect on how we live our lives, Sukkot enables us to contemplate the bounty we have been given, yet understand even further what we still need to do.

# Simchat Torah: From Deuteronomy to Genesis
## Traditional Haftarah Reading: Joshua 1:1–18

## Moving Through Difficult Times
### RABBI SANDRA J. COHEN

CAN YOU IMAGINE being Joshua? In the traditional haftarah reading for Simchat Torah, we read from Joshua 1:2, "My servant Moses is dead." Just as we finish the Torah by reading the end of the Book of Deuteronomy and then begin reading it again with the opening verses of the Book of Genesis, the haftarah reading for Simchat Torah reminds us that *B'nei Yisrael*, the "Children of Israel," also had to begin anew after Moses's death. Joshua, the appointed successor, had to move into an impossible role: How do you follow Moses?

God's words to Joshua give a hint. Three times, God says, "Be strong and of good courage" (Joshua 1:6, 7, 9). The people are frightened; they are preparing to enter the land of Canaan, with Moses gone. Joshua, their new leader, must show that he is confident, that he is up to the job at hand. This is not a time to show uncertainty, even if some things might go wrong. God reminds Joshua to have the Torah on his lips day and night. Thus will God be with him.

When we are leading, or even moving just by ourselves through difficult times, we can always turn to God for strength and to our tradition for wisdom. Thus we will never be alone in our endeavors.

## Carrying Our Legacy
### RABBI ETHAN PROSNIT

On Simchat Torah, we read the last words of Deuteronomy, marking the death of Moses, and then the first words of Genesis, beginning the Torah cycle anew.

It is fitting that the traditional haftarah reading for Simchat Torah is from the first chapter of the Book of Joshua. The Book of Joshua opens the biblical section called "Prophets" and continues the story of the Israelite people. In the first verses of the haftarah portion, we read about the death of Moses and how Joshua will be the one who will lead the Israelite people into the Promised Land. God then echoes that God will be with the Israelite people as God was with Moses and instructs Joshua and the people to be "strong and of good courage" (Joshua 1:6).

As Joshua leads the Israelites into the Promised Land, he carries on the legacy of Moses. The haftarah text makes us think about how we can carry on the legacy of our past leaders and loved ones. How can we be strong and brave as we navigate new journeys? What characteristics or aspects of their leadership do we carry toward the future?

The texts of our tradition remind us that we are part of a larger story. We stand on the shoulders of those who came before us.

## Alternative Haftarah Reading: Nehemiah 8:1–10

When the seventh month arrived—the Israelites being [settled] in their towns—the entire people assembled as one in the square before the Water Gate, and they asked Ezra the scribe to bring the scroll of the Teaching of Moses with which the Eternal had charged Israel. On the first day of the seventh month, Ezra the priest brought the Teaching before the congregation, men and women and all who could listen with understanding. He read from it, facing the square before the Water Gate, from the first light until midday, to the men and the women and those who could understand; the ears of all the people were given to the scroll of the Teaching.

Ezra the scribe stood upon a wooden tower made for the purpose, and beside him stood Mattithiah, Shema, Anaiah, Uriah, Hilkiah, and Maaseiah at his right, and at his left Pedaiah, Mishael, Malchijah, Hashum, Hashbaddanah, Zechariah, Meshullam. Ezra opened the scroll in the sight of all the people, for he was above all the people; as he opened it, all the people stood up. Ezra bless the Eternal, the great God, and all the people answered, "Amen, Amen," with hands upraised. Then they bowed their heads and prostrated themselves before the Eternal with their faces to the ground. Jeshua, Bani, Sherebiah, Jamin, Akkub, Shabbethai, Hodiah, Maaseiah, Kelita, Azariah, Jozabad, Hanan, Pelaiah, and the Levites explained the Teaching to the people, while the people stood in their places. They read from the scroll of the Teaching of God, translating it and giving the sense; so they understood the reading.

Nehemiah the Tirshatha, Ezra the priest and scribe, and the Levites who were explaining to the people said to all the people, "This day is holy to the Eternal your God: you must not mourn or weep," for all the people were weeping as they listened to the words of the Teaching. He further said to them, "Go, eat choice foods and drink sweet drinks and send portions to whoever has nothing prepared, for the day is holy to our God. Do not be sad, for your rejoicing in the Eternal is the source of your strength."

# The Essence of Simchat Torah Is Joy

*Rabbi Jan Katzew, PhD*

In keeping with the Rabbinic aphorism "Delve in it [the Torah] and continue to delve in it, for everything is in it" (*Pirkei Avot* 5:26), the unique Torah reading on Simchat Torah bridges the end of the Book of Deuteronomy to the beginning of the Book of Genesis. The *aliyot*, while always an honor, are given special names: *chatan/kallah Torah* (the groom/bride of Torah) and *chatan/kallah B'reishit* (the groom/bride of Genesis), respectively.

Nehemiah 8:1–10 is a fitting haftarah because it describes the earliest ritualized public reading of the Torah, complete with translation and interpretation: at the Water Gate, from a specially constructed wooden podium, Ezra the priestly scribe stands above the people, offering a blessing, and everyone present, men and women, respond, "Amen, Amen."

The Torah was and is to be democratized, read publicly, made understandable, interpreted, loved, and lived. On Simchat Torah, however, we access an even deeper emotional layer of our relationship with those scrolls—a layer that is captured exquisitely in the text from the Book of Nehamiah: the essence of Simchat Torah is joy.

Ezra tells the people not to cry and instead to eat and drink delicacies, provide for the people who lack sustenance, and celebrate the day by rejoicing in their relationship to God through Torah. His teaching is as timely as it is timeless.

## *Alternative Haftarah Reading: "Blessed Are You," by Ruhama Weiss, PhD*

Blessed are You, Shechinah, Source of Life,
Who bestows favor to the undeserving
Who granted me Torah and Talmud study
And being born to this generation of women
Who puts bread on my table with the crumbs of free time
Who bestowed the possibility of listening and being heard
And who gave me a community of now
Blessed are You, who bestows favor to the Undeserving.

# Joining the Circle

*Rabbi Naamah Kelman*

These words of Ruhama Weiss are written for our generation of women: the first who have studied Torah and who have cracked the Talmud open as well. Finally, we can carry our Written and Oral traditions forward, passing them on from woman to young girl to woman. We celebrate the never-ending fountain of stories, laws, lessons, mitzvot, and values that we receive from Torah, year after year. We must not forget that it is only recent history that has witnessed the yearning for and outpouring of commentary and creativity coming from women as well. It is a life-preserving and life-granting experience; we feel redeemed.

We rejoice as we join the circle, as we bring healing and redemption closer. Yes, we carry on the lessons of Torah; yes, we preserve and we evoke change; yes, we work for changes toward more equality and inclusion; yes, we seek to empower those who were excluded for generations.

# *Chanukah, Shabbat I*
## Traditional Haftarah Reading:
## Zechariah 4:1–7

## In Your Light Do We See Light
### *Rabbi Kerry M. Olitzky*

ON THE FIRST (and often, sole) Shabbat of the most widely celebrated Jewish festival in North America, Chanukah, the postexilic prophet Zechariah offers us *the* lesson that permeates all of Jewish prayer. His familiar teaching, which punctuates the traditional haftarah reading, is translated as "'Not by might, nor by power, but by My spirit,' says the God of heaven's hosts" (Zechariah 4:6).

For the Israelites returning to Jerusalem after the Babylonian exile—as for us today—this message is incomplete without the more concrete and embodied symbol of a golden seven-branched menorah, also described in this haftarah reading (Zechariah 4:2–3). This symbol is what explicitly makes the connection to the holiday:

- The menorah, later adapted for the Chanukah celebration, is housed in the ancient and in the future Temple envisioned by Zechariah.
- It was there to remind us of the divine light that illumines the world and casts no shadow.
- In this light, we are able to see ourselves most clearly.

We are charged to carry this divine light forward into the world, especially to its darkest places. As the Psalmist taught, "In Your light do we see light" (Psalm 36:10).

## Not by Might, Nor by Power, but by My Spirit Alone
### *Rabbi Donald B. Rossoff*

Every year, Jewish homes shine with the light of a *chanukiyah*, the nine-branched menorah that is the symbol of our Festival of Lights. In the traditional haftarah reading, the prophet Zechariah evokes the image of a menorah, which then serves as its central link to the holiday (Zechariah 4:2–3).

Zechariah addresses the community of returning expatriates (520–518 BCE), conveying divine encouragement as they struggle with limited resources and local opposition to build what would become the Second Temple. In a dreamlike vision, an angel of God shows the prophet a golden seven-branched menorah. Each lamp is linked to one of two olive trees, thus providing them with everlasting energy. When Zechariah asks the meaning of this vision, the angel replies, "'Not by might, nor by power, but by My spirit,' says the God of heaven's host" (Zechariah 4:6).

What exactly is "My spirit"? Given the context, God's spirit would be the spirit of perseverance and resilience during trying times, fortitude and courage in the face of the obstacles ahead, steadfast belief in the sacred importance of one's enterprise, and faith in one's ability to move mountains. And as God's spirit was then, so it is today and will be evermore.

## Alternative Haftarah Reading: "In Exile," by Emma Lazarus

"Since that day till now our life is one unbroken paradise. We live a true brotherly life. Every evening after supper we take a seat under the mighty oak and sing our songs."—Extract from a letter of a Russian refugee in Texas.

Twilight is here, soft breezes bow the grass,
Day's sounds of various toil break slowly off.
The yoke-freed oxen low, the patient ass
Dips his dry nostril in the cool, deep trough.
Up from the prairie the tanned herdsmen pass
With frothy pails, guiding with voices rough
Their udder-lightened kine. Fresh smells of earth,
The rich, black furrows of the glebe send forth.

After the Southern day of heavy toil,
How good to lie, with limbs relaxed, brows bare
To evening's fan, and watch the smoke-wreaths coil
Up from one's pipe-stem through the rayless air.
So deem these unused tillers of the soil,
Who stretched beneath the shadowing oak tree, stare
Peacefully on the star-unfolding skies,
And name their life unbroken paradise.

The hounded stag that has escaped the pack,
And pants at ease within a thick-leaved dell;
The unimprisoned bird that finds the track
Through sun-bathed space, to where his fellows dwell;
The martyr, granted respite from the rack,

The death-doomed victim pardoned from his cell,—
Such only know the joy these exiles gain,—
Life's sharpest rapture is surcease of pain.

Strange faces theirs, wherethrough the Orient sun
Gleams from the eyes and glows athwart the skin.
Grave lines of studious thought and purpose run
From curl-crowned forehead to dark-bearded chin.
And over all the seal is stamped thereon
Of anguish branded by a world of sin,
In fire and blood through ages on their name,
Their seal of glory and the Gentiles' shame.

Freedom to love the law that Moses brought,
To sing the songs of David, and to think
The thoughts Gabirol to Spinoza taught,
Freedom to dig the common earth, to drink
The universal air—for this they sought
Refuge o'er wave and continent, to link
Egypt with Texas in their mystic chain,
And truth's perpetual lamp forbid to wane.

Hark! through the quiet evening air, their song
Floats forth with wild sweet rhythm and glad refrain.
They sing the conquest of the spirit strong,
The soul that wrests the victory from pain;
The noble joys of manhood that belong
To comrades and to brothers. In their strain
Rustle of palms and Eastern streams one hears,
And the broad prairie melts in mist of tears.

# Songs of Revolt and Vanquishing Light

### CANTOR SHANI COHEN

Emma Lazarus (1849–87) was a fifth-generation American Jew of Spanish-Portuguese descent who gained her place in the chronicles of American history as the author of the iconic words inscribed on the Statue of Liberty: "Give me your tired, your poor, / Your huddled masses yearning to breathe free." An outspoken idealist and activist, Lazarus volunteered to support the Russian Jewish immigrants flooding New York in the 1880s. Even while facing antisemitism as well as the sexism of her time, Lazarus was able to use her education and considerable economic privilege to publish her poetry from a young age.

"In Exile" is part of a poetry collection exploring Lazarus's American Jewish identity, published when she was thirty-three years old. The poem is her response to a letter from a Russian refugee who relocated to Texas, far from his home country. Using biblical motifs of the Jewish people's exile from the Land of Israel, Lazarus opens her poem with imagery of the idyllic rural life that many Jews sought out in America: an "unbroken paradise." What is this paradise? Freedom, first and foremost, to practice Judaism, to sing our Jewish music, and to study Jewish texts from "Gabirol to Spinoza." Though technically just another "exile," America provides for the freedom that Jews had been praying for for thousands of years.

During the Chanukah season, we sing again our songs of revolt and vanquishing light. "They sing the conquest of the spirit strong, / The soul that wrests the victory from pain," Lazarus writes, and we can imagine Jewish immigrants huddling around the fire, singing of Judah the Maccabee. What were the Maccabees fighting for if not "freedom to love the law that Moses brought, / to sing the songs of David" in their land? Lazarus's contemporary version of this celebration lauds America as the promised land where our people can be free. Lazarus holds onto the hope and promise of America, not giving up on her values or faith in her country.

Today, we still espouse those values and work to make them a reality. May we carry forth the teachings of Chanukah, as well as the hope of Emma Lazarus, that "truth's perpetual lamp forbid to wane."

## Alternative Haftarah Reading:
### From "Some Notes on Jewish Lesbian Identity," by Melanie Kaye/Kantrowitz

As Jewish women, we need to look at our people with our own eyes. To see Judith, who saved the Jewish people; she flirted with the attacking general, drank him under the table; then she and her maid (whose name is not in the story) whacked off his head, stuck it in a picnic basket, and escaped back to the Jewish camp. . . . Judith set her maid free, and all the women danced in her honor. That's a Jewish princess.

Or Anzia Yezierska, who told, in Yiddish-like English, stories of Jewish immigrants, especially women's struggles for love, freedom, and education. Of her work, she wrote: "It's not me—it's their cries—my own people—crying in me! Hannah Breineh, Shmendrek, they will not be stilled in me, till all America stops to listen." That's a nice Jewish girl.

Or Violette Kaye, who recently when I asked, ashamed, to borrow money for an airline ticket back east, and she said, of course; and then told me they're retiring, and I said, this isn't a good time for any of us, and she said "Listen, if I have it, and I do, it's yours." That's a Jewish mother (mine).

# Our Herstory as Truthtellers, Advocates, and Resistance Fighters

*CANTOR ABBE LYONS*

The story of Judith, a young widow, assassinating Holofernes, the enemy general, has long been associated with Chanukah, yet was overshadowed by the stories of the Maccabees. While the violence in this story may feel uncomfortable, clearly Judith is just as fierce a freedom fighter as the much more well-known Maccabean men. The Torah reminds us over and over again of the economic vulnerability of widows, yet here Judith shows the opposite of vulnerability.

In "Some Notes on Jewish Lesbian Identity," Melanie Kaye/Kantrowitz celebrates Judith among many other Jewish women overturning modern stereotypes of Jewish princesses, nice Jewish girls, and Jewish mothers. She reveals our herstory as eloquent, passionate, practical, graceful, loving, and fierce truthtellers, advocates, and resistance fighters, countering the dysfunctional shame and blame we may have internalized.

On Chanukah, we celebrate Judith's courage and decisiveness while shifting our focus away from militarism. We listen to the voices of Yezierska's characters growing clearer as the light of the candles grows brighter each night. We seek to live our values even when that's a challenge—just like Violette Kaye.

# Chanukah, Shabbat 2
## Traditional Haftarah Reading:
## I Kings 7:40–50

## Bringing Light and Warmth
### CANTOR DR. EVAN KENT

WHEN I WAS a child, my family had a multivolume illustrated set of the Bible. I would spend hours looking at the wood engravings of biblical scenes as imagined by Gustave Doré. The drawings were intricate, with painstaking detail. Dore's engravings were filled with great emotion and drama, and aside from the drawings of Moses leading the Israelites through the Red Sea, it was the drawings of King Solomon's monumental Temple in Jerusalem that I found most fascinating. These were rich, detailed scenes of ancient Jerusalem, with the Temple decorated in all the opulence and richness we encounter in this week's haftarah reading.

When Chanukah begins on a Shabbat, we are fortunate to celebrate two Shabbatot over the course of the eight-day festival. The reading for the second Shabbat is I Kings 7:40–50. It begins with a description of the columns supporting the Temple and the capitals on top of the columns. Following this, we find descriptions of latticework, a gigantic water tank used for the purification ritual of the priests, and the altar for the Temple. The reading concludes with the description of the golden lamps that were positioned on either side of the entrance to the inner sanctuary.

These concluding verses present the connection to Chanukah: the importance of light and illumination, the spiritual message of this holiday. Chanukah occurs at the darkest time of the year, and through the successive lighting of candles the festival brings us light and warmth.

The kindling of the Chanukah candles reminds us that we as Jews have to bring righteousness into the world and to illuminate those places where intolerance and injustice are found. As we light the candles of Chanukah and recall the great Temple of Solomon, we must bring, through acts of justice and mercy, light into a world that is sometimes shrouded in spiritual and physical darkness.

# Between Abundance and Systemic Inequalities

*RABBI ANDREW BUSCH*

Chanukah's eight days always include at least one Shabbat, but when Chanukah starts on Shabbat, it includes two Shabbatot!

The second Shabbat's haftarah reading is I Kings 7:40–50, duplicating the Ashkenazic haftarah for *Parashat Vayak'heil* (Exodus 35:1–38:20). Both *Vayak'heil* and the *maftir* for the second Shabbat of Chanukah (Numbers 7:54–8:4) address the items required for Israelite worship.

I Kings 7:40–50 is quite specific regarding the necessary materials, utensils, and measurements required. For example, verse 49 clarifies that Solomon's Temple needed ten solid, golden lamp stands. Those lamp stands (*m'norot*) are a natural connection to the story and rituals of Chanukah. However, verse 47 is intriguingly vague: "the weight of the bronze was never determined." Everything else is carefully weighed, measured, and assigned. Why not the bronze? Was there simply too much bronze to measure it? Was there so much bronze that there was no need to measure it?

I Kings 7 is not granting permission for endless Chanukah gifts. Rather, this haftarah prods us to acknowledge real economic disparities. Beyond dedicating one Chanukah night to the giving of *tzedakah*, we are challenged to address societal economic disparities. One-time social action projects must give birth to continuous efforts addressing systemic inequalities.

## *Alternative Haftarah Reading: Jeremiah 31:27–40*

See, a time is coming—declares the Eternal—when I will sow the House of Israel and the House of Judah with seed of humans and seed of cattle; and just as I was watchful over them to uproot and to pull down, to overthrow and to destroy and to bring disaster, so I will be watchful over them to build and to plant—declares the Eternal. In those days, they shall no longer say, "Parents have eaten sour grapes and children's teeth are blunted." But every one shall die for their own sins: whosoever eats sour grapes, their teeth shall be blunted.

See, a time is coming—declares the Eternal—when I shall make a new covenant with the House of Israel and the House of Judah. It will not be like the covenant I made with their ancestors, when I took them by the hand to lead them out of the land of Egypt, a covenant which they broke, though I espoused them—declares the Eternal. But such is the covenant I will make with the House of Israel after these days—declares the Eternal: I will put My Teaching into their inmost being and inscribe it upon their hearts. Then I will be their God, and they shall be My people. No longer will they need to teach one another and say to one another, "Heed the Eternal"; for all of them, from the least of them to the greatest, shall heed Me—declares the Eternal.

> For I will forgive their iniquities,
> and remember their sins no more.

> Thus said the Eternal,
> who established the sun for light by day,
> the laws of moon and stars for light by night,
> who stirs up the sea into roaring waves,
> whose name is God of heaven's hosts:
> If these laws should ever be annulled by Me
>    —declares the Eternal—
> only then would the offspring of Israel cease
> to be a nation before Me for all time.

Thus said the Eternal: If the heavens above could be measured, and the foundations of the earth below could be fathomed, only then would I reject all the offspring of Israel for all that they have done—declares the Eternal.

See, a time is coming—declares the Eternal—when the city shall be rebuilt for the Eternal from the Tower of Hananel to the Corner Gate; and the measuring line shall go straight out to the Gareb Hill, and then turn toward Goah. And the entire Valley of the Corpses and Ashes, and all the fields as far as the Wadi Kidron, and the corner of the Horse Gate on the east, shall be holy to the Eternal. They shall never again be uprooted or overthrown.

# Effecting Change

### RABBI HOWARD STEIN

This alternative haftarah from Jeremiah reflects the historic themes of Chanukah, connecting the human rededication of the Temple with the light that God shines into the world. The prophet connects the light of the sun, moon, and stars and the roaring of the seas to the new covenant God will establish with Israel. This connection spans existence from Creation to messianic redemption. We are the agents who must sustain the route from Creation through the present to help us arrive at the future.

The root of the word *chanukah*, "to dedicate," is the same as the root for "to educate." When Jeremiah speaks about a new covenant sealed with God's teaching, we understand that learning leads to action. Our learning shows us how to use our power effectively. *Midrash Tanchuma* (*B'reishit* 1:5) teaches that God bound the sea so it would not flood the world; *M'chilta D'Rabbi Yishmael* (14:15) teaches that the sun and moon are testifying that God split the Sea of Reeds.

There are times to hold back, to act discreetly. At other times, we must release the floodwaters to effect the change we wish to see.

## *Alternative Haftarah Reading:*
## *"At Your Feet, Jerusalem," by Uri Zvi Greenberg*

Kings cast wreaths at your feet and fall upon their faces
    And they are then wonderful servants to you and your God.
Rome too sends its marble, crystal, and gold
    To build within you a summit sanctuary for fame and glory.
And we, we your barefoot sons and daughters
    Who come to you beggared from the ends of the world,
We are, as we here are, children
    Of Sovereignty: of the cactus growing by itself, of the waves of the cliffs.
We who leave Jewish community
    In the world, put our coat of many colors, like a lizard, into the bag.
Father scolded, mother wept, and the white bed was orphaned.
To you we have brought blood and fingers, love and muscles: unburdened
    Shoulders to carry the Hebrew globe with its open sores.
All our dreams and our ambitions we gave up
    That we might be poor laborers in the wasteland.
Where in the world can you find its like? Ask, you who were burned by Titus!
    Where do they love rusty sovereignty with eternal love?
Where is the wailing of jackals heard with great compassion?
    Where do they fever in red song, where do they shrivel and grow silent,
And cool flaming foreheads and kiss the cliffs?
The heatwind here slowly burns away our dear youth
    Whose dust is scattered daily over the crevices like gold
And we ask no compensation for our destruction.
And with our precious bodies we cover the swamps.
    As our hands drive into them the eucalyptus trees.
We who provide a feast for the worms of Canaan,
We are prepared with faithful bodies, fevering
    To be the warm bridge for the sovereignty that comes
Over the abyss of blood.
Should a sword be sharpened in Canaan against you —
    We would make for you a witness-pile of bodies like an outer wall.
And someone who denies the glory in pain and in your disaster
    Struggles from cliff to cliff here, cursing and reviling —
Yes, you will forgive him, and allow him to abuse:
    To pass from cliff to cliff because his spleen has risen up.
It is impossible to snap the head off the body with one's hands
    And throw it like a pot on one of the angry rocks.
But the hiss of this serpent is also the shadow of a melody!
And the soles of his feet danced a Hora here,

Crying, "God will build the desolation," in the light of the stars.
And until he goes to Jaffa, to the office of the émigrés,
   And puts his muddy coat, like a lizard, into the bag—
Yet many days
   Will he stand and quarry your rocks—at your feet—
And he will eat his bread in a sweat—the shew bread—
   Bitterly will he smoke a cigarette with his blood in his eyes.
Perhaps he will also dance another Hora
   With his dragging feet—one last time—
And shout "God will build" in the light of the great stars!

## Sowing Light amid Darkness

### Rabbi Douglas Kohn

The closing days of Chanukah merge multiple themes: the Temple reconsecration; the Jewish people's checkered history with leaders, notably noble and tyrannical kings; light sown amid darkness; and the centrality of Jerusalem in our canon, history, and lore. This is especially so when Chanukah includes a second Shabbat, and hence a second haftarah reading. The traditional reading from the Book of Kings stirs all of these themes concurrently.

Similarly, the early Zionist poet Uri Zvi Greenberg (1896–1981) captures these themes in his poem "At Your Feet, Jerusalem." An Israel Prize winner for literature and Bialik Prize awardee for poetry, Greenberg was among the most celebrated Israeli writers of the twentieth century, especially after he penned this poem in 1937. Weaving Hebrew phrases from Torah with allusions to kings and the destruction and rebuilding of Jerusalem, Greenberg transports us to the days of the British Mandate, telling a story of suffering as well as of dancing the hora. The children of *Eretz Yisrael* triumph, however, and Greenberg concludes that "'God will build' in the light of the great stars."

On this second Shabbat of Chanukah, the poet again brings the light of Jerusalem into every Jewish home. How can we preserve this light of hope and resilience throughout the year?

# Shabbat Sh'kalim
## Exodus 30:11–16

## Traditional Haftarah Reading:
## II Kings 12:5–16

## Collections and Distributions
### *Rabbi Barbara AB Symons*

IN THE TRADITIONAL haftarah reading for Shabbat Sh'kalim, which matches perfectly with the Torah portion's description of the half-shekel tax paid by the Israelites to build the *Mishkan* in the desert (Exodus 30:11–16), King Jehoash directs the priests to collect all the money brought in to the Temple in Jerusalem, whether through assessments or freewill offerings. When, twenty-three years later, he sees that no repairs have been made to the Temple, he changes course: no longer would the priests accept the money collected. It was not that the money was being inappropriately spent; it was that the money was inappropriately being unspent. King Jehoash speaks with the priest Jehoiada, and making the effort to gain the other priests' agreement, Jehoiada makes a new collection receptacle and comes up with a new plan. From that point on, the royal scribe and High Priest will collect the money offerings and then give the proper portion to those artisans in charge of repairing the Temple. Means and ends paid off.

Money given for specific purposes should be used that way in a timely manner. We know that our collections, be they dues or assessments, and the most righteous of giving, *tzedakah*, are not doing any good when trapped in their receptacles, whether in their electronic forms or in *tzedakah* boxes. After all, the important part of a *tzedakah* box is its opening for the distribution of the money for the sake of repairing the world (*tikkun olam*). Take a moment now, empty your *tzedakah* box, and use the funds to fix a broken part of our world.

## In Service
### *Rabbi Neil Janes*

The traditional haftarah reading for Shabbat Sh'kalim reminds us to hold people and organizations, even the Temple as a sacrificial "organization," to scrupulously high standards.

Shabbat Sh'kalim is one of the special haftarot read leading up to Pesach. The Torah reading is Exodus 30:11–16, which describes a census taken by collecting a half-shekel tax, used for the upkeep of the Tent of Meeting (the *Mishkan*).

The haftarah reading recounts that King Jehoash of Judah, in the ninth century BCE, instructs that money brought to the Temple be used for making repairs. After twenty-three years of minimal oversight, he discovers that the priests have made no repairs at all to the Temple. Under his renewed scrutiny, the priests change the system of tax collection by placing a money box at the entrance of the Temple. Distribution of the money is then overseen jointly by the royal scribe and the High Priest.

In this wonderful vignette, we see the danger of even accidental misuse of funds and the importance of scrupulousness by all those holding positions carrying out public and charitable service. The Babylonian Talmud (*Bava Batra* 9a) derives universal principles for the collection and redistribution of charity from these texts. From the Temple, to charity, to social justice—the prophetic readings bridge the worlds of institutional and political power and the lived experiences of the most vulnerable. We all must hold up and protect the highest standards.

## *Alternative Haftarah Reading: Babylonian Talmud, Sanhedrin 17b*

A Torah scholar is not permitted to reside in any city that does not have these ten things:

> a court that can mete out punishments;
> a charity fund for which monies are collected by two people and distributed by three;
> a synagogue;
> a bathhouse;
> a public restroom;
> a doctor;
> a bloodletter;
> a scribe;
> a ritual slaughterer;
> and a teacher of young children.

They said in the name of Rabbi Akiva: The city must also have varieties of fruit, because varieties of fruit illuminate the eyes.

# All Are Responsible for Supporting the Community
### RABBI DONALD P. CASHMAN

Shabbat Sh'kalim occurs on or before Rosh Chodesh Adar (Adar II in leap years) and takes its name from the additional Torah reading of Exodus 30:11–16. The chief feature of this *maftir* portion is a head tax of half a shekel for everyone age twenty and up, which was levied for expiation upon taking a census. The Torah assigns the proceeds to the service of the Tent of Meeting. Everyone, therefore, provides support for this required institution.

This passage characterizes a desirable dwelling place for a sage. The necessary institutions, personnel, and infrastructure of this city require everyone's financial support. Even if minimal, everyone has a stake in the well-being of the town.

This list comes from a time, place, and mindset different from our own. We don't need communal bathhouses, bloodletters, or public scribes-for-hire anymore, and foods are prepared or packaged elsewhere and shipped. Yet, we still need courts and schools that belong to everyone, water and sewage systems, doctors and hospitals, synagogues and supermarkets within a reasonable distance, and the assurance that our charitable dollars are used with integrity. These, and many more aspects of modern life, need to be underwritten by all for the benefit of all.

Each one of us has a stake in society, and we see in this passage the obligation to provide for the institutions, social services, and professionals we need. The Torah reading specifies a minimal amount for everyone to give to ensure that all feel the sense of belonging to the community. Yet we recognize this regressive head tax, where "the rich shall not pay more and the poor shall not pay less" (Exodus 30:15) as insufficient to handle all of our communal needs. A just society must admit all; but justice also requires that those blessed with more must provide more for the communal good.

## Alternative Haftarah Reading:
## From "Religion and Race," by Rabbi Abraham Joshua Heschel

In several ways man is set apart from all beings created in six days. The Bible does not say, God created the plant or the animal; it says, God created different kinds of plants, different kinds of animals (Genesis 1:11–12, 1:21–25). In striking contrast, it does not say, God created different kinds of man, men of different colors and races; it proclaims, God created one single man. From one single man all men are descended.

To think of man in terms of white, black, or yellow is more than an error. It is an eye disease, a cancer of the soul. . . . How many disasters do we have to go through in order to realize that all of humanity has a stake in the liberty of one person; whenever one person is offended, we are all hurt. What begins as inequality of some inevitably ends as inequality of all.

# Equality before God

### CANTOR MICHELE GRAY-SCHAFFER

In the Torah portion for Shabbat Sh'kalim, God imposes a half-shekel tax on Israelite men of military age for the maintenance of the people's worship space, then the Tent of Meeting. This sets a precedent that remains in place until the destruction of the Second Temple and beyond.

The traditional haftarah reading chronicles attempts of the boy-king Jehoash to reestablish the tax, as his indifferent predecessors have let it lapse and the Temple is in desperate need of repair. His attempts to reimpose the tax fail, but the High Priest Jehoiada installs a *tzedakah* box at the entrance to the Temple, and the people respond with great generosity.

Much commentary has centered on the concept of equality set forth in Exodus 30:15, "The rich shall not pay more and the poor shall not pay less than half a shekel when giving the Eternal's offering." One interpretation draws upon the concept that every person is equal in the eyes of God: because each of us is created in the image of God, our task is to emulate the Holy One's example.

Let me suggest that the failure of humanity to live up to God's example has long been a scourge of humanity. The Black Lives Matter movement has drawn attention to the unequal treatment of people of color in our time. Sadly, in my estimation, many people fail to recognize that the struggle of people of color is everyone's concern. On this subject, we may recall the words of Rabbi Abraham Joshua Heschel almost sixty years ago, given at the National Conference on Religion and Race held in Chicago in 1963.

Heschel's observations are no less relevant today. *Ki va mo-eid*—"it is time" for each of us to search our hearts for any traces of racism and thoughts of "the other." As a beginning, we can educate ourselves about the experiences of people of color by joining local Black Lives Matter groups and by studying and learning from germane documentaries, movies, and books. The need to heal this "ancient rupture in the human family," as attendees at the conference pledged, is pressing.

# Shabbat Zachor
## Haftarah Reading:
## Esther 7:1–10, 8:15–17

## Win-Win

*Rabbi Barbara AB Symons*

THIS HAFTARAH READING for Shabbat Zachor is unusual for two reasons. First, it connects not to the regular Torah portion but to an additional Torah reading from Deuteronomy 25:17–19, usually read from a second scroll, that tells of the ways that Amalek fought inhumanely against the Israelites, attacking the stragglers in the rear rather than the fighting forces in the front. Second, the haftarah reading in Rabbi W. Gunther Plaut's *The Torah: A Modern Commentary* is taken not from the Prophets section of the Hebrew Bible but from the Writings. More traditional Jewish communities read I Samuel 15:1–34, from the Prophets. The latter, like the additional Torah portion, speaks of Amalek and specifically of King Agag of the Amalekites. That is the Reform Jewish connection as well: Haman (boo!) was an Agagite and descendant of the Amalekites. Our haftarah gives us a preview of the Scroll of Esther, which we will read in the upcoming week as we celebrate Purim.

In Esther, since the decree to annihilate the Jews of the Persian Empire cannot be withdrawn, King Ahasuerus declares through an overriding decree that they may defend themselves. It is a bloody battle, with many lives lost at the hands of the Jewish community. In previous battles, such as the one described in Deuteronomy 20:10–14, the Israelites could either take all the plenty—including human beings—or destroy them. Yet by the time of Esther, we have evolved as victor. The Jews fight only those who seek to do them harm. Further, they do not even take the spoils. Instead, they translate their "gladness and joy" into feasting and merrymaking, sending gifts to one another and to the poor (Esther 9:17–19).

We are often winners—at games and sports, in winning a business contract or an award. But how do we celebrate the win? In Esther, we are given a model: We should celebrate joyfully, yet that is not enough. We must share our spoils with others, both with those in need and with those who have plenty. Per Esther, we are neither to gloat nor to turn inward. Rather, by celebrating in this way, we create a win-win situation. Even when there are two sides and a clear winner, let us ensure that ultimately all are victorious.

# Amaleikiyut

### RABBI DONALD B. ROSSOFF

"Remember [*zachor*] what Amalek did to you on your journey, after you left Egypt. . . . Therefore . . . blot out the memory of Amalek. . . . Do not forget!" (Deuteronomy 25:17–19).

The Torah commands that the Israelites never forget to wipe out the memory of Amalek. When in battle, Amalekites are to be wiped out and none of their spoil is to be taken. In I Samuel 15:1–34, the haftarah read by more traditional Jewish communities, King Saul battles Agag, an Amalekite king. But Saul spares Agag and allows the taking of his spoil. The prophet Samuel excoriates Saul for disobeying God's commands, kills Agag, and declares that Saul has lost the right of kingship.

The Scroll of Esther continues the battle between the descendants of Agag and Saul. Not wanting to use the name Amalek, the text identifies the villain as an "Agagite," a descendant of Agag, while Mordecai is subtly identified as a descendant of Saul. The Book of Esther ends with the death of Haman and his seed, bringing this battle to a "happy" ending.

My rebbe, Rabbi Frederick C. Schwartz, taught that in our day, we should avoid speaking about wiping out "Amalek," for this leads to demonizing people, which can have horrific consequences (e.g., the Cave of the Patriarchs massacre in 1994). Rather, we speak about wiping out *Amaleikiyut*, the forces that undermine Judaism and our ability to sustain a meaningful Jewish future. Externally, this can refer to antisemitism, racism, all forms of othering, and even economic downturn. Internally, it can take the form of assimilation, indifference, self-hatred, and *chilul HaShem*, the "desecration of God's name" by Jews whose unethical and immoral acts lead others to think that the Jews have no God.

As we remember to live affirmative and ethical Jewish lives through Torah, service to God and God's creation, and acts of *chesed* (love, kindness, and loyalty), we are wiping out *Amaleikiyut* and performing acts of *kiddush HaShem*, the "sanctification of God's name." Let us not forget!

## Alternative Haftarah Reading:
## Jeremiah 29:1-9

This is the text of the letter which the prophet Jeremiah sent from Jerusalem to the priests, the prophets, the rest of the elders of the exile community, and to all the people whom Nebuchadnezzar had exiled from Jerusalem to Babylon—after King Jeconiah, the queen mother, the eunuchs, the officials of Judah and Jerusalem, and the craftsmen and smiths had left Jerusalem. [The letter was sent] through Elasah son of Shaphan and Gemariah son of Hilkiah, whom King Zedekiah of Judah had dispatched to Babylon, to King Nebuchadnezzar of Babylon.

Thus said the God of heaven's hosts, the God of Israel, to the whole community which I exiled from Jerusalem to Babylon: Build houses and live in them, plant gardens and eat their fruit. Take wives and beget sons and daughters; and take wives for your sons, and give your daughters to husbands, that they may bear sons and daughters. Multiply there, do not decrease. And seek the welfare of the city to which I have exiled you and pray to the Eternal in its behalf; for in its prosperity you shall prosper.

For thus said the God of heaven's hosts, the God of Israel: Let not the prophets and diviners in your midst deceive you, and pay no heed to the dreams they dream. For they prophesy to you in My name falsely; I did not send them—declares the Eternal.

# Judaism as We Know It

### RABBI CHARLES MIDDLEBURGH, PhD

The Kingdom of Judah is nearing the end of its existence, and Jeremiah is convinced that Nebuchadnezzar will fulfill the will of God and destroy Jerusalem. One group of prominent people has already been exiled to Babylon in 597 BCE, and as the dark clouds gather over those who remain, he writes one of the most important letters in world history to those first exiles: he tells them to settle themselves properly, to build homes, have families, and grow orchards and vineyards. The very fact that all of these endeavors take years to accomplish is the clearest indication of the meaning of Jeremiah's words, the fact that they should make a life for themselves in their new land and establish new roots.

However, Jeremiah then tells the exiles something even more significant. He tells them to pray to God for the welfare of the government under whose rules they live, for its well-being will guarantee their own. With that instruction he effectively tells them that their former "national" God is no longer restricted to a Temple in Jerusalem or a kingdom of Judah—but a universal God who can be approached anywhere in prayer. His letter is revolutionary and, arguably, the beginning of Judaism as we know it.

Jeremiah started the Jewish people on the path of living constructively and happily in *galut* (exile). Even though few of us would consider ourselves to be living in exile, the message of rooting ourselves where we are is as relevant and meaningful as ever.

To understand where we are we must understand from where we have come. All the important things we remember need to be remembered right.

### *Alternative Haftarah Reading:*
### *Babylonian Talmud,* M'gillah 7b

Rava taught, "It is the duty of a person to drink so much on Purim that one cannot tell the difference between 'cursed be Haman' and 'blessed be Mordecai.'" It happened that Rabbah and Rabbi Zeira got together for a Purim feast. They got drunk, and Rabbah arose and killed Rabbi Zeira. The next day he prayed on his behalf and revived him. The following year Rabbah said to Rabbi Zeira, "Sir, would you like to celebrate Purim together again?" He replied, "A miracle does not happen every time."

# A Purim Murder Story

### RABBI SIMEON J. MASLIN, DMin, z″l

Rabbah killed Rabbi Zeira?! These were two of the greatest sages of fourth-century Babylonia. The idea that a great teacher of Torah would act like a drunken hooligan was so inconceivable to the seventeenth-century Venetian scholar Rabbi Azariah Figo that he examined the story in detail in his book of sermons *Binah L'Itim*, writing, "How is it possible to celebrate God's miracle with the kind of drunkenness that would cause a person to lose the power of common sense . . . and lead to injury?" Figo then goes on, page after page, describing the miraculous way that God interchanged the destinies of Mordecai and Haman, condemning the vizier Haman to the gallows and bringing the Jew Mordecai to royal favor.

How did Figo interpret the mitzvah of drinking on Purim? Performing a mitzvah, like the eating of matzah and bitter herbs on Passover, is intended to *increase* our understanding of God's miracles. But drunkenness on Purim would *decrease* our understanding of the miraculous process by which God interchanged the destinies of Haman and Mordecai. And so Figo interpreted the mitzvah of drinking on Purim as *only* up to that point when the distinction between "cursed be Haman" and "blessed be Mordecai" begins to blur. That is the Purim sobriety test.

But what about the murder of Rabbi Zeira? According to Figo, Rabbah did not physically kill Rabbi Zeira. Rather, as they were arguing the more abstruse points of the ascents and descents of Haman and Mordecai, Rabbah destroyed Rabbi Zeira intellectually. The next day, Rabbah felt so bad about the way that he had embarrassed his colleague that he went to him and apologized. The apology revived Rabbi Zeira's spirits but not so thoroughly that he was willing to celebrate Purim with Rabbah again.

Let us celebrate Purim with sober joy!

# Shabbat Parah
## Traditional Haftarah Reading:
## Ezekiel 36:22–36

## Through *T'shuvah* to Purity

*Rabbi Elizabeth Bahar*

S HABBAT PARAH is one of four special Shabbatot leading up to Passover. The *maftir* (final section of holiday and Shabbat Torah readings) is about the purification ritual of the red heifer. This ritual corresponds to the theme of purification in the haftarah reading, which reassures the Judeans exiled in Babylonia of their return. Even though God was angered by those Judeans who practiced idolatry, God will sanctify the holy name again by gathering the exiles back to Israel, where they shall observe God's law. They will "never again . . . be disgraced" (Ezekiel 36:30), their "ruins shall be rebuilt" (36:33), and God will repopulate the House of Israel (36:35).

However, the haftarah reading also speaks about our feelings of regret and shame for our failures: "Then you shall remember your evil ways, your dealings that were not good, and you shall loathe yourselves for your iniquities and your abominable deeds" (36:31). Brené Brown defines shame as "the intensely painful feeling or experience of believing that we are flawed and therefore unworthy of love and belonging—something we've experienced, done, or failed to do makes us unworthy of connection." If we allow our shame or self-loathing to overwhelm us, we will never be able to move toward a sense of healing and engage in a process of *t'shuvah* (repentance).

Yet, we know that "For not as humans see [does the Eternal see]; a human being sees only what is visible, but the Eternal sees into the heart" (I Samuel 16:7). We might feel ashamed of ourselves, but God values us already for being honest and open with ourselves. We can move beyond brokenness by following a path of *t'shuvah* leading to self-transformation and self-acceptance. This is God's gift of purity to us.

# A New Spirit

*Rabbi Dana Evan Kaplan, PhD*

Shabbat Parah is one of the special Shabbatot that necessitate variations in the Torah cycle. Shabbat Parah, the "Sabbath of the red heifer," takes place on the Shabbat preceding Shabbat HaChodesh. A special Torah reading (Numbers 19:1–9) describes the ritual of the red heifer, which is used to purify the entire Jewish people before they offer the Passover sacrifice. The haftarah reading from the Book of Ezekiel likewise focuses on the purification of the Children of Israel: God promises to sprinkle cleansing water upon them, which will cleanse them of all their impurities (Ezekiel 36:25).

God promises to give the Children of Israel "a new heart and a new spirit" (36:26). As a consequence of this new spirit within the Children of Israel, they will walk in the divine statues and faithfully observe the divine edicts.

Today, we do not possess any methods for purifying ourselves in a full ritual sense. But despite this dramatic change in the entire religious orientation of Judaism since the destruction of the Jerusalem Temple, God's promise to gather us from among the nations and from all the lands of our dispersion and bring us back to our land has indeed been fulfilled in our days. We can make a pilgrimage to the Land of Israel, not just as tourists but, as Ezekiel suggests, as active participants in the divine covenant with God. Our task now is to connect the State of Israel with our own spiritual development. With heartfelt focus on our personal character development, we can all learn to walk again in God's ways.

## *Alternative Haftarah Reading:*
## *"Esther," by Else Lasker-Schüler*

Esther—slim like a palm branch—
Lips—tasting like wheat stalks
And the holidays of Judah.

At night, her heart takes rest on psalms—
The gods are listening in their lofty chambers.

The king is smiling as she is approaching—
Because God has blessed her coming and going.

Young Jews sing songs for their sister
Engraved into the pillars of their reception halls.

# Blood Sacrifices

*Rabbi Sonja K. Pilz, PhD*

There are few moments in the Jewish calendar that seem more foreign to our contemporary religious sentiments than a Shabbat that recalls the ritual slaughter of a cow, leading up to Passover.

And yet, this is just one of many such days—as every day of the Jewish calendar recalls a yearly cycle of blood and food offerings: animals slaughtered in various sacred spaces by both groups and individuals, on both prescribed occasions and as spontaneous acts. Reading through the pages of ancient texts, we cannot ignore—and yet, we manage somehow to ignore—the descriptions of the steady stream of blood and sacrifice accompanying our most sacred, as well as our most ordinary, moments and stories. Shabbat Parah is one of the many moments throughout the Jewish year in which purification is achieved through shedding blood. The traditional *maftir* reading details the ancient ritual of slaughtering, burning, and sprinkling the ashes of a perfect cow as a purifying means. We know of many similar moments of blood-based purification rituals, from the rituals of Yom Kippur (Leviticus 16:1–34) to the "ordination" of the first generation of priests (Leviticus 1:1–8:36). A deep yearning for purity, relief, safety, and a clean conscience seems to have driven many of our ancient rituals—and has continued to do so to this day.

Jewish German poet Else Lasker-Schüler directs our attention to yet another sacrifice, often ignored by tradition—the sacrifice of young women. Similar to the Israeli playwright Hanoch Levin, who in 1970 called out the national sacrifice of every generation of young Israelis to the survival of the country by using the metaphor of the *Akeidah*, the binding of a young Jewish man, Lasker-Schüler shows us Esther, a young woman whose body and life are sacrificed by her uncle, her people, and her God, for the sake of the survival of us, her people.

Moving from Purim to Passover, still savoring hamantaschen, Purim plays, and many feminist stories about the queens Vashti and Esther, as well as the warrior Judith—may we take a pause, ever so shortly, to remember the bodies of young women who have been sacrificed on our way toward survival and freedom.

### *Alternative Haftarah Reading:*
### *"And You Shall Draw Water,"*
### *by Rabbi Sue Levi Elwell*
### *in* The Open Door: A Passover Haggadah

And you shall draw water in joy from the wells of redemption [Isaiah 12:3]
Throughout their desert wanderings,
The Israelites were refreshed by miraculous springs
that bubbled out of deep crevices
in the rocky landscape.
When Miriam died, the waters dried up.
The people mourned the slave child who waited by a river,
the woman who danced across a sea,
the leader who sang a nation to freedom.
When the springs flowed once more,
we named them Miriam's Well.
When fear blocks our path, when our travels deplete us,
we seek sources of healing and wells of hope.
May our questions and our stories nurture us
As Miriam's Well renewed our people's spirits.

## Miriam's Well

### RABBI REENA SPICEHANDLER

The Talmud links the description of the *parah adumah* (red heifer) ritual described in the special Torah reading for Shabbat Parah (Numbers 19:1–9) to the prophetess Miriam, whose death immediately follows. Instructions are given for using the ashes of a red heifer as a means of purification from transgression. Miriam's Well has also been described in midrash as a source of redemption and purification. It follows Miriam in the desert, providing life-giving water to the Israelites on their journey.

This Torah portion is one of the four special readings in the weeks leading up to Passover. It is a time when we attempt to purify our homes and our souls from physical and spiritual *chameitz*. Miriam's Well, which invokes the *mikveh*, is another means of ritual purification.

May we include at our Passover seder a *kos Miryam* (Miriam's cup), filled with pure water to remind us of the redemptive, cleansing powers of our ancestor, the prophetess Miriam, and her well.

# Shabbat HaChodesh
## Traditional Haftarah Reading:
## Ezekiel 45:16–25

## Preparing for Passover
## and Transforming Our Traditions
### Rabbi Eric L. Abbott, MARE

A S WE ENTER the month of Nisan, Shabbat HaChodesh prepares us to mean-ingfully celebrate Passover. In the traditional *maftir* reading (Exodus 12:1–20), God commands the Israelites to mark "this month" (*hachodesh hazeh*, the source of this Sabbath's name) as the first month of the year; God then further prescribes the inaugural Passover ritual. In the haftarah reading, set hundreds of years later in exile, the prophet Ezekiel foretells corresponding rituals of the future Temple.

These paired readings describe two historical poles: the initial Passover experi-ence and a future ceremony commemorating it. They depict preparations for the same festival, yet there are discrepancies in the rituals, such as the measurements of the festival's daily meal offerings.

These contradictions reveal that as history develops, our traditions can—and should—evolve. From Ezekiel's adaptation to post-Temple life to our modern efforts to expand our tent, our faith demands reshaping our tradition to meet the moment.

As we welcome the new month and prepare for Passover, let us bring this change into our homes. Let us retell the Passover story in ways that this generation can hear. May we, like Ezekiel, transform our traditions, reaffirming them to be radi-cally inclusive, spiritually powerful, and daringly hopeful.

## Rituals of Anticipation
### Rabbi Benjamin Altshuler

This haftarah reading from the Book of Ezekiel offers the prophet's vision for Jewish ritual in a future messianic era. We learn of a leader with both civic and religious responsibilities, tasked with preparing for the coming celebrations and eventual redemption. The human rites described here are performed in anticipation of a cosmic event to come; such prognostic structure mirrors the Torah portion for this Shabbat before the beginning of the month of Nisan.

In Exodus 12, the Israelites prepare for the final plague in Egypt prior to their anticipated flight from bondage. Here too, choice animals are sacrificed according to careful procedure in hopes that a better future will follow.

Overall, the haftarah reading radiates optimism. Ezekiel lives during a time of exile, yet he foresees a rebuilt Temple and a peaceful society governed with fairness. Like the Israelite slaves in Egypt, he retains hope for something out of reach but not beyond the realm of anticipation.

Today, we do not dream for a new Temple specifically, but we do dream of an era epitomized by rebuilding. Like the prophet, we live during a time of hardships, but if we take the time to plan the rituals of a future time of peace, we will be ready to usher in its arrival. We act first—then peace will come.

## Alternative Haftarah Reading:
### From "The First Day of Pesach, 1857," by Rabbi David Einhorn

Let your house be an altar of God. Our text tells us that the lintel and the doorposts were to be sprinkled with the blood of the paschal lamb... Our Ancients termed the lintel and the two doorposts as *mizbachot* [altars] and therefore no leavened bread was to come to this altar, the home. We have in these laws the Mosaic call: Your home is a divine altar!! Holy fire must be on it day and night! On days-of-God and the festivals, there was a special offering in the old Temple: Let it be thus in your home, devote those days to meditation, to praise of God and to worship. In short, devote those days to everything that belongs to enlightenment and self-sanctification, contemplate on the past and prepare for the future. The purpose of the usual week's activity is to enable us to live. Well then, on the rest-days—live!! In brief: Our couch is a Sanctuary, our tent is the dwelling place of God, our home is an altar, we are the offering priests, who always give *etzim baboker baboker* [wood for sacrifice every morning], and prepare anew daily the flame before God.

## Sacred Time—Sacred Space
### RABBI JORDAN HELFMAN

I am writing this essay while in isolation, awaiting the results of a COVID-19 test, days before the Yamim Noraim 2020. Rabbi Einhorn makes me question if I have done enough to make my own home into a *mikdash m'at*—an "echo of the sanctuary."

Though it is a basic idea in Judaism, I often struggle with the concept that our work should enable us to enjoy life. I struggle especially on the Festivals. There is always so much that seems more urgent than being present in the moment. This is even true now, in isolation, when I am realizing the truth of Hillel's teaching "Do not say, 'When I am free I will study,' for perhaps you will not become free" (*Pirkei Avot* 2:5). If, even when life slows down because of isolation, I am not able to turn to what I *say* is important, like reading, singing, studying, and enjoying my life and my family, are those things really important to me?

In the cycle of preparation before the days of Passover as outlined by Rabbi Einhorn, I personally find some comfort. It is after those days of preparation, when the seder is cooked, organized, and prepared, when we finally sit down together to read, sing, study, and enjoy, that I am finally able to connect with tradition, family, and the present—to create a sacred time in the year; to make my home an altar to God.

When is your sacred time of the year? How can we make our homes into altars to God?

## Alternative Haftarah Reading: "Book of Mercy #43," by Leonard Cohen

Holy is your name, holy is your work, holy are the days that return to you. Holy are the years that you uncover. Holy are the hands that are raised to you, and the weeping that is wept to you. Holy is the fire between your will and ours, in which we are refined. Holy is that which is unredeemed, covered with your patience. Holy are the souls lost in your unnaming. Holy, and shining with a great light, is every living thing, established in this world and covered with time, until your name is praised forever.

## The Name in the Dark

### Rabbi Mordecai Finley

Shabbat HaChodesh, the celebration of the beginning of the month of Nisan, alerts us to the beginning of spring—suddenly, between Purim and Pesach, we switch gears. Rosh Chodesh is celebrated each month when a sliver appears in the dark night sky, and this one announces the beginnings of a new journey toward greater freedom—be it embodied intellectually or spiritually.

I have an agreement with my Charedi son—he always calls on the day before every Rosh Chodesh to remind me. I always forget, especially when Rosh Chodesh falls on Shabbat. This Rosh Chodesh feels special. The quality of light is changing. As the light of Shabbat obscures the darkness and makes me forget the monthly festival, I seek to reconnect to the seemingly renewing Divine Name.

I can tell what the Name is, but I forget to mean it. I forget that days are ticking off, each day with its own holy Name, a Name that I am to find. I forget that I bonded with God by the meeting of fire forged by will—the will to know and be known, the will to hide and be sought, the will to remain and to renew. This Rosh Chodesh interrupts me. I try to mean the Name so deeply that the Name becomes Unnamed, that the bonding fire turns to a great light, greater than the sun, which disappears each night, and the moon, which disappears every month. Rosh Chodesh marks the days ticking off, spent immersed in light.

If I could only see in the dark.

Allow yourself to be interrupted.

# *Shabbat HaGadol*
## Traditional Haftarah Reading:
## Malachi 3:4–24

## Elijah Rock, Shout Shout;
## Elijah Rock Comin' Up, Lord!

*Cantor Rhoda J. Harrison, PhD*

I FIRST HEARD and sang the lyrics of "Elijah Rock" during the summer of 1977 at the URJ (then UAHC) Camp Harlam in Kunkletown, Pennsylvania. At the time, I had no idea I was singing a traditional African American spiritual made famous in the 1960s by Mahalia Jackson's powerful voice. What I did recognize was Elijah, the guy who, despite the annual invite, never actually shows up at the Passover seder. I should mention, I was eleven in 1977. My understanding of Elijah was limited.

The haftarah reading for Shabbat HaGadol, the Shabbat just before Pesach, reminds us that Elijah, that fanciful figure who appears on the doorsteps of the downtrodden in so many Jewish legends, will herald in *yom Adonai hagadol v'hanora*, the Eternal's "great and awesome day of redemption" (Malachi 3:23).

Redemption. What is redemption exactly? We often equate redemption with the freedom from Egyptian bondage we celebrate each Passover, but redemption requires far more than a release of the shackles of slavery. Redemption demands equality, peace, and harmony. Redemption is that time, as our prayer book *Mishkan T'filah* teaches, "when we grant everyone what we claim for ourselves" (269).

The composer who penned the spiritual "Elijah Rock" in the midst of the civil rights movement in our country surely understood this. When will we? We need to stop waiting for a mythical figure to herald in God's Great and Awesome Day. We need to show up! Let's be the Elijah of our legends—the Elijah who shows up without invitation. Let us be among those shouting out for justice in our world.

# A Persistent Sense of Hope

### RABBI KERRY M. OLITZKY

The haftarah reading from the prophet Malachi is read on the Shabbat before Pesach, referred to as Shabbat HaGadol (the Great Sabbath). This Shabbat was probably first called Shabbat Haggadah (the Shabbat of the Haggadah) since preachers often prepared their communities for their Passover seders on this day. Moreover, the powerful message of the prophetic reading also strengthens the connection to Pesach—whatever Torah portion is being read because of the calendar—with its reference to the prophet Elijah and the days of redemption he will herald in.

The redemption of the ancient Israelites from slavery holds within it a promise for our personal redemption, as well as for the future redemption of the world. And just in case you don't know what is impeding the redemption and the messianic era, Malachi lists the various shortcomings that will prevent such redemption. Once having acknowledged our shortcomings, we can then strive to discontinue these behaviors.

The penultimate verse (Malachi 3:23) is repeated at the end: a convention of not ending on a discouraging note and emphasizing a message of hope for us and for the world. This persistent and profound sense of hope is perhaps among the greatest gifts that the Jewish people has given to humanity, as well as the reminder to the self not to—never to—yield to despair.

## Alternative Haftarah Reading:
### "God's Beloved," Anonymous

The love of the princely daughter [of Zion]
has been most sweet and pleasant to Me.

Oh, ask and ask again: What have My
dear ones [the righteous] been doing?
Have they been longing for My return?
Soon, I shall swiftly fly [to the Temple]
to stand at My post forever.

And until your time comes, I shall
shield you from the clamour of those
who seek to betray you. By My life, I
shall not fail you nor speak in vain.

For I have long loved you with a love
that drew us close together, nurtured
the soul and gave the heart courage—a
love encompassed with love!

And I say to the prophets: "Have you
seen how the maiden, though battered
by storm, kept her troth to her
Friend?" And they answer: "This love
is a wonder surpassing all love."

# The Love of Zion

### RABBI MARK LEVIN, DHL

In the traditional haftarah reading for Shabbat HaGadol, the Shabbat prior to Passover, the seder, and the annual commemoration of the Exodus from Egypt, God promises Israel that good people will be rewarded despite their sins and the wicked punished before the "great and terrible day of the Eternal" (Malachi 3:23). The prophet Elijah will announce the end times and final redemption. Just as Passover celebrates the first redemption from Egypt, so the haftarah reading anticipates the final redemption and the end to history.

In our anonymous, medieval, poetic alternative haftarah reading, Israel lovingly longs for Zion and the return of God's indwelling presence, the *Shechinah*, to the sanctuary. As in the traditional haftarah reading from the prophet Malachi, the return of God's presence to the Land of Israel and the Temple Mount anticipates the final redemption. However, that glorious day is yet to come. Still, the *Shechinah* guarantees God's future presence and Israel's salvation.

The miraculous bond between God's presence and God's people is rooted in a love that has united them over time and space. The fidelity of those who "nurtured the soul and gave the heart courage" inspires even God's prophets, who express their awe at Israel's deeply embedded love.

As we share this haftarah reading, so may we share the love of return to our ancestral land in our own lives, either permanently or temporarily. To love Zion is a state of mind and affection, separate from the politics of the State of Israel. Love of Zion continues the two-millennia longing of the Jewish soul for the root of our inspiration and divine connection.

## Alternative Haftarah Reading:
## "Tefillah for Agunot," by Shelley Frier List

Creator of heaven and earth, may it be Your will to free the captive wives of Israel when love and sanctity have fled the home, but their husbands bind them in the tatters of their *ketubot*. Remove the bitter burden from these *agunot* and soften the hearts of their misguided captors. Liberate Your faithful daughters from their anguish. Enable them to establish new homes and raise up children in peace.

Grant wisdom to the judges of Israel; teach them to recognize oppression and rule against it. Infuse our rabbis with the courage to use their power for good alone.

Blessed are You, Creator of heaven and earth, who frees the captives.

# Freeing the Captives

### Rabbi Ariel J. Friedlander

The Shabbat before Passover is known as Shabbat HaGadol—"the Great Shabbat." Why does it have this name?

Maybe the name refers to the very long sermon the rabbi is required to give to ensure that everyone will prepare properly for Pesach. This Shabbat may also be named for its haftarah reading, which includes these words: "Behold, I will send you Elijah the prophet, before the coming of *yom Adonai hagadol v'ha-nora* [the great and terrible day of the Eternal]" (Malachi 3:23). This verse is emphasized by the custom of reading it a second time at the end of the haftarah portion. Finally, on the Shabbat before the Exodus, on the tenth of Nisan, the Israelites were given their first mitzvah, to set aside a lamb as a sacrifice. This required particular daring on their part, as the lamb was an Egyptian deity. Their courage was rewarded by a miracle, a *neis gadol*, for although this act could be seen as a public declaration of freedom, their Egyptian masters did not punish them.

Every morning, we begin our day with the blessing that we have been created *bat/ben chorin*, that we are "free." On Shabbat HaGadol, we look to the past and the redemption of our ancestors. Traditionally, we also read Malachi's vision of a future messianic era. However, we are not yet there and have much work still to do.

Each day that we enjoy our freedom, are we aware that there are those in our community today who remain in chains? The *agunot* are women trapped in a dead marriage, held hostage by their husbands, who refuse to write them a bill of divorcement. If a man abandons his wife or simply refuses to give her a *get*, then if she were to remarry, her children would be considered *mamzerim*, "cut off from the Jewish community."

No matter to which denomination we may belong, Judaism has a long-standing tradition of redeeming our captives. The *Shulchan Aruch* teaches that "every moment that one delays unnecessarily the ransoming of a prisoner, it is as if they were shedding blood" (*Yoreh Dei-ah* 252:3). *Agunot* are currently caught in a legal web, but inspired by the bravery of the Israelites on their day, we vow today to leave no one behind.

*Baruch atah, Adonai, matir asurim*—Blessed are You, Adonai, who frees the captives.

# *Pesach, Day 1*
## Exodus 12:21–51

## Haftarah Reading:
## Isaiah 43:1–15

## From Moses to Joshua
### RABBI NICOLE ROBERTS

THE HAFTARAH read by more traditional Jewish communities for the first day of Pesach (Joshua 5:2–6:1, 27) tells of the eve of the very first Pesach ever observed in the Promised Land. Now the completion of liberation was upon the Israelites, under Joshua. What did they do to prepare? They didn't make matzah ball soup! They circumcised themselves. The older generation, who were already circumcised, had passed on; so, to make themselves worthy in God's eyes of this miracle they were about to experience, the new generation had to circumcise themselves.

The tool used for this act was a flint, just like Moses's mother took to Moses's foreskin. This tool connects Joshua to Moses, as does the command to "remove your sandals from your feet" (Joshua 5:15)—a word-for-word echo of Moses's encounter with the Burning Bush (Exodus 3:5). Like the laying on of hands that transferred authority from Moses to Joshua (Numbers 27:23, Deuteronomy 34:9), this linguistic *s'michah* (laying of the hands) connects the two prophets— one who brings the people out of Egypt and the other who leads them into the Promised Land.

The haftarah reading affirms that *Adonai* is a God who can be trusted to keep promises and that the Jewish covenant continues from generation to generation.

## Sharing Our Truth
### CANTOR DAVID REINWALD

Because of its description of the Israelites crossing through the water of the Red Sea, Isaiah 43:1–15 is widely read by Reform Jews in North America as the haftarah on the first day of Pesach. It contains God's promise of continual protection of the people.

Today we know that "Isaiah's" prophetic voice varies so much throughout the Book of Isaiah because it was actually authored by a number of "Isaiahs." Here, Isaiah is a voice of reassurance to the people:

- He reminds the people of the Exodus from Egypt and of their own strength.
- His words are prayerful. He invokes the two names of our forefather as "Jacob" or "Israel," now synonymous with the name of our people. He reiterates that God will be with us when passing through water (Isaiah 43:2).
- He continues to affirm that we should not fear, for God is with us (43:5).
- He speaks about God as our redeemer from slavery, the theme of our holiday. God brought us out of Egypt and led us to redemption and freedom.

On Pesach, we were set free (Isaiah 43:8). Now we are the ones to gather and witness, and to share this truth (43:9–10).

## Alternative Haftarah Reading: "Reform Is Historical," by Rabbi Abraham Geiger

Reform is not a half-measure simply because it does not one-sidedly pay obeisance to some arbitrary principle and eliminate mercilessly everything that opposes it. Rather, our Reform is historical, and all of us serve as organs of history. As we draw from the past, we nourish the future; as we prepare ourselves for higher goals, we yet rejoice in our heritage and heighten its value for the present. I do not underestimate the difficult task which such procedure demands of us. Its conditions are devotion to the religious sentiment, supremacy of the religious idea, and at the same time a truly intimate connection with the history of Judaism. The history of Judaism is so vital, it has so many sprouts and shoots even in contemporary life, that once it is cleansed of weeds, its power of growth will not have diminished.

# Draw from the Past to Nourish the Future

### Rabbi Dana Evan Kaplan, PhD

The Torah reading for the first day of Passover describes the Exodus from Egypt and the Passover offering. Moses instructs the elders of Israel concerning the legal aspects of the holiday. Passover is a holy day not just for those assembled around Moses, but for all generations to come. The Torah specifically states that the children of future generations should be instructed as to why the festival has been and will remain of great religious significance.

In our alternative haftarah reading, Rabbi Abraham Geiger, one of the most scholarly European rabbis of the nineteenth century, draws directly on this same point—contemporary Reform Jews learn from the past and nourish the future. Rabbi Geiger argues that Reform Judaism is historical. He had seen how some early Reform Jews in Germany had rejected virtually the entirety of Jewish tradition for the sake of reverential religious services that could inspire the worshiper. While Rabbi Geiger was sympathetic to this goal, he wanted to create a coherent theological framework that could justify innovations in religious practice on the basis of historical precedent.

Reform Jews face the challenge of drawing on Jewish history and its extensive theological formulation and many legal decisions while developing an authentic approach to spirituality that feels right and true to each of us. Just in the past few years, synagogues throughout the country have had to make enormous, radical changes in their entire approach to worship, to Shabbat, to holy days (including Passover), and to the High Holy Days. Our goal is, as Rabbi Geiger puts it, to "rejoice in our heritage" while at the same time figuring out how it can speak to those living in a rapidly changing present.

### *Alternative Haftarah Reading: "Discovery," by Ruth Brin*

No one ever told me the coming of the Messiah
Could be an inward thing.
No one ever told me a change of heart
Might be as quiet as new-fallen snow.

No one ever told me that redemption
Was as simple as springtime and as wonderful
As birds returning after a long winter,
Rose-breasted grosbeaks singing in the swaying branches
Of a newly budded tree.

No one ever told me that salvation
Might be like a fresh spring wind
Blowing away the dried, withered leaves of another year,
Carrying the scent of flowers, the promise of fruition.

What I found for myself I try to tell you:
Redemption and salvation are very near,
And the taste of them is in the world
That God created and laid before us.

# A Change of Heart

*RABBI JILL PERLMAN*

The parting of the sea during the Exodus from Egypt is regarded as one of our greatest miracles. Imagine you had been there—what you would have experienced? There would be no doubt that redemption was revealing itself right there in our midst, with sea walls surrounding us on either side, as we marched away from trauma toward our freedom. In modern days like ours, with life's seemingly bigger miracles hidden away from us, how might redemption become manifest?

Ruth Brin's poem "Discovery" urges us to reconsider our notion of redemption and salvation. The miracle of redemption does not have to look big and dramatic like the parting of the sea or the eventual arrival of the Messiah. The miracles might look much smaller and less dramatic, but just as powerful, like the beauty of new-fallen snow and the awe of seeing birds return after the dead of the winter.

Even the poet's—or any other person's!—growing self-awareness might be experienced as redemptive, a stunning journey to self-discovery that she yearns to share. We, too, might realize that redemption and salvation are indeed very near if we only pay attention to the less obvious, but just as miraculous happenings within and around us.

This Passover, as we study and celebrate the great miracles of our past, let us also give thanks for the less big and dramatic, but just as miraculous happenings in our midst: a change of heart, the insight of the mind, the breath in our lungs.

# Shabbat Chol HaMo-eid Pesach
## Exodus 33:12–34:26

## Traditional Haftarah Reading:
## Ezekiel 37:1–14

## Intimacy and Comfort

### Rabbi Eleanor Steinman

Both the Torah and haftarah readings for Shabbat Chol HaMo-eid Pesach present dramatic encounters with God:

1. Moses, after a myriad of experiences leading the people out of Egypt, asks to see God's presence, literally *k'vodecha*, "Your [God's] glory" (Exodus 33:18). The Eternal instructs Moses to stand in the cleft of the rock, shielded "with My hand until I have passed by" (33:22) so that Moses can see God's back. This passage is incredibly intimate.

2. Ezekiel describes an experience with God that is simultaneously comforting and alarming to our modern Reform sensibilities: God places him in a valley of dry bones. God instructs Ezekiel to prophesy over the bones, and the skeletons come back to life, symbolizing the rebirth and hope for the Jewish future. Ezekiel's vision transmits a message of comfort for a people in exile.

These passages present us with two wildly different encounters with the Divine: one of intimacy and one of comfort. As people of faith with a diversity of theologies and experiences, we too seek intimacy with and comfort from the Holy One when the situation around us seems bleak. Many of us find comfort in knowledge, while others find solace in mystery. The prophet Ezekiel reminds us that knowledge and mystery can both be sources of truth. His prophecy presents hope for the Jewish people amid a valley of dry bones, a most unexpected place. Ezekiel's prophecy calls upon us to look for the divine spark in ourselves and in others, to remain hopeful, and to focus on building together toward a brighter future.

# Rebirth

*Rabbi Donald P. Cashman*

Bold and unusual imagery conveys God's goodness in the Torah and haftarah readings for Shabbat Chol HaMo-eid Pesach. God acquiesces to Moses viewing the Divine Presence by placing him in a rock, shielding him while passing by, and allowing him to "see My back" (Exodus 33:23). God's goodness is also described in the Thirteen Attributes (34:6–7); and in Exodus 34:10, God promises "wonders" (*niflaot*). Ezekiel's vision of the dry bones returning to life promises redemption to the Jewish exiles in Babylonia, just as Passover celebrates the redemption from Egypt.

At our seders earlier this week, we dwelt on the deliverance from Egypt. This haftarah reading aims to give hope to another group of exiles for the return to their Land. The redemptions from *galut Mitzrayim* (Egyptian exile) and *galut Bavel* (Babylonian exile) are cast in the *Tanach* as fulfillments of the covenant, accomplished with heretofore unseen divine power.

This haftarah reading inspires us to conceive of the national rebirth of the Jewish people in our time as something greater than its geopolitics. It is a watershed moment in Jewish history, on a par with the Exodus and the return from the Babylonian exile. Rising from the dead and returning home, the image from Ezekiel calls to us as a living allegory, just as our seders are living reenactments of the Exodus.

## *Alternative Haftarah Reading: Song of Songs 2:8–13, 5:2, 8:6–7, 13*

The voice of my beloved: Here it comes!
Leaping over the mountains, skipping across the hills.

My love is like a gazelle, a wild stag
He stands there on the other side of our wall, gazing
Through the windows, peering through the lattice.

My beloved calls to me:

Arise my friend, oh beautiful one,
Go to yourself . . .

For now the winter is past,
The rains are over and gone,
Blossoms appear in the fields,
The time for singing has come.

The sound of the turtledove
Echoes throughout the land.

The fig tree is ripening
Its new green fruit,
And the budded vines give of their fragrance,
Arise my friend, oh beautiful one,
Go to yourself . . .

I was asleep but my heart stayed awake.
There it is . . . the sound of my lover knocking:

Open to me, my sister, my friend,
My dove, my perfect one!
My head is wet with dew,
My hair drenched in the damp of night. . . .

Set me as a seal upon your heart,
A sign upon your arm,
For Love is as strong as Death
Its passion is as harsh as the grave,
Its sparks become a raging fire,
A Divine Flame.

Great seas cannot extinguish love
No river can wash it away,

If a man tried to buy Love
With all the wealth of his house,
He would only be scorned. . . .

Oh woman in the garden,
All our friends listen for your voice,
Let me hear it now!

# The Sound of My Lover Knocking

## Rabbi Shefa Gold

"The whole Torah is holy," says Rabbi Akiva, "but the Song of Songs is the holy of holies" (*Mishnah Yadayim* 3:5). The Torah commands that you must love God "with all your heart, with all your soul, and with all your might " (Deuteronomy 6:5). You are commanded to "to love your neighbor as yourself" (Leviticus 19:18); and you are asked to receive God's love in the form of Torah, community, history, and the wonders of nature. These commandments about love are at the heart of Torah. They constitute, at the same time, the simplest and the most complicated challenge of living a holy life.

The Song of Songs sings to all whose hearts lie awake, waiting to be roused by God, our true love, who is knocking, who calls us to become ourselves and to be connected in sacred union with all of creation, and with the Source of all. God is knocking with the reality of each moment.

One year I sat around a table at a Passover seder with a group of women. It was during the war in Bosnia, and we all felt helpless, knowing that the tragedy of genocide was unfolding while the world stood by. As Jews, imprinted with the history of the Holocaust, we felt despair. As we recounted the foundational story of our people, the Exodus from Egypt, we were sensitive to its violence, the fact of all those Egyptians who suffered from the plagues and the tragedy of their final drowning in the sea. Someone asked, "Don't we have any other story? Whenever we win, someone else loses. Do we have to win our freedom at the expense of another people?" "Isn't there any other way to freedom?" we asked. "Don't we have any other story?" As this question hung in the air between us, the silence felt like a great weight, and then the answer dawned.

"We do have another story!" I shouted. I explained that tradition calls us to read, study, and sing the Song of Songs during Passover. While the Book of Exodus tells the story of our outer journey from slavery to freedom, the Song of Songs tells the inner story. Rabbi Akiva hinted at this when he called the Song the "holy of holies." Just as the Holy of Holies occupied the very center of the Sanctuary, the Song of Songs stands at the center of the mystery of freedom.

## Alternative Haftarah Reading:
## From the writings of Rabbi Dr. Shmuly Yanklowitz

*One person dies every 40 seconds. . . .*

Risk factors may include: family history of mental illness and/or suicide, feelings of hopelessness, and history of clinical depression.

While these factors alone do not predispose an individual to suicide, others cannot be seen. For example, chemical changes in the brain, especially decreased levels of the neurotransmitter serotonin. . . . [And] even before our contemporary measurement of suicide through surveys and databases, there was an understanding that those who committed suicide suffered greatly. . . . So many suffer. Their pain is immense yet hidden. . . .

With the lamentable rise in suicide attacking our nation like a virus, the question from a Jewish perspective is: How do we respond to this crisis? . . .

Initially one who committed suicide was not to be mourned for.

No more. . . .

If you feel as if you might harm yourself or know someone who might, please call [this] number[: 1.800.273.TALK (8255)], staffed 24 hours a day, seven days a week.

Take care of each other. And know, please God always know, that you are never alone.

## The Hidden, Broken Piece

### Cantor Karen Webber, MSM, CPRS

It is all the brokenness we don't see that worries me.

The seder plate holds sadness. We dip twice in salty water because our grief is so large, once is not enough. Brittle, flat matzah sits still. The *maror* slaps us in the face, while the bitter lettuce just stuns. With *charoset*, we fashion our bricks to build walls of isolation.

For those who suffer from chronic depression, Egypt is real and ever present. Despair is constricting. Loneliness is exhausting, silent, and secret. The solitary confinement of the penultimate plague encourages delusions to take root: "I am unlovable . . . I am not worthy . . . I have no one." Cloaking our pain in darkness allows it to blossom.

Death of the firstborn is the last plague, yet, we know, even the Angel of Death can be redirected. Redemption is possible. The *afikoman*, though broken, is found. The last three foods provide the antidote: The egg, symbol of life, and the parsley, symbol of spring, mingle in life-giving waters. *Z'roa* points us toward possibility, extending an outstretched hand to lead us from darkness to light, from broken to whole, from narrow to wide-open spaces flowered with promise.

# Pesach, Day 7
## Exodus 14:30–15:21

## Traditional Haftarah Reading
## II Samuel 22:1–51

## Beginning a Time of Growth

### CANTOR KENNETH J. FEIBUSH

ON THE LAST DAY of Passover, we read the Song at the Sea, sung by Moses, Miriam, and the Children of Israel after passing through the Sea of Reeds. The Torah text itself has a special poetic layout, with the words spread out like the divided waters. In the song, the Israelites praise God for the miracle of parting the sea and the victory over Pharaoh's armies.

The haftarah reading from II Samuel is also called the Song of David. This poem has similar messages as the Song at the Sea: God as salvation, God defeating foes, and wonder at God's might. The structure and wording of these two songs are reminiscent of the works of the classical orators like Homer and Virgil.

Passover represents growth and rebirth. According to the biblical calendar, we begin counting the Omer on Passover, marking the growth of the barley crop, which ends on Shavuot. Today, many Jews use this time of the year, seven weeks altogether, to focus on inner work. As we look inward, reflect on our past, and start to work on self-improvement, we might, as David does, call out from our personal depths and despair and look to God as a rock of salvation.

We need the sense of joy and gratitude transmitted by this haftarah reading. David demonstrated how to offer praise to God even though he struggled with his son Absalom and warred with many neighbors. We can use his example of hope and praise when times are rough. Passover, a joyous holiday, ends with the seventh day, but we know that the growth of spring and summer has just begun. This allows us to offer praise for new moments in time—just like David did.

# Illuminate the Darkness

### RABBI ASHLEY BARRETT

At a moment of great joy and newly gained freedom, our people stand on the shores of the Sea of Reeds and sing out to God. The Israelites are thankful, not only for the gift of freedom, but also for the great miracle of splitting the sea. We remember the sweetness that is the miracle of freedom each year at Pesach.

The traditional haftarah reading offers a lengthy piece of poetry—a song of thanksgiving by King David. David expresses deep gratitude to God for the deliverance he received from the hands of his enemies. David's song offers a glimpse into the great power God wields. This power is used on David's behalf. God is referred to as David's "lamp," which illuminates the darkness (II Samuel 22:29).

In moments of deep darkness, when we are living through the trials that punctuate our lives, we must remember those moments and, more importantly, those people that help light up those moments. Then, as King David did, we can express our gratitude for those individuals even as we are still struggling to overcome those dark moments. This—the insistence on joy and gratitude in the midst of darkness, and the belief in the possibility of hope—is the formula to make our world into a little bit brighter place.

## *Alternative Haftarah Reading: Henrietta Szold's letter to Haym Peretz, on Saying Kaddish for Her Mother*

New York, September 16, 1916

It is impossible for me to find words in which to tell you how deeply I was touched by your offer to act as "Kaddish" for my dear mother. I cannot even thank you—it is something that goes beyond thanks. It is beautiful, what you have offered to do—I shall never forget it.

You will wonder, then, that I cannot accept your offer. Perhaps it would be best for me not to try to explain to you in writing, but to wait until I see you to tell you why it is so. I know well, and appreciate what you say about, the Jewish custom; and Jewish custom is very dear and sacred to me. And yet I cannot ask you to say Kaddish after my mother. The Kaddish means to me that the survivor publicly and markedly manifests his wish and intention to assume the relation to the Jewish community which his parent had, and that so the chain of tradition remains unbroken from generation to generation, each adding its own link. You can do that for the generations of your family, I must do that for the generations of my family.

I believe that the elimination of women from such duties was never intended by our law and custom—women were freed from positive duties when they could not perform them, but not when they could. It was never intended that, if they could perform them, their performance of them should not be considered as valuable and valid as when one of the male sex performed them. And of the Kaddish I feel sure this is particularly true.

My mother had eight daughters and no son; and yet never did I hear a word of regret pass the lips of either my mother or my father that one of us was not a son. When my father died, my mother would not permit others to take her daughters' place in saying the Kaddish, and so I am sure I am acting in her spirit when I am moved to decline your offer. But beautiful your offer remains nevertheless, and, I repeat, I know full well that it is much more in consonance with the generally accepted Jewish tradition than is my or my family's conception. You understand me, don't you?

# The Path to Meaning and Wholeness

### Rabbi Gila Colman Ruskin

I imagine Henrietta Szold going to shul on the last day of Passover to say *Kaddish* for her mother during the *Yizkor* service. As she stood, she pictured the welding of a link onto a long generational chain that she would not forgo because she was a woman, a daughter, and not a son. The letter she wrote to Haym Peretz in 1916 reveals the timeless feminist impulse that preceded the political. While Henrietta respectfully acknowledged the male authority of traditional halachah, she claimed her mother as her *poseket* (decider).

Her mother innately experienced the obligation of reciting *Kaddish* as a sacred call and psychological balm to the children of the deceased. Neither of those objectives can be met by hiring a surrogate. The Mourner's *Kaddish*, with its inscrutable Aramaic, must be recited with *kavanah* (intention) by the actual mourner whose heart bears the fissure of loss of a dear one. To reach true comfort and care, the body should physically stand, if possible, and the rhythmic chant be intoned aloud. This is the path to healing and wholeness.

Creating new ritual is a holy endeavor. As we create new ceremonies, let's imagine ourselves as links in the generational chain. Assessing the transformative power of ritual, we must be intentional in our crafting. Let's ask ourselves: Is this the best path to meaning and wholeness?

*Alternative Haftarah Reading:*
*"Passover's Peace Partners," by Rabbi Israel Zoberman*

Each drop of wine
Shed from joy's fullness
Is a human tear,
Dipped in shared bitterness
Of villain and vindicated.
For both are victims
Unless together they restore
Cup's sacred wholeness,
Extending to the vanquished
Victors' redemption.

## Celebrating Survival While Considering the Loss

*Rabbi Peter J. Haas*

The Torah reading for the seventh day of Pesach describes the miraculous splitting and returning of the Reed Sea, a miracle that both allowed the Children of Israel to cross safely over dry land and subsequently drowned the Egyptian army. This was a major miracle of salvation for the Jewish people.

The traditional haftarah reading, II Samuel 22:1–51, is a celebratory song by David expressing his gratefulness for being miraculously delivered from his enemies. On the one hand, this is a very personal psalm. On the other hand, it is also the haftarah reading associated with *Parashat Haazinu*, itself a celebratory song of deliverance from Pharaoh's army. So, the haftarah reading for this day refers us to both the great salvation from Egypt and the salvations that occur in our individual lives.

Such salvations come at a price. The seder, and this poem, remind us that also in our celebratory moments, we need to think of the price paid by others. How can the joy of Israel's and David's survival motivate us to help address the hurt that has lingered in their aftermath?

# *Shavuot*
## Exodus 19:1–8, 20:1–14

## Traditional Haftarah Reading:
## Ezekiel 1:1–28, 3:12 or Isaiah 42:1–12

## Describing God's Holiness

*Cantor Lauren Phillips Fogelman*

O N SHAVUOT, we celebrate receiving the Torah on Mount Sinai. This event is often considered to be one of divine revelation, meaning that God in heaven interacts with humans on earth. It is fitting, then, that one of the options for the haftarah reading assigned to this festival (Ezekiel 1:1–28, 3:12) tells another story about divine revelation. We read about the prophet Ezekiel, who lived during the period immediately before and after the destruction of the First Temple in Jerusalem. Exiled to Babylonia, he is famous for his use of imagery and symbolism in his striking vision of the divine chariot and the heavenly throne.

Ezekiel describes the chariot in vivid detail. Four winged creatures frame the chariot, each possessing various characteristics of humans and animals. The rim of each wheel is covered with eyes. The structure is cast in an amber glow made up of fire, lightning, and even a rainbow, which is often viewed as a sign of the covenant between God and humanity. Above the light is a sapphire throne that appears to have a human figure sitting upon it.

Medieval mystics have found endless meaning in the passages relating to Ezekiel's vision, similar to how we continue to find new interpretations of the Torah. This reading played a central role in the school of Jewish mysticism known as *Merkavah*, active approximately 100 BCE–1000 CE. *Merkavah* means "chariot," which comes directly from the chariot in Ezekiel's vision. The central text for this movement was known as *Maaseh Merkavah* (Work of the Chariot).

The haftarah reading ends with a line that we say as part of the *K'dushah*, the prayer acknowledging God's holiness in the *Amidah*: "Praised be the Presence of the Eternal from its place!" (Ezekiel 3:12). This aligns the haftarah text with the sanctity of prayer—another fitting reason why this reading helps us to celebrate our receipt of our holiest gift: the Torah.

Reform Judaism teaches that receiving Torah at Sinai is not celebrated as a singular mystical moment of divine revelation—and yet, many of us are yearning for spiritual moments like the one Ezekiel describes. How can we make more space for moments like these?

# A Light to the Nations?
### Rabbi Donald B. Rossoff

On Shavuot, Israel and its spiritual descendants once again stand at Sinai, the place where God covenanted with Israel and revealed God's Torah of life. But what was God's purpose in so covenanting and revealing? The answer is suggested in the haftarah reading for Shavuot from the Book of Isaiah (42:1–12), chosen by our teacher, Rabbi W. Gunther Plaut, z"l, for the first edition of the Reform Movement's *The Torah: A Modern Commentary*.

In one verse, Isaiah 42:5, the prophet harkens back before Sinai to the Creation itself, reviewing days 2, 3, 5, and 6 of the creation process in Genesis 1. Conspicuously absent in this retelling are references to days 1 and 4, the creation first of light and then of lights. This may be because Isaiah sees Israel as the light that God called forth to serve as *l'or goyim*, "a light of/to the nations" (Isaiah 42:6), opening eyes that cannot see, freeing those who sit in darkness (42:7). The implication is that God's call to Israel was part of the ongoing pursuit of the purpose of God's original Creation—that of realizing the potential of God's attributes of justice and mercy, righteousness and compassion in the world. God covenanted with Israel in righteousness so that Israel could covenant with humanity as *b'rit am*, "a covenant of the people," taking the world out of its darkness and enlightening it with the truth of God's oneness (Malbim) and the moral implications of that belief.

Is the description of Israel as a light to the nations actually descriptive—that is, factual—or prescriptive—that is, aspirational? Are we, as individuals, communities, and as a people, acting so as to become that which we are called to be?

## Alternative Haftarah Reading:
## "A Ketubah for Shavuot," by Rabbi Israel Najara

Friday, the sixth of Sivan, the day appointed by the Lord for the revelation of the Torah to His beloved people. . . . The Invisible One came forth from Sinai, shone from Seir, and appeared from Mount Paran unto all the kings of the earth, in the year 2448 since the creation of the world, the era by which we are accustomed to reckon in this land whose foundations were upheld by God, as it is written, "For He hath founded it upon the seas and established it upon the flood" (Psalms 24:2).

The Bridegroom [God], Ruler of rulers, Prince of princes, Distinguished among the select, Whose mouth is pleasing and all of Whom is delightful, said unto the pious, lovely and virtuous maiden [the people of Israel] who won His favor above all women, who is beautiful as the moon, radiant as the sun, awesome as bannered hosts: Many days wilt thou be Mine and I will be thy Redeemer.

Behold, I have sent thee golden precepts through the lawgiver Jekuthiel [Moses]. Be thou My mate according to the law of Moses and Israel, and I will honor, support, and maintain thee and be thy shelter and refuge in everlasting mercy. And I will set aside for thee, in lieu of thy virginal faithfulness, the life-giving Torah by which thou and thy children will live in health and tranquility.

This bride [Israel] consented and became His spouse. Thus an eternal covenant, binding them forever, was established between them. The Bridegroom then agreed to add to the above all future expositions of Scripture, including Sifra, Sifre, Aggadah, and Tosefta. He established the primacy of the 248 positive commandments that are incumbent upon all … and added to them the 365 negative commandments. The dowry that this bride brought from the house of her father consists of an understanding heart that understands, ears that hearken, and eyes that see.

# Entering the Covenant
### Rabbi Philip J. Bentley

Sephardic tradition for Shavuot includes the reading of this *ketubah* between God and Israel. According to the Torah, we stood "under" Mount Sinai; the mountain is imagined to be our chuppah with God imagined as the groom, while we, the people, are imagined to be the bride. This *ketubah* follows the language of the traditional wedding contract of the Sephardic tradition, whose language is much more romantic than the familiar Ashkenazic version.

This *ketubah* describes the conditions of the marriage. The Torah (the *ketubah*) and its traditions are described as a way of life that will sustain us forever. Marriage is envisioned as a covenant or contract between bride and groom rather than an oath made only by the groom. This covenant requires equal partners. God binds Godself to the conditions of the covenant with Israel, just as a human bride and groom.

The mitzvot include much more than ritual practices; they call us to be honest in business, to be kind and compassionate, to be fair and reasonable, and to pursue justice and peace. To fulfill these commandments, our "dowry" as Jews is to be able to see the world as it is and live according to the standards set by our tradition.

## *Alternative Haftarah Reading: "We All Stood Together," by Merle Feld*

*for Rachel Adler*

My brother and I were at Sinai
He kept a journal
of what he saw
of what he heard
of what it all meant to him

I wish I had such a record
of what happened to me there

It seems like every time I want to write
I can't
I'm always holding a baby
one of my own
or one for a friend
always holding a baby
so my hands are never free
to write things down

And then
As time passes
The particulars
The hard data
The who what when where why
Slip away from me
And all I'm left with is
The feeling

But feelings are just sounds
The vowel barking of a mute

My brother is so sure of what he heard
After all he's got a record of it
Consonant after consonant after consonant

If we remembered it together
We could recreate holy time
Sparks flying

# A Moment When Sparks Fly

*Rabbi Audrey S. Pollack*

On Shavuot, we listen to the words of *Aseret HaDib'rot* (the Ten Commandments), standing together to receive Torah as our ancestors did at Mount Sinai. According to Jewish tradition, it is not just the generation of Moses who stood at Sinai (*Sh'mot Rabbah* 28:6). All of us were there—men, women, and children, from the woodchoppers to the water-drawers. It is as if every generation, every soul, is present in that moment of the transmission of Torah. When we in our own synagogue communities stand and hear these words, we are connected to all of the Jewish communities around the world, throughout space and time, who embrace the teachings of Torah and walk in its paths.

Written out of the agony of exclusion, Merle Feld's poem reflects the gendered experiences that are present in our sacred texts. Her words express hope and expectation for a time when together we reimagine Jewish tradition to include the experiences and contributions of all of us. Her words call us to imagine what it felt like to stand at Sinai for all who have been othered. We ask: How do the voices and experiences of women, Jews of Color, the elderly, differently abled, queer and transgender, and Jewish-adjacent in our community enhance the tapestry of our tradition? What does it mean to remember that moment together, when, in a place where all of us have a place and a voice in Torah, we were "recreat[ing] holy time [and] sparks [were] flying"?

# Tishah B'Av
## Deuteronomy 4:25–40

## Traditional Haftarah Reading:
## Jeremiah 8:13–9:23 and Isaiah 55:6–56:8

## A Time and Space for Grief
### CANTOR JUDITH BORDEN OVADIA

ON TISHAH B'AV, traditionally, Jews observe a day of mourning, fasting, and refraining from any joyful behavior. The fast day marks the destruction of the First and Second Temples and the exile of the Jews from Zion. Additionally, a number of other tragic events are attributed to this day in history. The Torah portion (Deuteronomy 4:25–40) fittingly contains words of warning from Moses to the Israelites. In the morning haftarah reading (Jeremiah 8:13–9:23), Jeremiah laments and conveys God's wrath and sorrow over the destruction of Jerusalem and the exile of Israel.

The clear connection between the Torah portion and haftarah reading is the prophecy of Moses and its fulfillment in Jeremiah. Moses warns the Israelites that in the future they may turn away from God and God's teaching, specifically, by embracing idolatry; and Jeremiah reveals how this comes to pass. The destruction of the physical Temple and the geographic exile from the biblical Land of Israel, mourned for on Tishah B'Av, are representations of the spiritual chasm that has occurred between God and God's people, the rupture in the covenant.

To modern ears, the language of Jeremiah can sound both maudlin and grandiose. Where do we find meaning in the mourning for an ancient Temple? How can we hear Jeremiah's exhortations in a way that speaks to our twenty-first century Jewish practice?

> Thus says the God of heaven's hosts:
> Pay heed, and call to the wailing women to come!
> Send for the skilled ones, and have them come!
> Let them quickly raise a dirge for us,
> that our eyelids may run with tears,
> our eyes flow with water! (Jeremiah 9:16–17)

The text implies that effective grieving requires the support of both ritual and community. The sort of weeping and wailing that God ordains is rarely witnessed in our culture today. We avoid public displays of emotion. Each of us, however, experiences grief. Whether it is over the death of a loved one or the subtle kind that accompanies the transition from one stage of life to the next, grief is a part of our emotional reality. Tishah B'Av observances offer ritual spaces and times for grieving—whether we direct our consciousness toward the text or allow ourselves to express a more personal grief—through which we may exorcise some of the psychological barriers that stand between us and a true *cheshbon hanefesh*, an "accounting of the soul." This accounting is crucial if we are to make a meaningful attempt at *t'shuvah* (repentance).

# Tirades, Tears, *T'shuvah*

## CANTOR IDA RAE CAHANA

The COVID pandemic and Black Lives Matter protests have taught us to see many things more clearly. Among them are the sacrality, preciousness, and fragility of every human being; the need to respect nature in all its magnificence and terror; and the vastness of the task ahead to right the historic wrongs of injustice in our country. If ever the writings of prophets like Jeremiah resonated, that time is now. We literally cannot look away. Nor should we. Our eyes and ears are assaulted daily with images from cell phone videos, news coverage, and tweets. They remind us of the sickness of society, as well as—God forbid—the viral invasion of our bodies.

Jeremiah calls out to God in anguish and frustration; to the people around him, he calls attention to unfolding disaster. He sees the corruption of leaders and everyday people alike. Like them, our hearts are misguided—like them, we lie and deceive our sisters and brothers. And, like them, we use our power for ill (Jeremiah 9:2–4, 7).

When we read how they hoped for well-being though no good came, how they hoped for healing but instead terror came, Jeremiah 8:15 is eerily reminiscent of our current situation. In a weird twist, it seems the people Israel have become their own Pharaohs, with hardened hearts attuned only to their own desires (Jeremiah 9:20). Now it is we who abuse power, who take advantage of others.

But God doesn't want that. God mourns for the straying of the flock (Jeremiah 8:19–23). Witnessing creation profaning itself—again—tears apart the Creator, then as now. In a final plea, God calls on us to sound an alarm: "Send for the skilled women" (Jeremiah 9:16) to use their wisdom and skill to rouse people from their intransigence and stubborn clinging to evil! This is what God wants from us: to be kind, just, and merciful.

Maybe it is time for us to embrace our own pertinent understanding of Tishah B'Av. In our post-2020 vision, let us heed the prophet's words and help each other to be healers of our deepest psychic wounds.

## *Alternative Haftarah Reading:*
## *"For the Anniversary of the Destruction of Jerusalem,"*
## *by Rabbi David Einhorn*

With profound emotion, O Lord, we remember in this hour the dire day of desolation on which the enemy entered Your stronghold, giving over Your sanctuary a prey to devouring flames. . . . However deeply and painfully our soul is moved by the recollection of the unutterable grief . . . —in all these sore trials we recognize Your guiding, fatherly hand, means for the fulfillment of Your inviolable promises and the glorification of Your name and Your law before the eyes of all nations. Verily, not as a disinherited son, Your first-born went out into strange lands, but as Your messenger to all the families of man. Israel was no longer to dwell in separation from all the rest of Your children . . . he was to spread abroad the stream of his salvation, and become himself the carrier of the refreshing waters of healing powers. The one temple in Jerusalem sank into the dust, in order that countless temples might arise to Your honor and glory all over the wide surface of the globe. The old priestly dignity was taken away and the old sacrificial worship ceased, but in their stead the whole community, in accordance with its original distinction, became a priest and was called upon to offer up those sacrifices which are more acceptable in Your sight than thousands of rivers of oil, the sacrifices of active love to God and man, the sacrifices of pure and pious conduct, which, even in extremity and death will not deviate from the path of truth, the sacrifices of an unparalleled allegiance to God with which the centuries have become vocal. The true and real sanctuary, Your imperishable testimony, remained ours, untouched and undimmed. It assumed a new glory and emerged purer and in increased splendor from the flames. It was freed from the encircling walls which had shut it in and hidden its glory from the eyes of the millions of beings created in Your image. These to lift up to the recognition of their dignity as men and to bring them into the fold of Your spiritual people united in love and righteousness, Your priest, Israel, had to go out among them, and speak before them Your message of duty and righteousness. . . . Freed from the bonds of his childhood, in martyr heroism, Israel had to pilgrim through the whole earth . . . to deliver by his very fetters his own tormentors, by his wounds to bring healing to those who inflicted them. . . . Our trust remains firm in Your promise that one day all who are endowed with Your breath will bow down before You. Vouchsafe, O God, that all Israel may recognize this, the goal of its wanderings and pursue it with united strength and cheerful courage. Let his mourning end wherever he is still languishing beneath the oppression of hatred, and to the better thought open the eyes of those who deem Your messenger still cast out from before Your countenance, and would have him return to the narrow home where his cradle once stood, without his true aim as a prince of God and depriving him of his world-blessing duty. . . . Let the time speedily draw near when all the earth will become one atoning altar, from which all hearts and spirits shall flame up to You in burning love. Let Your message of truth and Your word of righteousness, like protecting cherubim, spread their wings over the sanctuary of mankind united in and with You. Let this brotherhood of man, like yon candlestick of pure gold, shine in seven-fold luster in the higher temple, and from the ruins of desolation, rise this new temple wide as the earth—and unwalled as its fresh air, the temple which will be a house of prayer and inspiration unto all the nations—the Sinai and Zion of all the world, the new Jerusalem on this earth, rebuilt in righteousness universal, and saved by justice flowing like a stream through all the lands.

# The Acceptance of the Unknown

### Rabbi Alexander Grodensky

Rabbi David Einhorn's reading has several important parallels to *Parashat D'varim*, which is always read on the Shabbat before Tishah B'Av. *Parashat D'varim* and Einhorn propose a perspective on God as the God of history who actively participates in the collective life of Israel.

Moses gives an overview on the wandering in the desert *toward* the Promised Land; Einhorn, in contrast, explains the meaning of the wandering *from* "the narrow home" into the wider world. Both wanderings are essential to the mission of Israel. Moses addresses the anxiety of the people in face of the unknown but promised land; he urges them to leave the comfort zone of the familiar for the sake of the next step in the development of Israel's collective mission. This transition is hard and at times painful, no less than the transition put in motion by the destruction of the Temple, addressed by Einhorn.

Leaving the limitations of the national and the ones who think and look like us toward an acceptance of an unknown, promised role in the redemption of humanity—from the walled temple to the "new temple wide as earth"—this is, according to Einhorn, the current task of the Jewish people worldwide.

## *Alternative Haftarah Reading: From* Listening to Battered Women: A Survivor-Centered Approach to Advocacy, *by Lisa A. Goodman and Deborah Epstein*

Kicked, slapped, shoved, and choked. Women are stalked and humiliated. They are isolated from friends and family, constantly monitored, and thwarted in their efforts to work.

Emergency battered women's shelters, victim advocacy, and crisis hotline programs were early services deeply rooted in a mutual self-help philosophy.

Now, another model has emerged. The survivor-centered approach to domestic violence is rooted in feminist theory, empowerment models, and a rights-based approach. The core of survivor centeredness is the act of giving voice and empowering women to make decisions about their lives and families.

The goal is to restore survivors' personal, interpersonal, and social power, which has often been intentionally diminished by abusers. Working respectfully with survivors helps them obtain their self-identified goals and ensures they have the knowledge, skills, and self-confidence to be in control of their lives again.

# Mourning Has Broken

### CANTOR KAREN WEBBER, MSM, CPRS

"Tears are my food day and night," said the Psalmist. "By the waters of Babylon, we lay down and wept" (Psalms 42:4, 137:1).

The challah dough is mixed with ash. The Ark draped in black, our Jerusalem sits bruised and battered, threading locks of hair through her fingers—a woman whose tunic has fallen to reveal scarring in places usually not visible. She is a shell of her old self. Her anguish is reflected in the destruction all around her. God's house has been razed. Front doors lay with uprooted trees and toppled stones. I weep.

> Her uncleanness clings to her skirts.
> She gave no thought to her future;
> she has sunk appallingly,
> with none to comfort her. (Lamentations 1:9)

The judgments are harsh.

We must be soft. We must comfort her. Let her not stand as victim, not stand alone. Let us cover and console her. She invites us into her pain, and into the pain of our lived, trauma-informed experience. We carry trauma in our bodies, in our bones. Old hurts turn hard and remain with us until we find those who will help us to systematically tease the memories out, tamp them down, and purge them forever.

# Haftarot for the American Jewish Calendar

# Martin Luther King Jr. Day
## JANUARY

*From "Why We Went: A Joint Letter from the Rabbis
Arrested in St. Augustine," 1964*

We came because we could not stand silently by our brother's blood. We had done that too many times before. We have been vocal in our exhortation of others but the idleness of our hands too often revealed an inner silence; silence at a time when silence has become the unpardonable sin of our time. We came in the hope that the God of us all would accept our small involvement as partial atonement for the many things we wish we had done before and often.

We came as Jews who remember the millions of faceless people who stood quietly, watching the smoke rise from Hitler's crematoria. We came because we know that, second only to silence, the greatest danger to man is loss of faith in man's capacity to act.

Here in St. Augustine we have seen the depths of anger, resentment and fury; we have seen faces that expressed a deep implacable hatred. What disturbs us more deeply is the large number of decent citizens who have stood aside, unable to bring themselves to act, yet knowing in their hearts that this cause is right and that it must inevitably triumph.

We believe, though we could not count on it in advance, that our presence and actions here have been of practical effect. They have reminded the embattled Negroes here that they are not isolated and alone. The conscience of the wicked has been troubled, while that of the righteous has gained new strength. We are more certain than before that this cause is invincible, but we also have a sharpened awareness of the great effort and sacrifice which will be required. We pray that what we have done may lead us on to further actions and persuade others who still stand hesitantly to take the stand they know is just.

## Act on What You Believe
### RABBI KERRY M. OLITZKY

The Chasidic rebbe Menachem Mendel of Kotzk exhorted his students not to just study Torah. Instead, he told them, "Be Torah." Thus, it comes as no surprise that at a CCAR Conference in 1964, sixteen Reform rabbis and one Reform lay social activist leader answered the call of Martin Luther King Jr. to join King in St. Augustine, where he would lead a nonviolent civil rights demonstration. Consequently, all of these men were arrested: two for sitting at a table with three black "youngsters" inside a restaurant; fifteen for praying outside of that same restaurant.

This letter, signed by all of those arrested and chiefly written by Rabbi Eugene Borowitz, PhD, *z"l*, took its lead from the piece that King himself penned, known as the "Letter from a Birmingham Jail." While the King letter chastises his fellow ministers for not standing with him, the rabbinic letter explains why this group of rabbis felt compelled to go to St. Augustine—and thus stands as reminder to us all. They wrote that they came " because we could not stand silently by our brother's blood." Their words are based on Leviticus 19:16 which instructs, "Do not passively stand by the blood of your neighbor." This text, which many Reform Jews read on Yom Kippur, comes from what is known as the Holiness Code.

In order to be *holy*, that is, *wholly different*, as Jews, we have to act on what we believe to be our own personal call to justice, our own personal call to "be Torah."

# Tu BiSh'vat
## JANUARY/FEBRUARY

### *Babylonian Talmud*, Taanit 5b

The Gemara relates: When they were taking leave of one another, Rav Nachman said to Rabbi Yitzchak, "Master, give me a blessing." Rabbi Yitzchak said to him, "I will tell you a parable. To what is this matter comparable? It is comparable to one who was walking through a desert and who was hungry, tired, and thirsty. And they found a tree whose fruits were sweet and whose shade was pleasant, and a stream of water flowed beneath it. They ate from the fruits of the tree, drank from the water in the stream, and sat in the shade of the tree. And when they wished to leave, they said, 'Tree, tree, with what shall I bless you? If I say to you that your fruits should be sweet, your fruits are already sweet; if I say that your shade should be pleasant, your shade is already pleasant; if I say that a stream of water should flow beneath you, a stream of water already flows beneath you. Rather, I will bless you as follows: May it be God's will that all saplings that they plant from you be like you.' So it is with you. With what shall I bless you? If I bless you with Torah, you already have Torah; if I bless you with wealth, you already have wealth; if I bless you with children, you already have children. Rather, may it be God's will that your offspring shall be like you."

## May We Be Like the Trees
### ILANA Y. SYMONS

The Torah is bookended by stories about trees. It begins with Adam and Eve eating the fruit of the Tree of Knowledge and their banishment from the Garden of Eden (Genesis 3). It ends with the Israelites marching into the Promised Land, where they are to plant trees; when these trees bear fruit, the Israelites will have a ceremony, an offering of all the first fruits of these trees to God (Leviticus 19:23–25). The Book of Proverbs (3:18) calls the Torah itself a Tree of Life; its fruits are sweet: laws and history, stories and values.

On Tu BiSh'vat, we celebrate the trees that appear throughout Jewish literature. This is a holiday of Rabbinic invention; clearly, the Rabbis noticed the orchard planted throughout the Torah. Trees are central to Judaism—so central, in fact, that the Rabbis declared Tu BiSh'vat one of the four new years of the Jewish calendar (Mishnah *Rosh HaShanah* 1:1). Like us, the trees merit renewal every year.

The Babylonian Talmud, *Taanit* 5b, explains that the highest blessing you can give to another person, higher even than Torah, wealth, and children, is that they be like a tree. The man in Rabbi Yitzchak's parable seeks to bless the tree for providing respite to a weary traveler, but he cannot find the right words; its fruits are sweet already, its shade is pleasant already, its place in the ecosystem is set. Instead, he blesses its saplings: may they grow into trees like the one from which they came.

Rabbi Yitzchak mentions only a twig of what trees offer us. They clean our air and provide oxygen to breathe. They are homes to all the forest's creatures and provide material for human shelter. They are a thing of beauty and mark for us the cycle of the year. Trees are the most versatile of nature's gifts, but only if we continue to plant and sustain them. They are even a model for us: Be unafraid to let your roots grow deep. Give generously of your fruit and teach your children to do the same. Be a respite for others from the forest of life.

May we continue to plant seeds so they may grow into saplings. May the generosity of the trees never change. May we always merit their gifts.

May we be like the trees.

# Black History Month

FEBRUARY

*From "All the Things We Can Do with Hope," by Evan Traylor, 2019*

And yet, in these most painful, heartbreaking moments, we must hold onto hope. Because with hope, we will create a more vibrant Jewish life and better world for all people. With hope, our congregations—from Albany to Austin, Boston to Sacramento—will gather unafraid in sacred community.

> With hope, we will celebrate the truly inspiring diversity of our Jewish community.
> With hope, Israelis and Palestinians will know a true and lasting peace.
> With hope, we will protect immigrants and refugees, and we will end the plague of gun violence in this country.
> With hope, young Jews will continue leading our community and world in remarkable ways.
> And with hope, we will empathize, organize, and mobilize to make our wildest dreams come true.

My friends, each and every day, we live in the world as it is. But when we choose to hope, to dream of a better future and to work to make it happen, we live in the world as it should be.

Yes, there will be challenges along the way. But the lessons of my ancestors—and all of our ancestors—is that hope is not a foolish wish. It is a powerful, radical force that will lead all of us, and all of the world, toward a better, brighter future.

## Storytelling as a Bridge between Past and Future and toward Hope, Equity, and Racial Justice

RABBI JAN KATZ

Elie Wiesel said, "Indeed I had dreamed of singing of memory and friendship in a world that sadly needs both."

At this point in my life, I am trying to remember the truths of all the stories of my past in order see more clearly where I could have been a better friend, where I could have taken another's story deeper into my heart and into my Jewish conscience, and where I could have practiced more of the love and acceptance that God intended for humanity to live together.

I remember my childhood friend Janet Jones, the Black Baptist preacher's daughter from diagonally across the street. We spend hours romping through the church parish hall and kitchen gardens. I eat at her table and even attend her prayer services on Sunday mornings. Adjacent to the church, my illiterate and oh-so beloved Russian carpenter grandfather, who lives across the hall from us, builds by hand, without so much as a measuring stick, the Chabad shul. Church and synagogue adjacent to each other, Black people and white people eating regularly at the same table. I live in blissful ignorance. I don't know anything about racial disparity and injustice. We are all poor. I am a child looking through the lens of the loyalty and love of friends and family. The Joneses are my family too.

In middle school, our lives diverge. I never get to ask Janet about her aspirations and her challenges as a Black woman. I am not present to her long enough. We miss out on taking on racial inequity together.

As undergraduates in the 1970s, during the Black Power movement, Annie Owens, my Black friend and co-conspirator in middle school through university, and I walk our separate ways.

Our friendship fades, until it cannot be restored—even when I, this very summer, reach out to her.

I yearn to restore that relationship. What would it have taken and what would it have meant if I stayed to listen to her stories and held the weight of her 400-years-lasting oppression with her? I'll never know.

Now, to simply—and finally!—sit steadfastly in sadness, struggle, protest, brokenness, and companionship with all people of color is already a sign of hope, a comingling of *tikvah* (hope) and *mikveh* . . . we must pool our resources equitably, moving together toward renewal and redemption.

# Presidents' Day

FEBRUARY

*Proverbs 16:15–31*

The ruler's smile means life;
their favor is like a rain cloud in spring.
How much better to acquire wisdom than gold;
to acquire understanding is preferable to silver.
The highway of the upright avoids evil;
one who would preserve their life watches their way.
Pride goes before ruin,
arrogance, before failure.
Better to be humble and among the lowly
than to share spoils with the proud.

One who is adept in a matter will attain success;
happy is one who trusts in the Eternal.
The wise-hearted is called discerning;
one whose speech is pleasing gains wisdom.
Good sense is a fountain of life to those who have it,
and folly is the punishment of fools.
The mind of the wise makes their speech effective
and increases the wisdom on their lips.
Pleasant words are like a honeycomb,
sweet to the palate and a cure for the body.
A road may seem right to a person,
but in the end it is a road to death.
The appetite of a laborer labors for them,
because their hunger forces them on.
A scoundrel plots evil;
what is on their lips is like a scorching fire.
A shifty person stirs up strife,
and a querulous one alienates their friend.
A lawless person misleads their friend,
making them take the wrong way.
One closes one's eyes while meditating deception;
one purses one's lips while deciding upon evil.
Gray hair is a crown of glory;
it is attained by the way of righteousness.

## May Leaders Rule Wisely

### Rabbi Jordan M. Parr

I once had the honor of giving the invocation at the inauguration of our city's mayor. We had been friendly, and I eagerly accepted the invitation. However, I had long worried that his ascension from television news anchor to mayor would lead to some errors (which I could accept) but also hubris (which I could not). I was glad when I came upon this passage in Proverbs that spoke to the moment: "The highway of the upright avoids evil; one who would preserve their life watches their way" (Proverbs 16:17).

All too often, we elect our leaders—mayors, governors, and presidents—without considering just how the job will change them. While the Hebrew prophets easily found their voice when criticizing and even excoriating kings, this passage calls for wisdom. While we must not always agree with the decision of a leader, we still must ensure that a leader rules wisely.

In the next verses, we read the following: "Pride goes before ruin; arrogance, before failure. Better to be humble and among the lowly than to share spoils with the proud" (Proverbs 16:18–19). The ultimate kingship is that of the Eternal. The writer of Proverbs is impressing upon a ruler that power does not emanate from one's innate talents, no matter how great, but rather from God. Even a king, especially one who rules as the scion of a dynasty, must remember that power is temporal and can easily be lost. It is only when one is subservient to God and keeps the welfare of the people in the forefront, that a ruler succeeds. In our time, let us act in the spirit of the writer of Proverbs and work to imbue ourselves—and our leaders—with the gift of wisdom.

# Women's History Month

### MARCH

*Esther 4:14; Speech by Rabbi Sally J. Priesand, Ordained as the First Female Rabbi at a Rabbinical Seminary, in June 1972*

One makes history at the intersection of innate talent, bravery, and persistence, gathered at the right moment, as Mordecai explains to Esther:

> And who knows, perhaps you have attained [this] elevated position for just such a time. (Esther 4:14)

Rabbi Priesand reflects on her groundbreaking role, describing how she did not seek this place in history:

I decided I wanted to be a rabbi when I was sixteen years old. Unfortunately, I don't remember why. I do remember always wanting to be a teacher, and my plans always seemed to call for me to teach whatever my favorite subject was at a particular time. . . . Fortunately, for me, my parents gave me one of the greatest gifts a parent can give a child: the courage to dare and to dream. As a result, I remained focused on my goal, unconcerned that no woman had ever been ordained rabbi by a theological seminary—and determined to succeed despite the doubts I heard expressed in the organized Jewish community. In those days, I did not think very much about being a pioneer, nor was it my intention to champion the rights of women. I just wanted to be a rabbi.

## To Recognize and to Lift Up

### RABBI MARY L. ZAMORE

The public seminary ordination of Rabbi Sally J. Priesand by Hebrew Union College–Jewish Institute of Religion in Cincinnati on June 3, 1972, opened a path for other women to be ordained as rabbis. Despite entering a world not entirely ready to accept women as rabbis, Rabbi Priesand and the women following her forged a path for female rabbis, cantors, and leaders in all the branches of Judaism. In remembering and celebrating this historic change, it is also important to recognize every woman who has not been afforded the opportunity to be ordained a rabbi, despite her efforts and longing. We especially think of Ray Frank (Litman), Martha Neumark (Montor), Irma Levy Lindheim, Dr. Dora Askowith, Helen Levinthal (Lyons), and Paula Herskovitz Ackerman, among the many who wanted to become rabbis but could not.

In celebrating Rabbi Priesand, we lift up every woman who has overcome limitations, contributing to the ever-widening acceptance of women as rabbis, cantors, scholars, Jewish professionals, thought leaders, and lay leaders. This haftarah reading links the verse from the biblical Book of Esther to Rabbi Priesand's own words. As Rabbi Priesand recounts, she just wanted to be a rabbi. Her aspiration was organic and ordinary, but her persistence met the right moment in history, making her ordination and rabbinate extraordinary.

May we all work to dismantle the societal structures that continue to disadvantage women in our communities.

# International Women's Day
## MARCH 8

### From "Brown v. Board of Education *in International Context,*" by Justice Ruth Bader Ginsburg

On a personal note, *Brown* and its forerunners, along with the movement for international human rights that came later, powerfully influenced the women's rights litigation in which I was engaged in the 1970s. Thurgood Marshall and his co-workers sought to educate the Court, step by step, about the pernicious effects of race discrimination. Similarly, advocates for gender equality sought to inform the Court, through a series of cases, about the injustice of laws ordering or reinforcing separate spheres of human activity for men and women. The ACLU's Women's Rights Project, which I helped to launch and direct, was among the organizations inspired by the NAACP Legal Defense and Education Fund's example.

*Brown* figured four years ago in a courageous decision by Israel's Chief Justice, Aharon Barak. The Israel Land Administration had denied the asserted right of Arabs to build their homes on land in Israel open to the general public for home construction. The Administration defended the denial on the ground that it would allocate land to establish an exclusively Arab communal settlement. Citing *Brown*, the Israeli Supreme Court ruled that such allegedly separate-but-equal treatment constituted unlawful discrimination on the basis of national origin. . . .

To sum up, *Brown* both reflected and propelled the development of human rights protection internationally. It was decided with the horrors of the Holocaust in full view, and with the repression of Communist regimes in the Soviet Union and Eastern Europe a current reality. It propelled an evolution yet unfinished toward respect, in law and in practice, for the human dignity of all the world's people.

# A Prophet in Her Own Time

*Susan Friedberg Kalson*

In this excerpt from a speech Justice Ruth Bader Ginsburg gave in the mid-2000s, she describes the concentric circles that continue to ripple out from the groundbreaking 1954 US Supreme Court ruling that "separate but equal" treatment on the basis of race is inherently unequal. Part of Ginsburg's genius as a lawyer in the 1970s was to apply the same principles used by the civil rights movement to persuade the Supreme Court that laws discriminating on the basis of gender were likewise unconstitutional. A student of international legal commentary, Ginsburg was interested and engaged in the world beyond the United States. In these remarks, she advocates for equity among all peoples and nations with the same passion that drove her American jurisprudence.

The daughter of Jewish immigrants, the discrimination Ginsburg experienced as a Jew and as a pioneering female lawyer drove her determination to fight discrimination of all kinds. In 1993, she became the second woman—and sixth Jew—appointed to the Supreme Court, where she redoubled the battle for equality under the law even after her views became the minority, dissenting opinion. By the time she died, Erev Rosh HaShanah 5781 (2020), she was hailed as a superhero, a feminist icon, and a prophet.

In her approach to life and the law, Ginsburg was shaped by her Jewish identity, values, and teachings. Emblazoned on the walls of her Supreme Court chambers were the words "*Tzedek, tzedek, tirdof*—Justice, justice you shall pursue" (Deuteronomy 16:20). On International Women's Day, may we take up her fight anew, building on her legacy to empower our call for justice, remembering Ruth Bader Ginsburg, a prophet in her own time—and for ours.

# Equal Pay Day

## LAST WEEK OF MARCH/FIRST WEEK OF APRIL

*From "The Women of Reform Judaism Resolution on Pay Equity," 2015*

Given the profound injustice of unequal pay, Women of Reform Judaism reaffirms its commitment to achieving pay equity and calls upon its sisterhoods to:

1. Urge the swift adoption of legislation that would provide women who face sex-based wage discrimination with a straightforward, accessible path for recourse, including but not limited to:
   a. Barring retaliation against workers who disclose their wages, so that workers can more easily determine whether they face wage discrimination, and
   b. Ensuring the right to maintain a class action lawsuit, providing women with the same remedies in court for pay discrimination as those subjected to discrimination based on race or national origin.
2. Work with synagogue leadership to enact just compensation policies for clergy and staff at all levels, or, where they already exist, to ensure that these policies properly guide the compensation, interviewing, hiring, firing and promoting of clergy and staff.
3. Implement sisterhood or congregational programs to empower women with tools to address pay inequity they may face in their professional lives outside the synagogue.
4. Take a leadership role to advocate for pay equity in their Jewish community and in their broader local community by forging partnerships with Jewish, other faith, and secular organizations in those communities.

## You Shall Not Defraud Your Fellow

### *Rabbi Liz P. G. Hirsch*

Not unlike our Jewish holidays, Equal Pay Day is not fixed to one calendar date of the year. It moves according to the specific calculations of the wage gap each year. Black Equal Pay Day, Latina Equal Pay Day, and Native Equal Pay Day are consistently later in the year, emphasizing the wider wage gap due to greater pay discrimination faced by women of color in the United States.

As the Religious Action Center of Reform Judaism notes, "Equal Pay Day is not a holiday to celebrate, but rather a day we use to bring attention to the ongoing injustice of pay discrimination in the United States . . . mark[ing] how far into the new year women must work to receive in wages what their male counterparts earned in the previous calendar year." The haftarah reading for Equal Pay Day is an excerpt from the Women of Reform Judaism's 2015 "Resolution on Pay Equity."

Our values, principles, and resolutions are the roots of the Reform Movement. With our text, we affirm our sacred commitment to gender equality and economic justice.

There is much work to be done. According to an analysis by the National Partnership for Women and Families, as of March 2020, "women in the United States are paid 82 cents for every dollar paid to men." The resolution first calls upon us to take a legislative strategy, supporting current bills and policies that work to reduce the gender wage gap. We can look to the work of our Religious Action Center for the most current legislation in need of our advocacy. Significantly, the resolution also requires us to hold up a mirror and examine the policies and practices of our own institutions to ensure we are modeling pay equity in every way. To that end, seventeen organizations have joined together to form the Reform Pay Equity Initiative, which is developing best practices for addressing the gender wage gap.

As we learn in the Holiness Code, the heart of our Torah, "You shall not defraud your fellow. You shall not commit robbery. The wages of a laborer shall not remain with you until morning" (Leviticus 19:13). May we work toward a day when all people are paid equally and justly.

# Transgender Day of Visibility

### MARCH 31

*"Invisibility in Academe," by Adrienne Rich*

Invisibility is a dangerous and painful condition. . . . When those who have power to name and to socially construct reality choose not to see you or hear you . . . when someone with the authority of a teacher, say, describes the world and you are not in it, there is a moment of psychic disequilibrium, as if you looked into a mirror and saw nothing. Yet you know you exist and others like you, that this is a game with mirrors. It takes some strength of soul—and not just individual strength, but collective understanding—to resist this void, this non-being, into which you are thrust, and to stand up, demanding to be seen and heard. And to make yourself visible, to claim that your experience is just as real and normative as any other . . . can mean making yourself vulnerable. But at least you are not doing the oppressor's work, building your own closet.

## We Must Reshape Our World

### ARIEL TOVLEV

Transgender Day of Visibility is not just a day of awareness. We have long been written out of history, as if we do not exist, as if we have never existed. And yet despite this invisibility, we have come to understand ourselves anyway. Transgender Day of Visibility is our collective call: we exist, we have always existed, and we will continue to exist.

But we cannot call out alone. We must come together in community to amplify our message, to declare to the world, "We are human beings! Our experiences are valid! Consider us not only in death and tragedy, but in life and joy! Celebrate with us in our life-affirming joy of gender euphoria!"

It is terrifying to be told you do not exist and to respond defiantly that you do. But in the midst of this vulnerability, there is strength and community. To every trans person who has felt invisible: you are valid, we see you, and you are not alone. To everyone, of every gender: we must reshape our world for it to include all of us. May we build a world that rejoices in everyone as they are, and may there be no need for closets anymore.

# Baseball Opening Day

### From "Kenneth Holtzman," Jewish Virtual Library

Kenneth Dale Holtzman is a former Jewish professional baseball player. He is still the winningest Jewish pitcher in [Major League Baseball] history. Holtzman (born November 3, 1945) was born in St. Louis. As a child, Holtzman would alternate eating Friday nights at the kosher homes of both sets of grandparents, who all immigrated to the United States from Russia. . . .

Holtzman signed with the Chicago Cubs . . . and made his major league debut at age 19 on September 4, 1965. . . . Holtzman was being called "another Sandy Koufax" as soon as he arrived in the big leagues. . . . The two greatest Jewish pitchers in history faced each other for the one and only time in their careers on September 25, 1966, the day after both had attended synagogue services for Yom Kippur. Holtzman was finishing his first full season in the majors while Koufax was winding down his final season. Holtzman [threw] a no-hitter for eight innings and [won] 2–1. . . .

When the second game of the 1973 American League Championship Series game against Baltimore fell on Yom Kippur, Holtzman—scheduled to pitch—did not play. That morning, a limousine took him to the Baltimore Hebrew Congregation, where he was escorted to the synagogue's front row and was seated next to Jerry Hoffberger, owner of the [Baltimore] Orioles.

# When Our Secular and Jewish Lives Come into Conflict:
# When Ken Holtzman Was Scheduled to Pitch on Yom Kippur

### Rabbi Stephen Weisman

Athletes, especially those at the higher levels of their sports, dedicate a great amount of their time to learning, training, and polishing their craft, often at the expense of being able to get involved in other things. In this, their experience is not very different from that of many young American Jews in the year of training leading to their celebration of becoming *b'nei mitzvah*. Preparation and training require sacrifice.

For most of us, most of the time, the secular and the Jewish elements of our lives complement each other, allowing our full involvement in both with little conflict. Sometimes, however, some of us find these elements working against each other, pulling us in two directions at once. At times like these, it is reassuring to know that we are not alone and to see how famous Jewish Americans have handled such conflicts. While the story of Sandy Koufax not pitching the first game of the 1965 World Series is much better known, Ken Holtzman experienced a similar conflict. Holtzman shared memories of that day with *Haaretz* in an article entitled "This Day in Jewish History, 1945: American Baseball Legend Who Struck Out in Israel Is Born":

> "I said to myself," recalled Holtzman, "'Oh my God, the owner of the opposing team. We're both missing today's game, and I have to pitch against his team in Oakland when I get home.'" Fortunately, Hoffberger turned out to be "the nicest guy in the world," and following services, he invited Holtzman back to his home. . . . Rested from his extra day off, Holtzman led his team to a 2–1 victory over the Orioles, and the A's went on to win the pennant and the World Series.

Not all of life's challenges work out so well, especially when two parts of our core being are thrown into conflict. Holtzman's decision—in this case, to put his Jewish identity and values ahead even of his support for his team in a playoff game, because he had faith in their ability to win without him—was handsomely rewarded.

# Yom HaShoah

## 27 NISAN (APRIL/MAY)

### *Ezekiel 37:1–14*

The hand of the Eternal was upon me, leading me out by God's spirit and setting me down in the middle of a valley. It was full of bones. God led me all around them. There were a great many of them spread on the surface of the valley, and they were very dry. God said to me, "Mortal, can these bones live?"

I answered, "O God Eternal, You [alone] know."

Then God said to me, "Prophesy to these bones, and say to them: You dry bones, hear the word of the Eternal. Thus says the Eternal God to these bones: Behold, I will cause breath to enter you, and you shall live. I will put sinews on you, and cover you with flesh, and spread skin over you. I will put breath into you, and you shall live. Then you shall know that I am the Eternal."

I prophesied as I had been commanded. And as I prophesied, there was a loud noise, a sound, and the bones came together, bone to matching bone. I looked and saw sinews and flesh and skin spread over them from above, but there was no breath in them.

Then God said to me, "Mortal, prophesy to the breath, O prophesy! And say to the breath: Thus says the Eternal God: Come, breath, from the four quarters, and breathe into these slain [bodies], that they may live [again]."

I prophesied as God had commanded me, and the breath came into them, and they came to life. They stood on their feet, an exceedingly great army.

Then God said to me, "Mortal, these bones are the whole House of Israel. They say: *Our bones are dried up, our hope is lost; we are cut off [from life]*! Therefore, prophesy to them and say: Thus says the Eternal God: I am going to open your graves, My people; I will lift you out of your graves and bring you [home] to the land of Israel. And when I have opened your graves and lifted you out of them, My people, you shall know that I am the Eternal. I will put My breath into you and you shall live [again], and I will place you in your own land. Then, says the Eternal One, you shall know that I, the Eternal, have spoken and have acted."

## Life and Death

### *RABBI JEFFREY GOLDWASSER*

On Yom HaShoah, we remember the six million Jews murdered in the Nazi genocide. We grieve the worst human-created catastrophe in history. Yet, we also recognize on this day that despite this catastrophe, the Jewish people still live. We have arisen, like the dry bones in Ezekiel's vision, and established a home in our own land. We cannot literally bring back those who were murdered, but we do recognize that our vision of God's presence in the world revives us, as a people, from death.

Yom HaShoah is a time for us to remember our past and to consider the present and future, too. Other peoples across the globe today are threatened by racial, nationalist, and religious hatred. As Jews, we stand up for justice, peace, and compassion. We continue to pursue Ezekiel's vision of restoring life where there has been death.

# The Shabbat between Yom HaShoah and Yom HaAtzma-ut

APRIL/MAY

### Zechariah 4:1–14

The angel who had been talking with me came back and wakened me as a sleeper is awakened. He said to me, "What do you see?" I said, "I see a lampstand all of gold with a bowl on its top; there are seven lamps on it, and, on its top, there are seven pipes for the lamps. By it are two olive trees, one on the right of the bowl, and the other on its left."

Then I said to the angel who had been talking with me, "What are these things, my lord?" And the angel who had been talking with me answered, saying "Don't you know what these things are?" "No, my lord, I do not," I said. Then he explained it to me, saying, "This is the word of the Eternal to Zerubbabel:

> Not by might, nor by power,
> but by My spirit
> —says the God of heaven's hosts.

"What are you, you great mountain? Before Zerubbabel, you shall become a plain. He shall bring out the topmost stone and [seeing it] all shall cry: Beautiful! Beautiful!"

And the word of the Eternal came to me: "Zerubbabel's hands have founded this House and Zerubbabel's hands shall complete it. Then you shall know that it was the God of heaven's hosts who sent me to you. Does anyone scorn a day of small beginnings? When they see the stone of the distinction in the hand of Zerubbabel, they shall rejoice.

"Those seven are the eyes of the Eternal, ranging over the whole earth."

"And what," I asked him, "are those two olive trees, one on the right and one on the left of the lampstand?" And I further asked him, "What are the two tops of the olive trees that feed their gold through those two golden tubes?" He asked me, "Don't you know what they are?" And I replied, "No, my lord." Then he explained, "They are the two anointed dignitaries who attend the Eternal of all the earth."

# Shabbat T'kumah: Idea and Content

### RABBI YEHORAM MAZOR

Many years ago, Rabbi Moti Rotem wrote an article on the days connecting Yom HaShoah, Israeli Holocaust Memorial Day, and Yom HaAtzma-ut, Israeli Independence Day. He compared this time of the Israeli year—seven days altogether—to the period of the High Holy Days between Rosh HaShanah and Yom Kippur in the fall, calling it "the Seven Days of the Testimony":

> During those Seven Days and every year anew, the Israeli people should, both as a community and individually, assess how far they have come in fulfilling the sacred commandment, calling, and historical responsibility to be witnesses in the face of the Shoah. In addition, we are also obliged to celebrate life in the form of Independence Day. During those ten days of *t'shuvah*, of "repentance," the people of Israel should do the necessary inner self-assessment to discern how they are coping with these responsibilities and their weight: are we building a future for our people? Even though this may also be an individual process, it is especially important for our public institutions. Our public institutions and their officials are called to do this sacred work between Memorial Day and Independence Day.

Rabbi Rotem's idea eventually gave the Shabbat between Yom HaShoah and Yom HaAtzma-ut a special name used in Israel: Shabbat T'kumah, "the Shabbat of Arising." On this Shabbat, we say prayers for those who were murdered in the Shoah and for those who were killed for or in the State of Israel and for the state and its mission as a shared "Jewish homeland" (Balfour Declaration) and as "a light to the nations" (Isaiah 49:6). It is a festive Shabbat on which we add special readings, poetry, prayers, and, of course, a rich *Kiddush*. In Israeli Reform congregations, we read from two Torah scrolls. From the first scroll, we read the regular seven *aliyot*. From the second scroll, we read as *maftir* a few verses from *Parashat Eikev*, Deuteronomy 8:1–10, and as the haftarah reading, we read Zechariah 4:1–14, about the prophet's vision of the golden menorah, adorned with two olive branches left and right. This vision is also captured in the insignia of the State of Israel.

Even though Shabbat T'kumah is an Israeli-Zionist-Reform creation, it has found its place also on the other side of the Atlantic Ocean. My vision is that we can celebrate it together.

# Yom HaAtzma-ut

## 5 IYAR (APRIL/MAY)

### The Israeli "Scroll of Independence" (M'gillat HaAtzma-ut)

Eretz-Israel [the Land of Israel] was the birthplace of the Jewish people. Here their spiritual, religious and political identity was shaped. Here they first attained to statehood, created cultural values of national and universal significance and gave to the world the eternal Book of Books.

After being forcibly exiled from their land, the people kept faith with it throughout their Dispersion and never ceased to pray and hope for their return to it and for the restoration in it of their political freedom.

Impelled by this historic and traditional attachment, Jews strove in every successive generation to re-establish themselves in their ancient homeland. In recent decades they returned in their masses. Pioneers, defiant returnees, and defenders, they made deserts bloom, revived the Hebrew language, built villages and towns, and created a thriving community controlling its own economy and culture, loving peace but knowing how to defend itself, bringing the blessings of progress to all the country's inhabitants, and aspiring towards independent nationhood. . . .

The State of Israel will be open for Jewish immigration and for the Ingathering of the Exiles; it will foster the development of the country for the benefit of all its inhabitants; it will be based on freedom, justice and peace as envisaged by the prophets of Israel; it will ensure complete equality of social and political rights to all its inhabitants irrespective of religion, race or sex; it will guarantee freedom of religion, conscience, language, education and culture; it will safeguard the Holy Places of all religions; and it will be faithful to the principles of the Charter of the United Nations. . . .

We extend our hand to all neighboring states and their peoples in an offer of peace and good neighborliness, and appeal to them to establish bonds of cooperation and mutual help with the sovereign Jewish people settled in its own land. The State of Israel is prepared to do its share in a common effort for the advancement of the entire Middle East.

We appeal to the Jewish people throughout the Diaspora to rally round the Jews of Eretz-Israel in the tasks of immigration and upbuilding and to stand by them in the great struggle for the realization of the age-old dream—the redemption of Israel.

## The Vision of the Proclamation

### RABBI GERI NEWBURGE

Yom HaAtzma-ut, Israel Independence Day, is one of the modern holidays instituted since the establishment of the State of Israel. The Israeli Proclamation of Independence was signed on 5 Iyar 5708, corresponding to May 14, 1948. In many ways the celebration of independence in Israel parallels the American observance of its independence on July 4, with picnics, fireworks, and public festivities.

The establishment of the modern State of Israel is considered by many Jews to be a miracle, and with it are unique opportunities to reconnect to a former expression of their "spiritual, religious and political identity." While Israel's right to exist has faced many threats, its establishment continues to be a source of Jewish pride for many of us.

The Proclamation of Independence itself is a powerful document. It recalls the message of the prophets, speaking to the preservation of rights for "all its inhabitants" regardless of any individual's personal identity. Moreover, the proclamation speaks to the "redemption of Israel"—something the ancient prophets sought to bring about with their messages of ethical behavior. In fact, some communities have the custom of reciting Isaiah 10:32–12:6 on Yom HaAtzma-ut, which discusses the divine promise of national redemption.

That said, the vision of the Proclamation of Independence calls upon Jewish communities all over the world to live according to the highest ideals of Judaism: to treat each other with dignity, with respect, and in the spirit of equality.

# Earth Day

## APRIL 22

### Pirkei D'Rabbi Eliezer *12:4, 6*

And (Adam) was at his leisure in the garden of Eden, like one of the ministering angels. The Blessed Holy One said: I am singular in My world and this one is singular in his world. There is no propagation before Me and this one has no propagation in his life; hereafter all the creatures will say: Since there was no propagation in his life, it is he who has created us. It is not good for the human to be alone, as it is said, "Then God Eternal considered, 'It is not good that the man be alone—I will make him a helpmate'" (Genesis 2:18).

When the earth heard this expression thereupon it trembled and quaked, crying before its Creator: Sovereign of all worlds, I have not the power to provide for the multitude of humanity. The Blessed Holy One replied: I and you will (together) feed the multitude of humanity. They agreed to divide (the task) between themselves: the night was for the Blessed Holy One, and the day (was apportioned) to the earth. What did the Blessed Holy One do? God created the sleep of life, so that the human lies down and sleeps while God sustains them, heals them, and gives them life and rest, as it is said, "I should have slept: then had I been at rest" (Job 3:13). The Blessed Holy One supports humanity with the earth, giving it water; and it yields its fruit and food for all creatures—but the first person's food "only through pain shall you eat of it, as long as you live" (Genesis 3:17).

# A Covenant of Mutual Reliance

*Rabbi Andrue Kahn*

On Earth Day we celebrate the marvels of nature, taking a moment to remember our reliance upon the earth as well as the earth's reliance upon us. This midrash illustrates the relationship between humanity, the earth, and divinity. Not only is humanity reliant upon God, but humanity is also reliant upon the earth, which itself is a partner with God in sustaining humanity. We, too, work with the earth to sustain ourselves.

This threefold symbiotic relationship between God, the earth, and humanity brings to mind a passage from the *Tanach*: "Two are better than one, for they get good reward for their toil. For if one should fall, the other will lift up their friend. But if the one alone should fall, there is no other to lift them up. If two lie together, they are warm, but as for one, how will they be warm? And if one should attack them, the two will stand against them. And the triple cord will not quickly be snapped" (Ecclesiastes 4:9–12).

Today, we are struggling mightily to find our proper balance in this triple cord with the earth and God. These passages tell us that it is not a mundane struggle but rather a sacred responsibility to uphold our part of this covenant. God's presence within this relationship reminds us that the earth itself is a divine creation, and just as we are responsible for upholding the divinity of all humanity, we are equally responsible for upholding the divinity of our sacred home. Not only for our species' survival do we strive to maintain an ecological equilibrium, but also as part of our ancestral covenant, part of fulfilling our sacred responsibilities as a people. The covenant that binds these three parties through mutual respect, care, and uplift is one we must mindfully uphold as partners in Creation.

# Lesbian Visibility Day

## APRIL 26

### *"I Shall Sing to the Lord a New Song," by Rabbi Ruth Sohn*

I, Miriam, stand at the sea
and turn
to face the desert
stretching endless and
still.
My eyes are dazzled
The sky brilliant blue
Sunburnt sands unyielding white.
My hands turn to dove wings.
My arms
reach
for the sky
and I want to sing
the song rising inside me.
My mouth open
I stop.
Where are the words?
Where the melody?
In a moment of panic
My eyes go blind.
Can I take a step
Without knowing a
Destination?
Will I falter
Will I fall
Will the ground sink away from under
me?

The song still unformed—
How can I sing?

To take the first step—
To sing a new song—
Is to close one's eyes
and dive
into unknown waters.
For a moment knowing nothing
risking all—
But then to discover

The waters are friendly
The ground is firm.
And the song—
the song rises again.
Out of my mouth
come words lifting the wind.
And I hear
for the first
the song
that has been in my heart
silent
unknown
even to me.

## Standing on Firm Ground

### RABBI HEATHER MILLER

This poem describes the feeling of insecurity whenever we step forward to fully become who we are. As Miriam approaches the parted waters of the Sea of Reeds, her story has not yet been written. She knows she needs to take steps forward toward her own freedom, but there are no assurances that she, or the other escaping Israelites, will make it through. Still, she feels called to sing the song within.

So many of us in the Queer community can relate to this feeling every time we come out. When we take the chance and step forward to present who we are, we wonder: Will we be accepted, supported, and loved? Or will we be rejected? Unsure, we bravely challenge ourselves to come out. And what an uplifting feeling it is when we find that the song of our souls is accepted. Then we are able to fully live our truth.

To come out is a sacred act where personal courage meets divine grace. How can we create communities where we encourage one another to live our unique truths? How can we assure others that when they step forward, they too will find that the ground is firm?

# Mental Health Awareness Month

MAY

*Jeremiah 20:7-18*

You enticed me, O Eternal, and I was enticed;
You overpowered me and You prevailed.
I have become a constant laughingstock,
everyone jeers at me.
For every time I speak, I must cry out,
must shout: "Lawlessness and rapine!"
For the word of the Eternal causes me
constant disgrace and contempt.
I thought, "I will not mention God,
no more will I speak in God's name"—
but [God's word] was like a raging fire in my heart,
shut up in my bones;
I could not hold it in, I was helpless.
I heard the whisper of the crowd—
terror all around:
"Inform! Let us inform against him!"
All my [supposed] friends
are waiting for me to stumble:
"Perhaps he can be entrapped, and we can prevail against him
and take our vengeance on him."
But the Eternal is with me like a mighty warrior;
therefore, my persecutors shall stumble;
they shall not prevail and shall not succeed.

They shall be utterly shamed
with a humiliation for all time,
which shall not be forgotten.
O God of heaven's hosts, You who test the righteous,
who examine the heart and the mind,
let me see Your retribution upon them,
for I lay my case before You.
Sing unto the Eternal,
praise the Eternal,
for God has rescued the needy
from the hands of evildoers!

Accursed be the day
that I was born!
Let not the day be blessed
when my mother bore me!
Accursed be the one
who brought my father the news
and said, "A boy
is born to you,"
and gave him such joy!
Let that one become like the cities
which the Eternal overthrew without relenting!
Let them hear shrieks in the morning
and battle shouts at noontide—
because they did not kill me before birth
so that my mother might be in my grave,
and her womb big [with me] for all time.
Why did I ever issue from the womb,
to see misery and woe,
to spend all my days in shame!

# When under Pressure

### RABBI CHARLES MIDDLEBURGH, PhD

We have a greater insight into Jeremiah's mental health than that of anyone else in the *Tanach*. Jeremiah shares his triumphs and disasters and his inner turmoil. At the height of his power as a prophet, his mood can change in an eyeblink. His depression is severe; he regrets having been born; he struggles with the sense that he has been seduced into prophecy by God, enticed into something that he would not otherwise have done.

It is worth considering the pressure that many in public life feel as they try to fulfill significant tasks that would be a challenge for anyone and the stress and depression that can come with real or perceived failure.

Jeremiah's testimony to his inner anguish should teach us to be kinder to those in authority and to acknowledge the emotional price they pay and the loneliness they endure even when they consider their role a calling. It is also a timely reminder to those in positions of leadership to make allowance for the mental illness of others and to support them as far as they are able on life's challenging path.

# Jewish American Heritage Month
### MAY

*"Prayer for Government" of the Reformed Society of Israelites,*
*Charleston, South Carolina, 1825*

Almighty God! sole ruler and governor of the whole universe! Thou who hast created countless systems for thy glory! Thou, who fillest all space with thy wisdom, truth, order and benevolence, in thy boundless mercy, bless, preserve and enlighten the President of these United States, together with his counsellors, and all the officers of the General and State Governments, executive, legislative and judicial. O, may a portion of thy divine wisdom fill the halls of their assemblies, and direct their hearts and understandings for the honour of thy holy name, and the prosperity of our beloved country. May the spirit of peace be ever in their counsels, and integrity be their leading principle.

We have reason to bless and extol thy goodness, O Lord! that thou hast numbered us with the inhabitants of this thy much favoured land, uniting us all into one great family, where the noble and virtuous mind is the only crown of distinction, and equality of rights the only fountain of power. We bless thy holy name, that thou hast removed the intolerance of bigotry far from out this happy republic, and hast relieved the people from the yoke of political and religious bondage. May thy redeeming spirit visit all the nations of the earth, and may the smiles of thy auspicious goodness be a light to the eyes of rulers, and the fear of thy justice awaken contrition in the heart of the oppressor. Graciously incline thine ear to the supplications of thy servants, assembled here this day. Bless the people of these United States. May sentiments of charity and friendship unite them as citizens of one common country. May the lights of science and civilization, as the flaming sword of Eden, defend them on every side from the subtle hypocrite and open adversary. Spread thy benign influence, great Author of existence! over all mankind. Grant this for the sake of thy supreme excellence and never ending mercies, and let us all say, Amen.

# Living up to the Ideals

*Rabbi Gary Phillip Zola, PhD*

The first organized attempt to reform Judaism in the United States occurred in Charleston, South Carolina. This historic initiative gave rise to the establishment of the Reformed Society of Israelites. In 1825, the members of this group began worshiping together, and in doing so, they introduced a significant number of liturgical innovations. These reforms led to the publication of American Judaism's first Reform prayer book: *The Sabbath Service and Miscellaneous Prayers Adopted by the Reformed Society of Israelites, Founded in Charleston, South Carolina, November 21, 1825.*

Three key members of the society's leadership composed several original prayers that sought to "preserve and perpetuate the principles of Judaism in their utmost purity and vigour." One of those original liturgical compositions, written by the distinguished educator and newspaper publisher Isaac Harby (1788–1828), was "Prayer for Government."

Harby's prayer constitutes the first attempt to pray on behalf of America's distinctly republican form of government, beseeching God to "bless, preserve and enlighten" the "executive, legislative and judicial" branches of government, as well as "the people of these United States." Despite the persistence of religious bias in America, Harby's prayer strikes an aspirational tone, expressing the fervent belief that in America "sentiments of charity and friendship" will ultimately prevail. Although Walt Whitman described the United States as "a teeming nation of nations," our Reform Jewish forebears prayed that all Americans would yet become "citizens of one common country."

During Jewish American Heritage Month, the government of the United States encourages its citizens to reflect on the many ways that American Jewry has influenced every facet of this nation's heritage. Despite its antiquated language, Harby's prayer inspires us to pursue justice so that one day the American nation will live up to the lofty ideals enshrined in its founding documents.

# Mother's Day

MAY

*"Women at the Head of the Class," by Jessica de Koninck*

Pitkin Avenue, walking with Mama,
Brooklyn, the Promised Land.
I push a shopping cart as big as me.
Mama stops to fix her stockings
near the rumbling el.
Everyone out this warm spring day,
Dodgers' opening day.
Only it's the Mets,
and they're in Queens.
Never as real
as Brooklyn or those Dodgers.
Now the internet news tells me
Bella Abzug died.
How can that be?
I'm on Pitkin Avenue.
She hasn't entered Congress yet.
Bella is Mama and Mama is Bella
Giant women in wide
brimmed hats—shouting
out each other with persuasion.
Mama says,
Bella doesn't know what she's talking about.
Bella is so argumentative.
Mama likes Bella.
Bella, what's wrong with Bella?
Doesn't she know it's opening day?

## Mothers and Matriarchs

RABBI ISABEL DE KONINCK

The origins of our American celebration of Mother's Day go back to the abolitionist and peace advocate Julia Ward Howe, whose 1870 "Appeal to Womanhood throughout the World" (later known as "The Mother's Day Proclamation") set forth a vision of an international congress of women "to promote the alliance of the different nationalities, the amicable settlement of international questions, the great and general interests of peace." Ann Reeves Jarvis, a peace activist who worked with Howe, took up the mantle of this cause, advocating for a Mother's Day dedicated to peace. It was her daughter, Anna Jarvis, who was finally successful in lobbying for the creation of the holiday, which was celebrated in every state by 1911. Quickly, the focus of Mother's Day shifted from the role of women in promoting peace and justice to a more general celebration of mothering and motherhood.

In the Jewish calendar, the American Mother's Day holiday falls during the Counting of the Omer. This calendrical position helps us link the original intent of the holiday (a celebration of women's roles in peace and liberation) to contemporary celebrations (honoring mothers for all they have taught us) and reminds us of the roles that every mother (whether by birth or choice) and every matriarch (whether by biology or history) play in helping each of us as individuals and the entire Jewish people march from freedom to understanding, from the most difficult times in our lives to the places of most learning, growth, and strength.

Our reading captures the timeless quality of our relationships with our mothers and matriarchs. Its image of Pitkin Avenue as the Promised Land reminds us that mothers and matriarchs help define a sense of home, safety, and belonging. These "giant women in wide brimmed hats—shouting out each other with persuasion" model living with passion and purpose. They are at once ordinary and extraordinary: like the feeling of opening day of baseball season, like the words shared between mother and child on the street, like the worlds spoken into being by our matriarchs when they declare, "This woman's place is in the House . . . the House of Representatives!"

At their deaths, the fabric of time and space tears: How can they be gone when we are still here, walking the streets of childhood? How can they be gone when there is so much left to learn from them? "Bella is Mama and Mama is Bella"— they live on in us, as we will be the parents and ancestors of the next generation.

# Harvey Milk Day

### MAY 22, MILK'S BIRTHDAY

*From "The Hope Speech," by Harvey Milk*

And in San Francisco, three days before Gay Pride Day, a person was killed just because he was gay. And that night, I walked among the sad and the frustrated at City Hall in San Francisco and later that night as they lit candles on Castro Street and stood in silence, reaching out for some symbolic thing that would give them hope. These were strong people. . . . They were strong, but even they needed hope.

And the young gay people who are coming out. . . . The only thing they have to look forward to is hope. And you have to give them hope. Hope for a better world, hope for a better tomorrow, hope for a better place to come to if the pressures at home are too great. Hope that all will be all right. . . . And you and you and you, you have to give people hope.

## The Ability to Imagine
### Rabbi Lisa A. Edwards, PhD

Harvey Milk delivered versions of his "Hope Speech" to various audiences after his election as the first out gay elected official in the United States. Milk was elected to the San Francisco Board of Supervisors in November 1977, began serving in January 1978, and was assassinated (along with San Francisco mayor George Moscone) in November 1978. Here is a prayer that can be read alongside his words:

Eternal One, You created us *b'tzelem Elohim*, in Your image, filling us—as You are filled—with hope; hope that we might yet bring to fruition Your vision of cooperation and harmony, of wholeness and peace.

You imagined such a world, Holy One, and then instilled within us the ability to imagine it too. You hope even now for such a world, Holy One, knowing You created us with the desire to give each other hope like Yours, hope that tomorrow will find us finally ready, finally able, to bring Your imagined world into being.

Blessed are You, Hopeful One, Creator of hope and of those who bring it to the world.

# Memorial Day
## MAY

### II Chronicles 10:1–11

Rehoboam went to Shechem, for all Israel had come to Shechem to acclaim him king. Jeroboam son of Nebat learned of it while he was in Egypt where he had fled from King Solomon, and Jeroboam returned from Egypt. They sent for him; and Jeroboam and all Israel came and spoke to Rehoboam as follows: "Your father made our yoke heavy. Now lighten the harsh labor and the heavy yoke that your father laid on us, and we will serve you." He answered them, "Come back to me in three days." So the people went away.

King Rehoboam took counsel with the elders who had served during the lifetime of his father Solomon. He said, "What answer do you counsel to give these people?" They answered him, "If you will be good to these people and appease them and speak to them with kind words, they will be your servants always." But he ignored the counsel that the elders gave him, and took counsel with the young men who had grown up with him and were serving him. "What," he asked, "do you counsel that we reply to these people who said to me, 'Lighten the yoke that your father laid on us'?" And the young men who had grown up with him answered, "Speak thus to the people who said to you, 'Your father made our yoke heavy, now you make it lighter for us.' Say to them, 'My little finger is thicker than my father's loins. My father imposed a heavy yoke on you, and I will add to your yoke; my father flogged you with whips, but I [will do so] with scorpions.'"

## A House Divided against Itself Cannot Stand

### Rabbi Jordan M. Parr

Today, we think of Memorial Day as the unofficial start of summer: pools and beaches open, grills are lit, we start wearing shorts and sandals, schools let out for the summer, and vacations begin. Indeed, we often forget the historical meaning of Memorial Day. Originally called Decoration Day, Memorial Day was instituted as a Day of Remembrance, a collective *Yizkor* if you will, for Union soldiers killed during the Civil War, a war that brought with it tremendous bloodshed and often pitted brother against brother, family against family. The carnage was immense. Recalling the Civil War, we read the passage from II Chronicles 10 differently:

- Jeroboam, one of Solomon's generals, had fled to Egypt after an attempted revolt.
- King Rehoboam, Solomon's son, ruled over the united Israel, guided by his father's elders and his own group of young, insolent courtiers. The elder counselors advised the young king to lighten the burden on the Israelites, broken after years of paying for Solomon's building projects, such as the Temple. The king rejected this advice, instead listening to his younger counsel, saying to the people, "My father flogged you with whips, but I [will do so] with scorpions" (II Chronicles 10:11).
- Not surprisingly, Jeroboam led a revolt of the Northern Israelites, chasing King Rehoboam back to Jerusalem. And, according to a subsequent text, "Israel has been in revolt against the house of David to this day" (II Chronicles 10:19).

This too was a civil war, brother against brother, family against family, tribe against tribe. The battles continued until 722 BCE, when the Assyrian army destroyed the Northern Kingdom and dispersed the Israelites to places unknown. The Bible would say that Israel was destroyed because they worshiped idols at Beth El and Dan. However, maybe more important for us is to take note of the great human cost of this centuries-long civil war between fellow Jews.

As Abraham Lincoln said, "A house divided against itself cannot stand." Indeed, he may have been thinking about Israel and Judah, not just North and South. At this time of strife in our country, it behooves us to attack each other neither with snakes nor scorpions, but rather with words of kindness, of love, and of wisdom, so that we can join together in unity. May the words of our mouths be acceptable to You, O God!

# Gun Violence Prevention Day
## JUNE 2

*Nachum 3:1, 3, 7, 18–19*

Ah, city of crime,
utterly treacherous,
full of violence,
where killing never stops! . . .
Charging horsemen,
flashing swords,
and glittering spears!
Hosts of slain
and heaps of corpses,
dead bodies without number—
they stumble over our bodies. . . .
All who see you will recoil from you
and will say,
"Nineveh has been ravaged!"
Who will console her?
Where shall I look for
anyone to comfort you? . . .
O king of Assyria;
your sheepmasters are lying inert;
your people are scattered over the hills,
and there is none to gather them.
There is no healing for your injury;
your wound is grievous.
All who hear the news about you
clap their hands over you.
For who has not suffered
from your constant malice?

## Senseless Violence

*RABBI GERI NEWBURGE*

National Gun Violence Prevention Day takes place in early June. While there is understandably no Torah portion that accompanies the day, as a Jewish community the preservation and sanctity of life is our primary obligation (mitzvah), so the day is a worthwhile religious observance for our communities.

The prophet Nachum lived in the seventh century BCE, likely in Jerusalem, and prophesied during the time of the destruction of Nineveh, the great Assyrian city, around 612 BCE. Nachum rails against the horrific violence the Assyrian rulers afflict on their citizens. His prophecy becomes especially poignant in chapter 3, where his powerful words convey the disturbing and haunting impact of violence on the residents of Nineveh, a result of their own destructive actions. The message is clear: destruction is sure to happen when violence is perpetrated, especially by those in powerful positions.

The senseless violence pointed out by the prophet seems to correlate to the senseless number of lives lost each year to gun violence in the United States. More and more people are directly impacted by gun violence, as firearms are used in more than half of suicides and more than two-thirds of homicides, while at the same time, mass shootings at schools, movie theaters, and concerts escalate in frequency and severity. Nachum's parting words leave a heart-wrenching impression: "For who has not suffered from your constant malice?" (Nahum 3:19).

In order to stop the suffering during our lifetimes and for subsequent generations, we must act now.

# Beginning of Summer Camp

*From* Next Generation Judaism, *by Rabbi Mike Uram*

The goal of having a greeter is to make new people feel more welcome, but something unintended can happen. When a new person arrives at some program, greeters often say things like "We are so happy you are here," "We want to welcome you," and "We have many great programs you will love." While explicitly the greeters are doing a wonderful job of welcoming a newcomer, implicitly they are repeatedly underscoring the distinction between "we" and "you." "We" are insiders. "You" are an outsider. "We" already feel comfortable. "You" need our help to feel comfortable. "We" have something to offer "you." "You" can help "us" by getting more involved or joining. Each time those words are used the impermeable boundary is accidentally reinforced.

There is another, more effective way to greet. Rather than using a greeting to make the event or organization the central focus of the conversation, a better approach is to make the person and the relationship the central focus instead.

## Welcome Home!

### AVIVA SYMONS

In his book *Next Generation Judaism: How College Students and Hillel Can Help Reinvent Jewish Organizations*, Rabbi Mike Uram shares his experiences as executive director of Penn Hillel. About one hundred miles north of the University of Pennsylvania is URJ Camp Harlam. Thousands of individuals have driven through its iconic gates with the same inexplicable feeling, summer after summer after summer—because there, each individual is welcomed *home* as their truest selves.

Within the realm of Relational Judaism, Rabbi Mike Uram analyzed the "magic" of overnight Jewish camp. One pitch is to welcome individuals as themselves, not as participants. The other pitch is to welcome these individuals *home*, not to a foreign Jewish organization. The phrase "Welcome Home!" has permeated the crisp air of the Pocono Mountains since 1958.

Let's welcome individuals *home* throughout the Jewish ecosystem: *home* to Jewish preschools and high schools, *home* to established congregations and informal gatherings, *home* to a warm smile and a relational conversation.

# Father's Day

### JUNE

### *"A Father's Blessing," from a Sermon by Rabbi Jerome Malino, 1974*

There is in our tradition and in the literature of our people something that I do not know the existence of in any other culture. It is called ethical wills. . . . These ethical wills are the message of one generation to the next. They were testaments of text, but more often they were testaments of example, and each generation both inspired and sustained the generation that came after it. And every generation of Jews—or we would not be here today—has been able to draw nourishment from those who lived before, has been able to draw guidance and inspiration, a set of values by which to live. . . .

Well what about today? Today life is different. I suspect most fathers would find themselves far too embarrassed to sit down and write a last will and testament that bequeathed to their children nothing but moral advice. Nowadays we feel impelled to leave things of substance which we hope will provide security for the next generation and perhaps for the one after that. We have no time for the written text, and we have no time for the spoken blessing, and we are altogether too self-conscious to indulge ourselves in this even if we had the time.

But . . . we must bless our children, placing our hands upon them and turning their faces toward God. Living, we must struggle for a better day. To foretell the future may be a patriarch's privilege, but to take the future in our hands is urgent and to make it good shall be our human glory . . . while yet we live, help us to guide our children in love and wisdom. Help us now to build a world of peace. . . .

It is not a matter of giving a blessing, but of being a blessing. It is not a matter of leaving a rich bequest of things, which more often than not will be dissipated with the passage of time, but of being a bequest, of being a blessing. And this is the challenge, really, that every Jew must confront: How can his [or her] own life be a blessing. . . .

We want our noble ideals to be the ideals of the best of the generations that lived before us and unless these ideals will be our ideals and unless we live by these ideals then they cannot be the ideals of our children and the goodness that motivated those who lived before us will not motivate those who will live after us. And if they do not live by that goodness then that goodness will not be able to bless them. But the thing is that we have done it and we can do it and there always have been enough Jews who have seen the past in all its splendor and all its nobility and have chose[n] to make themselves such blessings as will bequeath blessing to those who come after them.

There it is. The constant challenge to the Jew. The prodding and the urging; it is in a sense the wrestling which each Jew must have. And may it be true for each of us as it was true of Jacob that he did not cease the wrestling until a blessing had been his. Amen.

# Guarantors of Our Future

*Rabbi Gary Phillip Zola, PhD*

Jerome R. Malino (1911–2002) spent his entire professional life—sixty-seven years—serving one congregation: United Jewish Congregation in Danbury, Connecticut. Malino's rabbinical skill made him a beloved spiritual as well as a distinguished civic leader. He achieved national prominence for his impressive erudition and his compelling oratory, and in 1979, Malino was elected president of the Central Conference of American Rabbis, a title he held until 1981.

On Erev Shabbat, December 27, 1974, Malino preached on the weekly Torah reading, *Va-y'chi*, the final chapters of Genesis wherein the patriarch Jacob blesses his posterity. Exhorting his listeners to put themselves in Jacob's shoes, Malino urged parents to bequeath a meaningful ethical legacy to their children. "Every generation of Jews," the rabbi insisted, "has been able to draw nourishment from those who lived before, has been able to draw guidance and inspiration, a set of values by which to live."

On Father's Day, Rabbi Malino's spiritual message serves as a moving reminder that our children are, as the ancient Sages taught, the guarantors of our future. Fathers and mothers must therefore strive "to make themselves such blessings as will bequeath blessing to those who come after them." This lesson underscores one of Judaism's most ethical endowments: "It is not a matter of giving a blessing, but of being a blessing."

# Pride Shabbat

JUNE

*Isaiah 58:1-12*

Cry from the depth, says God—
do not hold back, lift up your voice like the shofar!
Tell My people their transgression, and the House of Jacob their sin.
Yes, they seek Me daily,
as though eager to learn My ways—
as if they were a nation that does what is right
and has not abandoned God's law.
They ask of Me the right way, eager for God's nearness:
They say, "Why did we fast, and You do not see it?
We afflict ourselves, and You do not know it?"
Because even on your fast day you think only of desire,
while oppressing all who work for you.
Because your fasting is filled with strife,
and with callous fist you strike.
No, your fasting this day will not lift up your voice before heaven.
Is this the fast I desire?
A day to afflict body and soul?
Bowing your head like a reed, covering yourself with sackcloth and ashes?
Do you call this a fast—a day worthy of the favor of Adonai?
Is not this the fast I desire—
to break the bonds of injustice and remove the heavy yoke;
to let the oppressed go free and release all those enslaved?
Is it not to share your bread with the hungry
and to take the homeless poor into your home
and never to neglect your own flesh and blood?
Then shall your light burst forth like the dawn,
and your wounds shall quickly heal,
your Righteous One leading the way before you,
the Presence of Adonai guarding you from behind.
Then, when you call, Adonai will answer,
and, when you cry, will respond "I am here."

If you remove the chains of oppression,
the menacing hand, the malicious word;
if you offer your compassion to the hungry and satisfy the suffering—
then shall your light shine through the darkness,
and your night become bright as noon;
Adonai will guide you always,
slake your thirst in parched places,
give strength to your bones.
You shall be like a well-watered garden,
an unfailing spring.
From you they will rebuild ancient ruins,
lay foundations for ages to come.
And you shall be called
"the one who mends the breach
and brings back the streets for dwelling."

# What Is the Pride You Desire?

### K. M. DiColandrea (DiCo)

In the midst of the pandemic, over ten thousand people marched in the streets of Brooklyn defending Black Trans Lives during Pride month in 2020. Since the organizers had requested that everyone wear white, looking out upon the massive crowd evoked memories of Yom Kippur.

You'll recall that on that most solemn day, we hear the prophet Isaiah's words, "Is this the fast I desire?" (Isaiah 58:5). Today, as we celebrate Pride month, consider a different question: "Is this the Pride you desire?" Is it about wearing rainbows and going to parades? Or is it an opportunity? An opportunity to recognize the legal policies still limiting the LGBTQ+ community, to hold up a mirror and reflect how homophobia and transphobia are perpetuated even in your own communities, to remember that Pride started when Black trans women fought back against police brutality at the Stonewall Inn?

Maya Angelou once shared, "The truth is no one of us can be free until everybody is free." We are so, so far from meeting Angelou's charge. This month is an opportunity to stand up against the homophobia, transphobia, and all other kinds of bigotry within your own communities. That should be the Pride you desire.

# Juneteenth

## JUNE 19

*From "Why Black Lives Matter to a People for Whom God Promised
a Holy Place," by Graie Hagans*

For those of us who live our lives through Blackness we cannot separate our duty as Jews from our fears of being strange in a land that though of our birth still does not recognize us fully as present. As Jews who cannot separate from our Blackness we inhabit spaces of silent loss. We struggle to rise as mourners in spaces that call for us to remember our time as slaves in Egypt. To remember that we are not safe as Jews. That are inhabited by the call "Never Again."

For we are the descendants of slaves with no great escape story. No great memorial to our suffering. No great God to intervene on our behalf, to choose us, to form us as a people. And yet for many of us who inhabit both Blackness and Jewishness we feel the deep divide, as the parting of the seas. For if our images of our great escape maintain the dichotomy of light versus dark would the sea fall in on us? Would we be cast aside, swept away in the great tide? Would we be held tight and carried with as much care as the bread we did not have time to rise? As so many with faces with skin so similar to mine remain in bondage, in isolation, removed from a people still struggling will we return to the voice of "we" in our demand to "Let my people go"?

## The Holy Duty of Advocating for Racial Justice

### CANTOR DAVID FAIR

Representation of Black Jewish voices is vital in any discussion of racial justice in Jewish spaces. Graie Barasch-Hagans is such a voice, boldly professing Blackness and Jewishness in a powerful, yet vulnerable way.

Many American Jews see Juneteenth as a holiday for Black Americans—quite unconnected to Judaism. Yes, Juneteenth celebrates Black freedom from American slavery, but it's not a holiday that White Jews have no relationship with. On the contrary, the concept of slavery is profoundly Jewish.

Slavery is one of the most discussed topics throughout the Torah. Exodus, Leviticus, and Deuteronomy are flooded with conversations concerned with the just and fair laws regarding the treatment of enslaved people. Even our liturgy is filled with references to slavery. In our daily morning blessings, we thank God, "who has made me free." At the end of the *V'ahavta*, we say, "I am Adonai, your God, who brought you out of the land of Egypt to be your God." *Mi Chamochah* is a prayer where we sing of our joy that we were freed from slavery. In the evening Kiddush, we say *zecher litziat Mitzrayim*, meaning "remembering the Exodus from Egypt." We Jews are no strangers to talking about slavery.

White Jewish Americans have an opportunity to be among the greatest advocates for Black American voices. If you are White, I invite you to let your children see you socializing with Black people—then watch them mimic this behavior. Buy books and watch movies with well-rounded Black protagonists. Find a way to ask your principal if your child can have a Black teacher. When you begin to anger people by voicing words of racial justice, only then will you truly be on your way to being a pursuer of justice.

# Independence Day

## JULY 4TH

### *Isaiah 1:11–17; Psalm 137:1–4*

In the words of the prophet Isaiah, we are called to acts of justice instead of empty ritual observance:

> "What are your many sacrifices to Me?"
> says the Eternal One.
> "I am sated with the rams you bring as burnt offerings,
> with the fat of your fine animals;
> I take no delight in the blood of bulls or lambs or goats.
> When you come to to seek My presence,
> who asked this of you,
> to trample My courts?
> Bring Me no more futile offerings;
> incense is an abomination to Me.
> New moon and sabbath,
> the calling of assemblies:
> I cannot endure festivities
> along with evil.
> I hate your new moons, your festival days:
> they are a burden to Me;
> I can bear [them] them no more.
> When you stretch out your hands,
> I will avert My eyes from you;
> however much you pray,
> I will not listen,
> while your hands are filled with blood.
> Wash yourselves; cleanse yourselves,
> put your evil doings away from My sight.
> Cease to do evil,

learn to do good,
seek justice; relieve the oppressed.
Uphold the orphan's rights;
take up the widow's cause."

The Psalmist makes us aware that true justice begins with the acknowledgment of pain and despair:

On the riverbanks of Babel
There we sat; we sobbed, as well,
When Zion came to mind.
On the willows in her midst
We hanged our lyres,
For there our jailers cajoled us: Join in song!
And our haranguers asked for jollity:
Join in jolly songs of Zion!

How shall we join in jolly song to Adonai
On foreign soil?!

## Our Unresolved Original Sin

*Rabbi Rick Jacobs*

For too long, the Fourth of July has only been a time of joyful celebrations, ignoring the unresolved trauma of slavery. On July 5, 1852, the former slave Frederick Douglass gave a now famous keynote address at an Independence Day celebration in Rochester, New York, asking, "What to the Slave is the Fourth of July? . . . This Fourth [of] July is *yours*, not *mine*. *You* may rejoice, *I* must mourn." Douglass anchors his soul-stirring address on two biblical texts: Isaiah 1:13–17 and Psalm 137. These texts offer a sobering counterbalance to the usual holiday fireworks and barbecues.

Centuries after independence was achieved, it is surely incumbent on all citizens to ask what the United States should do to finally address the unresolved original sin of slavery. In Psalm 137, our ancient Israelite forebearers—carried off as slaves to Babylon—asked how they could be expected to sing God's song in the land of their foreign oppressors. Frederick Douglass links this psalm to the experience of African American slaves: "To drag a man in fetters into the grand illuminated temple of liberty, and call upon him to join you in joyous anthems, were inhuman mockery and sacrilegious irony."

How can we today expect the descendants of slaves to feel anything but alienation at our annual rejoicing while racial injustice still plagues America?

In 1956, one hundred years after Douglass, a close associate of Dr. Martin Luther King Jr., Reverend Fred Shuttlesworth, anchored his generation's civil rights struggle in that same biblical text with this call to conscience: "Can we discern any difference between today's Birmingham and yesterday's Babylon? Nay, except that Babylon's might was her army, and Birmingham claims her strength in the sinews of coal and steel. Babylon thought more of her swinging gardens than the God of the universe; Birmingham prides her zoo more highly than she values her Negroes." Douglass chastises his listeners by adding the celebrations of July 4th to the prophet Isaiah's description of the festivals despised by the Holy One in favor of God's demand for acts of justice: "Put your evil doings away from My sight. Cease to do evil."

More than six decades after Reverend Shuttlesworth's soul-searching question, more than 150 years after Douglass penned his powerful words, and centuries after the "founders" gathered in Philadelphia, it is surely incumbent on all Americans to ask what the United States should do to finally address the unresolved original sin of slavery and genocide. To further awaken the conscience of our nation, on this holiday when we see the red, white, and blue all around us, let's consider Fannie Lou Hamer's reminder that "every red stripe in that flag represents the Black man's blood that has been shed."

# Opening the Olympic Games
## MID-JULY

*From "Exclusive: Aly Raisman Speaks Out on Sexual Harassment,*
*Judaism, and Her Future," by Aiden Pink*

Aly Raisman is a three-time Olympic gold medal-winning gymnast, a social media star with over 2.2 million followers on Instagram, and now a published author. But Raisman, age 23, proudly says that she still relies on her parents for guidance.

"I definitely go to my mom all the time for advice," Raisman told *The Forward* in an exclusive interview Tuesday. "I'm very, very close to my mom, so I'm very lucky to have her."

You even seek her out now, as an Olympic champion?

"Oh, yeah. Like, all the time. You're never too old to get advice from your mom."

Raisman spoke to *The Forward* before an event Tuesday . . . in Brooklyn. . . . In the past year, Raisman has found her voice. . . . Raisman reflected on the idea that there's something about Judaism that builds strong women who aren't afraid to make their voices heard.

"I think for me, being Jewish is all about being close with family," she said. "I think it's very family-oriented, which is something that's really important to me. And I think speaking out and being a strong female, I don't think you can be that without the support of your family." . . .

During the question-and-answer session . . . Raisman recounted similar advice that her parents gave her when she was a young gymnast: "People will always remember you for the kind of person you are, rather than the place you are on the podium."

Raisman also explained how she has come to realize "how important and how proud I am to be a Jew. . . . You not only get to represent the United States of America, you also get to represent the Jewish community all over the world. And I think that's really, really special and something that I take with a lot of pride." Indeed, she won one of her gold medals in 2012 doing her floor routine to "Hava Nagila."

## Faster, Higher, Stronger—In Life As on the Podium
### RABBI STEPHEN WEISMAN

Athletes, artists of all kinds, doctors, lawyers, engineers, and so many more disciplines and professions require years of study, training, and long practice before a person is prepared to take the public stage. For some, that moment of debut is private; for others, it happens under the glare of the spotlight, with cameras rolling to broadcast the performance to the world.

No one gets to such a moment of starting out—whether a career, or a new season, or a new job with a new company, or a promotion with their old company—without the support, mentorship, and sacrifice of many people in their lives, especially their immediate family. To be able to share such a start, to remain close with them, even after achieving fame, is a powerful statement. No matter how much we transform ourselves on the journey to starting out, as Raisman's parents taught her, the ability to stay true to who we are—how we were raised, the morals we were raised with—is critical to our ultimate success.

The Olympic gold medalist showed she is also a champion in fighting for the rights of those who have been abused by others, when she not only spoke out about her own sexual abuse by Dr. Larry Nassar, but raised her voice for so many others. As reported in a 2019 article entitled "Olympian Aly Raisman Talks about Surviving Sexual Abuse," about a conversation at her home congregation in Newton, Massachusetts:

> Throughout her nightmare, Raisman told her audience at Beth Avodah that her grandmother's Jewish values were a beacon of hope for her. "My Bubby instilled in me the value of kindness," she said. "If something weren't right, you would know, and I had to speak out if something wasn't right. She also said I had to be supportive of the people around me. The Jewish community embodies my Bubby's kindness, her caring and her goal of looking out for each other."

On any "Opening Day," any time we take on a difficult challenge or cause, these are valuable words to remember and carry with us to the starting line.

# Labor Day

## SEPTEMBER

### *Speech by Rose Schneiderman, April 2, 1911, after the Triangle Shirtwaist Fire*

I would be a traitor to these poor burned bodies if I came here to talk good fellowship. We have tried you good people of the public and we have found you wanting. The old Inquisition had its rack and its thumbscrews and its instruments of torture with iron teeth. We know what these things are today; the iron teeth are our necessities, the thumbscrews are the high powered and swift machinery close to which we must work, and the rack is here in the firetrap structures that will destroy us the minute they catch on fire.

This is not the first time girls have been burned alive in the city. Every week I must learn of the untimely death of one of my sister workers. Every year thousands of us are maimed. The life of men and women is so cheap and property is so sacred. There are so many of us for one job it matters little if 146 of us are burned to death.

We have tried you citizens; we are trying you now, and you have a couple of dollars for the sorrowing mothers, brothers and sisters by way of a charity gift. But every time the workers come out in the only way they know to protest against conditions which are unbearable the strong hand of the law is allowed to press down heavily upon us.

Public officials have only words of warning to us—warning that we must be intensely peaceable, and they have the workhouse just back of all their warnings. The strong hand of the law beats us back, when we rise, into the conditions that make life unbearable.

I can't talk fellowship to you who are gathered here. Too much blood has been spilled. I know from my experience it is up to the working people to save themselves. The only way they can save themselves is by a strong working-class movement.

## Still Wanting!

### *Rabbi Barbara AB Symons*

In the late nineteenth century, during protests of twelve-hour days and even seven-day weeks that still barely put food on the table, Labor Day came about first within states and then federally as a way not only to celebrate the achievements of laborers during the Industrial Revolution, but also to give the workers a day off. Its focus was on workers, not on white sales, the end of summer, and the annual stopping point for wearing white shoes.

Today, Rose Schneiderman would look at us "good people of the public" and, for all the advances since her time, still find us "wanting":

- Laborers who work full-time jobs still live below the poverty line, yet, we are commanded, "You shall not abuse a needy and destitute laborer" (Deuteronomy 24:14).

- People with disabilities cannot access adequate education, health care, and transportation and therefore cannot work to their fullest extent, and yet, we are commanded, "You shall not insult the deaf, or place a stumbling block before the blind" (Leviticus 19:14).
- Women do not have pay equity and yet we are admonished, "One who withholds the wages of a hired laborer, it is as though they take their soul from them" (Babylonian Talmud, *Baba M'tzia* 112a).

The very first laborer, about whom we will soon read in Genesis 2:15, was Adam, whose job description was "to work [the Garden of Eden] and keep it." He and Eve were God's first partners in Creation. We are called to carry on that legacy not only on the first Monday of September but throughout the year.

# September 11

### *"The Sandcastles," by Haim Gouri*

You remember,
it's like the afternoon wave that washed away
the sandcastle,
the tunnels and the fortress towers,
the patience, the seashells and the stalactites,
extra trimmings.
And didn't know.
The barbarism will return.
Insensitive to nuances, it doesn't hang back.
It thinks big.

## Communities of Humanity and Love

### *Rabbi Bill S. Tepper*

It was a day I will never forget: the agitated words of a teacher-colleague that "planes had hit buildings in New York"; the fretful assembly in front of televisions in our school library, gazing in disbelief at the unfolding catastrophe; and the near-unendurable moments until my family and I had gathered safely at home.

The memory and commemoration of September 11, 2001, were—and will always be—about obliteration, brutality, pain, and suffering. And, in the words of Haim Gouri, it is also about the "washing away" of the vulnerable and innocent. On September 11 a world of apparent strength turned, near-instantaneously, into one of fragility and fear.

As a soldier in pre-state Israel's Palmach and Haganah forces, rescuer of survivors of the Shoah, and journalist assigned to the trial of Adolf Eichmann, Haim Gouri understood the undercurrent of hatred, violence, and death threatening human existence. He had observed how a "tide of terror" easily overwhelmed aspirations to peace. Of Gouri's poetry it has been written, "Prophecy and poetry are parallel efforts. Like the prophet, the poet is acutely aware that most unhappy situations are beyond his (or any individual's) control. Both speak their words in the wind; both become self-doubting, vulnerable seers whose more lucid comprehension leads less to elation than to despair."

On this day—September 11—we recall the horror that struck America's "fortress towers": the World Trade Center buildings of New York City, the Pentagon in Washington, and the otherwise pastoral field of Shanksville, Pennsylvania. May our memories of those murdered be for blessings. And may we resolve to establish and nurture communities of humanity and love.

# Bisexual Visibility Day

SEPTEMBER 23

### Ruth 1:12–22

"Turn back, my daughters, for I am too old to be married. Even if I thought there was hope for me, even if I were married tonight and I also bore sons, should you wait for them to grow up? Should you on their account debar yourselves from marriage? Oh no, my daughters! My lot is far more bitter than yours, for the hand of the Eternal has struck out against me."

They broke into weeping again, and Orpah kissed her mother-in-law farewell. But Ruth clung to her. So she said, "See, your sister-in-law has returned to her people and her gods. Go follow your sister-in-law." But Ruth replied, "Do not urge me to leave you, to turn back and not follow you. For wherever you go, I will go; wherever you lodge I will lodge; your people shall be my people, and your God my God. Where you die, I will die; and there I will be buried. Thus and more may the Eternal do to me if anything but death parts me from you." When [Naomi] saw how determined she was to go with her, she ceased to argue with her; and the two went on until they reached Bethlehem.

When they arrived in Bethlehem, the whole city buzzed with excitement over them. The women said, "Can this be Naomi?" "Do not call me Naomi," she replied. "Call me Mara, for Shaddai has made my lot very bitter. I went away full, and the Eternal has brought me back empty. How can you call me Naomi, when the Eternal has dealt harshly with me, when Shaddai has brought misfortune upon me!"

Thus, Naomi returned from the country of Moab; she returned with her daughter-in-law Ruth the Moabite. They arrived in Bethlehem at the beginning of the barley harvest.

# On Gender, Generations, and Care

*Martin Rawlings-Fein, MAJS*

In the Book of Ruth (1:12–22), Ruth declares her commitment to Naomi in a vow that transcends gender and geographical boundaries as they start the journey to Judah from Moab to find Naomi's kinsman Boaz. Reading Ruth's words of devotion, we know that we are told a timeless love story regardless of the genders involved.

There are no wedding rituals codified in the *Tanach*, yet there we read two sets of vows of same-gendered couples that are used today as patterns for marital vows for all:

- In this haftarah reading, David's great-grandmother Ruth devotes herself to Naomi.
- In the book of I Samuel (18:3–4), just as in today's ritual exchange of vows and rings, Jonathan gives David his clothing, sword, and armor, and Jonathan "love[s David] as himself."

For bisexual, pansexual, or queer persons, the relationships of Ruth and Naomi and of David and Jonathan provide the most fitting examples for bisexuality in biblical texts and encourage us to look beyond gender expectations. These readings remind us that we can always find ourselves in the text, no matter how we identify.

Bisexual Visibility Day is part of the Jewish calendar, just as Ruth's story is part of a broader LGBTQ+ theology. However, the text also teaches us to respect and love our elders. We take our Jewish bisexual+ elders with us on our journey of self-discovery. The passage from the Book of Ruth has a clear message: regardless of gender, we all gain strength when we declare ourselves linked to others, especially our elders.

In their committed relationship to one another, Ruth and Naomi find connection and care. Both women are in mourning. They have lost much human life in such a short period. In our own lifetime, during the various pandemics from AIDS to COVID, we see people searching for that same kind of connection and care. Across generations, genders, and sexualities, we all need each other—to see who we are in our innermost hearts, to accept us fully, and to love us as themselves.

# Breast Cancer Awareness Month

OCTOBER

*Psalm 27*

Of David.

Adonai is my light and my victory—
From whom should I feel fright?
Adonai is the stronghold of my life—
From whom should I feel terror?

When evildoers approach me in battle to feed on my flesh—
My pursuers, my adversaries—
They have stumbled, they have fallen down.
If a camp encamps against me, my heart will not fear;
If a war arises against me,
In this I would trust:

One thing have I sought from Adonai—how I long for it:
That I may live in the House of Adonai all the days of my life;
That I may look upon the sweetness of Adonai,
And spend time in the Palace;
That You might hide me in Your sukkah on a chaotic day,
Hide me in the hiding places of Your tent,
Raise me high upon a rock.

Now my head rises high above my enemies roundabout,
And in Your tent I'll offer offerings to the sound of *t'ruah*.
I shall sing and chant praises to Adonai!

Hear, Adonai, my voice—
I am crying out!
Be gracious to me, answer me!
My heart has said to You: "Seek my face."
I am seeking Your face, Adonai—
Do not hide Your face from me.
Do not turn Your servant away in anger,
You have been my help—
Do not forsake me, do not abandon me, God of my deliverance!

# To Walk in the Land of the Living

*Rabbi Audrey R. Korotkin, PhD*

Psalm 27 is a traditional daily reading for the month of Elul, preceding the High Holy Days. Yet its themes of confidence in one's own powers of healing and of faith in God's powers of redemption speak clearly to breast-cancer patients and survivors. In fact, an examination of the Hebrew yields an even more personal connection.

In Psalm 27:2, the word *m'rei-im* means, as it does elsewhere in the Jewish Bible, "evildoers." But in ancient Aramaic, the word *m'ra* means "illness," "suffering," or "affliction"—a rendering used frequently in the *Targum*, the Aramaic translation of the *Tanach*. And what if we were to reimagine the phrase that follows in 27:3, as did the commentator Malbim, re-vocalizing the word *tachaneh* (camp, army) into *t'chineh*, "supplicatory prayer"?

Here, now, is how I would translate the beginning of this psalm:

> When illnesses assail me
>  to devour my flesh—
> it is they, the enemies within me,
> who will go down to defeat.
> If I were to offer up my prayer of supplication,
> seeking God's compassion,
> there would be no fear in my heart;
> no battle would shake my confidence.

My enemy is not outside of me; my enemy is within—this insidious disease that grows from the size of a pinpoint to consume the flesh of my breast, the symbol of my womanhood and the source of life and nourishment for my children.

So, I ask God not to abandon me, to give me courage so that I am consumed neither by this illness nor by despair. Others may look upon my affliction and see a dying woman—or one who is forever disfigured by this struggle. But I know that I am not my illness. And I know that God will keep my heart strong and my wits about me, so that I can look beyond these days of sickness to a time when I will walk "in the land of the living," on a path of wellness and wholeness in body and in spirit.

# Domestic Violence Awareness Month

OCTOBER

*From "In the Midst of History," by Martin Buber*

God carries on his dialogue with the creature to whom he has given power and it must render an account to him stating whether it has used this power in obedience to the given command. But he also carries on a dialogue with the other creature, that which suffers from the abuse of power. God hears its cry and himself renders an account in lieu of the wielder of power. . . . Thus, God is not a power, static in a region "above," from whom irresponsible potentates receive continual installments of authority. When they act contrary to the pact, when they afflict a creature entrusted to their power, and this creature sinks to the ground, then God is no longer up above, but down below, on the ground beside the afflicted. For he is "nigh unto them that are of a broken heart" (Psalm 34:19).

## We Will Listen to Your Story. We Will Believe You. We Will Support You. You Are Not Alone.

RABBI ARI S. LORGE

Martin Buber states that one of the ways humans are made in the divine image is through God's gifts of power and free will. We were given power so that we can use it for godly purposes.

However, since God also gave us the freedom to make our own choices, we may also choose to use power wickedly. When we turn our power upon one another, when we use it as a weapon to control and dominate another soul, we violate the covenant between ourselves and God. In those moments, God is not an impartial witness recording our deeds in some Book of Life. God moves unequivocally to stand alongside the abused and the afflicted. God becomes a partisan in that struggle on the side of victims and survivors. God stands to support, comfort, and strengthen those living in unhealthy and outright abusive relationships.

And so must we. In this month of October, we pledge that our community will be a *sukkat shalom*, a "shelter of peace," for those who are in relationships that hurt rather than heal. We will listen to your story. We will believe you. We will support you. You are not alone.

# Invisible Illness Awareness Week

## THIRD WEEK IN OCTOBER

*From* Tomer Devorah *(The Palm Tree of Deborah), by Moses Cordovero*

The quality of humility includes all qualities, since it pertains to *Keter* ["the highest aspect of God"]. Although *Keter* transcends all the other qualities, it does not exalt itself; on the contrary, it descends, constantly gazing below. Its emanator constantly gazes into it, bestowing goodness, while it gazes at those beneath.

God nourishes everything, from the horned buffalo to nits, disdaining no creature—for if [God] disdained creatures due to their insignificance, they could not endure for even a moment. Rather, [God] gazes and emanates compassion upon them all. So should you be good to all creatures, disdaining none. Even the most insignificant creature should assume importance in your eyes; attend to it. Do good to whomever needs your goodness. . . .

Your eyes should not gaze at anything disgraceful. Rather, they should always be open to notice those who suffer, to be compassionate toward them as much as possible. When you see a poor person suffering, do not close your eyes in the slightest. On the contrary, keep them in mind as much as you can; arouse compassion for them—from God and from people.

Your face should always be shining. Welcome each person with a friendly countenance. For with regard to *Keter Elyon*, the supernal crown, it is said: "In the light of the king's face is life." No redness or harsh judgment gains entrance there. So, too, the light of your face should never change; whoever looks at you will find only joy and a friendly expression. . . .

I have found an effective potion for the cure of pride. This consists of training yourself to do two things. First, respect all creatures, recognizing in them the sublime nature of the Creator. Second, train yourself to bring the love of your fellow human beings into your heart.

## Greeting Each Other with Dignity

### RABBI-CANTOR ELANA ROSEN-BROWN

Invisible Illness Awareness Week takes place each year during the month of October. It was established to draw awareness to chronic illness, injury, and pain. With this haftarah reading we honor and recognize all those who live with an illness that isn't easily visible to or understood by others. We welcome your voices and teaching.

By some reports 96 percent of all illness is invisible, and nearly half of all Americans live with a chronic disease. So, when we seek to raise awareness of invisible illness, we are truly seeking to become more compassionate for ourselves and our community. Those of us who live with an illness that is invisible know that it can have an additional devastating impact on emotional health. We may encounter misunderstanding and even doubt about the validity of our illness. Proving illness or explaining why some days are more difficult than others can become an additional burden and lead to feelings of isolation. Those with invisible illnesses face their own distinct challenges. At the same time, living with and learning to thrive with a chronic condition can bring deep spiritual teachings about loss, ego, humility, resilience, empathy, and more.

The haftarah reading from Moses Cordovero seeks to honor these hard-won qualities of wisdom. It is also a profound reminder of the familiar adage "Be kind, for everyone you meet is fighting a hard battle." When we incorporate this Mussar teaching from *Tomer Devorah* into our lives as a regular practice, we commit ourselves to listening more deeply, recognizing our own fragility, and greeting one another always with dignity.

# National Coming Out Day
## OCTOBER II

*From "Coming Out: An Act of Love," by Rob Eichberg*

What is important is to tell the truth about who we are—with all of our diversity.

This will be accomplished most effectively as more and more people who have been hiding stop hiding. It can also be done when we organize to present ourselves to the world more effectively and accurately rather than relying on others to present us. On October 11, 1987, well over half a million people gathered in Washington, D.C., for the march on Washington for lesbian and gay rights. In spite of this being the largest turnout for any demonstration in the history of the United States, and being peaceful throughout, the march was largely ignored by the mainstream media and by the Reagan administration. It was at that march that I found myself wishing that each of those marching had come out to their families, or to ten, fifteen, or twenty people on a personal basis. Our power cannot depend on the press alone—it depends on ourselves and on the risks we are willing to take in our personal lives. . . .

While some may see it as an asset, our ability to "pass" and to hide has perhaps been our greatest liability. More than anything else, the closet has kept us from being accepted and respected for who we actually are. . . .

In February 1988, when two hundred lesbian and gay leaders met in Virginia to consider the future agenda for the gay community it was obvious to all, and unanimously agreed on, that the time for a National Coming Out Day (NCOD) had arrived. October 11, commemorating the 1987 march on Washington, was selected as the date for this annual event.

## Who We Actually Are

*Rabbi Lisa A. Edwards, PhD*

Perhaps you looked at this passage and said, "I've never heard of National Coming Out Day! Do we really need such a thing?"

If you know LGBTQ+ people (or are one) who never hesitated to come out and live their lives freely and openly and in relative safety, that is at least in part due to the success of National Coming Out Day. Should the observance of this day become only a faint memory of a distant past? Don't let it. Ongoingly, perhaps increasingly, a day set aside to come out personally—to family, neighbors, coworkers, clubs, congregations—remains a viable and important step both in the life of LGBTQ+ people and for the ones to whom they come out. This national day of action is a vivid example of the phrase "the personal is political."

October 11 often falls on or near Rosh HaShanah, Yom Kippur, or Sukkot, any of which can be paired with the idea of "coming out":

- Rosh HaShanah, the "Day of the World's Conception," is the day when we remember God's choice to create a world filled with infinite variety.
- Yom Kippur calls us to return to our true selves.
- Sukkot emphasizes the importance of welcoming family, guests, and ancestors into an intimate conversation in a sukkah, a sheltered, yet fragile place.

# Indigenous Peoples' Day
### OCTOBER

*From the speeches of Justice Raquel Montoya-Lewis*

I was raised to remember that I come from those who survived. My ancestors on both sides of my family survived genocide, survived institutional boarding schools, survived attempts to eradicate their cultures, and yet as my father reminded me often "we survived." I am here because of their resilience, their courage, their intelligence, and their deep commitment to what is just.

I come from people who persisted, people who were lucky enough to survive, and my existence is dependent upon those people's persistence and resilience. That's something I hope I pass on to my own children. I hope they pass it on to their children because that's a very important concept for both the Jewish side of my family and the Native side of my family.

From both sides of my family, there is a very heavy emphasis on the importance of education, which is something that has really been the key to my ability to do what I've done. To take my education seriously, and to be able to go to college and beyond, that has absolutely been foundational to my success.

The best thing you can do is find someone—one or two people—whom you can talk to, who believe your experience, because in the absence of that, you can feel like you're isolated. Reaching out to those people, personally, and finding a sense of community—even if it is just one person—is really important. I had a couple people who have been critical mentors in my life, say to me when I felt like I couldn't keep going for whatever reason, "You should have a seat at that table. It's important, not just because of you, but if you don't do it, who is going to do it?"

For me, justice is not an abstract concept. Justice is a term of action and I believe as judges and justices that we are called to do justice.

## Through Justice to Peace
### RABBI JANE LITMAN

Justice Raquel Montoya-Lewis embodies the rich heritage of both Native Americans and Jews. She attributes her success to values passed down to her through these two traditions: the values of perseverance, of education, and most of all, of justice. Both cultures view justice as a restorative process, though which amends are made and the parties reconciled. The entire community has a stake in returning to balance and harmony.

Montoya's Indigenous culture equates justice with peace, so much so that "courts" are usually called "peacemaking circles." Her Jewish tradition shares this concept:

> Rabbi Shimon ben Gamliel said, "The world is maintained by three things, by justice, by truth, and by peace." Rav Muna added, "These three actually are one. If justice is present, then truth is present, and this makes peace. And all three are found in the same verse, as it is written: 'Judge with the justice of truth and peace within your gates.' Wherever there is justice there will be peace. And wherever there is peace there is justice."
> (*Derech Eretz Zutra*, section on Peace: 11-13)

From the biblical judge Deborah through Louis Brandeis and Ruth Bader Ginsburg, Jewish society has affirmed the worth of the judicial vocation. Raquel Montoya-Lewis is another such leader for both her peoples.

What can you do to uphold her values?

# Election Day
NOVEMBER

### *I Samuel 8:4-6, 10-20*

All the elders of Israel assembled and came to Samuel at Ramah, and they said to him, "You have grown old, and your sons have not followed your ways. Therefore appoint a king for us, to govern us like all other nations." Samuel was displeased that they said "Give us a king to govern us." Samuel prayed to the Eternal. . . .

Samuel reported all the words of the Eternal to the people, who were asking him for a king. He said, "This will be the practice of the king who will rule over you: He will take your sons and appoint them as his charioteers and horsemen, and they will serve as outrunners for his chariots. He will appoint them as his chiefs of thousands and of fifties; or they will have to plow his fields, reap his harvest, and make his weapons and the equipment for his chariots. He will take your daughters as perfumers, cooks, and bakers. He will seize your choice fields, vineyards, and olive groves, and give them to his courtiers. He will take a tenth part of your grain and vintage and give it to his eunuchs and courtiers. He will take your male and female slaves, your choice young men, and your asses, and put them to work for him. He will take a tenth part of your flocks, and you shall become his slaves. The day will come when you cry out because of the king whom you yourselves have chosen; and the Eternal will not answer you on that day."

But the people would not listen to Samuel's warning. "No," they said. "We must have a king over us, that we may be like all the other nations: Let our king rule over us and go out at our head and fight our battles."

## Vote! Vote! Vote!
### *Rabbi Ronald B.B. Symons*

Living as a twenty-first-century Jew in a democracy offers us the responsibility to cast a vote. I begin to assess candidates weeks before I cast my ballot. I make my decisions based on the political party, issues, character of the candidate, and the candidates' values alignment with my own. As modern a concept as the democratic voting process is, we can look to our ancestors for guidance in how to make our decisions as voters.

I Samuel 8 recounts the first time, in the eleventh century BCE, when the people of Israel realize they need a human leader different from the priests and prophets of the day. They demand of Samuel, "Appoint a king for us, to govern us like all other nations" (8:5). Dismayed by the apparent lack of faith in him, Samuel admonishes them for their apparently unfaithful desire and warned them that a king will enlist their sons in his chariot service, as local civic leaders, farmworkers, or weapon designers and that he will seize their daughters, slaves, and livestock for domestic service and their fields, vineyards, and a tenth of their produce and flocks for taxes. But even though Samuel warns the people, eventually he and God acquiesce. And so begin the reigns of Kings Saul, David, Solomon, and those who follow them in Judah and Israel.

All too often in our own day, politicians of all parties seem to fulfill all of Samuel's warnings. They believe their election gives them a license to take everything and everyone for themselves. Comparing Samuel with Moses, Jonathan Sacks writes:

> Israel enacted its social contract in the days of Samuel, when it voted for a monarchy. It entered its social covenant several centuries earlier: at Mount Sinai, when it accepted the sovereignty of God and the authority of his commandments. Israel was not yet a *state*: it had not even entered its land. But from that moment on, it was a *society*, bound precisely by the principle of shared responsibility.

As we cast our votes, let Samuel and Jonathan Sacks guide us in assessing our candidates on two levels: how greedy they are, and how responsible they will feel for all of us.

Vote! Vote! Vote!

# Kristallnacht (Night of Broken Glass)
## NOVEMBER 9–10

*"The Salty Taste of Tears," by Rabbi Joe Black*

She was a refugee with glass in her shoes
12 years old—scared and confused
Peeking through the curtains at American Jews
Who never walked in fear
The dread that lived within her bones
Was birthed on ancient cobblestones
And repossessed abandoned homes
And the salty taste of tears

The dreams that kept her up at night were vague and undefined
Boulevards where yellow stars marched lockstep in straight lines
Consonants and syllables that she had left behind
The smoke that never clears
With the salty taste of tears

She did what she was told to do

Minding all her p's and q's
As if compliance could undo
The past 2,000 years
She catalogued and turned the pages
A lifetime lived in different stages
Learning lessons of the ages
And the salty taste of tears

She lived with dread as if someday
Her fragile peace might go away
She knew God's grace just couldn't stay
It always disappears
And all this time I've tried to see
And understand her legacy
That she has now bequeathed to me
With the Salty taste of tears.

## Lessons from a Survivor

### RABBI ANDREA C. LONDON

This song by Rabbi Joe Black focuses on the experience of one Jew who lived through Kristallnacht: his mother. Sophie Black taught through her words and deeds the value of living the examined life. As a refugee from Nazi Germany, leaving shortly after Kristallnacht when she was just twelve, she was always haunted by and shaped by the horrors of the Shoah and the difficulty of immigrating to a new country.

She learned grit and perseverance during her first difficult year in school (they thought she was dumb because she didn't speak English) in this country and became a librarian in a college library, a voracious reader, a proud and loving mother, wife, and grandmother, and the matriarch of our congregation. Sophie's intellectual curiosity was insatiable, and she continued to study Judaism throughout her life and attend worship weekly. She never took the freedom to practice her Judaism for granted.

In contrast to the hatred of Nazi Germany, Sophie's love was boundless. She was the most devoted spouse even as her beloved, Sid, slipped away due to Alzheimer's disease, and she adored and was deservedly proud of all of her children and grandchildren. But her love extended beyond her family; Sophie's life was the definition of audacious hospitality. No one entered the doors of Beth Emet, regardless of age, skin color, gender identity, sexual orientation, or ability, without being doted on by Sophie. She knew how to make everyone feel welcome and cared about.

As with many refugees, despite her full and successful life, she was haunted by her early trauma. She was appreciative of her good fortune to flee Nazi Germany but always worried about bigotry. I feel blessed to have spent many years at Beth Emet with Sophie, learning from her, being challenged by her, and sharing a deep fondness and respect for each other. She was a true *Eshet Chayil*—"a woman of valor."

Would that we could all live like Sophie, able to show genuine love and respect for all human beings.

# Veterans Day

## NOVEMBER 11

### Judges 7:1-9

Early next day, Jerubbaal—that is, Gideon—and all the troops with him encamped above En-harod, while the camp of Midian was in the plain to the north of him, at Gibeath-moreh. The Eternal said to Gideon, "You have too many troops with you for Me to deliver Midian into their hands; Israel might claim for themselves the glory due to Me, thinking, 'Our own hand has brought us victory.' Therefore, announce to the men, 'Let anybody who is timid and fearful turn back, as a bird flies from Mount Gilead.'" Thereupon, 22,000 of the troops turned back and 10,000 remained.

"There are still too many troops," the Eternal said to Gideon. "Take them down to the water and I will sift them for you there. Anyone of whom I tell you, 'This one is to go with you,' that one shall go with you, and anyone of whom I tell you, 'This one is not to go with you,' that one shall not go." So he took the troops down to the water. Then the Eternal said to Gideon, "Set apart all those who lap up the water with their tongues like dogs from all those who get down on their knees to drink." Now those who "lapped" the water into their mouths by hand numbered three hundred; all the rest of the troops got down on their knees to drink. Then the Eternal said to Gideon, "I will deliver you and I will put Midian into your hands through the three hundred 'lappers'; let the rest of the troops go home." So [the lappers] took the provisions and horns that the other men had with them, and he sent the rest of the men of Israel back to their homes, retaining only the three hundred men.

The Midianite camp was below him, in the plain. That night the Eternal said to him, "Come, attack the camp, for I have delivered it into your hands."

# On the Value Behind the Service

### Rabbi Larry Freedman

In the United States, a military oath is sworn to the state, taking on the duty to follow the lawful orders of authorized commanders. The state and the rule of law is paramount. In Canada, the oath is to the Crown and (currently) "his heirs and successors according to law." It is uniformly understood that King Charles III or his successors represent the country, not an authoritarian monarch.

All this is to say that the military oath should never be to a single person. If that were the case, despots and dictators would arise. A military oath is an expression of commitment to a larger ideal, a sense of duty to defend not just territory but a unique culture, a multivocal democracy, and a unique way of life. The military oath is a sobering moment to stand determined to die if necessary to defend the country, the rule of law, and all of her inhabitants.

Let's see what God tells Gideon:

- First, God wants to be sure God gets credit for the military win. So the choosing of future warriors begins.
- Anyone who kneels to drink water is dismissed, the idea being that those who kneel are accustomed to kneeling before idols. They will not understand for what they fight or for whom they fight. They are not thinking about the big picture, the higher goals, the importance of their task.

The professional application of violence is the war fighter's task. Imbued with such responsibility and firepower, we want to be sure that our war fighters never forget what they fight for. The same applies to the exchange between God and Gideon: anyone who might kneel to an idol is not the person we want to carry forward with God's power.

On Veterans Day, we remember not just the service but the values behind the service, the meaning of the uniform every veteran wears. Jews have served in the United States armed forces since the Revolutionary War in large numbers. The best estimate is that today 1.5 percent of the American military is Jewish.

Jews have patriotically served the countries they lived in for thousands of years in many ways, often in uniform. You do not have to thank us for our service (although that's nice). Rather, ask us where we served and what we did. Soon enough, you'll hear about the values and meaning of our service. And be sure to offer a hearty "Happy Veterans Day."

# Thanksgiving
NOVEMBER

*II Samuel 22:17-20, 38-51*

In the Second Book of Samuel, King David offers a song of gratitude and grievances to God (II Samuel 22:17-20):

> You reached down from above and took me,
> pulling me out of the deep waters.
> You saved me from my powerful foe,
> from enemies too strong for me.
> They advanced on me in my time of calamity,
> but the Eternal was my support.
> You brought me out [from trouble] to the wide open space;
> because You cherish me, You rescued me.

Yet David's song is not only a song of gratitude. He also speaks with radical honesty about the bloodshed he committed for the sake of his own survival and the fulfillment of his ambitions. He describes a broken system (II Samuel 22:38-46):

> I chase my foes and destroy them,
> I do not turn back till they are no more.
> I destroy them, I shatter them;
> they cannot get up, they lie at my feet.
> You have girded me with strength for battle
> and laid low my foes beneath me.
> You make my enemies bare their necks;
> I rid myself of those who hate me.
> They cry for help, but there is none;
> [they cry] to the Eternal, but get no answer.
> Then I pound them like the dust of the earth,
> like mud in the streets I trample and pulverize them.
> You have saved me from strife with peoples,
> You have preserved me to be the leader of nations,
> [so that] a people I never knew [now] serves me.
> Foreigners shall cringe before me,
> obey as soon as they hear me;
> foreigners fade away,
> they come quaking from their strongholds.

The texts of the Bible often teach us about the hardships of the human condition (II Samuel 22:47–51):

> The Eternal lives! Praised be my Rock!
> God is exalted,
> the Rock of my salvation,
> the God who gives me revenge,
> who makes people subject to me,
> who frees me from my foes,
> who raises me above my enemies,
> who rescues me from the violent.
> So I thank You, Eternal One, among the nations,
> and sing praises to Your name.
> You are a tower of victory to Your king,
> You show love for your anointed,
> to David and his descendants forever.

## Beauty and Brokenness at Our Family Tables

### Amanda K. Weiss

Imagine David's song of thanksgiving playing out as a preemptive echo of Thanksgiving at Plymouth. Grateful for God's generosity, our Pilgrims might well have sung of being pulled out of the waters and rescued, rewarded for their beliefs. Their beautiful words and biblical metaphors for their gratitude do not leave any space for the Native American narrative: "They advanced on me in my time of calamity" (II Samuel 22:19). How many of our own Thanksgiving tales are shaped by our own biases and blurred by memory?

This alternative haftarah reading for Thanksgiving poignantly reminds us that history is written by the victors. Did our Pilgrims emulate David, pursuing their presumed "enemies" and "foes" until these peoples were utterly destroyed, trampled, and pulverized? The beginnings of European settlement set a precedent for a shockingly imbalanced system: invaders become "a leader of nations" (II Samuel 22:44), while the "foreigners" (22:45–46)—the original inhabitants!—are expected not only to serve, but to quake and cringe while doing so.

And still, at Thanksgiving, we envision our Pilgrims harmonizing this hymn: "The Eternal lives! Praised be my [Plymouth] Rock!" In order to be mindful of our historical contexts while singing God's praises, we are called, annually, to review our national narratives alongside the stories and identities we share.

# Kaf Tet B'November

## (UN vote in favor of the Palestine Partition Plan)

### NOVEMBER 29

*Psalm 47*

For the conductor: a psalm of the sons of Korach.

Sound t'kiah, O peoples—clap your hands!
Sound t'ruah for God—make a joyful noise in song!
For Adonai on high is awesome—
A great monarch over all the earth,
Whose words subdue people under us
And nations under our feet.

You choose our inheritance for us,
The pride of Jacob whom You love—selah!

God has ascended with *t'ruah*,
Adonai, through a sound of the shofar!
Sing: "God!" Sing!
Sing to our Majesty, sing!
For the Majesty of all the earth is God—sing a *maskil*-song!

God rules over peoples,
God sits on the holy throne.
The people's nobles have gathered together
The people of the God of Abraham;
For to God belong the Shields of the Earth—
God is surely in ascendance!

## A Founding Vision

### Rabbi Donald P. Cashman

A marvel of our age is the return to Jewish sovereignty in the Land of Israel through the vote of the world's nations. November 29 celebrates the 1947 United Nations vote on the partition of British Mandatory Palestine into two independent Jewish and Arab states, a watershed point in the establishment of the State of Israel.

The haftarah reading of Psalm 47 exhorts all the peoples to applaud our God (47:2). While the UN Partition Plan was not applauded by "all" (33 for, 13 against, 10 abstentions, 1 absent), its approval opened the door for the founding of a Jewish state half a year later. The psalm states that it is God who "rules over peoples" (47:9). However, in 1947, it was the UN delegates who were the "great of the peoples" and, with jurisdiction over the British Mandate, the "the people's nobles" who "to God belong" (47:10). In a seemingly ordinary parliamentary decision, humans can act as God's partners in redemption.

What may have been, had the Partition Plan been accepted by all? How can we treat those other Abrahamites righteously, who, if not "under our feet" (47:4), still lack independence or full equality?

Kaf-Tet B'November calls to us to press for a two-state solution, the founding condition of the Jewish State of Israel. While rejected by most Arab states, the Palestinian Declaration of Independence (1988) acknowledges the UN Partition Plan of November 29, 1947, as a legal basis for two states. How can we work on fulfilling this vision?

# World AIDS Day
### DECEMBER I

*"Wingsong: For All the Lovers and Friends Who Died of AIDS,"*
*by Maggid Andrew Elias Ramer*

I carry you on my back
I carry every one of you
who has died
on my back

You are not a burden
your weight is exalting
each one of you
is another feather
in my arched wings

You carry me
every one of you
carries me higher and higher
into my life
into the physical life
I live
for every one of you

When I sleep, you sleep too
when I dance, you dance too
when I pray, you are praying with me
and every time I kiss another man

each one of you
pressed up behind my lips
is drinking too
swan, hummingbird, egret, eagle
drinking

I drink for all of you
I live with all of you
together, together, together,
all of us are
drinking
living
flying

## Carrying Them with Us

*Rabbi Mychal Copeland*

The power of our gathering for World AIDS Day is not only to be found in the sobering statistics that report the millions who have died or are living with HIV. When we mark this day, we remember that each number is a person with a story. In Jewish tradition, one of the words for "person" is the same as "soul": *nefesh*. Each individual name sewn into the AIDS Quilt represents a unique, precious, pure soul.

The poem "Wingsong" was written for one gay man's lover who died of AIDS in 2004—but it was also written for all his friends who died, reminding us that AIDS has devastated whole communities. It is through our memories that these souls live on through those of us who loved them. They dance with us, they pray with us, they drink with us.

In Jewish tradition, we say of the dead that "their memories are for a blessing." They truly are. We carry them with us as an exaltation. Their memories propel us to educate about AIDS, reduce the number of new HIV patients, discover better therapies and cures. By carrying them lovingly on our backs and telling their stories, we honor their legacies and ensure that not one more human soul has to die this way.

The LGBTQI community has gained, at immense cost, collective wisdom about the value of honoring each soul, human dignity, loss, and perseverance in the face of disease and hate. On this World AIDS Day, let us hear the voices of individuals and communities touched by AIDS, and let us listen to what they have to teach us about moving forward with pride and strength.

# International Human Rights Day
## DECEMBER 10

*From the Universal Declaration of Human Rights Adopted by the General Assembly of the United Nations on December 10, 1948*

Whereas recognition of the inherent dignity and of the equal and inalienable rights of all members of the human family is the foundation of freedom, justice and peace in the world,

Whereas disregard and contempt for human rights have resulted in barbarous acts which have outraged the conscience of mankind, and the advent of a world in which human beings shall enjoy freedom of speech and belief and freedom from fear and want has been proclaimed as the highest aspiration of the common people, . . .

Whereas the peoples of the United Nations have in the Charter reaffirmed their faith in fundamental human rights, in the dignity and worth of the human person and in the equal rights of men and women . . .

Now, therefore, THE GENERAL ASSEMBLY proclaims this UNIVERSAL DECLARATION OF HUMAN RIGHTS as a common standard of achievement for all peoples and all nations to the end that every individual and every organ of society, keeping this Declaration constantly in mind, shall strive by teaching and education to promote respect for these rights and freedoms. . . .

> Article 1. All human beings are born free and equal in dignity and rights. They are endowed with reason and conscience and should act towards one another in a spirit of brotherhood.
>
> Article 2: Everyone is entitled to all the rights and freedoms set forth in this Declaration, without distinction of any kind, such as race, colour, sex, language, religion, political or other opinion, national or social origin, property, birth or other status. . . .
>
> Article 3: Everyone has the right to life, liberty and security of person.
>
> Article 4: No one shall be held in slavery or servitude; slavery and the slave trade shall be prohibited in all their forms.
>
> Article 5: No one shall be subjected to torture or to cruel, inhuman or degrading treatment or punishment.
>
> Article 6: Everyone has the right to recognition everywhere as a person before the law.
>
> Article 7: All are equal before the law and are entitled without any discrimination to equal protection of the law.
>
> . . .

## All Are Equal before the Law

*Rabbi Barbara Rosman Penzner*

International Human Rights Day is observed on December 10, the date when, in 1948, the General Assembly of the United Nations adopted the thirty articles of the Universal Declaration of Human Rights (UDHR). Following the devastation wrought by World War II, particularly the genocide of European Jewry fomented by Hitler and executed and accepted by multitudes of perpetrators and bystanders, this declaration proclaims a universal vision of the value of every human life. Though it is not a specifically Jewish text, the UDHR affirms the Jewish value that every human is created *b'tzelem Elohim*, "in the divine image," and therefore is deserving of basic rights. When congregations recite the UDHR on the Shabbat closest to Human Rights Day, it speaks in a moral voice as powerful as any Jewish prophet.

Like Hebrew prophecy, the UDHR calls all generations to strive *l'chavod ul'tifaret*, toward social justice and "for the honor and the glorification of God's name in the world." Some congregations hand out individual articles for each person to stand and proclaim the words, one by one, emphasizing its recognition of the uniqueness of every soul.

# Secular New Year

### DECEMBER 31–JANUARY 1

### *From "Three Calendars," by Shalom Aleichem*

It happened right here in Odessa, many years ago, at this time, during the intermediary days of Sukkos. Generally speaking, Odessa was still the same old Odessa. No one had heard of Tolmatshov, and a Jew could roam around free as a bird and sell his Yiddish books. Then, there weren't as many Yiddish papers as today. You weren't afraid of anyone, and there was no need to mess around with banned Parisian postcards. In the old days, I used to sell sabbath and holiday prayer books and Jewish calendars around Lanjerovski, Katerinenski, and Fankonin streets. You could always run into a Jew there, for that was the area where speculators, agents, and various other Jews hung around waiting for a miracle.

Just like you see me now, I was strolling along on Fankonin Street, the spot where our speculators wear out their shoe leather looking for business, and I said to myself: Where do I get a customer for my few Jewish calendars? Rosh Hashana and Yom Kippur are gone and forgotten and before you know it, Sukkos will slip right by and I still haven't gotten rid of my little bit of stock. God knows if I'll ever sell those bound calendars—for if they aren't sold before the holidays, you can't even give them away. Later, they're completely useless. And I had three of them left over from before the Jewish New Year!

I started off with a hundred and got rid of them on the street, mostly among the stock speculators. They weren't such fiery Jews—I mean, they didn't go for Yiddish books and all that. But when it came to a Jewish calendar for the entire year, well, even that sold. After all, you had to know when Passover or a yortsayt for a loved-one came. A Jew is a Jew, after all.

## Cherish and Preserve, Survive and Cope

*Rabbi Natalia Verzhbovska*

To understand the role of the secular New Year in the lives of Jews from the former Soviet Union, one must first understand the significance of this holiday for everyone living under the Soviet regime. New Year was the only holiday on the calendar that had nothing to do with the Soviet propaganda, the history of the Communist Party, or anything else political. It was a celebration that brought families and friends together and a moment of freedom—even if that freedom was an illusion. For this special day, we preserved the very valuable and hard to find mayonnaise to make the traditional salads Olivier, herring under the *shuba* (coat), and stuffed eggs. The even more scarce chocolates that children received as gifts at large New Year celebrations were hung on the *yolka* (what we learned to call "the Christmas tree"). That tree had never been a religious symbol for us, and it never occurred to anyone to associate it with any religious rituals.

After the collapse of the Soviet Union, many Jews returned to their religious roots. They implemented new holidays and rituals in their lives, began to celebrate Shabbat, gave gifts to their children on Chanukah, and arranged Passover seders—but the habits of cherishing and preserving anything that helps to survive and cope with life's hardships did not allow them to abandon the holiday that for several generations was a symbol of hope for a better life and belief in family values. The secular New Year celebration is still a part of the family life of many Jewish families from the countries of the former Soviet Union. Even if it seems sometimes strange, and even if nobody really can come up with any convincing arguments for keeping this tradition, it continues to be a sign of devotion and gratitude for every moment of goodness and happiness in an otherwise dark time.

And that seems to be very Jewish—doesn't it?

What do you do to light up the darkness?

# Sources and Permissions

THE CENTRAL CONFERENCE OF AMERICAN RABBIS expresses gratitude to the publishers and writers for the permission we have received to use their material in this book. Every effort has been made to ascertain the proper owners of copyrights for the selections used in this volume and to obtain permission to reprint copyrighted content where required. CCAR Press will be pleased, in subsequent editions, to correct any inadvertent errors or omissions that may be pointed out.

Except as noted below, Torah translations are taken from *The Torah: A Modern Commentary*, revised edition (New York: CCAR Press, 2006), edited by Rabbi W. Gunther Plaut. Translations of the traditional haftarot are by Rabbi Chaim Stern from the same volume. Translations of Psalms are from *Songs Ascending: The Book of Psalms in a New Translation with Textual and Spiritual Commentary* by Rabbi Richard N. Levy (New York: CCAR Press, 2018). Unless otherwise noted, translations of the Babylonian Talmud are from The William Davidson digital edition of the *Koren Noé Talmud* with commentary by Rabbi Adin Even-Israel Steinsaltz, adapted from Sefaria (Jerusalem: Koren Publishers). Other biblical translations are adapted from *Tanakh: The Holy Scriptures* (Philadelphia: Jewish Publication Society, 1985) and used with permission.

**69** Rabbi Regina Jonas as quoted in the German Jewish newspaper *Central Verein Zeitung*, June 23, 1938. See Elisa Klapheck, *Fräulein Rabbiner Jonas: The Story of the First Woman Rabbi* (San Francisco: Jossey-Ross, 2004), 58–59.

**72** Leah Goldberg, "Tel-Aviv: 1935," from *Im ha-Layla ha-ze (With This Night)*, Sifriat Poalim, 1964. Translation by Cantor Sarah Grabiner. Used by permission.

**74** "The Rainbow Haftarah," © 1993 by Rabbi Arthur Waskow. Used by permission. Additional versions, including Hebrew, trope, and background on the piece, are available at the Open Siddur Project, https://opensiddur.org/readings-and-sourcetexts/mekorot/non-canonical/exoteric/modern/the-rainbow-haftarah-by-rabbi-arthur-waskow-translated-by-rabbi-zalman-schachter-shalomi/.

**76** *The only thing we have*, Harvey Milk, "The Hope Speech," June 25, 1978; for the full text, see "You've Got to Have Hope" in *An Archive of Hope: Harvey Milk's Speeches and Writings* (Oakland, CA: University of California Press, 2013), 145-156.

**78** Rabbi Sheila Peltz Weinberg, "Traveler's Prayer," in *Kol Haneshamah: Limot Hol* [Daily Prayer Book] (Reconstructionist Press, 2006), 174. Used by permission.

**79** Alden Solovy, "Let Go," in *This Precious Life: Encountering the Divine with Poetry and Prayer* (New York: CCAR Press, 2020), 12. Used by permission.

**82** Maimonides, *Mishneh Torah, Hilchot Mat'not Aniyim*, trans. Joseph B. Meszler (Williamsburg, VA: 2003), 10:4. Adapted from Sefaria, https://www.sefaria.org/Mishneh_Torah%2C_Gifts_to_the_Poor.10?lang=bi.

83   Elie Wiesel, *Messengers of God: Biblical Portraits and Legends*, trans. Marion Wiesel (New York: Random House, 1976), 234–35.

87   Robert Frost, "Provide, Provide," in *The Poetry of Robert Frost* (New York: Henry Holt, 1969), 307.

89   Rabbi Chaim Potok, *The Chosen* (New York: Fawcett Crest, 1992), 204–5.

92   Alan Morinis, *Everyday Holiness: The Jewish Spiritual Path of Mussar* (Boulder: Shambhala Publications, 2008), 15–16.

93   Rabbi Ben-Zion Meir Hai Uziel and Rabbi Yitzhak Isaac HaLevi Herzog, "A Call to the Leaders of Islam for Peace and Brotherhood," December 4, 1947, trans. Rabbi Daniel Bouskila. The full letter is available at https://jewishjournal.com/commentary/opinion/110203/.

97   Y'hudah HaLevi, "Where Will I Find You," in *The Poetry of Kabbalah: Mystical Verse from the Jewish Tradition*, trans. Peter Cole (New Haven, CT: Yale University Press, 2012), 71. Used by permission.

99   *The You encounters me by grace*, Martin Buber, *I and Thou* (UK: Bloomsbury Academic Press, 2004), 62–63.

104  Rick Lupert, "God Wrestler," https://jewishjournal.com/commentary/blogs/308425/god-wrestler-a-poem-for-parsha-vayishlach/.

109  Translation by Rabbi Joseph B. Meszler.

114  Sefaria Community Translation, *Sh'mot Rabbah*, 18:12. Adapted from Sefaria, www.sefaria.org/Shemot_Rabbah.18?lang=bi.

119  *The prophet's utopian program*, Michael Coogan, ed., *The Oxford History of the Biblical World* (New York: Oxford University Press, 1998), 272.

125  *Be accustomed always*, Ramban, "Letter from Ramban to His Son," trans. Solomon Schechter (1892). The full letter is available at Sefaria, https://www.sefaria.org/Letter_from_Ramban_to_his_Son?lang=bi.

125  Translation by Rabbi Jessica K. Barolsky.

133  *You have to go the way*, James Baldwin, as quoted in Richard Goldstein, "'Go the Way Your Blood Beats': An Interview with James Baldwin," *Village Voice*, June 26, 1984.

138  Dahlia Ravikovitch, "Ga'ava (Pride)," from *Hasefer Hashlishi (The Third Book)*, trans. Chana Bloch and Ariel Bloch, Hakibbutz Hameuchad Publishing, 1991 (Second Edition).

139  Excerpted from the Americans with Disabilities Act of 1990, as amended by the ADA Amendments Act of 2008, https://www.ada.gov/pubs/adastatute08.htm#12101.

141  *All bodies are unique*, Patricia Berne, in Nomy Lamm, "This Is Disability Justice," The Body Is Not an Apology, September 2, 2015, https://thebodyisnotanapology.com/magazine/this-is-disability-justice/.

144  Rabbi Abraham Joshua Heschel, "Religion and Race," from a speech delivered at the National Conference on Religion and Race, January 14, 1963. Available online at BlackPast.org, https://www.blackpast.org/african-american-history/1963-rabbi-abraham-joshua-heschel-religion-and-race/. Used by permission of Prof. Susannah Heschel.

147  "My Parents' Lodging Place" from *Open Closed Open* by Yehuda Amichai. Compilation © 2000 by Yehuda Amichai. © 2000 by Chana Bloch and Chana Kronfeld. Used by permission of HarperCollins Publishers, Georges Borchardt, Inc., and Hana Amichai.

**148** Rabbi Abraham Isaac Kook, "*Shir M'ruba*: The Fourfold Song," in *Orot HaKodesh*, vol. 2, article 3, section 30 (Jerusalem: Mossad Harav Kook, 1985), 444–445. Translation by Rabbi Daniel Kirzane.

**153** Judith Plaskow, *Standing Again at Sinai: Judaism from a Feminist Perspective* (San Francisco: Harper San Francisco, 1991), 25, 31.

**153** *Reading texts against the grain*, Rita Felski, "Context Stinks," *New Literary History* 42, no. 4 (Autumn 2011), 574.

**157** Emma Lazarus, "The New Colossus," in *The Poems of Emma Lazarus* (New York: Houghton Mifflin Company, 1888), 202–203.

**158** "The low road" from *The Hunger Moon: New and Selected Poems, 1980–2010* by Marge Piercy, © 2011 by Middlemarsh, Inc. Used by permission of Alfred A. Knopf, an imprint of the Knopf Doubleday Publishing Group, a division of Penguin Random House LLC. All rights reserved.

**163** Adapted from *Orchot Tzaddikim: The Ways of the Tzaddikim*, ed. Gavriel Zaloshinsky, trans. Shraga Silverstein (Nanuet, NY: Feldheim Publishers, 1994), 2:6.

**168** We can be the hands of God, Rabbi Zalman Schachter-Shalomi, "The Hands of God," in *The Book of Miracles: A Young Person's Guide to Jewish Spiritual Awareness* by Rabbi Lawrence Kushner (Woodstock, VT: Jewish Lights Publishing, 1997), 67.

**171** Shaul Tchernichovsky, "Before the Statue of Apollo," 1899. Translation by Cantor Sarah Grabiner.

**173** *Paganism sees its gods*, Heinrich Graetz, "The Structure of Jewish History," in *The Structure of Jewish History and Other Essays*, ed. and trans. Ismar Schorsch (New York: Jewish Theological Seminary of America, 1975), 68.

**173** "K'hilah K'doshah," © 2000 by Dan Nichols. Used by permission.

**176** *What's more*: See Genesis 1:1–2:3, especially the account of the seventh day, including the parallel use of the words *vayaas*, *vay'chal*, and *ham'lachah*. This three-part parallel is most evident if we look ahead from *Vayak'heil* into *P'kudei*. Indeed, this Askkenazic haftarah selection is the Sephardic selection for *P'kudei*. For further references, see Michael Fishbane, *The JPS Bible Commentary: Haftarot* (Philadelphia: Jewish Publication Society, 2002), 138 and notes; and rabbinic commentaries *Tanchuma Vayak'heil* 5, *Tanchuma P'kudei* 2, and others.

**176** "To be of use" from *Circles on the Water* by Marge Piercy, © 1982 by Middlemarsh, Inc. Used by permission of Alfred A. Knopf, an imprint of the Knopf Doubleday Publishing Group, a division of Penguin Random House LLC. All rights reserved.

**178** Caroline Rothstein, "When We Make Art Together, We Dream a Better World into Existence," T'ruah, 2020, https://www.truah.org/resources/terumah-caroline-rothstein-torah2020/. Used by permission.

**182** "Gods Change, Prayers are Here to Stay" from *Open Closed Open* by Yehuda Amichai. Compilation © 2000 by Yehuda Amichai. © 2000 by Chana Bloch and Chana Kronfeld. Used by permission of HarperCollins Publishers, Georges Borchardt, Inc., and Hana Amichai.

**188** Rabbi Abba Hillel Silver, *Where Judaism Differs: An Inquiry into the Distinctiveness of Judaism* (Philadelphia: Jewish Publication Society, 1957), 181.

**190** Translation by Rabbi Amy Scheinerman.

**191** Translation by Rabbi Amy Scheinerman.

**193** *The Fathers According to Rabbi Nathan*, trans. Judah Goldin, Yale Judaica Series (New Haven, CT: Yale University Press, 1983), 32.

**195** Translation by Rabbi Amy Scheinerman.

**201** Translations by Rabbi Amy Scheinerman.

**203** *It is a great thing*, Robert Alter, *The Hebrew Bible: A Translation with Commentary*, vol. 2, *Prophets* (New York: W. W. Norton, 2019), 544.

**204** *No more than my space*, Alan Morinis, *Everyday Holiness: The Jewish Spiritual Path of Mussar* (Durban, So. Africa: Trumpeter, 2008), 51–54.

**204** Karl Marx, *Critique of the Gotha Program*, 1875, https://www.marxists.org/archive/marx/works/1875/gotha/index.htm.

**206** Translations by Rabbi Amy Scheinerman.

**209** Translation by Rabbi Ronald B.B. Symons.

**211** Translation by Rabbi Amy Scheinerman.

**213** Translation by Rabbi Jill Jacobs.

**215** Elie Wiesel, "To a Young Jew of Today," in *One Generation After* (New York: Random House, 1965), 163–66, 174.

**217** Translations by Rabbi Amy Scheinerman.

**220** "V'ahavta" from *The Art of Blessing the Day: Poems with a Jewish Theme* by Marge Piercy, © 1999 by Middlemarsh, Inc. Used by permission of Alfred A. Knopf, an imprint of the Knopf Doubleday Publishing Group, a division of Penguin Random House LLC. All rights reserved.

**222** Translation by Rabbi Amy Scheinerman.

**227** "Ready and Prepared," © 2021 by Trisha Arlin. Used by permission.

**233** *It is utterly impossible for us*, Ernestine Rose, address celebrating the 1834 emancipation of enslaved peoples in the British West Indies, Flushing, NY, August 4, 1853, in *The American Jewish Woman: A Documentary History*, by Jacob Rader Marcus (New York: Ktav, 1981), 167.

**237** Leah Goldberg, "Teach Me, O God," trans. Pnina Peli, in *Kol Haneshamah: Shabbat Vehagim* (Elkins Park, PA: Reconstructionist Press, 1996).

**238** Debbie Perlman, "For Complete Healing," in *Flames to Heaven: New Psalms for Healing and Praise* (Wilmette, IL: Rad Publishers, 1998), 10.

**244** *This is a textbook pattern*: "Understanding the Power and Control Wheel," Domestic Abuse and Intervention Programs: Home of the Duluth Model, https://www.theduluthmodel.org/wheels/.

**245** *Zohar* 1:15b, trans. Joshua Schwartz, in Joey Weisenberg, *The Torah of Music: Reflections on a Tradition of Singing and Song* (New York: Hadar Press, 2017).

**245** Moses Cordovero, *Pardes Rimonim*, gate 29, chap. 5, trans. Joshua Schwartz, in Weisenberg, *The Torah of Music: Reflections on a Tradition of Singing and Song* (New York: Hadar Press, 2017).

**251** Rabbi Abraham Joshua Heschel, "To Be a Jew: What Is It?," *Zionist Quarterly*, Summer 1951, reprinted in *Moral Grandeur and Spiritual Audacity*, ed. Susannah Heschel (New York: Farrar, Straus and Giroux, 1997), 7. Used by permission of Prof. Susannah Heschel.

**251** *A hopelessly communal people*, Rabbi Lawrence Kushner, "The Tent Peg Business: Some Truths about Congregations," *New Traditions*, Summer 1984.

**255** Rabbi Joachim Prinz, excerpted from a speech delivered at the March on Washington, August 28, 1963. Available at http://www.joachimprinz.com/civil-rights.htm.

**260** Natan Alterman, "The Silver Platter,"

*Davar*, December 19, 1947. Available online, https://zionism-israel.com/hdoc/Silver_Platter.htm.

263 Shimon Peres, *Ben-Gurion: A Political Life*, Jewish Encounters Series (New York: Schocken Books, 2011), 13–14.

265 Amos Oz and Fania Oz-Salzberger, *Jews and Words* (New Haven: Yale University Press, 2012), 1.

265 Rabbi Abraham Joshua Heschel, *Heavenly Torah: As Refracted Through the Generations*, ed. and trans. Rabbi Gordon Tucker (New York: Continuum, 2006), 667.

267 Laura Eve Engel, "Reciprocity," in *Things That Go* (Portland, OR: Octopus Books, 2019), 88. Used by permission.

269 Moshe Lavee, "You Are My Rock, " translated by Rabbi Jonathan Magonet. Used by permission.

271 Rabbi Chaim Stern, "When Evil Darkens Our World," in *Mishkan HaNefesh: Machzor for the Days of Awe; Yom Kippur*, ed. Rabbi Janet Marder and Rabbi Sheldon Marder (New York: CCAR Press, 2015), 506.

272 "Bein Kodesh L'chol"/"Between the Holy and the Mundane" by Amir Dadon and Shuli Rand. Translation by Sasha Dominguez. Available online at https://www.youtube.com/watch?v=sCJh9YcrL3k.

272 Translation by Sasha Dominguez.

277 From dedications to "Bashert" from *Her Birth and Later Years: New and Collected Poems 1971–2021* © 2022 by Irena Klepfisz. Published by Wesleyan University Press. Used by permission.

279 Excerpted from Rabbi Regina Jonas's halachic treatise "Can Women Serve as Rabbis?," in *Fräulein Rabbiner Jonas: The Story of the First Woman Rabbi*, by Elisa Klapheck, trans. Toby Axelrod (San Francisco: Jossey-Bass, 2004), 160.

281 *Half the kingdom*. This expression is used in Esther 5:3 to denote half of Ahasuerus' kingdom, offered by him to Esther.

281 Gertrude Stein, "Patriarchal Poetry," in *The Yale Gertrude Stein*, ed. Richard Kostelanetz (New Haven, CT: Yale University Press, 1980), 106. Used by permission of David Highman Associates Limited.

285 *. . . the time of year*: The period between the seventeenth of Tammuz, which marks the breaching of the walls of Jerusalem by the Romans in 70 CE, and the ninth of Av, when the Second Temple was destroyed. Jewish tradition holds that the First Temple was also destroyed on this same date in 586 BCE. Many other disasters have befallen the Jewish people on this date in the Hebrew calendar.

285 *T'filat HaDerech*, in *Mishkan T'filah: A Reform Siddur*, ed. Rabbi Elyse D. Frishman (New York: CCAR Press, 2007), 378.

286 "Trees," republished in Hebrew in Leah Goldberg, *Yalkut Shirim* [Collected poems], ed. Tuvia Rivner (Tel Aviv: Iachldav/Writers Association, 1970); translation by Rabbi Javier Cattapan.

292 Translation by Rabbi Kerry M. Olitzky.

293 Almog Behar, "Take This Poem and Copy It: Selected Poems and Stories in Hebrew and English Translation," 2017. Translation by Alexandra Berger-Polsky. Available at https://almogbehar.wordpress.com/english/. Used by permission of Almog Behar.

295 *And let them make Me a sanctuary*, translation by Rabbi Kerry M. Olitzky.

296 Aurora Levins Morales, "V'ahavta." © 2016 by Aurora Levins Morales. Used with the permission of The Permissions Company, LLC on behalf of Aurora Levins Morales, www.auroralevinsmorales.com.

298 Alden Solovy, "Tears, Too Close: A Prayer of Consolation," in *This Precious Life: Encountering the Divine with Poetry*

and Prayer (New York: CCAR Press, 2020), 54–55. Used by permission.

302 Howard Schwartz, "The Death of Adam," from *Midrashim: Collected Jewish Parables* (London: The Menard Press, 1976), 13. Used by permission of the author.

303 "A Holy Nation," from Elisa Klapheck, "Regina Jonas," *Jewish Women: A Comprehensive Historical Encyclopedia*, 31 December 1999, Jewish Women's Archive, https://jwa.org/encyclopedia/article/jonas-regina.

306 Translation by Rabbi Joseph B. Meszler.

308 Rabbi Joseph R. Black, "Blessing and The Curse," © 2003 Transcontinental Music, from the album *Sabbatical*. Used by permission of Rabbi Joseph Black.

311 Morris U. Schnapps, ed., *A Documentary History of the Jews in the United States, 1654–1875*, rev. ed. (New York: Citadel Press, 1952), 79–80.

313 Adapted from *The Septuagint with Apocrypha*, trans. Sir Lancelot C. L. Brenton, 1885, updated 2012. See https://ebible.org/eng-lxx2012/copyright.htm.

316 Translation by Rabbi Audrey R. Korotkin, PhD.

317 *One cannot be forced*: The forced conversion of the conquered Idumeans [Edomites] by John Hyrcanus I in the second century BCE is the only exception.

317 Maimonides, *Mishneh Torah, Hilchot Dei-ot*, trans. Simon Glazer (1927), 1:4, 1:7. Adapted from Sefaria, https://www.sefaria.org/Mishneh_Torah%2C_Human_Dispositions.1?lang=bi.

320 Rabbi Harold S. Kushner, *When Bad Things Happen to Good People* (New York: Schocken Books, 2004), 14, 34.

322 Rabbi Harold S. Kushner, "Would an All-Powerful God Be Worthy of Worship?," in *Jewish Theology and Process Thought*, ed. Sandra B. Lubarsky and David Ray Griffin (Albany: State University of New York Press, 1996), 89–91.

329 *I am almost demented*, Rabbi Stephen S. Wise, quoted in Carl Hermann Voss, *The Lion and the Lamb: An Evaluation of the Life and Works of Stephen S. Wise* (Cincinnati: American Jewish Archives, 1969), 14.

330 Yehuda Amichai, "The Place Where We Are Right" in *The Selected Poetry of Yehuda Amichai*, edited and translated from the Hebrew by Chana Bloch and Stephen Mitchell. © 1986, 1996, 2013 by Chana Bloch and Stephen Mitchell. Published by the University of California Press. Used by permission.

334 The translation has been adapted from JPS Tanach, with the last line translated by Rabbi David E. Ostrich.

335 Rabbi Zoë Klein, "Two Candles." Unpublished. Used by permission.

341 Translation by Rabbi Jessica K. Barolsky.

347 *Read in its entirety*: Orach Chayim 425:3; Mishnah B'rurah 4; as cited in Rabbi Isaac Klein, *A Guide to Jewish Practice* (New York: Jewish Theological Seminary of America, 1992), 265.

348 Excerpt from "Split at the Root: An Essay on Jewish Identity," from BLOOD, BREAD, AND POETRY: Selected Prose 1979-1985 by Adrienne Rich. © 1986 by Adrienne Rich. Used by permission of W. W. Norton & Company, Inc.

351 "Beautiful City" from *Godspell*, music and lyrics by Stephen Schwartz. © 1972 (Renewed), 1973, 1993, 2012 Grey Dog Music and S & J Legacy Productions LLC. Publishing and allied rights administered by Grey Dog Music. International Copyright Secured. All Rights Reserved. www.stephenschwartz.com. Reprinted by Permission of Hal Leonard LLC.

352 J. Sylvan, "Adoni" in *Beloved King: A Queer Bible Musical* © 2018, 2020, 2021 J.

Sylvan, Brandon Jackson, and Branuzsick Publishing. All Rights Reserved. Used by permission.

354 *The love Jonathan bore,* Saint John of the Cross (1542–1591), *A Spiritual Canticle of the Soul and the Bridegroom Christ* (Create-Space, 2013), 239.

356 *The problem with white people,* Robin DiAngelo, "Academic Robin DiAngelo: 'We Have to Stop Thinking about Racism as Someone Who Says the N-Word,'" interview by Nosheen Iqbal, *Guardian,* February 16, 2019, https://www.theguardian.com/world/2019/feb/16/white-fragility-racism-interview-robin-diangelo.

358 Rabbi Israel Zoberman, "The Shofar's Calling," *CCAR Journal: The Reform Jewish Quarterly,* Spring (2004), 48. Used by permission.

359 Aharon Berechiah of Modena, *D'rashit Ma'avar Yabbok* (Jerusalem: Ahavat Shalom, 2000), 102. Translation by Rabbi Phillip J. Bentley.

360 Melanie Kaye/Kantrowitz, "Jews in the U.S.: The Rising Costs of Whiteness," in *Names We Call Home: Autobiography in Racial Identity,* ed. Becky Thompson and Sangeeta Tyagi (New York: Routledge, 1996), 124.

361 Yehuda Amichai, "The Real Hero" in *The Selected Poetry of Yehuda Amichai,* edited and translated from the Hebrew by Chana Bloch and Stephen Mitchell. © 1986, 1996, 2013 by Chana Bloch and Stephen Mitchell. Published by the University of California Press. Used by permission.

364 Judy Chicago, "Merger Poem," © Judy Chicago/Artists Rights Society, New York. Used by permission.

365 Rabbi Aryeh Azriel, quoting Leonard Fein, "The Heart of Jewish Enterprise," sermon delivered at Temple Israel, Omaha, Nebraska, February 25, 2011,

reprinted in *The Jewish Press,* April 1, 2011, 9, https://issuu.com/jewishpress7/docs/040111.

366 *Their words are onslaughts,* Abraham Joshua Heschel, *The Prophets* (New York: Perennial Classics/HarperCollins, 2001), xii.

368 *Ring the bells,* Leonard Cohen, "Anthem," on *The Future,* Columbia, 1992.

370 Rabbi Joseph R. Black, "I Remember You," © 1998 Lanitunes Music. From the album *Leave A Little Bit Undone.* Used by permission of Rabbi Joseph Black.

372 *. . . there will be no more Canaanite*: Note that the Hebrew word כנעני translates to 'trader' or 'money-trader.' The word is also a homonym for 'Canaanite,' which is used here exegetically.

374 Sue Horowitz and Rabbi Lev Baesh, "Be the Change" in Horowitz's album *The Power and the Blessing.* Used by permission.

375 Alden Solovy, "Beauty Dances," in *This Grateful Heart: Psalms and Prayers for a New Day* (New York: CCAR Press, 2017), 58–59. Used by permission.

377 *Zechariah 14:16,* read as part of the haftarah for the first day of Sukkot. See Michael Fishbane, *The JPS Bible Commentary: Haftarot* (Philadelphia: Jewish Publication Society, 2002), 409.

378 Rabbi Leo Baeck, *The Essence of Judaism* (New York: Schocken Books, 1961), 143–44.

379 Yehuda Amichai, "A Man in His Life" in *The Selected Poetry of Yehuda Amichai,* edited and translated from the Hebrew by Chana Bloch and Stephen Mitchell. © 1986, 1996, 2013 by Chana Bloch and Stephen Mitchell. Published by the University of California Press. Used by permission.

383 Ruhama Weiss, "Blessed Are You," translated from the Hebrew by Rabbi

Naamah Kelman. Original Hebrew version at https://www.kibutz-poalim.co.il/so_woman_is_not_god.

386 Emma Lazarus, "In Exile," in *Songs of a Semite: The Dance to Death, and Other Poems* (New York: Office of the American Hebrew, 1882), 53–54.

387 *Give me your tired,* Emma Lazarus, "The New Colossus," in *The Poems of Emma Lazarus* (New York: Houghton Mifflin Company, 1888), 202–203.

388 Melanie Kaye/Kantrowitz, "Some Notes on Jewish Lesbian Identity," in *Nice Jewish Girls: A Jewish Lesbian Anthology*, ed. Evelyn Torton Beck (Watertown, MA: Persephone Press, 1982), 39.

393 Uri Zvi Greenberg, "At Your Feet, Jerusalem," in *Modern Hebrew Poetry*, ed. and trans. Ruth Finer Mintz (Berkeley: University of California Press, 1966), 120–24.

396 Translation by Rabbi Donald P. Cashman.

397 Rabbi Abraham Joshua Heschel, "Religion and Race," from a speech delivered at the National Conference on Religion and Race, January 14, 1963. Available online at Voices of Democracy, https://voicesofdemocracy.umd.edu/heschel-religion-and-race-speech-text/. Used by permission of Prof. Susannah Heschel.

402 Translation by Rabbi Simeon J. Maslin.

402 *How is it possible*, Rabbi Azariah Figo, *Binah L'Itim*, trans. by Rabbi Simeon J. Maslin.

403 *The intensely painful feeling*, Brené Brown, "Shame v. Guilt," *Brené Brown* (blog), January 14, 2013, https://brenebrown.com/blog/2013/01/14/shame-v-guilt/.

404 Else Lasker-Schüler, "Esther," in *Sämtliche Gedichte* (Frankfurt am Main: Jüdischer Verlag im Suhrkamp Verlag, 2004), 169. Translation by Rabbi Sonja

K. Pilz, PhD.

405 For the full text of Levin's *Akeidah* skit, performed in his play *Malkat Ambatiah* ("Queen of the Bathtub"), see *Ma Ichpat Latzipor* ("Why Should the Bird Care") (Tel Aviv: Hakibutz Ham'uchad, Siman Kria, 1987).

406 "And You Shall Draw Water," adapted from *The Open Door: A Passover Haggadah*, ed. Rabbi Sue Levi Elwell (New York: CCAR Press, 2002), 12–13.

407 *... there are discrepancies*: Michael Fishbane, "Haftarah for Shabbat ha-Ḥodesh," in *The JPS Bible Commentary: Haftarot* (Philadelphia: Jewish Publication Society, 2002), 355–60.

408 David Einhorn, "The First Day of Pesach, 1857," from *Sinai* 2: 522–33, in "Dr. David Einhorn's *Sinai* 1856–1862: An Evaluation and Partial Translation of His Writings," trans. Benno M. Wallach (Hebrew Union College–Jewish Institute of Religion, Cincinnati, 1950), 344. In the original text of Rabbi Einhorn's sermon, he uses Hebrew letters without transliteration. Like many of the early Reform rabbis, it is likely he felt comfortable writing in Hebrew and reading from sermon manuscripts without transliteration.

409 Excerpt(s) from BOOK OF MERCY by Leonard Cohen, page 43, © 1984 by Leonard Cohen. Used by permission of Villard Books, an imprint of Random House, a division of Penguin Random House LLC. All rights reserved.

412 "God's Beloved," from *The Penguin Book of Hebrew Verse*, ed. T. Carmi (London: Penguin Classics, 1981), 478–79. © T. Carmi 1981. Reprinted by permission of Penguin Books Limited.

414 Shelley Frier List, "Tefillah for Agunot," *JOFA Journal* 5, no. 4 (Summer 2005): 5, https://www.broydeblog.net/uploads/8/0/4/0/80408218/can_there_be_solutions_s.pdf.

417 Rabbi Abraham Geiger, *Nachgelassene Schriften*, vol. 1, 203ff.; translated in W. Gunther Plaut's *The Rise of Reform Judaism: A Sourcebook of Its European Origins* (New York: World Union for Progressive Judaism, 1963), 156–57.

418 Ruth F. Brin, "Discovery" from *Harvest: Collected Poems and Prayers*. © 1986, 1999 by Ruth Firestone Brin. Reprinted with the permission of The Permissions Company, LLC on behalf of Holy Cow! Press, www.holycowpress.org

421 © Rabbi Shefa Gold. Reprinted from *In the Fever of Love: An Illumination of the Song of Songs* (Teaneck, NJ: Ben Yehuda Press, 2009). Used by permission.

423 Adapted from Rabbi Dr. Shmuly Yanklowitz, "Comfort, Healing, and Talking Openly about Suicide," Medium, June 13, 2018, https://medium.com/@rabbiyanklowitz/comfort-healing-and-talking-openly-about-suicide-a4c62824c3d2; Shmuly Yanklowitz, "Intimidation, Alienation and Suicide: Creating Nurturing Communities Together," Times of Israel, October 25, 2013, https://blogs.timesofisrael.com/intimidation-alienation-and-suicide-creating-nurturing-communities-together/. Used by permission.

426 Marvin Lowenthal, *Henrietta Szold: Life and Letters* (New York: Viking Press, 1942), 92–93. Available online at Jewish Women's Archive, https://jwa.org/node/22356.

428 Rabbi Israel Zoberman, "Passover's Peace Partners," *CCAR Journal*, Summer 2015, 133. Used by permission.

430 From Israel Najara (ca. 1550–ca. 1625), "A *Ketubah* for Shavuot," quoted in Philip Goodman, "The Shavuot Marriage Contract: A Sephardic Agreement between God and Israel," My Jewish Learning, accessed August 5, 2021, https://www.myjewishlearning.com/article/the-shavuot-marriage-contract/.

432 Merle Feld, "We All Stood Together," *A Spiritual Life: A Jewish Feminist Journey* (Albany: State University of New York Press, 1999), 205. Used by permission.

436 Rabbi David Einhorn, "For the Anniversary of the Destruction of Jerusalem," in *Olath Tamid: Book of Prayers for Israelitish Congregations*, 2nd English ed., 1896, trans. Emil G. Hirsch, 141–46. Adapted with modernized English pronouns.

437 Adapted from Lisa A. Goodman and Deborah Epstein, *Listening to Battered Women: A Survivor-Centered Approach to Advocacy, and Mental Health and Justice* (Washington, DC: American Psychological Association, 2008), 1–2.

441 Excerpted from "Why We Went: A Joint Letter from the Rabbis Arrested in St. Augustine," June 19, 1964, Jewish Women's Archive, https://jwa.org/media/why-we-went-joint-letter-from-rabbis-arrested-in-st-augustine.

442 *Do not passively stand by*, translation by Rabbi Kerry M. Olitzky.

444 Excerpted from Evan Traylor, "All The Things We Can Do With Hope," ReformJudaism.org, December 18, 2019, https://reformjudaism.org/blog/all-things-we-can-do-hope.

444 *Indeed I had dreamed*, Elie Wiesel, "The Darkness of Chanukkah" (lecture archives, 92nd Street Y, New York City, December 7, 1999), 35.

447 Rabbi Sally Priesand quoted in *Rabbis: The Many Faces of Judaism*, ed. Michael Kress (New York: Universe Publishing, 2002).

448 *We especially think of*: Pamela S. Nadell, "The Long and Winding Road to Women Rabbis," in *The Sacred Calling: Four Decades of Women in the Rabbinate*, ed. Rabbi Rebecca Einstein Schorr and Rabbi Alysa Mendelson Graf (New York: CCAR Press, 2016), 31–43.

448 Excerpted from Justice Ruth Bader Ginsburg, *Brown v. Board of Education in International Context* (speech, Columbia University School of Law, New York, October 21, 2004), https://awpc.cattcenter.iastate.edu/2017/03/21/brown-v-board-of-education-in-international-context-oct-21-2004/.

449 *A student of*: Anne E. Kornblut, "Justice Ginsburg Backs Value of Foreign Law," *New York Times*, April 2, 2005, https://www.nytimes.com/2005/04/02/politics/justice-ginsburg-backs-value-of-foreign-law.html.

450 For the full text of the 2015 "Resolution on Pay Equity," see Women of Reform Judaism, https://wrj.org/what-we-believe/resolutions/pay-equity.

450 *Equal Pay Day is not a holiday*, Katie Wysong, "Equal Pay Day: Help Fight Gender-Based Wage Discrimination," Religion Action Center of Reform Judaism, March 31, 2020, https://rac.org/blog/equal-pay-day-help-fight-gender-based-wage-discrimination.

451 *Women in the United States*, "America's Women and Wage Gap," National Partnership for Women and Families, March 2020, https://www.nationalpartnership.org/our-work/resources/economic-justice/fair-pay/americas-women-and-the-wage-gap.pdf.

451 Excerpt from "Invisibility in Academe" from BLOOD, BREAD, AND POETRY: Selected Prose 1979-1985 by Adrienne Rich. © 1986 by Adrienne Rich. Used by permission of W. W. Norton & Company, Inc.

452 Excerpted from "Kenneth Holtzman (1945–)," Jewish Virtual Library, accessed August 7, 2021, https://www.jewishvirtuallibrary.org/kenneth-holtzman.

453 David B. Green, "This Day in Jewish History, 1945: American Baseball Legend Who Struck Out in Israel Is Born," *Haaretz*, November 3, 2015, https://www.haaretz.com/jewish/.premium-1945-baseball-legend-who-struck-out-in-israel-is-born-1.5416511.

456 Rabbi Moti Rotem. This extract is from a larger article first published in Hebrew on the *Keren Kayemet* website: hagim.org. See an alternative translation of the extract in an ARZA (Association of Reform Zionists of America) blog from 4.23.2020, reformjudaism.org/blog/tragedy-celebration-we-honor-state-israel.

457 Provisional Government of Israel, "Declaration of Independence," Tel Aviv, 5 Iyar 5708 (May 14, 1948), available in English at The Knesset, https://www.knesset.gov.il/docs/eng/megilat_eng.htm.

458 *Pirkei D'Rabbi Eliezer*, trans. Gerald Friedlander (London: 1916), 12:4, 6. Adapted from Sefaria, https://www.sefaria.org/Pirkei_DeRabbi_Eliezer.12?lang=bi.

459 *Two are better than one*, Ecclesiastes 4:9-12, in *The Hebrew Bible: A Translation with Commentary*, trans. Robert Alter (New York: W. W. Norton, 2018).

460 Rabbi Ruth Sohn, "I Shall Sing to the Lord a New Song" in *Kol Haneshamah: Shabbat Vehagim* [Shabbat and Holidays Prayer Book] (Wyncote, PA: Reconstructionist Press, 2014), 768–769. Used by permission.

463 Isaac Harby, "Prayer for Government," in *The Sabbath Service and Miscellaneous Prayers Adopted by the Reformed Society of Israelites, Founded in Charleston, South Carolina, November 21, 1825* (New York: Bloch, 1916), 25–26.

465 "Women at the Head of the Class," © 2020 by Jessica de Koninck. A version of the poem appears in the *Jewish Women's Literary Annual*, Vol. 4 (2001), 83. Used by permission.

**465** Julia Ward Howe, "Appeal to Womanhood throughout the World" (Boston, 1870). Available online at the Library of Congress, https://www.loc.gov/resource/rbpe.07400300/.

**466** *This woman's place is in the House*, "Bella Abzug for Congress," political poster (New York: 1971–76). Available online at the Library of Congress, Prints and Photographs Online Catalog, Yanker Poster Collection, www.loc.gov/pictures/item/2016648584/.

**466** Harvey Milk, "The Hope Speech," June 25, 1978. A version of the complete speech is available at ONE Archives Foundation, https://www.onearchives.org/wp-content/uploads/2019/02/one-archives-foundation-harvey-milk-v2.pdf.

**470** Rabbi Mike Uram, *Next Generation Judaism: How College Students and Hillel Can Help Reinvent Jewish Organizations* (Woodstock, VT: Jewish Lights, 2016), 71–72.

**471** "A Father's Blessing," sermon delivered by Rabbi Jerome Malino, December 27, 1974, DA-201, The Jacob Rader Marcus Center of the American Jewish Archives, Cincinnati, Ohio.

**475** Excerpt from "Why Black Lives Matter to a People for Whom God Promised a Holy Place" by Graie Hagans in *#BlackLivesMatter Haggadah Supplement* by Jews For Racial & Economic Justice. Used by permission of Graie Hagans. Available online at https://ritualwell.org/ritual/blacklivesmatter-haggadah-supplement/.

**477** *To drag a man in fetters*, Frederick Douglass, from a speech delivered July 5, 1852 in Rochester, NY. For the full text, see *ucl.ac.uk/USHistory/Building/docs/Douglass.htm*.

**478** *Can we discern*, Reverend Fred Shuttlesworth, quoted in Keith D. Miller, *Martin Luther King's Biblical Epic: His Final Great Speech* (Jackson, MS: University Press of Mississippi, 2011), 32.

**478** *Every red stripe*, Fannie Lou Hamer, quoted in Maegan Parker Brooks and Davis W. Houck, *The Speeches of Fannie Lou Hamer: To Tell It Like It Is* (Jackson, MS: University Press of Mississippi, 2013), 119.

**478** Aiden Pink, "Exclusive: Aly Raisman Speaks Out on Sexual Harassment, Judaism, and Her Future," *Forward*, October 26, 2017, https://forward.com/news/385903/exclusive-aly-raisman-speaks-out-on-sexual-harassment-judaism-and-her-future/.

**479** Judy Bolton-Fasman, "Olympian Aly Raisman Talks about Surviving Sexual Abuse," JewishBoston, January 7, 2019, https://www.jewishboston.com/read/olympian-aly-raisman-talks-about-surviving-sexual-abuse/.

**480** Speech by Rose Schneiderman at the Metropolitan Opera House meeting to protest the Triangle Shirtwaist Factory fire on April 2, 1911, in *Out of the Sweatshop: The Struggle for Industrial Democracy*, ed. Leon Stein (New York: Quadrangle/New Times Book Company, 1977), 196–97; first published in *The Survey*, April 8, 1911.

**481** Haim Gouri, "The Sandcastles," translated by Vivian Eden. © Vivian Eden, 2013. Permission donated in memory of Vivian Eden's cousin, Rabbi Elliot Stevens, z"l. Available at *Haaretz*, https://www.haaretz.com/life/books/premium-poem-haim-gouri-s-sandcastle-1.5346120.

**482** *Prophecy and poetry*, "Haim Gouri," in *Israeli Poetry: A Contemporary Anthology*, trans. Warren Bargad and Stanley F. Chyet (Bloomington, IN: Indiana University Press, 1986), 58.

**486** Martin Buber, "In the Midst of History," in *Israel and the World: Essays in a Time of Crisis* (New York: Schocken

Books: 1973), 81.

**487** From Moses Cordovero, "The Palm Tree of Deborah," in *The Essential Kabbalah* by Daniel C. Matt. © 1995 by Daniel C. Matt. Used by permission of HarperCollins Publishers.

**488** Rob Eichberg, *Coming Out: An Act of Love* (New York: Dutton, 1990), 186–87.

**489** Excerpts from speeches of Justice Raquel Montoya-Lewis, https://www.law.uw.edu/news-events/discovery/season-2/a-seat-at-the-table; https://www.king5.com/article/news/local/states-first-native-american-supreme-court-justice-sworn-in/281-3fb86244-266e-4d28-a4ba-9f555b5c3e06; https://www.kveller.com/native-american-jewish-justice-raquel-montoya-lewis-tells-us-how-she-made-history/.

**492** *Israel enacted its social contact*, Jonathan Sacks, *To Heal a Fractured World: The Ethics of Responsibility* (New York: Schocken Books, 2007), 125.

**492** "The Salty Taste of Tears" © 2020 Rabbi Joseph R. Black. Available online at rabbijoeblack.blogspot.com. Used by permission.

**498** Adapted by Rabbi Donald P. Cashman.

**499** Andrew Elias Ramer, "Wingsong: For All the Lovers and Friends Who Died of AIDS." © Andrew Ramer 2004. Unpublished. Used by permission.

**501** UN General Assembly, Resolution 217A, Universal Declaration of Human Rights, December 10, 1948, https://www.un.org/en/about-us/universal-declaration-of-human-rights.

**502** Shalom Aleichem, "Three Calendars," trans. Curt Leviant, *Jewish Currents*, September 15, 2017, https://jewishcurrents.org/three-jewish-calendars-a-story-by-sholem-aleichem/.

# Contributors

**RABBI BARBARA AB SYMONS** graduated from the University of Michigan and was ordained by Hebrew Union College–Jewish Institute of Religion in 1994. Having served other congregations, since 2006 she has been serving Temple David in Monroeville, Pennsylvania, just outside of Pittsburgh. She is deeply involved in the interfaith community primarily through her work with the Monroeville Interfaith Ministerium—of which she is past president—and through the Catholic-Jewish Education Enrichment Program. Engaged with the local community, Rabbi Symons has served as president of the hospital's clergy board and rabbinic groups, and she is active with the town council, school board, and library. She met her husband, Rabbi Ron Symons, during their first week in Jerusalem at HUC-JIR; she is daily and deeply proud of, and inspired by, him and their three children Aviva, Ilana and Micah, all of whom are not only committed Jews but learned, creative Jewish professionals. She is thrilled to have even a small part in raising up prophetic voices through the many diverse voices included in this book.

**RABBI ELIZABETH BAHAR**, ordained in 2009, is the rabbi at Temple Beth Israel in Macon, Georgia. She previously served Congregation Ahavath Chesed in Jacksonville, Florida, and Temple B'nai Sholom in Huntsville, Alabama. While promoting inclusion and innovation, she was recognized by *The Forward* as one of "America's 33 Most Inspirational Rabbis," (2015) and she has received multiple leadership awards in Alabama. Rabbi Bahar is an adjunct professor at Mercer University in Macon, Georgia, and is the proud mother of Aiden, David, and Daniel Bahar.

**RABBI JONAH DOV PESNER** is the director of the Religious Action Center of Reform Judaism and the senior vice president of the Union for Reform Judaism. Called one of the most influential rabbis in America, Rabbi Pesner has devoted his career to building interfaith and multiracial coalitions in successful campaigns for civil rights and social justice. Rabbi Pesner sits on the boards of the NAACP and the Leadership Conference for Civil and Human Rights, among others, and coedited *Moral Resistance and Spiritual Authority: Our Jewish Obligation to Social Justice* (CCAR Press, 2019).

**Rabbi Richard S. Sarason**, PhD, is the director of the Pines School of Graduate Studies and the Deutsch Family Professor of Rabbinics and Liturgy at Hebrew Union College–Jewish Institute of Religion. His academic writings are in the areas of classical rabbinic literature and thought and the history of Jewish liturgy. His books include *Divrei Mishkan T'filah: Delving into the Siddur* (CCAR Press, 2018).

**Rabbi Lance J. Sussman**, PhD, is the rabbi emeritus of Reform Congregation Keneseth Israel in Elkins Park, Pennsylvania, and the immediate past chair of the board of governors of Gratz College. Rabbi Sussman is a historian of the American Jewish experience and has published widely in the field, including a biography of Isaac Leeser (1995) and a biographical dictionary of Reform Judaism (1993). Currently, he is working on a book on Jews, law, and the American Revolution.

**Rabbi Rachel Timoner** is grateful and proud to serve as the senior rabbi of Congregation Beth Elohim (CBE) in Park Slope, Brooklyn. She is honored to stand with families at the moments of greatest joy and deepest sorrow in their lives, and she is delighted to be part of a flowering of creativity, community, learning, spirituality, and action at CBE. She is the author of *Breath of Life: God as Spirit in Judaism* (2011).

# Index of Commentary Authors

Abbott, Rabbi Eric L., 407

Adar, Rabbi Ruth, 121, 259

Alpert, Rabbi Tom, 87

Altshuler, Rabbi Benjamin, 407

Appell, Rabbi Victor S., 181

Axelrad, Rabbi Rachel, 270, 284

Baden, Rabbi Ilana Greenfield, 89

Baesh, Rabbi Lev, 374

Bahar, Rabbi Elizabeth, 3, 142, 204, 345, 403

Barolsky, Rabbi Jessica K., 125, 203, 279, 342

Barrett, Rabbi Ashley, 124, 426

Battis, Rabbi Jordana Schuster, 176, 285, 377

Bellows, Rabbi Lisa Sari, 92, 160, 310, 357

Bennet, Rabbi Debra, 150, 166

Bentley, Rabbi Philip J., 94, 214, 254, 359, 365, 431

Berger, Cantor David, 60

Berkowitz, Rabbi Leah Rachel, 82

Berman, Rabbi Sarah, 113

Binder, Rabbi Erin, 83, 152

Black, Rabbi Joseph R., 80

Blank, Rabbi Stacey, 124

Boxt, Rabbi Erin, 236, 367

Busch, Rabbi Andrew, 215, 391

Cahana, Cantor Ida Rae, 435

Caro, Cantor Susan, 146, 324

Cashman, Rabbi Donald P., 397, 421, 498

Cattapan, Rabbi Javier E., 287

Chaiken, Rabbi Max, 113, 250, 306

Citrin, Rabbi Paul J., 108, 131, 133, 198, 319

Clissold, Cantor Gabrielle, 150

Cohen, Rabbi Phil M., 367

Cohen, Rabbi Sandra J., 355, 356, 364, 381

Cohen, Cantor Shani, 99, 237, 387

Copeland, Rabbi Mychal, 500

Dana, Emily, 77, 301

Dantowitz, Rabbi Faith Joy, 79, 81

de Koninck, Rabbi Isabel, 231, 465

DiColandrea, K. M. "DiCo," 474

Dominguez, Sasha, 273

Dreskin, Rabbi Billy, 188

Dubin, Emma, 263

Edelheit, Rabbi Joseph, 371

Edwards, Rabbi Lisa A., 467, 489

Eger, Rabbi Denise L., 118

Fair, Cantor David, 475

Feibush, Cantor Kenneth J., 332, 425

Feingold, Rabbi Dena A., 256, 304

Feinstein, Rabbi Morley T., 260

Feshbach, Rabbi Michael L., 182, 205, 264

Finley, Rabbi Mordecai, 291, 409

Fogelman, Cantor Lauren Phillips, 429

Forman, Rabbi Sharon G., 72, 321, 369

Frank, Rabbi Samantha G., 55, 59, 111, 116, 122, 128

Freedman, Rabbi Larry, 495

Friedlander, Rabbi Ariel J., 414

Friedman, Rabbi Matt, 219, 248, 296

Frishman, Rabbi Elyse D., 309

Gibson, Rabbi Jamie, 138
Glasser, Rabbi Maya Y., 67, 131, 192, 267, 291, 352
Gluck, Rabbi Shira, 328, 331
Gold, Rabbi Shefa, 422
Goldberg, Cantor Margot E.B., 64, 175
Goldwasser, Rabbi Jeffrey, 454
Grabiner, Cantor Sarah, 73, 172, 187, 315, 350
Gray-Schaffer, Cantor Michele, 398
Greengrass, Rabbi Rachel, 274
Grodensky, Rabbi Alexander, 313, 318, 322, 327, 437
Gurvis, Rabbi Eric S., 324

Haas, Rabbi Peter J., 358, 428
Harris, Rabbi Cantor Kim, 350
Harrison, Cantor Rhoda J., 146, 234, 411
Helfman, Rabbi Jordan, 178, 319, 408
Henry, Rabbi Sharyn H., 173
Hirsch, Rabbi Liz P.G., 450
Hollie, Maggid Marques, 76
Hyman, Cantor Brad, 208

Jacobs, Rabbi Jill, 213
Jacobs, Rabbi Rick, 477
Janes, Rabbi Neil, 395
Joseph, Rabbi Rachel L., 192

Kahn, Rabbi Andrue, 459
Kalson, Susan Friedberg, 449
Kaplan, Rabbi Dana Evan, 189, 278, 337, 378, 404, 417
Katz, Rabbi Jan, 444
Katzew, Cantor Alane S., 239
Katzew, Rabbi Jan, 383
Keller, Sharon R., 86
Kelman, Rabbi Naamah, 384
Kent, Cantor Evan, 390
Kerber, Rabbi Justin, 257
Kipnes, Rabbi Paul, 376

Kirzane, Rabbi Daniel, 149, 221, 268
Kohn, Rabbi Douglas, 137, 157, 310, 312, 394
Korotkin, Rabbi Audrey R., 162, 301, 315, 317, 485
Kranjec, Danielle, 177
Kukla, Rabbi Elliot, 140

Levin, Rabbi Dan, 169
Levin, Rabbi Mark, 413
LeVine, Rabbi Jay Asher, 134, 246, 265, 337
Levine, Cantor Lisa, 160, 274
Lewis, Rabbi Michael F., 249
Lieber, Rabbi Valerie, 164, 244
Limmer, Rabbi Seth M., 67, 145, 153, 219, 271
Lisitsa, Rabbi Alona, 107, 253
Litman, Rabbi Jane, 490
London, Rabbi Andrea C., 493
Lorge, Rabbi Ari S., 486
Lyons, Cantor Abbe, 277, 348, 389

Maslin, Rabbi Simeon J., 402
Mazor, Rabbi Yehoram, 456
McCarroll, Rabbi Eliza, 69
Medwin, Rabbi Daniel B., 363
Memis-Foler, Rabbi Amy L., 326
Meszler, Rabbi Joseph B., 109, 199, 305, 308
Middleburgh, Rabbi Charles, 144, 401, 462
Miller, Rabbi Heather, 114, 460
Missaghieh, Rabbi Michelle, 197
Mühlstein, Rabbi Lea, 269, 300

Newburge, Rabbi Geri, 136, 164, 225, 266, 457, 470

Oler, Rabbi David, 163
Olitzky, Rabbi Kerry M., 292, 295, 385, 412, 441
Ostrich, Rabbi David E., 168, 245, 335
Ovadia, Cantor Judith Borden, 434

Parr, Rabbi Jordan M., 262, 446, 468

Penzner, Rabbi Barbara Rosman, 159, 502

Perlman, Rabbi Jill, 183, 294, 419

Perman, Rabbi Sara Rae, 272, 286, 336, 361, 380

Pesner, Rabbi Jonah Dov, xvii

Pilz, Rabbi Sonja K., 228, 405

Pogrebin, Abigail, 98, 226

Poland, Brandon, 71

Pollack, Rabbi Audrey S., 280, 333, 433

Prosnit, Rabbi Ethan, 381

Rawlings-Fein, Martin, 483

Regev, Rabbi Uri, 155

Reinwald, Cantor David, 416

Rigler, Rabbi Peter, 93, 180, 224

Robbins, Rabbi Debra J., 347

Roberts, Rabbi Nicole, 208, 416

Rosen-Brown, Rabbi-Cantor Elana, 282, 487

Rossoff, Rabbi Donald B., 385, 400, 430

Ruskin, Rabbi Gila Colman, 298, 353, 427

Samuels, Rabbi Ayala Ronen, 103

Sank Ross, Rabbi Jade, 97

Sarason, Rabbi Richard S., 25

Scheinerman, Rabbi Amy, 190, 195, 201, 206, 211, 217, 222

Schuman, Rabbi Burt E., 340

Schwartz, Rabbi Beth L., 303

Segal, Rabbi Emily E., 345, 377

Shaner, Rabbi Cantor Jordan, 96, 243, 372

Shribman, Rabbi Natalie Louise, 142

Singer, Rabbi Suzanne, 84, 366

Sirkman, Rabbi Jeffrey, 77, 251

Sloan, Sebastian, 170

Spicehandler, Rabbi Reena, 238, 406

Stein, Rabbi Howard, 392

Steinman, Rabbi Eleanor, 420

Sussman, Rabbi Lance J., 39

Symons, Aviva, 471

Symons, Rabbi Barbara AB, 64, 105, 255, 356, 395, 399, 480

Symons, Ilana Y., 88, 442

Symons, Micah, 102, 156

Symons, Rabbi Ronald B.B., 209, 491

Tepper, Rabbi Bill S., 119, 257, 481

Timoner, Rabbi Rachel, 49

Torop, Aaron DB, 101

Tovlev, Ariel, 451

Verzhbovska, Rabbi Natalia, 503

Wax, Rabbi Pamela, 148, 276

Webber, Cantor Karen, 360, 424, 438

Weisman, Rabbi Stephen, 230, 233, 453, 479

Weiss, Amanda K., 497

Winnig, Rabbi Paula Jayne, 373

Wise, Rabbi Stephen A., 330

Yanklowitz, Rabbi Shmuly, 91, 329

Zamore, Rabbi Mary L., 70, 447

Zemel, Rabbi Daniel G., 55, 59, 111, 116, 122, 128

Zola, Rabbi Gary Phillip, 464, 472

# Index of Alternative Haftarah Authors

Aleichem, Shalom, 502
Alterman, Natan, 260
Amichai, Yehuda, 147, 182, 330, 361, 379
Arlin, Trisha, 227

Baeck, Rabbi Leo, 378
Behar, Almog, 293
Berechiah, Aharon, of Modena, 359
Black, Rabbi Joseph "Joe" R., 308, 370, 492
Brin, Ruth, 418
Buber, Martin, 99, 486

Chicago, Judy, 364
Cohen, Leonard, 409
Cordovero, Moses, 245, 487

Dadon, Amir, 272
de Koninck, Jessica, 465

Eichberg, Rob, 488
Einhorn, Rabbi David, 408, 436
Elwell, Rabbi Sue Levi, 406
Epstein, Deborah, 437
Engel, Laura Eve, 267

Fein, Leonard, 365
Feld, Merle, 432

Geiger, Rabbi Abraham, 417
Ginsburg, Ruth Bader, 448
Goldberg, Leah, 72, 237, 286
Goodman, Lisa A., 437
Gouri, Haim, 481
Greenberg, Uri Zvi, 393

Hagans, Graie, 475
HaLevi, Yehudah, 97
Herzog, Rabbi Yitzhak HaLevi, 93
Heschel, Rabbi Abraham Joshua, 144, 251, 397
Horowitz, Sue, 374

Jonas, Rabbi Regina, 69, 279, 303

Kaye/Kantrowitz, Melanie, 360, 388
Klein, Rabbi Zoë, 335
Klepfisz, Irena, 277
Kook, Rabbi Abraham Isaac, 148
Kushner, Rabbi Harold S., 320, 322

Lasker-Schüler, Else, 404
Lavee, Moshe, 269
Lazarus, Emma, 157, 386
Levins Morales, Aurora, 296
List, Shelley Frier, 414
Lupert, Rick, 104

Maimonides, 82, 317
Malino, Rabbi Jerome, 471
Marx, Karl, 204
Milk, Harvey, 466
Montoya-Lewis, Raquel, 489
Morinis, Alan, 92
Moskowitz, Rabbi Michael, 173

Najara, Rabbi Israel, 430
Nichols, Dan, 173

Oz, Amos, 265
Oz-Salzberger, Fania, 265

Peres, Shimon, 263
Perlman, Debbie, 238
Piercy, Marge, 158, 176, 220
Pink, Aiden, 478
Plaskow, Judith, 153
Potok, Rabbi Chaim, 89
Priesand, Rabbi Sally J., 447
Prinz, Rabbi Joachim, 255

Ramer, Maggid Andrew Elias, 499
Rand, Shuli, 272
Ravikovitch, Dahlia, 138
Rich, Adrienne, 348, 451
Rose, Ernestine, 233
Rothstein, Caroline, 178

Schneiderman, Rose, 480
Schwartz, Howard, 302
Schwartz, Stephen, 351
Seixas, Moses, 311
Silver, Rabbi Abba Hillel, 188

Sohn, Rabbi Ruth, 460
Solovy, Alden, 79, 298, 376
Stein, Gertrude, 281
Stern, Rabbi Chaim, 271
Sylvan, J., 352
Szold, Henrietta, 426

Tchernichovsky, Shaul, 171
Traylor, Evan, 444

Uram, Rabbi Mike, 470
Uziel, Rabbi Ben-Zion Meir Hai, 93

Waskow, Rabbi Arthur, 74
Weinberg, Rabbi Sheila Peltz, 78
Weiss, Ruhama, 383
Wiesel, Elie, 83, 215
Wise, Rabbi Stephen S., 329

Yanklowitz, Rabbi Shmuly, 423

Zoberman, Rabbi Israel, 358, 428